*Party
Politics
in the
Continental
Congress*

Bicentennial of the American Revolution

CONSULTING EDITORS
Richard B. Morris

Jack P. Greene

Dumas Malone

John C. Miller

PUBLISHED

AMONG THE PROJECTED TITLES

H. James Henderson

NEW YORK   ST. LOUIS   SAN FRANCISCO   DÜSSELDORF
LONDON   SYDNEY   TORONTO   MEXICO   PANAMA   JOHANNESBURG   KUALA LUMPUR
MONTREAL   NEW DELHI   SAÕ PAULO   SINGAPORE

Party

Politics

in the

Continental

Congress

McGraw-Hill Book Company

LIBRARY OF CONGRESS CATALOGING IN PUBLICATION DATA

Henderson, Herbert James.
  Party politics in the Continental Congress.

  (Bicentennial of the American Revolution)
  Bibliography: p.
    1. United States.   Continental Congress.
2. Political parties—United States—History.
I. Title.   II. Series.
JK1033.H43   329'.02   74-12129
ISBN 0-07-028143-2

1 2 3 4 5 6 7 8 9 KP KP 7 9 8 7 6 5 4

This book was set in Garamond by University Graphics, Inc., and was printed and bound by Kingsport Press, Inc. The designer was Betty Binns. The editors were Nancy Tressel, Laura Givner, and Phyllis McCord. Milton Heiberg supervised the production.

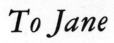
To Jane

Contents

Contents

Foreword

THE CONTINENTAL CONGRESS, that representative body which preceded the states in time, summoned them into existence, declared independence from Great Britain, established a Continental army and navy, conducted the military affairs of the American Revolution, and directed its foreign affairs, has long warranted a careful reappraisal. We now have just that from the pen of Dr. Henderson. In an extraordinary piece of research he has reexamined that immense documentation which is still extant for the Congress, judiciously evaluated the Congress's accomplishments, and pointed his finger at its frailities.

In the past, historians have usually laid stress upon the extralegality of the Congress, upon its instability and its deficiencies. These defects Dr. Henderson fully recognizes, while placing in proper perspective Congress's durable achievements. Dr. Henderson tells the story of a Congress that operated a viable national government until it was peacefully superseded by the federal government under the Constitution. Its stability and durability and its fifteen years of major legislative and administrative accomplishments may be contrasted with the relative impermanence of the revolutionary assemblies created in France during that nation's Revolution or in Latin America during that continent's wars for independence. Congress's climactic achievements were the two great land ordinances of 1784 and 1787, which admitted new states into the Union on an equal footing with the old, thereby striking a great blow against colonialism and permitting a republican system to attain continental limits.

While these notable accomplishments are widely recognized, what is far less known about the Congress is the fact that it laid the foundation for the first party system that emerged some years after the creation of the federal government. In fact, the distinctive feature of Dr. Henderson's book and its most original contribution is its focus on congressional politics and factions. Examining voting patterns, contests over control of appointments, personal and geographic divisions, the author uncovers all the elements of a concealed party system taking form as early as 1774. Lacking both national or grassroots organization, factions avoided party labels largely because of the implicit assumption at the time that a republican system of government depended for survival on the achievement of consensus in society and government. Thus political leaders like James Madison in his celebrated *Federalist* No. 10 and President Washington in his Farewell Address confessed that parties were an evil. It was the former's hope that a national government would create a consensus by channeling local and socioeconomic special interests into a central national legislature. Quite the reverse took place, for in fact the party system under the federal Congress soon displayed extraordinary vitality. Whether this was sparked by events abroad such as the French Revolution, which had a divisive impact in America or divisions at home over domestic policy pose questions historians still debate.

Others, notably Jackson Turner Main, have studied in some depth the rise of partisan politics in the States, but what is especially novel and remarkably persuasive about Dr. Henderson's argument is that through the use of statistical data on voting patterns he has demonstrated the existence of sustained and reasonably coherent legislative parties on a national level in the Continental Congress. There was an Eastern party attracting some support from the South, while the South and the Middle States managed to align a few adherents from New England to support their factional politics. There were localists and cosmopolites, states' righters and nationalists. The differences may have been primarily geographic, but they carried strong ideological overtones. Thus, as Dr. Henderson has shown, Congress provided a constitutional basis for a far more durable fabric whose erection brought about its supplanting; it also evolved a manageable system of partisan political controversy out of which a more permanent party structure emerged.

In short, we have here an insightful and compelling piece of historical analysis which will not only constitute a significant contribution to the historical scholarship of the era of the American Revolution but will also provide guidelines for interpretation and further research in the period in the years ahead.

Richard B. Morris

COLUMBIA UNIVERSITY

Preface

OUR UNDERSTANDING of the politics of the American Revolution has been distorted by a partially accurate but fundamentally misleading perception of the Continental Congress as a weak and ineffective precursor of the Federal Congress. From that perspective, the politics of the Continental Congress naturally seem either formless or dominated by a struggle over the desirability of stronger national power. In fact, the Congress was not impotent, nor was it totally preoccupied with the question of adjusting the balance between central authority and states' rights. Compared with national assemblies in other colonial revolutions, the Congress was extraordinarily successful. After all, it declared independence, managed the war, framed the alliance with France, concluded the peace treaty with England, and organized the West. These were substantial accomplishments; they were achieved in the face of heavy odds; and they produced a broad range of debates that deserve serious scrutiny if we are to gain a comprehensive view of the politics of the Revolution.

The partisan politics of the Continental Congress are of particular interest, for the most signal success of the American Revolution was the establishment of republican government over a vast span of territory—and the Continental Congress, while not so instrumental as the Federal Constitution in perpetuating that accomplishment, nonetheless provided crucial experience with the strains that accompany open, representative government. Paradoxically, to examine the politics of divisiveness in the Continental Congress is to assess the strengths as well as the weaknesses of the political culture that created and sustained it.

The best evidence that reveals the comprehensive structure of congressional politics is the roll calls that were recorded in the Journals from August of 1777 until the Congress was terminated in 1789. By comparing the way each delegate voted with the way all other delegates voted it is possible to uncover clusters of delegates who had a high level of agreement among themselves and who opposed, with varying degrees of intensity, other blocs of delegates. I have analyzed the voting records of 186 delegates on 1,069 roll calls and have constructed cluster blocs on an annual basis for the years 1777 to 1786. I did not include the years 1787 to 1789 because with the formulation of the Constitution the Continental Congress became a caretaking body that attacked few issues and recorded few roll calls. Nor did I include all votes and all delegates, for it was pointless to consider votes that were unanimous or near unanimous or delegates whose attendance was excessively sporadic. The resultant voting blocs, representing on the average 38 delegates voting on 107 roll calls each year, reflect, in my opinion, the basic configuration of the partisan politics of the Congress. I made no prejudgment about the kinds of issues that produced partisanship. I assumed only that delegates voted for meaningful rather than capricious reasons.

Voting analysis is a powerful tool, but it must be used in association with other sources and modes of inquiry. I have drawn extensively on the records of the Congress along with the correspondence of the delegates, newspapers, and pamphlets in an effort to capture the temper as well as the structure of congressional politics. Congress did not operate in a vacuum—it was the product of a resistance movement in the colonies; its proceedings were always affected by the war and by events in the states; and congressional partisan politics were sometimes intimately connected with local party politics, particularly those of Pennsylvania. Consequently, a comprehensive study of the internal structure of the politics of the Continental Congress has to be couched in the larger political history of the Revolution. I have attempted to do this without losing sight of the main subject.

I found that congressional politics were far from formless. There were coalitions of delegates, of states, and interests that lasted the entire life of the Congress. Further, while disagreements over the relationship between the national government and the states did affect partisan politics, regionalism was a more pervasive source of contention. That contention had such a patterned quality that I have concluded that congressional politics had advanced beyond the traditional factional politics of eighteenth-century legislative bodies. For that reason I have used the term "party politics" in the title of this study. I am not suggesting, however, that we should trace the organization of the first party system back to the Continental and Confederation Congresses. Without a direct relationship between the national legislature and the people, party politics in the sense that we understand them today were impossible. Still, the rapid emergence of political parties during the early 1790s in response to issues that were closely similar to those that had preoccupied the Continental Congress, and in a configuration that was remarkably like the structure of congressional politics during the Revolutionary period, warrants calling that era the germinal period of national party politics.

My conclusions might not be endorsed fully by some colleagues and friends to whom I am indebted, but I am compelled to acknowledge their influence and assistance. Robert Walker and Samuel Patterson, two political scientists, pointed out the utility of cluster-bloc analysis and Guttman scaling at the very outset of my research. Michael Kraus and

Preface

Virginia Harrington offered valuable suggestions concerning the earlier portion of this study when it was in the form of a dissertation. Edmund Morgan read this work at an earlier stage and has been unusually helpful with his comments and encouragement. My colleague Charles Dollar has generously assisted with problems associated with the computer. I also wish to thank the Research Foundation of Oklahoma State University for financial assistance that helped me complete the research and writing of the book. Some of the central arguments of the study were advanced at a symposium sponsored by the Institute for the Study of Early American History and Culture in 1971, when I benefited from the criticisms of Merrill Jensen, James Morton Smith, Cecelia Kenyon, and Alfred Young. Dan Lacy and Laura Givner of McGraw-Hill Book Company, and Tom Davis on a free-lance basis, helped to make the book more intelligible. I am indebted especially to Richard B. Morris who gave initial direction to the project, encouraged its completion, and throughout has set an example in his own work that all students of early American history can observe with profit.

My wife and children deserve condolences along with thanks, for they have endured as well as assisted the writing of the book. My greatest obligation is to Jane, my wife, whose help and understanding have made the book possible.

H. James Henderson

STILLWATER, OKLAHOMA

Abbreviations

Adams, *Works*	*The Works of John Adams*, Charles F. Adams (ed.)
AHR	*American Historical Review*
Amer. Arch.	*American Archives*, Peter Force (ed.)
CL	Clements Library
CRNC	*Colonial Records of North Carolina*
CUL	Columbia University Library
DAB	*Dictionary of American Biography*
HCL	Harvard College Library
HSP	Historical Society of Pennsylvania
JCC	*Journals of the Continental Congress*
JSH	*Journal of Southern History*
LC	Library of Congress
LMCC	*Letters of Members of the Continental Congress*, Edmund C. Burnett (ed.)
MHS	Massachusetts Historical Society
MVHR	*Mississippi Valley Historical Review*
NCHR	*North Carolina Historical Review*
NHHS	New Hampshire Historical Society
NYHS	New York Historical Society
NYPL	New York Public Library
PA	*Pennsylvania Archives*
PCC	Papers of the Continental Congress
PMHB	*Pennsylvania Magazine of History and Biography*
SRNC	*State Records of North Carolina*
WMQ	*William and Mary Quarterly*

1 Introduction

EW institutions in American history have been more frequently misrepresented or more often overlooked than the Continental Congress. Its accomplishments have been eclipsed by its limitations or by other more dramatic events. The Congress that declared independence has been overshadowed by the stirring military conflicts of the Revolution. The Congress that passed the land ordinances of the mid-1780s, some of the most important legislation enacted by any American law-making body, has been less noted for its actions than for its impotence. Inevitably, the Congress under the Articles of Confederation has been contrasted with the stronger federal government created by the Constitutional Convention. But natural as such a comparison is, it can be misleading. It is proper to view the Constitution as an alteration of the Articles, but to construe the history of the Continental Congress as a kind of confused journey toward the convention of 1787 is anachronistic. In actuality, the Continental Congress was primarily a revolutionary legislature, and in this context its record was strikingly successful.

Unlike the Congresses of the Federalist era, the Continental Congress began as an extralegal assembly with the difficult task of coordinating a group of relatively disjointed resistance movements. It subsequently became a revolutionary legislature without complete constitutional sanction even within the revolting colonies until the War of Independence was almost won. It was at once a national government that not only managed war and diplomacy but also had the responsibility of giving direction to a new nation-state that had to be fabricated from diverse colonial materials. Seldom has a legislative body coped with more complex and difficult problems. The very fact that it continued as a viable national government until it was peacefully superseded was remarkable. Its ability to organize an empire and its near success in solving the intricate problems of taxation and commercial regulation even at the moment of its demise call for scrutiny in an enlarged tapestry.

If the history of the Continental Congress is compared with that of revolutionary conventions and assemblies in other nations, its stability, not its impermanence, its accomplishments, not its limitations, are most noticeable. The constituent assembly established during the early stages of the French Revolution proved unable to control the revolution as it unfolded. Similar assemblies established in Latin America during its colonial wars for independence generally abdicated authority to juntas and military liberators who alone seemed capable of giving cohesion to the revolutionary movements. Still, the viceroyalty of Rio de la Plata succumbed to anarchy in a welter of provincial distrusts. Farther north, the viceroyalty of New Granada fragmented as Simón Bolívar's hopes for a united Latin America were dashed by similar strains. Provincial jealousies, regional distrusts, clashes between economic and social classes, and ideological conflicts have almost uniformly undermined representative political institutions in the crucible of revolution. To expect that the Continental Congress could have achieved what no revolutionary legislature ever has—the immediate creation of a powerful, representative, and responsible national authority sensitive to clashing interests in a widely dispersed nation—is to disregard both the historical record and contemporary events.

Actually, the Continental Congress was both more representative and responsible to popular sentiment than its formal constitution under the Articles would suggest. Under the Articles of Confederation the Continental Congress did not have the authority to tax, nor could it coerce the states into compliance with the requisitions it recommended. In fact, the Congress did tax the people through the issuance and subsequent devaluation of currency. The Congress could not regulate trade, but one of its first acts was to prohibit trade with England and the West Indies—an audacious measure that directly contributed to the movement toward independence. The Congress has been compared to a diplomatic assembly of sovereign states; clearly it was not a national legislature with a popular base, since each state had one vote. Nonetheless, the larger states dominated congressional deliberations, operations of critical standing committees, the diplomatic corps, and the executive departments created during the early 1780s.

It has been suggested that once the war began there was a flight of talented leadership from the Congress to the army and to the state governments. In fact, the Congress was a training ground in national government. The Congress and its administrative appendages gathered in most of the political leadership of the Revolutionary and Early National periods. The first five presidents, the first three chief justices, the first two secretaries of state, and the first two secretaries of the treasury were members of Congress. Virtually all the early post-Revolutionary appointments to the critical ministries in England and France went to men who had served in the Congress, including Thomas Jefferson, John Adams, Gouverneur Morris, James Monroe, and Rufus King. Over forty members of the Senate during the Federalist decade—almost exactly half of the entire membership from the original thirteen states—had been members of the Continental Congress. Many of the leaders of the House, including James Madison, Theodore Sedgwick, Elbridge Gerry, Roger Sherman, Richard Bland Lee, and Abraham Baldwin, had been members of Congress. Thomas Jefferson anticipated this nationalizing function of Congress when he suggested to James Madison that Virginia's "young statesmen" should be elected to Congress where "they see the affairs of the Confederacy from a high ground; they learn the importance of the Union and befriend federal measures when they return"[1].

The "high ground" of which Jefferson spoke in 1784 had been established during the previous decade. It was the first and second Congresses that accomplished the transformation of a disjointed colonial resistance into a reasonably cohesive colonial revolution between 1774 and 1776. The Patriot side of the ideological dialogue that was such an important part of the movement toward independence culminated in the resolves and proclamations of the Congress. Indeed, the Revolution was given its most succinct definition in the Declaration of Independence. It was the Congress that supervised the war of the Revolution, ineptly at times, but always with an awareness that civilian control over the military was necessary in the creation of a healthy republic. Nor was it accidental that the Congress designated a commander in chief who displayed that remarkable rectitude that must remain one of Washington's most admirable qualities. Had Washington used his military position for political purposes in the manner of a Napoleon or a Bolívar, he would have been removed from power. It was the Continental Congress that appointed a talented, if sometimes quarrelsome, diplomatic corps that negotiated a military alliance with France and a highly favorable peace treaty with England. The Congress was less than conspicuously successful in putting together the Articles of Confederation, but it established the framework from which the federal union could be made. Further, the fears of a centralized establishment that prevented the erection of a truly national government contributed in the most positive way to the creation of a national domain in the West, one of Congress's greatest achievements. In the land ordinances of 1784 and 1787, the Congress proclaimed that future states should be guaranteed a republican government and be admitted into the Confederation as equal members of the union rather than as colonial dependencies. These laws alone mark the decade and a half between 1774 and 1789 as one of the most important in American legislative history.

II

That the American Revolution did not founder in the manner of other colonial revolutions was not, of course, due solely to the influence of the Continental Congress. The North American colonies had a lengthy experience with representative government on both the provincial and local levels which distinguished them from the Spanish colonies in Latin America. The North American colonies were also distinguished by a relatively open society with a strong middle class and by a general commitment to republican ideology which was a natural product of their political traditions and social condition. Simón Bolívar, in addressing the Second Congress of Venezuela in 1819, insightfully ascribed the success of the United States more to the rectitude of its people than to the mechanics of its constitution[2].

At the same time, however, the United States was not immune to the divisive pressures common to colonial revolutions. The sense of national identity was imperfect; regionalism was a powerful force; and the very vitality of local political institutions made the establishment of a cohesive nation-state difficult.

Throughout its history the Congress had to cope with a variety of antagonistic interests. Before independence was declared, it was necessary to resolve the conflict between Patriots and Tories. This was done by the identification and ultimate suppression of the Tory force wherever and whenever possible. Although this was the most profound of the controversies faced by Congress, others persisted in the form of moderate and radical definitions of the purpose of the Revolution. These conflicts had to be compromised rather than suppressed, and compromise was not an easy matter. Political, diplomatic, and even military decisions were heavily freighted with social values and economic interests. A single measure such as the Continental Association adopted by the first Congress could produce a welter of disputes. The Association was meant primarily as a weapon against England, but it also was intended to separate Tories from Whigs in the enforcement of the boycott by local committees. Not all those who supported resistance against Britain were in favor of the repressive internal intention of the Association. The measure also had the incidental effect of dividing some congressional delegates representing areas with a stake in the carrying trade outside the empire. Many decisions having to do with military affairs provoked controversy, particularly the question of half pay pensions for officers. Some members of Congress saw this as a pragmatic necessity, while others believed it sacrificed the republican integrity of the Revolution. The contemplation of price controls as a means of curbing inflation tended to put merchant against consumer and moderate against radical. The definition of peace objectives created sectional frictions when it became apparent that Congress might have to defer to its allies who opposed American claims to rights in the Newfoundland fisheries and to the navigation of the

Mississippi. The ordinances organizing the West brought forth traditional tensions between speculator and settler, the East and the West, and the commercial and agrarian interests in the nation.

Such antagonisms led to the hesitant evolution of a rudimentary legislative party politics that could clarify and deal with disparate interests. These legislative parties should not, of course, be confused with the kind of organized politics that characterized the first party system of the 1790s. There were no party labels, no electoral tickets, no party platforms, and no extragovernmental grassroots organizations. Because the Continental Congress functioned in so many different capacities producing different kinds of thrusts and challenges, partisan politics within the Congress was complicated and often diffuse. Because the very notion of party or faction seemed to threaten the stability of the new nation in a time of revolutionary turmoil, partisan antagonisms were concealed when possible from outside scrutiny. Because party controversies involved both provincial jealousies and conflicts between social and economic classes, partisanship sometimes produced a confusion of regional interest and ideological commitment.

Unsurprisingly, historians have not generally recognized the existence of sustained and reasonably coherent legislative parties in the Continental Congress. Indeed, because the term "party" signifies the sort of extended organization associated with the first party system, there are compelling reasons not to use the word to describe the partisan politics of the Continental Congress. But the most acceptable alternative, factional politics, also raises definitional problems. Factions customarily refer to personal connections of limited duration cemented by the desire for political perquisites. This does not adequately describe the structure of congressional politics which rapidly produced sustained coalitions of delegates that were more than personal "connexions," to employ the pejorative eighteenth-century term often used to describe a faction. What will be referred to as the "Eastern bloc," or "party," can be discerned in the voting patterns during the entire history of the Congress. Delegates changed, but the bloc continued to exist. This Eastern "party" represented constituent as well as personal interests. Its ideological position was sufficiently coherent and recognized to be the subject of comment, usually of a critical nature, in the Philadelphia newspapers. Although primarily a New England phenomenon, the Eastern party attracted support from the Middle states and to a lesser degree from the South. Its opposition, formed primarily from the South and the Middle states (but not without a few adherents in the New England delegations), was also the subject of comment and criticism. In Pennsylvania, where state politics were powerfully influenced by another rudimentary although more extended party system, the composition of the Assembly which elected delegates to Congress was a remarkably accurate indication of the affiliation of the Pennsylvania congressional delegation. When the Assembly was controlled by the radically oriented "Constitutionalists," the Pennsylvania delegates could be relied upon to support the Eastern party. These were preparty politics to be sure, but they were postfactional politics as well. But rather than introduce a new nomenclature to describe them, terms such as "bloc," "faction," "party," and "interest" will be used—each where it seems most appropriate.

Predictably, congressional parties were primarily regional. National loyalty was only germinating, and the nation was expanding even as it cohered. Consequently, there were difficulties in communication and provincial distrusts that reinforced regional allegiances. But since none of the three major regions could single-handedly control national policy, intersectional alliances were necessary. Sometimes these alliances were forged out of pragmatic interest, and sometimes as a consequence of ideological factors. During the early stages of the Revolution, between 1775 and 1779, the ideology of regenerative republicanism was a powerful force in cementing a coalition between the New England delegations and the more radical elements in the Middle states delegations. During the remainder of the war a coalition was formed primarily of more conservative, nationalist delegates from the Middle states with the support of the South. Between 1784 and 1787 intersectional alliances were less structured at first and then became increasingly polarized along a North-South fault that had been implicit in the partisan politics of the Congress from the outset of the Revolution.

The Confederation ultimately succumbed to the two basic challenges the Congress had been coping with since the beginning, regionalism and the tension between social classes. In 1786 the Jay-Gardoqui negotiations threatened to sever the Confederation along a North-South axis, and in that same year the Shaysites in Massachusetts created a general alarm that the social order was threatened. But during the decade and a half of its existence the Continental Congress created the foundation for the new nation, both by laying out a constitutional base on which subsequent forms could be laid and by establishing the precedent of a manageable system of partisan political controversy.

Notes

1 Thomas Jefferson to James Madison, Feb. 20, 1784, in Julian Boyd (ed.), *The Papers of Thomas Jefferson* (Princeton, 1950–), VI, 548–549.

2 Simón Bolívar, address delivered at the inauguration of the Second National Congress of Venezuela in Angostura, Feb. 15, 1819, in Vincente Lecuna (comp.) and Harold A. Bierck, Jr. (ed.), *Selected Writings of Bolivar* (2 vols.; 2d ed., New York, 1951), I, 179.

2 Radical Whigs and the Resistance Movement

I N June 1776, John Adams wrote, "The last finishing strokes will be given to the politics of this revolution . . . nothing after that will remain but war"[1]. Adams proved a poor prophet; there was to be plenty of politics in the war just beginning. But his statement nonetheless illuminates a major obligation of the student of political factions in the American Revolution: to analyze the primary political struggle of the period before 1776, the controversy over the mode of resistance to Great Britain during the decade before the Declaration of Independence. Disconcertingly, the politics of that controversy are the combined politics of thirteen resistance movements and their interrelationships. Ultimately, those politics in their fullness are the causes of the Revolution and therefore are beyond the range of this study. But there is at least one respect in which the resistance controversy is particularly relevant to an analysis of congressional factionalism. This is the tendency of the resistance movement to bring together men from different colonies, thereby helping to firm interprovincial relationships that were the beginning of the partisan organization that developed in the Continental Congress. Forming political connections across provincial boundaries was a halting process, not achieved all at once, but by the early 1770s the nucleus of the radical faction that would emerge in the first Continental Congress had begun to take shape.

When it convened in 1774, the first Congress rapidly divided into three discernible groups. The first was the radical Whigs (or simply radicals, Samuel

Adams being an example), most of whom had continuously supported active resistance, even during the period of relative calm between 1770 and 1773. The second was the moderate Whigs (John Dickinson was one), who ultimately went along with independence but who from 1769 to 1776 favored a more temperate policy of resistance. Finally, there were the Tories (Galloway being a model), who often joined the moderates during this early period but whose prime loyalty remained with Britain. The three categories are suggested here strictly in a functional sense. Thus radical Whigs are understood as supporters of a policy which led to the Revolution and moderates and Tories as those who opposed that policy in two different degrees[2].

The three groups appeared unevenly in time and place. Crises in imperial relations such as those generated by the Stamp Act and the Townshend duties tended to blur the distinctions among them. Agitation over resistance policy was more pronounced in South Carolina, Virginia, New York, and Massachusetts than in Georgia, New Jersey, and New Hampshire. Yet out of the confusion of thirteen different resistance movements, each with its own characteristics, each with its own distribution of forces changing over time and in response to changing situations, there were several developments during the 1760s that influenced the pattern of factionalism in the Continental Congress.

Most noticeable were the basic splits in the provincial legislatures over how to react to measures like the Stamp Act. In Virginia, for example, Patrick Henry's aggressive prescription for the defense of colonial rights offered in his resolutions against the Stamp Act apparently produced a sharp cleavage in the rump session of the Virginia Assembly. Richard Henry Lee and other radicals joined Henry in opposition to moderates such as Richard Bland and conservatives such as Peyton Randolph. By 1766 Virginia's Governor Fauquier reported to the Board of Trade in London that everything had become "a Matter of heat and Party faction . . ."[3]. The sparse record of roll calls in the Massachusetts Legislature indicates that there was a small knot of opposition in 1765 when the overwhelming majority of delegates decided to assert that the provincial courts should be opened for business without stamps[4].

It is tempting to assume, as some historians have, that the Stamp Act disturbance and other imperial crises crystallized colonial party politics and that the radical and conservative forces in provincial legislatures moved inexorably toward factional alignment in the Continental Congress and toward the final battle over declaring independence. This assumption is correct only in an indirect and amorphous sense. The crises in imperial relations did, to be sure, produce a Patriot force within the provincial legislatures and in the provinces that ultimately provided both the leadership and the momentum for independence. At the same time there emerged a smaller and less effective opposition force which, alienated by the resistance tactics of the legislatures and groups like the Liberty Boys, provided a framework for factional opposition in the Continental Congress. But the march toward independence lacked both organizational and ideological clarity.

Imperial crises, for one thing, united colonials as well as divided them. Radicals and Tories alike disapproved of new taxes, as did indeed many Crown officials such as Thomas Hutchinson and Francis Bernard in Massachusetts. Months before the controversy sparked by Henry's resolutions, the Virginia Burgesses endorsed addresses to the King and both houses of Parliament protesting the proposed Stamp Act and stipulating that only Virginians could make internal policy for Virginians. Indeed, the Burgesses at that time used the extremist rhetoric so characteristic of the later resistance to voice their fear that the colonials would become slaves of Britain[5]. The committee that formulated these addresses included men of such differing political convictions as the conservative Peyton Randolph and the radical Richard Henry Lee. When Patrick Henry submitted his resolutions, Richard Bland opposed them, but the next year he suggested that the denial of civil rights might justify resistance to authority[6]. Bland's argument was as hedged as Henry's resolutions were open, and the difference between the two regarding the proper mode of defending colonial liberties, even though they agreed that those liberties were in danger, accounts in many ways for the partisan split over Henry's resolutions. But the issue separating Bland and Henry ceased to exist, for the moment at least, when Parliament repealed the Stamp Act. Likewise in Massachusetts, the vote to ignore the Stamp Act and to open the courts is notable both for the limited opposition it aroused (hardly 6 percent of the body voted against the resolution) and the fairly rapid subsidence of resistance. With the revocation of the act, both legislatures could rest content without generating organizational innovations to carry on the resistance effort. In the heat of a crisis, moderates and radicals tended to draw together, although they might disagree on the way of expressing the common discontent. When the crisis was over, organized resistance to Britain, radical and moderate, appeared to vanish.

The very existence of thirteen colonial governments, widely separated and concerned with disparate issues, was another factor complicating the development of organized resistance. At times the exigencies of local politics overrode concern for colonial rights, as when the Livingstons, DeLanceys, and even the Sons of Liberty used the Townshend Acts crisis in New York in order to secure office for themselves[7]. In Pennsylvania, politicians who had been conditioned by years of experience to perceive political issues in terms of the central question of proprietary rule responded to the Stamp Act in astonishingly irrelevant fashion. Benjamin Franklin and Joseph Galloway, who would be antagonists when it became clear in the 1770s that resistance policy transcended traditional parochial calculations, joined in support of the Crown and the Ministry in order to carry through their campaign against the proprietor Penn[8]. There were instances when the Crown was aligned with the proponents of radical resistance, as when Governor Fauquier hesitantly opposed the union of the speaker's and treasurer's posts in the Virginia Assembly along with Patrick Henry and Richard Henry Lee. Of course, factionalism never conforms neatly and solely to ideological tenets. But as the disparate and contradictory resistance movements began to be rationalized in terms of a common radical ideology, it became possible to organize resistance simultaneously in more than one colony. The largess of a colonial treasurer could not stimulate commitment across provincial boundaries, but ideology could bring about such cooperation, even if it was only temporary.

Yet, even when factional struggles did go along with resistance ideology as they did increasingly during the 1760s, provincial legislatures failed in that decade to achieve effective and durable coordination on an intercolonial level. The device of the circular letter and even the calling of the Stamp Act Congress and the formation of nonimportation associations did not supply the base for a sustained, coordinated interprovincial radical force. The function of the Stamp Act Congress and the early nonimportation associations was to persuade the Ministry to alter its colonial policy, not to construct a revolutionary mechanism. Thus, any partisan political formation that came out of these meetings would have to have been the result more of accident than design. The Congress and the associations were fashioned for specific purposes, and the more successful they were the less enduring they would be. Further, moderates and conservatives were not likely to erect knowingly an intercolonial faction, and it was largely moderates who controlled both the Congress and the nonimportation movement. The Massachusetts delegation to the Stamp Act Congress was led by Timothy Ruggles, who played such a temporizing role at the Congress that he was censured by the Massachusetts House. Virginia sent no delegation at all, its Assembly having been prorogued by Fauquier. The nonimportation associations were also largely controlled by moderate merchants. The radical Samuel Adams admitted he was "but as an Auxiliary in their Nonimportation Agreement"[9]. Neither of these interprovincial actions stimulated contacts between the major portion of the radical faction that emerged in the first Continental Congress. Patrick Henry and Samuel Adams were strangers when they first met in Philadelphia in 1774.

Of course, both Adams and Henry knew where the other stood, and they shared a common rubric of resistance that had been worked out during the previous decade. Although the resistance movement did not produce an enduring interprovincial organization, it did stimulate the formation of bodies of leaders who had developed channels of communication and who had acted in concert upon occasion as members of their various legislatures and as leaders of the Sons of Liberty. The Sons of Liberty in the North actually developed a correspondence union during 1765 and 1766, and whether or not radicals were in formal communication, the energetic activity of the press ensured that leaders of the resistance in one colony were aware of the arguments of their counterparts in the other colonies[10].

The pervasive colonial distrust of ministerial policy did not need to be nurtured by an interprovincial directorate. It grew in a spontaneous fashion. But the extraordinary coordination of the radicals in the first Continental Congress was the product of more than common attitudes toward British policy. It was the result of cooperation that was most fully developed in the alliance between Samuel Adams of Massachusetts, the master architect of the Revolution, and the Lees of Virginia and London.

II

The diffuse, but congruous, colonial effort to alter British policy lacked a geographic focus during the 1760s. Actually, if a center of communication existed for the proponents of radical existence at the end of the decade, it could be found not in New York where the Stamp Act Congress was held, but in London, where policy was made and colonial protests directed, where colonial agents were located and a community of Americans from the whole continent resided, and where a controversy over constitutional liberties within England already raged. In this sense London supplied what was lacking in the colonies— a location where opposition to innovations in British policy could be given continuous expression by Americans and colonial agents, where intercolonial contacts could be established and sustained both directly and indirectly. It is not at all coincidental that the origin of the faction centering on the Adams and Lee families that was so crucial to the radical Massachusetts-Virginia coalition in the first Continental Congress can be traced to London at the moment when the cause of John Wilkes, the well-known radical Member of Parliament, was reaching its climax.

It is not always appreciated that there were a number of Americans in London who played significant roles in the resistance movement. The presence and importance of Benjamin Franklin, of course, is well known. Franklin later contrived to leak some of Governor Hutchinson's correspondence to the Massachusetts radicals, an action which led to the widely publicized attack upon him before the Privy Council by Solicitor General Alexander Wedderburn for supposedly being an agent of a seditious Massachusetts faction. Less clearly recognized is the fact that years before Franklin's ordeal in the Cockpit at Whitehall on January 29, 1774, many colonials in London, such as Arthur Lee and his brother William Lee and Stephen Sayre (a business partner of William Lee and Dennys DeBerdt, the Massachusetts Agent in London), were involved in varying degrees in English radicalism, in colonial resistance, and in an attempt to fuse the two movements. Indeed, an impressive number of men who became delegates to the Continental Congress were in England for periods of time during the 1760s and 1770s, notably Franklin, Arthur Lee, Henry Marchant (temporarily Rhode Island's Agent), Joseph Reed of Pennsylvania, William Samuel Johnson and Eliphalet Dyer from Connecticut (agents of the colony and the Susquehanna Company respectively), the Englishman William Duer who settled permanently in New York by 1773, Benjamin Rush of Pennsylvania, Thomas Adams of Virginia, and a number of South Carolinians including Henry Laurens, William Henry Drayton, and Ralph Izard.

These individuals were by no means uniformly radical; rather, they represented many different political attitudes. The Lees, Sayre, Marchant, Rush, and Dyer were radicals. Franklin was ambivalent during the late 1760s as he shifted from his role in the antiproprietary party in Pennsylvania to defender of American liberties, particularly in the role of Agent for Massachusetts. Reed had radical leanings and played an important part as a link in setting up the Adams-Lee connection, but he later would become distracted by the opportunity offered by his friendship with Lord Dartmouth to play the role of conciliator. Thomas Adams and Henry Laurens might be called moderates, although Laurens joined Izard and Arthur Lee in defending the South Carolina Assembly's fund for the support of Wilkes when the Assembly was criticized in Sir Egerton Leigh's pamphlet *Considerations on Certain Political Transactions of the Province of South Carolina,* published in London in 1774. Duer, Johnson, and William Henry Drayton were conservatives, Johnson counseling moderation in response to the Townshend Acts and Drayton going so far as to criticize publicly the South Carolina Assembly in London newspapers[11]. Because the Americans in London represented different persuasions and interests, conflicts were bound to occur regarding the best response to British policy. In addition, there was some competition in the press and the colonial agencies for leadership of what was becoming the London wing of the resistance movement. Since these individuals represented different colonies and sections, and since communication between them and their colonial contacts received wide circulation in the colonies, London became a seedbed of intercolonial factionalism, particularly during the Wilkes controversy.

The colonials knew well the case of John Wilkes, convicted of seditious libel for his criticisms of the Crown in *Number 45 North Briton* and persistently denied his seat for Middlesex County in Parliament. American newspapers gave his cause voluminous coverage, and his works were published in the colonies. In some provinces, particularly those associated with the radical faction in the first Continental Congress, overt action was taken to demonstrate American support for Wilkes. In Virginia and Maryland patriot planters with appropriate symbolism contributed two collections of forty-five hogsheads of tobacco to aid Wilkes in his struggle with Parliament and the courts. The South Carolina Commons House of Assembly authorized a grant of £1,500 for the same purpose—an action that caused a protracted struggle between the Assembly and the Governor. In Massachusetts the Boston Sons of Liberty began a correspondence with Wilkes concentrating upon their common struggle in defense of constitutional liberty[12].

Americans were convinced in the late 1760s that they, and the English people through Wilkes, were suffering from the same invasion of the liberties of the individual (as in the writs of assistance in the colonies and Wilkes's arrest under a general warrant) and a similar violation of the principle of representative government established by the Glorious Revolution of 1688. Americans were convinced as well that Wilkes offered a good chance to bring pressure to bear on Parliament and the Ministry. These were the assumptions of the Boston Sons of Liberty who wrote admiringly to Wilkes in 1768 that "those generous and inflexible principles which have rendered you so greatly eminent, support our claim to your esteem and assistance. To vindicate Americans is not to desert yourself." Wilkes quickly replied from his cell in King's Bench Prison as "a friend to universal liberty" who would embrace the cause of the colonies as his own:

> As a member of the Legislature, I shall always give a particular attention to whatever respects the interests of America, which I believe to be immediately connected with, and of essential moment to, our parent country, and the common welfare of this great political system. . . . The only ambition I feel is to distinguish myself zealous for the preservation of this constitution and our Sovereign, *with all our laws and native* liberties that ask not his leave, if I may use the expression of Milton . . .[13].

As colonials were increasingly swept up in the Wilkes movement, the position of Americans in London became a matter of some moment[14]. The Lees, Sayre, and Marchant were Wilkes sympathizers, and Arthur Lee was an intense activist. Franklin, Drayton, and probably others, on the other hand, were repelled both by Wilkes personally and by the mob support he rallied in London. Indeed, Franklin published a rebuke to the workers who had participated in the Wilkes demonstrations, chiding them for being ungrateful for the poor relief which had been handed out to them by a charitable Parliament. Wilkes he called "an outlaw and an exile, of bad personal character, not worth a farthing. . . ." And he was astonished that a man with Wilkes's qualifications could win an election to Parliament[15].

Arthur Lee, who was in London to study law after having taken his doctorate in medicine from Edinburgh, was clearly the most active American supporter of the Wilkes movement. With a strong affinity for political dispute (as his later diplomatic and congressional career amply demonstrated), he wrote political pieces to present the American cause to the British public. He seized the Wilkes controversy as "a means of combining the complaints of the people of America and England." He was an early member of the Society for the Defense of the Bill of Rights formed in February 1769 to secure Wilkes's election to Parliament, and he succeeded in introducing a statement on American affairs in the protest resolutions drawn up by the society. He also placed a clause on the grievances of America in the Middlesex petition presented by Wilkes's constituency, and he published a series of articles on colonial affairs under the signature "Junius Americanus" that won him some recognition in the colonies[16].

It is clear that Arthur Lee was both a zealous American patriot and a very ambitious young man who wanted an important role in the movement for imperial reform. Perceiving the colonial agencies as one means of fulfilling that role, he worked to secure both the Virginia and Massachusetts appointments. In successive letters to his brother Richard Henry Lee he suggested that had he been Agent for Virginia in 1768 he "could have made the cause of America the cause of Middlesex [Wilkes's constituency]," that the present agents were "unknown here, of no abilities, no rank, or if any, of a bad character; some of them menials, all of them servile expectants," and that Richard Henry Lee should work to procure the post for him[17]. The faction of the Lees and Patrick Henry in the Virginia House of Burgesses supported Arthur Lee for the agency, but there was a three-way split in the House over Lee, Edward Montague, and Thomas Adams, and no decision was possible[18].

Lee's name was also put forth in connection with the vacancy left in the Massachusetts agency with the death of Dennys DeBerdt in 1770, thereby becoming entwined in a long-standing factional controversy in the Massachusetts House. The Otis-Adams radical faction there had persistently disagreed with the conservative Hutchinson group about the characteristics most desirable in an agent. While both factions understood the value of a merchant with connections in the British mercantile and official community, the conservatives who were usually allied with the colonial administration preferred an individual who would be conciliatory, politic, and circumspect in his behavior. The radicals generally supported types who could be expected to be more aggressive in defending the Assembly whenever it was in conflict with the Crown. Thus the radicals in 1762 secured the ouster of William Bollan, former Governor Shirley's son-in-law, for having cooperated with the chief justice in supplying the hated writs of assistance, permitting searches for contraband goods. They managed to appoint Joseph Mauduit, an elderly London draper and leading English Dissenter, in his place. Later on during the Stamp Act crisis there was a dispute over a replacement for the aged Mauduit, the Otis faction supporting the agent's son Israel, and the conservatives under the leadership of Thomas Hutchinson endorsing Hutchinson himself. A compromise candidate, Richard Jackson, the Agent for Connecticut and Pennsylvania and a friend of Governor Bernard, was appointed at this time. However, the radicals managed to name Dennys DeBerdt as Jackson's assistant, just as later they named Arthur Lee to assist Franklin. DeBerdt was a London merchant with American business connections who had opposed the Stamp Act. In a short time the House, through a committee dominated by James Otis, Samuel Adams, and Thomas Cushing, was dealing with DeBerdt, thereby bypassing Jackson, who was suspect for his connection with both Governor Bernard in Massachusetts and the Chancellor of the Exchequer, George Grenville, in England[19].

These partisan struggles between radicals and conservatives in Massachusetts carried important religious overtones. The Otis-Adams faction drew support from the Congregationalists, while the Hutchinson faction was tied up with the Anglican church. Neither of the radical candidates belonged to the Church of England, Mauduit being a noted Dissenter and DeBerdt a pronounced Flemish Huguenot. Bollan, on the other hand, was Anglican, and much of the criticism directed against him came from Congregationalists who were alarmed about the possibility that an episcopate would be established in the colonies. This juxtaposition of political and religious issues contributed greatly to the transformation of personal partisan politics to the politics of ideology which were to set the stage for revolution.

When DeBerdt died in 1770, the ensuing dispute in the Massachusetts House over the candidacies of Franklin and Lee for the post of agent was a muted extension of the same themes of aggression versus accommodation. Lee was personally unknown to the Massachusetts radicals, but his activities during the Wilkes controversy had attracted attention. He had been recommended, perhaps in preference to Franklin, by Joseph Reed, who had met Lee while visiting London in order to marry DeBerdt's daughter. On his return to Philadelphia, Reed stopped in Boston and there spoke to Adams about Lee[20]. Adams could not secure the agency for Lee, but he did manage to get Lee appointed Agent in case of Franklin's death or absence from London. (Lee in this capacity took over the Massachusetts agency when Franklin later returned to Philadelphia to attend the Continental Congress.) The product of all this maneuvering, then, was the beginning of the Adams-Lee radical alliance. The faction shortly grew larger with the inclusion of Richard Henry Lee and his supporters in Virginia.

Even after the Wilkes controversy died down, Samuel Adams kept up the connection with the Lees by steady correspondence and possibly through personal links such as Henry Marchant, who was entertained by Adams in Boston before he left America and was introduced by Lee to Wilkes and other English radicals after arriving in Britain. Both Lee's rivalry with Franklin and his friendship with Adams were reinforced during the early 1770s as Adams privately consulted Lee about British policy and Franklin's advice to Massachusetts. By 1771 it was rumored that the Secretary of State, the

Earl of Hillsborough, and the Ministry planned to put the Massachusetts Governor and judges on permanent salary, thus limiting the money-granting prerogatives of the House. Even worse, the Ministry wanted to break the sacred Charter of Massachusetts and deny the House its privilege of naming members of the province Council by having Council members appointed by the Crown. When Franklin suggested that Massachusetts need not worry about the rumors, Samuel Adams asked Lee what he thought of Franklin's advice. Lee, writing with a pen Peter Oliver described as "dipped in the Gall of Asps," replied, "This is just what I expected of him; and if it be true, the Dr. is not the dupe but the instrument of Lord Hillsborough's treachery"[21]. Lee accused Franklin of trying to protect his own interests. As a man who had a profitable office at will (the Postmaster Generalship) and a son in a high post at pleasure (William Franklin was Governor of New Jersey), surely Franklin wanted to keep on good terms with the Ministry. Lee also argued that the main object in Franklin's being in London was to convert Pennsylvania from a proprietary to a royal colony[22].

Lee's charges against Franklin were part of his attempt to secure the Massachusetts agency. They were also an expression of his conviction that urbane, compromising, and self-interested agents like Franklin and Jackson (who had entered the Imperial Administration as solicitor to the Board of Trade) were at best inadequate and at worst traitors to the colonial cause. It should be emphasized also that Lee's distrusts, although they sometimes bordered on paranoia, paralleled the growing belief among colonial radicals that a conspiracy to enslave America was being hatched in the recesses of Whitehall. Lee's suspicions reflected widespread eighteenth-century attitudes toward office holders. Hutchinson and Bernard were vilified repeatedly in Massachusetts, and Franklin himself believed the British electorate was so corrupted by politicians that only American virtue could save the empire[23]. It is likely that Lee found a ready audience in the Adams faction for his criticisms of Franklin, for word was circulated in Massachusetts that Franklin was the tool of Hillsborough. Probably only Franklin's delivery of Hutchinson's compromising letters to the Massachusetts House in 1772 served to redeem him in colonial eyes.

Lee, unlike Franklin, wanted to organize opposition in the colonies to defeat the threatened change in the Massachusetts charter. He suggested that it would be good strategy if "America in general appeared to be alarmed at it." This effect might be achieved, contended Lee, by informing the leading members of the colonial assemblies about the proposed change, gaining their support for a general protest, while Lee would work up petitions against the measure in London as he had done in the past. Lee proposed to take the first steps by writing John Dickinson in Pennsylvania and his brother Richard Henry Lee in Virginia. "The rest of the colonies, if properly prepared will have an opportunity of joining you in the opposition." Samuel Adams took up Lee's idea of a general union on this matter, suggesting that societies similar to the Supporters of the Bill of Rights in England should be formed in all the colonies and that these societies should send delegates to annual interprovincial meetings and correspond with a similar society in London. Adams's proposal never materialized in this particular form, but his promotion of local com-mitees of correspondence in 1772 was an expression of this general idea at the regional level[24].

Arthur Lee's hopes that the Supporters of the Bill of Rights society could be expanded into a trans-Atlantic organization of protest and resistance foundered for a number of reasons. First, the erratic Wilkes could not serve as a congenial symbol for Americans. Further, there were changes in the Ministry that made the administration less receptive to radical pressures. Finally, the petition movement in England had begun to decline. It became harder for the colonials to assume that reform was possible once the King had been sepa-rated from the influence of degenerate and designing ministers[25].

Lee was slower than Adams to discard the technique of trans-Atlantic resistance, partly because of his location in London, but also doubtless be-cause of the greater influence he was able to wield. By 1773 and 1774 he had established some important contacts with political figures of the stature of Lords Dartmouth and Chatham, and in early 1774 he became the prime Agent for Massachusetts when Franklin was forced by the Ministry to resign the post after the disclosure of his responsibility for divulging the Hutchinson letters. As Lee's authority increased, his counsel to his radical American correspondents moderated. In February of 1773 he wrote to his brother Francis Lightfoot Lee that New England was "precipitating matters too much," for "My Lord Dartmouth will not consent to violent measures, & tho he will not diminish, he will hardly increase the causes of complaint"[26]. Lee drew up a remonstrate against the Boston Tea Party for Parliament—his position had come very close to Franklin's.

Unaccountably, soon after becoming Massachusetts Agent, Lee decided to take a tour of the European continent at precisely the moment that the Coercive Acts were being passed, excusing this European caper on the self-serving grounds that feelings were so high at Whitehall that he could effect nothing until tempers subsided. It was Franklin who voluteered to remain in London to do what he could for Massachusetts in a private capacity while Parliament was in session and Lee was absent[27]. But Lee did have some advice for the colonials: to hold a congress and agree immediately upon the radical devices of nonimportation and, more punishing from the colonial point of view, nonexportation, for a period of one year. Perhaps it was not so much that Lee was slipping from the radical ranks as that he was functioning in what had clearly become the periphery of the resistance movement. Interprovincial organization quickly accelerated during 1773 and 1774 as committees of correspondence were begun and the network of private radical contacts was extended. The radical movement had begun with trans-Atlantic connections, but by the time of the Boston Tea Party, it no longer depended upon the London axis.

III

Historians often have assumed that the committees of correspondence set up to exchange information among various colonies on British infringements of colonial rights were the most formidable and indeed the most revolutionary instruments created during the resistance. If this assumption is correct, then the committees should have produced the nucleus of a continental radical faction. Yet while the committees helped establish certain valuable new contacts between radicals in New England, particularly between the Bostonians and the leadership in Connecticut, there were many factors that inhibited the new bodies in developing intersectional radical alliances. In the Middle colonies, for example, the committees often were controlled by moderates and conservatives. The chairman of the Pennsylvania committee, one of the last to be established, was Joseph Galloway, and he regularly tempered its communications. The New York committee, or the Committee of Fifty-one, was really a tool of the moderate faction of New York politics which, by seizing control of the machinery of resistance, attempted to stifle its revolutionary potential. At least nineteen of the fifty-one members later became Loyalists, and those who ended as Patriots were invariably moderates. The actions of the New York committee even found favor with Lieutenant-Governor Cadwallader Colden, who applauded the "cool tempers" of its members as well as their desire to avoid "all extravagant and dangerous measures"[28]. It is hardly surprising that the Boston committee was dissatisfied with the Committee of Fifty-one for its inaction and lack of patriotism. New York's committee seemed particularly lethargic during a season of high crisis in the summer of 1774, when there was vigorous action in New England and many parts of the South[29]. Yet even in the more radical regions the mere existence of the committees was no guarantee that continuous contacts among the members would be maintained. Massachusetts itself was no exception, for it took fully four months during the calm summer of 1773 to produce a circular letter from a subcommittee including Samuel Adams and John Hancock.

In those colonies where provincial committes were composed mostly of members of the assemblies and where their effectivess was therefore largely limited to the duration of the assembly session, activity was even less noticeable than usual during the period before the Tea Act furor. The Virginia committee could function only when the Assembly was in session, and the House of Burgesses sought to avoid this inconvenience by appointing a Select Committee of three who lived near Williamsburg to carry on most of the correspondence. The Select Committee consisted of Peyton Randolph, Robert Carter Nicholas, and Dudley Digges, all of whom were conservative or moderate. The radicals Richard Henry Lee, Patrick Henry, and Thomas Jefferson, who had sponsored the creation of the committee in the first instance, were named to a larger committee, but no one expected them to have as much influence as the conservatives on the Select Committee. Thus entirely fortuitous geographic factors inhibited the effectiveness of the committee of correspondence as a revolutionary mechanism in Virginia[30].

The outline of what was to become the radical congressional faction was indeed taking shape during the early 1770s. But its form was still rather indefinite—a fairly limited and increasingly conspiratorial network of correspondents reaching from New England to South Carolina, active not only in the committees of correspondence but also in town meetings and provincial legislatures and in the press. Contacts within this network were sometimes open, through legislative circular letters and official committee communications, but often they were private and thereby better adapted to bypass divisions in both the assemblies and the committees.

The Boston radicals may not have relied solely on letters and committees. Josiah Quincy, Jr., made a swing through the colonies from South Carolina back to Massachusetts in 1773, and he proposed the idea of a "continental correspondence" in both South and North Carolina to such people as Thomas Lynch, Miles Brewton, William Howe, and Cornelius Harnett[31]. Quincy could have been sent out on a clandestine errand to establish political rapport between Massachusetts and the deeper South. That South Carolina was the first colony to create a provincial committee of correspondence after Virginia may have been related to Quincy's soundings. Further, the Massachusetts–South Carolina contact was reinforced shortly after Quincy's trip by a journey to Boston undertaken by Thomas Lynch in the summer of 1773[32].

This faction, or "proto-faction," sometimes worked around as well as within the overt resistance organization. Richard Henry Lee provides an excellent example of the intricacy of resistance in his attempts to inform the Virginia Burgesses of the expected British retaliation for the Boston Tea Party. Lee was well informed about the crisis from beginning to end. Arthur Lee had written him about the impending Tea Act in February of 1773. At about the same time he had started a correspondence with Samuel Adams, a month before Virginia formed its official committee of correspondence, and from then on there was steady communication between the two radicals. Both Arthur and William Lee sent warnings from London of the impending Coercive Acts, coupled with urgent appeals that a general congress be held and that a system of nonimportation and nonexportation should be put into effect for one year. William Lee, in a letter either to Richard Henry Lee or Francis Lightfoot Lee (probably the latter), further advised that the staple-producing colonies should make no payments to London merchants[33]. Before going to the Assembly session in June 1774, Richard Henry Lee rushed a letter to Adams asking for any news Adams might have from Britain. He suggested as well that it would be "highly conducive to the general good" if the Boston committee of correspondence should write a public letter to the Virginia committee with information about any British movements in Boston. He was "led to suppose that something material may happen, in consequence of the well-deserved fate which befell the Tea in your quarter. . . ." He stressed that the letter should arrive while the Burgesses were sitting, a suggestion that had obvious utility. (He might also have been calculating that the general committee would be more receptive than the more conservative Select Committee of Correspondence[34].) A circular letter from Massachusetts arrived on May 30 containing recommendations by the Boston town meeting that the tea not be paid for and that a nonimportation and nonconsumption agreement, or "Solemn League and Covenant" in the Puritan terminology of the Boston radicals, be subscribed to by all the colonies. Lee prepared resolutions designed to achieve a boycott, but he was unsuccessful in promoting them in June because of opposition from the Burgesses' leadership who wanted to complete the regular business first. Virginia did not act as a colony until August, when an irregular convention of Burgesses approved nonimportation and elected delegates to the first Continental Congress[35]. Other colonies, notably Maryland, were more prompt in responding to the appeal from Boston.

The circular letter from Boston had earlier gone to Philadelphia on May 19 with Paul Revere, who was already functioning as a Revolutionary courier. Revere, moreover, took not only the formal circular letter but also private correspondence from Adams, Hancock, and Cushing to Reed and Mifflin, urging them to rally Philadelphia to the Boston plan[36]. Reed had known Adams as early as 1700, and he had been instrumental in obtaining Adams's support for Arthur Lee as Massachusetts Agent. Mifflin had met both Samuel and John Adams in Boston during the summer of 1773; possibly he came to an agreement with the Boston radicals then concerning resistance to the landing of the tea shipments and approved of the Boston Tea Party. Reed and Mifflin, along with Charles Thomson (also a private correspondent of Samuel Adams), followed advice from Boston to call a public meeting at City Tavern the very next evening. But John Dickinson prevented the radicals from putting nonintercourse into effect; unfortunately for the radicals Dickinson's prestige was necessary to give weight to the City Tavern assembly, but his moderation deflected the radicals' full intent[37]. Samuel Adams was also busy writing letters to South Carolina, pressing his own scheme of non-importation upon Christopher Gadsden, who with Peter Timothy, the publisher of the *South Carolina Gazette*, had been an Adams contact for some time in that colony[*38*].

Certainly it would be wrong to see some underlying radical master plan in the resistance movement leading to the Continental Congress. The South supported the resistance movement mainly for its own reasons, not because it was being manipulated by a national revolutionary elite. Virginia delayed responding to the circular letter from Massachusetts despite the efforts of Lee, while Maryland, on the other hand, developed strong support for Boston during the critical May–June days of 1774. A Maryland convention found common cause with Massachusetts on the Boston Port Act, and they agreed on the necessity of adopting stringent nonintercourse as the colonial response. Yet this position, which was more advanced than the radicals could manage in either Pennsylvania or Virginia, was taken by men of a moderate stamp who had had no discoverable relationship with what might be called the faction of national radical resistance. The leadership in the crucial areas of Annapolis and Charles County, as seen in the delegations chosen by those areas to the provincial convention held at Annapolis, was composed of Charles Carroll, Thomas Johnson, Jr., William Paca, Samuel Chase, Walter Hanson, Thomas Stone, Daniel Jenifer, and James Forbes—almost all moderates in terms of their behavior at the first and second Continental Congresses[*39*]. The Annapolis meeting's forceful response to the news of the Port Act on May 26 set the strong tone emulated in many other public meetings in Maryland. Annapolis decided to support nonintercourse enforced by an association with other counties bound by oath: "Ye emphatical sentence of ye Roman people against State criminals will not (only) be pronounced, but literally executed: *aqua et igne interdicatur*," as Charles Carroll described it[*40*].

In spite of the Annapolis meeting's radical rhetoric, it is not likely that the Marylanders were acting at Samuel Adams's instigation. Adams had few contacts in Maryland, and both Carroll and Chase opposed the radicals from other colonies on important issues at the first Continental Congress[*41*]. The Maryland Assembly members took a radical position in 1774 as part of their struggle with the Governor over the fixing of legal fees by administrative proclamation—Carroll, Johnson, Paca, and Chase were all involved in this dispute. Economic factors, particularly the indebtedness of tobacco planters in both of the Chesapeake colonies, also were important in the development of support for a boycott.

The rudiments of an intercolonial radical organization existed by 1774, but it was not yet in substantial command of the resistance movement, or movements, in the colonies. Actually, a number of well-known radical leaders were completely out of touch with one another, and they were not yet connected with the radical protofaction. John Adams, the Warrens, Hawley, Cooper, and Molineaux of Massachusetts had no discernible contact with Jefferson and Henry of Virginia, nor did any of these individuals know radicals from South Carolina. The New York radicals Alexander MacDougall, Isaac Sears, and John Morin Scott were primarily provincial in their attitudes and scope of action. It is at least incongruous that in Pennsylvania the cautious and moderate John Dickinson should have been approached by the most advanced radicals well into the 1770s. Arthur Lee automatically thought of him in 1771 as a good man to stir up resistance in Pennsylvania to the proposed change in the mode of electing the Massachusetts Council, and Samuel Adams two years later urged Dickinson to get back into print[42]—an appeal that demonstrates Adams's misunderstanding of Pennsylvania politics as much as his awareness of Dickinson's facility with the pen. In Reed, Mifflin, and Thomson the Boston radicals found true fellow spirits, but they were mistaken in pursuing George Clymer, the Philadelphia merchant who visited Sam Adams in Boston in the summers of 1773 and 1774 and who entertained Josiah Quincy, Jr., during his stay in Philadelphia. Clymer, despite his assertion that he had "ever been the advocate for the political conduct of the people of Boston," was not a radical of the Adams stamp in the summer of 1774, when he seemed to favor leaving control over colonial trade to Great Britain, and he was apparently not inclined to push for nonintercourse against the collective judgment of his merchant peers in Philadelphia[43]. Including Clymer in the intercolonial web of radical communication was especially futile when the Boston leaders neglected Pennsylvania's truly advanced radicals George Bryan, Joseph Fook, and Christopher Marshall.

Altogether, the limitations of the radical organization suggest that the resistance during the decade before the first Continental Congress was largely a federal phenomenon, a series of disconnected provincial grievances aggravated by a succession of British blunders. Yet it is important to note that while the radicals never completely controlled a formal resistance mechanism such as the committees of correspondence, they did establish a widely flung network which, when fused in the first Continental Congress, was in a position to command general resistance policy.

IV

The moderates and Tories failed to put together a unified opposition to the radicals at the outset; if they had done so, ironically, they might have stimulated their adversaries into creating a wider and more revolutionary organization. Actually, radicals were challenged only ineffectively within the separate colonies, and virtually not at all on an interprovincial basis. Indeed, a study of intercolonial factional organization during the decade before the first Congress can almost disregard both moderates and Tories.

Moderates like Dickinson were often active propagandists, and they sometimes got involved in organized interprovincial actions such as the Stamp Act Congress and the merchant associations. In no instance did they organize a sustained, intercolonial influence to challenge the radicals. This was due in part to the ambivalence of the moderate position: the moderates at once disapproved of radical tactics and supported radical grievances.

Tories, particularly during the earlier stages of resistance, experienced a similar dilemma, for they, too, generally opposed the Stamp Act and the Townshend duties. But the Tories, even after they had recognized the radical intent for what it was, seemed unable to offer effective opposition. Tory leadership, elitist and inbred like the Hutchinson-Oliver clique in Massachusetts, was incapable of establishing rapport with the population either through the press or through patronage. Instinctively conservative, and relying too much on Great Britain, they were disinclined or unable to offer constructive alternatives to the radical program. Joseph Galloway's plan of colonial union was a remarkable exception to the rule of Tory negativism, but Galloway's tactics, or lack of them, doomed the plan. He did not discuss the scheme even with William Smith, his counterpart in New York who later proposed a similar plan. Indeed, as William Nelson has suggested, "that Smith was not a delegate to the Continental Congress, was not in communication with Galloway, and seems never to have realized how close he and Galloway were in their views, is further evidence of the curious dispersion of the opponents of the Revolution"[44].

Intercolonial union under conservative auspices was the most promising constructive strategy available to the Tories, and their best opportunity for resisting the radicals lay in exploiting sectional antagonisms—a grave weakness of the Revolutionary front that was to persist throughout the war. It seems astonishing that the Tories did not seriously attempt to exploit the Southern and Middle colonies' distrust of New England radicalism—an uneasiness expressed in the coolness Josiah Quincy, Jr., encountered on his tour of the colonies in 1774. Boston's reputation for violence disturbed moderates and Tories alike; New England's leveling tendencies alarmed men of substance everywhere, just as her aggressive "Presbyterianism" (or Congregationalism) bothered many Anglicans, Quakers, and Baptists of all classes to the south. That Tories did occasionally play upon such sectional fears in the press makes the question even more relevant. In 1768, for example, a Tory writing under the pseudonym "An Englishman" warned Pennsylvanians and Southerners not to follow the rash course of nonimportation taken by Boston and New York. Should they do this, they would be throwing themselves into the arms of fanatics who intended to establish rule with the sword:

> Separate yourselves, then, ye men of prudence, ye wise considerate reasoners, from these boisterious and violent tempers—These heady and high-minded men, who formerly turned religion into rebellion, and faith into faction, and had, *in the name of God*, well nigh effected the utter ruin of our church and constitution[45].

Like many Tories, "An Englishman" saw the radicals as a "Presbyterian Party" "already numerous, headstrong violent and arbitrary," claiming to be "the unerring oracle of North America." The best method of countering the onslaught of these "Furious zealots" would be to organize a coalition of all other Christians and to establish a bishop or bishops. Such leadership would at once reinforce the anti-Presbyterian alliance and divert the attention of the "Puritans" who would otherwise be "more dangerously employed . . . in sowing dissensions, raising commotions, and disturbing the peace of the state. . . ." Whether this strategy was primarily political or religious is problematical. It does disclose, however, the common Tory perception of the resistance as a resurgence of Commonwealth philosophy and tactics led by New England puritans. Unfortunately for the Tories, an American episcopal establishment— the logical instrument of an anti-Presbyterian front—was anathema to most Anglicans as well as to the Puritans.

Of course, the Tories were at a great disadvantage in that their strategy was so dependent upon British policy. If New England was to be isolated and Great Britain's relationship with the Southern colonies made closer, the Crown should at least have eased off in the controversies over assembly prerogatives in South Carolina. The proposals for an American episcopate should also have been put to rest, and Boston should not have been given the opportunity to appeal for assistance against tyranny and privation. By 1774, when the Coercive Acts were passed, British ineptitude and Tory dependence on the mother country merged, with fatal results for the empire.

Middle colonies moderates such as Dickinson in Pennsylvania and John Jay and James Duane in New York were also very much compromised during the spring of 1774, but they did display some ingenuity in shunting aside what they (and indeed many radicals) understood to be the main current of radicalism. The Boston committee of correspondence sent out a general request in its circular letter for immediate cessation of trade with Britain and the British West Indies. Dickinson, Robert Morris, Thomas Fitzsimmons, and many other moderates in Pennsylvania joined Mifflin, Thomson, and Reed in forming an extralegal committee of forty-four members to consider the request. In New York the Sons of Liberty had been transformed by 1774 into the Committee of Fifty-one dominated by moderates joined by some Tories. Thus the opponents of radical resistance were well positioned in both colonies to frustrate the design of Sam Adams and the Boston radicals. This they did by rejecting the boycott and proposing instead a general congress to discuss the threat to colonial rights. By suggesting a meeting, they appeased the popular demand for action and also gave themselves the time and occasion to concoct a more temperate response to the British measures. Even the Tory Anglican minister Thomas Bradbury Chandler of New Jersey recalled that the Congress at first "raised our curiosity, but excited no terror." The results of the Congress, on the other hand, prompted Chandler to characterize it as "a mad, blind monster"[46].

It is one of the major ironies of the Revolution that the first Continental Congress, embraced by Middle colony moderates as a safe half-way house and accepted begrudgingly by the Boston radicals as a wispy substitute for the immediate enactment of their boycott, the Solemn League and Covenant, should have produced in the Continental Association precisely what the moderates hoped to avert and more than what the radicals expected to achieve. The ironic turn of events documents both the limitations of the moderates, who paid little attention to the construction of an intercolonial faction, and the persisting parochialism of the radicals, who, understandably perhaps, failed to realize how effective their preparations had been. It would seem that each had seized the other's weapon.

The explanation is fairly obvious. The moderate and conservative forces assumed (partly as an article of faith and partly as a result of their experience with the Stamp Act Congress) that an intercolonial assembly, composed in all likelihood of distinguished men, could be relied upon to recommend measured action. The radicals—particularly the Bostonians who felt most intensely the heavy hand of the new coercive British policy—distrusted a congress which would presumably do little more than dispatch additional petitions for the wastebasket at Whitehall. They swung almost by reflex action in the direction of the boycott as a means of supplying rapid pressure to relieve their suffering city. Samuel Adams was not averse to a congress—indeed, he believed that it was an "absolute necessity"—but he feared that "from the length of time it will take to bring it to pass it cannot answer for the present Emergency"[47]. Richard Henry Lee's communication in late June relating that the Burgesses had not acted on a boycott nor elected members to the Congress seemed to confirm Adam's fears. In actuality, even as Adams wrote at the end of May, sentiment was germinating throughout the South for strong economic counter-measures in support of Boston.

Clearly, the framers of the Solemn League wanted more than relief for Boston. They hoped to transform the boycott into a weapon of resistance that would be more effective than the previous nonimportation movements. The very name "Solemn League and Covenant" recalled the broadening of Puritan resistance to Charles I in 1643 during the initial stage of the English Civil War. Samuel Adams distrusted a boycott controlled by merchants for "the Trade will forever be divided when a Sacrifice of their Interest is called for." He preferred to "let the yeomanry (whose Virtue must finally save this Country) resolve to desert those altogether who will not come into the Measure"[48].

The idea of broad popular participation in a boycott, with the deprivation this would entail in the colonies, was oddly attractive in the South as well as in Congregational New England. Debt-ridden planters in the Chesapeake, resentful of their subservience to English and Scottish merchants, found common cause with the yeomanry in supporting nonimportation and nonconsumption as a means of reducing their dependence. Improvement of their economic position might be achieved not only by exporting without importing for one year but also through the encouragement of crop diversification and manufacturing. The Williamsburg Convention advocated just such a course in the resolutions it framed in August of 1774[49]. The reforming, regenerative element of the Solemn League, so congenial to the puritanical Samuel Adams, was not absent in the South. Samuel Purviance, a Baltimore merchant and long-standing correspondent of Adams, confessed in 1775 that if British oppression were ended too speedily, it would "only subject us to being divided, & render us an easier Prey to Luxury and Venality; Enemies that appear to me more formidible than Brittish Ministers"[50].

Yet although the Solemn League as recommended by the Boston committee represented a step beyond the old nonimportation associations, it would have been a weak structure dependent upon the willingness of the various provinces to subscribe to its terms and objectives. It is highly likely that the radicals' boycott would have had less uniform application than the Continental Association, voted by the Continental Congress, actually accomplished. There surely would have been resistance to it in the Middle colonies, with the result that the Patriot cause might have been fragmented at the outset of the Revolution.

Thus, the creation of the Continental Congress, the moderates' stratagem to avoid excessive economic countermeasures, provided the organization that carried out the American Revolution. The dozen years before the Declaration of Independence saw the radicals trying numerous means to bring together opposition to British measures in the colonies. Given the difficulties that thirteen locally oriented resistance movements provided, none of the various mechanisms used to organize and channel resistance was entirely successful. The Stamp Act Congress, the activities of colonials in London, and even the committees of correspondence failed to really unite the colonial resistance movements. But the activity of the radicals had hardly been futile. Whereas moderates and conservatives were in a kind of complacent disarray, the radicals assembled in Philadelphia with the habit of communication and with agressive intentions. The ultimate product of their labors would be American independence.

Notes

1 John Adams to John Winthrop, June 2 3, 1776, in Charles F. Adams (ed.), *The Works of John Adams* (10 vols.; Boston, 1850–1856), IX, 409. (Henceforth cited as Adams, *Works.*)

2 I do not intend at this point to use the terms "radical" and "conservative" in the sociopolitical sense that Merrill Jensen does, for example, in his *Articles of Confederation* (Madison, 1940, 3rd printing, 1959), p. 57n.

3 Cited in R. D. Meade, *Patrick Henry, Patriot in the Making* (Philadelphia, 1957), p. 209.

4 *Journal of the House of Representatives . . . of Massachusetts Bay* (Boston, 1765, 1766), p. 215. The vote was 81–5. See L. H. Butterfield (ed.), *Diary and Autobiography of John Adams* (Cambridge, Mass., 1962), 1, 264–265.

5 *Journal of the House of Burgesses* (Williamsburg, 1765), Dec. 18, 1764, pp. 90–91.

6 Richard Bland, *Inquiry into the Rights of the British Colonies* (Williamsburg, 1766). See especially pp. 26–27 for an example of Bland's circumlocution.

7 Roger Champagne, "Family Politics versus Constitutional Principles: The New York Assembly Elections of 1768 and 1769," *WMQ,* ser. 3, XX (1963), 57–59. See also Patricia Bonomi, *A Factious People; Politics and Society in Colonial New York* (New York, 1971), chap. VII and passim.

8 See William S. Hanna, *Benjamin Franklin and Pennsylvania Politics* (Stanford, 1964), chap. 11, esp. pp. 170–171.

9 Samuel Adams to Peter Timothy, Nov. 2 1, 1770, in Harry A. Cushing (ed.), *The Writings of Samuel Adams* (4 vols.; New York, 1904-1908), II, 64.

10 See Pauline Maier, *From Resistance to Revolution; Colonial Radicals and the Development of American Opposition to Britain. 1765-1776* (New York, 1972), for an excellent analysis of the growth of an intercolonial consensus of this sort.

11 Sketches of the Lees and Sayre can be found in Francis Warton (ed.), *The Revolutionary Diplomatic Correspondence of the United States* (6 vols.; Washington, D.C., 1889), I. Dyer, who was in London during 1763 and 1764, warned that Britain was determined to send troops "under pretence for our Defence; but rather as a rod and Check over us," quoted in George Croce, Jr., "Eliphalet Dyer: Connecticut Revolutionist," in Richard Morris (ed.), *Era of the American Revolution* (New York, 1939), pp. 293–294. It might be added that Dyer, like Franklin, did not perceive the full measure of colonial resentment over the acts of 1764 and 1765. On Marchant's stay in England see David Lovejoy, "Henry Marchant and the Mistress of the World," *WMQ*, ser. 3, XII (1955), 383; for Franklin's role during the 1760s see Hanna, *Benjamin Franklin and Pennsylvania Politics,* chap. 11, and Jack M. Sosin, *Agents and Merchants; British Colonial Policy and the Origins of the American Revolution* (Lincoln, Nebr., 1965), passim, esp. chaps. 5 and 6. William B. Reed, *Life and Correspondence of Joseph Reed* (2 vols.; Philadelphia, 1847), I, covers this stage of Reed's career and includes some of the Dartmouth correspondence; Johnson advised against noisy overt opposition to the acts: William Samuel Johnson to William Pitkin, Dec. 26, 1767, "The Trumbull Papers," Massachusetts Historical Society *Collections* (4 vols.; Boston, 1885-1902), ser. 5, IX, 249; Drayton published a letter under the title "R M to Speaker of South Carolina Commons" in the London *Lloyd's Evening Post,* Mar. 19-21, and the London *Publick Advertiser,* Mar. 20, 1770, as well as other newspapers. See Jack Greene, "Bridge to Revolution: The Wilkes Fund Controversy in South Carolina," *JSH,* XXIX (1963), 19-52.

12 Greene, "Bridge to Revolution"; Pauline Maier, "John Wilkes and American Disillusionment with Britain," *WMQ,* ser. 3, XX (1963), 373-395; Arthur M. Schlesinger, *Prelude to Independence; The Newspaper War on Britain, 1764-1776* (New York, Vintage ed., 1965), pp. 35-37.

13 Committee of the Sons of Liberty in the Town of Boston to John Wilkes, June 6, 1768; Wilkes to the Committee of the Sons of Liberty in Boston, July 19, 1768, British Museum, *Add MSS,* no. 30870. This correspondence has been published in Worthington C. Ford (ed.), "John Wilkes and Boston," Massachusetts Historical Society *Proceedings,* (Boston, 1914), XLVII, 190-215. The Boston letter was signed by Benjamin Kent, Thomas Young, Benjamin Church, Jr., John Adams, and Joseph Warren.

14 The names of colonials prominently involved in support for Wilkes would constitute an enormous list. In Massachusetts Thomas Young, Benjamin Church, Jr., John Adams, Samuel Adams, Joseph Warren, Richard Dana, and Josiah Quincy, Jr., all signed letters to Wilkes. In South Carolina Christopher Gadsden was the leader of a group of Charleston mechanics organized in the "Wilkes Club," and Gadsden, Thomas Lynch, James Parsons, John Rutledge, Thomas Ferguson, Benjamin Dart, and Peter Manigault formed a committee of the South Carolina Commons House of Assembly that directed money to the Supporters of the Bill of Rights in London, a group organized to defend Wilkes in which Arthur Lee was closely involved. (Greene, "Bridge to Revolution," pp. 23-24.)

15 See Franklin to John Ross, May 14, 1768, in Albert H. Smyth (ed.), *The Writings of Benjamin Franklin* (10 vols.; New York, 1905-1907), V, 133; Benjamin Franklin, "On the Laboring Poor," *Gentleman's Magazine,* April 1768; Franklin to William Franklin, Apr. 16, 1768, in Smyth (ed.), *Writings,* V, 121-122.

16 Arthur Lee, "Memoir," in R. H. Lee, *Arthur Lee* (2 vols.; Boston, 1829), I, 245-246; ibid., 22.

17 Arthur Lee to Richard Henry Lee, Aug. 15 and Sept. 18, 1769, in ibid., 192, 194.

18 Virginia was without an agent after 1770. Jack Sosin, *Agents and Merchants,* pp. 142-143.

19 Ibid., pp. 69–74. For a strong statement regarding the existence and continuity of political parties in pre-Revolutionary Massachusetts, see Stephen E. Patterson, *Political Parties in Revolutionary Massachusetts* (Madison, Wis., 1973).

20 Arthur Lee to Joseph Reed, Jan. 18, 1771, in William B. Reed, *Life and Correspondence of Joseph Reed,* I, 43.

21 Peter Oliver, *Origin and Progress of the American Revolution,* Douglas Adair and John A. Schutz, eds., (San Marino, Calif., 1963), p. 78; Arthur Lee to Samuel Adams, June 10, 1771, in R. H. Lee, *Arthur Lee,* I, 216–217.

22 Ibid. Lee's charges must have been aired in a veiled manner, for Samuel Cooper wrote to Franklin two months later that Cushing had shown him an anonymous letter "directed to him as from London in·a feigned hand, representing you as a tool of Lord H." Samuel Cooper to Franklin, Aug. 23, 1771, in Smyth (ed.), *Writings,* V, 357.

23 See Bernard Bailyn, *Ideological Origins of the American Revolution* (Cambridge, Mass., 1967), chap. IV.

24 Arthur Lee to Samuel Adams, June 10, 1771, in R. H. Lee, *Arthur Lee,* I, 216; Adams to Lee, Sept. 27, 1771, in Cushing (ed.), *Writings,* II, 234.

25 American uneasiness over Wilkes's personal character can be seen in the decision of the South Carolina Assembly to direct its fund of £1,500 to the Bill of Rights society rather than to Wilkes personally, an act that irritated Wilkes. On changes in the Ministry see Bernard Donoughue, *British Politics and the American Revolution* (London, 1964), p. 16. The American response to the failure of the Wilkes movement is interpreted by Pauline Maier, "Wilkes and American Disillusionment," as a major turning point in the road toward revolution.

26 Arthur Lee to Francis Lightfoot Lee, Feb. 24, 1773, Arthur Lee Papers, HCL. Lee, incidentally, rationalized his temperate advice in the same terms that Franklin had used —delay in the final settlement of colonial rights would work to America's advantage, for as she grew in strength, Britain steadily declined.

27 Arthur Lee to Francis Lightfoot Lee, Apr. 2, 1774, ibid.; R. H. Lee, *Arthur Lee,* I, 37; Benjamin Franklin to Thomas Cushing, Apr. 16 and June 1, 1774, in Smyth (ed.), *Writings,* VI, 229, 232. It might be added that Franklin's voluntary duty did result in a request for £200 spent "on the Province Acct. in various ways."

28 Edward D. Collins, "Committees of Correspondence of the American Revolution," American Historical Association, *Annual Report for 1901* (Washington, D.C., 1902), I, 250–258. H. B. Dawson, *Westchester County, New York, during the American Revolution* (New York, 1886), p. 11, asserts that twenty-one of the Committee became Loyalists, a figure set forth by Alexander C. Flick, *Loyalism in New York during the American Revolution* (New York, 1901), p. 22n. Becker notes that Flick included James Duane in the list of Loyalists, which was obviously wrong, and in his own count is able to find only nineteen. Cadwallader Colden to Earl of Dartmouth, July 6, 1774, in Peter Force (ed.), *American Archives* (ser. 4, 6 vols., ser. 5, 3 vols; Washington, D.C. 1837–1853), ser. 4, I, 517. (Henceforth cited as *Amer. Arch.*)

29 See the New York reply to the Boston committee of correspondence, ibid., 323–

324. For an excellent account of the Massachusetts committees of correspondence see Richard D. Brown, *Revolutionary Politics in Massachusetts, The Boston Committee of Correspondence and the Towns, 1772-1774* (Cambridge, Mass., 1970).

30 David Mays, *Edmund Pendleton* (2 vols.; Cambridge, Mass., 1952), I, 268.

31 Josiah Quincy, Jr., "Journal," Massachusetts Historical Society *Proceedings*, vol. 49, 457-458, 460. Samuel A. Ashe, *History of North Carolina* (2 vols.; Greensboro, N.C., 1908), I, 410, contends that Quincy visited North Carolina to secure united support for the resistance policy of Massachusetts. See also *CRNC*, IX, 610.

32 Thomas Lynch to Josiah Quincy, Jr., June 15, 1773, in Josiah Quincy (ed.), *Memoirs of Josiah Quincy, Jr.* (Boston, 1874), p. 115.

33 Arthur Lee to Richard Henry Lee, Feb. 14, 1773; Richard Henry Lee to Samuel Adams, Feb. 4, 1773; A. Lee to R. H. Lee, Mar. 18, 1774; A. Lee to F. L. Lee [?], Apr. 2, 1774; Wm. Lee to F. L. Lee [?], Apr. 2, 1774; Arthur Lee Papers, HCL; James C. Ballagh, (ed.), *Letters of Richard Henry Lee* (2 vols.; New York, 1911-1914), I, 106-108. The presence of two Lee brothers in London was a virtual guarantee that the London branch of the radical network would function even when one was absent, as Arthur was in the early summer of 1774. Although Arthur's letters show him to have been more completely interested in politics than William, whose correspondence is often filled with the family business of the Lees, the latter was not deficient in his commitment to radical resistance, which he found compatible with the tobacco trade.

34 Richard Henry Lee to Samuel Adams, Apr. 24, 1774, ibid., 106-107. For Lee's participation in the formation of the Virginia committee of correspondence, see William Wirt Henry, *Patrick Henry; Life Correspondence and Speeches* (3 vols.; New York, 1891), I, 160, and Hamilton J. Eckenrode, *The Revolution in Virginia* (Boston, 1916), pp. 32-33.

35 Richard Henry Lee to Samuel Adams, in Ballagh (ed.), *Letters*, I, 111-112; *Virginia Gazette* (Purdie and Dixon), Aug. 11, 1774.

36 Reed, *Life of Reed*, I, 66.

37 Kenneth Rossman, *Thomas Mifflin and the Politics of the American Revolution* (Chapel Hill, 1952), pp. 13-14; Mifflin to Samuel Adams, Dec. 27, 1773, Samuel Adams Papers, NYPL; Benjamin Labaree, *The Boston Tea Party* (New York, 1964), pp. 230-231.

38 S. Adams to Christopher Gadsden and L. Clarkson, July 18, 1774, in Cushing (ed.), *Writings*, III, 144.

39 *Amer. Arch.*, ser. 4, I, 352-353, 409.

40 Charles Carroll to William Graves, Aug. 15, 1774, *Maryland Historical Magazine*, V, 322-324. The Annapolis resolves also included a moratorium on debts to England until the Port Act was repealed.

41 Charles Carroll to Charles Carroll, Senior, Sept. 9, 1774, ibid., XVI, 33; James Duane to Samuel Chase, Dec. 29, 1774, in Edmund C. Burnett (ed.), *Letters of Members*

of the Continental Congress (10 vols.; Washington, D.C., 1921–1936), I, 88 (Henceforth cited as *LMCC*.)

42 A. Lee to S. Adams, June 10, 1771, in R. H. Lee, *Arthur Lee,* I, 215; S. Adams to John Dickinson, Mar. 27, 1773, in William V. Wells, *The Life and Public Services of Samuel Adams* (3 vols.; Boston, 1865), II, 59-60.

43 George Clymer to Josiah Quincy, Jr., June 14, 1774, in Peter Force (ed.), *Amer. Arch.,* ser. 4, I, 406-407.

44 William H. Nelson, *The American Tory* (London, 1961), pp. 50-51.

45 *An Address to the Merchants, Freeholders, and all other Inhabitants of the Province of Pennsylvania in particular, and the Southern Colonies in general* (Philadelphia, 1768).

46 Roger Champagne, "New York and the Intolerable Acts, 1774," *The New York Historical Society Quarterly,* XLV (April, 1961), suggests that partisan politics rather than the calculations of resistance may have conditioned the New York reaction to the crisis of 1774 as had been true earlier during the time of the Townshend Acts. Political factions sought popular favor in requesting a congress and in tolerating extralegal elections of delegates to the Congress; Thomas Bradbury Chandler, *What Think Ye of the Congress Now?* (New York, 1775), p. 48.

47 Samuel Adams to Charles Thomson, May 30, 1774, in Cushing (ed.), *Writings,* III, 124.

48 Ibid., 123-124.

49 *Virginia Gazette* (Purdie and Dixon), Aug. 11, 1774.

50 Samuel Purviance to Samuel Adams, Sept. 26, 1775, Samuel Adams Papers, NYPL.

3 Congressional Factionalism and the Decision to Revolt: 1774-1776

THE Anglican Tory Thomas Bradbury Chandler, in recalling the origins of the first Continental Congress, remarked that opposition to the acts of Parliament was "taken out of the hands of the people, whose imprudence already had much injured the cause, and it was committed to the conduct of a few Gentlemen of distinction and character, in whose wisdom, integrity and honour the greatest confidence was reposed"[1]. Had Chandler's hopes for an accommodation been realized, the first Continental Congress might have gone down in history as the Coercive Acts Congress, or some similar name reminiscent of the Stamp Act Congress. Instead, the Congress set the stage for a colonial revolution.

But it is difficult to scan the list of delegates to the Congress, or to read their instructions, without agreeing with Chandler's initial expectation. Certainly most of the delegates could not have given immediate alarm to conservatives who wished to make of the Congress an antidote for the radical contagion that had festered in Massachusetts. The brace of Adamses was present, to be sure, but so were many men of wealth and distinguished political station such as Peyton Randolph and Joseph Galloway, speakers of the assemblies of Virginia and Pennsylvania. The instructions drawn up by the Pennsylvania Assembly for Galloway and his fellow delegates specified that they should "form and adopt a plan for the purposes of obtaining redress of American grievances, ascertaining American rights upon the most solid and constitutional principles, and for establishing that Union & harmony between Great-Britain and the Colonies, which is indispensably necessary to the welfare and happiness of both"[2]. The Pennsylvania Assembly actually went further toward accommodation than the instructions recorded in the printed journal which Chandler apparently used as the source of his assessment of the Congress. The Pennsylvanians were "strictly charged to avoid every Thing indecent, or disrespectful to the Mother State." (Charles Thomson, the Philadelphia radical who was elected secretary of the Congress, deleted this deferential portion of the instructions from his record of the proceedings[3].) The instructions to the Massachusetts delegates spoke of "the restoration of union & harmony," as did those of New Hampshire and Virginia. The Delaware instructions urged the adoption of "prudent and lawful measures," and those of South Carolina stressed "lawful measures"[4].

Joseph Galloway, the most eminent and creative of the advocates of accommodation, was reassured by his early conversations with the delegates as they filtered into Philadelphia. After talking with the aristocratic Rutledges of South Carolina, he concluded that while Edward, the younger brother, was "rather warm," the sentiments of John Rutledge were similar to his own: "He is a Gentlemen of an amiable Character, has look'd into the Arguments on both Sides more fully than any I have met with, and seems to be aware of all the Consequences which may attend rash and imprudent measures." He found Nathaniel Folsom of New Hampshire "cool and moderate," and was confident that while Folsom's fellow delegate John Sullivan was "rather more warm," New Hampshire would not heedlessly support the Bostonians to the disadvantage of the rest of the colonies[5].

Galloway appears to have set forth his own views as well as sensing the attitudes of others in his early conversations with the delegates. He recognized from the beginning that it would be very unlikely that the British government would recognize the Congress as a legal body because it had not been elected in all instances by regular colonial assemblies, and because it was unwarranted either by law or custom. He accordingly hinted to several members that it would be necessary to send commissioners "home" to England to help in the transmission of accurate information from both sides of the Atlantic, to explain that a "regular" Congress could not be elected because of the dissolution of some of the colonial assemblies, to plead for the allowance of future congresses elected by duly constituted colonial legislatures, and to assure that such congresses would be "respectful and dutiful to the Mother State." Galloway clearly was preparing the ground for the plan of union that he later proposed to Congress, and so far as he could determine, his "intimations" were approved by the delegates[6].

Galloway and other conservatively inclined delegates to the Congress were poorly prepared. It seems to have been an axiom with Galloway that if the protest against the Coercive Acts were managed by gentlemen elected by regularly composed assemblies, the resistance could be contained within the margins of moderation. In fact, however, the New York delegation, probably the most uniformly conservative group in Congress, was elected by a handful of citizens without a shadow of legal authority[7], while many of the leading radicals in the first Congress were men of elevated political and social station who had been elected by representative, if not always legally constituted, assemblies. The highly radical Richard Henry Lee belonged to the Virginia gentry, and he was elected by a "very full" convention at Williamsburg that included many members of the House of Burgesses [8]. Thomas Lynch and Christopher Gadsden gave crucial support to the radical cause, and they were endorsed by the Commons House of Assembly of South Carolina. The Massachusetts delegation was also elected by the provincial legislature. Of course, the radicals often had to work covertly within the established government. General Gage would have dissolved the Massachusetts General Court, meeting in Salem, had he known it was electing delegates to Congress. Thus the agenda for the day was drawn up secretly by a Committee of Nine on the State of the Province chaired by Samuel Adams. The committee proposed that delegates be sent and named the slate that was approved by the Assembly behind locked doors [9].

Where radicals were in a position of strength they were able to penetrate the regular offices of government, so that in much of the South and in New England representative institutions were working to the advantage of the radicals rather than the conciliationists. This doubtless helps to explain the shock experienced by conservatives when they discovered that Congress was being manipulated by radicals at the very outset of the proceedings. Galloway offered the Pennsylvania State House as a location for the congressional sessions, but before the delegates even inspected the premises they voted for Carpenter's Hall as a meeting place. It was not a decision of grave importance, but it was a straw in the wind. The State House had an aura of legitimacy that Carpenter's Hall, a private guild house associated with the radical Philadelphia mechanics, did not. Another early decision that distressed Galloway was the selection of Charles Thomson, "the Sam Adams of Philadelphia," as secretary for the Congress. Galloway had long distrusted Thomson, whom he thought not only radical but also "void of principle and virtue." Galloway was quickly forced to change his mind about the climate in Congress. "I cannot say but from this day's appearance of proceedings I have altered very much my last sentiments," he wrote to Governor William Temple Franklin of New Jersey, to whom he had sent such reassuring remarks just two days before. "The Virginians and Carolinians (Rutledge excepted) seem very much among the Bostonians. . . . Both of these measures, it seems, were privately settled by an Interest made out of Doors"[10]. Galloway was almost certainly correct. It was not a Bostonian, but Thomas Lynch of South Carolina who moved that Congress sit in Carpenter's Hall and that Thomson record its proceedings.

The motions were the first of a series of well-coordinated moves by the radical faction which had been maturing during the previous four years, and which was prepared to take command. Lynch had met Josiah Quincy, Jr., and had corresponded with Samuel Adams. The two Adamses conversed with Lynch and Gadsden on August 29, a week before Congress opened. The next day John Adams recorded in his diary: "Walked a little about town; visited the market, the State House, the Carpenters' Hall, *where the Congress is to sit,* etc." Later in the morning Thomas Mifflin, the only radical member of the Pennsylvania delegation, invited the Adamses to his house, where they had "much conversation" with Charles Thomson[11]. It is unfortunate that other members of Congress were not the compulsive diarist that John Adams was, but it is evident that the Bostonians had been warned not to appear violent and that they were aware that there were Southerners who would play a leading role in setting forth the radical program[12]. The radicals had been working longer than the conservatives. They were more accustomed to mapping strategy together; they found it easier to make immediate plans; and it is not surprising that they caught the more complacent conservatives off guard. Their work, far from pacifying the people, would in the words of Chandler "inflame their minds with resentment against their lawful superiors, and animate them to rebellion"[13].

II

The first Continental Congress met in Philadelphia for almost two months, from September 5 to October 26. The struggle between radicals and conservatives centered upon four major issues: (1) the definition of colonial rights and grievances; (2) the endorsement of the inflammatory Suffolk Resolves hurried down from Massachusetts; (3) the disposition of Galloway's proposal that a general constitutional settlement be formulated in order to achieve greater harmony between the colonies and the mother country; and (4) the acceptance of the original radical tactic of a nonimportation, nonconsumption, and non-exportation agreement.

Assessment of the struggle over these questions is not a simple matter. The records of the first Congress contain neither roll calls nor debates, and so it is necessary to rely upon scattered and often insufficient information in the diaries, correspondence, and recollections of delegates. Further, delegates brought such different perspectives of the imperial crisis to Congress that similar postures could reflect different motives. It is highly probable, for example, that Samuel Adams viewed the congressional boycott as defined in the Continental Association as a revolutionary instrument which would aid in the local organization of the Patriot force. It is not at all clear, however, that Samuel Chase, the delegate from Maryland who supported a strenuous policy of non-importation, nonconsumption, and nonexportation, was also intent upon increasing tension between England and the colonies. Chase was willing to allow England to control external trade for nonrevenue purposes, and he opposed the use of economic coercion to force England to yield that right. Chase's support of the Association should be interpreted in the context of Maryland's initial response to the news of the Coercive Acts—a response that involved the dispute over Governor Eden's fixing of legal fees by administrative edict and the decision of many Maryland county conventions to stop debt payments until the repeal of the Coercive Acts. It is difficult to say with certainty that Maryland's firm support for the Association was not cultivated more by the prospect of a moratorium on debts at a time of economic distress than by an aggressive opposition to imperial regulation.

An evaluation of the outcome of the struggle between radicals and conservatives is also obscured by actions of the Congress which seem either inconsistent or contradictory. The Congress rapidly endorsed the highly radical Suffolk Resolves, but it also produced a statement of rights and grievances which reads like a restrained footnote to the resolutions of the Stamp Act Congress. This policy statement, along with the addresses to the King, to the people of England, and to the inhabitants of North America, can be interpreted as a conservative victory or as a concession by the radicals that had no relevance in their eyes for the confrontation with the mother country. All things considered, however, the record of the first Congress clearly indicates that the radicals achieved a genuine triumph as a result of their superior preparation and organization.

The conservatives had anticipated that a congress held in Philadelphia, 300 miles from the tempest in Boston, would be able to deliberate in an atmosphere of relative calm that would help the effort to reach an accommodation with England. But the Massachusetts radicals contrived to transport the mood of crisis from Boston to Philadelphia. Couriers regularly brought the latest news of General Gage's moves and the countermeasures taken by Massachusetts committees and county conventions[*14*]. The first news from Boston was more a rumor than an accurate report, but it was extraordinarily alarming and served to alert the Congress to the potential of the crisis with which they were coping. Word arrived on Tuesday, the sixth of September, that Gage was using troops and the fleet to bombard Boston. In actuality, the British had simply seized the provincial powder store at Cambridge without bloodshed, but the false report reached the whole city of Philadelphia and created great alarm. Silas Deane wrote, "All is confusion . . . every tongue pronounces revenge.

The bells toll muffled, and the people run as in a case of extremity, they know not where nor why"[*15*].

The "powder alarm," as it was called, stirred the Anglican minister Jacob Duché to deliver an electrifying reading of the thirty-fifth psalm along with an extemporaneous prayer which "filled every bosom present," according to John Adams. Duché had been nominated as a kind of chaplain for the Congress by Samuel Adams, who was aware of the criticism that New Englanders were intolerant religious zealots. The effect of a moving prayer for the victims of Gage's "horrid butchery" delivered by an Anglican (who ultimately became a Loyalist) was all that Adams could have desired. Christopher Gadsden declared that he was ready to take up arms and head straight for Boston, and apparently he made a resolution to attack Gage before reinforcements could be brought in. Joseph Reed, another long-standing connection of Samuel Adams, congratulated Adams upon a "masterly stroke of policy" during an evening's conversation at his lodging[*16*].

Two committees were appointed to state the rights of the colonies, their grievances, and the mode of redress, and to report on British acts of trade that affected the colonies. The great majority of conservatives wanted a petition that would be deferential in style, moderate in its demands, and couched in the traditional guarantees of the British constitution. But within two days the committee considering the rights of the colonists had decided to follow the radical tack suggested by Richard Henry Lee, Roger Sherman, Eliphalet Dyer, and others that colonial rights should be derived not only from the British constitution and the colonial charters but also "upon the broadest bottom, the ground of nature"[*17*]. The final definition of the colonial rights and grievances and the address to the King was not agreed upon for another month, but the early decision to revert to natural rights represented a major step away from the conservative expectation that the Congress should serve to dampen radical resistance.

Shortly after the "powder alarm" had subsided, two sets of resolutions framed by radicals in the Massachusetts counties of Middlesex and Suffolk arrived by courier. The Middlesex Resolves arrived first on September 14, but it was the Suffolk Resolves, framed by an illegal meeting in Milton under the direction of Samuel Adams's cohort Joseph Warren and carried into Philadelphia on September 16 by Paul Revere, that best accomplished the radical design. This remarkable set of resolves carried resistance almost to revolution. The framers advocated both nonconsumption and nonimportation, directed not only against England but also against the West Indies. In addition to this basic radical objective the resolves stated that the Coercive Acts were "gross infractions of those rights to which we are justly entitled by the laws of nature, the British constitution, and the charter of the province" to which "no obedience is due." Judges appointed in a manner not stipulated by the charter of Massachusetts should be paid "no regard." Tax collectors, constables, and all other officers who had public moneys should make no payment to the provincial county treasurer "until the civil government of the province is placed upon a constitutional foundation," or until ordered by the proposed extralegal provincial congress. The Quebec Act, in addition to the Coercive Acts, was also "dangerous in an extreme degree to the Protestant religion and to the civil rights and liberties of all America. . . ." Patriots should arm themselves and drill at least once a week. If Patriot leaders were apprehended, as it was rumored, all Crown officials in the county and the province should be seized and kept in safe custody until the resistance leaders were released. The first resolution referred to George III as "the rightful successor to the throne of Great Britain" to whom only conditional allegiance was due, subject to the stipulations in the original covenant between the Crown and the first planters.

To the Pennsylvania delegates who had been instructed by a conservative Assembly under the influence of Galloway to avoid anything indecent or disrespectful to the mother country, the language of the intial passage of the resolves seemed extreme:

> Whereas the power but not the justice, the vengeance but not the wisdom of Great Britain, which of old persecuted, scourged, and exiled our fugitive parents from their native shores, now pursues us, their guiltless children, with unrelenting severity. . . .

In this passage power was hypostatized and constitutional argument transformed into ideology. The resolves contained repeated references to God, natural law, the past, the future, forefathers, posterity, the streams of time, and the abyss of eternity. Couched in this framework, the determination of the conventioners of Suffolk to take defensive action "so long as such conduct may be vindicated by reason and the principles of self-preservation, but no longer" gave an ominous cast to the resolves[18].

Congress endorsed the Suffolk Resolves unanimously, recommending "a perserverance in the same firm and temperate conduct as expressed in the resolutions determined upon . . ."[19]. It was a major radical triumph and has to be attributed to the cultivation of a sense of urgency in Congress. Paul Revere brought alarming accounts of British military preparations in Boston which apparently seemed to justify the extreme action of the Suffolk convention. Galloway stated that the congressional radicals had actually provided a mob to threaten recalcitrant delegates with tarring and feathering. This may have been an exaggeration, but it is clear that the city of Philadelphia did not afford the tranquility that conservatives had expected. The very presence of Congress made Philadelphia a part of the rapidly nationalizing resistance movement.

But the radicals could not press too hard. Nor could they sustain indefinitely the sense of exigency that had characterized the early proceedings. This was understood by the radicals, and by the conservatives as well. Both Adamses wrote home to Massachusetts suggesting that a defensive strategy would be most likely to achieve sustained support from the other colonies. Samuel Adams advised against the creation of a provincial congress, while John Adams related in some detail the fear of hostilities in the Middle colonies[20]. It was shrewd counsel, for the more imaginative conservatives such as Galloway and Duane realized that if the radicals blundered it might be possible to bend resistance toward conciliation.

In the committee considering colonial liberties, conservatives under the leadership of James Duane were arguing for reconciliation through home rule, a concept which would allow Parliament the right to control imperial concerns while granting jurisdiction over internal matters to the colonial assemblies. Galloway's plan of union, which gave institutional embodiment to this arrangement, carried conservative policy to its most constructive, and for the radicals its most menacing, conclusion.

The Galloway Plan called for a unicameral interprovincial council which would initiate legislation regarading matters of common colonial concern, subject to the veto of a president appointed by the King[21]. The president could be dismissed by the King at will. If ever accepted by both the colonies and the Crown, the plan would have served the cause of reconciliation much more effectively than royal governors and redcoats. The intercolonial legislature, or "Grand Council," as Galloway labeled it, would have answered many of the colonial constitutional objections to Parliament's exercise of legislative authority in colonial affairs. The grand council, elected by provincial legislatures, predictably would have represented conservative rather than radical sentiment. As an established organ of interprovincial action, it could have remedied the alarming deficiency of communication between opponents of radical resistance throughout the colonies. Surely the radicals realized all this when they narrowly managed to defer consideration of the proposal on September 28, and when they later expunged the plan from the record of proceedings.

Although the radicals achieved a major triumph in the defeat of the Galloway Plan, they were unable to prevent a conservative drift during the early days of October when the definition of American liberties was being debated. A majority of Congress, for example, was willing to grant to Parliament the right to regulate external trade, so long as that regulation did not involve the raising of revenue. On October 3, James Duane was able to procure a resolve promising support of the British administration and defense of the colonies[22]. Three days later another express arrived from Boston, this time from the Boston committee of correspondence, conveying information that Gage was persisting in his fortification of Boston, that the city was likely to be made into a permanent garrison town, and that it might be necessary for the patriot population to evacuate the whole city. The Boston committee specifically requested congressional advice on this matter and promised to follow whatever Congress recommended. Thus Congress again was forced to consider critical questions of an immediate tactical nature rather than long-term constitutional issues.

It seemed clear to all that the Bostonians were precariously close to armed conflict with Gage, and it was not at all certain that the rest of the colonies, particularly the Middle colonies, would support open conflict. Thus the radical strategy of nationalizing the resistance would naturally dictate that Bostonians should accept the role of suffering victims of British oppression while obeying whatever directives the Congress chose to send. The more extreme conservatives, on the other hand, may well have aimed at *heightening* the military crisis in Boston and disassociating the Congress from it. Evidence in the cryptic Journals and surviving correspondence regarding the debates over the Boston communication is extremely sketchy, but it appears that George Ross and Joseph Galloway moved that Boston be left to its own discretion regarding not only defense but also holding the General Court and the administration of justice[23].

The policy adopted by Congress followed the radical program. It was resolved that the people of Massachusetts be applauded for their spirited and restrained resistance to the Coercive Acts, and if force were applied in administering the acts, all America would support Massachusetts in its opposition. (This resolution, though considered treasonable by Galloway and Duane, was entered in the Journals as the unanimous opinion of Congress.) Another resolution specified that all who cooperated with the administration in the enforcement of the acts would be stigmatized and ostracized. At the same time Congress resolved that the inhabitants of Massachusetts should submit to a suspension of justice where it was not legally available under British auspices and that Bostonians should behave peaceably[24].

The Declaration of Rights, which was to serve as the foundation of the various addresses framed by the Congress, was finally agreed to on October 14. Contrasted with the Suffolk Resolves, the declaration reads at first glance like an inconsistent afterthought. The fourth resolution, the heart of the document, stipulated that the colonials were entitled to a free and exclusive power of legislation in their several provincial legislatures . . . in all cases of taxation and internal policy, but that they would cheerfully consent to parliamentary regulation of external commerce for the commercial benefit of the empire. Legalistic rather than ideological in tone, the declaration contained little that had not been widely asserted in response to the Townshend Acts.

It is true that the declaration was tamer than the radicals would have wished, suggesting that the radicals felt it was necessary to placate moderates from the Middle colonies whose continued involvement in a largely unstitched series of resistance movements proceeding at different paces was essential. The declaration did, however, go further than conservatives wished. American rights were grounded not only on the British constitution and the colonial charters but also on the law of nature. Conservatives viewed the claim to exclusive legislative power in all cases of taxation and internal policy as an extreme denial of parliamentary authority. The inclusion of the Quebec Act as a grievance was strongly opposed by conservatives such as Duane who contended with undeniable logic that since the Congress was objecting to parliamentary intervention within the thirteen colonies, it was inappropriate for the Congress to meddle in the internal affairs of Quebec, particularly when most inhabitants of Quebec were satisfied with the religious provisions of the Quebec Act. But Richard Henry Lee's reply to Duane revealed the larger ideological framework of radical assumptions; he argued that the Quebec Act was "the worst grievance," citing the "cruelty of Roman Catholics" and the massacre of Paris, neither of which had much relevance for the ostensible purpose of the first Congress[25].

III

If the Declaration of Rights was less aggressive than the radicals wanted, they could afford the concession because of the dim prospect of the Crown's acceptance of any appeal from an irregular body such as Congress, and also because of the favorable attitude in Congress toward the original radical plan of non-importation. Contrary to the expectation of some of the radical leadership (and contrary to the analysis of some historians) there was little controversy about the desirability of some form of economic coercion against Britain. There is some evidence of a dubious nature that nonimportation was voted down early in the proceedings at the insistence of New York and New Jersey—or so Thomas Hutchinson contended from information he received from Thomas Pownall[26]. According to Pownall, Congress had rejected nonimportation and drawn up a petition to the King, and the delegates were ready to terminate the Congress, when some letters arrived in Philadelphia from Franklin which caused them to change their minds and carry their determinations to more radical lengths. Other evidence, or the lack of it, suggests that Pownall was incorrect. There is no mention of this in surviving correspondence of the members, nor is there any record of a vote turning down nonimportation during the interval between September 17, when Congress endorsed the Suffolk Resolves, and September 26, when Richard Henry Lee's resolution for nonimportation was considered favorably by Congress. There was, however, an inflamatory letter from London, dated July 27 and published in the *Pennsylvania Gazette* on

September 21, which doubtless goaded some members in Congress into decisive action. The letter suggested:

> The resolutions of Philadelphia, and those of Maryland and Virginia, I must however tell you, are esteemed, both by the Court and the Merchants of the City, as very *inoffensive,* and as the mere ebullitions of a set of angry men, whose force were spent the day they were made, and the proposed Congress is spoken of, and really considered both by Administration and all the Merchants of the City as a scheme that will produce no sort of security to the liberty of the Colonies, nor trouble to Administration . . . they *are assured by them* ("parricides" such as Hutchinson), and from both New York and Philadelphia, that it will produce nothing more than a remonstrance or petition of right (which, by the bye, it is already *determined not to receive*) and that you are so attached to your private interests, you will never stop either imports or exports. . . . And let me add, that if the Deputies of the several provinces, when convened in Congress, *do not* one and all firmly resolve to establish through every county and township, in their respective provinces, a solemn league and covenant, and under the obligation of an oath or affirmation, *not* to purchase or use the manufactures of this country . . . and if possible *not* to *export* any provisions to the West India islands, and at the same time they do not religiously resolve to meet again in Congress every six months . . . our children will be irremedially deprived of that inheritance of liberty, which our fathers carefully and piously *transmitted* to us[27].

Whether or not the members of Congress were stung by such provocation, even delegates from colonies which had not instructed them to seek a nonimportation agreement could not fail to comprehend a general expectation of some form of economic coercion. Merchants were beginning to buy up goods in anticipation of a stoppage of trade, and on September 22 the Congress unanimously issued a public statement instructing merchants to stop new orders and suspend orders not yet delivered until the Congress finally determined the precise means it would adopt to "preserve American liberties"[28]. Even techniques of enforcement of a boycott were anticipated outside Congress. The committees of correspondence of Boston, Roxbury, Dorchester, and other towns surrounding Boston Harbor agreed to prevent trade with the British troops through the creation of committees of observation and prevention, a decision which was also published in the Philadelphia newspapers[29].

There were sharp debates, on the other hand, over the concessions that were to be secured from Britain and over the extent of economic pressure to be applied. Conservatives wanted to confine the Association to importation and to ask for repeal only of the acts applying to Massachusetts. Radicals generally pressed for a broader statement of grievances that would embrace virtually all the offensive legislation passed since 1763, including the Quebec Act. Some radicals wanted to force Parliament to disavow its authority even to regulate colonial trade. Radicals advocated a severe boycott both to secure these larger objectives and to cleanse the colonial resistance movement of its lethargic elements.

There was greater disunity within the radical ranks over the terms and intention of the Association than over any other issue which came up during the first Congress. The translation of the idea of economic coercion into a workable system which did not unduly penalize any particular interest within a variety of sectional economies proved to be a problem that strained the unity of the Congress and forecasted future difficulties for the Revolutionary front. Another obstacle the radicals had to grapple with was the fusion of various provincial resistance movements; they did not always mesh harmoniously. Samuel Chase of Maryland, for example, argued that it was useless to think only of imposing nonimportation; nonexportation would be of vastly more importance, since it would affect merchants as well as manufacturers and trade as well as revenue in Britain[30]. Lynch of South Carolina agreed and emphasized that speed was necessary in order to gain the desired effect. The Virginian delegates, however, had been instructed not to agree to any nonexportation that would take effect before the next year. Gadsden of South Carolina advocated going ahead with nonexportation without Virginia, but this did not gain much support from Chase, whose colony raised the same staples as Virginia. The Congress consequently postponed nonexportation until September 10, 1775. Edward Rutledge and the other South Carolina delegates with the exception of Gadsden began to suspect Virginia's commitment to the cause, but they were more suspicious of the North. They argued that nonexportation of products to Great Britain would virtually destroy the trade of the staple-producing South while only slightly affecting the trade of the North. John Rutledge contended that just £50,000 out of the total £700,000 of Philadelphia's exports went to Britain and that "it was evident those Colonies were less intent to annoy the mother country in the article of trade than to preserve to them their trade as entire as possible"[31]. On this basis the South Carolina delegates demanded that rice shipments to Europe be exempted from the terms of the Association, although rice should have been interdicted as a dutiable product on the British list. South Carolina's demand momentarily endangered agreement on the Association, but it was granted, and the Association was approved by Congress in terms closely resembling the instructions the Virginians had brought with them. All importations from Great Britain and Ireland, and a number of goods including molasses, syrups, and coffee from the British West Indies, were to be stopped after November 1, 1774, provided that the thirteen acts of Parliament singled out as grievances had not been repealed by them.

Despite the postponement of nonexportation, the Continental Association must be viewed as yet another radical victory because of the broad list of grievances to be redressed before the Association would be lifted, and because of the provisions for aggressive enforcement. Not only were the revenue acts, the Tea Act, and the Coercive Acts cited as grievances; the Quebec Act and certain provisions of Admiralty jurisdiction in the enforcement of the Navigation Acts were also included. Since it was virtually certain Britain would not repeal the Quebec Act and almost as likely that she would not yield to the other demands, the implementation of the Continental Association was predictable.

Violators of the Association were to be publicly chastised as "enemies of American liberty" and boycotted by the public. An extensive system of committees charged with the enforcement of the Association was to be elected by the voters in every county, city, and town. Thus the implementation of the Association would involve thousands of individuals in a political infrastructure geared toward resistance, and it would also isolate open opponents to the radical cause. The impact of the Association cannot be exaggerated. Thomas Bradbury Chandler's characterization of the Congress as "a *mad, blind* monster" that aimed at a "total independency" was possibly more accurate than the members themselves realized.

The record of the first Congress, while by no means crystal clear, does permit some generalizations concerning the distribution of strength and the tactics followed by the radical and conservative forces. The radical faction was more cohesive, more thoroughly prepared, and more clever in its tactics than were the relatively disorganized conservatives. Thus while the radical core was probably a minority of the total membership, it was able to achieve the bulk of what it attempted. That core rested on a New England voting base but had important and effective members from Southern colonies as well. In the colonies of New York, New Jersey, and Pennsylvania support for the radicals was so faint as to be virtually nonexistent. The Adamses were important leaders of the radical faction. John was the more influential of the two in debate, but Samuel may have been the most important member of the whole faction, not to say the entire Congress, when his network of contacts within Congress and outside it is taken into consideration. Of course, our understanding of the events of the Congress is dependent upon fragmentary evidence. Beyond Charles Thomson's cryptic Journals, the major single source is the diary of John Adams, which not surprisingly makes John himself a rather commanding figure. Galloway, however, assigned more importance to Samuel than to John Adams, a logical assessment in view of Sam's more intensive involvement in the preparations for the Congress. According to Galloway, Sam Adams was a man who "eats little, drinks little, sleeps little, thinks much, and is most decisive and indefatigable in the persuit of his object"[32]. Galloway was impressed by Adams's ability to manage what he called "the faction" in Congress in conjunction with the actions of the Massachusetts radical organization so as to extract the greatest effort from the crisis in Boston. Ward of Rhode Island and Sherman and Dyer of Connecticut were important members of the predominantly radical New England delegations. Cushing and Paine of Massachusetts and Hopkins of Rhode Island helped split the votes of their provinces often enough to be put outside the core of the radical faction[33]. In the delegations from the Middle colonies only Mifflin and Thomas McKean of Pennsylvania clearly supported the radicals. In the Southern delegations the articulate and bold actions of Lee, Gadsden, and Patrick Henry probably made all the difference for the radicals. Chase and Lynch were other important Southern radicals, although they sometimes defected from the uniformly radical position established by Gadsden. Furthermore, the aristocratic Lynch was developing a distaste for what he regarded as the democratic tendencies of New England.

Although they had some support from the South, conservatives drew most of their strength from the Middle colonies. Duane and Galloway must be put at the vital center of the conservative bloc, and Duane carried his New York colleagues Alsop, Low, and, to a lesser degree, Jay[34]. Galloway was able to attract a majority of his Pennsylvanian colleagues in support of his Plan of Union, but none of them seems to have taken a leading role in the proceedings. John Dickinson was not elected to Congress until October 15 and attended only during the last ten days of the session, although he was responsible for drafting the petition to the King which Henry had already attempted to formulate. It is difficult to place Dickinson in the congressional spectrum. All things considered, he might be classified as a moderate conservative. At the end of the session he penned an urgent letter to Arthur Lee in England, imploring Lee to make the Ministry recognize the gravity of the crisis. This suggests that he thought the measures adopted by Congress were of a radical nature[35]. The main supporters of the conservatives in the South were the two Rutledges, although both Pendleton and Harrison were suspicious enough of radical intentions to give support now and then to the conservative cause. There can be little doubt about the posture of the Rutledges, who early discovered that their ideas were similar to those of Galloway and Duane. Edward Rutledge could find nothing at all wrong with Galloway's plan, which he pronounced "most perfect"[36].

These then were the general delineations of the radical and conservative groups in terms of their more active and influential members in the first Congress. For convenience they are schematized in Table 1.

IV

The first Continental Congress agreed to reconvene on the tenth of May in 1775, unless the grievances it had listed had been redressed. This resolution alone made the first Congress more than a protest convention similar to the Stamp Act Congress. Conservatives as well as radicals saw the necessity of fur-

TABLE 1

Radical and Conservative Factions in the First Continental Congress

State	Radical	Conservative
New Hampshire	John Sullivan*	
Massachusetts	John Adams	Thomas Cushing*
	Samuel Adams	Robert Treat Paine*
Rhode Island	Samuel Ward	Stephen Hopkins*
Connecticut	Eliphalet Dyer	
	Roger Sherman	
New York		John Alsop
		James Duane
		Isaac Low
		John Jay
New Jersey		
Pennsylvania	Thomas Mifflin	Joseph Galloway
		George Ross
		John Morton*
Delaware	Thomas McKean	John Dickinson*
Maryland		
Virginia	Richard Henry Lee	Edmund Pendleton*
	Patrick Henry	Benjamin Harrison*
North Carolina		
South Carolina	Christopher Gadsden	John Rutledge
	Thomas Lynch	Edward Rutledge

*Indicates probable affiliation with the faction.

ther intercolonial action; indeed, many leaders of both persuasions recognized the need for some sort of permanent North American legislature. Silas Deane wrote to Patrick Henry, "One general Congress has brought the Colonies to be acquainted with each other, and I am in hopes another may effect a complete and perfect American Constitution, the only proper one, for Us, whither Connected with Great Brittain, or Not—." Even conservatives who had been shocked by the prospect of separation from England hinted at in Deane's letter saw the desirability of intercolonial action as a means of completing what Galloway had unsuccessfully ventured in the first Congress. James Duane attempted to persuade Samuel Chase that New York and Maryland should join forces with other colonies whose politics were "the most consistent and rational" in the promotion of a plan of union.

Elections of delegates to the second Congress were held by provincial congresses and by regularly constituted assemblies from New Hampshire to South Carolina before the outbreak of hostilities at Lexington and Concord. The one exception was the colony of New York, whose legislature refused either to endorse the Association or to elect delegates to the second Congress. New York did, however, send a delegation elected by a provincial convention held on April 22, and Georgia, which had not been represented in the first Congress, elected delegates on July 7. Thus the assembling of the thirteen colonies that would ultimately declare independence was completed by the summer of 1775[37]. With the exception of a brief recess during August, the Congress was in continuous session for the next nine years.

The hostilities at Lexington and Concord displaced the resistance movement, and consequently the function of the Continental Congress. The second Congress assembled as a de facto national legislature with the responsibility of coping with a war against the British government. It was a situation that prompted many, but not all, of the prominent conservatives to abstain. Joseph Galloway of Pennsylvania and Isaac Low of New York, for example, refused to serve in a body they regarded as treasonable. Nonetheless, committed conciliationists such as James Duane and John Dickinson attended, and their ranks were enlarged by the presence of men such as the Rutledges and the deeply conservative Virginian Carter Braxton who were alarmed about the consequences of a civil war.

As in the first Congress, the most uniformly radical delegations came from New England. John Adams remarked that he "found this Congress like the last. When we first came together, I found a strong jealousy of us from New England, and Massachusetts in particular; suspicions entertained of designs of independency; an American republic; Presbyterian principles, and twenty other things—it has been so now"[38]. Yet some of the most effective radical leadership continued to emanate from the South. Virginia again sent talented members committed to the radical cause, such as Richard Henry Lee and the new delegate Thomas Jefferson. The Middle colonies continued to send the most conservative delegations.

As before, the radicals were better organized and more determined than were advocates of accommodation. In addition, however, the British followed a policy that constantly strengthened the hand of the radicals, so that even convinced accommodationists found it difficult to reconcile their desire for harmony with their commission to secure American liberties.

The predicament of James Duane is illustrative of the difficulties encountered by many conservatives who sincerely desired accommodation but who found themselves forced to advocate belligerent, even actively aggressive, resistance. Soon after Congress convened Duane stated that he viewed the hostilities as "a *family quarrel, disgraceful* and *ruinous,*" but he admitted ministerial policy had been "wicked" and "oppressive" and that the "innocent blood" that had been shed in Massachusetts was sacrificed in a common cause that bound the other colonies "by the most solemn engagements" to hazard their all in the conflict. Warning the delegates that they must restrain "every emotion of intemperate zeal, every sally of anger and passion" and that military actions must be defensive rather than revengeful, he felt compelled to advocate elaborate military preparation for his own province of New York both at its harbor and along its northern frontier. Duane suggested the maintenance of two large armies, one to contain Gage in Boston and the other to defend New York[39].

The dilemma of conservatives in Congress was the ironic product of British calculations that were militarily sound but politically blind. None of the thirteen colonies was more inclined toward conciliation than New York in 1775. The New York Assembly had refused to accede to the Continental Association, and delegates to the second Congress had to be elected as before by irregular convention. The colony was internally divided, militarily vulnerable, and receptive to a deftly contrived policy of accommodation. But a combination of factors—notably the loyalty of Quebec, the allegiance of the Iroquois, and the inviting invasion route along Lake Champlain—impelled the British to apply pressure in northern New York. On June 27 the Congress received word from the Albany committee of correspondence that Guy Carleton, governor and military commander in Canada, was mounting an invasion force of 600 men, ships and barges, and Indian allies. Congress immediately ordered General Philip Schuyler, previously appointed commander of Patriot forces in northern New York, to destroy Carleton's vessels. Congress had already resolved on June 1 not to allow any incursion into Canada, since it had nothing in view other than the defense of the colonies, but now it reversed itself, authorizing Schuyler to take St. Johns, Montreal, and any other part of Canada so long as an invasion was not disagreeable to the Canadians. (Congress already had addressed a letter to "the oppressed Inhabitants of Canada" intended to win that colony to the resistance[40].) The way was thereby paved for the invasion of Canada that took place during the fall and winter—an action that was applauded by conservatives. John Zubly, the Swiss-born delegate from Georgia who was a determined opponent of independence, approved of the invasion as a legitimate act of self-defense. After the campaign under Montgomery and Arnold foundered in the snows of Quebec, Robert Morris, the wealthy and powerful conservative from Pennsylvania who also opposed independence, wrote to Horatio Gates that Canada "must be ours at all Events; shou'd it fall into the hands of the Enemy they will soon raise a Nest of Hornets on our backs that will sting us to the quick"[*41*]. Duane, Zubly, Morris, and other advocates of reconciliation were drawn into an intolerable dilemma: they were forced simultaneously to profess their loyalty to the Crown while supporting military action against its authority.

The only way the conservatives could resolve this contradiction in their own minds was to assume that British policy was being manipulated by a corrupt and cunning ministerial clique and that both George III and the friends of the colonies in Parliament would force a change in men and measures once they correctly viewed the colonial resistance as a loyal defense of constitutional liberties. To encourage such a change, the conservatives were determined to try the hitherto unsuccessful tactic of petitioning the King.

Under the leadership of Dickinson the conservatives campaigned to win as many delegates as possible to the idea of a petition. John Adams recorded that they even approached some of the Massachusetts delegates (possibly Thomas Cushing and Robert Treat Paine) but that they concentrated their energies upon the South Carolina delegation to produce a majority in conjunction with the Middle colonies and Maryland. When the ground had been sufficiently prepared, according to Adams, Dickinson's so-called "Olive Branch Petition" was presented to Congress. The "humble petition" incorporated the only logic available to conservatives: the Ministry had compelled the innocent colonials to arm in self-defense, but the King was assured that his loyal subjects remained to "your Majesty's person, family, and government, with all devotion that principle and affection can inspire," and that they "ardently" desired the restoration of harmony and concord [*42*]. John Adams signed the petition along with all other members of Congress, but he grumbled to James Warren in Massachusetts that it gave "a silly cast to our whole Doings." Jefferson probably was correct in his autobiographical recollection that the petition was passed in order to indulge Dickinson and those who did not want "to go too fast"[*43*].

The passage of the Olive Branch Petition was an indication that there were more than a few members of the second Congress who did not want hostilities to lead to independence. John Jay and James Duane each offered a proposal for negotiation. Thomas Johnson, Jr., from Maryland argued that a reunion with Britain should be an objective of Americans second only to the preservation of their liberties, and if the petition were rejected by the Ministry, the effect would be to divide Britain and unite America[*44*]. His thinking probably reflected that of the majority of the Congress.

But the profound shock produced by Lexington and Concord throughout the colonies, and in England as well, virtually precluded a reenactment of previous crises when embargoes and petitions had brought about an adjustment of British policy. Before the news of hostilities reached England, the North Ministry was willing to placate the colonies to the extent of having Parliament forbear from levying taxes other than those necessary for the regulation of trade on the condition that the colonial assemblies would provide funds for defense and for the support of the royal administration and the judiciary. North's plan of conciliation would be applied individually for any colony that chose to comply. It was a transparent effort to divide the colonies, and in the aftermath of open hostilities, the radicals had little difficulty in defeating the plan both in the individual assemblies and in the Congress[45]. Subsequent British actions in the wake of the news that the colonists had taken up arms would make reconciliation almost impossible. George III proclaimed the colonies in a state of rebellion in August, rejected the Olive Branch Petition, and informed Parliament on October 26 that he would procure foreign mercenaries to help suppress the seditious colonials. Parliament passed the Prohibitory Act on December 22 forbidding all trade with the colonies and authorizing the confiscation of colonial ships at sea as of March 1, 1776. The Crown would take a stand that left no room for resistance.

V

It may seem in retrospect that the separation of the colonies from the mother country was inevitable after Lexington and Concord, but the news of the stiffening of British policy came in fragments over an extended period of time, and few members of Congress believed in July of 1775 that they would be declaring independence within a year. The very gap in communication that fed American suspicions of ministerial conspiracy helped keep alive hopes of moderates and conservatives for accommodation. Further, the movement toward independence lacked uniform provincial support. It was the continuing function of the Continental Congress to prod the reluctant, to restrain the enthusiastic, and to draw together the strands of separate resistance movements. Above all, the Congress had to provide programmatic and ideological coherence that would make the final decision to declare independence the act of a nation. It was, of course, the radical element in the Congress that most readily accepted this responsibility.

Almost simultaneously with the passage of the Olive Branch Petition, the second Congress issued a proclamation that gave a very different cast to military resistance. The "declaration . . . setting forth the causes and necessity . . . of taking up arms" issued by Congress on July 6 was drafted by Thomas Jefferson, a radical, and despite its modification by the conservative Dickinson, it emerged as a "Spirited Manifesto," in the approving words of John Adams[46]. In this statement calculated to explain the recourse to armed resistance "by obligations of respect to the rest of the world" rather than to the King (a phrase strikingly similar to the Declaration of Independence Jefferson would frame the next year), Parliament was reprobated for its "intemperate rage for unlimited domination," the Ministry for "its rapacity," and Gage for having "butchered our countrymen." While protesting that "we have not raised armies with ambitious designs of separating from Great Britain and establishing independent states," the Congress warned the mother country that "our cause is just. Our union is perfect. Our internal resources are great, and, if necessary, foreign assistance is undoubtedly attainable." Americans were of one mind "resolved to dye Free-men rather than live Slaves"[47].

The declaration was a "Spirited Manifesto" indeed, but its claim that the colonies were perfectly united was wide of the mark. On the same day that the declaration was passed, John Adams warned James Warren that some colonies were still unrealistically hoping to guarantee their liberties through negotiation. His plan was to avoid negotiation "like death," to throw away the scabbard once the sword was drawn, to establish provincial governments in all the colonies on the Connecticut model to "confederate together like an indissoluble Band, for mutual defence, and open our Ports to all Nations immediately." He admitted that the colonies were "not yet ripe for it—a Bill of Attainder, etc. may soon ripen them." He also confessed that while he preferred that most of the troops opposing Gage should be raised in New England, he found that other colonies were more interested in sending soldiers to Massachusetts than he had expected. His explanation was that they had "a Secret Fear, a Jealousy, that New England will soon be full of Veteran Soldiers and at length conceive Designs unfavourable to the other Colonies"[48]. Adams's comments reveal the difficulties the radicals faced in creating a united front both in the resistance against England and in the achievement of mutual trust between the colonies. His program also was a remarkably accurate prediction of the course of action the radicals would follow during the ensuing year.

The new measures proposed by the congressional radicals between June of 1775 and May of 1776 may be arranged in four general categories. First, the radicals constantly urged prosecution of the war. Second, they worked to use congressional influence to help create new constitutions in the provinces that would remove royal authority. Third, most radicals advocated opening American trade to other nations, and some advocated forming alliances with foreign powers, preeminently France. Fourth, they urged that a confederation be established among those colonies engaged in the resistance.

The radical program, if it may be called that, was only partially realized before the Declaration of Independence. For reasons that were very different, neither confederation nor foreign alliances could be undertaken before independence was formally declared. Visible alliances with foreign nations were impossible so long as the colonies professed allegiance to Great Britain. Further, to search for the most available allies, namely France and Spain, would be to commit the most grievous kind of treason against the mother country— an act of "independency," as the delegates viewed it in February of 1776 when

George Wythe of Virginia proposed such a course[49]. Radicals recognized the advantage of a strong confederation but were unable to carry the project forth before independence both because of the opposition of moderates and because of divisions among the radicals themselves. The framing of a constitution raised multiple problems concerning representation and the allocation of central authority that could only complicate the resistance movement. Benjamin Franklin, now an advanced radical, did offer a plan of confederation in July that provided for proportional representation and substantial congressional powers, but the plan was not even entered in the Journals. While the decision to drop the measure was prompted by opposition from conciliationists, the radicals were aware that the question of representation had already distracted the first Congress when it was agreed that each colony should have one vote. Judging from the course of action followed by the radicals, it is plausible to conclude that they wisely chose to promote national authority through Congress as it was then constituted rather than disturbing an often precarious coalition of large and small provinces, special economic interests, and disparate regional blocs[50]. Indeed, conservatives and moderates who opposed independence argued that separation from England was premature because the provinces would succumb to civil war without having previously created a strong national government[51].

The radical program thus of necessity unfolded over time, often in response to British acts of coercion in London and in the colonies. The hostilities in Massachusetts triggered the organization of a Continental army. The congressional decision to allow privateering and to open American ports to foreign powers was reached only after hostilities had expanded to Virginia and North Carolina and after news of the Prohibitory Act had reached the colonies. Nonetheless, the basic lines of the radical policy were articulated as early as June of 1775 by John Adams, Benjamin Franklin, Thomas Jefferson, and others. It was a policy that led logically to independence, but it is impossible to say that Adams or Franklin aimed at total separation during the early stages of the second Congress. Franklin's plan for confederation included a clause that would terminate the confederation upon the redress of American grievances. John Adams saw the desirability of foreign alliances in October of 1775, but he also saw the danger of French or Spanish influence should the colonies offer the kinds of concessions that would prompt the Bourbon powers to take action. Indeed, his doubts that the colonies could win an alliance from France or Spain revealed his abiding preference for England and its constitution when measured against the other powers of Europe[52]. It is plausible to speculate that Samuel Adams was working for separation from the outset of the first Congress, but he marched to his own drum and was conspicuously silent during the lengthy debates of the second Congress. In the last analysis, it was military resistance and British response that elevated the defense of colonial liberties to the assertion of formal independence. One senses that Samuel Adams anticipated the entire drama, but if he was a dedicated revolutionary from the outset, he was a rare British colonial. One senses also that the radicals were able to envision a program leading to complete independence from the beginning of the second Congress but that they were hesitant revolutionaries who insisted in effect that Britain legitimatize their policy by studied insults and outrages. It is perhaps less important that the British were mightily provoked than that they accepted the colonial challenge.

VI

United military resistance was crucial to the achievement of de facto confederation under the aegis of the Continental Congress. The New England radicals were aware that there were suspicions in the South that Massachusetts was "aiming at sovereignty over the other provinces," as Josiah Quincy, Jr., had discovered in South Carolina[53]. They attempted to overcome such sectional distrust by nationalizing the largely New England army which had surrounded Gage at Boston and by supporting George Washington as its commander in chief. In doing so they passed over the New England generals Artemas Ward and Israel Putnam (and possibly John Hancock, whose aspirations for national command were unrestrained by inexperience and lack of support from his fellow delegates). It was John Adams who moved on the tenth of June that the Continental Congress adopt the New England army; at the same time he gave broad hints that Washington should be the man to take over the command.

Adams's political prescience was not shared by all his fellow radicals, for Sherman spoke out in debate against the choice of Washington, arguing that the army already had a general in the person of Artemas Ward and was composed overwhelmingly of New Englanders who might resent a commander in chief from Virginia. Yet the majority was clearly in favor of Washington, and when Thomas Johnson of Maryland proposed Washington, he was unanimously endorsed by the Congress. Sherman's colleague, Eliphalet Dyer, was aware of the political motives in appointing Washington when he wrote to Joseph Trumbull that the choice of Washington "removes all jealousies" and "more firmly Cements the Southern to the Northern (colonies)." He noted as well that this would remove the fear that a successful New England general might march south to "give law to the Southern or Western Gentry"[54].

Sectional considerations determined a number of other appointments. There could be little doubt that the "first Major General" or second in command of the army at Boston would have to be a New Englander, and thus the choice went to Artemas Ward, commander of the army at Boston[55]. Since both the South and New England had representatives in the high command, it was necessary to give a slot to a representative of the Middle colonies as well. The man chosen was Philip Schuyler of New York, rich from his landed estates and business interests, and a member of Congress. Schuyler was commissioned a major general and was subsequently given command of the Northern army in the expedition against Canada.

Yet sectional calculations cannot account for all military appointments. The post of "second Major General" (i.e., third in command of the army at Boston) was given to Colonel Charles Lee, an Englishman by birth and a soldier of fortune by experience. Although he had been in America since 1773 and had land in Virginia, he had little real connection with any section. Rather, he was picked ostensibly for his great military experience, which included considerable service with the British army in America and Portugal during the Seven Years' War, in Poland under Stanislaus Poniatowski in 1769, and with the Prussian army in Turkey in 1770. Lee was articulate on almost any topic, especially military matters, and so there can be no doubt that he impressed many important people—including Washington himself—with his military abilities[56]. But there seems to be more to the Lee appointment than the hiring of a professed military expert. Lee had as pronounced ideas on politics as he did on military science. A fiery opponent of Toryism in England, he used his effusive and sometimes cogent pen during the pamphlet controversy that flourished before the Revolution. Less a provincial patriot than a zealous radical with an ideological commitment to the American cause, he had greatly impressed Richard Henry Lee, who in turn had recommended him to the Adamses[57]. The support of the Adams-Lee group in Congress (and indeed others in the radical force outside Congress) doubtless influenced the appointment of Lee [58]. "Sam and John fought for him," wrote John Adams in the third person, though "all the weapons, Dismal Bugbears were raised. There were Prejudices enough among the weak and fears enough among the timid, as well as other obstacles from the cunning . . ."[59].

Another appointment that had political overtones was the designation of James Warren, the Massachusetts radical stalwart, as paymaster general of the army at Boston. Again Samuel and John Adams were influential in securing the appointment, and again only over opposition, this time within the Massachusetts delegation from the moderate Cushing and the disgruntled Hancock[60]. It seems that the radicals, having supported Washington for tactical reasons, felt free to establish a cluster of political sympathizers in the leadership around Washington. The election of Horatio Gates as adjutant general with the rank of brigadier general added to the coterie, while Washington's own choice of Joseph Reed and Thomas Mifflin to be aides-de-camp brought up two more long-standing connections of the Adams-Lee faction. The partisan effects of these appointments were not immediately felt but would later contribute to the shadowy episode known as the "Conway Cabal."

The radicals wanted not only to prosecute the war with energy but also to aid the resistance movement by establishing new frames of goverment providing for provincial control of the executive and judiciary either in the absence of effective royal authority or in defiance of it. The supersession of royal authority was necessary, particularly in areas such as Massachusetts where hostilities were taking place. The maintenance of order and stability could best be effected through the creation of more regular systems of administration and law enforcement than were provided by the extralegal committees of correspondence and safety. Since some of the sharpest criticism of the resistance movement came from moderates who objected to the illicit activities of groups such as the Liberty Boys, the establishment of due process in law and administration was a sensible move that fused order and resistance.

It is apparent in this connection, as well as others, that neither the line of communications nor the tactical interplay between Congress and the New England provinces which Galloway resentfully noted at the first Congress was discontinued at the second Congress. John Adams related that the problem of setting up a new government for Massachusetts radicals was a constant topic of conversation during the interval between the two Congresses[61], and it cannot have been entirely coincidental that on June 2 the Congress received a letter from the Massachusetts Provincial Convention dated May 16 requesting the advice of the Continental Congress concerning its assumption of civil power in Massachusetts[62]. John Adams used this opportunity to suggest that Congress should recommend to each colony that it set up a constitutional convention to create a new government[63]. Congress established a committee composed of John Jay, James Wilson, Thomas Johnson, Richard Henry Lee, and John Rutledge to consider the Massachusetts letter, but the committee and Congress recommended nothing so drastic as what Adams proposed. They suggested instead that Massachusetts govern itself with a provincial assembly and a council elected on traditional principles until the Crown agreed to resume its prerogative under the old rules of the Massachusetts Charter[64]. Such a temperate recommendation irritated some radicals, but this was a marked step toward their ultimate goal of congressionally approved independent provincial governments. Scarcely six months earlier the first Congress had advised Massachusetts to submit to a suspension of justice rather than create new machinery to supplant the prorogued General Court.

After the August recess, the radicals raised the same issue in October when New Hampshire sent a similar request to Congress. Again, there is good evidence of interaction between Congress and the provinces, for the New Hampshire delegates, Josiah Bartlett and John Langdon, wrote home suggesting that the New Hampshire provincial convention petition Congress for permission to establish a government similar to that of Massachusetts[65].

The committee formed to consider the New Hampshire letter was more radical than its counterpart which had given the report on the Massachusetts letter. John Adams, Samuel Ward, and Roger Sherman were all advanced New England radicals, while Richard Henry Lee was their closest Southern connection. Only John Rutledge, the fifth member of the committee, was a conservative. Yet even the presence of Rutledge seems not to have disturbed the work of the committee. John Adams later recalled that Rutledge was one of his most "able coadjutors"[66]. The advice of Congress to New Hampshire was less specific and much more permissive than that given to Massachusetts six months earlier. It was suggested that New Hampshire call a "full and free representation of the people" and, if the representatives thought it necessary, "establish such a form of government, as in their judgement will best produce the happiness of the people, and most effectually secure peace and good order in the Province, during the continuance of the present dispute between Great Britain and the Colonies." As the New Hampshire delegates Bartlett and Langdon pointed out in a letter to Matthew Thornton, this was "power ample and full even to the choice of Governor, if the colony should think it necessary . . ."[67].

It seems apparent that the radicals were concentrating upon the creation of independent provincial establishments. If they had a larger scheme calling for political alterations above and beyond the removal of royal authority in the provinces, they were careful not to use the Continental Congress to promote it. Indeed, on more than one occasion they opposed congressional interference in decisions concerning the internal structure of the colonies. This was doubtless good strategy, but it reflected as well the general radical distrust of centralized authority and, probably no less important, a failure of the radicals to agree on the proper form of provincial government. Whether or not John Adams was correct in his autobiographical statement that "every one of my friends, and all those who were the most zealous for assuming governments, had at that time no idea of any other government but a contemptible legislature in one assembly, with committees for executive magistrates and judges," there is no doubt that Adams himself and a number of other radicals including Sherman, Rush, and Richard Henry Lee were dedicated opponents of such political innovations[68]. Only in the final stage of the Revolutionary movement, when a recalcitrant Pennsylvania Assembly stalled the achievement of independence, did the Congress take steps which it realized would materially alter the internal political structure of a province.

Having put the colonies on a war footing and having recommended the assumption of civil power in three colonies (for South Carolina had received advice similar to that given New Hampshire), the radicals had placed the colonies in a posture of practical independence. Were they to enlarge the war by carrying it to the high seas, and were they to seek foreign trade and military support, the colonies would be involved in a war for independence—in fact, if not in name.

As so often happened, events seemed to transform resistance into rebellion. It was readily apparent that the Association had not softened British policy. Furthermore, the colonials themselves found it increasingly difficult to obtain supplies such as arms, gunpowder, sulphur, and saltpeter—all of which were necessary for the prosecution of armed resistance, which even the conservatives agreed was essential. As early as July 15 Congress voted to relax the Association to permit importation of arms, and in September the Congress appointed a secret committee charged with the "importation and delivery of a quantity of gunpowder"[69].

By early October many of the delegates and others outside Congress began to question the efficacy of the Association (which now interdicted exportation in the empire). Charles Lee asked John Adams in a letter why the Congress shouldn't "invite ships of all nations into American ports." John Adams had already pondered the question, and he did not relish the prospect of seeing the Association turn America completely into "mere Husbandmen, Mechanicks, and Soldiers." Furthermore, he doubted that the people had the "virtue to do this for more than a year"[70]. New England wanted trade. Rhode Island had already sent a petition to Congress, which the Rhode Island delegates presented on the third of October, asking that the Continental Congress authorize the construction of an American fleet[71]. The Rhode Island proposal sparked a running debate in Congress which soon encompassed discussion of naval warfare, the Association, foreign trade, foreign alliances, and the desirability of breaking away from the British mercantile system[72].

Other factors entered the picture in a manner that produced a welter of factional and sectional crosscurrents. Parliament had passed the Restraining Act, which forbade trade outside Britain and the British West Indies—an act which mentioned only New England at first but which subsequently was applied to all colonies that agreed to be part of the Association. New York and North Carolina (as well as Georgia and Delaware) were not mentioned in the act and were, therefore, free to trade as usual as far as parliamentary restrictions were concerned. Virginia and South Carolina, the staple-producing colonies with markets in Britain, had been convinced from the beginning that the Association had penalized them more than the Northern colonies. Now that New York was not included in the Restraining Act, the Southern delegates were even more intent upon an equitable readjustment. Thus sectional tensions arose. There was also an ideological controversy between radicals and their opponents regarding violation of the Restraining Act. Conservatives were naturally hesitant about taking the drastic step of breaking out of the British mercantile system. Most radicals—particularly those from the Northern colonies—supported such a policy.

Conservatives generally agreed that the alternatives were either to open trade where the law allowed (that is to say Great Britain and the British West Indies) or to maintain general nonintercourse, with perhaps a few exceptions for strategic essentials. The New York delegate Robert R. Livingston, for example, was typical of the Northern conservatives when he advocated a relaxation of the restrictions on exports with the exception of tobacco and lumber. Tobacco was an important revenue-producing staple for Britain, while lumber was essential for crating sugar from the West Indies. Restricting these two exports would sharply curb British revenue and profits. The exportation of other goods was necessary, however, for otherwise it would be impossible to secure ammunition. Moreover, the colonies were in danger of losing their seamen to Great Britain if they were unable to find work at home. The South could sacrifice the tobacco and lumber trade, Livingston contended, because Southern planters were rich and could afford the loss, but the merchants and traders of the North would not be able to survive without trade. The Southern delegates naturally disagreed. In the words of Samuel Chase, "Merchants will not grow rich; there is the rub . . . we must give up the profits of our trade or lose our liberties"[73].

Chase was in favor of as tight an embargo as possible and was supported by most Southerners. Richard Henry Lee even advocated closing up the customs, thereby putting all the colonies on an equal footing[74]. Lee was supported by Gadsden and John Rutledge of South Carolina, Wythe of Virginia, Chase of Maryland, and McKean of Delaware. Only Zubly of Georgia, an extreme conservative, offered opposition in the Southern delegations. Radical and conservative divisions were frequently erased on this issue in both sections. Jay opposed Lee's tactic of putting all the colonies on an equal footing, arguing that if there was a necessity for all sacrifices to be absolutely equal, then New York should be burned because Charlestown was. Silas Deane, who generally joined the radicals, supported Jay[75]. But if the notes of these debates taken by Adams are full and accurate, New England radicals, by and large, refrained from entering the dispute. This probably was due to a desire not to cause a rift in the New England–Southern radical coalition. Certainly there is little doubt that New Englanders wanted to open the ports and revive their languishing trade[76].

The discussion of trade could not be separated from the question of maritime hostilities. The colonies had few warships, but they had a substantial merchant marine that could be armed, and they had the capacity to outfit privateers and build men-of-war. Furthermore, the Rhode Island motion to authorize naval construction coincided with a dispatch from Washington informing Congress that two British ships carrying munitions to Halifax could be intercepted. Military resistance on land invited resistance on sea.

Most New Englanders strongly supported the construction of a navy, but they could not win Congress to the idea in early October. The moderate Middle colony delegations naturally opposed such a drastic escalation of armed resistance, and while there was some support from Southern radicals, particularly

Gadsden of South Carolina and George Wythe of Virginia, even Richard Henry Lee had misgivings about a navy. He feared that no force the colonies could build would be sufficient to break the grip that the British fleet might clamp on Virginia's Chesapeake lifeline. According to John Adams, Southern moderates and conservatives thought the project was "the maddest idea in the world," as Chase put it[77]. Edward Rutledge led the conservative opposition, and did so with such effectiveness that Adams was certain that his arguments must have been supplied by the merchants of Philadelphia. Congress did take hesitant steps toward maritime defense, however, by authorizing ships to be outfitted to intercept the vessels bound for Halifax and, by the end of the month, by allowing the purchase of two more vessels at continental expense. On October 30 a naval committee with a decidedly radical complexion was formed with seven members, including Silas Deane, John Langdon, and Christopher Gadsden (originally the committee that considered Washington's dispatch), along with Stephen Hopkins, John Adams, Richard Henry Lee, and Joseph Hewes.

The decision to form an American fleet was prompted by subsequent intelligence from England and Virginia that indicated that Britain was intent upon crushing the resistance rather than negotiating with Congress. On November 9 Congress received news that George III had rejected the Olive Branch Petition and had declared the colonies to be in rebellion. Joseph Hewes of North Carolina, the most moderate member of the naval committee, reported on that day "we have but little expectation of a reconciliation . . . we have scarcely a dawn of hope that it will take place." Samuel Ward was convinced that the Ministry was determined to subdue the colonies and "extirpate" the New England colonies in particular[78]. It seems, however, that news from Virginia was more directly responsible for creating the necessary Southern support for an American navy. By early December Congress learned that Governor Dunmore had declared martial law, had raised an armed force, and had taken the intensely provocative step of offering freedom to all slaves who deserted their masters to join his army. Dunmore had ships at his disposal and was gathering his strongest support from the maritime town of Norfolk. On December 13, shortly after learning of the hostilities in Virginia, Congress authorized the construction of thirteen ships. By early January the naval committee had supervised the purchase of eight vessels, appointed Ezek Hopkins (the brother of the Rhode Island delegate Stephen Hopkins) commander in chief of the navy, and given him his first sailing orders to proceed to the Chesapeake and destroy Dunmore's fleet[79].

It is plausible that the Southern reluctance to launch an American navy was due not only to the recognition that the Southern coast was more vulnerable to the British fleet than was the coast of New England but also to the realization that the construction, and perhaps even the disposition, of a navy would be dominated by the Northern colonies. The naval committee of seven included four New Englanders. Its initial appointments showed the influence of sectional attachments and even nepotism. The commander in chief Ezek Hopkins was the brother of Rhode Island member of the naval committee Stephen Hopkins. Another important appointment to a captaincy was given to Abraham Whipple, commodore of the Rhode Island navy. Yet another went to Dudley Saltonstall, brother-in-law of Silas Deane, the member of the committee from Connecticut. It is thus not surprising that the day after Congress decided upon a larger program of naval construction, it created a marine committee with one member from each state to supervise the building of the thirteen frigates. But despite the allocation of contracts in the Middle colonies and the South, almost all vessels purchased or built after 1776 came from New England[80]. Although the marine committee took over the functions of the naval committee in early 1776, and although it was formally representative of all the colonies, actual power rested with the New Englanders who were more knowledgeable and more interested in its business. Two naval boards were created to administer naval affairs—one in Philadelphia in 1776 and one in Boston in 1777—and it was the Boston board that was given greater latitude in decision making. It was also the Boston board that handled the greater volume of business. After privateering was authorized, fully half of all prize ships were ordered to Boston for disposition. Despite being ordered to the Chesapeake, and then to Charleston, Ezek Hopkins took his force to Nassau in the Bahamas, and then to Newport, Rhode Island—an action which prompted a congressional censure later in the year. The South, in short, had reason to anticipate and even to fear Northern dominance of naval affairs.

Although the maritime weakness of the South would cause serious sectional tensions during the course of the war, it did not in the last analysis hamper the coalition between radicals from New England and the South during the months before the Declaration of Independence. Indeed, the vulnerability of the South helped cultivate support among Southern delegates for opening American ports to foreign vessels and for the search for European allies. Richard Henry Lee suggested as early as October that colonial goods might be exported in foreign ships. After the news arrived that George III had rejected the Olive Branch Petition, Congress appointed a five-man secret committee of correspondence to sound out foreign powers about assistance. The committee was composed largely of moderates and conservatives from the Middle and Southern colonies, including Benjamin Harrison from Virginia and Thomas Johnson of Maryland, along with Dickinson, Jay, and Franklin. Despite its conservative composition, the committee on December 12 delegated the radical Arthur Lee to contact European powers, especially France, about assistance. It was the radical Virginian George Wythe who proposed on February 16 that

Congress openly consider foreign alliances. His motion was rejected on the ground that "this was Independency," as Richard Smith noted in his diary[81].

George Wythe's resolution was premature, but within a month Congress would take steps that led directly toward independence. The stimulus, as before, was drastic new British policy which enormously strengthened the position of the radicals. On February 27 word arrived in Congress that Parliament had passed an act prohibiting all colonial trade effective March 1. The act was generally interpreted as making "the Breach between the two Countries so wide as never more to be reconciled." These words of Joseph Hewes were written with reluctance, but with the conviction that "nothing is left now but to fight it out . . ."[82]. John Adams was certain that the "restraining Act" should be called the "Act of Independency, for King, Lords, and Commons have united in sundering this country from . . . [Britain] I think forever"[83]. The resistance movement was thus again shunted to a more extreme position, and from this point on radicals were openly advocating independence, while conservatives preferred to hold back in the hope that British commissioners would arrive to negotiate. When this was no longer enough, they tried to delay the final break by pleading the necessity of first consulting their constituents[84]. In this new context there was enough support to enable passage of new measures providing for aggressive marine operations and trade with foreign nations. By the middle of March a privateering bill had matured sufficiently to gain acceptance from Congress over the opposition of the Pennsylvania and Maryland delegations, and by early April John Adams saw one of his most cherished steps toward separation consummated in the passage of a bill opening American ports to trade of the world—with the exception, of course, of the British Empire[85].

VII

By the early spring of 1776 the radical delegations from New England and the South were prepared for independence. Samuel Chase, who had opposed a navy in October, was the delegate who moved that privateering be allowed in March. Conciliationists had been either converted or removed. The Adamses had been hinting to their correspondents in Massachusetts that Thomas Cushing was not voting with them on critical measures, and he was replaced by the Marblehead radical Elbridge Gerry. Before long Gerry was writing to James Warren, the president of the Massachusetts Provincial Congress, that Massachusetts should send a resolution to Congress openly supporting independence. A month later (April 20) Richard Henry Lee suggested much the same thing in a letter to Patrick Henry[86].

Actually, popular sentiment in New England and much of the South indicated readiness for the final break. In April John Adams heard from James Winthrop that the Massachusetts people were becoming impatient waiting for Congress to act on independence. (Winthrop asked Adams what he thought of the idea of Massachusetts going ahead with a separate declaration of independence. Adams discouraged such a move, fearing that it might disjoin the movement.) On April 12 North Carolina instructed its delegates that they might join the other colonies in a resolution of independence. Some of the other provinces altered their instructions to allow for separation, and in May the Virginia Convention instructed its delegates to actually propose independence.

Realizing that the Middle colonies were the last major obstacle to independence and that Pennsylvania was the vital center of the Middle colonies bloc, the radicals closely scrutinized the political mood in the capital city of Philadelphia. Elections were scheduled for May 1 to fill seventeen new seats in an expanded Pennsylvania Assembly. Should the election be swept by the radicals, moderate control of the Assembly might be extinguished and the vital support of Pennsylvania won for independence. The results of the election dashed the hopes of the radicals, however, for moderates won most of the seats, ensuring that Dickinson, Robert Morris, James Wilson, and the other conciliationists would remain in Congress.

Confronted by this seeming impasse, the radicals altered their previous strategy of noninvolvement in provincial politics and used the Congress to spark what amounted to a coup d'etat in Philadelphia. A resolution sponsored by John Adams, passed on May 10 and subsequently modified on May 15, encouraged the people to turn out governments which still accepted any form of Crown authority. Pennsylvania still allowed royal justice in its courts, and within a week a mass meeting was held outside the Pennsylvania State House. The crowd acclaimed the congressional resolution, decided that the Assembly was incompetent "to the exigencies of our affairs," and approved a convention to frame a new constitution[87].

Moderates (or Revolutionary conservatives later to be referred to as Republicans) in Pennsylvania never forgave the congressional radicals for their responsibility in generating the Pennsylvania constitution of 1776, the most democratic of all the state constitutions. In 1779 it was rumored as far away as Massachusetts and Virginia that Samuel Adams was generally suspected by the "Gentlemen" of Pennsylvania of having "laid the Foundation of that Government" with the sole motive of turning Dickinson and Wilson out of Congress[88]. The record of Sam Adams's involvement in the Pennsylvania coup is as usual more obscure than the record of the role of his cousin John, but it is not difficult to credit Samuel with behind-the-scenes activities among the radicals in Congress and in Philadelphia which perhaps complemented the resolution sponsored by John. One of the major architects of the Pennsylvania constitution was Thomas Young, a transplanted Bostonian and a long-standing connection of Sam Adams. Further, Sam was on familiar terms with all the leaders of the radical party, and he was a frequent visitor in the house of Christopher Marshall, where the radicals often assembled[89]. The rumor of Samuel Adams's involvement in Pennsylvania radical politics also gains credence from the subsequent close relationship in Congress between the Adams-Lee faction and the radical delegates from Pennsylvania (or Constitutionalists, as they were known in state politics)[90].

By the time Richard Henry Lee's motion for independence was offered on June 7, the radical preparations in Pennsylvania were well advanced. The regularly constituted assembly did not go so far as to sanction independence, but on June 8 it relaxed its instructions so as to allow united action with the other colonies. The radical convention explicitly approved independence on June 24, and by that time the Delaware and New Jersey assemblies had succumbed to the rush toward what John Adams called "the promised land." Maryland came around by June 28, and so when the vote was taken on July 2, only New York was unable to support independence. The New York delegates abstained from voting and affixed their signatures later, as did Robert Morris and John Dickinson, who continued to oppose independence on the grounds that it was premature and impolitic.

The achievement of an agreement to support independence was the result of interrelated factors, some long-term and some short-range. There was a century of preparation for the decision to revolt, for the Revolution as it occurred would have been impossible in the absence of healthy provincial assemblies mindful of their prerogatives and experienced in defending them. In the short term the British government appears in retrospect to have committed stupid blunders that alienated moderates and impelled radicals toward independence. But from the vantage point of 1775, it is difficult to comprehend how the British government could have suffered the bulk of its colonial military arm to be incarcerated in Boston, not to mention an American invasion of Canada, without responding in force. If the parliamentary act stopping colonial trade on March 1 was severe, it was no more so than the boycotts legislated by the Congress. In truth, separation of the thirteen colonies from the mother country at one moment in time was in great measure the product of congressional leadership that legitimatized rebellion in the name of defense. Within Congress it was the cohesion and finesse of the radicals in overcoming moderate and conservative obstructionism that gave the resistance movement a revolutionary direction. Finally, while the radicals in Congress managed a wave of popular resentment, they also cultivated it in the press, in the provincial legislatures and conventions, in the Congress itself, and in the streets and the fields.

Notes

1 Thomas Bradbury Chandler, *What Think Ye of the Congress Now?* (New York, 1775), p. 6.

2 W. C. Ford, G. Hunt, and J. C. Fitzpatrick, (eds.), *Journals of the Continental Congress* (34 vols.; Washington, 1904–1937), I, 20. (Henceforth cited as *JCC*.)

3 Compare ibid. with Force (ed.), *Amer. Arch.,* ser. 4, I, 608–609, which includes the full account of the unpublished assembly proceedings. The instructions were printed in the newspapers in full and accurate form (see, e.g., the *Virginia Gazette* [Purdie and Dixon], Aug. 18, 1774), but Thomson's manuscript journal, PCC, microfilm roll 8, as reproduced in the *JCC*, I, and in the contemporary publications (see, e.g., *Journal of the Proceedings of the Congress, held at Philadelphia, September 5, 1774* [Philadelphia: William and Thomas Bradford, printers, 1774]), includes numerous variations and deletions. Compare also the Virginia instructions, *JCC*, I, 23, with the account in the *Virginia Gazette* (Purdie and Dixon), Aug. 11, 1774.

4 *JCC*, I, 15–16, 22–24.

5 Joseph Galloway to Governor William Franklin, Sept. 3, 1774, *LMCC*, I, 5–6.

6 Ibid., 6.

7 The credentials of William Floyd as they appear in the *Journals* illustrate the point: "By a writing duly attested, it appears, the County of Suffolk, in the Colony of New York, have appointed Col°. William Floyd, to represent them at the Congress." *JCC*, I, 19.

8 *Virginia Gazette* (Purdie and Dixon), Aug. 11, 1774.

9 William V. Wells, *The Life and Public Services of Samuel Adams* (3 vols.; Boston, 1865), II, 174–178.

10 Charles F. Adams (ed.), *The Works of John Adams* (10 vols.; Boston, 1850–1856), II, 358; Galloway to Benjamin Franklin, Sept. 27, 1770, in I. Minnis Hays (ed.), *Calendar of the Papers of Benjamin Franklin* (5 vols.; The American Philosophical Society, Philadelphia, 1908), II, 111; Galloway to William Franklin, Sept. 5, 1774, *New Jersey Archives*, ser. 1, X, 477; *LMCC*, I, 9.

11 John Adams, Diary, Aug. 29 and 30, 1774, *LMCC*, I, 1. Emphasis added.

12 The Adamses had been warned by Alexander McDougall in New York that they should not alarm delegates from the Middle colonies. George Clymer had earlier made the same point in a letter to Josiah Quincy, Jr. Adams, *Works*, II, 345–357; George Clymer to Josiah Quincy, Jr., June 13, 1774, in Force (ed.), *Amer. Arch.,* ser. 4, I, 406–407.

13 Chandler, *What Think Ye of the Congress Now?*, p. 14.

14 Governor Gage to Lord Dartmouth, Oct. 30, 1774, in Force (ed.), *Amer. Arch.,* ser. 4, I, 950.

15 Silas Deane to Mrs. Deane, Sept. 7, 1774, *LMCC*, I, 18.

16 Samuel Adams to Joseph Warren, Sept. 9, 1774, *LMCC*, I, 26–27; John Adams to Mrs. Adams, Sept. 16, 1774, *Familiar Letters of John Adams and His Wife Abigail Adams* (Boston, 1875), pp. 37–38. See also Silas Deane's comment on Duché's prayer, Sept. 7, 1774, *LMCC*, I, 18. Deane wrote that it was a prayer worth riding 100 miles to hear and that even the Quakers shed tears. John Drayton, *Memoirs of the American Revolution* (2 vols.; Charleston, 1821), I, 165; John Adams, Diary, Sept. 10, 1774, *Works*, II, 378.

17 Samuel Ward, Diary, Sept. 7, 1774; John Adams, Notes of Debates, Sept. 8; Ward, Diary, Sept. 9, 1774, *LMCC*, I, 19, 21.

18 The resolves are printed in *JCC*, I, 32–37.

19 Ibid., 39.

20 Samuel Adams to Joseph Warren, Sept. 15, 1774; John Adams to Joseph Palmer, Sept. 26, 1774, *LMCC*, I, 47–48.

21 *JCC*, I, 48–51.

22 Compare Duane's proposed resolve in *LMCC*, I, 61, with the resolution in *JCC*, I, 53–54.

23 John Adams mentioned such a motion offered by Ross and seconded by Galloway. Adams to Edward Biddle, Dec. 12, 1774, *Works*, IX, 349.

24 *JCC*, I, 58–60; *The Examination of Joseph Galloway before the House of Commons* (London, 1779), p. 63; *LMCC*, I, 66.

25 James Duane, Notes of Debates, Oct. 17, 1774, ibid., 77–78.

26 Peter Orlande Hutchinson (comp.), *The Diary and Letters of Thomas Hutchinson* (2 vols.; London, 1883–1886), I, 296.

27 "Extract of a letter from London, dated July 27," the *Pennsylvania Gazette*, Sept. 21, 1774.

28 This resolution was carried in the September 28 issue of the *Pennsylvania Gazette*.

29 Ibid., Oct. 12, 1774.

30 Chase's arguments as well as others which follow below can be found in John Adams's notes of debates for September 26 and 27 in Adams, *Works*, II, 382–386.

31 South Carolina delegates, "Report to the Provincial Congress," *LMCC*, I, 86.

32 Joseph Galloway, *Historical and Political Reflections on the Rise and Progress of the American Rebellion* (London, 1780), p. 66.

33 John Adams, Diary, Oct. 13, 1774, *Works*, II, 397; Samuel Ward, Diary, Oct. 22, 1774, *LMCC*, I, 80. Hopkins, for example, supported the right of Parliament to regulate trade in some instances, probably where revenue was involved.

34 Jay's position as a conservative does not emerge with quite the consistency of Galloway and Duane. He contended, for example, that colonial rights should be traced to the law of nature as well as constitutional sources, but he did join Galloway and Duane in the early unsuccessful maneuverings to prevent the selection of Carpenter's Hall as a meeting place and Charles Thomson as Secretary, and, further, he was one of the more vocal supporters of the Galloway Plan. John Adams, Diary, *Works,* II, 389-390.

35 John Dickinson to Arthur Lee, Oct. 27, 1774, *LMCC,* I, 83.

36 See Galloway's statements concerning John Rutledge in his letters to Governor William Franklin, Sept. 3 and Sept. 15, 1774, *LMCC,* I, 5-6, 9. John Rutledge's proposals concerning the basis of American liberties (centered upon the common law and maritime law of England and the colonial charters) were apparently used by Deane in his propositions. Ibid., 44n-45n. Edward Rutledge's statement is recorded by John Adams in his notes of debates, *Works,* II, 390.

37 JCC, II, 13-21.

38 John Adams to James Warren, July 6, 1775, Warren-Adams Letters, Massachusetts Historical Society, *Collections* (2 vols.; Boston, 1917, 1925), I, 75.

39 James Duane, "Notes on the State of the Colonies," May 25, 1775, *LMCC,* I, 98-100.

40 JCC, II, 15-16; Force (ed.), *Amer. Arch.,* ser. 4, II, 1048; JCC, II, 75, 109-110.

41 John Adams, Notes of Debates, Oct. 9, 1775, *Works,* II, 466; Robert Morris to Horatio Gates, Apr. 6, 1776, *LMCC,* I, 416.

42 JCC, II, 158-160.

43 Adams, *Works,* II, 410-414; Paul Leicester Ford (ed.), *The Works of Thomas Jefferson* (12 vols.; New York, 1904-1915), I, 17.

44 James Duane, "Notes on the State of the Colonies," May 25, 1775, *LMCC,* I, 98-101; Thomas Johnson, Jr., to Horatio Gates, Aug. 18, 1775, ibid., 190. It is apparent from Johnson's letter that Gates was opposed to the Dickinson petition.

45 Richard Henry Lee urged his brother Francis Lightfoot Lee, who was at that time a member of the Virginia Assembly, to refrain from taking action on the North proposal, should it reach the Virginia Assembly directly. R. H. Lee to F. L. Lee, May 21, 1775, in James C. Ballagh (ed.), *Letters of Richard Henry Lee* (2 vols.; New York, 1911-1914), I, 136. Congress rejected North's plan on July 31, 1775.

46 John Adams to James Warren, July 6, 1775, *LMCC,* I, 152.

47 JCC, II, 140-157.

48 John Adams to James Warren, July 6, 1775, *LMCC,* I, 152-153.

49 John Adams considered the possibility of foreign alliances as early as October of 1775 but dismissed it as unrealizable and dangerous. John Adams to James Warren, Oct. 7, 1775, ibid., 218-220. George Wythe's proposal was debated and postponed in February, the delegates recognizing that such an act would be tantamount to separation from England. Richard Smith, Diary, Feb. 16, 1776, ibid., 350-351.

50 Charles Thomson, Secretary of Congress, did enter Franklin's plan in a separate recording which he entitled "History of the Confederation." Copies of the plan were made public by some of the delegates, and it was considered by the New Jersey and North Carolina assemblies, both of which rejected it. Edmund C. Burnett, *The Continental Congress* (New York, 1941), p. 91. Franklin again moved that Congress take up the question of confederation in January of 1776, but this was opposed by John Dickinson and tabled by the Congress. Richard Smith, Diary, Jan. 16, 1776, *LMCC*, I, 313.

51 See, e.g., Carter Braxton to Landon Carter, Apr. 14, 1776, ibid., 420-421.

52 John Adams to James Warren, Oct. 7, 1776, ibid., 218-220. Adams speculated that both France and Spain would reason that the colonies would use them to gain independence, only to realign with England.

53 Josiah Quincy, Jr., Journal, Mar. 7, 1773, Massachusetts Historical Society, *Proceedings*, vol. 49, p. 445.

54 John Adams, *Works*, II, 416-418; Eliphalet Dyer to Joseph Trumbull, June 17, 1775, *LMCC*, I, 128.

55 *JCC*, II, 98.

56 See R. G. Adams's well-drawn portrait of Lee in the *DAB*, XI, 98-101; Douglas Southhall Freeman, *George Washington* (7 vols.; New York, 1948-1957), III, 441.

57 Charles Lee, *Strictures on a Pamphlet Entitled "A Friendly Address to All Reasonable Americans"* (Philadelphia, 1774). R. H. Lee to S. Adams, May 8, 1774, in James C. Ballagh (ed.), *Letters of Richard Henry Lee*, I, 110.

58 Lee had the support of Elbridge Gerry and Joseph Warren, for example. See James T. Austin, *Life of Elbridge Gerry* (2 vols.; Boston, 1828-1829), I, 79. Richard Henry Lee told Samuel Adams, "I take pleasure in introducing to your acquaintance General Lee, a most true and worthy friend to the rights of human nature in general, and a warm, spirited Foe to American oppression . . . I am sure his acquaintance will give you much pleasure." Lee to Adams, May 8, 1774, in Ballagh (ed.), *Letters*, I, 110. Apparently Lee did see Adams and the Boston radicals; the *Gazeteer and New Daily Advertiser*, Jan. 17, 1775, contains the following note on Lee: "extract of a letter from Boston, Dec. 10, 1774 . . . You asked me whether Colonel Lee . . . turned Liberty Boy? I can from the best authority assure you, that the very first person he enquired for on his arrival here, was Mr. Samuel Adams . . . the planner of all the measures of the rebels . . . and during the whole of his stay here, he was seldom, if ever, out of the company of one or another of our patriots, such as Adams, Young, Warren, Church and Hancock."

59 John Adams to James Warren, June 20, 1775, Warren-Adams Letters, I, 61. Adams goes on to assert he has "never formed any particular connection with Lee," and this may have been true for John Adams in a strict sense, but in view of other correspondence

of the Adamses and Richard Henry Lee, the conclusion that the Samuel Adams–Lee advocacy of Charles Lee did arise from a previous "connection" with Lee is almost inescapable.

60 See John Adams to James Warren, July 26, 27, and 30, 1775, ibid., 90, 93, 94. John Adams asserts in his autobiography that he had the support of Samuel Adams and Gerry, but not Cushing and Hancock, for this appointment. *Works*, III, 41.

61 Adams, *Works*, III, 13.

62 The letter is found in *JCC*, II, 76–78.

63 Adams, *Works*, III, 12–14.

64 *JCC*, II, 79, 83–84.

65 New Hampshire delegates to Matthew Thornton, Oct. 2, 1775, *LMCC*, I, 213. John Adams suggests in his autobiography that John Sullivan, who had strongly supported Adams when the latter made his suggestions in response to the Massachusetts letter of May 16, was instrumental in bringing about the New Hampshire petition. *Works*, III, 18.

66 Ibid.

67 New Hampshire delegates to Matthew Thornton, Nov. 3, 1775, *LMCC*, I, 246.

68 Adams, *Works*, III, 22.

69 *JCC*, II, 253.

70 Adams, *Works*, II, 414n.; John Adams to James Warren, Oct. 19, 1775, Warren-Adams Letters, I, 146–147.

71 *JCC*, III, 274.

72 Adams, *Works*, II, 452–457, 463, 469–486. Actually, the questions of a navy and trade were separate topics, but they became fused in congressional debates because of their natural relationship.

73 Ibid., 453, 455–456, 477.

74 Ibid., 469. Gadsden previously had advocated this policy on Oct. 5. Ibid., 456–457.

75 Ibid., 469–472. Silas Deane later became a *bête noire* for the Adams-Lee party in a dispute over the control of diplomacy. That he voted with the radical bloc at this time is an indication that the terms "radical" and "conservative" cannot be used categorically with regard to a continuum of time, though they do hold in the majority of cases. A fuller analysis of this point will be found in the following chapter.

76 See John Adams to James Warren, Oct. 7, 19, and 20, 1775, Warren-Adams Letters, I, 126, 146, 155.

77 Adams, *Works*, II, 463, 479–480, 463; ibid., III, 7; *JCC*, III, 283.

78 Joseph Hewes to Samuel Johnston, Nov. 9, 1775, *LMCC*, I, 251; Samuel Ward to Henry Ward, Nov. 11, ibid., 252.

79 For a description of the organization of the navy see Charles Oscar Paullin, *Paullin's History of Naval Administration, 1775-1911* (Annapolis, 1968), chap. 1.

80 Ibid., p. 19.

81 Richard Smith, Diary, Feb. 16, 1776, *LMCC,* I, 350-351.

82 Joseph Hewes to Samuel Johnston, Mar. 20, 1776, ibid., 401.

83 John Adams to Horatio Gates, Mar. 23, 1776, ibid., 406.

84 Hewes to Johnston, Mar. 20, 1776, ibid., 401.

85 Richard Smith, Diary, Mar. 18, 1776, ibid., 398. The final passage of a privateering bill came on March 19. *JCC,* IV, 257-259.

86 Gerry to James Warren, Mar. 26, 1776, in Austin, *Life of Gerry,* I, 174. Lee to Henry, Apr. 20, 1776, in Ballagh (ed.), *Letters,* I, 177.

87 Theodore Thayer, *Pennsylvania Politics and the Growth of Democracy* (Harrisburg, 1953), pp. 180-181.

88 David Hawke, *A Transaction of Free Men* (New York, 1964), p. 123. The crisis over independence in Pennsylvania is ably examined in more detail in Hawke's previous book *In the Midst of a Revolution* (Philadelphia, 1961), pp. 18-28. Hawke argues there was considerable interaction between congressional and provincial politics in this instance. See also J. Paul Selsam, *The Pennsylvania Constitution of 1776* (Philadelphia, 1936), esp. p. 101.

89 John Bradford to Richard Henry Lee, May 13, 1779, Samuel Adams Papers, NYPL.

90 In his diary, Christopher Marshall mentions Samuel Adams as a visitor more frequently than any other individual save James Cannon during the year before the Declaration of Independence. William Duane (ed.), *Extracts from the Diary of Christopher Marshall* (Albany, 1877), passim.

4 Factions and the Spirit of Seventy-Six

BEFORE the Declaration of Independence, the Continental Congresses were marked by profoundly serious struggles between radicals and conservatives over the resistance policy that led to separation from the mother country. It remains to examine the sources of those radical and conservative commitments. The examination is particularly interesting with regard to the radicals, since in the context of a colonial tradition of lawful change it is easier to explain the conservatives' hesitation to accept extralegal resistance than it is to account for the radicals' willingness to effect a violent revolution. It is important, however, to scrutinize all commitments, for to say that attitudes toward independence defined congressional factions is to set forth a tautology which obscures implications of early factionalism for subsequent partisan developments in the Congress.

Disconcertingly, the conventional broad-gauged determinatives such as the conflict between economic interest groups, between social classes, and between jarring political philosophies all produce disturbing anomalies when applied to congressional factions. John Adams and Samuel Adams had markedly different political philosophies, but they joined forces in support of violent revolution. Both were New Englanders, but they worked in concert with a number of Southerners without whose cooperation and leadership united endorsement of independence would have been impossible. Roger Sherman began as a bootmaker, while his radical cohort Richard Henry Lee was born into the upper ranks of the Virginia gentry. John Hancock was a radical merchant and Thomas Jefferson was a radical planter. But it will not do to insist upon the removal of all anomalies unless one is prepared to accept a kind of analytical anarchy by generating as many classifications as there were delegates in Congress.

The Revolutionaries themselves did not hesitate to describe their own qualities and those of the opposition. The radicals articulated their motives with complete assurance. They were simply forced to extremes in order to defend their just rights against a ministerial conspiracy to reduce the colonies to slavery. Their Tory opponents were, of course, less charitable. Peter Oliver, the eminent Tory who held many royal appointments in Massachusetts, charged that the radicals were activated by pride, resentment, passionate ambition, and other shabby impulses. Neither of the explanations can be dismissed, since the accuracy of a conviction has no relationship to the partisanship it inspires. There were, however, more considered judgments of the sources of factionalism. John Witherspoon, the notable Scotch Presbyterian divine who came to American in 1768 to become president of the College of New Jersey (now Princeton), warned against "the usual causes of division" shortly before he assumed his seat in Congress in the radicalized New Jersey delegation:

> If persons of every rank, instead of implicitly complying with the orders of those whom they themselves have chose to direct, will needs judge every measure over again, when it comes to be put in execution. If different classes of men intermix their little private views, or clashing interests with public affairs, and marshal into parties, the merchant against the landowner, and the landlord against the merchant. If local provincial pride and jealousy arise, and you allow yourselves to speak with contempt of the courage, character, manners, or even language of particular places, you are doing a greater injury to the common cause, than you are aware of[1].

Witherspoon was speaking to his congregation, but his words were printed and had application to the whole resistance, including the Congress.

Popular challenge of established authority, conflict between economic interests, and the opposition of one region to another had all contributed to congressional factionalism. Witherspoon's reflection that merchants might combine against planters had already materialized to some extent in the disagreements over the application of trade restrictions by Congress. Regionalism had been a constant problem as radicals attempted to bring the Middle colonies into line with the resistance effort. But before an assessment of these various influences can be made, it is necessary to classify as completely as possible the three factions as they stood regarding the movement toward independence.

In the absence of officially recorded votes and debates in Congress, it is

TABLE 2

Factions in the Continental Congress, May 1775–July 1776*

State	Radical	Moderate	Conservative
New Hampshire[2]	Langdon		
	Bartlett		
	Whipple		
Massachusetts[3]	Adams, S.	Cushing	
	Adams, J.		
	Gerry		
	Hancock		
Rhode Island[4]	Ward		
	Hopkins		
Connecticut[5]	Sherman		
	Wolcott		
	Dyer		
	Deane		
New York[6]		Lewis	Livingston, P.
		Floyd	Livingston, R. R.
		Wisner	Duane
			Jay
			Alsop
New Jersey[7]	Sergeant	Livingston, W.	Smith
	Clark	De Hart	
	Witherspoon		
	Stockton		
Pennsylvania[8]	Franklin		Dickinson
	Clymer		Willing
	Rush		Wilson
			Morris
Delaware[9]	McKean		Read
	Rodney, C.		
Maryland[10]	Chase	Paca	Johnson
			Tilghman
Virginia[11]	Lee, R. H.	Harrison	Braxton
	Lee, F. L.		
	Jefferson		
	Wythe		
North Carolina[12]	Penn	Hewes	
		Hooper	

State	Radical	Moderate	Conservative
South Carolina[13]	Gadsden	Lynch	Rutledge, E.
			Rutledge, J.
Georgia[14]	Bulloch		Zubly
	Hall		
	Gwinnett		

* Refer to the "Notes" section at the end of this chapter for the numbered references in the "state" column.

difficult to determine with assurance the positions of all members in the factional structure of Congress during this early period. This is particularly true of members who played obscure roles and therefore went unmentioned in the diaries and correspondence which have survived. Nonetheless, by piecing together odd references which indicate the positions of delegates in congressional proceedings, it is possible to construct a fragmentary representation of radical, moderate, and conservative forces as they related to the root question of active resistance and ultimately independence. The result, although impressionistic and incomplete, should be of use in interpreting the sources of factional commitments, particularly the radical commitment. Table 2 summarizes the configuration of the three blocs.

It is clear from careful examination of the factional structure of the second Congress that the ideological position of some delegates was not utterly consistent. Franklin had temporized during the Stamp Act crisis, but he was a firm radical in the first Congress and continued to be during the second Congress. Stephen Hopkins and Samuel Chase had been moderates in the first Congress, but they took the radical position during the second. George Clymer, while by no means as radical as the Bryans or Joseph Fook in the heated politics of Pennsylvania, was consistent enough in his support of the radicals to be included in the congressional faction. However, he would shortly veer toward the conservatives, as would Benjamin Rush. Rush was a committed advocate of independence and a convinced republican who was close to Thomas Paine, but he would subsequently join the conservative party in Pennsylvania as a result of his opposition to the Pennsylvania constitution and the radical party that formed to support it. Nonetheless, a majority of the delegates were consistent in their relationships with other delegates over time. With few exceptions the radicals in the Massachusetts and Virginia delegations continued to oppose the conservatives from New York and Pennsylvania throughout the Revolution. The question is, why?

II

Witherspoon's comments about economic interest serving as a catalyst for parties ring true for a number of conservatives. Robert Morris, Thomas Willing, Carter Braxton, and Benjamin Harrison all seem to have been wary of the effect a war would have upon their commercial investments. The division between radicals and conservatives in the Virginia delegation may well have reflected a division between agrarian and mercantile interests, since Harrison and Braxton had extensive commercial investments, while the radicals, Richard Henry Lee, Thomas Jefferson, and George Wythe, were primarily agrarians.

It will not do, however, to interpret the ideological configuration of Congress as a simple conflict between personalty and realty. Planter delegates from Virginia were frequently radical, but planter delegates from South Carolina were conservative. Individuals with mercantile interests in the Virginia delegation were conservative, but their counterparts in the South Carolina delegation were radical. The exigencies of business did not persuade merchants such as Christopher Gadsden, George Clymer, Eliphalet Dyer, Oliver Wolcott, Stephen Hopkins, John Hancock, Elbridge Gerry, William Whipple, and John Langdon to oppose radical resistance. Actually, merchants in the Continental Congress favored the radical cause by about 2 to 1. That ratio does not reflect a division between established merchants and expectant entrepreneurs, for Clymer and Hancock were as wealthy as most of the merchants in Congress who took the conservative position.

The intricate intercolonial and imperial connections between land company speculators probably also reinforced the formation of the conservative faction. Robert Morris, James Wilson, George Ross, and Thomas Johnson were all members of the Wabash Company. Yet whatever cohesive influence land speculation may have had on these delegates did not apply to Franklin and Samuel Chase, two radicals who were also members of the Wabash Company. Indeed, certain land investments might have contributed directly to radicalism. Andrew Allen of Pennsylvania charged that Connecticut land speculators were involved in "a deep laid Plot . . . to blow up the Constitution and Government of this Province which has hitherto been a Barrier against their dark Designs" [*15*]. Allen was suggesting that Susquehanna Company land speculators in Connecticut intended to use revolution to promote claims in the Wyoming Valley of Pennsylvania.

Robert R. Livingston and Carter Braxton were large landholders who may have opposed the Revolution because they feared that they would lose political and social power—an attitude to be expected from members of the landed aristocracy—but Richard Henry Lee and Thomas Jefferson were members of the landed aristocracy who did not hesitate to embrace the Revolution. Among delegates who derived the major portion of their income from the land, a slight majority seems to have favored the radical cause. Members of the professions did not show any overwhelming tendency toward radicalism or conservatism. Virtually all the New England lawyers in Congress were radical, but many from the Middle provinces, such as John Jay, James Duane, John Dickinson, and James Wilson, were conservative.

There are enough examples of delegates following a course ostensibly out of harmony with their economic interests to prompt further investigation. It is difficult to understand, for example, why John Hancock, already one of the richest men in New England, should advocate revolution in order to improve his fortune. Actually, Hancock lost money as a result of the Revolution. It is likely that he was captivated more by power and popularity than by the prospect of capital gains. Certainly this was the opinion of the Adamses, who found Hancock a staunch opponent in the contest for political power in Massachusetts. The Adamses themselves were intrigued more by the management of a revolution than by making money. Benjamin Franklin's steady drift toward radicalism after he became Agent for Massachusetts clearly jeopardized his place in the highly promising Grand Ohio Company land speculation. After the disclosure of his role in the imbroglio over the Hutchinson letters, he was forced to withdraw from the project, which had the support of no less than three members of the Privy Council[16]. William Floyd, the moderate New York delegate who was more sympathetic with independence than most of his delegation, knew that independence would place his property on Long Island in severe jeopardy—indeed, his estate was ruined by the end of the war[17].

The same consideration must have entered the thoughts of many others, and it undoubtedly contributed to the hesitation of men like Jay and his conservative friend Robert R. Livingston. John Adams speculated that "dread of confiscation" may have made men overly timid[18]. Some were willing to take the chance, however. Francis Lewis, another New York moderate, was deprived of his home and much of his wealth by the war[19].

If the calculations of economic interest are combined with attitudes toward the possibility of social and political unrest, the factional structure of Congress comes into somewhat clearer focus. Conservatives in the main were more closely attached to the colonial sociopolitical elites than were the radicals. There was no true representation of the ruling aristocracy of New Hampshire and Massachusetts in the strikingly radical delegations of those two colonies, for the Wentworths, Hutchinsons, and Olivers had become avowed Tories by this time. (This was less true, of course, in the chartered colonies of Rhode Island and Connecticut.) Jay, Duane, and the Livingstons, on the other hand, were part of the New York elite, either by birth or by marriage. (Duane was the son-in-law of Robert Livingston, Jr., Third Lord of the Manor.) The moderates Lewis and Floyd came from a distinctly lower echelon. Dickinson in Pennsylvania, Johnson and Tilghman in Maryland, and the Rutledges in South

Carolina were members of the social and political aristocracy. Even in Virginia the moderate Harrison and the conservative Braxton seem to have been more closely connected with the inner circle of political power than were the Lees and Jefferson, although, of course, the Lees were in the first rank of the gentry[20].

The correspondence of congressional conservatives often reveals uneasiness about actual or potential disturbance of the sociopolitical systems with which they were connected. Robert R. Livingston, writing shortly after independence, was alarmed that *"two thirds of our gentlemen fell off early in this controversy"* and that government would have to function "without that influence that is derived from respect to old families wealth age etc"[21]. Apparently John De Hart felt it more important to return to New Jersey to oppose the "levelling principles" in the New Jersey convention than to remain in Congress[22]. Conservative Virginians expressed the same fears. Landon Carter warned George Washington that the Virginia convention was composed of ambitious men and "inexperienced creatures," some of whom had the dangerous idea that government should be "independent of the rich man," with "every man . . . able to do as he pleased"[23]. Carter noted that these influences must eventually affect Virginia's representation in Congress. In the next election, the conservative delegates Braxton and Harrison were indeed eliminated. While the reasons for this are not entirely clear, Edmund Randolph wrote to Thomas Jefferson that "before the Day of ballotting arrived, no small Pains were taken to effectuate this Business," done on the pretext of saving money. William Fleming believed that a publication by Braxton containing suggestions for the Virginia constitution which "made him no friends in convention," as well as suspicions that his wife was a Loyalist, contributed to his rejection[24]. Braxton's *Address to the Convention of the Colony and Ancient Dominion of Virginia . . . By a Native of the Colony* was a warning against "all the tumult and riot incident to simple Democracy"[25]. Braxton advocated preserving as much of the English constitution as possible by having an elected assembly chosen for three-year terms, a council of state chosen by the assembly for life, and a governor and privy council elected by the legislature for good behavior[26].

Concern for social order was sometimes mixed with sectional distrust. Braxton was also alarmed about dislocation of the status quo as a consequence of confederation with the other colonies. In his *Address* he contended that any federal government should be prohibited from interfering in internal provincial affairs, a recommendation which should be understood in the context of his alarm over the egalitarian influence of New England. At just about the same time that he penned the *Address,* he wrote with irritation to Landon Carter that New Englanders were determined to accept the "best opportunity in the World now being offered them to throw off all subjection and embrace their darling Democracy"[27]. Edward Rutledge, a deep conservative, objected to the centralizing tendencies of Dickinson's work on a plan of confederation, partly because he viewed it as a vehicle for New England egalitarianism. In actuality, radical policy was more parochial than centralist, but observation of the radicals in Congress constructing a republican revolution did not disclose this fact. Thus John Adams ascribed part of the willingness of colonies to the south of New England to send troops to Boston in the summer of 1775 to a fear that a veteran army from New England might carry too much weight in the future [28]. Eliphalet Dyer of Connecticut believed that Pennsylvanian conservatives were trying to "possess the minds of Southern Gent of the Congress that we are a hardy daring enterprising people and if we prove successful against the Ministerial Army . . . we shall after that make our way by force into any of the Southern Colonies we please"[29].

It should be clear that no single factor can account for the complicated compound of individual and sectional interests and distrusts that contributed to the conservative force. Still, the most remarkable aspect of the controversy over resistance is not the existence of conservatism so much as the incidence of radicalism. The virtual unanimity of New England delegates in support of radical resistance, the role of the Southern radicals who seem to have violated all norms customarily associated with landed gentry by leading a revolutionary movement, and the willingness of radicals in Pennsylvania to stage what amounted to a coup d'état is less natural, and less understandable in a property-conscious society accustomed to gradual change.

In order to pursue these questions, particularly the sectional characteristics of partisan politics which were to become a fixed feature of congressional factionalism, it will be necessary to digress momentarily to investigate some of the broader aspects of the coming of the Revolution.

III

John Adams once compared the Revolutionary movement with "a large fleet sailing under convoy. The fleetest sailors must wait for the dullest and slowest"[30]. Resistance spread through the sections in stages. After Lexington and Concord, resistance was cauterized, and effective dialogue between radicals and conservatives was terminated in New England. Although the impact of Lexington and Concord stunned all the colonies, New England was at a more advanced stage of revolution than were the other provinces by the time the second Continental Congress convened. It was not until the fall of 1775 that the South experienced conflict. Dunmore's seizure of the powder at Williamsburg, his declaration of martial law, the burning of Norfolk, and, above all, his proclamation offering freedom to escaped slaves alienated all but the most conservative of the Chesapeake planters. The specter of a slave insurrection

helped persuade the gentry to lead in the overthrow of legitimate authority[31].
In North Carolina the battle at Moore's Creek Bridge in February of 1776
galvanized the determination of the Patriots and disclosed the internal danger
from Loyalists in the Carolinas. In Pennsylvania, on the other hand, the only
dispute that threatened to break out into armed conflict was between the Pennsylvanians and settlers from Connecticut in the Wyoming Valley.

Of course, the alliance between New England and the South antedated
Dunmore's blunders in Virginia and the battles at Lexington and Concord.
Indeed, the violence of 1775 was a product of earlier radical resistance. One
other possible general explanation of the sectional clusters of radicals in the
Congress, an explanation that can apply to the entire resistance movement,
is the ethnic and cultural homogeneity of the New England and Southern
societies relative to the Middle colonies.

On the surface, the social and economic characteristics of the three sections would seem to lead New England and the Middle provinces to combine
apart from the South. Both New England and the Middle colonies had stratified
but mobile urban societies surrounded by a self-sufficient property-owning
agrarian population. (There were immense landed estates in the Hudson River
Valley and a rich commercial farming region in southeastern Pennsylvania, but
these exceptions do not alter the generalization.) The South (again with an
exception in the major portion of North Carolina) contained fewer self-sufficient farmers, a larger agricultural laboring population, greater concentrations
of commercial agriculture, fewer urban areas, and in the tidewater region a
less mobile society[32]. The similarities between New England and the Middle
region did influence the merchant-controlled resistance of the 1760s and would
subsequently affect congressional partisan politics, but other influences seem
to have been more important when New England and the South combined to
promote the Revolution.

If the radical resistance is viewed as a product of a sense of separation, of
American community, of alienation from Britain, it is clear that New England
and much of the South shared common characteristics. Excepting the frontier
regions, both sections had developed a longer tradition of separateness from the
mother country than had the more recently settled Middle colonies. Richard
Merritt's massive analysis of symbols of American community in the colonial
press demonstrates that the perception of an American community separate
from England was first evident in the newspapers of New England and the
South, while the newspapers in the Middle colonies, and in particular New
York, were laggard in "recognizing the 'Americanness' of the colonies and
colonists" [33]. Ethnic homogeneity in the South and especially New England
also contributed to a sense of American community. It is noteworthy that
Virginia and Massachusetts, the two leaders of the Revolution, were the earliest
settled of all the colonies and were more purely English (excepting, of course,

the slave population of Virginia) than the Middle colonies. The presence of large enclaves of non-English populations in Pennsylvania, for example, seems ironically to have inhibited rather than enhanced consciousness of separation from England[34]. The more radical segments of the Middle colonies were those regions and population groups that by and large could identify with an older colonial tradition—the transplanted New Englanders of New Jersey and Long Island, the Scotch-Irish of Pennsylvania, and the "Presbyterian party" of New York whose Dissenter heritage harmonized with the Puritan message in the resistance literature. The evidence strongly suggests that cultural factors were of critical importance in the creation and reception of the rhetoric which helped legitimize violent revolution.

It is important in this connection not only to recognize the role of ideas in the coming of the Revolution, as historians again have, but also to distinguish between the constitutional argument regarding taxation and colonial liberties on the one hand, and what might be described as the broader holistic ideology of the Revolution on the other. The legalistic, argumentative character of much of the literature which condemned the Stamp Act, the Townshend Acts, the Tea Act, and the Coercive Acts as violations of constitutional liberties easily gives the impression that the resistance was a court case rather than a popular revolution. In truth the resistance was both, and in being both it had cohesive and divisive dimensions. Radicals and conservatives from all sections could and did support much of the legal brief against Parliament, but there was far less agreement about the moralistic reformative perception of the resistance which can be discerned at an early date in the pamphlets and correspondence of the resistance. Radicals may be distinguished from conservatives in terms of willingness to accept this latter broadly ideological meaning of the resistance. Further, while factors of individual psychology must in the final instance explain why some individuals such as Richard Henry Lee perceived the struggle with the mother country as ideologues while others such as John Dickinson did not, it is clear that sectional cultural environments did condition individual responses and therefore must be taken into account.

IV

In view of the emphasis historians have placed upon the admitted "uniqueness" of the British North American colonial polity, it is appropriate to stress that the work of political scientists and sociologists on the nature and force of ideology and the function of symbols in politics strongly suggests that the impact of ideology in the growth of a broadly based popular revolution in America resembled colonial revolutionary situations elsewhere. The characteristics of revolutionary ideological commitment, as summarized by Clifford Geertz (including the assumption that policy must conform to a "coherent, comprehensive set of beliefs which must override every other consideration," the doctrinaire tendency to claim "exclusive possession of political truth and . . . [abhor] compromise," the "alienative" tendency to distrust and attack established political institutions, the "totalistic" intention to "order the whole of social and cultural life in the image of ideals," and the "futuristic" promise to achieve "a utopian culmination of history"), were all present in varying degrees in the rhetoric of the radicals during the critical period of resistance and were obscured only by the argument of the radicals that they were attempting to restore the institutions they were attacking[35].

The widely held colonial belief that British policy was being formulated by a corrupt Ministry that was conspiring to reduce the colonies to a condition of "slavery" is an example of the alienation and distrust of established political institutions associated with ideological commitment[36]. Indeed, the assumption that British politics was corrupt was so widespread that it does not serve to discriminate between the radical and the conservative, the ideologue and the nonideologue, unless pains are taken to note the timing of such convictions and the implications which were drawn from them. Radical activists tended to stress British corruption earlier and in more extreme language than conservatives. They also seem to have become mesmerized by this notion, which was expressed again and again in private correspondence as well as public statements. Richard Henry Lee, for example, spoke of "tyrannical usurpation," of "systems calculated to destroy Human Liberty," and of Grenville's "infernal Crew of hireling Miscreants" in 1764 and 1765. As early as 1765 Lee was hopeful that "America can find Arms as well as Arts, to remove the Demon Slavery far from its borders. If I should live to see that day, I shall be happy; and pleased to say with Sidney, 'Lord now lettest now thy servant depart in peace'"[37].

While conservatives may have deplored ministerial corruption, they had faith in the recuperative faculties of British political institutions. The logic of John Dickinson's reliance upon petitions had to rest upon the expectation that policy makers in Britain might be persuaded to change their minds, or that the King and the people might force a change in ministers as a result of a legal remonstrance. Thomas Johnson, the delegate from Maryland, supported Dickinson's Olive Branch Petition, confident that it would help maintain a strong pro-colonial party in Parliament which would frustrate the "cunning Scotchmen" and Lord North[38]. Dickinson's urgent letter to Arthur Lee, written immediately after the adjournment of the first Congress, and predicting civil war unless "a few profligate men" leading a "brave and generous Nation" to "unmerited" distress were removed, reflects conservative and moderate assumptions about the extent of corruption in England[39]. What tended to separate the radical and the conservative (there were always exceptions of course) was differing attitudes about the depth of British corruption. While Dickinson was always careful to distinguish between "Mr. Grenville" and the "generous, sensible and humane nation, to whom we may apply"[40], Samuel Adams, Richard Henry Lee, and most radical activists believed that ministerial culpability was not isolated; rather, it was a generalized illness which had infected Parliament, as the Wilkes episode demonstrated, and which was spreading throughout all England. In the words of Samuel Adams, "there is no degree of vice, folly, or corruption now wanting to fill up any measure of iniquity necessary for the downfall of a state." Adams chastised not only the Crown and Parliament but also the freeman who sells his vote "for a belly full of porter" [41]. Samuel Chase voiced the same theme in 1775 in a letter to the conservative James Duane (whose correspondence characteristically does not reveal the same vein of alienation): "I consider [the British nation] as one of the most abandon'd & wicked People under the Sun," he charged. "They openly sell themselves & their Posterity to their Representatives who as openly traffic their Integrity & Honor to the Minister"[42].

In the mind of the radical ideologue the corruption that had infected British institutions and degraded the whole British nation threatened the colonies as well. The infection was evident not only in the presence of corruptionists in the customs service but also in the actions of virtually the whole of British officialdom. Worse still, increasing numbers of colonials were imitating British manners and succumbing to British vices. Indeed, as the Revolution drew closer, the radicals directed their attention increasingly upon the colonies rather than the mother country. Samuel Adams charged that his own Massachusetts had succumbed to "Levity Folly and Vice." This attitude was not peculiar to Adams or Massachusetts; Jefferson, Landon Carter, and many other leaders in Virginia deplored the luxurious tastes of the planter class, while Charles Thomson in Pennsylvania was shocked to find nineteen taverns on the 32-mile stretch of road between Philadelphia and Lancaster and chastised the "widespread debauchery and useless dissipation of time and money" which seemed so characteristic of the times[43]. The concern about the decline of colonial virtue antedated the period of active resistance against British policy.

Thomson's letter was written in 1764. Earlier, in 1761, John Adams wrote a statement which seems to have been intended as a letter to the press deploring the growing incidence of "public houses," with all their baleful effects: idleness, indebtedness, crime, incurable dissolution of manners, the corruption of government, enfeeblement of the race, in short, a pandora's box of "Plagues of every kind, natural moral and political"[44]. Adams opened the letter in a remarkable pose for a young man in his mid-twenties: "I am an old Man, seventy odd. . . ." After cataloging the evils of drink he proceeded to demonstrate "How different this is, from the state of Things in my Youth. Instead of unmanly Retreat to the Chimny Corner of a Tavern, the young fellows of my Age were out in the Air, improving their strength and Activity, by Wrestling, running, leaping, lifting, and the like vigorous Diversions, and when satisfyed with these, resorted every one . . . to virtuous Love . . . which these modern seminaries have almost extinguished or at least changed into filthiness and brutal Debauch . . ."[45]. Adams's puritanical compulsions may have been excessive, but the desire to reject the indulgences and promiscuity of the age was typical of the radical psychology[46].

The political consequences of moral degeneration could be as disastrous in the colonies as in the mother country. John Adams had seen the decline of political leadership in Massachusetts. The degradation of Daniel Leonard was an example. Leonard "wore a broad gold lace round the rim of his hat." wrote Adams, "He made his cloak glitter with laces still broader, but had set up his chariot and pair and constantly traveled in it . . . wealth and power must have charms to a heart that delighted in so much finery, and indulged in such unusual expense. Such marks could not escape the vigilant eyes of the two archtempters, Hutchinson and Sewall"[47]. It was Hutchinson in the guise of the "archtempter" who greatly contributed to the torrent of abuse which Samuel Adams poured upon this genial and scholarly native of Massachusetts. Hutchinson's alleged culpability was rooted in his having sold himself to the administration; it was augmented by his efforts to "tempt" others to commit treason against Massachusetts; and it culminated in his efforts to change the charter of Massachusetts by making Crown officials independent of the one check which arrested their total corruption—the power of the Legislature over the salaries of royal officials.

In Virginia there was a corollary concern about the corrosion of virtue in the planter leadership as a result of reckless consumption and consequent indebtedness. As Gordon Wood has noted, "Perhaps the importance of the Robinson affair in the 1760's lies not in any constitutional changes that resulted but in the shattering effect the disclosures had on that virtuous image [of the planter gentry]"[48]. The Loyalist who charged that Virginia's planter patriots should be compared with the first families of Rome who joined Cataline's rebellion because they were "slaves to luxury, and ruined by dissipation of every kind" may have been inexact in his analogy, but he also touched a sensitive nerve if the obsession with "corruption," "virtue," and "luxury" noted by Wood in the writings of the planter gentry is any indication of their attitudes[49]. The role of the planters in the enforcement of the Continental Association suggests that they were vitally concerned about internal reformation as well as resistance against Britain. The indictments delivered by the planter-controlled committees of inspection and observation were, if anything, more extreme in style and tone than those of Massachusetts. Further, the hostilities in 1775 between the Virginia militia and Dunmore's force suggest that the self-reforming planter leadership was striking at the most convenient external symbol of its decline—the concentration of Scotch merchants in the Norfolk region.

The broad support of radical resistance and ultimately revolution in New England and Virginia (and in their congressional delegations) may thus be explained in part by the need to reject the self-indulging tendencies of an increasingly wealthy planter and merchant social leadership which violated ancestral values and threatened economic and political disaster in these two older and homogeneous colonial societies[50].

It was natural for radical leaders in New England and Virginia, and indeed throughout the colonies, to attempt to lace the resistance movement with the reforming qualities of denial and austerity. Fast days were employed not only in New England, where they were a standing tradition, but also in Virginia, where they produced an effect "throughout the whole colony . . . like a shock of electricity, arousing every man, and placing him erect and solidly on his center," according to Jefferson, who with Patrick Henry and Richard Henry Lee was mainly responsible for the resolution[51]. The nonimportation movements were useful both as a means of applying pressure on Britain and as an attempt to induce reformation through self-denial and the separation of virtuous and corrupt segments of society. The failure of nonimportation in 1770 simply confirmed a general radical assumption that self-interest had contaminated vast portions of the mercantile community and that more drastic enforcement techniques should have been employed as they were in the implementation of the Continental Association through a vast system of committees of inspection and observation. The public confessions extracted from reformed violators of the Association accomplished this purpose, as did the boycott of merchants who refused to yield.

The well-known eighth article of the Association disclosed the wide employment of the appeal for austerity in prohibiting

> every species of extravagance and dissipation, especially all horse-racing, and all kinds of gaming, cock-fighting, exhibitions of shows, plays, and other expensive diversions and entertainments; and on the death of any relation or friend, none of us, or any of our families, will go into any further mourningdress, than a black crape or ribbon on the arm or hat, for gentlemen, and a black ribbon and necklace for ladies, and we will discontinue the giving of gloves and scarves at funerals [52].

The commitment to austerity was often infused with religious symbolism. Exhortations from the pulpit and the use of the fast day are obvious examples of this, but there were more subtle and perhaps unconscious uses of religious symbols. In North Carolina, the enforcement of the Continental Association resulted in a prohibition of horse racing on the grounds that "he only is a determined patriot who willingly sacrifices his pleasures upon the altar of freedom. . . ." Samuel Adams commented that he could live happily with poverty for the rest of his life if he could thereby contribute to "the Redemption of my Country"[53]. Governor Thomas Pownall noticed the fusion of religion, austerity, and partiotism in Massachusetts during the Townshend Acts nonimportation movement. He warned the British Parliament:

> The spirit of their religion will, like Moses' serpent, devour every other passion and affection; their love for the mother country, changing its nature, will turn to the bitterest hate; their affection of our modes and fashions (the present source of a great part of our commerce) will become an abomination in their sight[54].

Edmund Morgan has suggested that the resistance movement (and, indeed, the whole Revolutionary era) "was affected, not to say guided by a set of values inherited from the age of Puritanism"[55]. This was inevitable, given the vital influence of Puritanism in seventeenth-century colonial society, the persistence of Dissenter beliefs in the eighteenth century, the general tendency of national revolutions to draw upon past traditions, and the peculiarly rich potential of the Puritan tradition for the sustenance of a revolutionary ideology.

The Puritan value system provided an unmistakable standard for the evaluation of British political morality, and by encouraging the chastisement of corruption in England it contributed to a sense of alienation from the mother country. At the same time that it made the need for revolution almost compulsive, it nurtured, for New Englanders at least, an alternative identity, a prime function of revolutionary ideology. Its harmony with the Commonwealth tradition from which it drew inspiration provided a canopy of legitimacy which authorized defiance of constituted authority, even in terms that were familiar to the mother country herself. Its content was sufficiently specific concerning the symptoms of tyranny and the necessary checks against overweening use of power to apply to the precise points of the constitutional dialogue between Britain and the colonies; yet its generalized and evocative symbolism provided highly stimulating provocation for the general populace. It was conservative at its core in that it looked back to past values and sanctified property. It was thus a consolation to middle-class Revolutionaries, and indeed where necessary it elevated economic interest to high moral purpose. Yet its condemnation of profiteering helped gather the farmer and the mechanic into the Revolutionary fold. It institutionalized austerity through the Continental Association and thereby helped define the enemy while infusing a sense of solidarity and identification among those who accepted its commitments. Being many things to many men, it was a superb instrument of Revolutionary ideology.

The history of popular revolutions from the eighteenth century to the present has demonstrated that massive acceptance of an innovative political system can be greatly facilitated by endowing the new form with cultural attributes of older institutions. Thus President Sukarno of Indonesia, at the end of the Japanese occupation, drew upon ancient Indic tradition to frame the "sacred" ideological base for a newly independent nation[56]. That American revolutionaries should have incorporated Puritan values is entirely in accord with this nationalist revolutionary paradigm.

V

It is likely, on the other hand, that while the Puritan element of the Revolutionary ideology accentuated a sense of alienation from England, it also aroused sectional and class antagonisms within the Revolutionary coalition. In New England the Puritan message had a cohesive influence because of the preponderance of Congregationalists in that region. It is true, as Alan Heimert has pointed out, that many of the liberal, rationalist Congregational clergy were reluctant to urge the populace to support violent resistance[57]. Nonetheless, their reservations did not prevent the formation of a Revolutionary front in which orthodox and Arminian Calvinists as well as New Light evangelicals participated. The Coercive Acts muted theological differences and social distrusts, and there was general agreement about the corrupting influence of Great Britain, the need for moral regeneration, the profound danger of an American episcopate, the urgency of defending civil liberties as a means of preserving true religion, and the duty to resist British tyranny—if not as a commission from regicide Commonwealthmen, then at least from the Puritan forefathers. For many New Englanders, and clearly for many New England delegates to the Continental Congress such as the Adamses, Roger Sherman, Artemas Ward, Samuel Osgood, William Whipple, and Nathaniel Peabody, the Puritan revolutionary rhetoric was understood as a parochial, traditional, even curiously conservative force. The achievement of American nationality meant rejection of eighteenth-century corruption in its multiple aspects and the substitution of a republic of virtue as an updated version of the old wilderness Zion. The vision embodied many of the ingredients of conservative nationalism not simply because of the use of the past, but also because of the return to the conception of the covenanted community, an organic social system of collective sustenance and control. The Revolution would not wipe out social and political gradations, but the new order would be interdependent and virtuous, and thereby altogether different from the increasingly fragmented and sophisticated society of late eighteenth-century New England. It is not incongruous, therefore, that Massachusetts, the center of Revolutionary agitation in 1775, produced the most conservative of the state constitutions five years later.

Among the colonies as a whole, the Puritan rhetoric was devisive, a fact which helps explain the fractures in Middle colony delegations to the Continental Congress. In New York and Pennsylvania, more than in New England, the

Dissenter tradition tended to be rooted in the Great Awakening, in evangelical Calvinism, and correspondingly in a populist ethos. In New England the Puritan appeal could refer to the tradition of stewardship in the covenant theology as well as to the egalitarianism of the Commonwealth, but in the Middle colonies there was no harmonizing canopy comparable to the seventeenth-century wilderness Zion. Thus the Presbyterians were feared as populist revolutionaries, and New Englanders as aggrandizing Commonwealthmen.

It is, therefore, not surprising that when the Massachusetts delegates arrived in New York on their way to the first Congress, they were soon informed by radicals such as Alexander McDougall that the antagonism between the Livingston and DeLancey factions was also an encounter between Presbyterians and the Church of England. McDougall added that the Anglicans of New York had prejudices against New England which made them averse to extreme measures against England and that Episcopalian opposition to the resistance movement might well produce "a union of the Episcopal party, through the continent in support of ministerial measures"[58].

The Tory opposition in the Middle provinces echoed McDougall's analysis in different accents. Cadwallader Colden, the lieutenant governor of New York, believed that a "Presbyterian junto" was behind the Sons of Liberty and that Presbyterians had been the "chief and principal instruments" of all "flaming measures." Indeed, according to Colden, the resistance activists were outside agitators, mainly "independents from New England or educated there. . . ." Ambrose Serle, secretary to Admiral Lord Richard Howe, asserted that "Presbyterianism is really at the Bottom of the whole conspiracy, has supplied it with Vigor, and will never rest, till something is decided upon it"[59]. In Pennsylvania, the radical faction was also often referred to as "the Presbyterian interest." John Adams heard that "the Irish and the Presbyterian interest coalesce" in the support of liberty. One observer attributed the turnover of delegates to the Continental Congress elected from Pennsylvania in February of 1777 to the ascendancy of "the new light Presbyterian Party"[60].

The sectarian affiliations of congressional delegates from the Middle colonies do seem to show a connection between religion and politics. The conservative New York delegation was almost entirely Anglican. The New Jersey delegation which was removed just before independence contained a Baptist, a Quaker, and a Presbyterian, while the radical delegation that replaced it was heavily Presbyterian and under the leadership of John Witherspoon, a Presbyterian minister and president of the College of New Jersey. In the Pennsylvania delegation Benjamin Rush, who made the motion for independence in the Pennsylvania extraordinary convention, and Thomas McKean, who drew up the resolution with Rush, differed from the conservatives in their colony's delegation (such as Dickinson, Wilson, and Morris) both in politics and religion. Rush, although born an Anglican, turned to a rigid Calvinism. He leaned toward Universalism later in his life, but he was always a strong supporter of public worship and a believer in revealed religion, seeing no contradiction between that belief and his pursuit of science. He has been described as "unrelaxing" in his "earnestness and lack of self-indulgence" and completely lacking in the "lighter kind of humor"[61]. He had, in a word, the sort of zeal which characterized the Puritan, which he resembled, and the revolutionary, which he was and continued to be. James Wilson represented the opposite tendency. He had been a strong Whig and a Presbyterian, but perhaps because of his association with Robert Morris and other Philadelphia conservatives, he shifted to the conservative side, completing his conversion by joining the Episcopal church. It is clear from the Maryland delegate Tilghman's description of Thomas McKean, on the other hand, that McKean was a "true Presbyterian and joins the violents," while Dickinson was a Quaker[62].

Militant Puritanism was associated not only with revolutionary violence but with intolerance as well. Again, this caused more problems in the Middle colonies than in New England. Quakers and religious liberals from the Middle provinces saw religious authoritarianism darkly mixed with leveler tendencies in New England Congregationalism. Baptists from Massachusetts under the leadership of Isaac Backus could and did protest to a number of the delegates in the first Continental Congress that the Congregational establishment in Massachusetts was depriving them of their religious liberty, a complaint easily seized and enlarged upon by Israel Pemberton and other Philadelphia Quakers. Pemberton accused the Massachusetts radicals of intolerance and narrowmindedness and suggested that Massachusetts should follow the liberal example of more enlightened colonies. Noting the emphasis on liberty in the Revolutionary rhetoric, the Philadelphia Quakers asked whether "an upright, impartial desire to prevent slavery and oppression of our fellowmen, and to restore them to their natural right, to true Christian liberty, [had] been encouraged?" The Quakers suggested that corruption in the colonies could be eliminated by "showing mercy to the poor; and with true contrition and abasement of soul, to humble ourselves, and supplicate the almighty Preserver of men" for tranquility and peace, rather than arrogating the prerogative of God by "setting up and putting down Kings and Governments"[63].

The fears of Middle colony libertarian conciliationists seemed fulfilled by the radical coup d'état in Pennsylvania. The coup resulted in the Pennsylvania constitution of 1776 which required voters and officeholders to make a rigid profession of faith in Christ and in the Bible as the revealed Word of God. The man most responsible for this was the radical Presbyterian, Christopher Marshall[64]. In New York conservatives were able to retain control of the early stages of the revolutionary movement; consequently, the political radicalism and religious conservatism of the Presbyterian party was curbed. The cosmopolitan Gouverneur Morris and other influential members of the New

York convention insisted on a separation of church and state. Thus, the Church of England was disestablished, and an indulgent clause on religion was inserted in the constitution of 1777[65].

Southern reception of the Puritan element of the Revolutionary ideology was both mixed and inverted by comparison with the other regions in the Revolutionary coalition. In Virginia, for example, the influential Landon Carter joined a puritan distaste for the corruption of public virtue with liberalism in religion and conservatism in politics. Carter was as convinced as Samuel Adams that corrupt factions in England were plotting against American liberty, but he also feared that independence would result in democratic tumult and disorder. Thomas Jefferson, on the other hand, was as ardent as any New Englander in the support of independence, yet he had a deist's disdain for "enthusiasm" in religion. It is significant in this regard that Jefferson used the phrase "cooked up" when describing the unfamiliar strategy of the fast day resolution which would presumably arouse the populace of Virginia.

For the purpose of cementing a solid Revolutionary front, however, the Puritan appeal to austerity worked admirably with the Virginia aristocracy, which was deeply concerned about its indebtedness to Britain and inclined to think that social decay was spreading from England to the Chesapeake. If Carter Braxton and Landon Carter feared that men of wealth and virtue might be displaced by revolution, that fear was less intense than among the aristocracy in the Middle colonies[66]. The Virginia gentry was always in firm command of the Revolutionary process, a fact which in a sense supplied a comparable kind of stability that the stewardship tradition of the covenant theology did for New England conservatives. There was, moreover, a tradition of remarkable parish autonomy which encouraged opposition to the proposals for an American episcopate that was quite as intense as the opposition in New England. Many Southern Anglicans and probably all Southern radicals, whatever their religious persuasion, were prepared to applaud John Adams's warnings against ecclesiastical tyranny. Such general parallels help explain the alliance between Congregational and Episcopal radicals in the Continental Congress before independence. That there were pronounced differences between the two sects, on the other hand, is undeniable; indeed, such differences help explain some of the fractures in the alliance between New England and the South after independence.

The central secular and religious traditions of the South provided nurture for the principle of home rule, but they contained neither the leveler nor the antimonarchist tendency present in New England Congregationalism. Thus, while the maturity of Virginian society may have prepared that colony for independence, Virginians did not have the same traditionalist perception of the necessity and justice of the Revolution as did the Massachusetts radicals. The New Englanders stressed the independence of their Dissenter forefathers.

Virginians relied more upon constitutional principles and the history of the empire. But because the Revolution necessitated the rejection of the mother country, and since the achievement of an American nationality meant that the rationalization of independence should be articulated in terms outside the British experience whenever possible, Southerners often referred to the constitutional principles they drew from the British tradition in a-historical terms, however precisely located in British history. When Jefferson turned to the past, it was to "cook up" a fast day resolution or to find legal ammunition to refute British contentions that the colonies, having been established at public expense, owed allegiance to the Crown. If Jefferson discovered a golden age in the British past, it was in his *Summary View,* in which he expressed an attraction to Saxon England before simple democracy and liberty were contaminated by Norman feudalism[67] Jefferson's view of Saxon England was a romantic diversion rather than a meaningful historical appeal. In any event, it was too obscure to have ideological power. Samuel Adams was quite as guilty of utopian fantasy in his attraction to seventeenth-century Massachusetts, but Adams's historical symbols touched a past that was relevant for many inhabitants of New England.

Jefferson and Samuel Adams, and in varying degrees New Englanders and Southerners involved in the pre-independence alliance, faced the Revolution back to back, seeing it from different angles. The Revolutionary ideology was all-embracing enough to cover both orientations insofar as separation from the mother country was concerned, but it was not sufficiently cohesive to prevent later factionalism along lines of Revolutionary doctrine as well as in response to more tangible objects of sectional interest.

VI

Colonial resentment against the mother country had deeper causes not revealed in the emphasis on political morality in the Revolutionary rhetoric. Lawrence Henry Gipson has correctly stressed that the "Great War for Empire" radically changed the relationship between Britain and her North American colonies [68]. The removal of the French menace gave the colonies a new sense of security which lessened the need for British protection. (It was not coincidental that the geographic extremities of the colonial span were slower in supporting resistance, as in the case of Georgia and the other frontier areas, or were opposed to independence, as was Nova Scotia.) Seen from this perspective, the Revolution can be understood as a conflict over the requirements of imperial administration. Britain, sensing that her empire was so vast as to be unmanageable, temporarily halted continental expansion and tightened her imperial administration during the decade of the 1760s. The colonies, having already promoted imperial expansion on a smaller scale during the more lax period of British administration, chafed under the new restrictions. This source of conflict is well recognized and needs no elaboration, save perhaps to note that this constituted yet another dimension of Revolutionary ideology that conforms to the general model previously mentioned. The grandiose, utopian future could be seen not only as a puritan reformation, the intention of Samuel Adams, but also as an expanding America. Thomas Paine, whose sense of powerful ideological symbols was unmatched, sedulously used the word "continental" in his pamphlet *Common Sense:* "'Tis not the affair of a city, a country, a province, or a kingdome, but of a continent. . . . Now is the seed-time of continental union, faith and honor. . . . It is repugnant to reason, to the universal order of things, to all examples from former ages, to suppose, that this continent can longer remain subject to any external power"[69].

Practically all colonials, whatever their attitude toward resistance, accepted that America would ultimately outstrip the mother country in population and wealth. Thus this element of the Revolutionary ideology, like the contrast between the virtuous colonies and the corrupt mother country, had a cohesive influence. Yet again, as in the implications that were drawn from the ebb in political morality, there were divisive factors in attitudes toward expansion. Moderates and conservatives were less convinced than radicals that immediate separation was necessary to achieve this growth. Indeed, conservatives such as Carter Braxton anticipated that independence would result in civil war between the colonies as a result of conflicts over the unoccupied lands[70]. Land speculators in the Middle colonies which did not have charter rights in the West had worked through London to establish their claims. Revolution would erase the groundwork laid by speculative groups such as the Wabash Company, and it would prejudice the opportunity of the whole Middle region to participate in the westward movement. The South, with its vast claims to the West, could expect to gain from the Revolution. New England and New York also had claims, but there were differences between New England and the South in the way they viewed the West. These differences did not interfere with the establishment of a Revolutionary front, but they had the potential of splitting the radical bloc in Congress asunder.

The French and Indian War put these two radical sections in substantially different positions whether within the British Empire or outside it. The South was poised for extension into the interior. Virginians and North Carolinians were already probing the trans-Appalachian lands in the individualistic manner they had been accustomed to. New Englanders, however, were more separated from the West. Further, the Quebec Act had established a new jurisdiction over the New England claims (unlike the Southern claims beneath the Ohio)—a jurisdiction uncongenial in its political and ecclesiastical provisions. The Quebec Act reinforced the tendency of New Englanders to focus their attention more upon their own unoccupied spaces and upon unsettled areas in Pennsylvania and New York. Maritime interests also diverted the attention of New Englanders from the continental vision of the South. The expansionist thrust of Massachusetts had been north and east more than west, and policies had been based more upon the cultivation of commerce and the fisheries than upon staple agriculture. By 1779, when the Continental Congress was asked by France to stipulate its requirements for peace, the Southern and Eastern parties in Congress would pull in two different directions to the disadvantage of the radical coalition. But by then the coalition had already been subjected to severe strain.

Americans agreed that Britain had blundered in her imperial administration. Whether or not the Revolution would be successful would depend in turn upon how well the Revolutionary leadership could supply a better political framework for the vast continent with its disparate traditions and interests. Virtually all revolutionaries, whether radical or conservative in their attitude toward the pragmatic wisdom of independence, could agree that a republic was the most desirable form of government. The thrust of Revolutionary ideology led irresistibly to the conclusion that a republic was the only form which would embody the liberty toward which the resistance movement had been directed and which would at the same time cultivate the public virtue upon which a reforming society must depend. The emphasis of resistance literature on the specific corruptions of the British administration, the remarkable absence of any vital dialogue between radical and conservative Revolutionaries about even the possibility of a nonrepublican revolution, and the fact that the only influential attack against the institution of monarchy was written by Thomas Paine, an outsider, all testify to the deep republican commitment of the Revolutionaries[71]. The difficulty lay in the specific definition of a continental republic of virtue. Even if the republic could be defined, its achievement was another problem.

Notes

1 John Witherspoon, *The Dominion of Providence over the Passions of Men* . . . (Philadelphia, 1776), p. 47.

2 The New Hampshire delegation must have given regular support to radical measures for the radicals to have obtained as many votes as they did. They first set the stage for the recommendation by Congress for the assumption of civil government by the provincials, and although they were acting under instructions from the New Hampshire provincial convention, the letters from Bartlett and Langdon to Matthew Thornton (Oct. 2, 1775, *LMCC*, I, 213) and the New Hampshire Committee of Safety (Oct. 26,

1775, ibid., 241–242) indicate that the delegates took the first steps to forward this design. (See also the letter from Bartlett and Langdon to Matthew Thornton, Nov. 3, 1775, ibid., 246.) Bartlett and Whipple also suggested that New Hampshire authorize its delegation to vote for independence; Bartlett and Whipple to President of New Hampshire, May 28, 1776, ibid., 466.

3 The radicalism of John and Samuel Adams needs no documentation. Elbridge Gerry was elected to fill the place of the moderate Cushing, who was not prepared to advocate independence; Gerry's radicalism is evident in his letter to James Warren in which he suggested that Massachusetts instruct her delegates to declare for independence. Gerry to Warren, Mar. 26, 1776, ibid., 409–410. Cushing's moderation is evident from John Adams's complaint to Joseph Hawley that Cushing regularly split the Massachusetts vote. Adams to Hawley, Nov. 25, 1775, ibid., 260, See also Samuel Adams to John Adams, Dec. 22, 1775, ibid., 284. It is difficult to place John Hancock anywhere other than in the ranks of the radicals, but if John Adams's memory served him well, Hancock "courted Mr. Duane, Mr. Dickinson, and their party. . . ." Adams, *Works,* III, 34–35. Harrison seems to substantiate Adams in his letter to Washington; Harrison to Washington, July 21, 1775, *LMCC,* I, 170.

4 Ward was one of the stalwarts of the Adams-Lee faction within the radicals. See Adams, *Works,* III, 35. Hopkins was also a radical, although there had been a long-standing political feud between Ward and Hopkins in Rhode Island. Hopkins' radicalism was most pronounced on naval matters in which his colony and he himself were materially concerned.

5 Sherman's radicalism also needs no substantiation, but see Christopher Collins, *Roger Sherman's Connecticut* (Middletown, Conn., 1971), passim. Wolcott seems to have been ready for independence in February of 1776. Wolcott to Samuel Lyman, Feb. 19, 1776, *LMCC,* I, 356. Deane was radical on issues involving the creation of a navy, outfitting privateers, and opening American ports to foreign trade. Adams, *Works,* II, 452–453, 463. Yet Deane was not within the radical nucleus and would later become an archenemy of the Adams-Lee faction. He probably belongs on the fringe of the radicals because of his attitudes toward the resistance in 1775.

6 Little need be mentioned about the conservatism of Duane and Jay. Duane seconded Galloway's plan of union and supported Dickinson's conciliatory plans. Jay's conservatism is evidenced in his vote on March 22, 1776, opposing a motion to name the King rather than Parliament as the cause of colonial ills. Richard Smith, *Diary, LMCC,* I, 404. Alsop and Wisner made little impact upon Congress and apparently voted along with the majority of their colleagues. Wisner was most insistent that the New York Provincial Congress reconsider its instructions. Wisner to New York Provincial Congress, July 2, 1776, ibid., 525. It does appear, however, that Wisner favored independence before the New York Provincial Congress altered its instructions to the New York delegation. Thomas McKean asserted many years afterward that Wisner actually voted for independence. E. C. Burnett is skeptical of this in view of the fact that the New York delegates were not authorized to vote on the question. McKean to A. J. Dallas, Sept. 26, 1796, ibid., 533, 525n. Alsop's conservatism can be seen in his reisgnation of his seat after the New York convention endorsed the Declaration of Independence. Alsop to the

New York convention, July 16, 1776, ibid., II, 12–13. Floyd may have shown more moderate tendencies. Benjamin Rush relates that he "always voted with the zealous friends to liberty and independence." George W. Corner (ed.), *The Autobiography of Benjamin Rush* (Princeton, 1948), p. 146. Lewis had been one of the dissenters on the Committee of Fifty-one in New York (Force [ed.], *Amer. Arch.,* ser. 4, I, 113–114) and probably was more favorable to independence than most of the New Yorkers. His subsequent record shows him as a moderate, but there is little evidence of his position in Congress at this time.

7 The fact that New Jersey sent a new delegation just before independence was declared, and that after that New Jersey swung away from the conservatism characteristic of the Middle colonies, indicates both that the previous delegation (William Livingston, John De Hart, and Richard Smith) was rather conservative and the newer one more radical (J. D. Sergeant, Clark, Witherspoon, Hopkinson, and Stockton). This is substantiated by Witherspoon's general reputation as a radical and by Sergeant's position on the vote of March 22 referred to in note 6. W. L. Whittlesey asserts Abraham Clark was sent to Congress as an outspoken advocate of independence; *DAB,* IV, 19. It is nevertheless difficult to call William Livingston and De Hart conservatives in spite of the election of the newer, more radical delegates. Livingston may not have wanted independence, but he is mentioned by Paul Wentworth, a New Hampshire Loyalist who had a good deal of accurate information on the colonies, as "a violent Presbyterian and Independent" who was a leader of radicalism in New Jersey. B. F. Stevens (ed.), *Facsimiles of Manuscripts in European Archives Relating to America, 1773–83* (26 vols.; London, 1889–1895), no. 487, pp. 7, 19.

8 Dickinson and Wilson were leaders of the conservatives in Congress, as is well known. Willing joined Wilson and Duane against the radicals on the debate of February 21, 1776, concerning Congress's desire to continue dependence upon Great Britain. Richard Smith, Diary, Feb. 21, 1776, *LMCC,* I, 359. Robert Morris, also a conservative, would not vote for independence. See also ibid., 271, 416. Franklin's radicalism needs no substantiation; nor does Rush's. Clymer is customarily classified in the left wing of the Pennsylvania Whigs. He was introduced to Samuel Adams in April of 1773 in connection with the resistance movement (William V. Wells, *Samuel Adams* [3 vols.; Boston, 1865], II, 61), was chairman of the committee which forced the tea merchants to resign (*DAB,* IV, 235), and voted for independence.

9 McKean's radicalism is well accepted. John Adams records that he denied parliamentary authority over America as early as September 1775. Adams, *Works,* II, 426. McKean was also instrumental in securing Delaware's repudiation of the Crown and support of independence by his personal appearance in the Delaware Assembly. *DAB,* XII, 79. Caesar Rodney's 80-mile ride to vote for Lee's resolution for independence is a symbolic capstone to his career of radicalism in Delaware, while George Read's conservatism is attested to by Delaware's divided vote, on July 1, on independence (Read canceling out McKean).

10 Chase is an example of a moderate who turned radical during the latter phase of the resistance. By 1776 John Adams thought enough of Chase's radicalism to urge him privately to campaign in Maryland for instructions to the congressional delegation to

vote for independence; *LMCC,* I, 503. Adams also records that Chase was one of those in favor of the recommendation to the colonies to form their own governments; Adams, *Works,* III, 21. Paca took a moderate position, apparently not protesting Maryland's instructions to vote against independence, and being willing earlier to grant Parliament the authority to regulate trade. Adams, Diary, Sept. 23, 1775, ibid., II, 426. Thomas Johnson, Jr.,'s conservatism is testified to by his support of the Olive Branch Petition (Johnson to Horatio Gates, Aug. 18, 1775, *LMCC,* I, 190), his opposition to the outfitting of privateers in March of 1776 (ibid., 386), as well as his vote on March 22, 1776, when he opposed naming the King rather than Parliament as the source of colonial troubles. Tilghman was a strong conservative. See his letter to his father, Feb. 4, 1776, in Charles Stillé, *Life and Times of John Dickinson* (Philadelphia, 1891), p. 30.

11 No documentation is necessary to establish the well-known radicalism of Richard Henry Lee, Francis Lightfoot Lee, and Jefferson. Wythe strongly supported confederation as early as January 1776, when the Congress stalled on this issue. Samuel Adams to John Adams, Jan. 15, 1776, in Harry A. Cushing (ed.), *The Writings of Samuel Adams* (4 vols.; New York, 1904-1908), III, 260. See also Samuel Adams to James Warren, Oct. 3, 1775, Warren-Adams Letters, Massachusetts Historical Society, *Collections* (2 vols.; Boston, 1917, 1925), I, 124. Benjamin Harrison supported more than one radical measure (see Richard Smith, Diary, *LMCC,* I, 350, for his position on foreign alliances, e.g.), but nevertheless was an opponent of the Lees and Adamses. Benjamin Harrison to George Washington, July 21, 1775, ibid., 169-170; Adams, *Works,* III, 35. John Adams believed Harrison was trying to slow down the movement for independence; ibid., 41-42. Carter Braxton called independence a "delusive bait" in April of 1776; *LMCC,* I, 420-421.

12 Hooper was not ready to recommend constitutions for New Hampshire and South Carolina in 1775 and wanted reconciliation in February of 1776. Adams, *Works,* III, 21-22; Hooper to Samuel Johnston, Feb. 6, 1776, *LMCC,* I, 348n. Yet Hooper argued for confederation in January of 1776 along with Franklin against Dickinson. Richard Smith, Diary, July 16, 1776, ibid., 313. Penn, like Hooper, wanted both freedom and reconciliation, but he also suggested the radical step of considering foreign alliances in early 1776. Penn to Thomas Person, Feb. 14, 1776, ibid., 349. Hewes's suspicions that the radicals in Congress were scheming for independence, which he hoped would not come too soon, seem to place him with the conservatives. Hewes to S. Johnston, Dec. 1, 1775, ibid., 266-267. But Hewes was a firm Patriot in the North Carolina resistance.

13 Gadsden's radicalism is proverbial. Lynch seems to have joined the radicals early in the first Congress (remembering his recommendations of Carpenter's Hall and Charles Thomson), but he definitely was not on good terms with the New England radicals as well as his own radical colleague Gadsden. Lynch to Washington, Dec. 8, 1775, in Force (ed.), *Amer. Arch.,* ser. 4, IV, 218; Lynch to P. Schuyler, Jan. 20, 1776, *LMCC,* I, 323. Lynch supported independence, and it seems he should be a radical, but not as a member of the inner core of the group. Both Rutledges generally supported Dickinson. See, e.g., Jefferson's comments on the proceedings in the June 8 meeting of the Committee of the Whole concerning Lee's motion for independence, in Julian Boyd (ed.), *Papers of Thomas Jefferson* (Princeton, 1950-), I, 309-313. South Carolina also voted against independence on July 1. ibid., 314. See also Edward Rutledge's letter to John Jay, June 29, 1776, *LMCC,* I, 517.

14 Zubly's adamant opposition to independence is well known. Bulloch, Hall, and Gwinnett's arrival in Congress swung Georgia to the cause of independence.

15 Andrew Allen to Philip Schuyler, Mar. 17, 1776, *LMCC,* I, 398.

16 Bernard Donoughue, *British Politics and the American Revolution* (London, 1964), pp. 116–117.

17 *DAB,* VI, 481.

18 John Adams to Mrs. Adams, July 23, 1775, in Charles Francis Adams (ed.), *Familiar Letters of John Adams and His Wife Abigail Adams during the Revolution* (Boston, 1875), p. 83.

19 Examples of individuals violating economic interest in supporting the Revolution could be vastly enlarged by reference to activities outside Congress. The merchants of Newburyport, Massachusetts, appear to have participated in radical resistance and Revolution throughout the whole period 1764–1776 for political rather than economic reasons. Indeed, according to Benjamin Labaree, *Patriots and Partisans* (Cambridge, 1963), the Newburyport merchants who helped bring about independence were ruined by the Revolution (p. 43).

20 Carter Braxton and Benjamin Harrison, for example, were close enough to the Virginia Treasurer John Robinson to have been implicated in Robinson's generous but scandalous lending of the colony's funds. Harrison owed £150, while Braxton was one of the major debtors, owing £3,848. Richard Henry Lee is listed for just £12, probably a minor personal debt, while Francis Lightfoot Lee, Jefferson, and Wythe owed nothing. Since Robinson was perhaps the most powerful political figure in Virginia immediately before the resistance period, the list of major debtors is suggestive of the dimensions of the Virginia oligarchy. The list of debtors to the Robinson estate can be found in David Mays, *Edmund Pendleton* (2 vols.; Cambridge, Mass., 1952), I, 358–369. As Mays points out, the Lees and Patrick Henry (who owed Robinson just £11) could have had funds from Robinson if they chose (p. 184), and so their not being indebted to any significant amount does not necessarily exclude them from the ruling establishment. Yet it is worth noting that Richard Henry Lee and Henry were political antagonists of Robinson and were in this sense outside the inner circle.

21 Robert R. Livingston to Edward Rutledge, Oct. 10, 1776, Livingston-Bancroft Transcripts, NYPL, I, 229, quoted in George Dangerfield, *Chancellor Robert R. Livingston* (New York, 1960), p. 87.

22 Jonathan D. Sergeant to John Adams, Apr. 11, 1776, quoted in John Hazelton, *The Declaration of Independence* (New York, 1906), p. 58.

23 Landon Carter to George Washington, May 9, 1776, *Amer. Arch.,* ser. 4, VI, 389–391.

24 Edmund Randolph to Thomas Jefferson, June 23, 1776; William Fleming to Jefferson, July 27, 1776, in Boyd (ed.), *Papers of Thomas Jefferson,* I, 407, 475.

25 *Amer. Arch.,* ser. 4, VI, 751.

26 Ibid., 752–753.

27 Braxton to Landon Carter, Apr. 14, 1776, *LMCC*, I, 421.

28 John Adams to James Warren, July 6, 1775, ibid., 153.

29 Dyer to William Judd, July 13, 1775, ibid., 172–173.

30 John Adams to Mrs. Adams, June 17, 1775, ibid., 132.

31 The Virginia convention framed a declaration contending that since Dunmore had offered freedom to the slaves and armed them for the destruction of Virginians, it was the duty of the convention to protect their constituents. One of the prominent members of the committee which framed the resolution was Carter Braxton. Force (ed.), *Amer. Arch.,* ser. 4, IV, 81–82. See also "Letter from a Clergyman in Maryland to the Earl of Dartmouth," Dec. 20, 1775, ibid., 361, in which it is asserted that Dunmore's proclamation "made the breach infinitely wider;" also the pamphlet *An American,* Jan. 5, 1776, calling Dunmore's plot a "base and inhuman strategem," and "a savage war" which would "cut the Gordian knot which has hitherto so firmly bound us to Britain;" ibid., 539–540.

32 Jackson Turner Main, *The Social Structure of Revolutionary America* (Princeton, 1965), pp. 37, 51, 62, 184, 187, 189, 192, 193. For a discussion of the tendency toward greater stratification in Boston see James Henretta, "Economic Development and Social Structure in Colonial Boston," *WMQ,* ser. 3, XXII (1965), 75–92.

33 Richard Merritt, *Symbols of American Community* (New Haven, 1966), esp. p. 137.

34 William H. Nelson, *The American Tory* (London, 1961), p. 89.

35 Clifford Geertz, "Ideology as a Cultural System" in David Apter (ed.), *Ideology and Discontent* (Glencoe, 1964), p. 50.

36 Bernard Bailyn, *Pamphlets of the American Revolution* (Cambridge, Mass., 1965), I, 86–89. Bailyn has shown that this attitude permeated the literature of the resistance. See also Gordon Wood's impressive *Creation of the American Republic, 1776–1787* (Chapel Hill, 1969), passim.

37 Richard Henry Lee to a gentleman in London, May 31, 1764; Lee to Landon Carter, June 22, 1765; Lee to Arthur Lee, July 4, 1765; Lee to Carter, Aug. 15, 1765; James Ballagh (ed.), *Letters of Richard Henry Lee* (2 vols.; New York, 1911), I, 6, 8, 10–12.

38 Thomas Johnson to Horatio Gates, Aug. 18, 1775, *LMCC*, I, 190. Johnson also argued that if the petition were rejected, the colonials could then achieve greater unity against an intransigent Ministry. Yet it is evident to me that Johnson was inserting this notion mainly to make the petition more palatable to radicals.

39 John Dickinson to Arthur Lee, Oct. 27, 1774, *Amer. Arch.,* ser. 4, I, 947.

40 John Dickinson, "Letters from a Farmer in Pennsylvania" (Letter No. 111), in Paul Leicester Ford (ed.), *The Writings of John Dickinson* (Philadelphia, 1895), p. 327.

41 "A Religious Politician," Wells, *Samuel Adams,* II, 371-372.

42 Samuel Chase to James Duane, Feb. 5, 1775, Duane Papers, NYHS. In marking the distinction between a revolutionary and a moderate or a "radical" and a "conservative" at this particular point, it is instructive to compare the papers of James Duane and Samuel Adams. While Adams's correspondence for the year 1775 is studded with letters which in their entirety stitch together a revolutionary fabric with the strands gathered at the first Continental Congress, this letter from Chase is the only letter in the existent Duane correspondence at the NYHS from a delegate at the first Continental Congress which deals with the resistance movement. There is a letter from Thomas Wharton (Mar. 18, 1775) which presumes upon the acquaintance struck up between Duane and Wharton at the first Congress, but interestingly enough, the letter is entirely concerned with a request by Wharton that Duane should execute a commission to sell 20,000 acres of land which had been used as security for a debt owed by George Croghan to Wharton which Croghan was unable to pay. Thomas Wharton to James Duane, Mar. 18, 1775, Duane Papers, NYHS.

43 Samuel Adams to William Checkley, June 1, 1774, in Cushing (ed.), *Writings,* III, 128; Wood, *Creation of the American Republic,* p. 109; Charles Thomson to Benjamin Franklin, Dec. 18, 1764, in I. Minnis Hays (ed.), *Callendar of the Papers of Benjamin Franklin,* (5 vols.; Philadelphia, 1908), II, 36.

44 Lyman H. Butterfield (ed.), *Diary and Autobiography of John Adams* (Cambridge, 1962), I, 190-192. This piece is in Adams's Diary but was apparently intended for publication. It did not appear in any of the Boston newspapers, however. Butterfield calculates the date as January of 1761.

45 Ibid., 190, 192.

46 Adams's Diary also contains a lengthy list of suggestions for his nieces, penned at about the same time as the statement on taverns, in which he berates English women for being the most slovenly in Christendom and expresses such a keen interest in tidy cleanliness that he promises that if his daughters do not take proper care of themselves when reaching "the Years of Discretion," he would "throw [them] into a great Kettle and Boil till they are clean . . ."; ibid., 193-194.

47 Adams, *Works,* II, 194-195.

48 Gordon S. Wood, "Rhetoric and Reality in the American Revolution," *WMQ,* ser. 3, XXIII (1966), 3-32. The magnitude of planter consumption is examined in Emory G. Evans, "Planter Indebtedness and the Coming of the Revolution in Virginia," ibid., XIX (1962), 511-533.

49 *Amer. Arch.,* ser. 4, II, 14. Wood, "Rhetoric and Reality."

50 That the attack upon merchant corruption in Massachusetts was executed by radicals outside the center of power, while the Virginia planter radicals were in part involved in the excoriation of their own class, helps explain the greater presence of moderate and conservative elements in the Virginia resistance.

51 Paul Leicester Ford (ed.), *The Works of Thomas Jefferson* (12 vols.; New York, 1904–1905), I, 9–10.

52 JCC, I, 78.

53 Proceedings of the Wilmington Committee of Public Safety, *CRNC,* IX, 1091; Samuel Adams to William Checkly, June 1, 1774, in Cushing (ed.), *Writings,* III, 128.

54 Speech of Governor Pownall before Parliament, 1769, reprinted in the *London Chronicle,* Sept. 19, 1776, by "An American." *Amer. Arch.,* ser. 5, II, 390–391.

55 E. S. Morgan, "The Puritan Ethic and the American Revolution," *WMQ,* ser. 3, XXIV (1967), 3. Morgan emphasizes the "Puritan ethic" as a refinement of Weber's conception of the Protestant Ethic, but the ideological significance of the Puritan tradition can be construed in the broadest manner, as will be suggested below.

56 See Geertz, "Ideology as a Cultural System," in Apter (ed.), *Ideology and Discontent,* p. 67.

57 Alan Heimert, *Religion and the American Mind* (Cambridge, 1966), pp. 419–420.

58 Adams, *Works,* II, 348–350. See also John Webb Pratt, *Religion, Politics, and Diversity: the Church-State Theme in New York State History* (Ithaca, N.Y., 1967), p. 77. Pratt asserts, "The religious grievances of New Yorkers became rooted in the protest movement leading on ultimately to hostilities and independence."

59 Cadwallader Colden to the Earl of Hillsborough, quoted in Claude Van Tyne, *Causes of the War of Independence* (Boston, 1922), p. 365; Ambrose Serle to Admiral Howe, quoted in Charles H. Metzger, *Catholics and the American Revolution* (Chicago, 1962), p. 126. According to a letter from Boston in the Jan. 19, 1775, issue of the *Gazeteer and New Daily Advertiser,* it was the general belief of the British colonial officialdom that "Presbyterians everywhere are not only inimical to us, but determined to break off all connections with us as soon as they can." Governor Martin of North Carolina echoed this notion when he advised Lord Dartmouth that "distinctions and animosities of a purely religious nature between the Anglicans and Presbyterians had become transferred to politics" and that Presbyterians "in general throughout the continent are not of the principles of the Church of Scotland, but like the people of New England, more of the leaven of the independents, who have been ever unfriendly to Monarchical Government." *CRNC,* IX, 1086.

60 Edward Tilghman to his father, Feb. 4, 1776, in Stillé, *Dickinson,* p. 174; Adams, *Works,* II, 426; James Allen, Diary, *PMHB,* IX (1885), 279.

61 Corner (ed.), *Autobiography of Benjamin Rush,* pp. 233, 10.

62 Note that Tilghman used the term "Presbyterian" as a definition of antiestablishmentarian commitment. Tilghman to his father, Feb. 4, 1776, in Stillé, *Dickinson,* p. 173.

63 "Ancient Testimony and Principle of the People called Quakers, renewed, with respect to the King and Government; and touching the Commotions now prevailing in these and other parts of America, addressed to the people in general," *Amer. Arch.,* ser. 4, IV, 785–787. The patriot response was to stress that while the colonies were indeed corrupt, Britain was more so, and that while the tribulations being endured at the moment might very well be retribution for past iniquities, "it would be rendering ourselves unworthy of His future protection to throw ourselves back upon her." Further, the colonial role in the collapse of the British Empire was clearly that of serving as God's instrument; "A Religious Politician," Wells, *Samuel Adams,* II, 374.

64 William Duane (ed.), *Extracts from the Diary of Christopher Marshall* (Albany, 1877), June 28, 1776, pp. 79–80. The statement went "I _____ do profess faith in God the Father and in Jesus Christ, his Eternal Son, the true God, and in the Holy Spirit, one God, blessed for evermore, and do acknowledge the Holy Scriptures of the Old and New Testament to be given by Divine Inspiration" (p. 79n). Obviously, this profession would be unacceptable to many Quakers and Deists.

65 Pratt, *Religion, Politics, and Diversity,* pp. 85–86.

66 Landon Carter's Diary is particularly instructive with regard to the attitudes of the conservative Virginia Revolutionary gentry. See especially Jack Greene's introduction in Greene (ed.), *The Diary of Landon Carter* (2 vols.; Charlottesville, 1965), I, 38–39, 42–45.

67 Thomas Jefferson, "Summary View of the Rights of the British Colonies," in Boyd (ed.), *Papers of Thomas Jefferson,* I, 121–122, 132–133.

68 Lawrence Henry Gipson, "The American Revolution as an Aftermath of the Great War for Empire, 1754–1763," *Political Science Quarterly,* LXV (1950), 86–104.

69 Thomas Paine, *Common Sense* (Dolphin Books ed.; New York, 1960), pp. 27, 34.

70 Carter Braxton to Landon Carter, Apr. 14, 1776, *LMCC,* I, 421.

71 See Wood, *Creation of the American Republic,* chaps. 2 and 3.

5 The Politics of War, 1776-1778

WAR usually unites a nation, but it may divide or even destroy an imperfectly formed colonial nation engaged in a disorganized revolt. In Latin America, for example, provincial loyalties overrode national loyalties, even in the crucible of conflict. At times, the war of liberation became a civil war, as in Venezuela in 1815, when there were bloody clashes between regions and between classes. The American Revolution was not immune to such divisive influences. Independence was declared before a confederation was framed. Support for independence in the Middle colonies had been hesitant, and the loyalty of substantial elements of the population there was uncertain. The South was plagued by internal divisions, particularly between the eastern tidewater and the interior regions of the Carolinas, where there had been insurrections during the previous decade. Christopher Gadsden warned the Congress that the greatest danger to America came "from whence she was little aware," from "the extreme back parts of Virginia, North & South Carolina, Georgia & Florida, where were a numerous Sett of Banditti of no Property or principles whatever & ready to be made the Tools of power for the Sake of plunder wherever they could do it with impunity." Gadsden reminded Samuel Adams of this prediction in early 1779 when South Carolina was threatened both from the interior and from the sea. By then the old Carolina-Massachusetts radical axis seemed to have broken, for Congress was unable or unwilling to send aid to the threatened Southern state. Gadsden reminded Adams that "I am the same man, my Friend with the Same Principles I set out with at First, and American *at large,* anxiously wishing for the Happiness & confirmed Independency of the whole. . . ." He implored Adams to remember the support Massachusetts had received in her moment of peril and to consider that a half-dozen frigates were desperately needed to defend the Carolina coast: "If You can't give us effectual Assistance by Land & You will make no Attempts by Water, what Advantage have we by the Confederacy & what must we think then, but that we are intended to be sacrificed to make a better Bargain for the other states?"[1]

As things turned out, a land force under General Benjamin Lincoln was dispatched to help the South Carolinians momentarily turn back the English moving up from Savannah under General Provost, and later in the year a French fleet under Admiral d'Estaing attacked the British at Savannah in conjunction with Lincoln. But Savannah was not captured, and South Carolina's precarious position in the southern extremity of the union was unchanged. It was clear that military policy would mightily affect the political coalitions established before independence and that John Adam's expectation that the war would bring an end to congressional politics was unrealistic.

By 1776 it was apparent to the British that the Revolution was not an isolated phenomenon restricted to New England as they had first thought. Between the summer of 1776 and 1779 Lord George Germain, Secretary of State for the Colonies who was responsible for military strategy, and Generals Sir William Howe, Sir Henry Clinton, John Burgoyne, and Lord Cornwallis fought a different kind of war. The British command decided to make New York its base of operations because it was more centrally located than Boston, and because there seemed to be more Loyalist support in the Middle region than in New England. In the fall of 1776 the British mounted a huge 30,000-man invasion force under Howe that captured New York City without great difficulty and then pursued the Continental army under Washington into New Jersey. Two American generals, John Sullivan and the highly touted Charles Lee, were captured, and the American army was nearly destroyed. In the meantime the American invasion of Canada had failed, and Benedict Arnold was forced to fall back to Ticonderoga with his weary men to face an invading force from Canada under Sir Guy Carleton. The lateness of the season forced Carleton back into Canada after he was delayed by a spirited American defense at Valcour Bay on Lake Champlain, but an invasion from the north remained an annoyingly persistent threat which materialized during the following year when Burgoyne marched south with an army of over 7,000 men. Despite Washington's victories at Trenton and Princeton during the winter of 1776–1777, victories which had vastly greater psychological importance than tactical significance, Howe invaded and occupied Philadelphia during the late summer of 1777. Philip Schuyler and the Pennsylvanian general Arthur St. Clair were unable to prevent Burgoyne from seizing Fort Ticonderoga, the vital defensive post at the southern end of Lake Champlain. Only after Schuyler was replaced by Horatio Gates, who mustered a large force of New England militia, was Burgoyne stopped and defeated at Saratoga. The victory at Saratoga during the fall of that year brightened the gloom that had prompted the characterization of 1777 as "the year of the hangman." (The three 7s were seen as symbolizing the gallows.) But the victory at Saratoga, while of critical importance (for it brought France into the war), did not materially ease the condition of the Continental army under Washington. The winter of 1777–1778 was the agonizing season of Valley Forge.

In addition to conducting a conventional war aimed at seizing major cities and attacking the major army of the enemy, the British launched a campaign of pacification. General Howe offered royal pardon to all who would lay down their arms and take an oath of allegiance to the Crown. In New Jersey, thousands accepted the offer, including Richard Stockton, a signer of the Declaration of Independence who was captured by the British. Howe also released General John Sullivan, who had been captured in the Battle of Long Island, to convey an offer of a cease-fire to the Americans on the condition that all extralegal conventions and congresses be dissolved and the Declaration of Independence rescinded. A conference was held at Staten Island in September of 1776 between the British commanders and a delegation from the Continental Congress shortly after the British triumph at Long Island and just as Washington was preparing to evacuate Manhattan. The delegation refused to consider Howe's first condition that the Declaration of Independence be rescinded, but the very fact that a meeting was held at all was a sign of weakness in the eyes of many radicals.

The British capture of the two major cities of the Middle region did not prove to be decisive because the United States had no political capital in the European sense of the term, and because popular resistance could spring up almost anywhere at any time among a widely dispersed people at arms. But the continuation of the war depended upon the will to fight, and the early successes of the British in pacifying New Jersey as well as conquering New York City and Philadelphia seemed to raise questions about American resolution.

II

The republican ideology of the Revolution had many direct implications for the waging of the war. The reforming expectation of the radicals was dependent upon broad self-denying public support and involvement in the war. If a healthy republic depended upon public virtue—that is, the willingness of the citizen to subordinate his private interest to the larger good of the whole—the successful prosecution of the war was even more dependent upon individual sacrifice. The general who cared too much for his rank and reputation, the commissary officer who was overly concerned with his profits, the contractor with his commission, the soldier with his bounty, the officer with his pension, all threatened the integrity of the Revolution. It had been battles and bloodshed that had galvanized the resistance in 1775. Battles and bloodshed, austerity and denial could purify the young republic.

Characteristically, it was the radicals who saw most clearly the ideological implications of the war effort. Having been responsible for the decision to revolt, the radicals now felt compelled to protect the Revolution against compromise. The war must be fought with total commitment by the whole people. Indifference and neutrality had become treason. The "power of resentment," about which Samuel Adams spoke glowingly, had to be cultivated, particularly in the backward Middle states. There could be no early settlement with England short of complete independence. Allies should be sought, but American interests and particularly the republican character of the Revolution could not be jeopardized in diplomatic arrangements with European monarchies. By assuming the role of guarantors of the Revolution, the radicals became, in their own eyes at least, what might be called the Party of the Revolution.

The radical bloc continued to be an intersectional coalition during the years 1776–1779, but because of changes in congressional delegates and in the political situations within the states, especially in Pennsylvania, and because of certain differences within the radical coalition regarding the composition of the military, that coalition lost its strikingly New England–Southern character. Christopher Gadsden returned to South Carolina in early 1776, and although Henry Laurens, who arrived in Congress in the middle of 1777, became an important ally of the radicals, the South Carolina delegation during the rest of the Revolution was less radical than it had been in 1774. Patrick Henry did not return to Congress after 1774, and Thomas Jefferson left in September of 1776 to spend the war years in Virginia. George Wythe also left Congress by the end of 1776. Richard Henry Lee and his brother Francis Lightfoot Lee were present during much of the period between 1776 and 1779, but they were often outvoted in a large and mixed Virginia delegation. Moreover, the Southern radicals and the New Englanders, while in substantial agreement on many issues related to the prosecution of the war such as opposition to profiteering and to foreign influence in American policy making, differed sometimes in positions on military policy. Henry Laurens and Richard Henry Lee were vigilant in their opposition to Robert Morris's profit-making ventures, and they were pronounced antagonists of the French minister Conrad Alexandre Gérard in 1778 and 1779—particularly when Gérard tried to manipulate congressional definition of American peace terms. They did not, however, generally agree with the New England radicals on the matter of lifetime half pay pensions for officers.

The most sustained representation of the pre-independence radical bloc was in the New England delegations. Josiah Bartlett, William Whipple, Samuel Adams, John Adams, Elbridge Gerry, William Ellery, Roger Sherman, Oliver Wolcott, Eliphalet Dyer, and Samuel Huntington all served fairly constantly between 1776 and 1779. Thus the radical bloc came to be dominated by New England in a way that was impossible during the very early Congresses, when the New England radicals had to tread softly for fear of antagonizing the conservatives from the Middle colonies. The New England dominance of the radical party was furthered by the fact that much of the cross-sectional voting support came from new men from the Middle states who had been elected by more radical assemblies in New Jersey and Pennsylvania. John Witherspoon and Thomas McKean were the only long-term radicals from the Middle states; most of the radical voting strength from the Middle region came from more obscure men such as Nathaniel Scudder of New Jersey and Joseph Searle, James McLene, and William Clingan from Pennsylvania. It was not difficult for the more experienced New Englanders to lead the newcomers, who seem to have spoken little and made few motions but who regularly voted with the New Englanders—even on practical issues in which Pennsylvania had negligible interest, such as rights to the fisheries as a condition of peace.

A major reason for the ability of the radical New England leadership to draw support from the newly elected radicals from the Middle states was the ideological similarity between the two groups regarding military policy. The Pennsylvania radicals who promoted the constitution of 1776 drew much of their strength from the militia which resented the Continental army's pretentions to superiority. New Englanders in general, and the radicals in particular, were suspicious of a standing army, and they were concerned about the maintenance of civil control over the military. They supported higher pay and bounties for common soldiers and correspondingly lower allowances for officers. They distrusted arrogant Continental generals such as George Schuyler and Benedict Arnold and were adamantly opposed to half pay pensions for officers, believing that this would lead to the creation of a military aristocracy wholly incompatible with republican society. At the same time, they wanted an aggressive prosecution of the war, and they were critical of Washington for having failed to win victories against Howe when he invaded Pennsylvania. Their position was not inconsistent, given the principles to which they adhered. The military was a potentially aggrandizing influence that had to be curbed in a republic, but a republican revolution against royal mercenaries required the full commitment of a citizen's army.

Contrary to the prejudice of some radicals, the pre-independence conservatives who went along with the Revolution were as thoroughly committed to the prosecution of the war as were the radicals. Conservatives did accept the fact, if not the wisdom, of independence. Realizing, however, that in the heterogeneous Middle states there was a danger that the Revolution might create internal divisions, they tended to fear rather than exhort massive participation in a people's revolution, and they tended to view the Revolution less as an opportunity for reformation than as a crisis which made imperative the creation of military and political structures to stabilize and control the revolutionary process. In this context it was appropriate that the conservative delegates elected to Congress from Pennsylvania should group in opposition to the radicals, as indeed they did.

Pre-independence conservatives such as Robert Morris and the Rutledges were put in an awkward position by the claim of the radicals that they were the only authentic party of the revolution. They were hampered as well by turnovers in those delegations in which they had enjoyed strength, for the same contrast between sustained and interrupted tenures obtained between New England and the Middle states as between New England and the South. As can be seen from Table 3, the conservatives of 1775 disappeared from Congress by early 1777, with the exception of a few members such as James Duane, Robert Livingston, and John Jay, whose attendance was sporadic to say the least. The conservatives did not abdicate power, for some such as John Rutledge returned to important positions in the states. Moreover, and perhaps more important, conservatives such as Robert Morris and Jay continued to exert a powerful influence upon congressional politics from positions outside Congress—Morris in finance and Jay in diplomacy. Further, vacancies in the conservative ranks were often filled by able, articulate newcomers such as Gouverneur Morris from New York and John Mathews from South Carolina. Clearly, however, the radicals had the advantage of seniority and continuity of leadership—an advantage that was reflected in the composition of a number of standing and special committees[2].

A number of factors combined to make the period 1776-1779 an era of New England ascendancy. One was the preponderance of sustained tenures among the New Englanders in the Congress between 1775 and 1780. Another was the fact that the attention of the Congress during the early years of the Revolution was fixed upon military combat even more than upon the framing of the Confederation and the negotiation of alliances abroad. Yet another was the military reputation of New England, which stood higher than that of the other sections which were less successful in turning back the British. But as the Revolution progressed, it became less and less clear that the New England party, or "Eastern Party" as it was often called, was necessarily a party of undiluted republican radicalism. As the war progressed the Eastern party pursued pragmatic interests that were unconnected with the prosecution of a republican revolution. There was a large investment in Continental moneys in New England that made the region conservative on fiscal matters such as interest

TABLE 3

Subsequent Congressional Tenures of Delegates Classified As Radical and Conservative during 1775 and 1776

	1776	1777	1778	1779
Radicals				
Bartlett (N.H.)	xxxxxxxxxx		xxxxxxx	
Langdon (N.H.)				
Whipple (N.H.)	xxxxxxxxxxxxxxxxx		xxxxxxxxxxxxxxxxxx	
Adams, S. (Mass.)	xxxxxxxxxxxxxxxxxxxxxxxxxxxxxxxxxxxxxxxxxx			
Adams, J. (Mass.)	xxxxxxxxxxxxxxxxxxxxxxxx			
Gerry (Mass.)	xxxxxxxxxxxxxxxxxxxxxxxxxxxxxxxxxxxxxxxxxxxxxxxxx			
Ellery (R.I.)	xxxxxxxxxxxxxxxxxxxxxxxxxxxxxxxxxxxxxxxxxxxxxxxxxx			
Hancock (Mass.)	xxxxxxxxxxxxxxxxxxxxxxxx			
Hopkins (R.I.)	xxxxxxxxxx			
Ward (R.I.)	xxx			
Deane (Conn.)	x			
Dyer (Conn.)	x	xxxxxxxxxxxxxxxxxxxxxxxx		
Sherman (Conn.)	xxxxxxxxxxxxxxxxxxxxxx		xxxxxxxxxxxxxxxxxxx	
Wolcott (Conn.)	xxxxxx xxxxxxxx		xxxxxx	
Clark (N.J.)		xxxxxxxxxxxxxxxxxxxxxxx		
Sergeant (N.J.)	xxxxx xxxxxxxxxx			
Stockton (N.J.)		xxxxx		
Witherspoon (N.J.)		xxxxxxxxxxxxxxxxxxxxxxxxxxxxxxxxxxxxxxxxxxxxx		
Clymer (Pa.)		xxxxxxxxxxxxxxx		
Franklin (Pa.)	xxxxxxxxxx			
Rush (Pa.)		xxxxxxxx		
McKean (Del.)	xxxxxxxxxx		xxxxxxxxxxxxxxxxxxxxxxxxxx	
Rodney (Del.)	xxxxxxxxxx			
Chase (Md.)	xxxxxxxxxxxxxxxxxxxxxxx		xxxxxxxx	
Jefferson (Va.)	xxx			
Lee, R. H. (Va.)	xxxxxxxxxxxxxxxxxxxxxxx	xxxxx	xxxxx	
Lee, F. L. (Va.)	xxxxxxxxxxxxxxxxxxxxxxxxxxxxxx		xxxxxxx	
Penn (N.C.)	xxxxxxxxx	xxxxxxxxx	xxxxxxxxxxxxx	
Gadsden (S.C.)				
Bulloch (Ga.)				
Hall (Ga.)	xxxxxxxxxx			
Gwinnett (Ga.)	xxxx			

	1776	1777	1778	1779
Conservatives				
Alsop (N.Y.)	xxxxxxx			
Duane (N.Y.)	xxxxxx	xxxxxxxxx		xxxxxxxxxx
Jay (N.Y.)				xxxxxxxxxxx
Livingston, P. (N.Y.)	xxxxxxxxxxxxxx			
Livingston, R. R. (N.Y.)		xx		xx
Smith (N.J.)	xxx			
Dickinson (Pa.)	xxxxxx			xxxxxxx
Morris (Pa.)	xxxxxxxxxxxxxxxxxxxxxxxxxxxxxxxxxxxxxxxxxx			
Willing (Pa.)	xxxxxx			
Wilson (Pa.)	xxxxxxxxxxxxxxxxxxxxxxxx			
Read (Del.)	xxxxxxxxxxxxxxx			
Johnson (Md.)	xxxxxxxxx			
Tilghman (Md.)	xxxxxx	xx		
Braxton (Va.)	xxxxxxx			
Rutledge, E. (S.C.)	xxxxxxxxxx			
Rutledge, J. (S.C.)				
Zubly (Ga.)				

rates on Continental loan office certificates. The definition of peace terms stimulated by the possible mediation of Spain in 1779 exposed the economic interest of New England in the Newfoundland fisheries. Thus the New England party included members such as Elbridge Gerry and Oliver Wolcott, who cannot be called Revolutionary ideologues in the manner of Samuel Adams. Nonetheless, partly because of fortuitous factors (such as the predominance of Middle states men in the trade and financing of the war and the consequent distrusts of central finance men among New England conservatives) and partly because of the very real military and political involvement of Easterners in the resistance and early stage of the Revolution, it is not amiss to use the terms "radical" and "Eastern" almost interchangeably. It will be useful, however, to occasionally distinguish between "Old Radicals" such as Samuel Adams, Roger Sherman, and Richard Henry Lee, who conspired to transform resistance into revolution, and the somewhat more pragmatic Eastern party in which the Old Radicals could usually be located.

Party development in the other segments of the union was less pronounced during the first stage of the Revolution. There was a rather loosely organized Southern alliance composed of delegates from Maryland, Virginia, the Carolinas, and Georgia[*3*]. This alliance was not a cohesive legislative party but a congeries of like-minded individuals at this stage of the Revolution. The most cohesive delegations in the Southern alliance were from Maryland and North Carolina because of the divisive impact of Old Radicals in the Virginia delegation and the pro-Eastern tendencies of Henry Laurens in the South Carolina delegation. In the Middle states there was a three-way division among conservatives, moderates, and radicals which was in essence a continuation of the old pre-independence factionalism, largely because of provincial reinforcement, as in the struggles over the Pennsylvania constitution. Yet here too there was a second dimension of sectional interest which at times subdued ideological differences. Sectional interest was the major force behind the formation of the moderate faction which included delegates from New York, New Jersey, and Pennsylvania. The moderates attempted to avoid entanglement in ideological issues which excited the Pennsylvania Constitutionalists, such as the drive to curb profiteering through price controls, but on the other hand they were less impressed than conservatives with the necessity of generating strong central power to stabilize the Revolution, and they could sometimes be found with the Eastern interest in opposition to contracting arrangements made by Robert Morris. They constituted a weak "third force" during the period up to 1778, reflecting the inability of the Middle states to coalesce as a sectional bloc, but by 1779 they exerted considerable influence.

Obviously, in the light of these generalizations about factional structure during the period of New England ascendancy, it will not do to talk about a dichotomized Congress. Even the labels "radical" and "conservative" are often ambiguous when applied to the post-independence extensions of the independent and conciliationist factions. Thus the terminology used below will be somewhat more complicated, perhaps less convenient, but, it is hoped, more precise[*4*].

III

Having done their utmost to secure the Declaration of Independence, and having argued that American arms could vanquish the British even in the face of the ominous defeats at Long Island, the radicals were in no mood to compromise in September of 1776 when General Sullivan (who had been captured and was now out on parole with a message from General Howe) brought Howe's suggestion that an informal meeting should be arranged to discuss an accommodation. Howe made it clear that he could not officially recognize Congress, a treasonable body in the eyes of the Crown, but this should not prevent attempts to bring about a cease-fire. Sullivan thus brought no concrete proposals or terms from Howe. A controversy arose in Congress over whether or not to pay any attention to Howe's suggestion. John Adams was irritated at Howe for having made the offer, which he considered "insidious, ridiculous, but delicate and troublesome," and even at Sullivan for having conveyed it. John Witherspoon thought that the very willingness of Congress to consider the proposal was an indication that it "had not yet acquired the whole ideas and habits of independence"[5]. The meeting was also opposed by Benjamin Rush and James Ross, two of the Pennsylvania radicals, while it was supported by Edward Rutledge, Thomas Lynch, and Thomas Stone (of Maryland). The Congress did send a deputation composed of John Adams, Benjamin Franklin, and Edward Rutledge to confer with Howe. Predictably, nothing came out of the talks.

If radicals, now the "Party of the Revolution," were disturbed about a faint receptivity in Congress to Howe's temptation, they were much more upset about the failure of the Middle states to adequately defend themselves against the invading British. Samuel Adams confided to James Warren that "Nothing can exceed the Lethargy that has seized the People of this State [Pennsylvania] and the Jerseys." Independence had been declared, but it had not been won—indeed, it was endangered from within. Adams was not willing to charge Pennsylvania as a whole with disaffection, but he was indignant that while "non-Resistance is the professed Principle of Quakers . . . the Religion of many of them is to get money and sleep, as the vulgar Phrase is, in a whole Skin"[6]. Adams believed that while the proprietary interest and the Loyalists were also partly to blame, the root of the lethargy could be found in one man, John Dickinson, who had argued for accommodation with Great Britain from September of 1774 to July of 1776: "He has poisoned the Minds of the People, the Effect of which is a total Stagnation of the Power of Resentment, the utter loss of every manly Sentiment of Liberty and Virtue"[7]. Adams was being unfair. Dickinson was a complex man of refined intelligence, irreconcilable ideas, and conflicting loyalties. He felt compelled to take to the field in command of a brigade, in defense of "unkind countrymen whom I cannot forbear to esteem as fellow-citizens amidst their fury against me"; yet all the while he hoped for a negotiation which would end the conflict. Sam Adams could not understand this, for like most Revolutionaries he was a man of a single idea, unquestionable commitment, and corresponding strength. Full of resentment, he was ready to "give up this City and State for lost until recovered by other Americans"[8].

As is often the case in revolutions, the inner threat loomed larger than the external one. Samuel Adams believed "much more is to be apprehended from the secret Machinations of these rascally People [the Loyalists], than from the open Violence of British and Hessian Soldiers, whose Success had been in a great Measure owing to the Aid they have received from them . . . can a man take Fire into his Bosom, and not be burned?"[9]. With these assumptions, every loss on the battlefield, every breakdown in supply, and every drop in the value of the Continental currency became suspect as the possible work of anti-Revolutionaries, making it imperative that the Old Radicals hang together to protect the Revolution in the "soft" Middle states. For those who had taken the conservative position on independence the explanation was quite different. The attitude of Robert Morris was typical. He argued to Horatio Gates that the difficult and confused days of late 1776 were "the fruits of a certain premature declaration which you know I always opposed. My opposition was founded in the evil consequences I foresaw . . . and the present state of several Colonies justifies my apprehension"[10]. Morris was referring primarily to Pennsylvania, which was then not only threatened by invasion but also locked in a sharp internal struggle over the radical Pennsylvania constitution of 1776.

The political turmoil and lethargic military performance of the Middle states prompted New England delegates to assume an aggressive stance in Congress. New England militia had forced Howe out of Boston. There was no reason why the same thing could not be done in New Jersey and Pennsylvania. "They are completely in our Power," argued John Adams in the winter of 1777, after Congress had felt that it was necessary to move from Philadelphia to Baltimore to avoid capture by the invading British. He went on to contend that "if We do not embrace the Opportunity, We shall not only in dust and ashes repent of our Sloth, but it will be Justice that We should Suffer the wretched Consequences of it . . ."[11].

New England delegates privately urged their home states to lead the way by filling army quotas and meeting the British with vigor. Samuel Adams told James Warren, "It is necessary that New England should maintain her Character and Firmness." John Adams agreed: "It may be depended upon, that our State is the Barometer at which every other looks." This was indeed generally understood to be true. William Smith, the New York Tory, hoped for a collapse of the New England states, for then

> The Opposition will be at an End, for tho' I do not estimate their Soldiers beyond others yet as they furnish more and are higher toned and have the best Coast for introducing Foreign Supplies with least Obstruction, I consider their Spirit as the political Barometer of the Power of the whole Confederacy[12].

The British presence in Rhode Island was humiliating for New England's reputation, and when Congress authorized an expedition to oust the British, John Adams pressed upon James Bowdoin the urgent necessity of destroying the enemy. "If it costs us Thousands of Lives it ought to be done," he concluded[13].

The arrogant and often pious belligerence of the New England radicals sometimes estranged other delegates. In February of 1777, when Congress decided to order reinforcements for Washington, the radicals wanted to attach a declaration to the effect that Washington should be commanded "not only to curb and confine the enemy within their present quarters, but with the blessing of God, entirely to subdue them before they are reinforced"[*14*]. To Thomas Burke, a recently arrived delegate from North Carolina, this was a pompous, "unworthy gasconade" which might make the Continental Congress look ridiculous and which implied as well an insult to Washington. (Burke was convinced the Eastern delegates had "a great desire . . . to insult the General.") The four New England states, Virginia, and Georgia voted to retain the paragraph, while New Jersey, Pennsylvania, North Carolina, and South Carolina voted to expunge it[*15*]—a division which shows a rough continuation of the alignment of 1775–1776. Conservatives such as Edward Rutledge, who had a genuine fear of New England military ambitions, were somewhat distressed by the strongly worded directions for military contributions which the Continental Congress pressed upon the states. Rutledge seemed alarmed that in order to "*compel*" New Jersey to provide more assistance for the defense of New York, it had "directed (not permitted)" Washington to move 2,000 men from that state to New York City[*16*].

There was also much opposition to the high bounties and wages advocated by New Englanders for the army. This sentiment was particularly strong in the Southern delegations, which disapproved of what they saw as leveling influences in the structure of the New England militia. Even William Hooper of North Carolina, who had been born in Massachusetts and educated at Harvard, and who inclined toward the radicalism of New England, was irritated by the New England policy—sheer extortion as Hooper saw it—and it made his "blood boil"[*17*]. This was part of a general anti-New England spirit that had spread among many of the Southern delegates. William Williams, the Connecticut delegate, wrote at this time to his brother-in-law Joseph Trumbull that the chance of Trumbull's obtaining a purchasing contract would suffer because he was a New Englander[*18*].

New England influence was predominant after Congress hurried out of Philadelphia to Baltimore in December of 1776 under the threat of Howe's advancing troops. Attendance in Congress was very thin, dwindling at times to less than twenty-five members, and despite the location, the Middle states were the least represented. There were times in January when New York, Delaware, and Maryland were simultaneously unable to vote because they did not have two members in Congress. Although this was unfortunate for the general cause, it was not without advantage for the Easterners. As Francis Lewis noted, the New England states were never without representation, and with a bloc of four votes out of ten at ready command, the Old Radicals in the New England cluster did not need much outside support to control any vote. It was at this time that Benjamin Harrison complained to his friend and business connection Robert Morris (who was in Philadelphia on congressional business) that "the Yankeys . . . Rule as absolutely as the Grand Turk does in his own Dominions." It is likely that a succession of committee appointments from November through early January which were weighted in favor of the Old Radicals antagonized Harrison[19]. The most conclusive partisan triumph of the Old Radicals seems to have provoked virtually no debate or comment in the correspondence of the delegates. On October 22, Arthur Lee was made Commissioner to France when Jefferson declined the post because of having to attend to the needs of his family. Lee's appointment reinforced the radical network of the resistance period. William Hooper's comment to Robert Morris that "if there are two Interests in America, that must necessarily prevail which has always had its advocates on the spot to support it"[20], while not directed at this decision, was an apt explanation of it.

IV

While opposition to New England expanded and became firmer in the Southern delegations, changes occurred in the Middle states which promoted the formation of an Eastern alliance. By 1777 both New Jersey and Pennsylvania had delegations composed of men who had taken the radical position on independence and who were consequently inclined to align with the New England delegates. Some, such as Rush from Pennsylvania and Witherspoon from New Jersey, had joined the radicals in Congress before the Declaration of Independence. Others, such as Daniel Roberdeau of Pennsylvania and Abraham Clark of New Jersey, were new men who aligned with the Easterners because of congruent social and political beliefs[21].

New York, on the other hand, remained under conservative control during the early part of the Revolution. The New York convention promulgated a constitution which did not seriously alter the status quo, and it sent delegates to Congress who formed a northern center of opposition to the Eastern alliance [22]. While the New York–New England antagonism had roots reaching back long before the Revolution, in 1776 and 1777 it focused in Congress on the "Northern Department," or theater of war, along the historic invasion route from Canada stretching from Montreal to Lake Champlain and Lake George, down to Albany and the Hudson. Contention over the military command of this theater was accompanied by dispute over control of supplies—an issue which involved many friends and relatives of congressional delegates. Another issue which pitted New Yorker against New Englander was the controversy over Vermont, or the Hampshire Grants, as the area was called, where both New York and New Hampshire (and to an extent Massachusetts as well) had land claims.

An indication of just how closely congressmen were related to these disputes is the fact that James Duane, who was a very effective worker for the New York claims in Vermont, was at the same time an extensive speculator in those lands. Joseph Trumbull, commissary general, was a brother-in-law of William Williams, a delegate from Connecticut. The commissary of stores and provisions for the Northern Department in 1776, on the other hand, was Walter Livingston of the powerful Livingston family, which was represented in Congress by Robert R. and Philip Livingston. The question of control of supplies of the Northern army was complicated by the fact that Morgan Lewis, the son of the New York delegate Francis Lewis, had been appointed deputy quartermaster general for the Canadian expedition by General Gates and was displaced by Schuyler when the Canadian expedition fell back to New York[23].

Walter Livingston and Joseph Trumbull became natural antagonists, and the two blocs divided in Congress on the issue of supply much as they did on the issue of military command. Samuel Adams charged that all difficulties concerning supplies could be traced to Walter Livingston and suggested to Trumbull that he bring the matter to Congress through a remonstrance to Washington, using arguments supplied by Adams[24]. Both Livingston and Trumbull were interested in the possibility of supplying the army by contract rather than through the older style of the commissary, and both had their protagonists working for them in Congress[25]. Williams even referred to a regular political club in connection with this matter: "We have a Club once a week . . . I intend to sound them, and prepare the Matter as well and as soon as may be"[26].

The most celebrated controversy in the New York theater of war was the struggle between Schuyler and Gates over command in the Northern Department. Philip Schuyler had the general command in 1776, but he was encountering building opposition from the New Englanders in Congress who preferred their political ally Gates. The hostility toward Schuyler seems to have developed largely as a result of Schuyler's contemptuous treatment of New England officers and men under his command during the Canadian expedition of 1775. Alexander Graydon, who shared Schuyler's distaste for New England militia officers, nevertheless understood why Schuyler should have been displeasing to the Yankees, for "he certainly was at no pains to conceal the extreme contempt he felt for a set of officers who were both a disgrace to their stations and the cause in which they acted"[27]. Even Governor George Clinton of New York wrote to James Duane that "our friend Phil has good qualities, but he has contrived to make himself disagreeable and suspected by the Yankees . . ."[28].

Gates, while constantly seeking preferment, and occasionally displaying that concern for honor and rank criticized as unrepublican by the Old Radicals, was professedly and probably sincerely more democratic than Schuyler in his political and military attitudes. In any event, he won the allegiance of the New England militia. This support was the crucial argument in the ultimate decision to put him in charge of the Northern Department during the middle of Burgoyne's invasion. In addition, however, Gates had served with some distinction as adjutant general under Washington at Cambridge, and perhaps most important, he had been on intimate terms with the radicals since the earliest meetings of Congress.

Resentment against Schuyler among New Englanders magnified when the first Canadian campaign failed in the spring of 1776 and the army was forced to fall back into New York, thereby exposing the northern New England frontier[29]. Gates was then given command of the field army in Canada, a fuzzy commission since there was no army in Canada, and, predictably, a jurisdictional dispute broke out between the two generals, each the favorite of a congressional faction. Although Schuyler won this argument, and Gates was forced to accept a subordinate position, criticism of Schuyler intensified during the summer. It was charged that he was a do-nothing general who stayed behind the lines seeking profits from army supplies[30]. The sensitive Schuyler demanded a hearing and offered his resignation in September. The Congress rejected both, but it did send a commission of two men, Clymer of Pennsylvania and Stockton of New Jersey, to consult with Gates at Ticonderoga about reformation of the Northern Department. The report of the commission was submitted to a congressional committee balanced evenly between the conservatives Harrison and Philip Livingston and the radicals Wythe and Samuel Adams, with Clymer occupying a middle position. (Stockton had returned to New Jersey, where he was captured by the British.) When Congress fled from Philadelphia, Livingston and Wythe returned home, and in the subsequent appointments to the committee the radicals achieved control through the addition of Richard Henry Lee and William Whipple, a New Hampshire merchant of the Old Radical persuasion[31]. The committee recommended, and Congress resolved, that the old system of supply through a commissary general rather than through contracts be maintained and that a number of specific defense measures, such as the creation of two large floating batteries on Lake Champlain to cover the boom and the bridge, be undertaken during the winter by General Schuyler or "the commanding officer of the northern army"[32]. Gates was not satisfied with his status under Schuyler, however, and after bringing some New Jersey and Pennsylvania troops to assist Washington in the New Jersey campaign, Gates excused himself on the grounds of ill health and repaired to Congress and the Eastern party. Gates had no difficulty winning the key support of Samuel Adams, who shortly wrote to John Adams that "General Gates is here. How shall we make him head of that army?"[33]

After three months Gates's lobbying was partially successful as a result of congressional irritation over a letter from the imperious Schuyler. Congress had removed one Doctor Stringer from Schuyler's command without consulting the general. Insulted, Schuyler protested in what Congress chose to style an "ill-advised" letter which was "highly derogatory to the honor of Congress." The delegates resolved that Schuyler should be cautioned to write future letters "in a style more suitable to the dignity of the representative body of these free and independent states . . ."[34]. Ten days later Gates was appointed to the command of the army at Ticonderoga.

The New York delegates, at the behest of Schuyler and the New York convention, sedulously worked for Schuyler's reinstatement as sole commander in the Northern Department for the summer campaign of 1777. The New York delegation was strengthened in number and talent by the spring; it included not only James Duane, Philip Livingston, and William Duer but also Schuyler himself. In a close vote on May 15, they succeeded in reinstating Schuyler by gaining most of the votes from the Southern delegations. Duane reported that this was not an easy task at the outset, since "several of our old friends—Hooper, Hughes, E. Rutledge, Harrison, Reade, Stone, Chase etc. etc. were absent and most of their seats filled with strangers." By "cultivating the friendship of the members from the Southern states," as Duer put it, and, according to Duane by sparing no expense, "for it was no time to consult parsimony," they were able to carry the issue[35]. Votes were not yet recorded in the Journals, but according to Duer's description the New Yorkers gathered the votes of Maryland, Virginia, and the Carolinas with the sole exception of Richard Henry Lee. Georgia was split, as was New Jersey, the latter only because of the absence of Jonathan Dickinson Sergeant and Abraham Clark, whose "political line of conduct lies to the Eastward of Biram's River" (near the New York–Connecticut boundary), in the words of Duer. The presence of transplanted Connecticut men in the Georgia delegation explained its deviation[36].

If the campaign for the reinstatement of Schuyler helped mature the anti-Eastern coalition between conservative Middle states delegates and the Southerners, Gates's clumsy response to his "disgrace" hardly impeded its growth. Gates hurried down to Congress and arranged for a hearing through Roger Sherman, and when he was admitted to the floor of Congress on June 18, he launched into a personal attack against James Duane, charging him with having masterminded the changes in the Northern Department. According to Duer's description of the angry debates, Duane first protested mildly that Gates was out of order; then Paca of Maryland heatedly moved that Gates be ordered to leave the building, and Duer seconded Paca's motion. Sherman, who was responsible for Gates's presence on the floor, rose to defend the general, as did "his Eastern Friends," whereupon Middleton, Burke, Harrison, and others of the Southern party attacked Sherman and Gates's defenders[37]. Gates left after venting his spleen, and probably damaging his case.

Actually, Schuyler's assumption of the command at the very moment

Burgoyne was leading a powerful army down the lakes worked to Gates's advantage in a way no lobbying in Congress could possibly match. The Americans suffered decisive and humiliating defeats at Crown Point and Ticonderoga. The defeats prompted the radicals to demand a court-martial for Arthur St. Clair, the field commander, and for Schuyler as well, for he bore the ultimate responsibility, although he was positioned behind the front. The Easterners pressed for the removal of Schuyler and the appointment of the "honest and true" Gates, who was *"always present"* with his men *"in Fatigue and Danger"*[38]. The New Englanders now received important assistance from their Middle states radical allies. Jonathan Dickinson Sergeant of New Jersey moved on July 26 that Schuyler be recalled. He was seconded by Daniel Roberdeau of Pennsylvania and supported in debate by Abraham Clark of New Jersey[39].

The Eastern party missed the assistance of Richard Henry Lee, who was not in Congress at that moment. He had been forced to return to Virginia in order to mend political fences that were in such disrepair that he had been left out of the newly elected delegation. His opponents in the Assembly charged that he had favored New England to the disadvantage of Virginia. Duer had been "credibly inform'd" that Lee would not be elected, and he had to confess to John Jay, "The mere contemplation of this event gives me pleasure" [40]. As it turned out, Lee was finally included, but the radicals had been able to gain the day in his absence anyway.

The main problem the radicals had to overcome in ousting Schuyler and putting Gates in command was the accusation that the evacuation by Schuyler and St. Clair was necessitated by the failure of New England to contribute to defense. Thomas Burke of North Carolina reported home that "the loss was certainly occasioned by the want of sufficient well appointed force, and as the Eastern states were to supply the Troops for that station . . . the officers . . . could not have done more than they did"[41]. Burke was irritated that New England was "unwilling to admit that any of our misfortune has happended through a weakness which they only share in common with the rest" [42]. Samuel Adams and other radicals anticipated this criticism and sent urgent messages to Massachusetts for a full account of all New England militia and regular troops sent to the Northern Department. But they maintained that even if it were true that Schuyler was short of troops, it was because of a fact which the radicals had always stressed: Schuyler was unable to get New England troops to serve under him. Had Gates been given the command this could not have happened[43]. John Adams was much more forceful, at least in a letter to his wife: "We shall never defend a post until we shoot a general. After that we shall defend posts. . . . No other fort will ever be evacuated without an inquiry, nor any officer come off without a court martial. We must trifle no more" [44].

Overriding an objection by James Duane that Schuyler was being victimized by an alarming combination of four states—an accusation that was as accurate as it was indignantly denied by New Englanders—the Eastern party managed a recall of Schuyler and an instruction to Washington to appoint a new commander[45]. Both factions immediately contacted Washington in support of their candidates, and Washington demurred, turning the decision back to Congress. The Easterners then completed their triumph by electing Gates. Only New York opposed[46].

Not long after Schuyler was removed a massive people's army overwhelmed Burgoyne's dwindling force at Saratoga in early October. It was the most electrifying triumph of the Revolution thus far, and it vindicated the reputation of New England, which had supplied most of the men for the battles, and of the Party of the Revolution, which had put Gates in command. The victory was all the more striking by contrast with the lethargic defense put up against Howe, who at that very time was sweeping all before him in his drive from the Chesapeake to Philadelphia. Congress was again forced to flee in mid-September, this time to the interior of Pennsylvania at York. John Adams was disgusted at what he perceived was a morass of cowardice and Toryism[47]. Elbridge Gerry was convinced that had Howe come anywhere other than Maryland, Delaware, and Pennsylvania (the old self-interested proprietary seats of the opposition to the Revolution), he would have been defeated[48].

The Schuyler-Gates imbroglio reveals many of the overlays which made up the factional structure of Congress. At the base of the controversy there was a thoroughly provincial competition between New York and New England. The solid backing Schuyler received from New York and the united opposition he encountered from New England can be ascribed to this parochial component. At the same time, Schuyler's elitism contrasted with Gates's cultivation of the militia raised the issue of the relationship between a professionally oriented army and a people's army. As Henry Marchant pointed out in the debate of July 26, both Congress and the armed forces depended upon the generally pure, uncorrupt, and well-founded judgment of the people. The unpopularity of Schuyler with the New England militia therefore became profoundly important[49]. Southerners, chary of the expansion of the New England brand of republicanism, and more inclined to accept military professionalism, entered the lists on the side of Schuyler, while the anti-elitist Middle states delegates joined the Eastern party. Indeed, some Middle states delegates (Sergeant, Clark, Roberdeau, and later Shippen, Clingan, McLean, and Searle are examples) aligned more closely with New England Old Radicals of the Adams-Sherman school than did some stalwart defenders of New England interests such as Elbridge Gerry and Francis Dana.

The Schuyler-Gates affair, viewed in terms of Revolutionary ideology, thus contributes to an understanding of the formation of interstate factions which both subsumed and transcended the calculations of sectional interest. New Englanders realized this, for in order to be consistent they had to privately chastise their own generals who exhibited military punctilio and treated Congress with disrespect. James Lovell went so far as to devise a model form for John Trumbull of Connecticut to use when petitioning Congress for an earlier date of commission. Lovell warned Trumbull that his threat to resign if his demand were not granted would certainly be accepted unless Congress received a more respectful request[50]. Lovell and the Massachusetts delegates opposed another New England general, Benedict Arnold, in a controversy involving precedence and rank. James Lovell was disgusted by Arnold's putting "self-love" above "the general interest" and interpreted the dispute as one "between Monarchical and Republican principles put at a most critical time"[51]. A year later, almost the entire Eastern alliance would turn against the talented but abrasive Arnold when he disregarded the civil authority of the Constitutionalist government of Pennsylvania.

It is in this light that two other events of the period 1777–1779 dealing with military policy should be examined: the so-called Conway cabal, and the issue of granting officers half pay for life.

V

Gates's reputation was so elevated by the Saratoga victory that comparison with Washington himself was natural at a time when the commander in chief was suffering humiliating defeats at the very doors of Congress. By the end of November, James Lovell was of the opinion that Gates, the proven hero, was needed in many places where things were not going well, but mostly "near Germantown," where Washington had been unable to deter Howe. "Good God!" exclaimed Lovell to Gates, "what a situation we are in! How different from what might have been justly expected! You will be astonished when you come to know accurately what numbers have at one time and another been collected near Philadelphia to wear out stockings, shoes, and breeches. Depend upon it for every ten soldiers placed under the command of our Fabius, five recruits will be wanted annually during the war"[52]. Although many of Lovell's comments are cryptic and ambiguous, there is little doubt of his dissatisfaction with Washington: "If it was not for the defeat of Burgoyne, and the strong appearances of an European war, our affairs are Fabiused into a very disagreeable posture"[53].

The severest critics of Washington belonged to the Radical party. Most of them were from New England, but many were from the Middle states. James Lovell was perhaps his strongest critic, but Jonathan Dickinson Sergeant (whose connections with Congress were still close, although he was at this time attorney general of Pennsylvania) was hardly less acidulous in his confidential criticisms to Lovell: "Two battles he has lost for us by two such Blunders as might have disgraced a Soldier of three months standing . . ."[54]. Samuel Adams wrote to Richard Henry Lee on January 1 that "a miserable set of General officers" must be to blame for the fact that "a promising Campaign has . . . ended ingloriously"[55]. Adams was critical of Washington by inference, anticipating that he "may one day suffer in his own Character by Means of these worthless Creations," and adding that it would be difficult to attribute Washington's failure entirely to misfortunes suffered as a consequence of incompetent generals[56]. Gerry, Ellery, Dyer, and Sherman were other New Englanders who reprobated Washington in varying degrees. Abraham Clark of New Jersey believed that "we may talk of the Enemy's cruelty as we will, but we have no greater cruelty to complain of than the Management of our Army," a statement that could very well include Washington[57]. The decision of Congress to reconstitute its military committee by naming a Board of War with Gates as president in October and November of 1777 also seemed to betray a lack of confidence in Washington within the Congress.

Congressional criticism was linked with strictures against Washington within the army and its appendages. Elias Boudinot of New Jersey, commissary general of prisoners and later a member of Congress, complained of a very confused rush to prepare for the defense of Philadelphia, only to allow the enemy to enter the city without firing a shot[58]. Benjamin Rush, previously a member of Congress who was at this time in charge of the hospital service in the Continental army, sent an unsigned letter to Patrick Henry charging that "America can only be undone by herself." He went on to argue that "the northern army has shown us what Americans are capable of doing, with a General at their head. The spirit of the southern army is in no way inferior to the spirit of the northern. A Gates, a Lee or a Conway, would in a few weeks render them an irresistible body of men"[59]. Quartermaster General Thomas Mifflin also was an opponent of Washington, as was Thomas Conway, an Irishman in French service whom Congress had elevated to brigadier general, to the distress of many American officers, including Washington. Conway sharply criticized the commander in chief in a letter to Gates which was related to Washington. The conjunction of congressional and military condemnation of Washington's generalship persuaded many of Washington's adherents (and most of his biographers) that a "cabal" existed to substitute Gates for Washington as commander in chief.

It is interesting, and relevant in certain ways, that virtually all the criticisms cited above came from individuals who were connected with the Old Radicals who viewed Washington's initial appointment as a matter of political expediency rather than military wisdom. It is also interesting that none of the statements quoted above, and they have been selected as about the most extreme examples of criticism of Washington in each case, substantiate the allegation that a plot or cabal existed to remove Washington. When the criticism of Washington is compared with that leveled at Schuyler earlier the same year, it becomes immediately apparent that if there was a cabal, it was so embryonic as to deserve another name. Certainly the Journals reflect no move to displace Washington, yet his ouster would have to have been approved by Congress in the same way that Congress removed Schuyler from command of the army facing Burgoyne. The assumption that an organized conspiracy to oust Washington either existed in Congress or between a cabal in Congress and a cabal in the army needs much more evidence than has yet come to light. All we are really able to assume is that in spite of considerable muffled criticism, Washington's reputation was strong enough to stifle any possible move to displace him on the part of those who preferred his more successful competitor.

Conway shortly resigned his commission, and Gates, along with others, did all they could to cover up any connection they might have had with the "cabal." In retrospect, the greatest significance of the Conway affair is its implication that the American Revolution was not immune to the charismatic personalism that frequently crops up in colonial wars for independence. Benjamin Rush contended in a letter to David Ramsay that Conway, Mifflin, and Charles Lee were "sacrificed to the excessive influence and popularity of One Man. . . . Where is the republican Spirit of Our country?"[60] Rush's confidence may have been misplaced, but his criticism was natural, and the tendency to view it as suspect was unworthy of the Revolution.

In more than one instance debates over military appointments and policies involved an implicit dilemma over expediency and revolutionary purity, or put differently, between pragmatic and ideological approaches to the Revolution. Never was this more true than in the controversy over lifetime half pay pensions for officers.

The half pay pension was customary for English officers, and it is not surprising that the officers of the American army should have wanted a comparable settlement from the Continental Congress. Washington, looking for ways to stabilize his officer corps, was in favor of half pay, and he recommended it to a congressional committee at Valley Forge as a means of toning up the army during the bleak winter of 1777–1778. The congressional "Committee at Camp" was composed of Nathaniel Folsom of New Hampshire, Francis Dana of Massachusetts, Joseph Reed, and Gouverneur Morris, who had just arrived from New York. Both Folsom and Dana generally voted with the Eastern alliance, but neither was a member of the Old Radical party. Joseph Reed was associated with the radical Pennsylvania Constitutionalists and had been an old connection of the Adamses and Lees, but his involvement in congressional politics was sporadic, and his instincts were those of a practical politician rather than a doctrinaire revolutionary. The youthful and brilliant Gouverneur Morris was a conservative in every sense of the term. A member of the New York aristocracy, he saw more to fear than applaud in the resistance movement. He accepted independence but did not approve of it, and he could be relied upon to temper social radicalism in whatever capacity he served. A close connection of Schuyler, Duane, and other members of the moderate and conservative New York political establishment, he would quickly make contacts with Middle states conservatives and anti-Eastern members of the Southern bloc in Congress. No one in Congress had a more lively wit or a more ready answer in debate. It was inevitable that Morris should rapidly become a dominant force in the anti-Eastern coalition.

Whether because of Morris's presence on the committee, or because of Washington's persuasion, or because of firsthand experience with conditions in the field, the Committee at Camp recommended to Congress that some of Washington's suggestions be accepted[61]. At first the committee submitted a report suggesting the establishment of a half pay pension for officers' widows. Nothing came of the proposal at this time, but it was renewed in an altered fashion on March 26 when the committee recommended in addition that commissions be made vendible. From then until May 15, when a compromise measure was passed providing for half pay for officers for a term of seven years (rather than life), the issue was energetically debated in Congress.

The argument of Washington, the army officers, and even the New Englanders Folsom and Dana was that the army would lose its experienced officers unless they were offered more than a rapidly depreciating currency for the hazards and deprivations of the service. Even assuming these officers could be replaced, which was highly unlikely, it would be more economical to offer them half pay for life than to recruit a whole new force.

The practicality of the case set forth by the committee was sufficiently compelling, and the crisis of the winter sufficiently urgent, so that the case won substantial support in Congress. There were, however, a number of delegates who were unconvinced of the justice and the economy of establishing half pay pensions. They argued, with what seemed to their opponents hypocritical cant, that no true patriot should need financial inducement to serve his cause and country. Henry Laurens, the wealthy Charleston merchant who had arrived in Congress during July of 1777, refused to believe officers would desert without the lure of half pay. Speaking as one who had "already lost a great Estate and am in a fair way to part with the *present* small remainder," he was confident that "there are many Thousands whose hearts are warm with the reasonings which induced the original Compact and who have not bowed the Knee to Luxury nor to Mammon." This was the posture that endeared Laurens to the Eastern Old Radicals and made him their second most important connection in the Southern delegations[62].

Thomas Burke was unconvinced: "The arguments drawn from Patriotism and public spirit may be fine and specious[*sic.*], but I choose to trust to some principle of more certain, lasting and powerful influence," meaning, of course, half pay for life. Opponents of half pay also argued that pensions and vendible commissions might result in a standing army or a peacetime military interest that would endanger all the gains won during the Revolution. Burke dismissed this prediction as well, despite the fact that he was second to none in his distrust of national coercive authority[*63*].

With the exception of the South Carolinians Laurens, Hutson, and Drayton, Southerners agreed with Burke, while New Englanders, excepting Gerry, opposed the establishment of half pay. Even the Lees departed from their New England cohorts on this issue. It is certain that Francis Lightfoot Lee—never more than a marginal member of the Eastern alliance—supported half pay, as can be seen from Table 4. Richard Henry Lee (not included in the table because of sparse attendance) was present for the vote on May 15 and gave his assent to the final compromise, but so did most of the New Englanders. The one other vote he cast was not by itself particularly illuminating, unfortunately, but it is probably safe to say that he was less alarmed by the threat of the military than was James Lovell, for example.

Voting on this issue was particularly close. While the South Carolina delegates sometimes followed Laurens's lead into the opposition, Gerry, the least doctrinaire of the Old Radicals, generally opposed the ardent antimilitarist James Lovell, and Dana of the Committee at Camp vacillated enough to make the Massachusetts vote unpredictable. The position of the Middle states was therefore crucial, and they in turn tended to split down the center with New Jersey opposing, New York supporting, and Pennsylvania dividing internally.

After defeating the motion for half pay for life when it was first brought forth, the opponents of the measure tried to refer it to the states for their consideration, a tactic that was almost certain to kill the measure. After a month of debate and jockeying and either narrowly or equally divided voting, supporters of half pay were apprehensive that it would be lost by referral to the states because the Pennsylvania delegation was shifting to the opposition. Jonathan Bayard Smith, who can be classified as a marginal radical on the basis of his entire voting record, had first opposed half pay, then supported it, and was now opposed again.

The struggle for half pay prompted significant partisan organization. Gouverneur Morris, the tactical leader of the half-pay bloc, reminded Robert Morris, who was then a Pennsylvanian delegate but not in attendance, that James Smith, an advocate of half pay, would be counterbalanced by Clingan, who was "of the true Eastern Stamp and Clay. . . . Think one Moment and come here the next." William Duer added a postscript to Morris's letter urging Robert Morris "to be here by Eleven o'Clock to Morrow"[*64*]. The crucial vote

TABLE 4

Voting Blocs on Half Pay for Officers for Life, April 1-May 15, 1778*

		Con								Pro							
		1	2	3	4	5	6	7	8	1	2	3	4	5	6	7	8
Radical Center	Lovell (Mass.)	x	x	x	x	x	x	x	x								
	Wolcott (Conn.)	x	x	x	x	x	x	x	x								
	Ellery (R.I.)	x	x	x	x	x	x	x		x							
	Huntington (Conn.)	x	x	x	x	x	x	x		x							
	Scudder (N.J.)	x	x	x	x	x	x	x		x							
	Hutson (S.C.)	x	x	x	x	x		x		x							
	Laurens (S.C.)	x	x	x	x	x		x		x							
	Sherman (Conn.)	x	x	x	x					x							
	Clingan (Pa.)	x	x	x	x					x							
Radical Fringe	Drayton (S.C.)	x	x	x	x						x						
	Dana (Mass.)			x	x		x	x		x	x	x			x		
Conservative Fringe	Smith, J. B. (Pa.)	x					x			x		x		x	x		
	Gerry (Mass.)				x					x	x	x	x		x	x	
	Burke (N.C.)					x					x	x		x		x	x
	Henry (Md.)						x			x	x	x	x	x	x		
Conservative Center	Banister (Va.)										x	x		x	x		x
	Smith, J. (Pa.)									x	x		x			x	x
	Mathews (S.C.)									x		x	x	x	x		
	Plater (Md.)									x		x	x	x	x		
	McKean (Del.)									x		x	x	x	x	x	
	Chase (Md.)										x	x		x	x	x	
	Adams, T. (Va.)									x	x	x	x	x	x		x
	Carroll (Md.)									x	x	x	x	x	x		x
	Morris, G. (N.Y.)									x	x	x	x	x	x		x
	Lee, F. L. (Va.)									x	x	x	x	x	x	x	x
	Langworthy (Ga.)									x	x	x	x	x	x	x	x
	Duer (N.Y.)									x	x	x	x	x	x	x	x

*Votes are not chronological, but scaled to reveal attachment or opposition to the issue.

was taken on May 13, and Robert Morris appeared in Congress to defeat referral to the states. Morris and James Smith tipped Pennsylvania against Clingan, and the measure was defeated by the close margin of 6 to 5. Jonathan Bayard Smith was not recorded as present on the thirteenth of May, and it is possible only to conjecture whether his absence was the result of persuasion by Morris.

The struggle over officers' pay was resolved for the time being with a compromise on the fifteenth of May: half pay would be granted to officers who served the duration of the war, but for a term of only seven years after the peace treaty. The compromise also included a provision that enlisted men who remained in the service for the duration should receive a bounty of eighty dollars along with other bounties in land to which they might be entitled[65].

The question of half pay was one of the more critical issues in the early history of the Congress. Not only was it a crucial factor in defining the increasing Eastern-Southern antagonism which would dominate partisan politics during the middle years of the Revolution; it produced as well a major reinforcement of the New York–Southern coalition. Further, the position of Clingan in the radical ranks was an early indication of the emerging New England–Pennsylvania Constitutionalist alliance that would blossom in 1779. Both the radical Constitutionalist and the New England Old Radicals viewed the half pay measure as a symptom of antirepublican tendencies which, in the words of the Massachusetts radical Joseph Ward, would "debase human kind, and lay waste the *Natural* and *moral* World . . ."[66]. Ward's seemingly extravagant characterization was actually quite typical of the attitude of members of the Party of the Revolution. Given the universal importance of the struggle against tyranny in all its subtle forms, the commission to curb "the Gentlemen of the Blade"[67] as James Lovell termed them, was just as important as victory in the battlefield.

Notes

1 Christopher Gadsden to Samuel Adams, Apr. 4, 1779, Samuel Adams Papers, NYPL.

2 See George Wood, *Congressional Control of Foreign Relations during the American Revolution, 1774–1789* (Allentown, Pa., 1919). Although Wood focuses on foreign relations, he has also surveyed the general composition of the hundreds of standing and special committees attending to other types of business. The composition of thirty selected committees during 1775 and 1776 selected by Wood shows the radical thrust and corresponding alienation of Middle states members which can be inferred from delegate tenures. During 1775 delegates from the Middle colonies held 46 of 105 memberships on ten important committees, while in 1776 on a sampling of 20 committees with 66 memberships the representation of the Middle states dropped to 14, a decline

from 44% to 21%. Representation from the other two sections rose, of course, particularly New England membership, which rose from 28 of 105 (27%) in 1775 to 29 of 66 (44%) in 1776. Wood notes that in the latter year at least one of the trio of Samuel and John Adams and Richard Henry Lee was on each of the 20 committees selected at random. Wood concludes on the basis of this and other data that by late 1776 the radicals under the leadership of the Adamses and Lees were controlling the course of the Revolution (pp. 32–36).

3 While Maryland is often classified as a Middle state, the voting tendencies of Maryland delegates—not to mention her commitment to the tobacco staple—suggest that she belonged in the Southern Alliance.

4 See Chapter 7 for an extended analysis of factional structures during the period 1777–1779.

5 John Adams to James Warren, Sept. 4, 1776, Warren-Adams Letters, Massachusetts Historical Society, *Collections*, (2 vols.; Boston, 1917, 1925), I, 272; Adams, *Works*, III, 80–81. Witherspoon, speech in the Continental Congress, Sept. 5, *LMCC*, II, 72–73.

6 B. Harrison to Robert Morris, Sept. 13, 1776, "Confidential Correspondence of Robert Morris," Stan V. Henkels, *Catalogue*, No. 1183 (Philadelphia, 1917), p. 11.

7 Samuel Adams to James Warren, Dec. 12, 1776. Warren-Adams Letters, I, 279–280.

8 Ibid., 280.

9 Samuel Adams to James Warren, Feb. 16, 1776, ibid., 291–292.

10 Robert Morris to Horatio Gates, Oct. 27, 1776, *LMCC*, II, 135.

11 John Adams to Abigail Adams, Sept. 8, 1777, quoted in Page Smith, *John Adams* (2 vols.; New York, 1962), I, 340.

12 Samuel Adams to James Warren, Apr. 17, 1777; John Adams to James Warren, Feb. 3, 1777, Warren-Adams Letters, I, 314–315, 289; William Smith, *Memoirs*, William H. W. Sabine, ed. (2 vols.; New York, 1958), I, 81.

13 *JCC*, VII, 272–273; John Adams to James Bowdoin, Apr. 17, 1777, *LMCC*, II, 327.

14 Thomas Burke, Abstract of Debates, Feb. 24, 1777, ibid, 274.

15 Ibid., 275.

16 E. Rutledge to R. R. Livingston, July 20, 1776, ibid., 17.

17 William Hooper to Joseph Hewes, Nov. 16, 1776, ibid., II, 155.

18 Williams to Trumbull, Aug. 7, 1776, ibid., 41–42.

19 A committee to report on the Northern army was appointed on November 27 and consisted of the conservatives Harrison and Philip Livingston, along with the radicals Wythe and Samuel Adams (as well as the moderate Clymer). Richard Henry Lee was added on December 9 and William Whipple, the New Hampshire radical, on December 24. *JCC*, VI, 985, 1013, 1037. On the same day that Whipple was appointed to the

committee on the Northern army, a committee of five was appointed to prepare a plan for obtaining foreign assistance. This committee was entirely radical, being composed of Gerry, Samuel Adams, Witherspoon, Abraham Clark (a New Jersey radical), and Richard Henry Lee. Harrison seems to have felt that even the information available to Congress was being manipulated by the radicals. On December 25 he wrote to Morris, "For God's Sake send us some News we have none here but what a *Purviance* or a Rush Deal out to us . . ." (*LMCC,* II, 183). Rush, with Richard Henry Lee and Francis Hopkinson, made up a Committee of Intelligence appointed October 17 to report war news received by Congress. (*JCC,* VI, 886.) Samuel Purviance was a Baltimore merchant, a radical, a member of the Baltimore Committee of Safety, and a contact of Samuel Adams from pre-independence days.

20 William Hooper to Robert Morris, Feb. 1, 1777, *LMCC,* II, 232. Hooper, the transplanted New Englander, had shown some sympathy for the radical position during the resistance. He was by now beginning to resent New England domination in Congress. See his letters of Nov. 8 and 16 to Joseph Hewes, ibid., 147, 155. See also Thomas Burke to Richard Caswell, Feb. 4, 1777, ibid., 235, and Benjamin Harrison to Robert Morris, Jan 8, 1777, ibid., 208.

21 W. L. Whittlesey describes Clark as a seventeenth-century English Leveller, *DAB,* IV, 118. His voting record in Congress tends to confirm that characterization. For a sample of Roberdeau's puritan compulsions, see his letter to Washington, May 26, 1777, *LMCC,* II, 376.

22 The New York radical John Morin Scott (whom the New Englanders had contacted on their way to the first Continental Congress) contended in June of 1777 that an aristocratic faction composed of Duane, Philip Livingston, Duer, Robert R. Livingston, Jay, and Gouverneur Morris had combined to dominate the government. He charged the first three in particular with the responsibility for his not obtaining a position on the bench. See Duane to Schuyler, June 19, 1777, *LMCC,* II, 382–383; Duer to Schuyler, June 19, 1777, quoted in Don R. Gerlach, *Philip Schuyler and the American Revolution in New York, 1733–1777* (Lincoln, Nebr., 1964), pp. 305–306.

23 See Francis Lewis to Mrs. Gates, Aug. 13, 1776, *LMCC,* II, 48–49. It is interesting to speculate whether or not Lewis's position as a moderate in the New York delegation was anything more than coincidental with his being displaced by Schuyler, whose sympathies were definitely with the New York conservatives.

24 Samuel Adams to Joseph Trumbull, Aug. 3, 1776, ibid., 35–36.

25 William Williams to Joseph Trumbull, Oct. 7 and 10, 1776, ibid., 118, 122; Elbridge Gerry to Joseph Trumbull, Oct. 8, 1776, ibid., 120.

26 Williams to Trumbull, Oct. 7, 1776, ibid., 118; *Amer. Arch.,* ser. 5, III, 1308.

27 Alexander Graydon, *Memories of a Life, Chiefly Passed in Pennsylvania* (Harrisburg, 1811), p. 122.

28 George Clinton to James Duane, Aug. 27, 1777, Sparks Papers, HCL.

29 Late in May of 1776 a convention of the committees of safety and inspection in the towns of ·Berkshire County in western Massachusetts sent an address to Washington which contained complaints·against Schuyler. Benson J. Lossing, *The Life and Times of Philip Schuyler* (2 vols.; New York, 1872-1873), II, 63.

30 These criticisms were not confined to New Englanders, by the way. See Joseph Reed to Robert Morris, July 18, 1776, in Henkels, *Catalogue,* No. 1183, p. 151, and George Clinton to James Duane, Aug. 27, 1777, Sparks Papers, HCL.

31 JCC, VI, 985, 1013, 1037

32 Ibid., 1047-1048.

33 Adams, *Works,* IX, 449.

34 JCC, VII, 180-181.

35 Duane to R. R. Livingston, June 24, 1777; William Duer to R. R. Livingston, May 28, 1777, *LMCC,* II, 387, 377.

36 Ibid. Nathan Brownson, who was in attendance between January 3 and May 1, 1777 (Burnett, *LMCC,* II, xliii), is referred to by Thomas Burke and Benjamin Harrison as "a Connecticut man . . . Georgia was of no use in Congress but to vote with Connecticut. . . . Since then Mr. Walton has given his attendance.. . . . Georgia is now frequently divided. . . ." Burke to the Governor of North Carolina, May 23, 1777, ibid., 371. "You may as soon change the Devil into an Angel of Light as a Connecticut man into anything else . . . ," Harrison reported to Robert Morris. NYHS, *Collections,* Revolutionary Papers, I (1878), 410.

37 William Duer to Philip Schuyler, June 19, 1777, *LMCC,* II, 384-385.

38 Samuel Adams to Richard Henry Lee, July 15, 1777, ibid., 424.

39 Charles Thomson, Notes of Debates, ibid., 424.

40 William Duer to John Jay, May 28, 1777, in Henry P. Johnston (ed.), *Correspondence of John Jay* (4 vols.; New York, 1890-1893), I, 137.

41 Thomas Burke to the Governor of North Carolina, July 30, 1777, *LMCC,* II, 431-432.

42 Ibid.

43 Samuel Adams to James Warren, July 31, 1777, and Samuel Adams to R. H. Lee, July 15, 1777, ibid., 434, 413.

44 Charles F. Adams (ed.), *Familiar Letters of John Adams and His Wife Abigail Adams, during the Revolution* (Boston, 1875), pp. 292-293.

45 Charles Thomson, Notes of Debates, July 28, 1777, and James Lovell to William Whipple, Aug. 4, 1777, *LMCC,* II, 427-428. 437.

46 James Lovell to William Whipple, Aug. 4, 1777, ibid.

47 Adams, *Works,* II, 437.

48 Gerry to Joseph Trumbull, Oct. 2, 1777, *LMCC,* II, 505.

49 Charles Thomson, Notes of Debates, July 26, 1777, ibid., II, 425.

50 James Lovell to John Trumbull, Mar. 22, 1777, ibid., 308–309.

51 James Lovell to William Whipple, Aug. 11 and 8, 1777, ibid., 445, 442.

52 Lovell to Gates, Nov. 27, 1777, in George W. Greene, *Life of Nathanael Greene* (3 vols.; New York, 1867–1871), II, 7–8. E. C. Burnett, who describes Lovell as a "fomenter" of the Conway cabal in his article on Lovell in the *DAB,* XI, 438–439, interprets the statement "we want you most near Germantown" as a way of saying to "supplant Washington." *LMCC,* II, 570n. It might as well indicate that Lovell wanted a victorious general to help win a battle without necessarily supplanting Washington. Since Gates was elected to the Board of War on the same day that Lovell was writing to him, the statement could even more easily have referred to that appointment.

53 Lovell to Gates, Nov. 27, 1777, in Greene, *Life of Nathanael Greene,* II, 8.

54 Sergeant to Lovell, Nov. 20, 1777, Samuel Adams Papers, NYPL.

55 Cushing (ed.), *Writings,* IV, 1.

56 Whether or not Adams was a real opponent of Washington, he got the reputation of being one. See his letter to James Warren, May 25, 1778, Warren-Adams Letters, II, 77.

57 Clark was also critical of Washington in letters to John Hart and Elias Dayton, Feb. 8 and Mar. 7, 1777, *LMCC,* II, 242–243, 291–292.

58 Elias Boudinot to Elisha Boudinot, Sept. 23, 1777, quoted in Bernard Knollenberg, *Washington and the Revolution: A Reappraisal* (New York, 1940), p. 195.

59 Henry sent the letter to Washington, who recognized the handwriting as that of Rush. The letter is included in Jared Sparks (ed.), *The Writings of George Washington* (12 vols.; Boston, 1839), V, 496.

60 Rush to David Ramsay, Nov. 1, 1778, Rush MSS, quoted in Kenneth Rossman, *Thomas Mifflin and the Politics of the American Revolution* (Chapel Hill, 1952), p. 164.

61 JCC, X, 18–20.

62 Henry Laurens to James Duane, Apr. 7, 1778, *LMCC,* III, 154. Shortly after Laurens's arrival John Adams described him as a man whom he admired, "a gentleman of great fortune, great abilities, modesty and integrity, and great experience too. If all the States would send us such great men, it would be a pleasure to be here." John Adams to Abigail Adams, Aug. 19, 1777, in Adams (ed.), *Familiar Letters,* p. 292.

63 Thomas Burke to Governor Richard Caswell, Apr. 9, 1778, *LMCC,* III, 163.

64 Gouverneur Morris to Robert Morris, May 11, 1778, ibid., 230.

65 *JCC,* XI, 502. The radicals had demanded that enlisted men receive consideration if officers were to be given any additional emolument—a position which confirmed the conservative opinion of New Englanders and radicals as "levellers" who had no proper comprehension of the status and authority of an effective officer corps.

66 Joseph Ward to James Lovell, Jan. 26, 1778, Samuel Adams Papers, NYPL.

67 James Lovell to Samuel Adams, Jan. 20, 1778, ibid.

6 Confederation

THERE is an impressive foundation of historical scholarship supporting the notion that the fundamental issue that divided Congress was the allocation of authority between the national and the state governments. During the nineteenth century historians such as George Bancroft and Francis Wharton regarded congressional politics as a contest between enlightened advocates and benighted opponents of central authority. Bancroft, who wrote a national epic, and Wharton, who analyzed Revolutionary diplomacy, both deplored the seeming incapacity of the Continental Congress to direct the war and the diplomacy of the Revolution. The federal Constitution provided a convenient measurement of the fragility of the Articles of Confederation, and congressional delegates could be divided into political camps in terms of their receptiveness to the principles of national competence finally established at the Constitutional Convention.

The narratives of these "Nationalist" historians did not stand unchallenged. Their analyses were almost exclusively political in emphasis and therefore were decidedly limited in scope. Historians of the "Progressive" school such as Carl Becker and Charles Beard, who wrote during the early twentieth century, broadened their inquiry by scrutinizing more closely the social and economic forces that affected the politics of the Revolution and the Congress. They concluded that the Patriots disagreed about the purpose and even the desirability of the Revolution and consequently split into opposing radical and conservative camps once independence had been declared. The conservatives, after accommodation with England was no longer possible, wanted a stable transfer of power that would not significantly alter the pre-Revolutionary social and political order, while the radicals sought more sweeping changes.

The most impressive treatment of the internal politics of the Revolution from the Progressive angle of vision has been provided more recently by Merrill Jensen, who published two complementary works: *The Articles of Confederation* in 1940, and *The New Nation* in 1950. Jensen concluded that while most radicals were Revolutionaries, a sizable number of Revolutionaries were not radical—that is, they were not committed to social, economic, and political alterations of the pre-Revolutionary order. Because radical reform could be achieved most effectively—perhaps exclusively—in the states, it was axiomatic that radicals should support a weak confederation of sovereign states and that conservatives should rely, with certain exceptions, upon a strong national government to preserve the status quo. The Progressive historians thus contradicted the Nationalist historians in almost every respect. Nonetheless, each discerned two parties with the same basic membership; each unraveled the tangled skein of Revolutionary politics along the main thread of confrontation between nationalists and particularists; and each incorporated the Constitution as the consummation of the essential political struggle of the Revolution, albeit in utterly different terms[1].

Close inspection of the actual formulation of the Articles of Confederation during 1776 and 1777 does not support either of these interpretations. Paradoxically, however, each has some validity, and the theme they share—the idea that the struggle between advocates of centralism and federalism was the basic component of congressional politics—also rings true, but only with important qualifications.

The difficulty with the nineteenth-century Nationalist interpretation is that many of the most "enlightened" advocates of increased central authority were less than committed Patriots in 1776—a point correctly emphasized by the Progressive historians. Robert Morris, James Wilson, and John Dickinson of Pennsylvania, and Robert R. Livingston, James Duane, William Duer, and Gouverneur Morris of New York are all examples of men who opposed independence and supported national consolidation in varying degrees. There were, of course, Patriot nationalists such as John Adams, Benjamin Franklin, and Benjamin Rush in the Congress, and nationalists within the military were legion. But nationalists in the Congress such as John Adams subordinated confederation to independence, and nationalists within the army were with a few exceptions more concerned with war than politics during the early stages of hostilities.[2].

The Progressive argument also suffers from several inconsistencies and anomalies. Logically, the radical proponents of independence should have taken a parochial position on the issue of confederation. Many delegates such as Samuel Adams and James Lovell of Massachusetts did; indeed, the Progressive interpretation is generally sounder on the question of ideological continuity of factional membership than is the Nationalist interpretation. But there is little evidence that radicals were indifferent to the formulation of the Articles of Confederation, as has been suggested[3]. Quite the contrary, they were active proponents of confederation, believing that it was just as important in the support of the war as the conservatives believed it was important as a tactic to be used in delaying independence. A number of radicals, preeminently Patrick Henry in 1774 and Richard Henry Lee thereafter, favored proportional representation in the Congress. This was sine qua non for significant national authority that even conservative nationalists such as Robert Morris and John Dickinson did not insist upon. There were other anomalies in radical postures over time that are difficult to dismiss simply as the inevitable exceptions to the rule. Thomas Paine was unequaled as a propagandist for the radical cause, but his pamphlet *Common Sense* that helped persuade so many colonials to accept independence contained a plan of continental union that was in some respects more centralist than the measures nationalists advocated in Congress. Thomas Burke of North Carolina was unequaled as a jealous defender of states' rights when the Articles were given their final modification before being submitted to the states in 1777, but at one point he advocated a conservative two-house Congress, and he subsequently became a strong advocate of executivism when supporting Robert Morris's office of the Superintendent of Finance in 1780 and 1781. The reason for Burke's last turnabout is sufficiently clear: his state of North Carolina was being overrun by the British, and he saw new and compelling arguments for consolidated power.

In short, the postures of delegates regarding the distribution of national and state powers was dependent not only upon abstract ideological commitments but also upon changing circumstances in the movement toward independence, in the fortunes of war, and in the political and economic interests of states and individuals at different moments in time. Consequently, there were odd inconsistencies in the behavior of individuals and delegations that prevented the crucial question of the allocation of powers within a federal republic from assuming the central significance it might have had in the definition of partisan politics in the Continental Congress during the 1770s.

II

The first practical circumstance to confuse the matter of confederation was the question of independence. Radicals were more interested in separating from England than they were in framing a confederation—although they were hardly indifferent to the latter concern. John Adams's position as he spelled

it out in a letter to Patrick Henry shortly before the Declaration was approved
is illuminating:

> It has ever appeared to me that the natural course and order of things was this:
> for every colony to institute a government; for all the colonies to confederate,
> and define the limits of continental Constitution; then to declare the colonies
> a sovereign state, or a number of confederated sovereign states; and last of all,
> to form treaties with foreign powers. But I fear we cannot proceed systematically,
> and that we shall be obligated to declare ourselves independent States, before
> we confederate . . .[4].

The statement reveals the characteristic logic of Adams's methodical mind,
but it also shows a tendency to subordinate theory to act, and constitution
making to revolution. It may have been an inadvertence, but Adams seemed
not to have decided upon, or thought it vital to distinguish between, the alternatives of continental union through a single state or a number of sovereign
confederated states. In any event, Adams and other radicals tended to minimize
the problems of continental union, from both an overriding conviction that
engagement in the Revolution would provide a catalyst for a general reformation of popular virtue and the comfortable assurance that the established provincial governments would form an acceptable political base for republican
revolution. Adams suggested to Horatio Gates that thirteen popular governments in the style of Connecticut (or something a little less democratic)
might defy all Europe.[5].

Conservatives used the absence of a confederation as an argument against
independence in the spring of 1776. Carter Braxton was convinced that "the
Continent would be torn in pieces by Intestine Wars and Convulsions" unless
controversies between the colonies over boundaries and land claims were healed
and a "grand Continental league . . . be formed and a superintending Power
also"[6]. Edward Rutledge contended that the chance for foreign aid would
be negligible without a confederation, contemptuously adding that "a Man must
have the Impudence of a New Englander to propose in our present disjointed
state any Treaty (honorable to us) to a Nation now at peace"[7]. But such
arguments did not mean that conservatives were in favor of confederation.

After independence was declared, conservatives such as Braxton and
Rutledge had reservations about a strongly centralized confederation. The
suspicions of the "democratical" and aggrandizing New England colonies continued among Southern conservatives who feared that the Easterners were
"Lugging us into Independence" in order to create thirteen democracies on the
Connecticut model. Thus Braxton urged Virginia both to preserve as much of
the monarchic element in her constitution as was possible and to confederate
with careful safeguards against central manipulation. Edward Rutledge warned
John Jay that the early draft of the Articles of Confederation had the vices
of its major author—their fellow conservative John Dickinson. It "refined"

things too much and tended to destroy "all Provincial Distinctions . . . making every thing of the most minute kind bend to what they call the good of the whole." This could mean only that "these Colonies must be subject to the Government of the Eastern Provinces." Rutledge wanted to vest the general government with no more power than was absolutely necessary and "to keep the Staff in our own Hands"[8]. His statement was ironic, for Dickinson's "refined" production included little more consequential power for the Congress than was allowed after the Articles were curbed by the explicit assertion of state sovereignty at the insistence of the exquisitely sensitive states' righter Thomas Burke. Above all, the original draft as well as the subsequent ones provided that each state should have one vote—a clause that severely inhibited significant national power. It was not only that Southern conservatives feared Eastern egalitarianism, but also that conservatives from small states feared the disproportionate influence of the larger states in a Congress apportioned on the national principle.

The achievement of a coherent conservative nationalist movement was made somewhat easier by another change in events by 1780 when financial distress and a British invasion of the South prompted a coalition of Middle and Southern delegates with some support from New England. But this co-alition (which will be covered in detail in a subsequent chapter) lasted only until the ratification of the Treaty of Paris in 1783. Peace created still another set of circumstances that shaped a different sort of nationalist front—one that was not without internal tensions between competing state and private interests and, in a more profound sense, between different perceptions of the kind of nation that should emerge from the Revolution.

Just as the Revolutionary movement swelled with a sense of common cause which was crucial for the success of the resistance and the war, so too the Revolution produced an unmistakable spirit of particularism. While Revolution-ary ideology contained visions of a republican utopia of continental dimensions, it also depended upon alienation, "the power of resentment," and distrust of authority, thereby generating tendencies toward political diffusion. Even if this had not been so, the disintegration of Crown authority left a psychological void which no confederate contrivance could possibly fill. Indeed, provincial loyalty became stronger rather than weaker with the substitution of a new central al-legiance. The spirit of particularism was even felt within the states. John Win-throp complained in 1776 that some towns in Massachusetts were applying revolutionary arguments for provincial independence to justify demands for county legislatures and town probate courts. Such extreme decentralization distressed John Adams, who had little patience with these "narrow notions"[9].

It was inevitable that the formulation of the Articles of Confederation should have reflected these divergent tendencies of nationalism and parochial-ism. Most delegates, and probably most Americans, were drawn at once toward the new nationality and the older provincial allegiance. It was the parochial-ist Patrick Henry who called himself "an American" and declared that pro-vincial distinctions were erased. Richard Henry Lee, an anti-Federalist in 1787, argued for the nationalist mode of proportional representation in the Conti-nental Congress in 1777. William Duer, presumably a conservative advocate of national executive consolidation, voted for equal representation of the states, knowing full well that this would frustrate the creation of any effective national sovereignty over the states. Samuel Adams, who believed above all else in the manners and principles of New England, struggled in Congress against Middle states conservative opposition for a broadly nationalist foreign policy which included not only American rights to the fisheries but also rights to the navigation of the Mississippi. Even Thomas Burke, whose parochial arguments were the apotheosis of states' rights philosophy, supported a continental post-war military establishment in the form of half pay for officers and went so far as to move for increased powers for the Superintendent of Finance.

Thus while it was inevitable that the controversy between centralism and federalism should be an enduring theme during the Confederation era, few individuals were so unaffected by changing circumstances and ambivalent loyalties as to make that controversy the basis for the stable partisan alignments necessary for a coherent pattern of congressional politics.

III

The immediate history of the formulation of the Articles of Confederation began with Richard Henry Lee's motion on June 7, 1776, that "these United Colonies are, and of right ought to be, free and independent States. . . ." Lee's resolution sensibly also called for consideration of foreign alliances and the creation of a confederation. A committee composed of one member from each state was appointed on June 12, and in exactly one month—actually before the Declaration of Independence was engrossed and signed—a plan of confederation was laid before the Congress. The draft was debated in committee of the whole until late August, but agreement on important questions such as representa-tion and the definition of congressional powers was impossible to come by, and the question was dropped by and large until April of 1777. After that it was periodically considered, debated, and postponed until the fall, when the final draft—altered in many details from the original 1776 draft—was finally ap-proved by Congress in November. Ratification by all the states did not occur for over three years, primarily because of the opposition of Maryland to the large claims of states with charter rights to territory in the West—above all the claims of Maryland's powerful neighbor Virginia. After Virginia agreed to cede her lands north of the Ohio River in January of 1781, thereby diminishing her imperial stature within the union, Maryland promptly ratified the Articles, and they went into effect on March 1, 1781.

Nationalist historians of the nineteenth century sometimes criticized Virginia for her seemingly selfish refusal to give up her western claims and for her responsibility for the lengthy delay in the ratification of the Articles. Progressive historians, particularly Merrill Jensen in his study *The Articles of Confederation,* saw the matter differently. Jensen emphasized the differences between the first and final drafts of the Articles and contended that the first draft was drawn up by a committee dominated by conservatives who wished to create a powerful national government that could curb the democratic thrust of the Revolution. There was circumstantial evidence that the committee was also responsive to the interests of land speculators from the landless Middle states and that under the leadership of John Dickinson, the man most responsible for the phraseology of the draft, the committee sought to clear the way for the land speculators by curbing the claims of states with charter rights to the West. It seemed plausible that the year's delay in finishing the draft was due to the insistence of the radicals that the independence and sovereignty of the states be guaranteed and that the territorial integrity of the states be secured. Finally, from the Progressive angle of vision, the delay of three years in securing ratification was just as attributable to the private interests of speculators from the landless states as to the demands of the yeomanry of Virginia[10].

While there is much merit in the Progressive interpretation of the framing of the Articles, it should be recognized that both the Dickinson draft and the final draft of November 1777 created a league of sovereign states equally represented in a Continental Congress that expressly denied to the central government the crucial power of direct taxation. There were certain ambiguities in the language of the Dickinson draft that might have been used by a centralist-minded Congress to usurp power at the expense of the states, but for that to have taken place, conservatives in the Congress needed far greater cohesion and unity of purpose than they exhibited between 1776 and 1780. Furthermore, even the final draft granted substantial authority to the Congress in the areas of war, diplomacy, and the management of the West. Finally, both radicals and conservatives disagreed among themselves on so many issues that it is difficult to reduce the struggle over the Articles to differences in political philosophy.

The committee designated on June 12, whether by accident or design, was almost evenly balanced between radicals and conservatives of various hues. John Dickinson, the chairman of the committee and its most influential member, along with Edward Rutledge and Robert R. Livingston, provided a powerful conservative force in the committee. The radicals, on the other hand, had important representation, including Samuel Adams, Stephen Hopkins, Roger Sherman, and Thomas McKean. All told, the radicals of varying persuasions probably outnumbered the conservatives by a margin of seven to six, although the conservatives had the edge in talent and influence[*11*].

Oddly enough, the only real criticism of the actual substance of the Dickinson draft from within the committee came from a conservative, Edward Rutledge[*12*], while the major grievance of the radicals was that Congress was tarrying on the critical matter of confederation. Josiah Bartlett of New Hampshire worried that the final settlement of this "important business" was delayed because of difficulties that had arisen within the committee. A whole year later Samuel Adams deplored the fact that two days were wasted in debate on Vermont, concluding that "a kind of Fatality still prevents our proceeding a Step in the important affair of Confederation"[*13*]. His correspondent, the radical Richard Henry Lee, agreed about the urgency of confederation, asserting that it should be the great object of American policy and the surest way to establish American independence—a fact "clearly discerned by the friends of Dependence, because it is obvious, that those generally, who were marked foes to the declaration of independence, are the men that now thwart and delay Confederation"[*14*]. Although radicals had placed independence above confederation, they had become the "Party of the Revolution," and it was only natural that Lee and others who had forced independence and who were favoring energetic prosecution of a war that was going badly at the time should have favored completing the Confederation with as much haste as possible. Radicals differed among themselves over certain fundamental questions, most importantly the problems of representation and the basis of taxation, but these differences and the delays they engendered were a source of dismay among the radicals. John Witherspoon, a member of the radical camp from the small state of New Jersey, naturally supported equal representation, while Richard Henry Lee argued strenuously for proportional representation; but Witherspoon was convinced that all were in agreement that "there must and shall be a confederation for this war"[*15*].

The only delegate who seemed reluctant even to frame a confederation was Thomas Burke of North Carolina, an articulate Irishman who first arrived in Congress in February of 1777 and who believed that the proper moment for deciding about the terms of confederation was not during a time of crisis, but during a period of "peace and tranquility." He freely admitted, however, that he differed "very widely on this subject with a majority in Congress." Burke's colleague from North Carolina, Cornelius Harnett, suggested that Burke's isolation was complete. "Every member of Congress seems to wish for a Confederacy except my good friend Burke, who laughs at it as a chimerical project; it does not strike me in that point of view"[*16*]. The difficulty in establishing ideological categories in terms of attitudes toward confederation at this moment is illustrated by the fact that both Burke and Harnett were inclined toward democracy, if one is to judge from their positions in the formulation of the North Carolina constitution[*17*]. In Congress, on the other hand, Burke (as well as Harnett) could usually be found voting on the side of the Middle states conservatives. To conclude that his objections to the Articles were representative of the full range of radical sentiment would be misleading, for the radicals were united only in their opposition to uncontrolled central authority—and not in the way in which national authority should be constituted. Further, Burke himself was motivated by complicated drives, some of which had very little to do with ideology, whether radical or conservative, nationalist or states' rightist.

Dickinson's draft of the Articles of Confederation was not uniformly centralist; rather, it reflected the characteristically ambivalent nationalist and parochial loyalties of American Revolutionaries. The Confederation was described in Article II as a "firm League of Friendship" between the colonies "for their common Defence, the Security of their Liberties, and their mutual and general Welfare . . ."[*18*]. Representation and voting were equal, but in Article VIII the Congress was given substantial national powers, including "sole and exclusive" power over war and peace; the settlement of disputes between states over boundaries, jurisdictions, "or any other Cause whatever"; the adjustment of colonial claims in the West; the disposition of western lands separated from the states or purchased from the Indians; and the emission of bills and the borrowing of money. Yet the national government was prohibited in that same article from ever laying any taxes or duties except in the management of the Post Office. Further, the exercise of those powers was constrained not only by the rule that each state had one vote, but also by the stipulation that the consent of nine states had to be secured for a comprehensive list of important decisions and by the requirement that an absolute majority of seven states was necessary for all other matters. Article XI stipulated that all charges for the common defense or general welfare would be paid out of a common treasury in proportion to population (including slaves but excluding Indians who did not pay taxes), but the collection of a state's proportion, or quota, would be left to its own discretion. Separate states were prohibited in Article IV from entering into treaties with Britain or any other foreign country, unless by consent of Congress. If Congress approved, they might also establish subconfederations, or alliances, one with another. The Congress clearly had preeminent authority to make treaties, but in Article VIII the states were individually allowed to lay tariffs on imports if such duties did not conflict with treaties entered into by the Congress. The states were guaranteed sole and exclusive regulation of their internal police, but not in cases that interfered with the Articles of Confederation—a clause that Thomas Burke found particularly menacing. The states were prohibited from maintaining standing armies in time of peace, but they were allowed to appoint all officers below the rank of general for contingents they raised for the common defense (Article X).

The Dickinson draft, despite its ambivalence, despite the haste with which it was formulated, and despite the novelty of independence (states were referred to as "Colonies" in the Dickinson draft and as "States" in the final draft of 1777), contained some provisions of enduring importance that were ultimately included in the Constitution. In accord with the republican philosophy of the Revolution, it was provided in Article IV that neither the United States nor any state could grant any title of nobility. In Article VI it was stipulated that the inhabitants of each state were entitled to the same "Rights, Liberties, Privileges, Immunities and Advantages" in another state that the inhabitants of the other state enjoyed. The Congress was given authority to regulate relations with the Indians, to dispose of western lands for the benefit of the whole union, and to create and to admit new states (Article XVIII). In granting powers related to the declaration of war, the issuance of letters of marque and reprisal, the regulation of land and naval forces, the disposition of prizes taken on the seas and coasts, the punishment of crimes at sea, and the establishment of a post office system, the draft anticipated many of the provisions of the Constitution. It was a remarkable step in the direction of a national government.

Still, the Dickinson draft was in many respects a concession to the smaller, landless states. With regard to what William Williams called "the great Question" and to what Henry Laurens called the "One vast point" of representation in Congress, Dickinson and the committee adopted the particularist position of one vote for each state. There is no reason to think that the committee was bound by the unit rule of voting already established in Congress, for in other respects precedents were discarded. Furthermore, both the Galloway Plan and Franklin's plan of confederation put before Congress a year before had provided for proportional representation. Since the Dickinson draft also stipulated that any amendment would have to be ratified by all the states, modification of the equal vote provision was impossible in view of the small states' fear of engulfment by the large states. Given irrevocable equal representation, a truly national government was impossible in principle and in fact. While the rather loosely defined congressional authority in boundary disputes between states and in western lands occupied only by Indians did enhance the power of the national government, it is probable that these provisions reflected the interests and fears of the small landless states rather than a nationalist conspiracy.

Criticism of the Dickinson draft came from all angles, but general controversy focused upon the problems of representation, the mode of calculating state contributions to the general treasury, and the connected issues of boundary disputes and western claims. The debates over these questions indicated, not unsurprisingly, that provincial loyalties overrode virtually all other considerations for a vast majority of the delegates. The question of representation pitted delegations from large states against delegates from small states. The determination of quotas separated Northern delegations from Southern delegations. The problem of the control of western lands divided delegates from states with claims to the West from the delegations from the states that did not have such claims. Thus state and regional interests did not conform to an orderly and consistent pattern, and because of this, the disputes over the Dickinson draft did not in the main reinforce the old division between radicals and conservatives—nor did those disputes create at this time a new basis for partisan politics.

It is apparent, even from the sketchy notes of the early proceedings before roll calls were recorded in the Journals, that the Old Radicals divided on the question of representation. The radicals John Adams, Benjamin Franklin, and Benjamin Rush from the populous states of Massachusetts and Pennsylvania joined the conservative Arthur Middleton of South Carolina in support of proportional representation during August of 1776, while radicals and moderates such as Sherman, Hopkins, Witherspoon, and Chase from the small states aligned in opposition[19]. When the confederation was finally hammered out in the fall of 1777, Virginians of all persuasions continued to support proportional representation—by that time clearly a losing cause. With unfailing cohesion Richard Henry Lee (the Old Radical), Francis Lightfoot Lee (a moderate radical who was drifting away from the Eastern alliance), Joseph Jones (a moderate), and John Harvie (a conservative) continued their opposition to the equal vote. By then most of the Congress, including conservatives such as James Duane and Robert Morris, who later supported the nationalist cause, had become reconciled to the inevitability of equal representation. Only Adams, Middleton, and John Penn of North Carolina voted with the Virginians[20].

The mode of apportioning state quotas, or contributions to the general treasury, also stimulated much controversy, but along rather different lines. The Dickinson draft provided that quotas should be figured on the basis of the total population of a state, excluding non-taxpaying Indians but including slaves. The Southern states naturally objected to this clause and cast about for an alternative. Samuel Chase of Maryland moved that quotas be levied on the basis of white population only—a notion that resulted in a rigorous division between the North and the South[21]. As finally determined in 1777, quotas were to be established on the basis of land values—a decision that was opposed strenuously by all New Englanders who represented states with relatively concentrated populations and high levels of land improvement. When the New Englanders proposed a plan that would count all property, including slaves, the Southern delegations marshaled enough support from the Middle states to put it down. In the last vote on the issue on October 14, 1777, the New England delegates voted uniformly against the land value proposal and were supported only by the votes of the conservative Duane of New York and the radical Roberdeau of Pennsylvania[22]. Both Lees and Witherspoon voted with conservatives against radical New Englanders on this roll call.

The agreement between the Middle states and the Southern delegations on quotas broke down on the third major divisive issue—the matter of congressional authority over conflicting boundaries and claims to unoccupied lands in the West. Virginia and Pennsylvania disagreed about their boundary line in the southwestern portion of Pennsylvania, and Virginia had massive claims to western lands, while Pennsylvania had none. Land speculators in both states were active in the westward movement, however, so disagreements were bound to crop up. There were other conflicting boundaries and claims that complicated attitudes toward the congressional authority that had been included in Article XVIII of the Dickinson draft. Connecticut settlers had come to blows with Pennsylvanians in the Wyoming Valley of Pennsylvania, where the Susquehanna Company of Connecticut had planted some people. New York and New Hampshire, and to a lesser degree Massachusetts, had claims to Vermont, or the Hampshire grants, as that region was known. While the Southern states —particularly Virginia, North Carolina, and Georgia—had relatively exclusive claims below the Ohio River to the Mississippi, Virginia, New York, Connecticut, and Massachusetts had a number of overlapping claims west of the mountains and north of the Ohio.

The Dickinson draft included a provision in Article XVIII for settling boundary disputes as well as a number of other references to undetermined boundaries, the limitation of western claims, the purchase of Indian lands, and other matters which, although not specifically granting control of western lands to Congress, implicitly cast doubt upon the validity of the charter claims of the landed states. Virginia, which had the largest claim, took the lead in attempting to include a constitutional sanction of the western claims of the landed states. Virginia was generally supported by the other landed states and opposed most strenuously by the landless states Maryland and Pennsylvania [23]. This division persisted into October of 1777, when three attempts to encroach on the landed states were voted down by Congress[24]. The first attempt was a motion to grant the Congress power to review the territorial claims of each of the states in order that Congress might decide upon proper boundaries. The second motion was a simple grant of authority to Congress to limit the western boundaries of the states claiming to the South Sea [the Pacific], while the third involved a grant of authority to Congress to determine western boundaries and create new states from those lands separated from the older states.

All these motions of the fifteenth of October were soundly defeated, but just as on the issues of representation and taxation, the voting predominantly reflected state self-interest. Roll-call votes were taken on the first and third motions, and all support for the measures came from the Middle states which were largely landless. New York, which backed Maryland and Pennsylvania on the first motion, did have western claims, but at the moment she was involved in the dispute with Vermonters who had settled in the Hampshire grants under warrants issued by New Hampshire, and the New York delegates who had been trying to secure a full-scale investigation of the Vermont problem were doubtless convinced that the review of original grants would work to their advantage in Vermont. By the second roll call, resistance within the Middle states began to crumble. On that question providing for congressional authority to establish western boundaries and create new states from separated lands, Maryland stood virtually alone. The other landless states (excluding Delaware, which was not represented at the time) must have compromised their interests in favor of the overall objective of confederation in somewhat the same way that the larger states—excepting Virginia—were willing to accept equal representation a week earlier. Not only did the landless states fail to secure these resolutions; the ambiguities of the Dickinson draft were clarified to the advantage of the landed states by the inclusion of a clause offered by Richard Henry Lee specifically stating that "no State shall be deprived of territory for the benefit of the United States[25].

Thus it is apparent that the main determinant of voting on the three main problems of confederation was state self-interest, sometimes overridden by a desire to complete the long-delayed confederation. It is not at all apparent that partisan loyalties as they emerged during the period 1774–1777 played any significant part in either the original positions of the delegates or in the subsequent compromises which occurred. The basic tendency of factionalism during this period of the Revolution was toward a division between the New England delegations on the one hand and a coalition of conservatives from the Middle states and an increasingly self-conscious Southern bloc on the other. This was an antagonism that could not be reduced to any particular factor involved in the construction of the Articles of Confederation, but of the three issues just discussed, the alignment on the debate over appointment of quotas (which incidentally had the least to do with the definition of federal relationships) most nearly approximated the partisan division of the mid-Revolution [26].

IV

The revision of the Dickinson draft included more than the three major questions of representation, taxation, and management of the West. The volatile and talented delegate from North Carolina, Thomas Burke, saw many dangerous centralizing tendencies in the Dickinson draft, and he ultimately persuaded Congress to make other alterations. Even the final draft failed to satisfy him. Although it allowed no taxing authority to the Congress, Burke detected "an unlimited power over all property . . . a power to Tax at pleasure" in the congressional power to borrow money and emit bills[27]. He distrusted the provision for a Council of State that would sit when Congress was not in session, despite the fact that the Council had no legislative power whatsoever. While agreeing that Congress might frame commercial treaties with other nations, Burke was distressed that Article VI prohibited the separate states from entering into an agreement, alliance, or treaty with a foreign power, since this imposed "very unnecessary restraints upon the States"[28]. Although he was willing that the states should be prohibited from entering unauthorized alliances and confederations with each other, he did not agree with the provision in Article VI which also eliminated treaties between states that were unsanctioned by the Congress[29].

Burke was particularly alarmed by the provisions in Article III of the Dickinson draft that guaranteed to the states only their present laws and customs and control over matters of internal police that did not conflict with the Articles. He felt that this article was in effect a blanket grant of sovereignty to the national government in all future nonpolice matters[30]. To remedy this oversight—or, less graciously, this surreptitious, centralist design—Burke moved to attach an amendment to the Dickinson draft stipulating that the states should retain all powers not specifically granted to the Confederation— a proposal that was included as Article II in the final draft of the Confederation.

Interestingly, Burke found so little concern with the danger his proposal was designed to countervail that he found it difficult to secure a second for the motion[31]. After South Carolina did second his amendment, Burke encountered opposition in the ensuing debate not only from the nationalist James Wilson but also from Richard Henry Lee, a radical. Lee's opposition has caused some puzzlement to historians who have been aware of his famous essays in opposition to the Constitution of 1787. Two factors can explain this seeming inconsistency: first, Lee was at this moment attending to the interests of a large state and had not yet given up on the possibility of proportional representation; second, and most important, it is unlikely that Lee (or for that matter Dickinson) anticipated that the Articles as they emerged from committee would ever be used as an instrument of central aggrandizement. Actually, Lee was frustrated with the time-consuming debate over details of the Dickinson draft. In a letter to Samuel Adams in the summer of 1777 he objected strongly to the congressional penchant for "excessive refinement, and pedantic affectation of discerning future ills in necessary, innocent, and indeed proper establishments. . . ." As already mentioned, he suggested that obstruction of the confederation was a Tory maneuver[32].

It is highly unlikely that Dickinson harbored covert designs leading toward an ultimate centralist coup through the phraseology of Article III. Dickinson added a number of queries in the form of footnotes to his draft that help illuminate his intentions. His questions regarding the first three articles were directed at the possibility of providing a national guarantee of each state's constitution and form of government—a guarantee that would hardly support nationalist consolidation. In other queries Dickinson anticipated some of Burke's objections, as under Article VIII, where he wondered (1) whether the establishment of garrisons and fortifications in a state should be undertaken for the general defense if that state objected and (2) whether the general government should try persons in the Continental service without first applying to the government of the concerned state. Of course, interpretation of Dickinson's motives depends greatly on what the queries signify. It is at least plausible to infer in the absence of direct evidence that they reflected Dickinson's own ideas which the committee did not accept—although the reverse could be true. Since Dickinson also added a question about the advisability of a general guarantee against new religious establishments which was more in accord with his own libertarian beliefs than with the sectarian attitudes of some of the Old Radicals such as Samuel Adams, the inference that the queries were Dickinson's rather than those of the committee seems reasonable.

Assessing Burke's motivation in objecting to the nationalist implications he perceived in the Dickinson draft is no less difficult than penetrating Dickinson's motives. Burke was an interesting, but complicated, individual. Clearly, as Elisha Douglass has shown, he was an egoist, highly sensitive, quick to take affront—but able, aggressive and ambitious[33]. He seems as well to have been notably unstable in his political convictions. He took a radical position during the resistance and the early part of the Revolution in North Carolina, but he became increasingly conservative. Indeed, by the end of the war, when he served as Governor of North Carolina, he had become, in Douglass's words, "a hopeless reactionary"[34]. Even his opposition to the Dickinson draft of the Articles showed inconsistencies that are so mystifying in retrospect as to cast doubt upon the genuineness of his commitment to the principle of states' rights at the very time he seemed to be defending those rights most strenuously.

Soon after Burke moved that the states be guaranteed their sovereignty, freedom, and independence, he made a proposal, apparently in May of 1777, that would have transformed the Council of State—a housekeeping body in Dickinson's proposal that Burke subsequently found objectionable—into an upper house of the Congress strikingly similar to the Senate that was created ten years later in the federal Constitution[35]. The motion was prefaced with a justification: "For the better managing the interests of the united States, Shall be instituted a general Council and Council of State to form a Congress"[36]. The Lower House, or General Council, would be constituted by some measure of proportional representation, while the states would be equally represented in the Council of State[37]. Consistent with his insistence upon the sovereignty of the states, Burke left the mode of election to the two houses entirely to the states, but there were anomalies in his design, just as there were in Dickinson's earlier draft. All Continental legislation would have to originate in the lower house, but the approval of the Council of State was necessary for the bill to become a law. With the exception of a declaration of war, congressional bills would become law with the assent of an absolute majority of the membership of both houses—that is to say, seven votes rather than the nine votes required for most important measures in the Dickinson draft. In this respect the Burke proposal was more nationalist than Dickinson's. The plan also provided that all ordinances passed by the Congress would be "binding on all and every of the United States" so long as they did not exceed the powers expressly given to the national government under the Articles. There was one exception: Compliance with a declaration of war (which required the consent of three-fourths of the General Council and nine votes in the Council of State) was not obligatory for states which in effect chose to remain neutral. Such states would be exempt from taxes and other obligations associated with the war, but they would be excluded from all benefits accruing from victory. Burke anticipated not only the Constitution but also the discontents that produced the Hartford Convention of 1814.

Burke's motion was summarily rejected by the Congress. A few cryptic comments in a different hand on the cover of the motion provide a convincing explanation why the Congress dismissed the motion: "Delays in Execution. Congress Executive Body resembling King &c; 2. No combination Except one or the other[.] Idea of Distinctions resembling British Constitution"[38]. It is clear that while the whole thrust of the Revolutionary constitutional brief was directed toward the notion of divided sovereignty, the members of Congress still adhered to a simplistic view of the nature of sovereignty in the new nation. The Confederation had to be either a collectivity of sovereign states or a unitary system menacingly similar to the imperial structure that the colonies had just rejected. The "Distinctions" reminiscent of the British constitution were similarly unacceptable because Burke's recommendation resembled the aristocratic principles underlying the separation of the Houses of Commons and Lords. Burke's proposal more closely resembled the Constitution than any other design offered before the compromise that was effected at Philadelphia ten years later. But what was logical and obvious at the Constitutional Convention was almost incomprehensibly innovative in 1777.

Other revisions of the Dickinson draft, whether accepted or rejected, were less drastic. The original reciprocal guarantee of liberties and privileges for citizens of one state in another was qualified to include only free inhabitants and to exclude paupers, vagabonds, and fugitives from justice. A clause was added providing for the extradition of persons charged with treason, felony, or other high misdemeanors. Further, "full faith and credit" was to be given to the acts and judicial proceedings of one state in another—a clause that also found its way into the federal Constitution. In these respects the Dickinson draft was actually further nationalized rather than decentralized. A related attempt to allow suits for recovery of debts in one state in the courts of another state was rejected, however.

Although national unity was enhanced by such interstate agreements, there were regional suspicions that helped curb national power in the final draft. One restriction was the clause added to Article VI prohibiting the states from keeping vessels of war during peacetime, except in numbers allowed by Congress. While direct evidence about the reasons for this amendment (passed on October 23) is lacking, the insecurity felt by Southern delegates as early as the first Congress regarding their vulnerability to naval attacks and blockades was very likely the source of the restriction[39].

V

Most of the revisions just referred to appear to have been made without great discord. In any event, they did not in the main prompt recorded roll calls— an innovation that began in August of 1777. The major problems of representation, tax quotas, and the management of western lands, on the other hand, did produce a series of roll calls that revealed the complicated and often contradictory pattern of the dispute over the Articles of Confederation.

Eleven votes on amendments to the Dickinson draft which revealed centralist and states' rightist attitudes have been arranged in Table 5 in a fashion resembling a Guttmann scalogram[40]. The object of the scalogram is to rank legislators in terms of their voting on a particular issue. The scalogram should reveal clusters of like-minded delegates and also disclose how those clusters were postured in relation to the issue. Ideally, the scalogram should result in a series of voting blocs that range from complete support to complete opposition to the issue—in this case the matter of congressional power. Thus, on the eleven votes nationalist-minded delegates should have supported proportional representation as well as congressional authority to fix state boundaries and control western territory. They should also have supported an indefinite term for the president of the Congress, for that would have added at least a small amount of direction to a body lacking central authority. Likewise, nationalists (or "centralists") should have opposed an amendment to Article XIV providing that no treaty concluded by the Congress might prevent the states from laying imposts on foreign goods.

The clusters of delegates reveal that there was a distinct tendency for members of Congress to form blocs in response to the issue of centralism. Bloc II, for example, included six delegates who cast a total of 52 votes, only two of

TABLE 5

Voting Scale on the Articles of Confederation: October–November 1777

Bloc	Delegate	Votes (x-Centralist vote; o-States' rightist vote)																						
		1	2	3	4	5	6	7	8	9	10	11	1	2	3	4	5	6	7	8	9	10	11
I	Jones (Va.)	x	x	x	x	x	o	o	o	o	o	o											
	Lee, F. L. (Va.)	x	x	x	x	x	o	o	o	o	o	o											
	Lee, R. H. (Va.)	x	x	x	x	x	o		o	o	o	o											
	Harvie (Va.)				x		o	o	o	o	o	o											
	Adams, J. (Mass.)	x	x	x			o		o		o		o			o							
	Penn (N.C.)	x	x		x		o		o	o	o	o				o		o		x			
II	Adams, S. (Mass.)						o	o	o		o	o	o	o	o	o							
	Gerry (Mass.)							o	o	o	o	o	o	o	o	o							
	Lovell (Mass.)						o	o		o	o				o								
	Harnett (N.C.)						o	o	o	o	o	o	o	o	o	o	o						
	Heyward (S.C.)						o		o		o	o	o	o	o	o	o						
	Roberdeau (Pa.)	x					o	o	o				o	o	o	o				x			
III	Duane (N.Y.)						o		o	o		o	o	o	o	o	o		x		x		
	Duer (N.Y.)						o		o			o	o	o	o	o	o		x		x		
	Morris, R. (Pa.)						o				o				o	o			x		x		
	Smith (Md.)						o		o	o			o	o	o	o			x				x
IV	Marchant (R.I.)							o	o		o	o	o	o	o	o	o	x		x			
	Folsom (N.H.)							o		o	o	o	o	o	o	o	o	x	x				
	Laurens (S.C.)							o		o	o	o	o	o	o	o	o	x	x				
	Witherspoon (N.J.)									o	o	o	o	o	o	o	o	x	x				
V	Williams (Conn.)										o	o	o	o	o	o	o		x		x	x	
	Law (Conn.)							o	o		o	o	o	o	o	o	o	x	x	x			
	Dyer (Conn.)							o	o		o	o	o	o	o	o	o	x	x	x	x		

NOTES:

Votes 1–5 deal with representation, the centralist position reflecting support of proportional representation and the states' rightist position reflecting opposition to proportional representation. Votes 1–4 were taken on Oct. 7; vote 5 on Oct. 28, *JCC,* IX, 779–782, 849.

Vote 6 deals with right of states to levy imposts. Opposition is interpreted as support of centralism. Oct. 23, *JCC,* IX, 835.

Vote 7 is an amendment to Article 14 specifying that no person may serve as President more than one year in three. Support is interpreted as an anticentralist position. Nov. 7, *JCC,* IX, 879.

Vote 8 is concerned with the establishment of machinery for the adjudication of disputes between states by Congress, provided that no state is deprived of territory by such adjudication. Support is interpreted as an anticentralist position, since the Dickinson draft had been more permissive. Oct. 27, *JCC,* IX, 843.

NOTES, Table 5 (Cont.)

Vote 9 deals with the use of the courts of one state for recovery of debts in another state. While this motion is somewhat ambivalent, support is taken as an implicitly centralist position. Nov. 12, *JCC*, IX, 896.

Vote 10 stipulates that definite territorial bounds should be established for all states, which should submit proofs of claims. Support is interpreted as a centralist position. Oct. 15, *JCC*, IX, 807.

Vote 11 also deals with western lands, giving Congress power to fix western boundaries. Support is taken as a centralist position. Oct. 15, *JCC*, IX, 808.

which deviated from the general pattern. Bloc III consisted of four delegates from three Middle states who cast a total of 36 votes, only one of which was deviant. But while there were five rather distinctive blocs, there was a remarkable lack of consistency in their commitment to the principles of centralism outlined above. Blocs I and V cast more nationalist votes in proportion to their numbers than did the other three blocs (39 percent and 32 percent respectively, as contrasted with 23 percent for Bloc III and 19 percent for Bloc IV and just 5 percent for Bloc II). But incongruously, Blocs I and V were the two clusters that agreed least, while Bloc II, the consistently states' rightist cluster, had a higher level of agreement with Bloc I, the most nationalist cluster, than did any other bloc.

These data bear out the observation that Thomas Burke made in a letter to Governor Caswell of North Carolina that while there were divisions in Congress over the issue of central authority, the sides shifted and, moreover, seemed unaware of the implications of their positions[41]. But Burke was accurate only in an abstract sense. He failed to appreciate the particular interests of the states that affected their postures as the debate over the Articles unfolded, and he seemed unaware that the basic thrust of the Congress was toward states' rights rather than centralism. Actually, 77 percent of all the votes cast on the 11 roll calls favored states' rights, and the nationalist votes were largely the consequence of pragmatic and distinctive calculations that did not comport with a consistent ideological division.

Bloc I, the most nationalist of all the clusters, was essentially a large-state bloc dominated by Virginians who supported a national rather than a confederation Congress[42]. Since the question of representation was tackled before the other issues having to do with central powers, and because proportional representation was defeated, it was natural that the Virginians should have refused to submit to central authority regarding questions such as the disposition of western lands in a legislature in which they were severely underrepresented.

By contrast, Bloc III was a Middle states cluster with discernible nationalist inclinations that emerged most clearly in the votes on the questions of executive tenure and congressional authority to resolve controversies over state boundaries. Duane, Duer, and Morris represented states with strong cases in boundary disputes with their neighbors. It is notable, however, that the New York and Pennsylvanian delegates, including Robert Morris, voted against giving Congress the power to fix western boundaries of states with extensive western claims. In that instance the desire to consummate the Confederation seems to have overrruled calculations of individual and state interests. Only Smith of Maryland, who represented the state that was to offer the most persistent opposition to the claims of the landed states, voted affirmatively on that roll call.

Blocs IV and V were composed for the main part of smaller states with powerful neighbors whose commerce was often dependent upon those stronger states. The issue that drew these two blocs together was the desire for congressional authority to make commercial treaties that overrode treaties negotiated by the states (vote 6). The Connecticut delegation showed more consistent nationalism than the assortment of delegates in Bloc IV by also opposing restrictions on the tenure of the president of Congress.

Bloc II was a consistently parochial cluster. With the exception of Roberdeau's two votes on representation and debt settlement, the bloc voted consistently antinationalist. Even Roberdeau's vote on representation was canceled with four subsequent antinationalist votes (2-5). The presence of Samuel Adams, as well as Lovell, Roberdeau, and, to a lesser extent, Gerry, gave this bloc an Eastern coloration. To the degree that the Eastern party represented an ideological extension of resistance radicalism, its states' rights position was consonant with the thesis that congressional factionalism was a derivative of states' rights democratic opposition to conservative nationalism.

The main difficulty with establishing the roots of congressional partisanship in the dispute over the structure of the Confederation is that the blocs which emerged in connection with this issue correspond only roughly with the general voting patterns when all issues—foreign affairs, military decisions, and finance, as well as the Confederation—are taken into consideration. The states' rights bloc (II), for example, split in two in the overall voting. Harnett and Heyward voted much more closely with Jones and Harvie of Virginia than they did with the Easterners[43]. Richard Henry Lee of Bloc I had a higher rate of agreement in the general voting with Samuel Adams, Gerry, Lovell, and Roberdeau of Bloc II than he did with Harvie and Jones of Bloc I. In the general voting Dyer agreed more often with Marchant than he did with Law, his fellow delegate from Connecticut. Duane of Bloc III agreed more often with Penn of Bloc I than he did with Smith. The examples could be multiplied.

Nationalist historians, in focusing their attention upon the weaknesses of the Confederation, overlooked the vitality of the states and the significance of the steps that were taken toward interstate cooperation, such as in the "full faith and credit" clause of the Articles. Progressive historians better appreciated the strength of the states and the appropriateness of the Articles of Confederation as a national framework during the early stage of the Revolution. But there were limitations in their analysis as well. They failed to see that while the United States was unlike most other new nations in the strength of its provincial political institutions, it was not immune to the strains common to colonial revolutions—strains that had to do with conflicts not only between economic classes but also between provincials and cosmopolites and between differently situated sections and states.

VI

Comparisons between colonial revolutions are admittedly precarious, but virtually all such revolutions have been marked by divisions between regions that retained different colonial identities, between commercial and agrarian populations, between the port cities and remote interiors, and between cosmopolitan and provincial-minded populations. Such tensions in the Latin American wars for independence not only produced contending centralist and federalist ideologies but also helped to shred the larger administrative provinces that had existed under the Spanish empire. The viceroyalty of La Plata, which had been settled as long as most of the British colonies and which had some fifty years of history as an administrative unit, broke into three distinct nations during the protracted war for independence. The revolutionary leadership in Buenos Aires, the *portenos* as they were called, had to send troops against Montevideo, the major city on the eastern shore of the wide opening of the La Plata River—a distance that was shorter than the mileage between Philadelphia and Boston. Even within the territory that was to become the nation of Argentina there were sharp cleavages that threatened the establishment of a single nation-state. Farther north, Simón Bolívar helped to preserve a united front whenever and wherever he was able to exert influence, but he could not prevent the viceroyalty of New Grenada from collapsing in a heap of parochial animosities that pitted loyalist against revolutionary inside the present nation of Colombia as well as in the more geographically extended regions that emerged as Venezuela, Colombia, and Ecuador.

This disintegrative process in Latin America did not conform to an entirely uniform pattern. In much of the Spanish empire the federalists were the cosmopolitan urbanites, but in Argentina the *portenos* of Buenos Aires were centralists. Certain generalizations can be made, however, one of which is that the large administrative units that functioned with generally acceptable results within the framework of a highly centralized and paternalistic empire did not serve as viable polities during the transition from colonial dependencies to nation-states. Put another way, boundaries that were drawn for administrative convenience in an imperial system proved to be inadequate in the enlivened politics of independence.

Another generalization is that centralists usually had to struggle against a formidable opposition that drew strength from many sources. To the extent that trade patterns had been artificially structured by imperial edicts—a factor that had inhibited the trade of Buenos Aires during much of the colonial period—natural readjustments created provincial tensions and jealousies. To the extent that the colonial revolution drew upon the sovereignty of the people as a source of legitimacy to replace the old imperial structure, and to the extent that the revolution translated that sovereignty into actual popular participation in the political process, it led inexorably to political diffusion. In the process, larger political units that had been legitimized through imperial prescription rather than popular acquiescence tended to break down.

Seen in this comparative context (a comparison that could be enlarged to include a number of Third World colonial revolutions during the twentieth century), one of the most remarkable aspects of the American Revolution was that virtually all the British North American colonies remained intact as a single nation. All the contiguous colonies that had had the opportunity to develop a British identity by forty years before the Revolution remained within the Confederation. (Florida, Nova Scotia, and Canada were brought into the empire only shortly before the Revolution, and both Florida and Canada had populations that were alien to British culture and institutions.)

It is something of a truism to note that the success of the United States in maintaining its national integrity was due to the unusually thorough experience in self-government enjoyed by the colonials. There was a paradox involved in that success that has not always been appreciated, however. The Constitution could not have been formulated at the outset of the Revolution. Nor did the most confirmed centralists among the Patriots contemplate anything of the sort. The whole thrust of the Resistance was against innovative centralism. The decision to declare independence was presumptive evidence against the immediate creation of anything more than a loose confederation. Patriots anticipated that the Revolution would bring about changes, to be sure, but those changes would involve a return to past virtue rather than a search for a different and strange future; they would affect the behavior of men more than the structure of government; and to the degree that alterations in government were necessary in order to fulfill the reforming expectations of the Revolutionaries, they would involve the states more than the national government. The Articles of Confederation gave constitutional expression to the inevitable diffusionist thrust of the colonial revolution. The paradox lay in the capacity of the state governments, because of their vitality and resilience, to absorb that diffusionist thrust. It was precisely the power of the states that preserved the Confederation by forming a base for halting steps toward federal union. Thus the nation could be built simultaneously from the bottom up and from the top down. The federal compromise could not have occurred otherwise.

This did not happen harmoniously, of course. Just as the initial grappling with the problem of confederation stimulated controversy, but not enduring partisan divisions, so too the gradual restructuring of the Confederation along more nationalist lines produced increasingly pronounced national and parochial interests. The struggle between those interests would become a main theme of congressional politics during the years 1780–1783 and 1786–1787.

The conflict between nationalists and parochialists was never well defined, however, for reasons that also had to do with the vitality of the states and the complicated tensions associated with colonial revolutions. There were three problems that lent themselves naturally to a coalition of nationalist-minded leaders—Continental finance, the disposition of western lands, and foreign policy. Had all the states been equally situated with respect to these three questions, a coherent struggle between nationalists and states' righters might have evolved, but in fact there were sharp differences between the relative positions of the states that prevented such a struggle. Virginia, for example, had a stable provincial political system led by a set of highly talented leaders, along with claims to a western domain that was as sizable as many European nations. But while these advantages made her a veritable Prussia of the Confederation, she lacked a well-developed commercial class capable of managing the public debt—another important payoff of the Revolution. Pennsylvania lacked chartered claims to western lands and for this reason sympathized with the objections of Maryland regarding Virginia's claims to the West. But she also had a growing population, a thriving port, an aggressive commercial class, and a central location that inevitably placed her in the center of Confederation finance and private land speculation in the West. Massachusetts also had a large investment in the Continental debt, but she was largely outside the power center of Confederation finance during the superintendency of Robert Morris, and she harbored deep and long-standing suspicions of France that prevented her from arriving at an accord with either the Middle states or Southerners who tended for different reasons to befriend the French.

Because of the vitality of the states, there were some in Virginia who contemplated assuming unilateral control of the West; the Clark expedition and the sale of western lands during the Revolution seemed to substantiate such a policy. Merchants and holders of the public debt in Pennsylvania, Massachusetts, and other states had the alternative of working through relatively stable state fiscal systems, and some of them did. Ironically, some of the stronger nationalists emanated from small states that lacked the capacity to go it alone.

Finally, because the United States was such an extended polity embodying markedly different cultural traditions, like-minded individuals frequently found it difficult to communicate with each other sufficiently well to break free from the ties of parochialism. Even the calculus of common interests failed to overcome the kinds of regional suspicions that had retarded the movement toward independence.

Notes

1 George Bancroft, *History of the United States* (10 vols.; Boston, 1834–1874). Bancroft's description of the delibertaions of Congress in 1778 is entered under the chapter heading "A People Without A Government" (X, 168–180). Francis Wharton (ed.), *Revolutionary Diplomatic Correspondence of the United States* (6 vols.; Washington, D.C., 1889). Wharton's labels for the two "parties" or "schools" of congressional politics are revealing: the states' righters were "expulsionists," or "liberatives," while the nationalists were "constructivists," (See Wharton's lengthy Introduction in vol. I, esp. pp. 252, 257.) Carl Becker, *The History of Political Parties in the Province of New York, 1763–1776* (New York, 1917); J. Franklin Jameson, *The American Revolution Considered as a Social Movement* (New York, 1926); Merrill Jensen, *The Articles of Confederation* (Madison, 1940), *The New Nation* (New York, 1950).

2 In his communication with the Congress, Washington frequently pleaded for a stronger Confederation to support the war effort, but he did not take his case to the people, as was done so frequently by commanding generals in other wars for colonial independence. By the early 1780s, a number of generals served in the Congress, but even they did not uniformly support nationalist measures. General Varnum of Rhode Island did, for example, but General Ward of Massachusetts did not.

3 Jensen, *The Articles of Confederation*, p. 110.

4 John Adams to Patrick Henry, June 3, 1776, Adams, *Works,* IX, 86–87.

5 John Adams to Horatio Gates, Mar. 23, 1776, *LMCC*, I, 406.

6 Carter Braxton to Landon Carter, Apr. 14, 1776, ibid., 421.

7 Edward Rutledge to John Jay, June 8, 1776, ibid., 476–477.

8 Edward Rutledge to John Jay, June 29, 1776, ibid., 517–518.

9 John Winthrop to John Adams, June 1, 1776, Winthrop Papers, Massachusetts Historical Society, *Collections,* ser. 5, IV, 307–308; John Adams to John Winthrop, June 23, 1776, ibid., 310.

10 Jensen, *The Articles of Confederation*, chap. V, pp. 150–160, and chap. VII, esp. p. 170.

11 Ibid., p. 126. Jensen uses different criteria to distinguish radicals from conservatives and finds only two members of the committee (Adams and Hopkins) who were unquestionably radical. An objection might be raised against excluding Gwinnett of Georgia from the radical ranks apparently because he was English-born, for example. Gwinnett was part of the Georgia contingent which voted for independence, and he was described by Benjamin Rush as a "zealous Democrat" who took the Pennsylvania constitution of 1776 back to Georgia and pressed for its use as a model for the Georgia constitution. George Corner (ed.), *The Autobiography of Benjamin Rush* (Princeton, 1948), p. 153. I am in agreement with Jensen's central conclusion that the draft produced by the committee reflected Dickinson's ideas in the main.

12 Edward Rutledge to John Jay, June 29, 1776, *LMCC*, I, 495.

13 Josiah Bartlett to John Langdon, June 17, 1776, ibid., 517; Samuel Adams to R. H. Lee, June 26, 1777, ibid., II, 388-389.

14 Richard Henry Lee to Samuel Adams, July 12, 1777, in James C. Ballagh (ed.), *The Letters of Richard Henry Lee* (2 vols.; New York, 1911-1914), I, 308.

15 Adams, *Works*, II, 496.

16 Thomas Burke to Governor Richard Caswell, Nov. 4, 1777, *LMCC*, II, 542. See also Harnett's letter in *SRNC*, XIII, 386.

17 Samuel A. Ashe, *History of North Carolina* (2 vols.; Greensboro, 1908), I, 564. Both Burke and Harnett were important figures in the construction of the North Carolina constitution.

18 References are to the printed version in *JCC*, V, 546-554.

19 Adams, *Works*, II, 496, 499-501; William Williams of Connecticut asserted in July of 1777, "It is most strenuously contended in behalf of the larger states that their votes shall be proportionate to their population. . . ." Williams to Governor Jonathan Trumbull, July 5, 1777, *LMCC*, II, 399-400. How many delegates this statement embraced at the time is impossible to determine.

20 *JCC*, IX, 779-782.

21 Adams, *Works*, II, 496-498; Paul Leicester Ford (ed.), *The Works of Thomas Jefferson* (12 vols.; New York, 1904-1905), I, 42.

22 *JCC*, IX, 801.

23 Adams, *Works*, 11, 492-496, 501-502.

24 *JCC*, IX, 806-808.

25 Ibid., 843; PCC no. 47.

26 On this vote of October 14, 1777 (*JCC*, IX, 801), the Eastern states were entirely in accord, and they drew support from Daniel Roberdeau of Pennsylvania, a delegate who would subsequently align quite closely with that alliance. Two Southern delegates who also were connected with that alliance—Richard Henry Lee and Henry Laurens, newly arrived from South Carolina—did not support the Easterners, but they had little alternative on this particular issue that so clearly involved Southern interests. One other interesting deviation of a Middle states delegate might be pointed out: James Duane, the New York conservative, sided with the New Englanders on this issue. While this may be construed as an anomaly, Duane's subsequent voting record indicated that he was far from being a central adherent to the nationalist party that later rallied around Robert Morris.

27 Thomas Burke, "Notes on the Articles of Confederation" (Nov. 15, 1777), *LMCC*, II, 555.

28 Ibid., 553.

29 Ibid.

30 Thomas Burke to Richard Caswell, Apr. 29, 1777, ibid., 345-346; Jensen, *The Articles of Confederation,* p. 131.

31 Thomas Burke to Richard Caswell, *LMCC,* II, 346.

32 Richard Henry Lee to Samuel Adams, July 12, 1777, Samuel Adams Papers, NYPL.

33 Elisha P. Douglass, "Thomas Burke, Disillusioned Democrat," *NCHR,* XXVI (1949), 152. Another article on Burke is Jennings B. Sanders, "Thomas Burke in the Continental Congress," ibid., IX (1932), 22-37.

34 Douglass, "Thomas Burke," 162.

35 *JCC,* VII, 328-329. Ford included this motion in the *Journals* under the date May 5, 1777, without any particular reason. The motion written in the hand of Thomas Burke is located in the PCC, no. 47, f. 37, along with other materials modifying the Dickinson draft in the committee of the whole, the only date being a separate reference to August 20, 1777. Burnett, *Continental Congress,* p. 239, speculated that the motion was offered around May 5, a dating accepted by Jensen, *The Articles of Confederation,* pp. 179-180. Burke's correspondence during May substantiates the conjectures of Ford and Burnett, for it reflected his concern that "the difficulty of preserving the Independence of the States, and at the same time giving to each its proper weight in the public Council, will frustrate a Confederation." Burke to Governor Caswell, May 11, 1777, *LMCC,* II, 360. See also his letter of May 23 to Caswell, ibid, 370-371.

36 PCC, no. 47, f. 37.

37 Ibid. Burke's motion provided for representation in the General Council "in the following Proportions," after which there was a blank where the respective numbers would presumably be delineated. The Council of State (consistently capitalized in Burke's manuscript, whereas the General Council was referred to as the "general Council," just as were the "united States" at the outset of the motion) was clearly to consist of "one Delegate from every State. . . ." (ibid.). The variations in capitalization were not reproduced in Ford's editing of the *JCC,* by the way.

38 PCC, no. 47, f. 37.

39 John Adams pointed out the situational differences between New England and the rest of the union in a letter to James Warren when he commented that all the trade of Pennsylvania, Delaware, Maryland, and Virginia could be stopped at the necks of the Delaware and Chesapeake Bays, and that because of this, there was "great Objection" to the construction of an American fleet that would protect New England trade while denying such protection to the Southern colonies. John Adams to James Warren, Oct. 19, 1775, *LMCC,* I, 236. As previously mentioned (Chap. 5), John Adams had been responsible for the creation of a naval board at Boston in April of 1777 which gathered in more business in contracts and prizes than the first board in the Middle Department at Philadelphia. This may have contributed to a sense of "Jealousy" that Thomas Burke believed was responsible for the prohibition in Article VI. The always unpredictable Burke was not alarmed that the fleet of one state would endanger the security of another state, but he felt that such fears would "forever prevent the United States from having a powerful Navy. . . ." Thomas Burke, "Notes on the Articles of Confederation" [Nov. 15, 1777], ibid., II, 554.

40 For an explanation of the adaptation of the Guttmann scale, see George Balknap, "A Method for Analyzing Legislative Behavior," *Midwest Journal of Political Science,* II (November 1958), 377-402.

41 Thomas Burke to Governor Richard Caswell, Mar. 11, 1777, *SRNC,* XI, 419. (Burnett includes a major part of this letter in the *LMCC,* but deleted this particular passage.)

42 Of course, Bloc I emerged as the most nationalist bloc because of the fact that five roll calls were taken on the one issue of representation, whereas only three votes dealt with western lands, and only one vote with tariffs. Nevertheless, since proportional representation was the sine qua non of effective national authority, its weight in the scale was not far out of line.

43 Harnett agreed with Jones 84% of the time and with Harvie 81% of the time, while his level of agreement with Samuel Adams was 38% and with Lovell 43%.

7 Congressional Parties, 1777–1779

THE Articles of Confederation and the procedural conventions that governed the Continental Congress before their adoption in 1781 rested upon certain assumptions regarding sovereignty, representation, and the resolution of conflict that had a powerful influence upon the structure of congressional partisan politics. Article II specifically stated that the states retained their sovereignty and independence, and every power not expressly delegated to the Continental Congress. Congressmen represented states rather than popular constituencies within the states. Differences of opinion over the major congressional concerns—namely, war, diplomacy, and western lands—were resolved by majority vote (and under the Articles the votes of nine states); and in the casting of votes the powerful state of Virginia had no more weight than its diminutive neighbor Delaware. An inevitable result of these constitutional arrangements was that like-minded states grouped together in order to secure their interests in a manner often resembling the bloc allignments of diplomatic assembly such as the United Nations.

For a number of reasons, however, the Congress did not function simply as an assembly of sovereign states. Although constitutionally equal, the states were in fact quite unequal in size, wealth, and power, and in the influence they brought to bear in the Congress. Each delegation could consist of from two to seven delegates, and the large states generally maintained larger delegations than did the poorer small states, thereby augmenting their influence when congressional business was channeled into committees. The most articulate and influential leaders on the floor of Congress generally came from the larger states, and virtually all the major diplomatic appointments were given to men from the big important states—notably Virginia, Massachusetts, Pennsylvania, New York, and South Carolina. The fact that Pennsylvania sent 48 delegates to Congress between 1774 and 1789 meant not only that the influence of Pennsylvania in congressional proceedings was greater than that of Delaware (which sent only 18 delegates, three of whom were actually connected with Pennsylvania through business, residence, or office holding) but also that the more dispersed and variegated population of Pennsylvania could be given something resembling proportional representation. It would be stretching the truth to say that the ampler delegations from the large states changed the mode of representation. Delegates collectively had to cast one vote regardless of their size and the number of people they represented. It is a fact, nevertheless, that congressional delegations reflected the kind of politics that obtained in the states that elected them. Where the political process was sensitive to a diversified polity, as in Pennsylvania, the congressional delegation tended either to reflect antagonistic interests or to mirror the party that momentarily held power in the Assembly. Consequently, divisions within delegations did occur. Partisan politics in the Congress were, therefore, marked both by struggles between blocs of states and by conflicts between ideological and socioeconomic interests that transcended state and regional boundaries. In short, the Continental Congress, despite its formal composition, began very early to function as a legislature of a nation as well as an assembly of sovereign states.

That congressional politics were affected by popular influences as well as by the strategic interests of sovereign and independent states can be attributed in part to the fact that it was impossible to divorce national politics from the ferment of partisan struggles within the states. That ferment, and its extension into national politics, was most noticeable in Pennsylvania, where the Congress resided during most of the Revolution. But even in South Carolina, where politics had been dominated by the Charleston aristocracy, politics were markedly broadened by mass meetings in Charleston that began during the resistance and continued into the Revolution[1].

Throughout the colonies, the Revolution, while hardly erasing the politics of deference, contributed to the decline of elitist, factional politics. Traditionally, partisan politics had been the politics of faction—a process dominated by relatively transitory clusters of notables and placeholders linked by familial and social ties who strived for political office because of the honors and perquisites that were attached to it. Although factions persisted in state politics after independence was declared, they tended to be discredited by the republican ideology of the Revolution. Recent studies have indicated that factions were often undermined (or overridden as the case might be) by conflicts among representatives of broader interests in the lower houses of the state legislatures—interests that were enlivened by the Revolutionary movement. While the exact contours of those struggles varied from state to state, it seems that representatives of cosmopolitan, densely populated commercial regions often collided with representatives from the remoter populations of the less developed and poorer areas[2]. Elitist factions were giving way to a broader interest-oriented politics that in certain instances began to take the shape of organized parties, particularly in Pennsylvania[3].

Congressional politics was a mixture of the old and the new. There were factional alignments such as the Adams-Lee connection that guarded favorites in the diplomatic service and in congressional committees. There was likewise a faction that formed around Robert Morris that had direct pecuniary interests in the financing of the Revolution. But the Lee-Adams faction espoused a puritan republican ideology, and the Morris faction formulated a program that was in effect an ideology of national consolidation. In these respects, both transcended the limited, nonprogrammatic characteristics of traditional factions. Further, each was able to draw support from interest-oriented partisan aggregations in the Congress and in the states.

The politics of the Continental Congress thus showed the marks of a transition from the politics of factions to more modern forms of partisan organization. It will not do, of course, to call such organizations political parties in the modern sense of the term. The modern party has a sustained life that depends upon an elaborate and extended organization reaching from the national committee to workers in the precincts. It is capable of mobilizing the electorate so as to place its candidates in office; it is also capable of maintaining a reasonable degree of discipline among its members and promoting the program it offers to the voters. Such organization obviously could not exist under the Confederation because members of Congress had little direct contact with the electorate in the states and, perhaps more significantly, because organized efforts to gain political office were frowned upon as being incompatible with the kind of disinterested public service required of republican revolutionaries[4].

All things considered, congressional politics are best characterized as a politics of interest that took the form of contention between regionally oriented nascent legislative parties. It will not do to make too much of the organization, or even the self-awareness, of the congressional parties. They lacked any significant organization beyond the confines of Congress because the Articles of Confederation did not establish a direct relationship between the national legislature and the people. Only the popular election of the House of Representatives and the President would create a stage for national, extended political parties. Partisan organization was generally deplored, and so the very people who contributed to the formation of congressional parties were loath to admit their existence. Oliver Ellsworth, for example, felt constrained to assure his Connecticut constituents that the bloc voting of New England delegates in support of rights to the fisheries as an ultimatum for peace was the consequence of individual decisions rather than an organized design[5]. Moreover, the transition from the traditional politics of faction was uneven in that the coordination and cohesion of the New England–based Eastern party tended to be more perfected than that of the more loosely joined Southern party. Nonetheless, the behavior of partisan aggregations in the Congress during the period 1777–1779 was sufficiently advanced beyond factionalism to warrant a different term.

The argument that there were nascent congressional parties has been based on deductions from the correspondence of members of Congress, from descriptions of congressional partisanship, and from quantitative analysis of congressional voting. Because of the emphasis placed on the voting analysis, it is necessary to digress momentarily to consider the methods used in analyzing congressional roll calls.

II

In August of 1777, the Continental Congress began to record and publish roll-call votes as they were cast by individuals and by states. This seemingly routine procedural innovation actually marked an important transition in the history of the Congress. During the resistance it was important that congressional decisions, however disputatious, be publicized as the unanimous judgment of the delegates; by 1777, disagreement could be admitted and publicized. In retrospect, one can only admire the assurance of the delegates as well as respect their commitment to the principles of open, representative government, for this was a decision that was reached before the military victory at Saratoga, and before the consummation of the French alliance.

For the historian, the decision to record roll calls was particularly fortunate, since the roll calls are a rich body of data that can be quantitatively analyzed so as to disclose the configuration of congressional partisanship. By matching the votes of one delegate against another, it is possible to discern clusters of delegates who voted in substantial agreement with each other, and accordingly separate them from other clusters of delegates with whom they rather consistently disagreed. "Substantial agreement" has been defined in this study as 67 percent agreement between delegates on non repetitive roll calls on which there was at least 10 percent disagreement in the legislature as a whole[6]. The cluster blocs portrayed in Tables 6, 7, and 8 (in the next section of this chapter) are composed of delegates who had that relatively high level of agreement, one with another. Naturally, there were some delegates who had over 67 percent agreement with a majority of a cluster, but not with all the members of the bloc. Rather than to exclude such delegates, the practice here has been to establish two categories of membership in the voting bloc—"core" members who uniformly agreed with each other at least 67 percent of the time, and "marginal" members who agreed with at least half of the core members of the bloc at the same level of agreement. The blocs have been calculated on an annual basis in order to include as many delegates as possible in a body that had a large annual turnover. Even so, not all delegates were included in the analysis because of the extremely sporadic attendance of some. In no instance, however, was a delegate who voted in 40 percent of the roll calls excluded.

The analysis that follows places strong reliance on voting blocs as meaningful partisan aggregations. Theoretically, of course, the voting clusters could have been the result of coincidence rather than organization or even shared interests. In addition, because of erratic attendance, the ratios of agreement versus disagreement between any given three delegates do not necessarily reflect an equal number of votes on the same issues. Thus the possibility exists that the blocs were entirely fortuitous. Almost certainly the delegates themselves, if we could interview them, would deny that they belonged to a "party." It is therefore appropriate to ask two questions: Were the voting blocs fairly accurate replications of a structure of partisan politics in the Congress, and, despite the attitudes of the delegates toward factionalism, did legislative parties exist in the Congress?

In answer to the second question, it should be recalled that factionalism of any sort was considered reprehensible because of the traditional stigma attached to it during the colonial era and because it seemed prejudicial to the common cause during the Revolution. No delegate would admit that he belonged to a party, but he might very well charge that a group of opponents had formed a party, or a "junto," or a "set." At the same time that delegate likely as not would insist that he and those delegates who regularly voted with him were nonpartisan "true Whigs" who were disinterestedly defending the republic. Partisan politics, in short, were both practiced and deplored.

With regard to the question of whether or not the blocs accurately represented the structure of congressional politics, it is significant that the cluster blocs were basically sectional, and this is precisely what one would expect in a newly formed national legislature that represented widely flung populations that had some basically different economic and social characteristics. As previously mentioned, virtually all colonial peoples experience regional tensions during their transition into a nation. This was true of the Dutch at the turn of the seventeenth century, the Argentineans in the early nineteenth century, and the Nigerians in the mid-twentieth century. The pervasive impact of sectional division in the United States was evident in the fact that legislative parties in the Congress retained their original cast throughout the whole revolution and Confederation regardless of the identity of the delegates. Indeed, even after the Articles of Confederation were replaced by the Constitution, the sectional structure of partisan politics did not immediately change. The Federalist party began as an essentially Northern party, and the Republicans as a Southern party[7].

The regional cluster blocs were not entirely uniform; nor were they static in their strength and composition. Individuals and entire delegations deviated from their state and section, an indication that while parties were basically sectional, there were other factors that affected the structure of congressional politics. Richard Henry Lee, Henry Laurens, and some other Southerners frequently joined the Eastern party, for example. The entire New York delegation tended to align with the Southern party rather than with their New England neighbors, and the Pennsylvania delegation abruptly changed its position on a number of occasions.

All the important exceptions to the rule of regional parties can be explained; moreover, they help to illuminate the shape of congressional politics. In addition, comments about deviant members and delegations substantiate the fact that members of Congress and outsiders in the state assemblies were aware that legislative parties existed in the Congress. Virginian assemblymen knew that Richard Henry Lee had joined the Easterners when they initially voted against his reelection to the Congress in 1777. Lee was forced to argue that he had not "favored New England to the injury of Virginia"—not because he had not voted with the Easterners, for he had, but because in Lee's mind the interests of Virginia and New England were harmonious[8]. The assemblymen seem to have thought differently, for they reelected his brother Francis Lightfoot Lee, who had not aligned with the Eastern party. Duer wrote to John Jay that "the mere contemplation" of Lee's being excluded "gives me pleasure"—as indeed it should have, for Duer was then working to improve the already cordial relationship between New York and the Southern states. When Lee was ultimately reinstated, Duer warned Robert R. Livingston that "he will return here more rivited than ever to his Eastern friends; I assure you they lost in him no contemptible ally"[9]. James Lovell of the Eastern party could agree in at least one respect, for he informed William Whipple of New Hampshire (an Old Radical who would soon return to Congress) that Lee's reelection would help to protect Congress against "the prevalence of a certain set"[10]. Neither the supporters nor the opponents of Lee saw themselves as a "party," but each viewed the opposition as a party.

Occasionally an entire delegation would shift from one party to another. This was particularly true of Pennsylvania, which turned from the Eastern to the Southern interest in 1781. The shift was immediate and complete and can be explained only by taking into account the fact that control of the Pennsylvania Assembly had slipped from the hands of the radical supporters of the constitution of 1776 into the grasp of their conservative opponents. Clearly, the assemblymen who elected the new delegation understood both the attitudes of their representatives and the partisan cast of congressional politics.

Some close observers of congressional politics wrote about "juntos" and "alliances" in Congress that unmistakably referred to the cluster blocs revealed by the voting analysis. An anonymous letter writer in the *Pennsylvania Gazette* who used the signature "O Tempora! O Mores!" complained that a congressional party, or "junto," had formed during the early war years when the Northern and Southern states suspected some Middle states "on many real grounds as well as some pretended ones" of being unsympathetic with the Revolution. The writer (probably a displaced delegate from Georgia, Edward Langworthy) provided an accurate description of the Eastern party when he contended that the "junto" was made up of "certain of the delegates from New England, New Jersey, and this state [Pennsylvania], and of two or three members southward"[11]. According to Langworthy, or whoever wrote the piece, the junto was highly cohesive and had skillfully manipulated congressional policy, particularly in the area of foreign affairs.

Descriptions of congressional party politics were colored by the particular perspective of whoever happended to be doing the observing, but there was a notable agreement about the composition of the parties. Louis Fleury, a French officer who paid close attention to Congress because of his efforts to win a promotion, believed that the Eastern party was led by Generals Horatio Gates and Charles Lee. Fleury may have been wrong about the leadership of the party, but he was largely correct when he contended that the party was composed of delegates from Pennsylvania, New Jersey, South Carolina, and New England and that it was formed "on the platform that no man of influence should have power over all the forces of the state"[12]. Fleury saw a two-party division, the opposition coming from Virginia, Maryland, New York, North Carolina, and Delaware. One of the more elaborate interpretations of congressional factionalism by an outside observer during this period was provided by the French minister to the United States, Conrad Alexandre Gérard, in his dispatches to the foreign minister, the Comte de Vergennes. While Gérard's analysis, like Fleury's, was influenced by his particular perspective (so that he often referred to the Southern party as "the Friends of the King"), the general tenor and specific content of his statements coincide neatly with the bloc analysis[13].

Finally, off-hand comments of members of Congress and others who where close to it usually reinforce the conclusions that can be drawn from the quantitative analysis. Robert Hanson Harrison, a member of Washington's staff and a close friend of Alexander Hamilton, spoke disapprovingly of a congressional "Eastern alliance" in 1780 while applauding the independent postures of the generals, John Sullivan and Ezekiel Cornell, who then represented New Hampshire and Rhode Island in the Congress[14]. Even the seemingly unrelated remarks of Benjamin Rush in his autobiography about the characteristics of members of the Massachusetts delegation conform with the bloc configuration during 1777–1779. Rush, when commenting upon Samuel Adams, remarked, "In some parts of his conduct I have thought he discovered more of the prejudices of a Massachusetts man than the liberal sentiments of a citizen of the United States." Rush's characterization of Elbridge Gerry was quite different, for Gerry had "no local or state prejudices"[15]. The recollections of Rush illuminate Adams's position in the core of the parochial Eastern party and Gerry's tendency to take an independent course during 1778 and 1779.

Thus, the cluster analysis not only corroborates but also enhances other types of contemporary evidence, such as newspapers, correspondence, and memoirs. It is appropriate in this connection to stress that quantitative analysis must be used imaginatively in order to understand better other more conventional types of evidence. After all, it is not necessary to employ roll-call analysis to demonstrate the existence of a connection between Richard Henry Lee and the New Englanders—something about which we are already amply informed. The quantitative approach is most useful in uncovering some of the nuances of the relationship between the Adamses and the Lees not readily apparent from other evidence. For example, the Adams-Lee coalition was primarily a factional connection between Samuel Adams and Richard Henry Lee, rather than between all the Adamses and Lees in Congress. John Adams, judging from the small number of votes available for analysis in 1777, was less closely affiliated with Lee (63 percent agreement) than was Samuel Adams (71 percent). Francis Lightfoot Lee, while voting with the faction in support of his brother Arthur Lee, never belonged to the Eastern party. Indeed, in 1778 he was a core member of the Southern party.

III

Tables 6–8 show the pattern of congressional blocs between August of 1777, when roll calls were first recorded, and the end of 1779. Although the tables speak largely for themselves, a few interpretive comments are necessary. The cluster blocs for 1777 are smaller than they might have been had roll calls been taken during the whole year. As it was, sufficient data were available for only 24 delegates, as contrasted with 47 delegates for 1778 and 1779. Nonetheless, there is a strong likelihood that the Eastern-Southern division revealed by the limited number of delegates was representative of the legislature in its entirety, for that pattern continued in terms of the positions of states and individuals during the following two years. The blocs in 1778 seem more

TABLE 6

Congressional Blocs, 1777

	Eastern Party	Southern Party
N.H.	Folsom*	
Mass.	Adams, J.	
	Adams, S.	
	Gerry	
	Lovell	
R.I.	Marchant	
Conn.	Dyer*	Williams*
N.Y.		Duane
		Duer
N.J.		Elmer*
Pa.	Roberdeau	Morris, R.
Md.		Smith, W.
Va.	Lee, R. H.	Jones, J.
N.C.		Harnett
		Penn
S.C.	Laurens	Heyward

* Marginal membership.

Independents (members included in the analysis, but not members of either bloc): Law (Conn.), Chase (Md.), Harvie and Lee, F. L. (Va.).

complex than those of the other two years because of overlapping memberships in a large number of blocs. It would have been possible to portray only three of the blocs and thereby simplify things, but because the parties varied in cohesion over time, and because they always tended to be coalitions of intra-regional blocs, the 1778 pattern was left untouched.

Tables 7 and 8 illustrate that both parties had internal northern and southern wings. This was particularly true of the Southern party, which constantly tended to divide into Chesapeake and Carolina components. The Eastern party always seemed to muster greater cohesion, particularly in its New England base, but Connecticut and the Middle states sometimes did not follow the lead of Massachusetts. There was in addition a constant tendency for delegates from the Middle states to form a separate bloc—one which was associated generally with the Southern party. Still, the deepest and most enduring division was between the North and the South.

TABLE 7

Congressional Blocs, 1778

	Eastern Party		Southern Party		
	Mass. Bloc	Conn.–Middle States Bloc	Chesapeake Bloc	N.C. Bloc	Ga. Bloc
N.H.	Bartlett				
	Whipple				
Mass.	Adams, S.	Adams, S.*			
	Holten				
	Lovell				
R.I.	Ellery*	Ellery*			
Conn.	Dyer	Dyer*			
	Ellsworth	Ellsworth*			
	Huntington, S.*	Huntington, S.			
	Sherman*	Sherman			
N.Y.			Morris, G.	Morris, G.*	
			Duer*	Duer*	Duer*
N.J.		Scudder			
	Witherspoon*	Witherspoon			
Pa.	Clingan	Clingan			
		Roberdeau*	Morris, R.*	Morris, R.*	Morris, R.*
Del.	McKean*				
Md.			Carroll		
			Chase		
			Henry		
			Plater	Plater	
Va.			Adams, T.	Adams, T.	
			Lee, F. L.		
				Griffin	
				Smith, M.*	Smith, M.
N.C.			Burke*	Burke	
			Harnett*	Harnett	
			Penn*	Penn	
S.C.					Mathews
Ga.			Langworthy*	Langworthy*	Langworthy*
					Telfair
					Walton

* Marginal membership.

Independents: Gerry and Dana (Mass.); Marchant (R.I.); Wolcott (Conn.); Lewis (N.Y.); Elmer and Fell (N.J.); Forbes (Md.); Harvie and Lee, R. H. (Va.); Laurens, Drayton, and Hutson (S.C.).

Congressional parties were no more than prefigurations of the organized parties that developed later in the first party system, and so there were few pressures to follow a "party line"—although such pressures did exist. Some delegates thus appeared in the party voting blocs during one year and not another. There were many reasons for this seemingly erratic behavior. One was the relationship between the kinds of issues that occupied the Congress on the one hand, and the interests of the state that the delegate represented on the other. Further, most delegates who moved in and out of a bloc did so in a marginal capacity. William Ellery is a good example of both tendencies. Rarely did a delegate move from a Southern to an Eastern bloc or vice versa. The only member who came close to doing this between 1777 and 1779 was Jonathan Elmer of New Jersey. Elmer was a marginal member of the Southern party in 1777 and almost qualified as a member of the Connecticut-Middle states bloc of the Eastern party the next year. Elmer's behavior may illustrate yet another factor that affected the composition of congressional parties—the fact that certain delegates were able to influence other members. According to James Lovell, James Duane was successful in winning Elmer away from the Eastern orientation that prevailed with the New Jersey delegation in 1777. "You must know," Lovell wrote to William Whipple, "that Jemmy D. [James Duane] has got E---e [Lovell's abbreviation for Elmore—actually Elmer] fast"[16].

The Eastern party enjoyed an ascendancy during the early portion of the Revolution, including the years 1777-1779, that is not totally apparent from a cursory examination of the cluster blocs. Close inspection of Tables 6-8 will reveal two distinctions between the Eastern and Southern parties that help account for the Eastern ascendancy, however. The Easterners drew more general support from the Middle states and the South than the Southerners were able to draw from other sections. (This was particularly true during 1778 and 1779, although the full voting record of 1777 might very well have shown the same pattern.) Secondly, the Eastern party was more cohesive than was the relatively loose coalition of Southerners and their allies from New York. Both parties had the potential of mustering six or possibly seven votes, so that the vote of a single delegate such as McKean or Dickinson of Delaware might decide an issue. Under these conditions, cohesion within the delegations that formed the centers of the parties was crucial. If cohesion within blocs is scored as a ratio between core and marginal membership versus nonmembership for delegations and sections, it is clear that the New England component of the Eastern party was more cohesive than the Southern segment of the opposition party (71 percent over 61 percent).

There were a number of reasons for the failure of the South to match the cohesiveness of the New Englanders. The divergence between the Chesapeake region and the lower South has already been mentioned, but it warrants additional stress. Maryland and Virginia—particularly its Northern Neck—were in

TABLE 8

Congressional Blocs, 1779

		Southern Party	
		---	---
	Eastern Party	*Middle States Bloc*	*Southern Bloc*
N.H.	Peabody*		
	Whipple		
Mass.	Adams, S.		
	Gerry*		
	Holten		
	Lovell		
R.I.	Marchant		
Conn.	Spencer		
	Huntington, S.*		
	Sherman		
N.Y.		Duane	
		Floyd	Floyd*
		Jay	Jay*
		Morris, G.	
N.J.	Houston	Fell*	
	Witherspoon*		
Pa.	Armstrong*	Atlee	
	Muhlenberg*		
	Searle		
	Shippen		
	McLene		
Del.		Dickinson*	
Md.		Carmichael	Plater*
		Plater*	Paca*
Va.	Lee, R. H.		Griffin
			Smith, M.*
N.C.			Burke
			Harnett
			Hill
			Penn
			Sharpe*
S.C.			Drayton
Ga.			Langworthy

* Marginal membership.

Independents: Ellery and Collins (R.I.); Root (Conn.); Lewis (N.Y.); Scudder (N.J.); Forbes, Henry, and Jenifer (Md.); Laurens and Mathews (S.C.).

certain respects more akin to their close neighbor Pennsylvania than to distant South Carolina. It was thus not entirely surprising that when the Middle states later played a strong role in shaping congressional policy, there were three Southerners who in 1783 joined a Nationalist party from the Middle states—the Virginians James Madison and Joseph Jones, along with Daniel Carroll of Maryland.

If the South Carolinian and Virginian delegations often saw things differently because of different locations and interests, they were similar in many respects. One was that both states sent some tenaciously independent individuals to Congress, men who seemed to prize their individuality so much that they almost delighted in disagreeing with delegates from their own region and state. Richard Henry Lee's defection from the Virginians was the most striking example of this kind of posture, but Henry Laurens of South Carolina was in some ways more fiercely independent. Lee joined the Eastern party, but Laurens, although he frequently supported the Easterners, was more inclined to follow an independent course. One of the purest of republicans, Laurens once went so far as to attempt to disqualify votes that had been cast by the sole Georgia delegate, Edward Langworthy, on the grounds that his credentials were not in order. Most Southerners did not share Laurens's concern for legality at a time when Langworthy's vote had been important in resisting the demand of the Eastern party that fishery rights be included in America's peace terms. Partisan feelings were so high at this juncture that Laurens appears to have dueled with John Penn of the North Carolina delegation[*17*]. Thus regional separativeness and errant talent combined to deprive the Southern interest of cohesion and direction. Virginia was the natural leader of the Southern party, but it was unable to assume that role during the late 1770s[*18*]. Only during the 1780s did Virginia take command under the direction of Madison, Jefferson, and Monroe.

Because of the diffusion in the Southern delegations, the leadership of the Southern party often came from the Middle states during the late 1770s and early 1780s. While it is true that the Eastern party won more votes from the Middle states during the late 1770s, New York generally voted with the South, and so did some Pennsylvanians. Influential members such as John Jay and the Morrises provided important leadership that the Southern party could support in opposition to the Easterners. This direction, along with the clever intervention of the French minister, Conrad Alexandre Gérard, was particularly important during the struggle over the definition of peace terms in 1779.

The sectional character of congressional politics as well as the edge that the Eastern party had because of its cohesiveness were reflected in the control of standing committees during this period. From the very first days of Congress, there had been an attempt to allocate committee appointments evenly among the three sections. This arrangement initially had favored the Eastern interest because of the coalition between New England and the South. With the realignment of forces during 1776 and 1777, however, representation of the Eastern and Southern forces was much more even. Appointments to the permanent committees of commerce, treasury, foreign affairs, war, and marine during the period 1777–1779 were remarkably balanced between the two interests. In 1777, 12 appointments were given to members of the Eastern party, while 11 went to the Southern interest. In 1778 the ratio was 15 to 13, and in 1779 it was 10 to 8, although in the latter year there were 4 appointments to the Middle states bloc in the Southern interest which tipped the scales against the Eastern party[*19*]. Easterners dominated the treasury committee and the important marine and foreign affairs committees. The Southern party had a larger representation in the committees on war and commerce.

Cohesion and continuity of tenure were extremely important in the committees, just as in the roll-call votes. Here again, the Easterners had the advantage in some committees, although not in all of them. James Lovell, whose tenure on the foreign affairs committee ran through this entire period, and whose knowledge of French gave him a special influence in the correspondence of the committee, dominated its activity. The highly important commerce committee, which handled foreign supply contracts, was largely under the influence of the mercantile group connected with Robert Morris—a group supported by the Southern interest. Morris was on the committee during 1777 and part of 1778, and he either directly or indirectly dominated its actions during the entire period, with the exceptions of an interval between December of 1778 and November of 1779. Still, since the committee system was closely linked with Congress—more so than the executive departments that were created in 1780 and 1781, for example—the Easterners enjoyed greater power. John Jay noted this when he complained about the inordinate influence of the Eastern party (or the "family compact," as he called it) in the marine committee, an agency that was important because of its authority over prize cases, among other things:

> The Marine Committee consists of a Delegate from each State. It fluctuates, new Members constantly coming in and old ones going out. Three or four indeed have remained in it from the Beginning, and have a proportionate Influence, or more properly *Interest* in it. Very few of the Members understand even the State of our naval Affairs or have Time or Inclination to attend to them. But why is not this System changed? It is in my opinion convenient to the Family compact[*20*].

Jay was correct, for Whipple, Marchant, Sherman, and Richard Henry Lee were all influential Eastern members, while only Harvie and Philip Livingston (who was not included in the bloc analysis) represented the Southern interest.

This was symptomatic of an ascendancy that the Easterners were reluctant to part with.

IV

Both the voting clusters and contemporary testimony indicate that factions were basically sectional. But the existence of deviants and independents, along with the splits and fluctuations in the delegations from the Middle states, suggests that nonsectional factors helped to structure congressional partisan politics and that sectional blocs had socioeconomic and ideological characteristics that both reinforced sectional antagonisms and influenced the alignment of Middle states delegations and sectional deviants. If a rigid North-South sectionalism had obtained, New York should have joined New England rather than the South, and Pennsylvania should have been more inclined toward the South than New York was. The behavior of the Pennsylvanians is particularly interesting in this regard, for the orientation of a given Pennsylvania delegation could be predicted with almost complete accuracy on the basis of whether it was elected by the radical Constitutionalists or their more conservative "Republican" opponents in the Pennsylvania Assembly.

Constitutionalists uniformly sided with the Eastern party during this period. The more conservative Republicans who controlled the Assembly by 1780 chose delegates who joined either the Southern party or a Middle states–Southern coalition. Since Pennsylvania had the best approximation of a two-party system at the time of the Revolution, it may be inferred that congressional parties had ideological as well as sectional characteristics.

There is little doubt that the Constitutionalists and the Eastern party shared a programmatic outlook for the most part. Both extolled the militia and were distrusftul of policy associated with a standing army, such as lifetime half pay pensions for officers. Both were alarmed about wartime profiteering by merchants with government contracts. Both advocated stern treatment for monopolizers, profiteers, and others who seemed to lack commitment to the Revolutionary cause. Yet, in varying degrees, both distrusted consolidated political authority. Both were discernibly anti-Gallican when it became apparent that the French officials Gérard and Holker were combining with Robert Morris, Silas Deane, Gouverneur Morris, and other opponents of the Eastern interest in the formulation of foreign policy and in the promotion of contracts for supplies from abroad. Conversely, the Republicans and the Southern interest supported French diplomacy, the fiscal policy of Robert Morris, and officers' pensions.

The two major alliances did have somewhat different occupational attributes and economic interests. Table 9 summarizes the occupational orientation of the two parties, although it is difficult to categorize some delegates such as Samuel Chase, who was a lawyer with extensive mercantile investments.

Agrarian occupations and interests were more prevalent in the Southern party than in the Eastern party, as might be expected, while professional and officeholding occupations were most noticeable among the Easterners. If the lawyers were divided into two groups signifying mercantile and agrarian orientations, the Southern party would be roughly half agrarian (planters, landowners, and lawyers with significant agricultural investments, including Duane, Jay, Jones, and Heyward, amounting to 12 delegates out of 25, or 48 percent), while less than one-fifth of the Eastern party would be agrarian (namely Ellsworth and the physician Peabody, who speculated in the Masonian Patent lands in New Hampshire, along with Lee and Laurens—just 4 out of 23 delegates, or 17 percent of the total). Interestingly, when mercantile-oriented lawyers are added to the two interests, the Eastern party becomes only slightly more mercantile in composition than the Southern. (Adding John Adams, Marchant, Ellery, Sherman, and Samuel Huntington to the merchants of the Eastern interest produces a total of eight delegates, or 35 percent of the party, while the addition of Gouverneur Morris and Chase to the five merchants among the Southerners yields a ratio of 28 percent.) Thus it is difficult on the surface of things to construe the opposition of the two parties as an agrarian-mercantile dichotomy. Indeed, as one examines the composition of the two interests more closely, it is apparent that the mercantile wing of the Southern party, because of the presence of individuals such as Robert Morris and William Duer, was more powerful than that of the Eastern party. It is possible to argue that by 1779 the Eastern party was more united in opposition to the mercantile operations of Robert Morris and his connections than to the agrarian interests of the landed states of the South.

The Southern party strenuously opposed the Eastern objective of fishing rights off Nova Scotia and Newfoundland during the debates over peace terms in 1779. This represented an agrarian objection to the continuance of the war for a parochial maritime-mercantile interest, but the reaction of one New England delegate, Nathaniel Peabody of New Hampshire, disclosed another dimension of the Eastern-Southern antagonism which in the eyes of the delegates themselves was probably more important than a conflict of agrarian and mercantile interests. Peabody spoke of "the Tyrannic strides of Certain Aristocratical Genrty . . . Using their Hostile influence to Subjugate the E.[ast] and force them to a Compliance with Measures injurious degrading, and Contrary to every republican principal"[21]. Years before, Josiah Quincy and John Adams had expressed suspicions about the willingness of the Southern planter gentry to adapt to a republican revolution. These attitudes were consonant

TABLE 9

Occupational Classification of Delegates, 1777-1779

	Merchants	Lawyers	Professionals*	Office-holders	Land-holders†	Planters
Eastern Party	3 (13%)	8 (35%)	7 (30%)	3 (13%)	0	2 (9%)
Southern Party	5 (20%)	9 (36%)	2 (8%)	1 (4%)	2 (8%)	6 (24%)

*Includes teachers, physicians, and ministers.

†Includes farmers and individuals who derived their main income from investments in non-slave land enterprise.

SUMMARY:

Merchants: Whipple, Gerry, Roberdeau (Eastern party); Duer, R. Morris, T. Adams, Harnett, Telfair (Southern party).

Lawyers: J. Adams, Ellery, Marchant, Dyer, Ellsworth, S. Huntington, Sherman, McKean (Eastern party); Duane, Jay, G. Morris, Chase, Henry, Jones, Penn, Burke, Heyward (Southern party).

Professionals: Bartlett, Peabody, Lovell, Holten, Scudder, Witherspoon, Houston (Eastern party); Elmer, Langworthy (Southern party).

Officeholders: Folsom, S. Adams, Clingan (Eastern party); Carmichael (Southern party).

Landholders: Floyd, Hill (Southern party).

Planters: R. H. Lee, Laurens (Eastern party); Carroll, Plater, Paca, F. L. Lee, M. Smith, Mathews (Southern party).

with the general belief at the time that Southern society was much less egalitarian than that of the North[22].

Such a disparity was reflected in the Congress, especially in the contrast between the planter contingent in the Southern interest and the professional group of physicians and teachers among the Easterners. Peabody was himself a physician, as was his correspondent Josiah Bartlett. The difference in wealth and social status between Peabody and Bartlett and Chesapeake planters such as Carroll, Paca, Plater, and Meriwether Smith was extreme. Before the Revolution, Carroll had been collecting probably twenty times Peabody's annual income in rents from his estate alone. Delegates could not have been unaware of the contrast between professionals such as Peabody, Lovell, Bartlett, Holten, Scudder, Witherspoon, and Houston, who rarely earned more than £100 a year, and planters such as Carroll, Paca, Plater, Smith, Drayton, and Mathews, who owned from 50 to 300 slaves along with 1 to 10,000 acres of land representing estates of from £4,000 to £30,000. Lawyers generally fared better than physicians; indeed, Thomas Burke had shifted from medicine to law, "which promised much more profit and yet less Anxiety," because of this fact, but it appears that most of the lawyers in the Eastern party were less affluent than most of the members of the Southern coalition[23]. John Adams was quite successful, but Sam Adams was much more interested in politics and shielded his revolutionary virtue in the armor of poorly paying offices. Ellery also turned from the law to officeholding, while Ellsworth, shortly before the Revolution, was averaging by his own count just £3 per year as a struggling young lawyer[24]. Ellsworth soon did remarkably well, but Roger Sherman left the law for business before the Revolution, without evident success, and was at this time slipping toward insolvency[25]. Marchant and Dyer were wealthier, but neither could match the social or economic status of the eminently successful New York lawyer James Duane and the well-positioned Jay and Gouverneur Morris. Nor were they on a par with Southerners such as Joseph Jones, Paca, Heyward, Drayton, and Mathews, who had extensive wealth in land and slaves. Dana, Law, and Williams were more substantial lawyers, but they were not members of the Eastern party. Indeed, judging from the scanty data of 1777, Williams sided with the Southerners.

There were, of course, wealthy individuals in the Eastern party and relatively poor delegates who were part of the Southern interest. Elbridge Gerry was engaged in lucrative war contracts as a Marblehead merchant just as William Duer was in New York. Gerry's investments in government securities during the war and after made him the largest security holder in the Constitutional Convention. William Shippen clearly belonged to the Philadelphia elite. His quota in the effective supply tax of the city in 1779 was £592—a figure that was inflated, to be sure, but it was the eleventh-highest tax of approximately 3,960 entries in the tax list of that year [26]. Ironically, two of the most wealthy and prestigious Southern delegates—Richard Henry Lee and Henry Laurens—supported the Easterners. Henry Laurens was one of the largest slaveholders in the entire list of congressional delegates. Richard Henry Lee had a higher social and political status than any Virginian in the Congress at this time, and Virginians were not unmindful of such matters. (Richard Henry Lee's affiliation with the Eastern party may be explained in part as an attempt to seize control of Revolutionary policy—as a power play involving Arthur Lee in Paris as well as the Easterners—but the question still remains why Lee chose to operate in association with the Eastern interest rather than through the more natural Southern base.) In the North Carolina delegation, Penn and Burke were successful lawyers, and Penn, who had moved from Virginia to North Carolina shortly before the Revolution, had an important connection in his Virginian relative and mentor, Edmund Pendleton. Yet they and the other North Carolinians, including the influential merchant Cornelius Harnett, were less wealthy than either Lee or Laurens, or Shippen and Gerry in the Eastern party. The North Carolinians were nonetheless a persistently cohesive delegation that formed an important foundation for the Southern interest.

Perhaps the most that can be said about the differences between the New England and Southern membership of the two parties is that the Southerners by and large mirrored the conventional conception of an economic and social colonial aristocracy, while the Easterners reflected the middle-class character of the New England region.

This point was of some consequence in the establishment of intersectional links between the Middle states and the two parties. It is surely more than coincidental that with the exception of Elmer of New Jersey in 1777 and Floyd of New York in 1779, all the delegates from the Middle states who joined the Southerners were substantial merchants or landholders. Duane, Duer, Jay, and Gouverneur Morris of New York fit into this category—particularly Jay and Morris, who were members of elite New York families. Duer was a major contractor and speculator whose mercantile activities were comparable to those of John Langdon in New Hampshire, Daniel Parker in Massachusetts, and Robert Morris in Pennsylvania. James Duane had been a leader of the New York bar before the Revolution, had married into the Livingston clan, and was an extensive land speculator. Gouverneur Morris was second in line for the inheritance of the baronial Morrisania estate. He had received a patrimony of £2,000 rather than the land, but in due time he managed to secure title to the estate[27].

Francis Lewis was the one New York delegate who remained unattached to either the Southern party or to the Middle states bloc. Lewis is less well known than the other New Yorkers and deserves some attention because of his more independent position in the delegation. He was older than the other delegates. Duer, Jay, and Morris were thirty-two, thirty-four, and twenty-six, respectively, in 1779. Duane and Floyd were somewhat older—forty-six, and forty-seven—but they were still a generation apart from the sixty-six-year-old Lewis. Lewis had retired from his mercantile business in New York City to Whitestone on Long Island well before the Revolution, after having built up "a considerable fortune," according to his biographer in the *Dictionary of American Biography*[28]. Lewis's early career had not been conspicuously successful. He appears to have failed in a number of business enterprises and once was reduced to taking in boarders. Thomas Jones, the Tory justice of the supreme court of the province of New York, in a violently critical summary of Lewis's career in his *History of New York during the Revolutionary War*[29], contended that Lewis had secured his fortune through shady manipulation of moneys from recaptured prizes during the French and Indian War in the capacity of admiralty court claimant. Other biographers of Lewis have challenged Jones's charges[30], but it does appear that Lewis was an upstart who was not fully accepted by the New York aristocracy. Lewis carried on considerable commerce as a private merchant during the Revolution, but outside the Duer, Duane, Schuyler, Robert Morris mercantile connections. Lewis's son Morgan, for example, had been appointed deputy quartermaster general for the Canadian expedition by Horatio Gates in the fall of 1775 but was removed by Schuyler in the summer of 1776[31]. Perhaps as retribution against the Schuyler-Morris axis, Lewis confided to Henry Laurens that Robert Morris had shifted a cargo from private to public account in order to cover its loss at sea[32].

It is apparent on the other hand that George Plater of Maryland, the owner of a vast plantation with a labor force of almost 100 slaves, quickly established a close relationship with Gouverneur Morris, while Francis Lewis, actually a friend of the family, did not. The correspondence between Morris and Plater was sprinkled with intimacies that are difficult to conceive between Morris and his fellow delegate Lewis, and impossible to imagine between Morris and an Adams or a Sherman[33].

In the New Jersey delegation three of the members, Scudder, Witherspoon, and Houston, were linked with the Eastern faction. All three were professionals. Scudder was a physician, Witherspoon a clergyman and college president, and Houston a professor of mathematics at Princeton. None of the three appears to have had business or landed investments of any consequence. One New Jersey delegate, Elmer, was aligned with the Southern party in 1777, but in 1778 he was unaffiliated, and actually inclined toward the Eastern party, as his high ratios of agreement with Samuel Adams, Henry Marchant, and Roger Sherman indicate. Elmer was also a physician without substantial property. The one New Jersey delegate who jointed the Southern-oriented Middle states bloc in 1779 was John Fell. Fell was the only merchant among the New Jersey delegates, and probably the richest of the group. He was the senior member of the New York firm of John Fell and Company, which owned several armed ships during the French and Indian War. Fell owned a 220-acre tract in Bergen County, where he established his residence during the 1760s. He sold the estate in 1793 for £2,000 and before that had enough surplus capital to invest over $1,000 in state bonds and stock of the Bank of New York[34].

In the Pennsylvanian delegations of 1777–1779, the same pattern held, with some exceptions. The majority of the delegates who were closely affiliated with the Eastern party were small landholders or small merchants by contrast with the massive mercantile operations of Robert Morris of the Southern interest. William Clingan, who was listed as a shopkeeper in the 1768 Chester County rates owned 144 acres, 3 horses, and 4 cattle in 1781[35]. James Searle was a merchant who was mentioned in the Pennsylvania tax lists only in connection with a 90-acre tract in Middletown Township, Bucks County, during the middle 1780s[36]. James McLene was a frontier farmer who had taken up 100 acres of land in Antrim Township, Cumberland (later Franklin) County. He also may have purchased 400 acres in Westmoreland County, for there are two 200-acre surveys listed under his name in 1773, but in any event McLene's total estate cannot have been worth more than a few hundred pounds [37]. Frederick Muhlenberg, a fringe member of the Eastern party in 1779, was a renowned minister of negligible estate. John Armstrong, also a marginal member of the Eastern party that year, was a fairly substantial land-holder. Muhlenberg owned a 56-acre farm, while Armstrong held over 1,000 acres in four locations in Cumberland County, as well as two Negro servants. Both Daniel Roberdeau and William Shippen were connected with the Eastern faction, and they had more wealth and higher social status than the other Pennsylvanians—except Robert Morris. Roberdeau, a susbtantial businessman (and, like Armstrong, a general in the Pennsylvania militia), had a number of properties in the city and county of Philadelphia valued at over £1,300 in 1782. Shippen was a physician by profession but was also a member of a wealthy and prestigious Philadelphia family. As already pointed out in the listing of the effective supply tax for the city in 1779, Shippen's estate ranked eleventh in almost 4,000 entries[38].

The two Pennsylvanians who aligned either with the Southern or Middle bloc were Robert Morris and Samuel Atlee. Morris's holdings in mercantile property were sufficient to buy out the entire Middle states contingent of the Eastern interest. Atlee, a member of the Middle states bloc of 1779, spent eleven years in the military before the Revolution, serving as a captain during the French and Indian War. He secured a medium-sized farm in Lancaster County for his services in the war and was assessed 12 shillings from his 130-acre farm with three horses, two cows, and one servant in 1773. By 1782 he had acquired 166 acres and an extra horse and cow, but had released his servant. Atlee seems as out of place with Gouverneur Morris, Jay, and Duane as Shippen does with McLene[39]. It is likely that Atlee, who had eleven years' military experience, and who had been captured by the British at the Battle of Long Island, related more naturally to the Southern interest because of its stress on profesionalism in the military. (The Constitutionalists of Pennsylvania, on the other hand, always cultivated the militia, which was a major source of electoral strength for the party[40].)

There was also a split in the Delaware delegation that did not reflect a socioeconomic disparity. John Dickinson, the famous author of the *Farmer's Letters,* was the son of Samuel Dickinson, who owned a 1,300-acre estate in Kent County dating back to 1715. John had studied law at the Inns of Court and by the time of the Revolution had an annual income of at least £2,000 in lawyer's fees and rents from the estate[41]. Dickinson's place on the fringe of the Middle states bloc seems entirely appropriate, but that the powerful and wealthy lawyer and officeholder Thomas McKean, chief justice of Pennsylvania, should have often aligned with the Eastern party seems incongruous.

Of course, a perfect dichotomy along the lines of wealth and status need not have been a necessary condition for the existence of tension between the two sets of political leaders who had popular and aristocratic perceptions of the Revolution. Nor, for that matter, is it necessary to accept the thesis set forth by "A True Patriot" in the *New Jersey Gazette* that "*riches* and *wealth* ever lay human nature under the strongest temptations to grasp at the reigns of government; and, when obtained, to lord it over the honest commonalty in society"[42]. Yet that "A True Patriot" and many others, including Samuel Adams and the Old Radical group in Congress, believed that this was true is not to be disregarded. "A True Patriot" argued that the Confederation was composed of states with different types of constitutions, some leaning toward democracy, as did that of New Jersey, and some toward aristocracy, as did the constitution of New York.

> In perusing the New York constitution, it appears evident to me that the powers of government are thrown into the hands of the rich and wealthy in the two cities. . . . It appears highly probable to me, that men, who have thus carried their point against the commonalty in their own state, being delegated to the august Council of the empire, will endeavor to favour every scheme which may have the same tendency in the other states. . . . Hence I would almost venture to assert, that if you enquire of your delegates you will become sensible that individuals in the Supreme Council of this empire have already discovered symptoms of such ambitious designs.

The writer went on to urge citizens to carefully watch their representatives in Congress to see that they remained faithful to the welfare of their constituents, that in constructing financial policy and promoting foreign loans they be prevented from securing personal advantage, and that they behaved in a manner "calculated to procure the continuation of the kind interposition of Providence in our favor"[43].

This was a sentiment much more characteristic of the Eastern than the Southern party. The Calvinist tenets that had been so influential in the psychology of the radical resistance still served to differentiate perceptions of the Revolution. William Whipple was concerned about the pernicious influence of privateering in New Hampshire. "No kind of business can so effectually introduce luxury, extravagance, and every kind of dissipation that tend to the destruction of the morals of the people." Josiah Bartlett was convinced that "our cause is as just as any the Israelites were ever engaged in," but he was "sorry to find that like them we are a crooked and perverse generation, longing for the fineries and follies of those Egyptian task masters from whom we have so lately freed ourselves . . .[*44*]. Samuel Adams, Roger Sherman, and, indeed, every Old Radical echoed these sentiments and joined in attempts to induce the expected behavioral reformation through sumptuary legislation. Members of the Southern party on the other hand, tended not only to oppose legislation to curb profanity in the army and theatergoing in Philadelphia but also to ridicule the crypto-Commonwealthmen in Congress. George Plater, when informed by Gouverneur Morris of a congressional resolution against theatrical performances, could not understand why the puritanical Easterners had objections against amusement. Plater found congressional life austere, dour, and uncivilized. He and his wife were usually at the center of an informal society of congressmen who attempted to relieve the tedium of congressional business with polite diversion. The Virginia delegate John Banister wrote that the "thick atmosphere" of the "Bestian Land" at York was relieved by the sociable efforts of the Platers and some other congressmen—"Men of the World" and "not natives of this Soil." He went on to say in a letter to Mrs. Bland, "Beside this particular Society we have a Saturday's Club composed of about fourteen very agreeable Members. Here we sometimes have a few Ladies to drink Tea, on an Island which for its beauty and enchanting situation we have honoured with the Name of Daphne"[*45*]. Anyone familiar with the correspondence of the Morrises, Platers, Banisters, and certain other adherents of the Southern party would not be surprised at this attempt to emulate the arcadian diversions of the French Court. Banister did not list the fourteen congressmen, but one may be assured the group did not include the Whipples, Adamses, and Shermans, who advocated living on mussels and clams like the Puritan fathers.

These distinctions were symptomatic of different attitudes toward the Revolution that could and did exacerbate partisan tensions. Such factors are, of course, extremely difficult to assess either in their incidence or influence. It is worth mentioning, however, that the Eastern party was overwhelmingly Congregational and Presbyterian, as had been true of the resistance radicals, while the Southern interest was predominantly Anglican. This was strikingly true of the Middle states delegates who split more in accord with religious denomination than social and economic status.

Congressional parties were stitched by sectional tradition and interests, by social and economic status, and also by familial and business relationships. Robert Morris was William Paca's brother-in-law; James Duane and John Jay were connected by marriage with the Livingstons, who often represented New York in the Congress and who were always involved in congressional politics and business whether present in Congress or not; William Shippen was the father-in-law of Alice Lee, the sister of Richard Henry Lee, Francis Lightfoot Lee, and Arthur Lee; William Shippen's granddaughter Susan Shippen Blair married Daniel Roberdeau's son Isaac. (Later on there was a connection between the Eastern and Middle states blocs when Anne Hume Shippen, the daughter of William Shippen, Jr., and Alice Lee, married Henry Beekman Livingston, the son of Robert R. Livingston and brother of Chancellor Livingston[46]. The Stockton, Rush, and Boudinot families also were interrelated, although none of them was in Congress during this period.

Business connections were even more notable, particularly in the Southern interest. William Duer, Gouverneur Morris, James Duane, Robert Morris, Charles Carroll, Samuel Chase, William Paca, and John Harvie were either directly or indirectly related in enterprises in commerce or land speculation. Benjamin Harrison, Jr., Carter Braxton, William Hooper, Joseph Hewes, Edmund Pendleton, John Penn, and James Wilson were associated in business either separately or, more often, with Robert Morris[47]. Such personal contacts, which made the first national legislature more tightly knit than any given Congress in this century, were extremely important in smoothing over the difficulties that were bound to occur in the fusion of a cluster of parochial cultural traditions. At the same time, personal connections related to the taking of profits from the Revolutionary effort generated profoundly divisive effects.

One further distinction between the two parties deserves mention. If the characteristic Easterner was less wealthy and less socially prestigious than the characteristic Southerner, he was also older. The average age in the Eastern membership in 1779 was forty-seven, while that in the Southern interest was forty-one. While this difference is hardly remarkable, the disparity between the ages of the leaders of the parties was more striking. Eastern leaders, including the Adamses, Gerry, Ellery, Witherspoon, McKean, and Richard Henry Lee, were on the average the same age as the membership of the party—that is, forty-seven. The leaders of the Southern and Middle states blocs of the Southern party (men such as Jay, the Morrises, Duane, Dickinson, Meriwether Smith, Burke, and Mathews) had an average age of just thirty-six[48].

The fact that Easterners tended to be older than their opponents, and Southerners younger, was symptomatic of (although not the cause of) yet another difference between the parties. The Eastern party was led by an extension of the leadership of the radical movement during the days before independence. The Southern interest, on the other hand, was led either by latecomers to Congress (such as Smith and Burke) or by men such as Duane and Dickinson who had attended the first Congress but who had taken a conservative position.

Thus the Eastern party, as it functioned during 1777–1779, was in a better position to claim Revolutionary authenticity, and it did exactly that. In the formulation of military policy, in the definition of the meaning of a republican revolution during the debates over the structure of the Confederation, and, somewhat later, in the formulation of foreign policy and the conduct of fiscal affairs, the Easterners claimed to be the Party of the Revolution, protecting it against the uninformed and the misguided, and against the predators who would use it to selfish advantage.

V

The evolution of a system of congressional parties was inevitable, but it was an uneven and at times confused development. Partisanship was intense in 1778 and 1779, but during the next two years it subsided when the Middle states with Southern support began to direct congressional policy. There were a number of reasons for the ebb in party tensions that will be discussed in subsequent chapters, but one reason that deserves mention at this point was the mounting volume of newspaper criticism of factionalism in the Congress and in some of the states. (It was a criticism that was sometimes planted by congressmen and others connected with Congress, such as the French minister Gérard, but it lost none of its force because of that fact.)

Commentary about partisanship often clouded the nature of legislative conflict and thereby inhibited the growth of legitimate, organized contention. "O Tempora! O Mores!" had chastised the Eastern party as a self-interested junto. Another writer, "The Impartial American," called parties "the dangerous disease of civil freedom; they are only the first stage of anarchy. . . ." They were "the thermometer of virtue; as their zeal rises the latter is diminished; as the former decreases, virtue becomes genuine"[49]. Conservative critics often condemned partisan strife as an inevitable consequence of mass participation in politics. The more popularized lower houses of state assemblies, according to this view, inherited the "factions and disorders" of a tumultuous democracy. In Pennsylvania, which had no upper house, conservatives such as William Bingham deplored the absence of an upper house "unpolluted" by faction that could check the influence of "individuals possessed of popular Talents" in the Assembly[50]. Pennsylvania radicals such as Timothy Matlack, a dedicated Constitutionalist and subsequently a member of the Congress, were equally suspicious of organized opposition. Matlack suggested that the conservative Republican Society should reexamine its criticism of the constitution.

> Let some cool and dispassionate Member of your club look on the path in which you are treading, and count how many steps there remains before you, between you and the line on which is marked Conspirators, and I suspect that he will be induced to think you have gone far enough[51].

Congress, too, was sometimes linked with conspiratorial partisanship. "Gustavus Vasa" complained that a "*factious few*" in Congress had very likely been bribed by Governor Johnstone of the Carlisle Commission that had been sent from England to appease the rebellious colonies and that the Congress of 1779 was "a wandering star" that had been "hurled out of the political vortex of former Congresses" as a result of the "furious and incessant concussions and percussions of party collisions"[52]. Thus, congressional parties were more than factions, but they had factious effects.

There were other reasons for the persistence of factional "concussions," for the parties themselves had lingering traces of factionalism. The loosely joined Southern interest in particular lacked the cohesion, discipline, and self-awareness of a developed legislative party. Not only did it contain a number of members who took pride in their independence; but its most active leaders sometimes behaved in the manner associated with the traditional faction—that is, they sought office for perquisites and power rather than to serve a broad constituency or to promote a policy. There were some Easterners who were similarly motivated, but William Whipple, Samuel Adams, and Roger Sherman were more concerned with protecting the Eastern interest than with advancing their careers on the new national stage. Gouverneur Morris, Robert Morris, and Meriwether Smith, on the other hand, were criticized in their states for paying more attention to their own concerns than to those of their constituents[53].

Paradoxically, Easterners such as Samuel Adams whose loyalties were to state and region were more responsible for the development of congressional parties—an innovation in the political process—than were more cosmopolitan congressmen such as Gouverneur Morris, who used "connexions," so typical of traditional factionalism, to carve a career in the new national politics. The paradox revealed a problem that was inherent in the structure of the confederation. Winning the Revolution within the framework of the "firm league of friendship" proclaimed in the Articles of Confederation required either unanimity of purpose or a mechanism for the definition and compromise of conflicting interests.

It was the Easterners who offered the ideology based on public virtue that seemed to offer the best hope for achieving a unanimity of purpose, but that ideology depended upon a behavioral reformation that had corroded by 1779. Since Sam Adams's Christian Sparta failed to materialize, some means of resolving conflict had to be found. The Congress was the obvious stage, and congressional parties a less obvious and clearly less palatable mechanism, for the definition and resolution of conflict. It was the Easterners again who succeeded best in forming a cohesive congressional party, but their posture as the "Party of the Revolution" precluded the existence of a legitimate opposition. Further, so long as parties were markedly sectional in composition, their existence prejudiced the success of a revolution that had depended from the outset on the nurture of a united effort. It was in part a recognition of this fact that prompted the members of Congress to try to still party passions during the next two critical war years.

Notes

1 Pauline Maier, "The Charleston Mob and the Evolution of Popular Politics in Revolutionary South Carolina, 1765-1784," in Donald Fleming and Bernard Bailyn (eds.), *Perspectives in American History* (1970), published by the Charles Warren Center for Studies in American History, Harvard University, IV, 182-183.

2 See Van Beck Hall, *Politics without Parties: Massachusetts, 1780-1791* (Pittsburgh, 1972), for the "preparty" struggles in Massachusetts during the 1780s. Jackson Turner Main, who kindly allowed me to look at the manuscript of his study of partison politics in the lower houses of the states, finds a cosmopolitan-parochialist antagonism in a number of the state legislatures.

3 See Robert L. Brunhouse, *Counter-Revolution in Pennsylvania* (Harrisburg, Pa., 1942). For the less developed party politics of New York see Alfred F. Young, *The Democratic Republicans of New York* (Chapel Hill, 1967).

4 For a good analysis of the characteristics of party as distinguished from faction, see William Nisbet Chambers, *Political Parties in a New Nation: The American Experience, 1776-1809* (New York, 1963), esp. chaps. 1 and 2. This analysis, it might be noted, does not agree with that of Chambers in certain substantive details regarding the 1770s and 1780s, but his definitions of different kinds of partisan organization are sound and helpful. See Richard Hofstadter, *The Idea of a Party System* (Berkeley and Los Angeles, 1969), for an articulate summation of the pervasive aversion to the notion of an organized political party.

5 *Connecticut Courant*, Sept. 1, 1779.

6 Unanimous and near-unanimous roll calls were not included, since the intention of this study was to discover the configuration of disagreement. The level of 10% disagreement was chosen arbitrarily on the assumption that no faction would be uncovered only if votes on which less than 10% disagreement occurred were counted. Repetitive roll calls, i.e., those which were duplications of the previous roll call both with regards to issue and voting configuration, were not included because they would have resulted in the inflation of certain issues—such as the fisheries debates of 1779, which were characterized by ineffectual parliamentary maneuver.

7 Mary P. Ryan, "Party Formation in the United States Congress, 1789-1796: A Quantitative Analysis," *WMQ*, ser. 3, XVIII (1971), 523-542.

8 Richard Henry Lee to Governor Patrick Henry, May 26, 1777, *LMCC*, II, 374.

9 Duer to John Jay, May 28, 1777, in Henry P. Johnston (ed.), *Correspondence of John Jay* (4 vols.; New York, 1890-1893), I, 137; Duer to Livingston, May 28, 1777, in ibid., 377.

10 Lovell to William Whipple, July 7, 1777, *LMCC*, II, 402.

11 "O Tempora! O Mores!" *Pennsylvania Gazette,* June 23, 1779.

12 Fleury's statement is reproduced in B. F. Stevens (ed.), *Facsimiles of Manuscripts in European Archives Relating to America, 1773-83* (26 vols.; London, 1889–1895), vol. XVII, no. 1616. Fleury was not on particularly good terms with Henry Laurens, with whom he corresponded about a promotion, a fact which may have encouraged him to link South Carolina with the Eastern interest. (See Henry Laurens to Louis Fleury, Apr. 28, 1778, *LMCC*, III, 196.)

13 Comments about congressional factionalism occupy a prominent place in Gérard's reports. See, for example, his letter to Vergennes, June 12, 1779, in John J. Meng (ed.), *Despatches and Instructions of Conrad Alexandre Gérard* (Baltimore, 1939), pp. 717–724.

14 Robert H. Harrison to Alexander Hamilton, Oct. 27, 1780, in Harold C. Syrett and Jacob E. Cooke (eds.), *The Papers of Alexander Hamilton* (New York, 1960–), II, 490.

15 George W. Corner (ed.), *The Autobiography of Benjamin Rush* (Princeton, 1948), pp. 140, 144–145.

16 LMCC, II, 403. Elmer subsequently drifted away. In 1778 his highest levels of agreement were with members of the Eastern position.

17 Laurens's dispute with the North Carolina delegates can be traced in an exchange of letters in Burnett, ibid., IV, 129–158, and his duel with John Penn in Samuel Sterett to General Mordecai Gist, Jan. 13, 1779, Gist Papers, Maryland Historical Society, vol III, and *LMCC*, IV, 39n. On Laurens's challenge of Langworthy's eligibility, see Henry Laurens, "Notes of Debates," May 8, 1779, ibid., 201–202, Laurens's penchant for engaging in disputes with his fellow Southerners was almost limitless, for he was involved in a controversy with Meriwether Smith as well. (See "Brutus," in the *Pennsylvania Packet*, May 29, 1779.)

18 While the defection of Richard Henry Lee was instrumental in weakening Virginian leadership of the Southern party, it should be stressed that there was no massive defection from the Southern interest among the Virginians. Some historians, in noting the Lee-Adams faction, have failed to appreciate that the Eastern party in which the faction was lodged was overwhelmingly Northern. Thus Thomas P. Abernethy, in his very good book *Western Lands and the American Revolution* (New York, 1937), contends that the natural line of cleavage in the Continental Congress was between North and South but that this sectional division "was cut across and largely submerged by the alliance between the Virginia Lees and the Massachusetts Adamses . . ." (p. 205). Jennings B. Sanders, *Evolution of Executive Departments of the Continental Congress 1774-1789* (Chapel Hill, 1935), p. 96, asserts, "There is abundant evidence of sectional feeling in the Continental Congress, but so far as the form of government to be set up was concerned, it appears that the line of cleavage was political more than sectional. Otherwise, the Adams-Lee alliance is accounted for with some difficulty."

19 A number of independents were also on these committees.

20 John Jay to George Washington, Apr. 26, 1779, *LMCC*, IV, 176-177. (Burnett interprets the term "Family compact" to mean the Lee family [p. 177n], but in the context of factional politics of 1779 as well as the sectional interests in marine affairs, the meaning would seem to be the Adams-Lee faction.)

21 Peabody to Josiah Bartlett, Aug. 17, 1799, ibid., IV, 382.

22 Jackson Turner Main, *The Social Structure of Revolutionary America* (Princeton, 1965), pp. 227-228.

23 Burke to Mrs. Sydney Jones, c. 1778, quoted in ibid., p. 101.

24 William G. Brown, *The Life of Oliver Ellsworth* (New York, 1905), p. 23. Ellsworth had inherited a parcel of land along the Connecticut River which he wanted to dispose of to pay the costs of his education at Yale, but being unable to find a purchaser he was reduced to cutting wood for sale in Hartford. Ultimately, Ellsworth developed a thriving law practice and invested successfully in land, businesses, and securities, but this was largely after his 1778 tenure in Congress.

25 Forrest McDonald, *We The People* (Chicago, 1958), p. 48.

26 *PA*, ser. 3, XIV, 516.

27 Edward P. Alexander, *James Duane* (New York, 1938), chaps. II–IV; Anne Cary Morris (ed.), *Diary and Letters of Gouverneur Morris* (2 vols.; New York, 1888), I, 16-17.

28 C. W. Spencer, "Francis Lewis," *DAB*, XI, 215.

29 Thomas Jones, *History of New York during the Revolutionary War* (2 vols.; New York, reprinted for the New-York Historical Society, 1879).

30 See Julia Delafield, *Biographies of Francis Lewis and Morgan Lewis* (2 vols.; New York, 1877); C. W. Spencer, "Francis Lewis," *DAB*, XI, 214-215.

31 Francis Lewis to [Mrs. Gates?], Aug. 13, 1776, *LMCC*, II, 48-49, 49n.

32 Henry Laurens, "Minutes of Proceedings" [Jan. 9, 1779], ibid., IV, 20-21.

33 See the extensive exchange of letters between Morris and Plater in the Gouverneur Morris Papers, CUL.

34 See the article on Fell in the *DAB*; also the note by William Nelson in the *New Jersey Archives,* ser. 2, I, 54n-55n, and Forrest McDonald, *We The People,* p. 128.

35 *PA*, ser. 3, XI, 497, and XII, 468.

36 Ibid., XIII, 500, 540, 601. See also Mildred E. Lombard, "James Searle: Radical Businessman of the Revolution," *PMHB*, LIX, 284-294.

37 *PA*, ser 3, XXV, 31, and XXVI, 464-465. There is a biographical sketch of McLene in the *PMHB*, IV, 93-94.

38 *PA*, ser. 3, XVI, 116, 315, 349, 539; XIV, 516.

39 Ibid., XVII, 722. See the sketch of Atlee by Samuel Pennypacker in the *PMHB*, II, 74-84; see also Lancaster County Historical Society, *Historical Papers,* II (1898), 140-145; John B. Linn, "Samuel J. Atlee," Benson J. Lossing, (ed.), *The American Historical Record,* vol. III, no. 34 (1874), 448-449.

40 Brunhouse, *Counter-Revolution in Pennsylvania,* p. 69. Atlee was captured during the battle of Long Island and subsequently released through a prisoner exchange in late 1778 (see Samuel J. Atlee, "Extract from the Journal of the Battle of Long Island, August 27, 1776," *PA*, ser 2, I, 512–516). Atlee then petitioned for a reappointment to the army as a brigadier general in early 1779, but despite Reed's recommendation, he failed to get the slot. Atlee's record in Congress during 1779 offended the Constitutionalists, who removed him in the election of 1779.

41 Charles Stillé, *The Life and Times of John Dickinson* (2 vols.; Philadelphia, 1891), I, 14–25; McDonald, *We The People*, p. 65n.

42 "A True Patriot," no. VII, reprinted in the *Pennsylvania Gazette*, June 16, 1779.

43 Ibid.

44 William Whipple to Josiah Bartlett, July 12, 1778, *Historical Magazine*, VI (1782), 75; Bartlett to Whipple, May 29, 1779, Bartlett Papers, NHHS.

45 John Banister to Mrs. Bland, June 19, 1778, HSP. (Banister is not included in the bloc analysis because of infrequent attendance.)

46 The Roberdeau-Lee-Shippen-Livingston connection is traced in Roberdeau Buchannan, *Genealogy of the Descendants of Dr. William Shippen, the Elder* (Washington, D.C., 1877); see esp. p. 6.

47 See below, Chapter 9.

48 Leadership is a difficult thing to measure, particularly from the rather sparce records of the Continental Congress. In this instance, motions as recorded during 1779 are used as an index. The year 1779 was the first year in which the movers of motions were recorded in the *Journals*, and so with some exceptions, delegates who were not present for a sufficient part of the year to be included in the voting blocs cannot be assessed. Thomas McKean was in Congress for only a portion of the year and is not included in the voting blocs, but because of his great activity he did make more motions than average, and he is thus included—the inference being that he was also active in 1778. Four other members not in the blocs of 1779 are ranked as leaders because of their indisputable prominence: John Adams, William Duer, Samuel Chase, and Robert Morris. Finally, Richard Henry Lee, who is included in the 1779 blocs, but who was not present sufficiently long while motions were being recorded to have qualified under this test, also has been inserted in the leadership group.

49 "The Impartial American," *Pennsylvania Gazette*, Feb. 24, 1779.

50 *Continental Journal* (Boston), May 27, 1779. William Bingham to Biddle, May 3, 1784, Gratz Collection, HSP.

51 *Pennsylvania Gazette*, Mar. 24, 1779. See also ibid., Mar. 31, 1779.

52 "Gustavus Vasa," ibid., Sept. 1, 1779. Paul Wentworth, the famous American who served as a British agent during the war, supplied a lengthy intelligence report to the British Ministry based on just such principles. His "Minutes respecting political Parties in America, and Sketches of leading Persons in each Province," in Stevens (ed.), *Facsimiles,* no. 227, includes frequent references to the fortune, rank, and susceptibility to temptation of each of the individuals he examines.

53 See below, p. 205.

8 The Second Resistance: The Politics of Foreign Affairs, 1778–1779

THE party politics of the middle period of the Revolution cannot be understood apart from the major issue of those years, the control of policy and personnel in foreign affairs. The controversies of earlier years had dissipated or were quiescent. The Articles of Confederation were completed and in the hands of the states. The Old Radicals had tested the substance of Washington's power, and they had to rest content with their hero Gates taking a subordinate position. Technical questions of finance related to the volume of currency in circulation and the interest rate on loan office certificates were more perplexing than disputatious at this moment. But the related question of mismanagement of public funds, particularly the misuse of American funds abroad, was growing into a major controversy in 1778. There were calls for congressional investigation of the actions of Robert Morris, Benedict Arnold, and, above all, Silas Deane. Deane became the main target of charges of financial mismanagement as a result of the accusations of Arthur Lee in Paris. Because of his role in the procurement of French financial and military assistance —including the negotiation of the alliance with France—it was inevitable that criticisms of Deane would affect the relationship between the United States and its ally France.

It is impossible to exaggerate the significance of the Lee-Deane controversy. With the introduction of Arthur Lee into the center of congressional politics, the old Massachusetts-Virginia-London axis of the resistance was again established as an integral part of intersectional politics. The controversy also reactivated the rhetoric of the resistance. Liberty was again threatened, less by the overt enemy Britain than by the corruption of "interested" men such as Deane (and his American connection Robert Morris) and the subtle duplicity of America's new ally France. For the core of the Adams-Lee faction, this was the period of the "second resistance," with the Adams-Lee group assuming the role of Patriots, the Deane-Morris group functioning as Tories, and France playing the Old World menace contaminating New World virtue. France, through her adroit emissary Conrad Alexander Gérard, attempted to persuade Congress to scale down the American peace objectives to a simple recognition of American independence by Britain, thereby undermining both New England's hopes for the rights to North Atlantic fishing grounds and the Southern concern for guarantees of navigation of the Mississippi. The resulting furor over foreign policy threatened a revival not only of the Adams-Lee axis but also of the full New England–Southern Patriot coalition. But that coalition failed to mature fully; the antagonism between the Eastern and Southern parties was heightened rather than diminished by the controversy. Eastern influence actually reached a peak and then began to decline during 1778 and 1779. The Eastern party was unable to apply convincingly the old resistance paradigm to the circumstances of the mid-Revolution.

Although the Lee-Deane dispute did not have any appreciable effect upon Congress until 1778, the conflict was rooted as far back as 1769, when Arthur Lee first set out on his turbulent career of European service. Lee first gained the attention of Americans, of course, when he attempted to bring the colonial resistance together with the British reform movement at the time of Wilkes furor. Intensely ambitious, thoroughly convinced of his own abilities and patriotic virtue, and by nature excessively suspicious, Lee had little tolerance for competition in the management of American affairs across the ocean. He showed the fullness of his misanthropy in harsh criticisms of Franklin while he was serving as subagent for Massachusetts. This criticism created the distrust and animosity that characterized the relationship between the two men when they, along with Deane, served as commissioners to France.

Lee was jealous of Franklin, but he could appreciate the older man's wide influence and stature and thus understand his appointment as commissioner to France. He was much less inclined to accept the choice of Silas Deane as commercial agent of the Committee of Secret Correspondence in 1776. It is not difficult to comprehend Lee's feelings. He had just been left as America's only quasi-official representative in London, after Franklin departed to sit in the second Continental Congress. In December of 1775 he was charged by Congress with obtaining as much information as he could gather secretly about the attitudes of European powers toward the rebellious colonies. Earlier he had traveled widely on the Continent, had become fluent in French, Italian, and

Spanish, and he made important contacts in both England and France. He met Beaumarchais in London in 1775 when the French agent was covertly probing politicians of the opposition to see what potential the colonial conflict had for France. Lee had reason to believe his work was important to the colonial cause; this initial contact with French diplomacy led to Vergennes's memoir, recommending intervention in the American conflict, which was presented indirectly to Louis XVI[1].

It was inevitable that Lee should resent the appointment of Silas Deane, a Connecticut Yankee who had never crossed the Atlantic and had only recently become known outside his native state. The son of a Connecticut blacksmith, Deane had managed to graduate from Yale. He acquired some capital from a fortunate marriage and used it shrewdly enough to become a merchant of some note by the time of the early Revolutionary agitation. Able and, like Arthur Lee, extremely ambitious, he plunged into the politics of the resistance. He was an early spokesman for the Liberty Boys, engaging in correspondence with Samuel Adams, and later he was made a delegate to the first Continental Congress. For reasons which are not entirely clear, he was not reelected to the second Congress, but having used his time in Philadelphia to good advantage in making contacts with Robert Morris, Jay, and other conservatives from the Middle colonies, he was put up for office under the auspices of the Congress. Thus, in making his fortune, Deane transformed himself from a little-known Connecticut radical into a national figure with important connections in the Middle states. The latter persona was bound to be repugnant to the suspicious Old Radicals.

Deane was nothing if not enterprising. By the fall of 1776, he was associated with Robert Morris in a plan to form a company capitalized at £400,000 and intended to engage in trade between England and the newly independent United States via France. The cargoes were to exclude arms and ammunition, but even so the mere contemplation of such a scheme would have offended the Old Radical group, had they known of it. This project did not materialize, but others did, including speculation in insurance in conjunction with Samuel Wharton, the Philadelphia merchant[2]. Another speculator was Edward Bancroft, Deane's secretary and former pupil in Connecticut, who managed to combine speculation in American employ with spying in the service of the British. Deane helped seal the success of the insurance enterprise by using his access to confidential shipping information.

Deane's connections with Middle states merchants were extensive, beginning with such business leaders as Wharton and Robert Morris. Deane also dealt with Thomas Morris, Robert's brother, who was a commercial agent at Nantes until he was discharged because of incompetence, and then he traded with Morris's replacement Jonathan Williams, a nephew of Benjamin Franklin. Deane's brother Simeon was a merchant in Virginia with many business connections throughout the United States[3]. Deane's connections were solid; consequently his support in Congress was impressive—particularly in the Middle states and the Chesapeake delegations.

Lee criticized not only Deane's speculation, which involved use of public funds as well as confidential information, but also his role in a vitally important question regarding the nature of French assistance to the United States. Deane contended that French aid during the early part of the Revolution had been given as a loan, an interpretation that coincided with the official position of the French government. Lee, however, insisted on the basis of his early understanding with Beaumarchais that the moneys and supplies sent by France had been granted outright as a gift. With this difference of interpretation, the personal antipathy of Lee and Deane spread out into the series of political issues involved in the French alliance.

Unknown to Lee and the Eastern party that supported his position, Deane actually was a traitor as well as a speculator. Through his secretary Edward Bancroft, Deane was leaking secrets to England. As Julian Boyd has put it: "Deane . . . had in effect handed the British ambassador a key to the confidential files of the American commissioners. Whitehall saw almost every move that was taking place between them and the French government"[4]. Deane had more than one channel of communication with the British government. Through the most important of these, Bancroft also was passing information to a former employer, Paul Wentworth. This member of the prominent New Hampshire family had moved to England from his plantation in Surinam, where Bancroft had served as his physician, in order to sell whatever information he possessed or could obtain about the colonies to the British administration.

Shortly after Deane arrived in France, and apparently before he had decided to channel secret information to the British, he was warned by Arthur Lee not to trust a number of individuals in commercial and government circles, including Sir James Jay, Dennys DeBerdt (the son of the former Agent of Massachusetts and brother-in-law of Joseph Reed), William Mollesan, John Langdon (the delegate to the first Congress from New Hampshire), Colonel George Mercer, and Wentworth. Some of Lee's charges were wide of the mark, including an assertion that Joseph Reed was a "Dangerous man," but the warning about Wentworth was absolutely sound. Lee also may have told Deane in a separate letter that Bancroft was not to be trusted, but Deane rejected all of Lee's advice as unfounded and proceeded to rely upon Bancroft for counsel[5].

Profiteering, misapplication of public funds (for Deane used public funds for purchasing in his own name shares in privateering ventures), and outright treason were charges that could justly be laid against Deane; the crimes awaited discovery by the jealous and suspicious Arthur Lee. Unlike Lee, Benjamin Franklin, who shared his suspicions about Deane, was urbane enough not to lose his composure when he became aware that there were security leaks involving someone close to the commissioners. He was also shrewd enough to understand that the information reaching the British Ministry concerning the not-so-secret French aid to America could only work to America's advantage, should a rift between England and France occur as a result[6]. The sophisticated restraint Franklin employed in this situation places him immediately a world apart from Lee and the Eastern party, who regarded the idea of a purge as a good tonic for patriotic virtue.

Lee discovered some of the irregularities in Deane's conduct, and then he found one of Deane's insurance premiums, part of the speculative scheme with Wharton and Bancroft, inadvertently mixed in with the public accounts. This document, coupled with his conviction that Deane and Beaumarchais were charging the United States for supplies which had originally been arranged as gifts, prompted Lee to present charges against Deane to the Congress.

Because of their numerical superiority, the Easterners were able to recall Deane in 1777 and put John Adams in his place. Lee was given a mission to Spain, where he was to seek aid—fruitlessly as it turned out. The Spanish were unwilling to accept Lee, but he retained his commission until late 1779, spending most of his time in Paris, to the distress of Franklin. Other commissions were handed out by Congress. One went to Ralph Izard, an aristocratic South Carolinian, who was directed to the Grand Duchy of Tuscany, and one went to William Lee, the brother of Arthur, who was sent to the Courts of Vienna and Berlin. These appointments were a clear instance of what Samuel Flagg Bemis has termed "militia diplomacy"[7], and they also represented an enlargement of the influence of the "Eastern party" in the execution of American foreign policy. Both Izard and William Lee were connected with Arthur Lee rather than Deane.

Franklin's position was less clear than the positions of the other commissioners, both abroad and at home. Not an unqualified advocate of Deane, he nonetheless felt more affinity with the Deane group in Congress than with the partisans of Lee. There can be no doubt about the existence of ill feeling between Lee and Franklin. The animosity between them stemmed from their encounter in 1770 when Lee served, as he seemed forever destined to serve, in a position subordinate to Franklin as agent for Massachusetts Bay. By February of 1778 Lee was complaining that while he had been scurrying about Europe on "toilsome & most disagreeable journies," Franklin and Deane "were living in luxury receiving homage . . . tho not one appointment, nor contract, nor one livre of the millions expended has gone by my recommendation and patronage"[8]. Lee struck out at Franklin directly, too, sending acidulous messages to Franklin complaining about being left out of the business of the mission in Paris. Franklin was so distressed that he composed a letter to Lee suggesting that he should control his "sick mind, which is for ever tormenting itself with its jealousies, suspicions, and fancies . . ." and that if he did not cure himself of this tendency "it will end in insanity"[9]. Franklin did not send the letter, but even if he had, such advice was not likely to dissuade Lee from complaining about Franklin to his cohorts in Congress. Lee's charges about stockjobbing with public funds were aimed mostly at Deane, but by late 1778 he also suspected Franklin of misdeeds. He did not fail to note that Franklin's landlord, Chaumont, from whom Franklin enjoyed a rent-free residence, contracted for American supplies and bought and sold American prize ships. Franklin's grandnephew was a business connection of Chaumont, and Franklin's associates in the Vandalia scheme, Thomas Walpole and Samuel Wharton, speculated in stocks on the London market with information which by general assumption was leaking from Paris[10]. Lee's reports reinforced the distrust Samuel Adams already felt for Franklin as a suave self-interested manipulator, lacking in virtue and unworthy of the Revolution.

It appears that in spite of Lee's accusations, Franklin was able to maintain a foot in both congressional camps. James Lovell of the Massachusetts delegation was virtually single-handedly managing the correspondence of the foreign affairs committee, and he was favorably disposed toward Franklin. Further, Franklin was raised to the post of Minister Plenipotentiary to France in the fall of 1778 with what must have been the support of the Eastern party, although the vote was not recorded in the Journals[11]. The elevation of Franklin put John Adams out of a job, but it was expected that Adams would be sent to Holland on a mission to obtain a loan and perhaps a treaty of amity and commerce.

By 1778, when Deane returned from France after having tarried long enough to participate in the formulation of the alliance, the foreign service was highly skewed in favor of the Eastern bloc. During the next year, however, there was mounting pressure for an adjustment of the balance of power. This was partly because Deane, after arriving in Philadelphia to defend himself before Congress, took the offensive in a series of statements to the Congress, and ultimately in the press, complaining that Lee was a troublemaker who was distrusted by the French—perhaps with good reason, in view of Lee's having been patronized by Lord Shelburne when he was in England[12]. Lee's opponents in Congress, stimulated by Deane, contended that the wrong man had been brought back and that the Lees and Izard were disrupting American diplomacy and should be recalled. The stage was set for one of the bitterest and most pervasive conflicts in the history of the Congress.

II

It is clear that from the outset the Lee-Deane controversy fused with the pre-existing party system of Congress. As a consequence, the quarrel was magnified from a personal dispute into a national controversy in a manner that would be difficult to explain unless there had existed an established structure of party politics. Also, partisanship was intensified in a pattern of reciprocal impacts: As the Lee-Deane imbroglio grew more bitter on being merged with congressional politics, it in turn exacerbated partisan antagonisms by bringing up a whole range of related issues, such as the formulation of America's peace aims and even the question of price controls to curb profiteering.

The sharpening of existing partisanship in Congress under the pressure of the Lee-Deane controversy can be explained from a number of angles. This was a highly charged personalized conflict rather than a dispute over technical problems of military policy or finance. It involved members of Congress such as the Lee brothers, Joseph Reed, and those who had connections with Robert Morris and the Deanes. It further implicated the French alliance and, more immediately, the French Minister in Philadelphia, Gérard, who planted propaganda with newspapers and directed statements prejudicial to Lee to chosen delegates such as Morris, Paca, and Drayton, and thus infuriated the Lee faction.

Ideologically, the contest was a struggle between the imperatives of revolutionary purity and the dictates of pragmatism. Of course, neither side would have seen it quite that way. The Lee partisans were convinced they were the guardians of the integrity of the Revolution, and they saw in Deane and his cohorts not realism but a tainted self-interest, hardly distinguishable from Toryism, that would destroy the Revolution whatever the outcome of the war. The defenders of Deane either saw as inevitable some private involvement on the part of those charged with the execution of commercial affairs or else refused to believe the accusations of illegitimate activities leveled by Lee against Deane. All Deane's supporters proceeded from a basic assumption that the French alliance had to be carefully nurtured and that the campaign of the Lees and Adams to control Revolutionary policy constituted a menace to amicable relations between the United States and France. There was a measure of sincerity on both sides and some truth in both perceptions.

At least in part, the Revolution acted as a catharsis for the Eastern party. Having declared independence and having begun to fight a war to rid America of the corrupt influence of the royal administration, the Old Radicals now had to maintain the Revolution by stamping out internal contamination. Had Lee's partisans known the full story of Deane's operations in France, their opposition would have been more inspired and successful. As it was, Deane was able to cover most of his trail. But even without conclusive proof of peculation or treason, Deane was guilty in the minds of the Old Radicals of desecrating the Revolution by having used it to his own advantage. Samuel Adams, who scrupulously guarded his poverty and thereby kept pure his revolutionary ardor, could not forgive Deane for having moved out of his Connecticut origins to a new stage where "he very early attached himself to Men of different Sentiments from those which most if not all [the exception doubtless being Hancock] your

Delegates brought with them from your Country & strenuously maintained."
Deane was unworthy of the Revolution: "What Mr. D's political Principles
were if he had any I never could learn. His Views always appeared to me commercial & interested"[*13*].

The Lee partisans saw only the darkest of intentions in the party supporting Deane. According to Francis Lightfoot Lee, the group was composed of
"Tories, all those who have rob'd the public, are now doing it, and those who
wish to do it, with many others, whose design, I fear, is of a much more alarming nature, and a few who wish to succeed to Offices abroad." Doubtless,
Deane's supporters thought it "necessary to their designs, to remove all the
old friends of Liberty and Independence. . . ." Lee later suspected that there was
a desire "in some" (the allusion being almost unmistakably to the Deane party)
to stall the operations of Congress in order to bring about such disorder in
finance and foreign policy that the public would wish for a return of British
rule. Samuel Adams was certain that "the vigilant Eye of so consistent a Patriot
[as Lee] may be formidable to a Combination of political and Commercial Men,
who may be aiming to get the Trade, the Wealth, the Power and the Government of America into their own Hands. He must therefore be hunted
down . . ."[*14*].

In the minds of the Eastern party, the struggle pitted old patriots against
new enterprisers. Arthur Lee wrote to Samuel Adams that "we have the battle
to fight all over again against the Tories, strengthened by all the Defaulters
& the new men, who are ambitious of rising upon the ruin of those, who have
hitherto fought the battle at every hazard." Richard Henry Lee reassured his
brother, "Tis remarkable that the uniform, fixed, invariable Whigs are for
you"[*15*].

Given the fusion of the Eastern party with the Lee partisans and the
longer tenures of the Old Radicals within the Eastern interest, Lee's generalization could seem credible. The assumption of Lee's supporters that they were
a band of unflinching Patriots struggling to prevent the Revolution from being
corrupted was also encouraged by what Americans construed to be a general
dissolution of virtue during the middle period of the war. This was a period
of hyperinflation accompanied by a surge of buying that was deplored by all
factions, but especially by the Easterners. The correspondence of Samuel
Adams was filled at this time with even more than the usual amount of moral-
izing. He was convinced that "a general Dissolution of Principle & Manners
will more surely overthrow the Liberties of America than the whole Force of
the Common Enemy. While the people are virtuous they cannot be subdued;
but when *once* they lose their Virtue they will be ready to surrender their
Liberties to the first external or *internal* Invader." Adams was particularly
concerned to protect his own Massachusetts against that "Innundation of Levity
Vanity Luxury Dissipation & indeed Vice of every kind which I am informed

threatens that Country which has heretofore stood with unexampled Firmness in the Cause of Liberty and Virtue." This warning went to James Warren, who replied that he was "Sensible the torrent you mention should be Stemmed. . . ." Warren was doing his best to sound the alarm, but as a result "in some Companys I get the Character of an old Fashioned Fellow & in others of a strong Party Man . . ."[*16*].

While the Easterners perceived the Lee-Deane struggle as a reenactment of the resistance drama with all its ideological manifestations, the Deane partisans operated from different assumptions. Those Middle states delegates who were sensitive to commercial interests or who were linked to the funding system newly established between France and the United States naturally saw Lee and his associates as wild troublemakers, or possibly as mere power-hungry amateurs. Thus, Robert Morris, Gouverneur Morris, John Jay, James Duane, John Fell, and some others looked askance at Lee, and their anxiety to safeguard business interests only tended to confirm the suspicions of the Lee party. But the bulk of Deane's support lay in the Southern delegations. This group not only brought more votes but also adhered more consistently to the Deane strategy than some delegates in the Middle states bloc of the Southern interest such as Duane and Fell.

Why the South should support a Connecticut Yankee in preference to a Virginian from a prominent planter family is one of the more interesting questions raised by the Lee-Deane episode. Some members of the Southern party were connected directly or indirectly with the Morris financial community, but the great majority of Deane's Southern adherents were hardly attached to him by interest.

On the surface, it seems that Deane's protestations of innocence were more convincing to Southerners than Lee's campaign to establish Deane's culpability. Cyrus Griffin of Virginia, in a letter in which he chastised Congress for being composed of men who "proceed upon the interested Principle" (and thus agreed with the Easterners), nevertheless charged the Adams-Lee group with trying to "ruin an inocent Character" in attacking Deane[*17*]. Besides, the Lees and all their projects were suspect in Southern eyes because of the long-standing connection between Arthur and Richard Henry Lee and the Eastern party.

Griffin also was convinced that Deane was mainly responsible for the French alliance, believing that "he alone has the great merit of concluding that valuable Treaty with the Minister of France . . ."[*18*]. This opinion was carefully fostered by Deane and emphasized by Gérard, who made it emphatically clear that Lee was *persona non grata* with the French Ministry. For the Deep South, suffering a British invasion in late 1778, good relations with France were crucial. Thus, the Carolina bloc in particular and Southerners in general chose Deane essentially because of pragmatic calculations. There were the expected exceptions to the Southern position, of course: the Lees and the obstinate Henry Laurens.

Deane's partisans displayed impressive organization and tactics. Shortly after Deane arrived in Philadelphia, Joseph Reed sensed that a strong party was forming in Congress with the primary purpose of ousting Lee. Richard Henry Lee was astonished at the support Deane was finding, and he could attribute it only to "envy, selfishness, and Deane's arts"[*19*]. Francis Lightfoot Lee charged that the Deanites were "circulating their insinuations and falsehoods thro' the Country with great Industry . . ." and with considerable success because they had "dependencies thro' the Continent by means of their new formed commercial Establishments." Samuel Adams also made reference to "Mr. D's political Friends, some of whom I suppose are in Boston . . ." and who were "disposed to give him great Eclat. . . ." Adams's intuition was prophetic. He heard from James Warren six months later that a campaign had been launched in Massachusetts to "prejudice the People against the Lees & to propogate that you are a friend to them." Warren also related that opponents of the Lees had persuaded the Massachusetts Legislature to create a committee to consider the propriety of replacing three members of the congressional delegation[*20*]. These movements testified to the increasing organizational sophistication of the opponents of the Eastern party in Congress.

III

It is unlikely that the campaign against Lee and his cohorts would have been as successful as it was if it were not for the influence on Conrad Alexandre Gérard. The French Minister arrived with D'Estaing's squadron in company with Deane, whom he had known in Paris as a participant in the negotiation of the treaties of alliance and commerce. Gérard also knew Lee, who had complained about provisions in both treaties, and from the outset there can be no doubt that Gérard was hopeful that the bothersome Lee could be flushed out of the foreign service. Again and again Gérard made the telling point that Lee was *persona non grata* in Paris, and he grew particularly insistent on Lee's unacceptability to his government when Congress was considering revoking Lee's commission in the Spring of 1779. Gérard concentrated to good effect on several members distributed about the Southern interest, including Thomas Burke of North Carolina, William Paca of Maryland, and William Henry Drayton of South Carolina[*21*].

While Gérard's opposition to Arthur Lee and his cohorts in Paris surely reflected a true French distaste for Lee, it is plausible that Gérard's assistance in discrediting Lee was in part his reward to the Southern leaders for cooperating in the formulation of American peace terms. Vergennes had warned Gérard not to become involved in the Lee-Deane dispute[*22*], but Gérard quickly perceived that he could use partisan divisions in Congress to support French policy. Gérard expected that Spain, France's Bourbon ally, would soon mediate or enter the war against the British. He was determined that Congress should set minimal peace terms and not clog peace negotiations or the common war effort. Excessive demands for territory or rights would only stiffen British resistance, alienate the Spanish, and encroach upon French interests.

The interests that Gérard sought to protect were not inconsequential. France had lost a vast empire in 1763 as a result of the Treaty of Paris that terminated the Seven Years' War. She did not wish to recapture Canada, which had never been a profitable colony, but she had a distinct interest in the fisheries off Newfoundland and Nova Scotia. Access to fisheries was a major concern in the eighteen century, when fisheries were commonly regarded as a nursery of seamen and one of the keys to a powerful maritime force. French interest in the Grand Banks off Newfoundland was apparent in a paper drawn up by the French foreign office shortly before France entered the war in 1778. The paper stressed, "We shall shake her [England's] power . . . we shall extend our commerce, our shipping, our fisheries . . ."[23]. Although France renounced any territorial ambitions upon the continent of North America in the treaty of alliance with the United States, the northeastern islands were not mentioned. Arthur Lee recorded in his journal that he, Franklin, and Deane pressed for an additional clause wherein France would renounce the right to conquest "in the islands of Newfoundland, Cape Breton, St. John's Anticosti, and the Bermudas," but only the Bermudas were mentioned in the treaty[24]. The right which was not renounced by France in the treaty with the United States was made explicit in the treaty France subsequently concluded with Spain. Article V of the Convention of Aranjuez stated that the expulsion of the English from the island and fisheries of Newfoundland was one of the advantages sought by France, and in Article VI it was stipulated that if France acquired Newfoundland, the Spanish were to be admitted to the fisheries.

Gérard also was an indirect representative of France's ally Spain. Like France, Spain had suffered losses to the British during the eighteenth century, but she could not look with favor upon a rebellion in the Western Hemisphere, where she had a vast and ancient empire. Nor could she countenance American expansion to the Mississippi and the Floridas.

Thus, Gérard had to oppose New England's desire to acquire Nova Scotia and possibly all of Canada, along with a guarantee of rights to the Newfoundland fisheries. Southern interest in the Floridas and the navigation of the Mississippi also had to be discouraged. Gerard made much of this clear to the delegates, though of course in veiled language. He assured Congress that both France and Spain were too generous to desire an increase of territory at America's expense, that Spain had shown her good intentions toward the United States in her mediation offer, and that America should respond by asking for independence alone rather than impeding the efforts of her allies with extensive demands[25]. Thus, Gérard's intervention brought the composition of the foreign service into a far wider arena. Not only did the Lee-Deane dispute have to be resolved, perhaps through the recall of the Lees and Izard; now a peace commissioner would have to be appointed and peace terms formulated.

Congress had already created a special committee of thirteen on January 20 to investigate the disagreements among the foreign commissioners. Another committee of five, consisting of Gouverneur Morris, Samuel Adams, John Witherspoon, Meriwether Smith, and Thomas Burke, was appointed to draw up preliminary peace terms. The latter committee reported quickly on February 23 with a set of rather ambitious recommendations that revealed how much work Gérard had yet to accomplish. The committee suggested that American boundary demands should exclude Canada but embrace territory west to the Mississippi south of the Great Lakes and north of the thirty-first parallel—that is, as far south as the southern boundary of Georgia. Free navigation of the Mississippi was recommended as far south as the thirty-first parallel, along with free commerce with some port or ports below the boundary in Spanish Louisiana. The committee also proposed that "a right of fishing and curing on the banks and coasts of the island of Newfoundland, equally with the subjects of France and Great Britain," should be reserved to the subjects of the United States. Nova Scotia and its dependencies were to be ceded to the United States or declared independent, provided that the allies of the United States were willing to continue the war to attain that objective[26].

The recommendations of the committee met Gérard's requirements only on the matters of Canada and the Floridas, but the stipulation that the cession of Nova Scotia was dependent upon allied cooperation effectually nullified that demand[27]. Leaders of the Southern interest soon revealed that they did not intend to include other demands of the Easterners in the essential peace terms. When the fisheries were debated again on March 22, Gouverneur Morris moved to place the Nova Scotia fisheries in the same category as those of Newfoundland, except that the highly important question of rights to cure fish on the shores of Nova Scotia should be added, subject to the same provision that had been inserted in the original recommendation that the peninsula be ceded to the United States: curing rights were to be demanded only if "the allies be in circumstances to support them in carrying on the war for such acknowledgement. . . ." The Eastern party was confused, for it divided over the motion and enabled it to pass. Then, as soon as Morris's motion was adopted, Smith and Burke moved to strike out the right of curing fish on the shores of Nova Scotia. The Easterners at that point marshaled their forces, but they could not prevent Smith's motion from passing. New England unanimously opposed the motion, and so did the Pennsylvania Constitutionalists, but New Jersey divided because of the vote of John Fell of the Middle bloc, and, curiously, Laurens did not vote on the roll call[28].

The Southern party cooperated with Gérard in every respect. On at least one occasion, Gerard induced Morris and Smith to introduce a resolution that he had been formulating behind the scenes. This provided that in the event Great Britain continued the war the fisheries should be divided "equally between France, Spain and America" to the exclusion of England[29]. While this motion failed, Gérard's diplomacy succeeded regarding the free navigation of the Mississippi. Burke and Drayton moved that American rights to the navigation of the Mississippi also should be contingent upon the willingness of the allies to assist in securing this right. The motion failed, and when the demand was voted on in its more extreme original form, it was rejected altogether. The Southern party unanimously opposed the demand, despite the fact that the South had a greater stake in western expansion than the New Englanders. Nonetheless, the scant support that the motion aroused came largely from the Eastern party[30].

It is difficult to account for the Southern submission to the will of the French minister. It may have been that Burke and Drayton were attempting to create a precedent for excluding the Eastern demand for rights to the fisheries. But if this was so, their commitment to the West was faint indeed by comparison with the attachment of the Eastern delegates to the fisheries. The explanation may lie in the fact that the Carolinians were alarmed about the mounting British pressure in Georgia and South Carolina. Although the South did not become a major theater of the war until 1780, the British under Prevost and Campbell occupied Georgia in December and January, 1778–1779. Securely established in Savannah, they constituted a major threat to nearby Charleston. The Southerners naturally looked to powerful France for assistance, as did most Americans. Gérard was well aware of this and accordingly established close relationships with various delegates within the Southern interest.

Gérard's success in working with the Southern interest underscores as well the fact that the loosely joined Southern party contained some ambitious delegates who were interested in achieving prominence on the national stage as well as protecting their constituents. While the Carolinians, Burke and Drayton, had good reason to placate the French Minister because of the impending British threat in the lower South, Gouverneur Morris and Meriwether Smith could not have been similarly motivated. The evidence is strong that both were interested in securing a post overseas and that they calculated that Gérard's influence would further their ambitions.

IV

Coincident with the debate over the peace terms, there was an equally bitter struggle over the closely related question of the composition of the foreign service. On March 24, the committee of thirteen which had been appointed January 20 delivered its report on the foreign commissioners, stating the obvious situation that "suspicions and animosities" had arisen among the commissioners. Their report contained ten articles. The first identified the individuals and their commissions currently at foreign courts. Franklin was recognized as Minister Plenipotentiary to France, a position to which he had been elevated in September 1778 in what might be termed the first attempt at an adjustment in the balance of power between the Lee and Deane forces. It had been anticipated then that Lee would have a mission to Spain and John Adams, sent over to replace Deane, a post in Holland. But the Paris mission was by far the most important, and Franklin's appointment actually diminished the influence of the Eastern faction. The report went on, naming Arthur Lee commissioner to Spain, William Lee commissioner for Vienna and Berlin, Izard commissioner to Tuscany, and Adams commissioner to France in place of Deane, "but . . . the said commission of Mr. Adams is superseded by the plenipotentiary commission to Dr. Franklin." Two other articles suggested that ministers plenipotentiary were necessary only at Paris and Madrid and that only one minister or commissioner need reside at any court. The crucial parts of the report were articles four and five. Article four stated that "suspicions and animosities have arisen among the said Commissioners, which may be highly prejudicial to the honor and interests of these United States." Article five resolved "that the appointments of the said commissioners be vacated, and that new appointments be made[31].

Other motions were offered requiring the fourth article to specify the "commissioners" whose "suspicions and animosities" were in question. James Duane and Gouverneur Morris were active in promoting this over the objections of the Easterners, and theirs was a remarkable maneuver since they allowed the name of their ally Franklin to be included. Franklin might have been passed over because he was a minister plenipotentiary rather than a commissioner[32]. Duane and Morris called for a vote on each of the five emissaries, along with Silas Deane. There was almost unanimous agreement about including Deane in the list of names in article four, along with the two Lees and Izard. John Adams was not branded with the stigma of article four, while Benjamin Franklin was. Interestingly, the Adams-Lee faction in the Eastern party wanted to include Adams in the list, and they were voted down in this instance by the majority of the Southern interest. Franklin seems to have been exempted at first, but he was included in a subsequent vote. Neither roll call was recorded, but it is virtually certain that the inclusion of Franklin was the work of the Southern interest rather than the advocates of Lee[33]. Thus, both the Lee faction and the partisans of Deane and Franklin seem to have acted against their best interests, but both groups saw two or three moves ahead in the contest. Clearly, article four was to be a springboard for recall, and the Easterners—or those among them most committed to Lee—wanted to maneuver Adams's name into the fourth article as a prop for Lee. Probably the Southerners were inclined to placate the Easterners by excluding Adams in hopes of winning support for the recall of Lee. The strategy behind the naming of Franklin was more complicated and remains somewhat obscure, but it is very likely that most Southerners calculated that Franklin could be used as a stalking horse because he would be retained, despite the wording of article five (which specified that the "said commissioners" be removed and new appointments be made). Some members of the Southern interest favored vacating all the slots, and at least two of them—Morris and Smith—seem to have been personally interested in stepping into a post.

After what the delegate John Fell of New Jersey termed a "very warm loud and long debate" which lasted until five in the afternoon on April 20, it was resolved in the last of nine recorded roll calls to have article four read as follows: "That suspicions and animosities have arisen among the late and present commissioners, namely, Dr. Benjamin Franklin, Mr. Silas Deane, Mr. Arthur Lee, Mr. Ralph Izard, and Mr. William Lee, highly prejudicial to the honor and interest of these United States"[*34*]. Between April 22 and June 20, a bitter partisan struggle took place over the execution of the fifth, or recall, article. It was decided that Benjamin Franklin should not be recalled and, despite the intervention of Gérard, that Arthur Lee also should not be recalled. The decision on Lee was by the narrowest of margins—four yeas, four nays, four divided, and one state absent—and had the question been put asking for Lee's continuance rather than recall, the divided vote would have gone for his dismissal. Still, considering that Gérard had informed Congress through Paca and Drayton that Lee was not trusted by Vergennes, the failure of the motion was a notable demonstration of the strength that the Lee faction still wielded. The Adams-Lee faction could not prevent the removal of William Lee and Ralph Izard from their posts, on the other hand, although the Congress agreed on June 8 that they need not return to the United States. Two days later Deane was allowed to return to Europe, but he was not assigned any official post.

By allowing Deane to leave the United States and by not requiring William Lee and Izard to return home, the Congress chose to subdue—insofar as it could—the contention between Lee and Deane that had roiled Congress for the better part of a year. Deane went to Paris, where he spent some time without any congressional appointment. He became disillusioned with the possibility of independence by 1781, and then journeyed to England. He died in 1789 while embarking on a voyage to Canada. Izard returned in 1780 and was elected to Congress from South Carolina. His voting record placed him in the Southern party during 1781 and 1783. William Lee went to Holland, where he dabbled in diplomacy, drawing up a treaty of commerce with a lesser Dutch official, John De Neufville, which was never ratified but which the British used as a pretext for declaring war on Holland. He returned to Virginia in 1783.

But because the peace terms had not yet been fixed, and because a peace commissioner had not yet been designated, the larger question of the definition and fulfillment of American diplomacy was in uneasy balance between the Eastern and Southern parties. It is in this context that the maneuverings over the recall motions should be examined, particularly because the series of votes between April 22 and June 10 strongly suggests that there was a serious move to recall Franklin on the part of the inner core of the Deane group.

Table 10 displays most of the roll calls dealing with the recall motions in a scaled arrangement that discriminates both in terms of factions and issues. The table provides a clear picture of the configuration of what may be termed the Adams-Lee and Deane "factions" or partisans—both their centers, or "cores," and their support groups. Four delegates—Gerry, Wynkoop, Jenifer, and Laurens—did not fit into the scale because their voting was so erratic. This indicates that the Adams-Lee faction was not precisely identical to the Eastern party, of which Gerry was a marginal member. Nonetheless, the convergence of the faction and the party was very close. Laurens's deviation from the Adams-Lee faction was an anomaly. He was clearly one of Lee's most articulate and aggressive advocates, but his votes on Deane, which place him out of the Lee faction in the scale, were forced on him by a position he had taken in debate with Thomas Burke[35]. Jenifer was an independent, and Wynkoop was unidentifiable because he was not present in Congress long enough to be classified.

The Lee core can be separated from all other groups by its opposition to the final form of the resolution in article four stating that suspicions and animosities existed and by its opposition to the recall of Izard and William Lee on June 8. The second bloc, or the Lee support group, did not oppose the recall of Izard and William Lee but did join the Lee core in opposition to the recall of Arthur Lee, in support of the detention of Deane, and on all other issues. The Deane support group joined the Lee faction in not demanding the return of William Lee and Izard, contrary to the position of the Deane core. The two support groups thereby helped partially to defuse the Lee-Deane controversy, the Lee support group by agreeing that William Lee and Izard should be removed, and the Deane support group by agreeing that they should not be required to return home to face an investigation.

The larger core groups were less conciliatory. Composed almost wholly of members of the Eastern and Southern parties, their involvement in the workings of Revolutionary diplomacy was accordingly more intense. (The Lee and Deane cores were roughly 90 percent Eastern and Southern respectively.) The core of the Lee faction attempted to retain the whole of the Lee-Adams

TABLE 10

Recall of the Foreign Commissioners and Disposition of Silas Deane, April 20-June 10, 1779

	1	2	3	4	5	6	7	8	9	10	1	2	3	4	5	6	7	8	9	10
Lee Core																				
Whipple (N.H.—E)	x	x	x	x	x	x	x	x	x	x										
S. Adams (Mass.—E)	x	x	x	x	x	x	x	x	x	x										
Lovell (Mass.—E)	x	x	x	x	x	x	x	x	x	x										
Armstrong (Pa.—e)	x	x	x	x	x	x	x	x	x	x										
Searle (Pa.—E)	x	x	x	x	x	x	x	x	x	x										
Shippen (Pa.—E)	x	x	x	x	x	x	x	x	x	x										
Scudder (N.J.—U)		x	x	x	x	x	x	x	x											
McLene (Pa.—E)		x	x	x		x	x	x	x											
Huntington (Conn.—e)	x		x	x	x	x	x	x						o						
Holten (Mass.—E)	x	x		x	x	x	x	x	x		o			o						
Lee Support																				
Ellery (R.I.—U)	x		x	x	x	x	x	x	x		o	o								
Sherman (Conn.—E)			x	x	x	x	x	x			o	o								
Spencer (Conn.—U)			x	x	x	x	x	x			o	o	o							
Deane Support																				
Fell (N.J.—m)				x		x	x	x			o	o	o	o		o				
Duane (N.Y.—M)						x	x	x			o	o	o		o	o	o			
Floyd (N.Y.—Ms)						x	x	x			o	o	o		o					
Dickinson (Del.—m)						x	x				o	o		o						
Collins (R.I.—U)				x		x	x				o		o	o	o	o	o			
Deane Core																				
Drayton (S.C.—U)	x	x								x	o			o	o	o	o	o	o	
Muhlenberg (Pa.—e)	x									x	o	o	o	o	o	o	o	o		
Plater (Md.—Sm)										x	o	o	o					o	o	
Jay (N.Y.—Ms)										x	o	o	o	o	o	o	o	o	o	
Carmichael (Md.—s)										x	o	o	o	o	o	o	o	o	o	
Sharpe (N.C.—s)										x	o	o	o	o	o	o	o	o	o	
Fleming (Va.—*)											o	o	o	o	o	o	o	o	o	
Deane Inner Core																				
Paca (Md.—s)											o	o	o	o	o	o	o		o	o

TABLE 10 *(Continued)*

Recall of the Foreign Commissioners and Disposition of Silas Deane, April 20–June 10, 1779

	1	2	3	4	5	6	7	8	9	10	1	2	3	4	5	6	7	8	9	10
G. Morris (N.Y.—M)											o	o	o		o			o	o	o
M. Smith (Va.—s)											o	o	o	o	o	o	o	o	o	o
Griffin (Va.—S)											o	o	o	o	o	o	o	o	o	o
Burke (N.C.—S)											o	o	o	o	o	o	o	o	o	o
Penn (N.C.—S)											o	o	o	o	o	o	o	o	o	o
Unaffiliated																				
Wynkoop (Pa.—*)	x			x	x	x		x		o		o	o							
Laurens (S.C.—U)	x	x	x					x			o		o	o	o	o				
Gerry (Mass.—e)				x		x	x				o	o	o		o					o
Jenifer (Md.—U)					x	x					o	o	o	o			o	o		

CODE:

E = core membership in Eastern faction on all issues during 1779, e = marginal membership in Eastern faction; M = core membership Middle states faction, m = marginal membership; S = core membership Southern faction, s = marginal membership; U = unaffiliated with any faction; * = not present often enough during 1779 for inclusion in general bloc analysis; x = vote supporting Lee position; o = vote supporting Deane position.

KEY TO VOTES:

(1) Apr. 20, Suspicions and animosities arisen among present and late commissioners (Franklin, Deane, A. Lee, W. Lee, Izard) highly prejudicial to honor and interest of the U.S. Agreed. x = nay, o = ay. *JCC,* XIII, 487. (2) June 8, Shall Ralph Izard be recalled? Agreed. x = nay, o = ay. *JCC,* XIV, 701. (3) June 8, Shall William Lee be recalled? Agreed. x = nay, o = ay. *JCC,* XIV, 704. (4) June 10, Postponement of debate on Deane until further investigation of his defense. Agreed. x = nay, o = ay. *JCC,* XIV, 711. (5) May 3, Shall Arthur Lee be recalled? Rejected. x = nay, o = ay. *JCC,* XIV, 542. (6) June 10, Deane not to leave U.S. without permission of Congress. Previous question. Rejected x = ay, o = nay. *JCC,* XIV, 712. (7) June 10, Deane not to leave U.S. without consent of Congress. Rejected. x = nay, o = ay. *JCC,* XIV, 713. (8) June 8, William Lee need not return to U.S. Agreed. x = nay, o = nay. *JCC,* XIV, 705. (9) June 8, Izard need not return to U.S. Agreed. x = ay, o = nay. *JCC,* XIV, 703. (10) Apr. 22, Shall Franklin be recalled? Rejected x = nay, o = ay. *JCC,* XIII, 500.

interest in their allotted posts, while the committed partisans of Deane tried to send their man back to Europe and bring all the Eastern-oriented Lee-Adams diplomats home for investigation, except John Adams. The evidence suggests that they planned to place Adams either in Holland or Spain while controlling all the other slots, including the post of peace commissioner. There is good reason to suspect that the inner core of the Deane faction contemplated recalling Franklin as well in order to "make room" for some of their own members[36].

Both Gouverneur Morris and Meriwether Smith would like to have been assigned a foreign mission, and both happened to be under fire from their home constituencies. The Virginia burgesses were criticizing Smith for mixing private with public business. After he managed to squeak through the election of June 18, 1779, they forced him to take an oath that he would not engage in commerce during his term as a delegate. Gouverneur Morris, even though he rushed back to New York in the late of summer of 1779, could not prevent his defeat in the September congressional elections[37]. Perhaps their troubles at home prompted both men to become intrigued with the hope of representing the United States in Europe. Meriwether Smith suggested to Thomas Jefferson that while he felt that his responsibility to his family and private affairs compelled him to return to Virginia, he was "induced both by Duty and Inclination, to acquaint you that I will cheerfully undertake any Negociations which the Exigency of the State may make it necessary for you to attempt in Europe"[38]. With a more direct approach, Gouverneur Morris sedulously cultivated a foreign post. After Jay was appointed Minister to Spain at the end of the extended imbroglio over terms and ministers, he wrote from his new post to Robert R. Livingston and Morris with his regrets that the latter had not been sent to Europe: "But it seems that period has not yet arrived, and Congress must for some time longer remain his field"[39]. Jay's remark reflected more than a momentary fancy on Morris's part, and Morris's ambition is reflected in correspondence between members of the Eastern party. Nathaniel Peabody was a New Hampshire delegate who arrived in Philadelphia in late June, early enough to become thoroughly infected with the factional contagion. Later in the year after Henry Laurens had been appointed Minister to Holland, Peabody wrote to William Whipple that "the tall man from N.Y. [Gouverneur Morris] who has in your hearing often proposed selling his vote upon the disposition of important matters for a Pinch of Snuff, from first to Last in this affair took every Method to make the appointment and mode of Conducting it so far as it could respect those Gentlemen indelicate & disgustful, as I imagine with intent to Get rid of both by their refusing to accept any public appointment in order to make room for himself"[40]. Earlier, James Lovell expressed his conviction that Morris was angling for the secretaryship under the peace minister John Adams or, if Adams refused, for the ministry itself[41].

Smith had no chance for a congressional appointment. Morris, on the other hand, was generally recognized as a man of unusual intelligence and great promise. Just twenty-six years old in 1779, he was, in Gérard's words, a *"Jeune homme . . . très considéré pour ses talens"*[42]. Morris had been chairman of two important committees on foreign affairs, and he had established close contact with the French minister. He proposed more resolutions than any other member of Congress during 1779 and was possibly the most articulate and able member of the pro-Deane faction in Congress. It is certain that Morris would have enjoyed having the mission in France, and it is plausible that he voted to recall Franklin in order to replace him[43].

Throughout the Lee-Deane imbroglio and the controversy over the peace terms, Morris seems to have taken his cues as much from Gérard as from any other source. He proposed at least one motion that had been formulated by Gérard, and he even broke with the Southern delegates, his main supporters, when he advocated that the fisheries be required as a sine qua non, not for a peace treaty, but for a treaty of amity and commerce with Britain. Since the fisheries proviso would doubtless impede negotiations for a commercial treaty, the South opposed and Gérard supported Morris's proposal. In no instance does Morris appear to have run counter to Gérard's suggestions. Morris's close cooperation with Gérard raises a question about Gérard's own role in the recall episode, and there are reasons to believe that the French minister himself was not averse to the recall of Franklin[44].

Morris and his Southern cohorts in the Deane nucleus may have split in July over the fisheries, but during the period before the vote on Franklin's recall, they were not only in perfect accord but also the most active of the delegates in the Deane faction. During the period March 22 to June 10, there were thirteen resolutions proposed by delegates opposed to the fisheries and navigation clauses which resulted in roll-call votes on those two issues. Two resolutions came from the five members of the Deane support group, one resolution from the eight members of the Deane core, and ten resolutions from the six members of the Deane nucleus. Thus, those delegates voting for Franklin's recall were those most active in promoting French aims, those most intimate with Gérard, and, at least with regard to Morris and Smith, those most interested in an overseas post.

V

Meanwhile, debate on the terms of the peace treaty continued in Congress. After six months of reports, resolutions, counter resolutions, and roll calls, the fisheries were eliminated as a sine qua non for peace. The reduction took place by stages. First, the demand of free access to the fisheries was made contingent upon support from the allies; then the right was not to be demanded, but in no case given up; then the fisheries were to be a sine qua non for a treaty of commerce but not of peace; finally, they were made not an ultimatum for a commercial treaty, but in no case were they to be given up in a treaty of commerce. At long last, on August 14, it was agreed that the instructions to the peace commissioner (not yet appointed) should include the following provision:

Although it is of the utmost importance to the peace and Commerce of the
United States that Canada and Nova Scotia should be ceded, and more particularly
that their common right to the Fisheries should be guarantied to them, yet a desire of terminating the war hath induced us not to make the acquisition of these
objects an ultimatum on the present occasion[45].

With regard to the negotiation of a treaty of commerce, the commissioners,
also not yet appointed, were instructed that the right of fishing was not to be
given up, that it was essential to the welfare of the United States that they have
free and undisturbed access to the fishing banks of the North Atlantic, and that
molestation of that right would constitute a breach of the peace and a common
cause of the Union. The faith of the Congress was pledged to the states: without their unanimous consent no treaty of commerce nor any trade could be
carried on with Britain unless she explicitly stipulated she would not molest or
disturb Americans in the Newfoundland banks and other fisheries 3 leagues or
more off the shores of British possessions[46].

Navigation rights on the Mississippi had been eliminated from the peace
terms with little difficulty in March, but during September news arrived that
Spain was entering the war. In these new circumstances, Congress agreed that
navigation rights on the Mississippi had to be agreed upon in return for an
American guarantee of Spain's acquiring the Floridas[47]. This condition was
the product of a week and a half's debate in Congress over what the United
States should demand from Spain in return for a treaty of alliance and commerce with her. At one point Huntington of Connecticut and Smith of Virginia
proposed that the United States guarantee Spain's possession of the Floridas
on the condition that the United States received both free navigation of the
Mississippi and the right of deposit at a free port or ports, as well as a subsidy.
McKean of Delaware moved that the ports and subsidy provisions be eliminated, and this motion passed without a roll call. Meriwether Smith then
moved that a free port or ports be demanded, but in the vote that followed
Virginia and North Carolina found little support. Peabody of New Hampshire,
Jay and Lewis of New York, and Atlee and Muhlenberg of Pennsylvania delivered the only votes in favor of Smith's proposition—not enough to carry
the issue. Thus, for the second time, the navigation demand was reduced, and
the issue was removed from discussion even more effectively than the matter
of the fisheries.

Although the two issues of the fisheries and navigation rights were no
longer part of the peace terms to be presented to Great Britain and the allies
of the United States, they, along with other objectives, were left to the discretion and abilities of the men to be chosen peace commissioner and minister to
Spain. Consequently, attention focused increasingly on the elections. (Indeed,
Jay's endorsement of the free ports resolution quite probably was a move to
cultivate support for his candidacy for one of the posts.)

The Easterners were in perfect agreement about candidates for the two posts. They desperately wanted flinty and aggressive John Adams as peace commissioner, and, with slightly less enthusiasm, they were committed to Arthur Lee for the Spanish post, assuming he would make a "staunch negotiator." Since Congress had agreed that the vote of seven states would be necessary for important appointments, the Eastern party was in a good position to obstruct an anti-Eastern commissioner, though the specific appointment of Adams was another matter. Yet the concessions the Easterners had made on the fisheries issue in the exhaustive debates of the spring and summer had given them a heavy lien on the post. Since Franklin was a Middle states man, the ever-present ideal of sectional balance could be used to enhance Adams's claim. Gérard had left little doubt but that Arthur Lee was unacceptable to the French, but to appoint Lee to Spain could be defended as removing him from France. Even if this stratagem should fail, the Eastern faction could maintain that the pro-French Franklin should be balanced by the more independent Lee. While these ideas probably were assumptions held rather than arguments made, the case for Lee was enhanced by his having been appointed commissioner to Spain once before—in a different context, of course. While the Eastern faction probably realized they could not muster seven states' votes for Lee, they hoped that Lee's previous appointment could be deemed sufficiently broad to give him the new responsibility under it and so entrust him with the procurement of a treaty of alliance with Spain. The Middle-Southern opposition also had a candidate for the peace commissioner slot: John Jay, whom Gérard had suggested for that post in a message to Vergennes as early as February[48].

Again, as in the preceding debates over peace terms and the report of the committee of thirteen, the tactics of faction were amply evident and tortuously complex. It appears from the cryptic comments of Laurens, Lovell, Gérard, and the Journals (1) that the Lee partisans attempted unsuccessfully to confirm his commission to Spain on either Thursday the twenty-third or Friday the twenty-fourth of September[49]; (2) that with the designation of an envoy to Spain still unsettled, nominations were taken for the peace commissioner on Saturday the twenty-fifth (not only were Adams and Jay nominated, but also Franklin and Lee); (3) that Jay ruled Franklin's name out of order as a sole peace commissioner and objected to him as a joint commissioner with Adams[50]; (4) that Arthur Lee's name was put forth frequently in debate, apparently by James Lovell, as a proper man for the commission[51]; (5) that John Mathews of South Carolina and Peabody of New Hampshire, with the support of Elbridge Gerry, tried unsuccessfully to disqualify any man (including Jay) who had sat in Congress during the previous nine months from accepting a salaried appointment from Congress[52]; (6) that on the same day (the twenty-fifth) Adams was nominated by Laurens and Jay by Meriwether Smith, without result; (7) that two ballots were taken on Sunday, September 26, with Adams receiving six votes to Jay's five—again not a decisive result; (8) that on the same day Lee lost his prior claim to the Spanish post through a resolution to appoint a minister plenipotentiary rather than a commissioner to treat with Spain[53]; (9) that also on the twenty-sixth nominations were taken for the post of Minister to Spain, Lee's name being offered by Laurens, Adams's by Paca, and Jay's by Mercer of Virginia[54]; and (10) that finally Jay was elected Minister to Spain (his own vote being necessary) and Adams was named peace commissioner on September 27[55].

Some of the factional calculations which terminated this lengthy controversy over foreign policy are perfectly clear; other aspects of the maneuvering are shrouded indeed. It is certain that the Middle-Southern coalition and Gérard were willing to accept Adams in one of the posts as long as Jay also was included and Lee eliminated. It is almost as certain that the coalition wanted Jay as peace commissioner and Adams as minister to Spain, since Smith nominated Jay for peace commissioner on September 25, and Adams's name was placed in nomination for the Spanish post by Paca on the twenty-sixth[56]. Gérard told Vergennes that he would have preferred the elections reversed[57]. The Deane inner faction that had cooperated with Gérard and voted for the recall of Franklin was still mapping policy with the French emissary. Of the six delegates who originally composed that group, three were present in Congress during the deliberations of late September: Griffin, Paca, and Smith. It was Smith who nominated Jay for Paris and Paca who nominated Adams for Madrid. And it was Smith seconded by Paca who offered the resolution to change the Spanish slot from commissioner to minister plenipotentiary—the crucial ploy in the elimination of Lee. It is not entirely certain whether this Deane core was involved in the final settlement giving Adams the post of peace commissioner and Jay the post of Minister to Spain. Lovell contended that a compromise definitely took place, asserting that the final elections were the result of an "accommodation scheme . . . proposed in Whispers early in the Morning . . ."[58]. Jay was nominated for the Spanish post, after Laurens had nominated Adams, by James Mercer of Virginia. Mercer had arrived in Philadelphia only on September 9, so it is unlikely that he was running an independent course on such an important issue. Probably Smith and Paca persuaded Mercer to put up Jay, and then they voted for him in the roll call. The election of Adams was counted unanimous; the only dissent came when John Dickinson voted for Franklin (whose name wasn't even in nomination at that point). Dickinson was still smarting from Adams's publicized characterization of him as a "piddling Genius."

Doubtless the majority of the Eastern party was so keen on having John Adams in the peace commissioner's position that they were willing to sacrifice Lee. James Lovell and a few other extreme partisans of Lee refused the compromise, however; he, Peabody, Marchant, Laurens, and some of the Pennsylvania delegates voted against Jay[59]. Moreover, Lovell or some other

Lee advocate actually nominated Lee for peace commissioner, despite the preference for Adams in the Eastern party.

The struggle over foreign appointments did not come to an end until October 21, when Henry Laurens was elected a commissioner to negotiate a loan and a treaty of amity and commerce with Holland. Laurens's appointment fulfilled the requirements of sectional representation and factional equipoise, but even so, it was not accomplished without some partisan stress. Some delegates advocated that John Adams, who was not yet actively involved in peace negotiations, be given the assignment. Gouverneur Morris, back in Congress until the expiration of his unrenewed term, attempted to make the commission so disagreeable that Laurens would not accept it. Nathaniel Peabody corroborated the suspicion that Morris wanted the commission himself[60]. In the actual balloting, Laurens received the votes of all the states except Connecticut, New York, and Maryland. At first sight, it seems anomalous that the Southern faction should endorse a man who was regarded almost in the same light as Richard Henry Lee. Possibly, though, Laurens's election was a secondary matter in the general factional settlement of September. At one crucial point Laurens wavered in his support of Lee; he voted with the Deane group to substitute a minister plenipotentiary for a commissioner to Spain, knowing full well that this would eliminate Lee. He also opposed the motion by his fellow delegate Mathews to prevent members of Congress from serving in remunerative posts under congressional appointment—a rule that would have excluded Jay as well as himself. Thus, despite Laurens's vocal defense of Lee, and even his nomination of Lee for the post of Minister to Spain, it is plausible that the South Carolinian was cultivating Southern support for the impending election of the commissioner to Holland. The compromise that removed Lee and put Jay in his place may have involved Laurens as well as Adams.

VI

The great debate over foreign policy and appointments left deep wounds. Gérard's tampering with congressional business reinforced all the Easterners' parochial distrusts of the traditional enemy, Catholic and monarchical. Even before the alliance with France was signed, Samuel Adams's correspondence, both that received and that sent, reflected muted suspicions. Samuel Mather, the descendant of New England's most illustrious Puritan family, warned Adams: "The Benevolence, generous Benevolence, tendered from France, must needs be as acceptable as it was Seasonable. But you know, my honoured Friend, that, as Kings govern Kingdoms, Interest governs Kings." Sam Adams needed no such warning. Even before he received Mather's letter, he wrote a letter of his own (he may never have sent it) to James Warren stressing that

America must depend only on herself and that the politics of Europe rested to such a degree on "Whims and Refinements" that it would be perilous for the United States to rely upon France or other European states. "When it suits the Interest of foreign Powers, they will aid us substantially. That some of them will soon find it their interest to aid us I can hardly doubt, but there seems not to be virtue enough left in the world, from generous and disinterested Motives to interpose in Support of the common Rights of Mankind"[*61*]. Such pious and fearful attitudes were endemic in the Eastern party.

It is thus readily understandable that James Lovell should have urged in August 1779 to inform *"good Men"* in Boston what had caused the delay in formulating America's peace demands: "that France and Spain indeed seemed earnest to know *our* ultimata, especially in points which were nearly allied to their Interests—Florida and Newfoundland." Indeed, Lovell was on record as favoring writing the treaty of peace "with the Bayonett" rather than the subtler means of diplomacy[*62*]. The Eastern resentment against Gérard was more pointed still. Richard Henry Lee complained at one point that the Deane party was receiving "prodigious aid . . . from the whispers of G—d," and that "a doctrine quite new in the history of politics is broached now, which is, that it becomes the dignity, and consists with the interests of Sovereign powers to consult foreign Courts, and less than that, foreign Ministers. . . . And this altho such resident Minister shall clearly and unequivocally engage in faction, and party doings . . ."[*63*].

When France entered the Revolution the specter of Old World contamination arose once again for the Old Radicals who had long maintained that America must disengage herself from corrupt Britain in order to recapture her New World innocence. The fear that the Revolution was being infected by an interested alliance between Gérard and the Deane partisans lay behind Lovell's indictment of the "Lickspittles of the Plenipotentiary." Similarly, Nathaniel Peabody saw in the foreign policy dispute many "melancolly Considerations." Regarding the fate of Arthur Lee, Peabody remarked that Congress "adjudged that no Patriotic efforts in the Cause of the Country [—] no Acts of Political or religious Virtue could be Esteemed Meritorious"—Lee, the "Honest man & faithful Servant," was utterly destroyed. But Jay, "the most Perfidious of the whole Race of Jesuits whose Sole View had been to divide the Councils of america" and "Bannish a Spirit of republicanism from his land to introduce and establish a general aristocracy or perhaps the Domination of a British Tyrant, & who had wholly joined himself to Idols," was elected, and thus was "Taken into the Bosom of this beautiful, once Chast, Virgin america there like a vulture to prey without control upon her vitals"[*64*].

The partisan struggles over foreign policy and appointments abroad illustrate the intricate overlay of factionalism and the politics of legislative parties that characterized much of the history of the Continental Congress.

Easterners were committed to Arthur Lee because of the Adams-Lee connection, a factional tie, and also because they believed that Lee would serve the Eastern interest better than the candidates for the post of Minister to Spain from the Southern party. The supporters of Deane sometimes paid more attention to the suggestions of Gérard than to the best interests of their constituencies. This was understandable, for just as the alliance with France gave added stature to the Revolutionary cause, so did the presence of the French minister elevate the stage on which the Congress deliberated—and to have been a confidant of such a personage was exhilarating for some. A few members of the Southern interest appear to have attached themselves to Gérard in the hope of gaining preferment for a foreign mission. Peabody's condemnation of Jay for having "wholly joined himself to idols," although extreme, was partially true. It was a charge that could have been directed with more accuracy toward Gouverneur Morris and Meriwether Smith, both of whom were engaged in classical factional politics. But then, Henry Laurens, too, engaged in factional politics and possibly worked to secure a foreign post. The strivings for place and preferment were not confined to the circle of Congressmen who surrounded the French minister.

Jay understood the depth of resentment his election occasioned among the Lee partisans. He hastened to assure Lovell that he expected the New Englander's allegiance only while he continued "to do honestly"[65]. Jay's rapid estrangement from Gérard during the lengthy trip to Europe they undertook together, as well as his unexpectedly aggressive defense of American interests in Madrid, could have been a direct consequence of his understanding the situation.

If partisan resentments helped prod Jay into an independent course of diplomacy, the resolution of the Lee-Deane imbroglio also terminated the Adams-Lee alliance as an effective force in Congress. In the end there had been too many defections from the Eastern bloc over the question of Lee's continuance for the faction to continue to operate unimpaired. Indeed, when Lee's fate hung in the balance for the second and final time, neither Sam Adams nor Richard Henry Lee was on hand to rally the faithful. The battle over the fisheries was led by Elbridge Gerry, who was a deviant on the Lee-Deane issue. Nor did the Eastern party muster sufficient force to save free navigation on the Mississippi. In the last analysis, the ideological cement of the Old Radical Massachusetts-Virginia axis could hold only with the additional adhesion of sectional self-interest. Sadly, the failure of the Old Radicals had more important repercussions than its effect on the members themselves: the inability of the Eastern party to carry the fishery and Mississippi objectives worked great damage. That the two issues were set up in debate as matters of national integrity, and even national survival, merely made the failure more catastrophic.

Arthur Lee returned to America and visited Boston, where he was embraced by the Eastern Old Radicals, and in 1782 he began a term as a Virginia delegate in Congress. In 1783, he did join a small New England–Southern coalition composed of himself and Theodorick Bland from Virginia and David Howell and William Ellery from Rhode Island. The coalition was as short-lived as it was ineffective. Like the old Adams-Lee alliance, this group was stridently opposed to Robert Morris's influence, but unlike the old faction, the members of this coalition were unremittingly parochial, and, predictably, they foundered on the issue of western lands. Perhaps the "neo-radicals" of 1783 were nothing more than a logical extrapolation of the Old Radicals of 1776. Certainly, the events of 1778–1779 transformed the Revolution for those in Congress who had been most responsible for its inception.

Notes

1 Henri Doniol, *Histoire de la Participation de la France à l'Etablissement des Etats Unis d'Amerique* (5 vols.; Paris, 1886–1892), I, 133–134, 159.

2 Deane comments on his fortune at having used this transaction to good effect in a letter to his wife (Mrs. Elizabeth Saltonstall Deane), in Charles Isham (ed.), *Deane Papers,* (5 vols.; New-York Historical Society *Collections,* XIX–XXIII [New York, 1887–1891]), I, 121–122.

3 Some of the aspects of mercantile relationships affecting congressional factionalism are discussed in the following chapter.

4 Julian Boyd, "Silas Deane: Death by a Kindly Teacher of Treason?" *WMQ,* ser. 3, XVI (1959), 324. It is Boyd's intriguing suggestion that Bancroft may have poisoned Deane in order to save himself from exposure.

5 Arthur Lee to Silas Deane, July 28, 1776, Auckland MSS, in B. F. Stevens (ed.), *Facsimiles of Manuscripts in European Archives Relating to America, 1773–1783* (26 vols.; London, 1889–1895), no. 467. Lee also asserted, "I have good reason to fear that Joseph Reed in Philadelphia is a Dangerous man" *(ibid.).* This is a strange comment, considering Reed's early admiration for Lee and Reed's part in bringing Lee to Samuel Adams's attention. Lee's suspicions of Reed may have arisen from the latter's correspondence with Dartmouth suggesting modes of reconciliation between Britain and the colonies at the same time the radicals were pressing for independence. Reed was not the only American proposing reconciliation to Dartmouth at that time, it might be noted. Cyrus Griffin, also a member of Congress, presented a plan of reconciliation in December of 1775. Griffin to Dartmouth, Dec. 30, 1775, *Virginia Magazine of History and Biography,* XIX (1911), 417. Boyd points out that Deane made no mention of Lee's charges to Congress on the ground that there was no proof but that he did report George

Mercer to Gérard and Hugh Williamson to Congress as both being untrustworthy, on unsupported information from Bancroft. Actually, Lee did mention Mercer in his letter of the 28th. Boyd does not mention this letter but makes reference instead to a letter of July 20, which has not been preserved. Inasmuch as the information obtained from other sources as in the letter of the 20th seems to be exactly that which is in the letter of the 28th, it is possible that the date on the undiscovered letter is incorrect. If this is so, then Boyd's supposition that Deane was warned as well against Bancroft by Lee is unfounded, for Bancroft's name does not appear in the letter.

6 Boyd, "Silas Deane," pp. 328–329.

7 Samuel Flagg Bemis, *The Diplomacy of the American Revolution* (New York, 1935; 1957 ed., Bloomington, Ind.), p. 114n.

8 Arthur Lee to Samuel Adams, Feb. 16, 1778, Samuel Adams Papers, NYPL.

9 Benjamin Franklin to Arthur Lee, Apr. 3, 1778, in Albert H. Smith (ed.), *The Writings of Benjamin Franklin* (10 vols.; New York, 1905–1907), VII, 132.

10 Carl Van Doren, *Benjamin Franklin* (New York, 1938; Compass Books ed., 1964), pp. 583–584; E. James Ferguson, "Business, Government, and Congressional Investigation in the Revolution," *WMQ*, ser. 3, XVI (July 1959), 307; Thomas Abernethy, "Commercial Activities of Silas Deane in France," *AHR*, XXXIX (April 1934), 477–485.

11 *JCC*, XII, 908.

12 "To the Free and Virtuous Citizens of America," *Pennsylvania Evening Post*, Dec. 11, 1778. Deane used his own name under this address, which appeared in other newspapers as well.

13 Samuel Adams to Samuel Cooper, Jan. 3, 1779, in Harry A. Cushing (ed.) *The Writings of Samuel Adams* (4 vols.; New York, 1904–1908), IV, 112.

14 Francis Lightfoot Lee to Arthur Lee, Dec. 10 and 15, *LMCC*, III, 530, 536; Samuel Adams to James Warren, Jan. 6, 1779, in Cushing (ed.), *Writings*, IV, 115.

15 Arthur Lee to Samuel Adams, Mar. 6, 1779, Samuel Adams Papers, NYPL; Richard Henry Lee to Arthur Lee, May 23, 1779, *LMCC*, IV, 227.

16 Samuel Adams to James Warren, Feb. 12, 1779; to James Winthrop, Dec. 21, 1778, in Cushing (ed.), *Writings*, IV, 123–124, 104; James Warren to Samuel Adams, Feb. 28, 1779, Samuel Adams Papers, NYPL.

17 Cyrus Griffin to Thomas Jefferson, Oct. 6, 1778, *LMCC*, III, 445

18 Ibid.

19 Richard Henry Lee to Arthur Lee, Sept. 16, 1778, ibid., III, 414.

20 Francis Lightfoot Lee to Arthur Lee, Dec. 10, 1778, ibid., 530; Samuel Adams to James Warren, July 20, 1778, in Cushing (ed.), *Writings*, IV, 48; James Warren to Samuel Adams, Feb. 28, 1779, Samuel Adams Papers, NYPL. Samuel Cooper, the

Congregational divine and close friend of Samuel Adams, may have been responsible for some of the anti-Lee sentiment in Massachusetts. Cooper was a strong proponent of the French interest and wrote a number of pieces in Boston newspapers favoring the alliance at the behest of Gérard. For a good treatment of propaganda favoring the French see William C. Stinchcombe, *The American Revolution and the French Alliance* (Syracuse, 1967), chap. IX.

21 For Gérard's statements to Burke, Paca, and Drayton, see *LMCC,* IV, 168–170, 167n, 177–178, 177n.

22 Vergennes to Gérard, Apr. 22, 1778, in John J. Meng (ed.), *Despatches and Instructions of Conrad Alexandre Gerard* (Baltimore, 1939), pp. 136–137.

23 "Considerations upon the Necessity of France Declaring at Once for the American Colonies, Even without the Concurrance of Spain," Jan. 13, 1778, quoted in Edward S. Corwin, *French Policy and the American Alliance of 1778* (Princeton, 1916), pp. 400–401. The document was unsigned, but it contained expressions from earlier papers by Vergennes.

24 Richard Henry Lee, *Life of Arthur Lee* (2 vols.; Boston, 1829), II, 378–379, 383.

25 Gérard's address was on Feb. 15, 1779 (*JCC,* XIII, 185–186); William Henry Drayton's report of the address is in *LMCC,* IV, 69–71. See also Gérard to Vergennes, Feb. 17, 1779, in Meng (ed.), *Despatches,* pp. 525–529.

26 *JCC,* XIII, 241–242.

27 James Lovell to Horatio Gates, Mar. 1, 1779, *LMCC,* IV, 84.

28 *JCC,* XIII, 241–242.

29 Ibid., XIV, 581; Gérard to Vergennes, May 21, 1779, in Meng (ed.), *Despatches,* p. 657.

30 *JCC,* XIII, 369–370. Samuel Adams was not present that day.

31 Ibid., 364, 487.

32 The anti-Lee force would subsequently employ the distinction when the choice of a plenipotentiary for the Spanish court was made.

33 Gérard reported to Vergennes that a motion to include Franklin was first voted down but then put back in discussion. Gérard to Vergennes, May 4, 1779, in Meng (ed.), *Despatches,* pp. 615–616. James Lovell wrote to John Adams that he opposed the motion to name Franklin, and it is evident from the voting scale (see Table 10) that Lovell's vote was a key to the position of the group favoring Lee. James Lovell to John Adams, June 13, 1779, *LMCC,* IV, 262.

34 John Fell, Diary, *LMCC,* IV, 164, *JCC,* XIII, 487.

35 See Laurens's note, June 11, 1779, *LMCC,* IV, 258.

36 H. J. Henderson, "Congressional Factionalism and the Attempt to Recall Benjamin Franklin," *WMQ,* ser. 3, XXVIII (April 1970), 259–263.

37 See Jay to George Clinton, Aug. 27, 1777, *LMCC,* IV, 390. In this letter Jay refers to efforts in New York to injure Morris in the eyes of his constituents. The effect was evident in the election of October 1, when Morris was tied with Ezra L'Hommedieu for a poor fifth in the election of five delegates by the New York Assembly. In a subsequent run-off, Morris lost. *Journal of the Assembly of the State of New York* (Fish-Kill, 1779), p. 45. Morris's loss of support in the New York Assembly was precipitous. In 1778 he won 32 of a possible 40 votes; in 1779, 23 of 42 votes; and in 1780, 3 of 39 votes.

38 Meriwether Smith to Thomas Jefferson, June 25, 1779, *LMCC,* IV, 286.

39 John Jay to Robert R. Livingston and Gouverneur Morris, Sept. 29, 1779, ibid., 460.

40 Nathaniel Peabody to William Whipple, Nov. 1, 1779, Peabody Papers, NHHS.

41 James Lovell to Richard Henry Lee, Oct. 26, 1779, *LMCC,* IV, 498.

42 Gérard to Vergennes, July 19, 1778, in Meng (ed.), *Despatches,* p. 175.

43 If Morris did not expect to be offered the Paris post, he may have calculated that John Adams would fill the vacancy, and this would open the pending mission to Holland for which Adams was intended and which Laurens would later fill. If Morris wanted any of the major posts, including the Spanish mission, Franklin's removal was necessary. Clearly, the necessity of balancing the sections would allow no more than two representatives from the Middle states in the four missions. John Jay was a certain candidate for one of the slots. Gérard, whose opinions in this matter carried great weight with the Southern party, had already advocated Jay as peace commissioner.

44 H. J. Henderson, "Congressional Factionalism," 265–267.

45 *JCC,* XIV, 959–960.

46 Ibid., 960–961.

47 Ibid., XV, 1046–1047.

48 Gérard to Vergennes, Feb. 25, 1779, in Meng (ed.), *Despatches,* p. 542.

49 Gérard to Vergennes, Sept. 25, 1779, in ibid., p. 895.

50 Ibid.; James Lovell to John Adams, Sept. 27, 1779, *LMCC,* IV, 446.

51 John Fell, Diary, Sept. 25, ibid., 438–439; James Lovell to John Adams, Sept. 27, 1779, ibid., 446.

52 *JCC,* XV, 1105–1106.

53 Henry Laurens, "Notes of Proceedings," Sept. 25 and 26, 1779, *LMCC,* IV, 437.

54 Ibid., 438.

55 *JCC,* XV, 1113.

56 Laurens, "Notes of Proceedings," Sept. 25 and 26, 1779, *LMCC,* IV, 437–438.

57 Gérard to Vergennes, Sept. 26, 1779, in Meng (ed.), *Despatches,* p. 896.

58 James Lovell to John Adams, Sept. 27, 1779, *LMCC,* IV, 447.

59 Laurens, "Notes of Proceedings," Sept. 26, 1779, ibid., 438. There was no recorded roll call on this vote, merely a summary of the vote by states in Laurens's notes. Nevertheless, the identity of those who voted against Jay can in most instances be inferred.

60 Nathaniel Peabody to William Whipple, Nov. 1, 1779, Peabody Papers, NHHS.

61 Samuel Mather to Samuel Adams, Apr. 22, 1777; Samuel Adams to James Warren, Apr. 17, 1777, Samuel Adams Papers, NYPL.

62 James Lovell to Samuel Adams, Aug. 12, 1779; Lovell to Horatio Gates, Apr. 19, 1779, *LMCC,* IV, 164, 363-364.

63 Richard Henry Lee to Francis Lightfoot Lee, Apr. 26, 1779, ibid., 179.

64 Peabody to Whipple, Nov. 1, 1779, Peabody Papers, NHHS. Peabody does not mention Jay by name, but there is no question about his identity. Peabody used some of the same terms as Lovell in describing this event. Lovell, in speaking of Lee's removal and Jay's election, used the phrase "the Sacredness of the Approbation or Disapprobation," while Peabody, in another portion of this letter, referred to "the Great & fundamental Doctrine of *Election & reprobation.*"

65 Lovell to John Adams, Sept. 28, 1779, *LMCC,* IV, 450.

9 Currency Finance and Corruption, 1776–1779

I T is unlikely that the Lee-Deane imbroglio would have been so convulsive had Deane not been accused of profiteering and fiscal mismanagement, for public finance, in its many manifestations, was a powerful source of controversy during the era of the Revolution. As historians have frequently noted, the policies of Robert Morris when he was Superintendent of Finance aroused heated debate. Possibly most historians, regardless of their sympathies, have assumed that the public debt was a decisive factor in the dispute over the sufficiency of the Articles of Confederation and in the movement toward the Constitution. The Continental debt, according to most accounts, helped to form a group of nationally minded men who wished to strengthen the Articles so that the central government could handle the debt more effectively. Thus Continental finance divided nationalists and their opponents who wished to preserve the powers of the states as they existed under the Articles. While there is much validity in this interpretation of the relationship between finance and partisanship during the 1780s, it does not adequately describe the controversies over finance during the early years of the Revolution. Dickinson's draft of the Articles did not even hint at the possibility of national taxation, and most congressional disputes over finance had to do either with sectional economic interest or with alleged mismanagement of public moneys. It was the administration of public finance rather than the philosophy behind it that had the greatest impact upon congressional politics.

Because the Congress lacked taxing authority, it decided very early to meet its financial obligations by issuing paper money and bonds that would be redeemed ultimately by the states. This decision to resort to currency finance rather than direct taxation was reached as early as the summer of 1775 when $2,000,000 in bills of credit were printed to pay the Continental army[1]. Paper money flotations were common in the colonies during the eighteenth century, so the delegates were not acting without precedent. There appears to have been no disagreement over this question, and in any event the Congress had neither the authority nor the inclination to levy direct taxes upon a population that had commissioned it to oppose imperial taxation. Likewise, Congress turned with little hesitation to the flotation of domestic loans under national auspices in the form of interest-bearing government bonds of large denomination called loan office certificates. The certificates initially carried an interest rate of 4 percent—an indication that the delegates expected that they would be widely accepted.

There was a difference, of course, between the currency finance employed by the Continental Congress and the previous colonial experience with paper money. The colonies had been able to retire money through taxation—and often did so quite successfully[2]—but the Congress had to rely upon the states for redemption of the Continental bills. It was difficult to set up rules for the apportionment of the debt among the states, and naturally each state thought itself unfairly treated when Congress established its annual schedule of contributions. For this reason, and because of real distress, the states never met their full quotas, and the value of the continental declined—gradually at first, and then precipitously. By late 1779, when well over $200,000,000 of bills had been issued, the continental was almost worthless. Loan office certificates also declined in value, but not so drastically because Congress did its best to make the interest payments on the certificates.

By the end of 1779 congressional finance was in such disarray that many delegates advocated granting taxing powers to Congress, but during the important debates over the structure of the Confederation during 1776 and 1777 that was not seriously considered. Most of the disputes over finance during the early Revolution—and there were many of them—involved the implementation of the original decision to use currency finance as delegates tried to reconcile critical national fiscal problems with the interests of their states.

Disagreements over finance between 1776 and 1779 reinforced the basic cleavage between the North and the South. Unlike the divisions over the Lee-Deane imbroglio and the definition of peace terms, however, conservatives from the Middle states often aligned with New England rather than the South. There were exceptions to the rule that usually had to do with populist legislation such as price regulation, or with factional matters such as charges of profiteering on the part of Deane and Morris. But on many basic decisions, such as the interest rate on loan office certificates, the delegates from all the Northern states found a common cause. Interestingly, the radicals of the Eastern party tended to follow what could be called a conservative course on fiscal policy; they favored the interests of the investing and commercial community rather than those of the yeomanry. There were good reasons for their position: they had commercial constituencies to protect, and because the war was located in the North at this time, a very large portion of the Continental moneys gravitated in that direction for the payment of troops and supplies. Thus radicals from Massachusetts were exceptionally concerned about the value of the continental and the earnings from loan office certificates.

In February of 1777 an effort was made to raise the interest rates on loan office certificates from 4 percent to 6 percent. Support for the measure, which passed on February 26, came predominantly from the North. All the states from New Hampshire to Pennsylvania voted in the affirmative, with the exception of Rhode Island; New York was unrepresented at the time but probably would have supported the measure. Ellery of Rhode Island opposed the increase because he thought it would result in a larger national debt, not because he opposed the basic idea of loan office certificates that would bring profit to investors who were able to buy government bonds in large denomination. He had previously urged Governor Cooke of Rhode Island to see that the Assembly encouraged the sale of certificates when they brought 4 percent in hopes that this would persuade Congress that the higher rate was unnecessary[3]. Virginia and Georgia voted in favor of the 6 percent figure, but this did not represent the true Southern position, for Richard Henry Lee had originally favored 4 percent, but was converted to the higher rate by his Eastern friend, John Adams; and Nathan Brownson, the sole Georgia delegate, was a Connecticut man who, according to Thomas Burke, always voted with the state of his birth and was of "no other use in the Congress"[4].

Opposition to the higher interest rate for certificates came largely from the Carolinas, whose delegates best reflected the Southern interest. William Hooper of North Carolina contended that most of the Continental securities would gravitate to the North—as indeed they did—and that favorable arrangements for investors would do nothing for the South[5]. Congress reexamined the interest rate in September of 1777, and an attempt was made to lower the rate from 6 percent to 5 percent. The Easterners again defended the higher figure almost to a man, and while there were four Southerners who supported them, two of the four were Richard Henry Lee and Henry Laurens, both of whom were sympathetic with the Eastern interest[6]. Because of the close connection between finance and the military effort (which affected the North more directly than the South at this time), Southerners who allied with the members of the Eastern party may have voted with them on financial issues as well as matters pertaining to the war.

The Eastern party did not achieve perfect unanimity on fiscal policy. At the same time that the interest rate was being reexamined, Congress attempted to buttress the value of loan office certificates by paying interest on them with money borrowed from France. This resolution, passed shortly before the alliance was concluded, helped to strengthen the certificates, but it also caused some delegates to fear that the United States might fall under French influence. John Adams and Henry Laurens favored taxation and economy rather than foreign loans, and when the issue came to a vote, the two delegates broke with the Easterners. Laurens was of the opinion that paying interest on loan office certificates with French livres would mortgage American soil to a "foreign Crafty power" and that "if we have not virtue enough to Save our Selves, easy access to the Treasury of France will only hasten our ruin." John Adams stressed that Americans should pay taxes to their states rather than borrow abroad, and he urged his wife Abigail to pay every tax, even if she had to sell his books and her cows to raise the money[7]. Laurens's suspicions were an early indication of the anti-French sentiment that later permeated the Eastern party when peace terms were hammered out in 1779, but in 1777 most Easterners did not share his fears.

Despite occasional disagreements, the New Englanders generally agreed on measures to uphold the value of bills and certificates—often in collaboration with Northern conservatives. This was true even in late 1778, when the Lee-Deane controversy was prompting sharp divisions between the Eastern and Southern parties. In December of 1778, for example, most Northerners agreed upon a complicated plan to reduce the number of Continental bills in circulation by converting them into loan office certificates. The Congress accomplished this design by invalidating over $40,000,000 in severely depreciated bills of credit that had been printed in May of 1777 and April of 1778 on the pretext that these two emissions had been extensively counterfeited. Hoping to convert the depreciated currency into more stable bonds, Congress offered holders of the bills the alternative of receiving either loan office certificates or new bills of credit in exchange for the old bills. The transfer had to be made by June 1, 1779. In the meantime, the bills to be exchanged could be used in payment of Continental obligations either to the national treasury or to the states[8].

The opposition to the recall and exchange of the 40 millions of continentals centered in North Carolina, although the South as a whole opposed the exchange against overwhelming support for the measure in the North. Thomas Burke voiced the most extreme opposition on both constitutional and pragmatic grounds. He contended that Congress could not unilaterally invalidate a currency which had been made legal tender by state legislation, for this implied an unwarranted national power to repeal state laws. For this reason he, his colleague Whitmill Hill, and Meriwether Smith of Virginia opposed even the initial resolution to recall the two issues. But Burke's major objection to the measure had to do with the welfare of North Carolina. He believed the people of his state would not have sufficient notice to bring in the old bills to the loan

TABLE 11

Ratios of Support for Transfer of Bills of Credit, December 1778

New England		Middle States		South	
N.H.	12/0	N.Y.	11/7	Md.	4/8
Mass.	17/1	N.J.	12/0	Va.	3/6
R.I.	12/0	Pa.	8/0	N.C.	0/12
Conn.	18/0	Del.	6/0	S.C.	14/4
Total	59/1	Total	37/7	Ga.	0/3
				Total	21/33

NOTES:
The ratios show the total individual votes cast in the six roll calls by the delegates from each state expressed in terms of support over opposition. The delegates were Whipple and Frost, N.H.; Adams, S., Gerry, and Holten, Mass.; Collins and Ellery, R.I.; Dyer, Ellsworth, and Root, Conn.; Duane, Jay, Lewis, and Morris, G., N.Y.; Fell and Witherspoon, N.J.; Roberdeau and Searle, Pa.; McKean, Del.; Carmichael and Henry, Md.; Lee, F. L., and Smith, M., Va.; Burke and Hill, N.C.; Drayton, Hutson, and Laurens, S.C.; Langworthy, Ga. The votes are recorded in *JCC,* XII, 1232-1233, 1236-1238.

office before the June 1 deadline, and even if they did, the conversion of a depreciated currency into a 6-percent loan would penalize those Southern states where money was scarce, while at the same time rewarding the commercial states of the North where most of the continentals were held[9].

As can be seen from the summary of votes in Table 11, New England in particular and the North in general gave overwhelming support to the six roll calls relating to the exchange of the bills of credit. Except for South Carolina, the South was almost as uniformly opposed. The South Carolinians did not share the reservations of their fellow Southerners—probably because of the preponderant influence of the city of Charleston in the South Carolina delegation. All three of the South Carolinians who were in Congress at this time—William Henry Drayton, Henry Laurens, and Richard Hutson—were from that city, as were no less than twenty-six of the thirty delegates South Carolina sent to the Continental Congress between 1774 and 1789. It is, therefore, not surprising that South Carolina joined the North on many matters of public finance during the Confederation era, just as South Carolina would later join Northern Federalists in support of Hamilton's fiscal program. But just as remarkable as the posture of South Carolina was the fact that it was entirely possible for Samuel Adams and James Duane to see eye to eye on matters of currency finance.

TABLE 12

State Delegation Agreements by Section, on Roll Calls Dealing with Finance, 1777–1779 (54 roll calls)

	New England	Middle	South
New England	82%		
Middle States	67%	76%	
South	38%	52%	66%

The accord reached by the Northern delegations on the transfer of the bills of credit was simply symptomatic of a larger commonalty of interest on financial questions between 1777 and 1779. Table 12 summarizes the way state delegations (not individual delegates) cast their votes on fifty-four roll calls dealing with finance during these years. Not only did the New England states have a remarkably higher level of agreement with the Middle states than with the Southern delegations; they even had a level of agreement slightly higher than the Southern delegations did among themselves (67 percent as opposed to 66 percent). One further statistic might be added to those on the table: the North as a whole (New England and the Middle states combined) had a regional level of agreement of 71 percent on the fifty-four roll calls—higher than the 66 percent agreement within the Southern states—and as a section it had a ratio of only 44 percent agreement with the South.

The evidence indicates that fiscal policy during the early years of the Revolution both accentuated and clouded the partisan politics of the Continental Congress. The basic division between the North and the South was sharpened by decisions related to currency finance, but Easterners and conservatives from the Middle states who differed on so many other issues were often able to agree on this one. Before 1780 hostilities were located largely in the North, causing a flow of Continental paper into that region, and the Eastern party was just as attentive to the interests of a substantial investing community as its opponents from New York and Pennsylvania were.

II

The harmony between the Eastern party and the conservatives from the Middle states on the basic decisions of currency finance did not extend to the management of all economic problems during the early war years. There were disagreements over speculation, the use of public office for private gain, appointments to the Commissary and Quartermaster Departments, the establishment of price controls, and other issues related to the use of public funds. Some of these controversies in Congress were the product of relatively uncomplicated sectional competition for the plums of wartime procurement; others had ideological implications. Sometimes disagreements over economic matters were limited in scope and consequence, but at other times they had disturbingly broad ramifications that touched the diplomacy of the French alliance, the constitutional relationship between Congress and the states, and even the character of the Revolution.

Appointments to the major commands in supply for the Continental army, for example, had a markedly sectional cast that revealed the Northern focus of hostilities and the Eastern ascendancy in Congress. The first commissary general appointed by Congress was Joseph Trumbull, the son of Governor Jonathan Trumbull of Connecticut and the brother-in-law of the Connecticut delegate William Williams. Joseph Trumbull's elder brother, Jonathan (the younger), was paymaster general of the army in the Northern Department—that is, in the New York theater of operations. Thomas Mifflin of Pennsylvania, the first quartermaster general, also was connected with the Eastern interest in Congress during the early years of the Revolution.

The Trumbulls and Mifflin did not escape criticism for their management of supply. Considering their inexperience and the novelty of many of the problems they encountered, such criticism was predictable. All three resigned between 1777 and 1778. But it is notable that after Joseph Trumbull died in 1778 at the early age of forty-one, the voting on the compensations to be granted to his estate closely resembled the general partisan configuration[10].

The New England–Pennsylvania connection continued after the resignations of the Trumbulls and Mifflin. Mifflin was appointed to the newly formed Board of War, and Jonathan Trumbull was elected the first comptroller of the treasury. Mifflin's replacement as quartermaster general was General Nathanael Greene of Rhode Island. Greene was recommended by a congressional committee under the chairmanship of Joseph Reed of Pennsylvania that had been appointed to investigate the Quartermaster and Commissary Departments. Greene accepted the post only on the condition that his recommendations for appointments to two new posts of assistant quartermasters general that had been advocated by the committee and legislated by Congress be accepted. It is more than coincidental that Greene's choices for the two offices were two Philadelphia merchants—Charles Pettit to handle accounts and John Cox to manage purchases. Both were close friends of Reed. Pettit, in fact, was Reed's brother-in-law, his associate in some land speculations, and a former business partner of Reed's father, Andrew Reed. Since Greene knew Pettit at this time only by reputation, Reed's role in the appointment must have been influential[11]. Yet another indication of the weight of the Eastern interest in Congress was the appointment of the profit-minded Connecticut merchant Jeremiah

Wadsworth to succeed Trumbull as commissary general. These appointments cannot be regarded simply as partisan victories, for the allowances voted for Wadsworth were not seriously challenged. Only Nathaniel Scudder of New Jersey, Jonathan B. Smith of Pennsylvania, and Burke opposed the commissions arranged for Wadsworth upon the recommendation of a predominantly Eastern committee[*12*]. Wadsworth and Greene, unlike Gates, had little involvement with the broader concerns of the Eastern party. (Indeed, they formed a partnership with Simeon Deane, the brother of Silas Deane.) But all the appointments illustrated the power of the Eastern party, and some of them—particularly those from Pennsylvania—had partisan overtones.

Partisan politics during this period were fueled less by sectional squabbles over congressional appointments than by strong prejudices against profiteering and by sharp suspicions of men who mixed private business with their public offices. This was somewhat anomalous, since wartime profiteering, no less than currency finance, was a common practice in the eighteenth century. Indeed, many colonial fortunes were built upon trade and speculation, which during the wars with France was at best unpatriotic and at worst completely illicit. Further, given the relatively undeveloped structure of business and government at that time, a fusion of public and private business was actually necessary. Congress had to use the services of established merchant capitalists such as Trumbull, Wadsworth, and Morris in order to supply its army. The ready-made mercantile connections of these men were indispensable in the absence of a bureaucratized procurement system. Members of Congress themselves sometimes became involved in governmental commercial transactions, either while holding office or after a term in Congress. Wadsworth, Pettit, and Mifflin were delegates either before or after holding positions in the Quartermaster and Commissary Departments, while Joseph Trumbull was connected with Congress through his brother-in-law, William Williams, and also as an alternate for Roger Sherman. John Langdon, William Duer, Silas Deane, James Lovell, and many other delegates held positions as shipbuilders, commercial agents, army contractors, or collectors of revenue after terms in Congress. Robert Morris, of course, was at once chairman of the Secret Committee of Commerce and a partner in the firm of Willing and Morris, which handled almost a fourth of the committee's disbursements[*13*].

But profit taking in the Revolution, particularly when connected with public business, stimulated more criticism than had occurred during the earlier colonial wars. This happened not so much because American colonials had less commitment to Great Britain during the intercolonial wars than American Revolutionaries had to the struggle for independence, though this was very probably true, but because the Revolution was in part a civil war—a fact which prompted Patriots to stand guard against a hidden Loyalist menace. Because the Revolution was a people's revolution, its success seemed dependent upon what

Patriots liked to call public virtue. The plea for austerity during the nonimportation movements was an early expression of this dependence, and the legislative proscriptions against engrossing and monopolizing during the war continued to emphasize the need for public sacrifices and to warn of the danger of internal subversion. The public response was encouraging, but incomplete. As early as December of 1776 an anonymous writer from Worcester, Massachusetts, complained that "a great number of forestallers and regraters have infested the country, and are the plagues and pests of society"[*14*]. The Pennsylvania Legislature contended that rising prices were due to "the practices and combinations of evil and designing men . . . ," while the Continental Congress proclaimed that depreciation of the currency could be traced to a failure of morality, to the "shameful avidity of too many of our professional friends," as well as to "the arts of our open and secret enemies . . ."[*15*]. The numerous attempts to enforce price controls upon commodities and wages demonstrate that in many instances Patriots were inclined to legislate against violations of revolutionary morality. Almost every price control law contained a preamble condemning the "avaritious conduct" of the public[*16*]. The pamphlet literature of the Revolution is likewise studded with assertions, such as those of "A Jersey Farmer," who contended that "the depreciation of our paper money . . . *proceeds in the first place from a want of virtue* or patriotism. . . ." The Jersey Farmer went on to advocate legislation on both the provincial and national levels to put a stop to the "monstrous extortion now prevailing . . ."[*17*].

Many were disturbed by the social and economic flux accompanying the Revolution. "A True Patriot," commenting in the *New Jersey Gazette* upon "malignant disorders in the body politic," deplored "the unequal division of property in the space of so short a time."

> Thousands of the most honest and respectable citizens of America, who obtained their possessions by the hard industry, continued sobriety and economy of themselves or their virtuous ancestors, must now behold many men, whom they looked upon in the commencement of these troubles (if I may be permitted to use the language of the most patient of men), as such *whose fathers they would have disdained to have set with the dogs of their flock,* raised to immense wealth, or at least to carry the appearance of a haughty, supercilious and luxurious spendthrift; while they much look upon their estates as devoted to enrich such, or mortgaged to support their extravagance[*18*].

In a series of seven essays printed in the New Jersey and Pennsylvania newspapers during the spring of 1779, "A True Patriot" feared that the Revolution suffered from a malignancy. He deplored the failure of the states to match the exertions of the thirteen colonies when Boston was under attack in 1775; he saw libertinism and Epicureanism in the disregard of congressional fast day proclamations, in the profanation of the Sabbath, and in the "balls, assemblies, extravagant dress and unaccountable fashions." The "efficient cause" of such general calamities was the depreciation of paper money. "A True Patriot" was confident that the generality of farmers and mechanics behaved honestly, but they were being victimized by the quartermasters, commissaries, and their deputies who were the worst of "the harpies which have preyed upon our vitals . . ."[*19*]. By the spring of 1779, public sentiment was so inflamed against merchants, particularly those connected with public procurements, that Quartermaster General Nathanael Greene urged Commissary General Jeremiah Wadsworth that they and Simeon Deane should keep a projected business partnership completely quiet, "for however just and upright our conduct may be, the World will have suspicions to our disadvantage." Greene and Wadsworth went so far as to use fictitious names and a code system for their business correspondence[*20*].

The political implications of these calamitous commercial practices were especially disturbing. "A True Patriot" perceived a loss of confidence in the Congress. The new aristocracy of profiteers and corruptionists was engrossing political power in the states and in the Congress. The result might be to change America from a democracy to an aristocracy[*21*]. The Eastern party had no alternative, if indeed it desired one, other than to guard the Revolution against the forces described by "A True Patriot." For ultimately, according to the very prescription of the Puritan rhetoric of the Resistance, this was what the Revolution was being fought to prevent.

It would be nonsense to contend that Congress was divided into squadrons of puritans and corruptionists. Speculation was deplored by all and practiced by some members of all parties—sometimes by those who condemned it most loudly. In 1775 Silas Deane had joined Samuel Adams and Thomas Lynch in criticizing the high cost of a powder contract Congress was arranging with the firm of Willing and Morris; shortly afterward Deane joined forces with Morris. When Congress was discussing whether or not to break the Continental Association, Samuel Chase contended, "We must give up the profits of trade or lose our liberties." Three years later he was sharply critized for speculating in flour. In the same debate in the second Continental Congress, Richard Henry Lee charged, "Money has debauched States, as well as individuals, but I hope its influence will not prevail over America. . . ." Yet later Lee, who deferred to no one in defining republican virtue, was accused of refusing paper money payments from his tenants[*22*].

The fact remains, however, that as prices skyrocketed with the large emissions of paper money, charges of profiteering began to permeate the partisan dialogue in Congress. Richard Henry Lee whispered to Samuel Adams that he had reason to suspect "jobbing" in both Massachusetts and Virginia. "The public concerns & the public money are perhaps sacrificed to private purposes. Congress should interfere," he concluded[*23*]. As the Lee-Deane controversy began to flower, the Lees were quick to accuse the supporters of Deane, and particularly Robert Morris and his many commercial connections, of improper handling of public money. While neither the Lees nor the Easterners were the sole practitioners of public virtue in Congress, there was enough truth in the allegations to lend credibility to their charges, and there was enough difference between the mercantile activities of the delegates in the New England coalition, and the Middle states–Southern alliance to prompt serious debate.

It would be wrong to interpret this debate, as some historians have, as a controversy between agrarian and mercantile interests[24]. Such an interpretation misconstrues the composition and objectives of both parties. Actually, there were more agrarians in the Southern bloc which threw its support to Morris and Deane than there were in the Eastern party. Indeed, the delegates in the Eastern party, including the central membership of the Adams-Lee faction, were predominantly merchants and lawyers, such as Whipple, Ellsworth, and Laurens, who represented mercantile interests. Those Easterners who were neither merchants nor lawyers, such as the schoolteacher James Lovell and the politician Sam Adams, generally came from urban constituencies with commercial interests.

There was, however, a difference between the wartime activities of commercially oriented delegates in the Eastern party during 1776–1779 and comparable delegates in the Middle states and Southern blocs of the opposition. In the former group, only Elbridge Gerry, a marginal member of the party for the most part, profited from public and private trade during the Revolution[25]. John Langdon of New Hampshire, a very active merchant, had been a member of Congress previously, but he was not in Congress during the controversies of 1777–1779 precisely because he was intent upon taking advantage of profit-making opportunities. When Whipple's nomination of Langdon to head an agency for prizes was defeated in the spring of 1776 on the grounds that Langdon was a member of Congress, Langdon threatened to resign his seat rather than relinquish the agency. He did not return for another term. Whipple chided Langdon, arguing that this would "have an avaricious appearance . . . there cannot be a greater evidence of patriotism than preferring the public good to one's own private interest"[26]. Whipple, also a merchant, was entirely different from Langdon. Whipple contended that anyone "who increases in wealth in such times as the present must be an enemy to his Country, be his pretentions what they may"[27] Whipple's purity made him proof against criticism, guarded as he was by his "impenetrable shield" of selfless patriotic commitment. Indeed, he said just this in a letter to Langdon, whom he continued to chastise for dealings with men he considered Tory speculators in Philadelphia. (Langdon had asked Whipple to negotiate a payment to Thomas Wharton in paper money which, much to Whipple's indignation, Wharton was reluctant to accept.) Whipple in a rather patronizing manner recommended that Langdon undertake a study of republicanism: "This will have a tendency to abate your anxiety for the acquirement of wealth and prepare the mind to meet adversity with a smile"[28].

Most Easterners during this period affected the posture so strikingly assumed by Whipple. Samuel Adams seems to have welcomed his chronic lack of funds—to have been possessive only about his poverty. Of course, not all the New Englanders were able to carry this off with equal effectiveness. James Lovell became increasingly disenchanted with austerity as time went by. In November of 1779, he wrote to John Hancock (with whom, unlike Sam Adams, he seems to have been on fairly good terms), confessing that he hoped he would never hear *"invincible arguments"* leading him to "repent of having preferred the Public Good to my private Emolument," particularly since he had already thought of a number of compelling reasons why he should[29].

Daniel Roberdeau of Pennsylvania was another merchant who generally supported the Easterners, and he too campaigned against profiteering. It was Roberdeau who, with Christopher Marshall, presided at a mass meeting which launched a committee movement to check rising prices and probe into engrossing in Philadelphia in 1779. Roberdeau's campaign against profiteering was irritating to Pennsylvania merchants not only because of the extralegal character of the committees but also because of the sanctimonious approach of Roberdeau and his associates, who tended to sit in judgment in matters of Revolutionary morality. In the sarcastic words of Gouverneur Morris, who doubtless voiced the sentiments of the Robert Morris coterie, Roberdeau conceived of himself as "the chosen among ten thousand" leading a "chosen Band of Patriots" in an attempt to rescue the "shipwreck'd Morals" of the people and "check the rapid Progress of Vice." Morris had little sympathy with this "blessed work of Reformation," which in his estimate was designed to promote "public Hatred and public Shame"[30].

Henry Laurens, one of the few Southerners drawn toward the Eastern party, is yet another example of a merchant who was uninvolved in public commercial transactions and also acted as a public inquisitor. It was Henry Laurens, acting upon information supplied by Francis Lewis, the sometimes deviant delegate from New York, who accused Robert Morris of writing off a private loss of Morris's firm, Willing and Morris, by shifting a cargo of tobacco which had been seized by the British from private to public account and then receiving compensation through the Secret Committee of Correspondence, of which Morris was a member[31]. The charge was proved inaccurate, but Laurens's readiness to deliver the accusation is indicative of his disposition to oppose Morris and others who were handling public moneys. His basic philosophy was actually antimercantile—at least as he articulated it in the Congress. His prescription for public virtue was reminiscent of the attitude of William Whipple and Samuel Adams:

> Reduce us all to poverty and cut off or wisely restrict that bane of patriotism, Commerce, and we shall soon become Patriots, but how hard is it for a rich or covetous Man to enter heartily into the Kingdom of Patriotism[32].

Morris was, in fact, so involved in both public and private trade and so closely connected with congressional decision making on the Secret Committee of Correspondence and the Secret Committee of Commerce that criticism was bound to occur. Further, a remarkable percentage of the membership of the Southern interest had business connections with Morris. Morris, who was heavily engaged in the flour and tobacco trades, had a network of business correspondents in Pennsylvania, Maryland, and Virginia. In Virginia, Carter Braxton and Benjamin Harrison, Jr., John Harvie, and John Banister were all associates of Morris to one extent or another. Morris also had connections with Simeon Deane, the brother of Silas Deane, who was located in Virginia—largely through John Holker, the French consul and purchasing agent, who was himself so deeply involved in private trade that the French government later gave him the alternatives of severing his business activities or resigning his official post. Simeon Deane in turn had a partnership with the Virginia delegate Thomas Adams. A number of Maryland delegates were connected with Morris through land speculation. Samuel Chase, Charles Carroll, and William Paca were members of the Illinois-Wabash Company, as was Morris. Paca, incidentally, was Morris's brother-in-law[33].

The Middle and Southern delegations were also linked by ties of friendship and favor. Robert Morris was on particularly good terms with Gouverneur Morris and William Duer of New York, both of whom became part of Morris's financial system after he assumed office as Superintendent of Finance. Gouverneur Morris appears not to have been engaged in trade or land speculation before 1780, but his notions regarding finance and government and his friendship with Robert Morris made him a constant supporter of the financier both in the press and in the Congress. Robert Morris later selected Gouverneur Morris as his assistant when he was Superintendent of Finance. William Duer, another close friend of Robert Morris (who was the godfather of Duer's son), apparently was not directly involved in business with Morris during the early years of the war, but he later had investments in Morris's Bank of North America and was able to outbid Wadsworth for a provisioning contract in 1783 because of credit extended by Morris from the public purse[34]. Morris also lent money to at least one congressional delegate, Thomas Burke of North Carolina. Burke seems to have overcome his parochialist scruples during 1778 and 1779, for he later led in the struggle for Morris's pet plan for a nationally controlled impost[35].

The conviction that well-positioned officials were using public office for personal profit energized partisan politics in an extraordinarily complicated fashion on almost all levels of government. The Lee-Deane controversy, as perceived by the Adams-Lee faction, was a morality play which pitted the genuine Party of the Revolution against the "Yellow Whigs" in every conceivable manner. The charges of profiteering abroad that were brought against Deane and his cohorts were duplicated in domestic affairs, particularly in 1779 during the period of runaway inflation, and especially in Pennsylvania, where Continental procurements were supervised by the Congress, and where state partisan politics were most polarized. In Philadelphia popular resentment against high prices and against supposed engrossing and forestalling resulted in the formation of extralegal committees that assumed responsibility for the maintenance of price stability. Ultimately, the city militia, reinforced by a mob, took arms against those who chose to stay at home and make profits rather than fight.

III

The activities of the price control committees and the Philadelphia militia can be regarded as a generalized radical thrust, for these outbursts embodied more than purely local grievances; they were directed against a mercantile complex which reached far beyond the city of Philadelphia; and they had repercussions that were felt throughout the country and abroad. The resentment of the protesters was both economic and political. The Constitutionalist party which had elected Searle, Shippen, and McLene to Congress in 1779 was unquestionably the "Party of the Revolution" in Pennsylvania because it had agitated for independence when moderates had temporized, and because it drew support from the traditionally underrepresented interior farmers and from the Philadelphia mechanics[36]. Constitutionalists and the New England radicals developed close connections during the early part of the Revolution and shared many viewpoints regarding Revolutionary policy. As already suggested, both groups extolled the militia rather than the more professional Continental army and opposed half pay pensions for officers. In varying degrees both groups distrusted consolidated political authority and tended to oppose moves to centralize the national administration. Both groups, but especially the Constitutionalists, were disturbed by the influence of Robert Morris in finance and by the power exercised in the Continental establishment by Morris and his anti-Constitutionalist connections. Joseph Reed, despite his role in the appointments of Pettit and Cox, found that there was discrimination against Constitutionalists in the allocation of Continental offices in Pennsylvania. According to Reed, militiamen loyal to the Constitutionalist government saw "all the appointments of Commissaries, Quartermasters, and other officers of Continental establishment bestowed almost without exception on persons opposed to the present government. Many of these are profitable; all give an influence of which they are never like to participate; on the other hand, it is employed to support opposite measures"[37]. It was thus inevitable that controversies over profiteering that involved Constitutionalist state authorities, the Continental Congress, and the Continental army should have inflamed partisan politics in Congress.

One such dispute concerned General Benedict Arnold, who had been appointed military commander of Philadelphia upon the evacuation of the British in June of 1778. The Pennsylvania Council charged that he had issued passes to suspicious persons for trips to British-held New York. Another charge (not actually included in the final presentment) was a complaint that Arnold had been elevated to the position of major general over Pennsylvania's John Armstrong (subsequently a Pennsylvania delegate in Congress, where he was a marginal member of the Eastern bloc). The central charges, however, were that Arnold had arrogantly neglected the Patriots of Pennsylvania when allocating preferments and had imposed menial offices upon them against their will. Tories, on the other hand, had received favorable treatment—indeed, Arnold had engaged in speculative schemes with "disaffected persons." Arnold had invested in the cargo of a ship, the *Charming Nancy,* which had been seized by an American privateer operating under papers issued by Arnold and had been taken to Egg Harbor, New Jersey. Arnold ordered a group of wagons in Continental service from Chester County to bring the cargo from Egg Harbor so that he could put it on the Philadelphia market. In January of 1779 the Chester wagonmaster presented a formal complaint about this usage to the Pennsylvania Council. When the Council made an inquiry, Arnold retorted with considerable insolence that he was responsible only to Washington and the Congress. Reed, president of the Council, then asked Congress to investigate[38].

Congress appointed a committee of five under the chairmanship of William Paca to look into the complaint against Arnold. The committee hesitated to recommend action against Arnold; consequently, Reed and the Council felt that Congress was allowing the military to subvert the state government of Pennsylvania. The issue, as it was debated and voted upon in Congress, thus involved not only charges against Arnold but also the federal relationship between Congress and a state. Yet delegates seem to have voted not in accord with what we know about their attitudes toward federal politics but rather in terms of factional attachments. John Floyd and Thomas Burke usually defended states' rights, for example, but both supported Arnold against the Council[39]. Neither James Lovell nor Henry Laurens was a states' righter, but both supported the Pennsylvania position. This can be seen in the scale of six votes recorded between March 26 and April 3, 1779, arranged in Table 13. Virtually all the six votes related to procedural matters regarding the conference between

TABLE 13

Arnold Speculation Scale, March–April, *1779*

	Anti-Arnold						Pro-Arnold					
	1	*2*	*3*	*4*	*5*	*6*	*1*	*2*	*3*	*4*	*5*	*6*
Whipple (N.H.—E)	x	x	x	x	x	x						
Frost (N.H.—*)	x	x		x	x	x						
Adams, S. (Mass.—E)	x	x	x	x	x	x						
Holten (Mass.—E)	x	x	x	x	x	x						
Dyer (Conn.—*)	x	x	x	x	x	x						
Root (Conn.—U)	x	x	x	x	x	x						
Armstrong (Pa.—e)	x	x	x	x	x	x						
Muhlenberg (Pa.—e)	x	x	x	x	x	x						
Shippen (Pa.—E)	x	x	x	x	x	x						
Van Dyke (Del.—*)	x	x	x	x	x	x						
Henry (Md.—U)	x	x	x	x	x	x						
Lee, R. H. (Va.—E)	x	x	x	x	x	x						
Lewis (N.Y.—U)	x	x		x	x	x						
Lee, F. L. (Va.—*)	x	x		x	x	x						
Laurens (S.C.—U)	x	x		x	x	x						
Duane (N.Y.—M)	x	x			x	x						
Searle (Pa.—E)	x	x	x	x								
Fell (N.J.—m)		x	x	x	x	x	o					
Lovell (Mass.—E)		x	x	x	x		o					o
Paca (Md.—s)	x		x	x	x		o	o				
Plater (Md.—sm)			x	x	x	x	o	o				
Nelson (Va.—*)			x	x	x	x	o	o				
Hill (N.C.—S)				x	x	x	o	o				
Adams, T. (Va.—*)			x		x	x	o	o		o		
Morris, G. (N.Y.—M)			x				o	o				
Griffin (Va.—S)					x	x	o	o	o	o		
Floyd (N.Y.—Ms)						x	o	o		o		
Burke (N.C.—S)				x	x		o	o			o	o
Ellery (R.I.—U)	x							o	o	o	o	o
Collins (R.I.—U)							o	o	o	o	o	o
Jay (N.Y.—Ms)							o	o	o	o	o	o
Carmichael (Md.—s)							o	o	o	o	o	o

TABLE 13 *(Continued)*

Arnold Speculation Scale, March–April, 1779

	Anti-Arnold						Pro-Arnold					
	1	2	3	4	5	6	1	2	3	4	5	6
Penn (N.C.—S)							o	o	o	o	o	o
Drayton (S.C.—U)							o	o	o	o	o	o
Langworthy (Ga.—S)							o	o	o	o	o	o

CODE:
E = core membership in Eastern faction on all issues during 1779, e = marginal membership in Eastern faction; M = core membership Middle states bloc of the Southern interest, m = marginal membership; S = core membership Southern interest, s = marginal membership; U = unaffiliated with any faction; * = not sufficiently present during 1779 for inclusion in general bloc analysis; x = vote supporting position of Pennsylvania Council; o = vote supporting Arnold.

VOTES:
1: Mar. 26, 1779 (*JCC*, XIII, 375); 2: Mar. 26 (ibid., 377); 3: Mar. 27 (ibid., 380); 4: Mar. 29 (ibid., 389); 5: Apr. 3 (ibid., 415); 6: Apr. 3 (ibid., 416).

Congress and the Pennsylvania government, but they also reflected attitudes toward Arnold and his Constitutionalist critics.

The irrelevance of constitutional imperatives and the force of partisan loyalties in the Arnold controversy did not escape the vigilant scan of Henry Laurens. He noted in debate that those supporting Arnold were irate over the publication of charges by the Council in the Philadelphia newspapers because this was an insult to Congress, but that the same men had previously refused to consider Silas Deane's "affrontive Publication" involving Congress. Laurens concluded, "Nothing can more clearly demonstrate Party spirit of the most dangerous tendency than this consistency of conduct"[40]. Lauren's charge that there was a connection between the Arnold affair and the Lee-Deane imbroglio proved to be remarkably accurate. There were eight members of the core of the anti-Arnold bloc who were present later on for the struggle over the recall of the foreign commissaries, and seven of the eight supported Lee. Excluding the two Rhode Island delegates who were bound to defend Arnold because he was a resident of that state, all the delegates who supported Arnold subsequently opposed the Lee faction. The same high correlation existed between the divisions on the Arnold incident and the general alignments on all issues during 1779. As can be seen from Table 13, virtually all members of the anti-Arnold core who aligned with a major bloc belonged to the Eastern party. Conversely, the pro-Arnold groups were attached to the Middle and Southern blocs within the Southern interest.

The Arnold affair was a prelude to heightened radical activity in Pennsylvania during the spring and summer. Extralegal committees to detect Tories and to set and enforce price ceilings were established. Daniel Roberdeau and Christopher Marshall, the former a member of the Eastern party in Congress during 1777 and 1778, presided over the mass gathering at which the committees were formed. Marshall had previously suggested that Joseph Reed and the city officials stay "out of the way" on that day[*41*]. This was a turbulent moment in the politics of Pennsylvania, and indeed in the unfolding of the Revolution. The address of the "Committee of the City and Liberties of Philadelphia" to their "fellow citizens throughout the United States," published in the *Pennsylvania Evening Post* on June 29, gave notice that "the additional opportunities which a state of war affords to the subtile, the selfish, and disaffected, together with the impossibility of describing the numerous kinds of disaffection practicable in an invaded country, render the revival of committees, during the present war, not only a convenient but a necessary appendage to civil government"[*42*]. Somewhat paradoxically the committee contended that the state government should not be given this authority because it might not relinquish such extraordinary powers. It is possible that the committee was in reality persuaded that the state government would be unwilling or unable to effect the catharsis it had in mind.

Urged on by the city militia, which threatened to take up arms if the committee could not secure a reduction in prices, it investigated charges that Robert Morris had secured control of a cargo of wheat on the *Polaris,* a ship that was reported to be the property of Silas Deane, and that he had postponed sale of the cargo for an extended time. The committee acknowledged in a letter to Morris that

> enquiries of this kind are attended with niceties and difficulties, which would be innovations on the rights and freedom of trade at any other time than this, but, embarked in a cause which has been in a great measure supported by generously surrendering individual ease & advantage, we are persuaded that Mr. Morris can but approve the principle which the public, and we by their authority, have proceeded on, and to which himself on many occasions has contributed[*43*].

It is doubtful that radicals such as Timothy Matlack, Thomas Paine, and other signers of the letter were as much concerned about violating the rights and freedom of trade as they were intent upon chiding Morris for not surrendering his ease and advantage. A related incident that had particular relevance for the Continental Congress, and indeed the French alliance, revealed their intentions.

The Philadelphia Committee accepted 168 barrels of flour that had been seized by a Wilmington price control committee under the leadership of one Patrick O'Flinn from a merchant by the name of Jonathan Rumford. Rumford had violated price ceilings established by the Wilmington committee when purchasing the flour under consignment for Robert Morris. Morris was in

turn acting as agent for John Holker, the French commercial agent in Philadelphia, who intended the flour for d'Estaing's naval squadron[44]. Holker
complained of the seizure in letters to the committee, the Pennsylvania Council, and the Continental Congress. The committee, unmoved, assured Holker
it was acting in the best interests of the war effort and the French government.
Reed and the Congress recognized that the committee was creating a diplomatic
problem and requested that the flour be returned. On July 21 the town meeting
of Philadelphia ordered that a committee report charging both Morris and
Holker with private trading in flour contrary to the laws of Pennsylvania and
Delaware be published. This was done in the July 24 issue of *The Pennsylvania
Packet,* much to the annoyance of Gérard[45]. Gouverneur Morris in Congress
in turn attempted to have the congressional rebuke of the committee published,
but this was voted down in a strongly partisan roll call[46].

The committee campaign thus joined a class conflict between the militia
and the merchant elite with the party battles in Congress over the politics of
the French alliance. Gérard did not fail to recognize this. Meriwether Smith
reported to Jefferson that Gérard interpreted the extralegal committees as
"instruments in the Hands of designing Men, who are not Friends to the Alliance, and wish to throw all Government into the Hands of the People by those
means, the better to attain their favorite purpose"[47]. Gérard was prone to
interpret all obstructions such as the Holker incident as a British-connected
subversion of the alliance. Gérard's reaction was perhaps natural, but Meriwether Smith and other supporters of the Deane interest also had their doubts
about the intentions of the Constitutionalists and their congressional sympathizers in the Eastern party.

The confrontation between the radical extremists and the force represented by Robert and Gouverneur Morris, Holker, Gérard, Deane, and their
Southern allies reached a dramatic focus on July 24, the day of the *Packet* article chastising Morris and Holker. That evening a delegation from the committee led by Charles Wilson Peale and John Bull, accompanied by a body of
citizens and militia, assembled outside the residence of Whitehead Humphreys,
the presumed author of a series of letters in the *Pennsylvania Evening Post*
signed "Cato." The "Cato" essays were part of a lengthy chain of charges and
countercharges involving fiscal policy, the alliance, and partisan conflict in
Congress and Pennsylvania[48]. "Cato" had attacked Thomas Paine, a member
of the Philadelphia committee who, as the author of "Common Sense," had
previously responded to "Americanus"—very probably Edward Langworthy,
the pro-Deane Georgia delegate whose commission had expired[49].

The newspaper controversy had been initiated by "Americanus," who
published his first essay in the *Pennsylvania Gazette* on May 19. At the outset
the emphasis of the letters was on inflation. "Americanus" contended that
inflation was to be expected so long as the Continental Congress did not "fix

property" and so long as taxation and foreign loans were neglected. He suggested that patriotism sustained currency at the outset, but once new governments were established, public virtue, like religious miracles, became "superfluous"[50]. "Americanus" was utterly opposed to writing off the debt at a depreciated scale, since this would be immoral and unjust to France, who had come to America's assistance without asking for any territory in return[51]. In short, "Americanus" was as disconcertingly skeptical about American revolutionary ardor as he was solicitous about the welfare of France.

"Americanus" shifted his attention to foreign affairs and factionalism in Congress in his essay of June 23, chastising the Eastern party for obstructing the formulation of the peace terms because of a selfish desire for fishery rights. This brought a rejoinder from Paine, who was attacked in turn by "Americanus" and "Cato" in subsequent issues of the *Gazette* and the *Evening Post.* At this point the newspaper controversy was connected with the committee actions against Holker and Harris.

It is not clear whether the armed delegation from the committee which assembled menacingly before Humphreys's house suspected that Langworthy was the author of "Americanus." "Common Sense" had contended that Deane was the author and that Langworthy had carried the essays to the press, and so in any event Langworthy was associated with the letters. It seems hardly coincidental that Langworthy was staying at the Humphreys residence. Langworthy, moreover, wrote to Congress protesting the incident and charged that the delegation from the committee attempted to break into the house and threatened to seize both Humphreys and himself. Langworthy added that he had heard and believed it true that there was a committee plan to force Drayton, Gouverneur Morris, Deane, and himself to appear before the committee for an investigation. Langworthy appealed for congressional protection: ". . . when I see the Arms and Troops of these States, turned by one part of the Subjects, acting without any legal Authority, on the other, I am very apprehensive for the Consequences"[52].

IV

The outburst of popular resentment against self-interested merchants and persons suspected of Toryism brought Revolutionary radicalism in Pennsylvania to a climax—and indeed in the nation as a whole, in the sense that it coincided with the peak of the influence of the Eastern party in Congress. In retrospect, it would seem that if an internal revolution was to occur, the summer of 1779 was the moment for it. The committee movement displayed symptoms of urban class conflict and mob action reminiscent of the disturbances of the 1760s[53]. In addition to the committee actions against Morris,

Holker, and others and to the intimidation of Humphreys and Langworthy, plans were made to neutralize suspected Tories and to chastise opponents of the Constitutionalist party. On October 4 a mob attacked the residence of James Wilson, hated for his defense of disaffected persons in court. One man was killed, and Wilson was forced to flee. Within a few days Benedict Arnold appealed to the Continental Congress for a guard of twenty men commanded by a competent officer to defend him against "a Mad Ignorant and deluded Rabble"[54].

There was a possibility that the committee movement might spread to other states. The Philadelphia Committee never intended to function in isolation. At the first organizational meeting chaired by Roberdeau on May 25, a subcommittee was appointed with the charge of executing the Philadelphia design "in all other parts of the United States"[55]. The Wilmington Committee involved in the case against Morris and Holker existed as the result of an appeal from the Philadelphia subcommittee. The Philadelphia movement was not unnoticed in New England and Virginia. In Boston, where the proclamations of the Philadelphia Committee were reprinted in the *Continental Journal,* a pamphleteer urged his fellow citizens to assemble at the Old Scotch Meeting House on June 17 in order to "catch the Philadelphia spirit"[56]. Meriwether Smith sent letters to Governor Thomas Jefferson and other friends to warn them to discourage the formation of committees in Virginia[57]. In the context of runaway inflation and widespread resentment against profiteering, Smith's concern that the committee movement might become a powerful, even revolutionary, force was not overly exaggerated.

Smith's alarm was reinforced by Gérard, who believed from the outset—even before the action involving Holker—that the movement was highly dangerous. In short time Gérard, as already suggested, would become convinced that the committees, "a monsterous power . . . subversive of all principles of society and government"[58], were antagonistic to the alliance—a conviction which, although exaggerated, had some foundation. Gérard and Meriwether Smith did not regard as implausible the possibility of a national coalition of the Pennsylvania Constitutionalists and the Eastern party resting upon an urban popular base strategically located in the Middle states.

Ironically, the frenzied activities of 1779 were the harbinger of a new era of conservative rather than radical Revolutionary politics. That year was a watershed between a phase of the Revolution when national politics was deeply influenced by a leadership that hoped for fundamental behavioral change and a phase dominated by new leaders searching pragmatically for the techniques of success in military, fiscal and political administration. The quasi-religious expectation of a reformation had become increasingly elusive by 1779. Newspaper and pamphlet rhetoric sedulously reported the decline of public virtue, but no "True Patriot" stated the case more succinctly than the New

Hampshire delegate Josiah Bartlett in a letter to William Whipple in the spring of 1779: "Where is the spirit that actuated us in the beginning" he lamented. "Gone alas! I fear forever!" was his answer. In a later letter Bartlett, writing from New Hampshire, used a biblical analogy to describe the times:

> I have no doubt that our cause is as just as any the Israelites were ever engaged in, and am sorry to find that like them we are a crooked and perverse generation, longing for the fineries and follies of those Egyptian task masters from whom we have so lately freed ourselves. . . . I wish we may not travel in the wilderness in which we are at present, till the present generation are gone off this stage and a more virtuous one risen in its stead[59].

But, of course, the Revolution could not wait for a new generation. The stage was thus set for the substitution of bureaucracy and order for virtue and enthusiasm under elitist rather than popular auspices.

That such a change should have taken place was probably in part a natural consequence of the dynamic revolution which often seems to course from the flush of enthusiasm to the search for stability. More concrete reasons can be assigned, however. In all likelihood the influence of the French alliance helped redirect the Revolution both because of a relaxation of the militia effort that had been so noticeable in 1776 and at Saratoga and because of the requirements of French diplomacy which tended to internationalize the Revolution. The Puritan general Joseph Ward could provide a cosmic explanation of the agonies of Valley Forge by referring to "Providence . . . administering political and moral physick to this people"[60]—a consoling message so long as America fought alone. Losses after the entry of the French, such as the failures at Newport and Charleston, were still susceptible to cosmic interpretation but were far less palatable. The Spirit of Seventy-six was the product of a solitary challenge of British military might.

French opposition to American demands for the fisheries, the Mississippi, and Canada likewise undermined the politics of enthusiasm. Finally, sectionalism—the constant of congressional politics—thwarted both autonomous reformation and unified radical reform. There was no effective coordination of the committee movement between Philadelphia and Boston, despite the fact that Samuel Adams returned to Boston in June of 1779, for example. But the best illustration of the corrosive effect of sectionalism on the radical front can be found in the difficulties that followed the British invasion of Georgia and South Carolina in 1779.

The British capture of Savannah on December 29, 1778, naturally distressed South Carolina, which appealed for both land and naval support from the North to prevent the feared invasion of that state. Although Congress recommended that Virginia and North Carolina send reinforcements, and although a corps of Continental troops was dispatched by Washington under

General Benjamin Lincoln, the South Carolina authorities felt insecure against the threat of an advance by General Augustine Prevost. For one thing, the troops from Virginia and North Carolina were slow in materializing. Lieutenant-Governor Thomas Bee (subsequently a member of Congress) complained on April 5 in a letter to the South Carolina delegate William Henry Drayton that word had just arrived that Virginia would be sending only 1,000 men "at some Distant Period . . . & most of those without Arms. . . ." Bee reminded Congress through Drayton that when Boston, New York, and Philadelphia were attacked, "theirs was made a common cause," but now South Carolina was receiving different treatment. Bee candidly disclosed the mood of the government: "If Congress mean we should make the best Terms for ourselves we can, I wish they would be Explicit—Genl. Prevost would gladly Accept us now, on our own Terms"[61]. The South Carolina government did indeed ask for a neutral status when the British invaded Charleston—a request denied by Prevost.

It will not do, however, to ascribe the South Carolina action wholly to the fear of conservative planters such as the Rutledges that resistance would threaten disturbances in the backcountry or, worse, a slave insurrection. This was indeed true of Governor John Rutledge and the Council, which unanimously rejected a congressional suggestion that South Carolina raise a force of 3,000 Negroes, and both Bee and Rutledge feared uprisings in the interior[62]. Virtually the same sentiment was held, however, by Christopher Gadsden, the old radical cohort of Sam Adams. In a letter to Adams written at this time he pointedly assured Adams that "I am the same Man my Friend with the Same Principles I set out with at First, an American *at large,* anxiously wishing for the Happiness & confirmed Independency of the whole, not having, indeed scorning, a Thought in Favour of *any one* State to the Prejudice of the Rest." Reminding Adams that South Carolina was one of the first provinces to answer the distress call from Boston, he asked why she was not receiving succor now. His conclusion was similar to that of Bee: "if You can't give us effectual Assistance by Land & You will make no Attempts by Water, what Advantage have we by the Confederacy?" Gadsden added that he, as one who had defended New England in the early days of the Revolution, was taunted continually with the fulfillment of the argument he had opposed: that New England had entered the Revolution for its own advantage[63].

The distant location of South Carolina would have made coordination in a radical front (a problem quite different from cooperation in the movement toward independence) difficult under the best of circumstances, and impossible in 1779. Ironically, the best chance for an internal revolution such as that advocated by Paine and the supporters of the committees would have come from the separation of Georgia and South Carolina, resulting in a smaller, more hard-pressed republic.

The defense of a vast confederation, the coordination of diplomacy with an often implacable ally, and the salvage of the system of currency finance proved to be problems for which the Old Radical leadership had no effective answers. A centralized fiscal system which recognized and tolerated private advantage, along with the brokerage of separate interests not always compatible with the radical ideology that was set forth at the outset of the Revolution, would characterize the second phase of Revolutionary politics—dominated no longer by the Eastern party, but by a coalition of Middle and Southern delegates.

Notes

1 Paradoxically, the plan for state redemption of the bills of credit was based upon a memorial sent by the New York Provincial Assembly and drawn up by Gouverneur Morris, who would later become one of the strongest proponents of national taxing authority. *Amer. Arch.*, ser. H, II, 1262.

2 Historians have disagreed over colonial money emissions. Writers of the late nineteenth century tended to deplore paper money expedients in their own time or any other; see, e.g., Albert S. Bolles, *The Financial History of the United States, from 1774 to 1789*, (New York, 1884), pp. 27-31. More recently historians supported the usefulness and general success of colonial currency finance. See E. James Ferguson, *The Power of the Purse* (Chapel Hll, 1961), chap. 1. It is instructive to note that a contemporary historian, David Ramsay, in his *History of the American Revolution*, published in 1789, argued that the recourse to paper money was "in some degree owing to a previous confidence, which had been begotten by honesty and fidelity, in discharging the engagements of government" (II, 132).

3 Benjamin Rush recorded the vote in his diary, *LMCC*, II, 228-229; Ellery to Governor Cooke, Feb. 15, 1777, ibid., 254-255.

4 Thomas Burke, Abstract of Debates, Feb. 24 and 26, 1777, ibid., 275, 282.

5 William Hooper to Robert Morris, Feb. 1, 1777, ibid., 232. Hooper was also a transplanted New Englander, but he better reflected the interest of his constituency than did Brownson.

6 *JCC*, VIII, 726.

7 Ibid., 725. Henry Laurens to John Gervais, Sept. 5, 1777; John Adams to Mrs. Adams, Aug. 19, 1777, *LMCC*, II, 477-478, 455.

8 *JCC*, XII, 1238.

9 Thomas Burke to Governor Richard Caswell, Dec. 20, 1778; North Carolina delegates to Governor Caswell, Dec. 22, 1778, *LMCC*, III, 542-543, 547-548.

10 *JCC*, XIII, 398-401. The New England delegations drew support for a generous compensation from the Pennsylvania radicals, Witherspoon (but not Fell) of New Jersey, the New York moderates Floyd and Lewis (but not Jay and Morris), Van Dyke of Delaware, the Lees of Virginia, and Laurens of South Carolina. Other Southern delegates opposed the Easterners on almost every roll call.

11 Nathanael Greene to the President of Congress, Mar. 26, 1778, in George Washington Greene, *The Life of Nathanael Greene* (3 vols.; New York, 1871), II, 53–55; John F. Roche, *Joseph Reed; a Moderate in the American Revolution* (New York, 1957), pp. 21, 22, 65, 127.

12 JCC, X, 327

13 Ferguson, *Power of the Purse*, p. 77, and chap. 5, passim.

14 Force (ed.), *Amer. Arch.*, ser. 5, III, 1176–1177.

15 *Pennsylvania Statutes at Large*, IX, 177–180; *JCC*, IX, 954, XV, 1052–1054.

16 For a summary of price control legislation see Ralph V. Harlow, "Aspects of Revolutionary Finance," *AHR*, 35 (1929), 46–68.

17 *New Jersey Gazette*, Feb. 10, 1779.

18 Reprinted in the *Pennsylvania Gazette*, Mar. 31, 1779.

19 Ibid., April 14, 1779.

20 Nathanael Greene to Jeremiah Wadsworth, Apr. 14 and 30, 1779. *PMHB*, XXII (1898), II, 14.

21 *Pennsylvania Gazette*, Apr. 21, 1779.

22 John Adams, Notes of Debates, *Works*, II, 448–449, 477–478.

23 Richard Henry Lee to Samuel Adams, Oct. 30, 1777, Samuel Adams Papers, NYPL.

24 Thomas P. Abernethy, *Western Lands and the American Revolution*, (New York, 1937), p. 205.

25 Robert East, *Business Enterprise during the American Revolution*, (New York, 1938).

26 William Whipple to John Langdon, Apr. 29, 1776, Force Transcripts, LC.

27 William Whipple to Josiah Bartlett, May 21, 1779, ibid.

28 William Whipple to John Langdon, June 21, 1779, ibid.

29 James Lovell to John Hancock, Nov. 8, 1779, CL.

30 This piece of acidulous satire was meant for the newspapers, but Morris decided not to publish it because the style was too severe and the object "too contemptible." Gouverneur Morris Papers, folder 816, dated 1780, CUL.

31 Clarence Ver Steeg, *Robert Morris*, pp. 22–23.

32 Henry Laurens to William Livingston, Apr. 19, 1779, *LMCC*, IV, 163.

33 Abernethy, *Western Lands,* pp. 215, 213, 239. The correspondence of Robert Morris at the Library of Congress contains evidence of these relationships; see also the Holker papers in the Library of Congress and the Clements Library—Morris to Holker, Oct. 6, 1778, and Oct. 8, 1778, LC, shows connections between Morris, Harrison, Holker, Banister, and John Hancock as well.

34 Ver Steeg, *Robert Morris,* pp. 81, 160-161; Duer to Morris, May 12, 1782, Morris Papers, LC.

35 Thomas Burke to Robert Morris, Nov. 4, 1780, ibid. For Burke's role in the impost proceedings see Chapter 10.

36 See Brunhouse, *Counter-Revolution in Pennsylvania,* passim.

37 Joseph Reed to Washington, May 8, 1779, in William B. Reed, *Life and Correspondence of Joseph Reed* (2 vols., Philadelphia, 1847), II, 104.

38 The complaints of the Council can be found in letters from President Reed to the Continental Congress, Jan. 20 and 29, 1779, Pennsylvania State Papers, PCC. See also the proceedings of the Council reprinted in the *Pennsylvania Gazette,* Feb. 10, 1779, and John F. Roche, *Joseph Reed* (New York, 1957), pp. 167-170; John Fell, *Diary,* Jan. 26-28, *LMCC,* IV, 44; *JCC,* Jan. 28, 1779.

39 Burke's attitude toward states' rights was well known; Floyd's concept of states' rights can be discerned in his letter to George Clinton, Jan. 3, 1779, *LMCC,* IV, 4-5. Burke, incidentally, was possibly beginning his shift to a nationalist position. (See Chapter 10 for Burke's later career in Congress.)

40 Henry Laurens, Notes of Debates, Mar. 29, 1779, *LMCC,* IV, 123.

41 Christopher Marshall, *Diary,* Duane (ed.), p. 217; See Brunhouse, *Counter-Revolution in Pennsylvania,* pp. 68-70, for a description of the formation of this and other committees.

42 *Pennsylvania Evening Post,* June 29, 1779.

43 Letter signed by T. Matlack, David Rittenhouse, Thomas Paine, Charles Wilson Peale, and B. Smith to Morris, July 21, 1779. Robert Morris Papers, Mis. Col., LC.

44 The Holker affair can be traced in the PCC.

45 Gérard to Vergennes, Aug. 8, 1779, in John J. Meng (ed.), *Despatches and Instructions of Conrad Alexander Gérard* (Baltimore, 1939), pp. 828-833.

46 *JCC,* XIV, 923.

47 Meriwether Smith to Jefferson, July 30, 1779, *LMCC,* IV, 348.

48 Edward Langworthy to John Jay, July 25, 1779; ibid., 344-345n.

49 Paine, Bull, and Peale believed "Cato" was Humphreys, as does the editor of the Deane Papers (NYHS, *Collections,* Deane Papers, IV, 4). Richard Henry Lee believed

"Cato" was Gouverneur Morris; James C. Ballagh (ed.), *The Letters of Richard Henry Lee* (2 vols., New York, 1914), I, 92. See also Burnett's comment (*LMCC*, IV, 278–279n). The identity of "Americanus" remains something of a puzzle. It was assumed at the time that Gouverneur Morris was the author, but "Cato" categorically denied that on the authority of Morris (*Evening Post,* July 9), and Paine as "Common Sense" in the *Gazette* of July 21 asserted he did not believe the author was Morris, since "the manner is not his . . . (a correct assessment). Paine asserted he had heard that Deane was the author and that "his friend Mr. Langworthy carried it to the press" (ibid.). In all probability Langworthy was the author. Stylistically the "Americanus" articles resemble Langworthy's correspondence—in the heavy use of semicolons and an unusually long sentence structure, for example. Further, the concern of "Americanus" about the impediment of the fishery demands in the formulation of peace terms betrays Langworthy's anxiety about cordial relations with France while Georgia was under invasion; his intimate knowledge of the proceedings in Congress and his insistence in the July 7 issue of the *Gazette* that he is not a member of Congress but rather a private citizen of moderate circumstances all fit his position as a delegate momentarily retired but vitally concerned in congressional affairs. It is true that almost the same characteristics described Deane, but the "Americanus" articles reveal more anxiety about the peace terms than about Deane's case.

50 *Pennsylvania Gazette,* May 19, 1779.

51 Ibid, June 2, 1779.

52 Langworthy to John Jay, July 25, 1779, *LMCC*, IV, 344n–345n.

53 Artisan resentments against wealthy merchants were evident in an article directed "To the Inhabitants of Pennsylvania in general, and particularly those of the city and neighbourhood of Philadelphia. . . . Signed by order of a meeting of tanners, curriers and cordwainers, held at the Committee-Room, 11th day of July, 1779." *Pennsylvania Packet,* July 15, 1779.

54 Arnold's letters, located in the PCC, are reprinted in Burnett, *LMCC*, IV, 476n–477n.

55 *At a General Meeting of the Citizens of Philadelphia, and Parts adjacent, at the State-House Yard in this City, on Tuesday the 25th of May 1779* . . . (Philadelphia, 1779).

56 *Sons of Boston! Sleep No longer!* (Boston, June 16, 1779).

57 Meriwether Smith to Thomas Jefferson, July 30, 1779, *LMCC*, IV, 348.

58 Gérard to Vergennes, May 29, 1779, in Meng, (ed.), *Despatches,* pp. 692–693.

59 Josiah Bartlett to William Whipple, Apr. 24 and May 29, 1779, Bartlett Papers, NHHS.

60 Joseph Ward to Samuel Adams, Dec. 17, 1777, Samuel Adams Papers, NYPL.

61 Thomas Bee to William Henry Drayton, Apr. 5, 1779, South Carolina Papers, PCC.

62 John Rutledge to the South Carolina Delegates, Apr. 24, 1779, South Carolina State Papers, ibid.

63 Christopher Gadsden to Samuel Adams, Apr. 4, 1779, Samuel Adams Papers, NYPL.

10 Crisis, Confederation, Consolidation

B
Y 1780, the war of the Revolution had reached an impasse in the North. General Sir Henry Clinton, the British commander in chief who was headquartered in New York, was too weak to attack Washington and the Continental army in New Jersey. At the same time, Washington's Continentals were far from able to take New York. In New England, the British, after withstanding a combined French-American attack on Newport, withdrew of their own accord in 1779. A French fleet and army under Admiral Charles de Ternay and General de Rochambeau arrived at the Rhode Island port in July of 1780, but the force was contained by British naval superiority for almost a year. As had been forecasted in 1779, the major actions of 1780 and 1781 were in the South.

Clinton, who had failed to take Charleston in 1776, vindicated himself by capturing the South Carolina capital on May 12 after a four-month seige. It was one of the major victories of the entire war for the British. Benjamin Lincoln was forced to surrender an army of over 5,000 men, including 2,000 Continentals. Burgoyne had lost fewer men when he was defeated at Saratoga. From their base in Charleston, the British moved up into North Carolina, inflicting other staggering losses upon the Americans, the most striking being the defeat of a full army under Horatio Gates at Camden in August of 1780.

Washington, who remained in the North, hoped that the events in the South might enliven Americans who had slipped into what seemed to be an unaccountable lethargy. But only in the Battle of King's Mountain in the Carolina interior could the Patriots take comfort. The British under the capable command of General George Cornwallis won a series of victories which, though inconclusive, was nonetheless stunning.

In Congress the psychological impact of the major losses in the South was profound. It seemed the warnings of Bull and Gadsden had materialized. Without aid from the North, South Carolina would have to secure the best terms she could from the British. General Ezekiel Cornell from Rhode Island, one of the many new members sitting in Congress in 1780, reported back to Governor William Greene that Georgia and South Carolina had submitted to the British and that he expected North Carolina would follow their example. He complained that "we have but little to expect south of Maryland. The once patriotic state of Virginia weighs but little at present, in the scale of defence or the furnishing of men or supplies." As disdainful of Southern resistance in 1780 as Sam Adams had been of the defense put up by Pennsylvanians in 1777, Cornell's reaction to such distressing failures of revolutionary nerve was different from that of Adams. Eschewing rhetorical appeals to patriotic virtue, he advocated consolidation of authority both in Congress and in the military. Indeed, he thought a dictatorship might be necessary to save the Union and the Revolution[1]. Cornell, though in a minority, was not the only delegate who proposed rash measures. John Mathews, the aggressive member from South Carolina, after criticizing his home state for the poor performance of its militia and the Congress for its inattention to the plight of South Carolina, also supported a centralization of authority[2].

The attitudes of Cornell and Mathews, although extreme, were symptomatic of a different mood in Congress in 1780. After five years of hostilities and fifteen years of resistance, the era of the Party of the Revolution had passed, and the day of the technician had come. The majority of Congress decided the war was to be won with a professional army nurtured by conventional rewards for officers rather than through spasmodic exertions of the militia; diplomacy was to be joined with allied policy rather than relying upon heroic self-sufficiency; fiscal affairs were to be established on the pragmatic base of commercial expertise and even self-interest rather than patriotic denial; the common cause was to be reinforced by the coercive power of the Confederation rather than divinely ordained, spontaneous local efforts; the Articles were to be ratified and either amended or used flexibly; Congress was to rationalize its administration through the creation of executive departments; and, above all, the war was to be won and independence achieved—even if the delegates could not agree upon exactly what the Revolution was to accomplish.

II

The shift of congressional attention from ideology to the strategy of victory was made easier by changes in the composition of Congress during 1780 and 1781. New men with new orientations appeared in the Eastern delegations. John Sullivan of New Hampshire, who attended during the latter part of 1780 and during most of 1781, was more a Continental army man that he was an Easterner, for example. Both Ezekiel Cornell and James Varnum, who dovetailed terms as Rhode Island delegates during 1780 and 1781, believed that executive energy and central authority were necessary at this critical juncture of the war[3]. Sullivan, Cornell, and Varnum were all generals whose perception of the Revolution was formed more by military than political experience. Of the three, only Sullivan had served previously in Congress, and then only during the brief session of the first Congress in 1774. All three were distressed by the concern in Congress for parliamentary detail; all three found Congress rooted in tradition and unwilling to innovate. Cornell was appalled by the "langour that attends all our conduct. . . . The greatest part of our time is taken up in disputes about diction, commas, colons, consonants, vowels, etc." Varnum contended that "the kind of Government sufficiently energetic to obtain the Objects of Peace when free from invasion, is too feeble to raise and support Armies, fight Battles, and obtain compleat Victory. . . ." It is understandable, therefore, that Cornell contemplated granting dictatorial powers to Washington for a limited period in order to garner the supplies and men for a military coup that would finish the war. Varnum went further by advocating a convention that would suspend the Articles of Confederation in favor of a thoroughly centralized regime for the duration of the war[4].

From the Middle states, yet another general, Philip Schuyler, took a seat in Congress as a delegate from New York during the spring of 1780. Schuyler could be relied upon to resist parochial, militia-oriented policy. Pennsylvania sent a radical delegation in 1780, but by the time of the elections for the 1781 delegation, the conservative Republican party had secured control of the Pennsylvania Assembly. Consequently, the radical Constitutionalist trio consisting of James McLene, William Shippen, and James Searle—all of whom served during at least part of 1780—was replaced by Samuel Atlee (the deviant of 1779 who had been left out of the 1780 delegation probably as a result of Constitutionalist dissatisfaction with Atlee's role in the Lee-Deane affair), George Clymer, and Thomas Smith, among others. Clymer was a wealthy Philadelphia merchant who became receiver of funds for the Bank of North America promoted by Robert Morris in 1781[5]. Clymer and Smith were members of the conservative Republican Society, a group which announced its opposition to the radical Pennsylvania constitution of 1776 in the *Pennsylvania Gazette,* March 24, 1779; and by this point in the Revolution, the politics of Pennsylvania and the Continental Congress were so closely interlocked that the affiliations of Clymer and Smith were predictable. The changes in the Pennsylvania delegation were alarming to Arthur Lee, who had returned from Europe at last. He wrote from Philadelphia that "Toryism is triumphant here. They have displaced every Whig, but the President. Atlee, Wincoop, Clymer, Montgomery and Smith brother to the Tory Doctr are chosen members of Congress"[6].

In the Southern delegations, three able and articulate nationalists were present during 1780 and 1781: John Mathews of South Carolina (who had first arrived in 1779) and James Madison and Joseph Jones of Virginia. All three were young, energetic, willing to innovate, and convinced of the necessity of action. Mathews, who had first arrived in 1778, was immediately "disgusted" by the "thirst for Chattering," "the loss of so much precious irretrievable time," on the floor of Congress[7]. By 1780, he had become probably the most influential and certainly the most controversial member of the newly formed Committee to Headquarters, which was supposed to streamline communication between Congress and the army. Mathews did his utmost to transfer decision-making power regarding the procurement of supplies and other matters directly related to the military campaign from Congress to the committee and to the army[8]. James Madison, one of the most talented members of Congress during the 1780s, gave new stature and cohesion to the Virginia delegation, which had been distinguished by internal divisions and the inability to assume its natural role as leader of a Southern coalition. Madison and his fellow delegate, Joseph Jones, regularly espoused a flexible interpretation of the Articles of Confederation which stressed the presumed inherent power of Congress to coerce the states into compliance with national policy[9].

But it would be a mistake to conclude that these men were solely responsible for the changes that occurred in congressional policy. A number of Easterners, including Samuel Adams, James Lovell, Oliver Ellsworth, and Roger Sherman, along with their radical allies from Pennsylvania, served during part or both of the transitional years 1780–1781. Nor were all the new delegates from New England advocates of centralism and executivism. The puritanical general from Massachusetts, Artemas Ward, who was present during both years, never cast a vote in opposition to Samuel Adams. Daniel Mowry of Rhode Island, a delegate in 1781, did not share the attitudes of Cornell and Varnum. Nor could one have expected uniform support for the new policies from the Southern delegations. Richard Henry Lee was absent, but his doctrines were defended during both years by the Virginian Theodorick Bland. Finally, Thomas Burke of North Carolina, the most ardent of all states' righters, served in both 1780 and 1781.

In fact, the policy innovations that occurred during those two years were brought about with the partial assistance of Easterners, Old Radicals, and

Southern advocates of states' rights. All were present in sufficient numbers to have prevented passage of the legislation. That they did not organize to block the innovations testifies to the pervasiveness of congressional concern over the war and the critical condition of Confederation finance. There was little inclination among the delegates to re-create the partisan disputes of the previous two years. Even the return of Arthur Lee and Ralph Izard from France in 1780 did not rekindle party animosities. Izard arrived in Philadelphia first, planning to justify his conduct before Congress. His case was presented to a committee composed of James Lovell, Thomas McKean, and James Madison, which handled it with more dispatch than Izard probably expected or desired. The altered mood of Congress was reflected in Lovell's remark to Elbridge Gerry that he hoped the reception of Lee might "get through as quickly as Izard"[10]. It appears not only that the Lee-Deane imbroglio was a thing of the past but also that the Adams-Lee connection had ceased to be a significant element in congressional politics.

The diminution of the power of the Adams-Lee compact illuminates more than a conciliatory mood in Congress. It helps to show how factions, in the classical sense of the term, differed from the kind of legislative parties that were germinating in the Continental Congress. Factions tended to depend upon personal connections, and Richard Henry Lee and Samuel Adams never again served in Congress at the same time. Adams left the Congress in April of 1781, never to return, while Richard Henry Lee did not appear again until 1785. The Adams-Lee connection and the Lee-Deane imbroglio were frenzied manifestations of congressional partisanship, but they were not the source of that partisanship. The basic division in the Congress was between the North and the South; it had existed from the outset and would continue throughout the history of the Confederation.

The configuration of voting blocs during 1780 (Table 14) illustrates that regional differences persisted at the same time that changes were taking place in the structure of congressional parties. Eastern and Southern parties continued to exist, but they lacked the cohesion and ideological coherence of previous years. In 1779 the Eastern party was composed of a single bloc which controlled six northern states and drew important support from Virginia and South Carolina as well. In 1780 the party fell apart, becoming a loosely joined coalition of three blocs. The vital center of the party remained in New England, but the Massachusetts delegation no longer drew consistent support from the radical Pennsylvanians. While there was a marginal connection between the Pennsylvanians and the delegates from Connecticut, that connection was established on issues such as the constitution of the court of appeals on maritime cases, state troop quotas, and the fixing of prices for provisions rather than on ideologically volatile matters such as the Lee-Deane controversy and the definition of peace terms.

TABLE 14

Congressional Blocs, 1780

	Eastern Party			Southern Party	
	Massachusetts Bloc	Pennsylvania Bloc	New England-Virginia Bloc	New York Bloc	Southern Bloc
N.H.	Folsom	Adams, S.*	Folsom*		
Mass.	Gerry				
	Holten				
	Lovell		Lovell		
	Partridge				
	Ward				
R.I.	Collins*		Collins	Collins*	
			Cornell		
Conn.	Ellsworth*				
	Huntington, S	Huntington, S.*			
	Sherman	Sherman*			
N.Y.				Duane	
				Floyd	
				Hommedieu	
				Livingston	
				Schuyler	
				Scott*	
N.J.	Clark*				
			Fell*		
Pa.	McLene*	McLene			
		Matlack			
		Muhlenberg			
		Searle			
		Shippen			
Del.		McKean			
Md.		Hanson			
					Forbes
					Plater
Va.					Griffin
			Jones, J.		
			Madison		

TABLE 14 *(Continued)*

Congressional Blocs, *1780*

	Eastern Party			Southern Party	
	Massachusetts Bloc	Pennsylvania Bloc	New England–Virginia Bloc	New York Bloc	Southern Bloc
N.C.					Burke
					Jones, N. W.
					Penn
S.C.				Kinloch*	
				Mathews*	

* Marginal membership.

Independents: Peabody (N.H.); Ellery (R.I.); Bland, Henry, Walker (Va.); Hill (N.C.).

Significantly, the Massachusetts bloc included Elbridge Gerry but not Samuel Adams. While Adams's remarkable separation may be attributed to technical factors such as sparse attendance during 1780, it also is likely that it reflected changes in the ideological accents of congressional politics. Adams continued to vote in agreement with the Pennsylvanian radicals, while Gerry, a loyal but pragmatic New Englander who did not become seriously involved in the Lee-Deane imbroglio, was a core member of the Massachusetts bloc in 1780 (he was only a marginal member of the Eastern party in 1779). Gerry's relationship with the Eastern party was a kind of temperature gauge of the incidence of partisanship.

New England drew support from Virginia in 1780, but it was support that was altogether different from the Adams-Lee connection. The alliance between the New Englanders—Nathaniel Folsom, James Lovell, John Collins, and Ezekiel Cornell—and the Virginians—Joseph Jones and James Madison—was formed as a consequence of shared opinions regarding questions such as the disposition of troops and the management of depreciated loan office certificates. It was an alliance that indicated that Lovell was not the ideologue that Sam Adams was and that Madison and Jones were less parochial than other Southerners such as their colleague Cyrus Griffin, but it did not mean that a new connection was being forged between New England and the South. Madison and Jones, both committed nationalists, soon established more durable bonds with centralists from the Middle states who were close to Robert Morris and who endorsed consolidationist programs associated with the public debt. The New Englanders subsequently either departed from Congress or shifted away from the nationalists in accordance with the provincial sentiments of their constituencies.

Among the Middle states and Southern delegations, there was also a basic continuation of previous factional patterns accompanied by novel developments. New York again joined the South rather than New England, but it drifted from its traditional connection with Maryland to a position closer to South Carolina. One reason for this was alterations in the New York and Maryland delegations. Jay and Morris had left the Congress, while the new delegate from Maryland, John Hanson of Frederick County in the interior of the state, tended to find more in common with the radical Pennsylvanians than with the New Yorkers. A second reason was New York's deliberate cultivation of broad Southern support for its claim to Vermont (a boundary dispute that had constantly operated to separate New York from its New England neighbors). New York found that it was difficult to placate the entire South on matters which had to do with land claims, and thus as New York cultivated the deeper South, she tended to lose the support of Maryland. Despite this, however, New York was able to maintain reasonably good relations with both the upper and the lower South.

Like the Easterners, the Southern party did not achieve the kind of cohesion during most of 1780 that it had in 1779. This was partly attributable to the controversy over western lands and partly due to disagreements over the proper allocation of troops and supplies in the face of mounting presure from the British in the South. Jones and Madison were inclined to guard the Middle states and the Chesapeake, for example, while the Carolinians naturally wanted to divert as many men and supplies as possible farther south.

But if the British threat triggered disagreements, it also, more importantly, constituted a powerful force drawing the traditionally disunited Southern delegations together. The full effect of the Southern campaign was not felt until late 1780, and it was not registered in the voting alignments until 1781. Thus in 1780 the Southern coalition included only eight delegates from the South, but in 1781 there were eighteen Southerners associated with a closely linked group of blocs from the Middle and Southern states. During the winter months of 1780 there were rarely more than five delegates on the floor of Congress from the four states of Virginia, the Carolinas, and Georgia, but by the fall that number had risen to twelve. American arms had suffered another disastrous defeat under Gates at Camden, South Carolina, thereby exposing North Carolina to a British onslaught under Cornwallis. The Confederation treasury was bankrupt, and the Congress was forced to ask for contributions in kind rather than for money from the states. The North Carolina delegate Whitmill Hill wrote to Thomas Burke, recently elected Governor of North Carolina, that the only recourse "the army had was to secure bread with commissary certificates, of which the people are quite tired, and when it is to grow better I know not, as I am very apprehensive the new Emission will not have a Circulation when the attempt is made. Are you not alarmed at our Situation? Must confess I am exceedingly." He concluded, "In short, I know not what is to become of us"[*11*]. It was a situation that impelled Southern delegates to unite among themselves—and, indeed, with all others who would help throw back the invader.

The deep penetration of British troops into the South was a novel development in the war, but the problems that prompted Hill's alarm were familiar enough —a shortage of soldiers, supplies, and sound money. Congress, in the face of these problems, was not inactive; it was simply increasingly ineffective.

Faced with the hyperinflation during the winter of 1779–1780, Congress toyed with the idea of imposing general price controls, as had been advocated by the committees in Pennsylvania and by a convention held at Hartford in October of 1779. Congress recommended that the states meet in a general convention on January 5 to pass a broad limitation of prices to go into effect on February 1, but the convention did not materialize. It was clear that more drastic steps were necessary.

By March, Congress decided to accept the inevitable, and on the eighteenth of that month it virtually repudiated $200,000,000 in Continental money by ordering that it be exchanged for new currency at a ratio of 40 to 1 of specie—a measure long advocated by those who traced inflation not to the machinations of evil men but to an excess of money[*12*]. The plan called upon the states to retire the old money through taxation. As it was delivered to Congress, the new money would be emitted, guaranteed by both Congress and the states, with 40 percent allocated for congressional expenditures and the remainder for the states in proportion to the amount each retired. The program had little success. Its reception in the states was uneven. Virginia, for example, at first refused to ratify the act—a move which John Walker told Thomas Jefferson produced as much "uneasiness" in Congress as did the loss of Charleston. William Grayson, a member of the Board of War and Ordnance who had previously served as a delegate from Virginia, wrote to General William Smallwood that if Virginia did not rescind her determination, "we are all undone." Virginia did comply by July, but the substitution of new money for old without any alteration in the financial powers of Congress could not curb depreciation. By June of 1781, when the whole amount of the old currency was supposed to have been retired, just $31,000,000 had been withdrawn from circulation— not enough to cut depreciation in half[*13*].

Worthless old money and the scarcity of any substitute meant that some delegates experienced personal distress. William Ellery of Rhode Island was completely out of money and was unable to sell a warrant on the treasury even at a discount—a sacrifice he was willing to make simply to avoid being dunned by his creditors. Writing to Governor William Greene of Rhode Island, he added that he was not the only poor delegate in Congress: "Many are in the same circumstance"[14]. Money was short everywhere. Samuel Johnston told the Governor of North Carolina he would be unable to accept his appointment to Congress unless the Board of Trade supplied him with money to meet his expenses.[15].

Despite the dearth of funds in the South, some Eastern delegates were resentful that their states had contributed more money to the war effort than the South had. Ellery's colleague Ezekiel Cornell advised Governor Greene to "pay no more money on Continental account than is absolutely necessary for the salvation of the country." According to Cornell, Rhode Island had lent more money to the Continent than every state in the South and would find great difficulty in securing reimbursement for its loan office certificates. Cornell was particularly irate about the Southern contributions when he considered the lethargic defense put up by the Carolinas and the selfish Virginian distraction with her western lands[16].

But if monetary problems sometimes sharpened the division between Eastern and Southern delegations, there were times when the two sections joined against the security-rich Middle region. Such was the case when the issue of a depreciation scale for loan office certificates was raised. After the decision to devalue Continental currency in March of 1780, Congress turned its attention to the revaluation of outstanding loan office certificates and, as E. James Ferguson has pointed out, proceeded to greatly overrate them in setting up a scale for conversion to specie value in terms of depreciation of the purchase money. The final date decided upon to begin the scale was September 1, 1777, by which time a substantial depreciation already had taken place[17]. Furthermore, interest was paid on the face value of all securities dated before March 1, 1778, despite the acknowledged depreciation before that time. Actually, a number of motions were made to place the cut-off date for the acceptance of face value of purchase money even later than September 1. Matlack and Muhlenberg moved that the date be March 1, 1778, and when this was rejected, Houston and Schuyler moved December 1, 1777. When this, too, was voted down, McKean and Schuyler suggested September 10, and finally September 1, 1777[18]. The September 1 date was voted in by a count of 7 to 5, so there was substantial opposition even to the final arrangement. The positions of the delegates on the four votes are arranged in Table 15.

The convergence of such disparate delegates as the conservative nationalist Schuyler and the radical parochialists James Searle and Timothy Matlack on such a highly charged issue as speculation in public securities is another demonstration of the breakdown of the politics of republican purity. Clearly, the Pennsylvania radicals simply were voting according to the interests of their security-holding constituents in departing implicitly from the position they

TABLE 15

Voting on Depreciation Scale for Loan Office Certificates, June 22, 1780

Bloc	Delegate and State	0634	0633	0632	0631	0634	0633	0632	0631*
I	Folsom (N.H.)	x†	x	x	x				
	Lovell (Mass.)	x	x	x	x				
	Holten (Mass.)	x	x	x	x				
	Ward (Mass.)	x	x	x	x				
	Cornell (R.I.)	x	x	x	x				
	Ellsworth (Conn.)	x	x	x	x				
	Sherman (Conn.)	x	x	x	x				
	Clark (N.J.)	x	x	x	x				
	Jones, J. (Va.)		x	x	x				
	Madison (Va.)	x	x	x	x				
	Jones, N. W. (N.C.)	x	x	x	x				
	Hill (N.C.)	x	x	x	x				
	Few‡ (Ga.)		x	x	x	o†			
II	Huntington (Conn.)		x	x	o	o			
	Fell (N.J.)		x	x	o	o			
	Henry, J. (Va.)		x	x	o	o			
	Walker (Va.)		x	x	o	o			
	Walton (Ga.)		x	x	o	o			
III	Armstrong‡ (Pa.)		x		o	o	o		
	Schuyler (N.Y.)				o	o	o	o	
	Houston (N.J.)				o	o	o	o	
	Searle (Pa.)				o	o	o	o	
	Muhlenberg (Pa.)				o	o	o	o	
	Matlack (Pa.)				o	o	o	o	
	Ingersoll (Pa.)				o	o	o	o	
	McKean (Del.)				o	o	o	o	
	Hanson (Md.)				o	o	o	o	
	Bee (S.C.)				o	o	o	o	
	Kinloch (S.C.)				o	o	o	o	

*Numbers refer to designations of votes in Clifford Lord (ed.), *The Atlas of Congressional Roll Calls* (New York, 1943), vol. I.

†In all cases x represents a negative vote; o, a positive vote.

‡Few and Armstrong may be included in blocs I and III.

had taken during the previous year. The significance of this shift cannot be fully understood apart from the realization that Matlack was a bitter opponent of Robert Morris in Pennsylvania state politics and that John Armstrong was the most dedicated advocate of price controls in Congress. If it is assumed, as many historians assume, that the nationalist thrust of 1781 coalesced around the public debt, it is at least anomalous that parochialists and nationalists should have been in such disarray during 1780. Just as there were Constitutionalists supporting speculators in loan office certificates, there were delegates who advocated a strongly nationalist policy in the opposition bloc, notably Cornell, Sherman, Joseph Jones, and Madison. It was not until the Articles of Confederation were ratified, the office of the Superintendent of Finance created as part of a reformation of the congressional executive apparatus, and Robert Morris appinted to the post that the public debt could become an instrument of national consolidation.

It was the army, of course, which suffered most from the dearth of funds. The collapse of the continental meant that Congress had to ask the states to provide supplies directly to the army. Quotas of beef, bacon, flour, horses, and so forth were set up for the states north of Virginia, while the South was expected to do its best to supply the armies in the Southern campaign. This system of requisitions, apart from being a last resort, seemed to offer certain advantages: it would, it was hoped, reduce private speculation and abuses in the Commissary Department; it would provide supplies without heavy public debts and the inequities which flowed from the use of an inflating currency; and it promised to reduce a complex supply system to a simple and ideologically attractive formula whereby the nation's resources would be as inexhaustible as its industry[19].

But complications rapidly appeared. It was difficult to agree upon equitable quotas. Massachusetts, for example, successfully argued that her contributions should be reduced because of the expenses she had incurred during an unsuccessful expedition launched under her own auspices against the British at Penobscot Bay. Since some monetary value had to be affixed to contributions in order to establish credits in a general accounting, inequities still existed because of differing prices for provisions in the various states. Some states — a very few — met their quotas, while others were more laggard. Finally, no satisfactory administrative mechanism existed to enforce the system, and to the degree that it was implemented, congressional power was undermined. As Joseph Jones put it, "As to the Army the Congress is at present little more than the medium through which the wants of the Army are conveyed to the States"[20].

The collection of specific supplies from the states, as well as other matters related to the military, such as the recruitment of troops, the reformation of abuses in procurements, and the general improvement of communication and coordination between the army and Congress, was entrusted by a wary Congress to a committee of three which was sent to Washington's camp. Consisting of Philip Schuyler, John Mathews, and Nathaniel Peabody, the "committee at headquarters" set out on April 12. The committee had a stormy history during the spring and summer of 1780 until it was finally disbanded on August 11[21]. In its recommendations for organizational changes, the committee followed the suggestions of Washington and Quartermaster General Nathanael Greene, to the distress of many members of Congress who had become upset with Greene's demands for more control. Relations between the committee and Greene, on the one hand, and Congress on the other became so strained that the irritated Greene resigned, and Congress disbanded the committee—not without some sharp exchanges with the excitable Mathews, whose patience was exhausted.

This episode, which was part of the prelude to broader executive reorganization in the spring of 1781, was not marred by recognizable factional divisions. Nathanael Greene was a Rhode Islander who initially had been the candidate of Joseph Reed, a marginal Constitutionalist. Greene had anti-Morris subordinates such as Charles Pettit, later the chief architect of the Constitutionalist fiscal policy in Pennsylvania. Despite this, Greene did not win the united support of the Eastern party in the struggle over the reorganization of the Quartermaster Department. Congress commissioned the original Quartermaster General, Thomas Mifflin, a Republican in Pennsylvania politics, to draw up a new plan, which won the support of those who disliked either the structure of Greene's proposed revision or the manner in which he presented it to Congress. Mifflin, an Eastern connection from Resistance days, was backed by the Old Radicals, Sherman and Lovell[22].

The divisions within New England on this issue were curious in one sense but intelligible in terms of the distinction between the "Old Radicals" and newer delegates such as Peabody of New Hampshire and Cornell of Rhode Island. Both Peabody and Cornell were sympathetic with the mode of military operations practiced by Washington and Greene. They did not distrust the military as the Eastern party had, and, in any respects, did.

The new mood of Congress did not go so far as to tolerate John Mathews's proposal that Washington be granted dictatorial powers[23]. On the other hand, another request of the committee which Washington had long advocated and Congress persistently denied was granted—half pay to officers for life. After sidestepping the issue in 1779 by recommending on August 17 that the individual states make whatever allowances for pensions they saw fit, Congress finally voted through a half pay settlement in October of 1780. The Old Radicals, Samuel Adams and James Lovell, predictably opposed what they construed to be a measure for the creation of a military aristocracy. Connecticut and New Jersey also voted against the resolution as did, surprisingly, General Cornell of Rhode Island. But another New England general, John Sullivan, cast New Hampshire's vote in support of the measure, and so did the Pennsylvania Constitutionalist delegate James McLene. The military crisis of 1780 made it impossible for the Eastern bloc to draw support from the South on this measure. The Virginia vote was cast by the single delegate, Theodorick Bland, who was closely tied to the Lees, but Bland voted against Sam Adams on half pay[24].

Neither finance nor military policy during the critical days of 1780 sustained the party lines that had been drawn during the years of Eastern ascendancy.

IV

The problems related to finance and the army could be ameliorated, though hardly eliminated, by the completion of the Confederation. The delegates did not need to be reminded as they were by the French Minister who succeeded Gérard, Chevalier de La Luzerne, that the American cause would gain added stature and power if the Articles of Confederation were ratified. The major obstacle preventing the completion of the Confederation was the vast claim of Virginia to the West—a claim that antagonized "landless" states lacking comparable claims and, in particular, the state of Maryland, which had refused to ratify until Virginia ceded her western lands to the general government. Brought firmly under national authority, the West would at the very least provide Congress with future revenue from land sales to help cope with the national debt. In a more profound sense, the West constituted a lure holding the Confederation together, for only a united confederation could successfully exploit its resources—unless a single state or section, of necessity Virginia or the South, dominated its development. During 1778 and 1779, Virginia seemed to be attempting precisely such dominance. Maryland's refusal to ratify the Articles of Confederation out of fear that it might be absorbed by Virginia, made powerful by a vast interior domain, was natural[25].

But the western problem was vastly complicated by speculative interests which had been contending for access to the western lands along the Ohio since the 1740s. The history of the disputes between Virginia and Pennsylvania-Maryland land companies is much too lengthy to be discussed here[26]. It may suffice to suggest that just before the Revolution, the land speculators from Pennsylvania, preeminently Samuel Wharton, George Croghan, and William Trent, in conjunction with highly placed English politicians such as George Grenville and Thomas Walpole, along with Benjamin Franklin, had very nearly succeeded in displacing the claims of the older group of Virginian speculators organized in the Ohio Company to most of the present state of West Virginia. The advent of the Revolution demolished the plans of the Walpole Associates, as they became known, to establish a proprietary colony of "Vandalia," but the appetites of the Pennsylvania speculators, as well as associates in New Jersey and Maryland, were not diminished in the least. Organized as the Vandalia and Indiana Companies claiming territory to the south of the Ohio, and as the Illinois and Wabash Companies with claims to the north of the river, the Middle states investors, reinforced with Indian treaties, pressed for congressional jurisdiction over the region west of the Alleghenies and for validation of their claims.

As the Revolution progressed, controversies between landed and landless states; between rival groups of speculators in Virginia, North Carolina, Pennsylvania, and Maryland; and between states with disputed boundaries continued unabated. Such disputes delayed the initial formulation of the Articles as well as their ratification[27]. The celebrated George Rogers Clark expeditions in the Ohio Valley were calculated to enhance Virginia's claim to the region as well as to expel the British. Clark's force set out in the fall of 1777 against Colonel Henry Hamilton, who had been raiding frontier settlements with Loyalist and Indian support. Clark captured Kaskaskia by July of 1778, and by late February he forced Hamilton's surrender at Vincennes.

Shortly after, in June of 1779, Virginia set up a land office to issue warrants and sell land in the West—an action which prompted protests from Pennsylvania speculators, including William Trent and George Morgan. Congress created a committee of five to investigate the problem, and in a report considered by Congress on October 29 and 30, 1779, the committee advocated that Virginia reconsider its act and that "every other State in similar circumstances . . . suspend the sale, grant, or settlement of any land unappropriated at the time of the declaration of independence, until the conclusion of the war"[28]. The report passed by a sizable margin, eight states to two, dramatizing Virginia's isolation not only from Maryland and the landless states but also from Massachusetts and Connecticut, which had their own claims in the Northwest, and from Congress in general. Only North Carolina supported the Old Dominion, and even the North Carolina delegates, in concert with Gouverneur Morris, attempted at one point to confine the restriction to Virginia.

Undaunted, the Virginia Assembly, under the leadership of George Mason, who had substantial investments in the West, adopted a "Remonstrance . . . to the delegates of the United American States in Congress Assembled" on December 14, to be presented to Congress by the Virginia delegates at their discretion. Virginia agreed to halt the sale of land north of the Ohio but continued to sell land south of the river. Furthermore, the Assembly pointedly reminded Congress that it had no jurisdiction over the western lands and, therefore, must disregard the petitions from the speculators of the Vandalia and Indiana Companies[29].

Virginia's policy of continuing to sell lands south of the Ohio won the state no sympathy from Congress, particularly from delegates such as Ezekiel Cornell, who grumbled that Virginia was paying more attention to the sale of her "out lands" than to the battle against the British[30]. Cornell's irritation was exacerbated by the fact that proceeds from the western lands went to Virginia; in Cornell's judgment, that state was not contributing its share to the common cause. His angry suggestion that Rhode Island contribute no more to the Continental account than was "absolutely necessary for the salvation of the country" was a natural consequence of this resentment. That Cornell was a strong centralist is suggestive of how divisive the West, a potentially nationalist influence, could be.

It was during 1780 that Virginia assured its weaker sister states that it did not intend to establish its own western empire when it yielded its claim to the area north of the Ohio. On September 6, the Virginia delegates moved in Congress that all ceded lands should be formed into new states and constitute a common fund for members of the Confederation. Thus was the Northwest, at least, transformed into a "payoff." The effect was immediately apparent. Maryland ratified the Articles; the Confederation was a legal fact; and the consolidation of the nation could commence.

There were a number of reasons for this breakthrough, all of which had importance for the transitional phase of congressional partisanship during 1780. First, the military situation in both the South and the Northwest worsened, placing Virginia in an entirely different relationship with the West. During the early part of 1780, Joseph Jones and James Madison joined the Easterners in ensuring that military forces in the North should not be weakened in order to liberate the South. They resisted motions for the removal of troops or provisions to the north of Virginia; opposed the reallocation to the South of funds which had been designated to complete the hull of the seventy-four-gun frigate "America" being built by John Langdon at Portsmouth, New Hampshire; and supported a clarification of Washington's orders so as to allow him to conduct military operations outside the limits of the United States—a revision which the New Englanders endorsed as a means of legitimizing a Canadian campaign[31]. The Virginians seem to have been as much concerned with protecting the northern and northwestern frontiers as with defending the South during the early part of the year, but by late 1780, things had changed. The Chesapeake itself was jeopardized by General Alexander Leslie's raids—a fact which prompted Virginia and Maryland to cooperate with each other.

Related to military pressures, but separate nevertheless, was the question of relations with France. French assistance in the final stages of the war was critical, and Luzerne, Gérard's competent and more successful replacement, stressed that French aid would be much more effective if the Confederation were completed. The traditional pro-Gallican posture of the South made both Virginia and Maryland eager to overcome the western problem.

Military and diplomatic pressures were not the only reasons for Virginia's decision to cede the Northwest. Jones and Madison were more continental in their outlook than were many of their compatriots at home. Both urged the wisdom of ceding the Northwest well before the fall. Jones told Jefferson in June that the New York cession of her western claim earlier in the year was "worthy of imitation" and that Virginia should "moderate her desires"[*32*]. Jones actually lobbied in the Virginia Assembly for the cession.

That the West was an extraordinarily complex problem that confused rather than harmonized the movement toward stronger union in 1780 is illustrated in yet one other factor contributing to the Virginia cession—the vexing question of Vermont.

The "New Hampshire Grants," as they were often called at that time, were closely tied with the issue of the West, since boundary disputes even over settled lands would create precedents for congressional action in resolving western claims. Moreover, a secessionist movement such as that launched by the Vermonters, who had created their own government and were pressing for separate status as a state by 1777, particularly disturbed Virginians and North Carolinians who were concerned about their settlements beyond the mountains. Finally, the question of admitting another New England state had thorny sectional implications which were not lost upon Southern delegates.

New York, New Hampshire, and Massachusetts all had claims to the Vermont region. While Massachusetts never seriously pressed its case, which was not a good one, it did oppose New York jurisdiction. New York claimed the land under an Order in Council of 1764, and New Hampshire by usage. Governor Benning Wentworth of New Hampshire had allotted some 130 townships on the tenuous grounds that the boundary adjustment with Massachusetts in 1738 had established the New Hampshire border as a northward extension of the western boundaries of Connecticut and Massachusetts[*33*]. During the early 1770s, many settlers on the west side of the Green Mountains held their lands by New Hampshire warrant, while others held title from New York under Governors Cadwallader Colden and William Tryon. New York speculators received a million acres from Colden, including a large tract given to James Duane in 1765. Those who held the New York titles were harrassed by the Green Mountain Boys under Ethan Allen (who had organized a land company along with Thomas Chittendon and Abidad Pratt of Salisbury). Armed conflict broke out in 1774 and continued sporadically beyond the Revolution[*34*].

The struggle over Vermont involved conflicting claims of land speculators, much as did the dispute in the Ohio region. The struggle inevitably became entwined with congressional politics, as was clearly demonstrated in the very composition of the New York and New Hampshire delegations as the issue came to a head in 1779 and 1780. The prolonged presence of James Duane in the New York delegation can be attributed in part to his desire to secure his vast claims in Vermont. Samuel Livermore, who had been attorney general of New Hampshire, was chosen as a delegate for 1780 specifically to act as agent in the Vermont affair. Delegates often were judged mainly in terms of their position on the dispute. Woodbury Langdon was aghast that Nathaniel Folsom should also have been sent to Congress in 1780, because his attitude toward the Vermont lands apparently was not compatible with New Hampshire speculative interests[35].

New York strategy on Vermont was both complicated and difficult to execute. Clearly that strategy explains in part the alliance between New York and the Southern delegations. New York could rely upon the Southern interest, both in validating state claims and in preventing an addition to the Eastern weight in the scale of congressional factionalism. The strategy contributed to the reluctance of Duane and Livingston to move relocation of the Maryland line for the defense of New York—a move that in Livingston's words would have "lost us the confidence of the Southern States and . . . deprived us of the power of being useful upon other occasions"[36]. At the same time, there was the problem of Maryland, whose antagonism toward the western policy of Virginia made it difficult for New York to secure united Southern support, which she needed to counter New England opposition.

The New York Legislature ceded its claim to the Northwest in February 1780. The cession was unencumbered by reservations about military bounties and Indian treaties concluded by outside speculators, such as those stipulated later by Connecticut and Virginia. Thus New York broke the logjam that had prevented western cessions, thereby placating Maryland. Should Virginia follow suit because of embarrassment over the liberality of New York's precedent, the Confederation might be consummated. Once this was effected, the jurisdiction of Congress over the Vermont dispute would be strengthened and, accordingly, the case of New York fortified.

The New York precedent increased pressure on Virginia to cede her western claims. Realizing the great expense of administering the sale of such remote lands and recognizing further that governing a vast territory would be virtually impossible by one state, Virginia was not entirely disposed to cling doggedly to her western claims. By the summer of 1780, Joseph Jones had returned temporarily to Virginia to be with his ailing wife and to lobby in the Burgesses for cession of the western lands. By September of that year, back in Congress, he was able to present Virginia's terms for cession of her lands north of the Ohio: (1) that states be established in the ceded lands no less than 100 nor more than 150 miles square "or as near thereto as circumstances will admit," and that remaining territory not ceded be guaranteed to the parent state; (2) that expenses incurred in ousting the British from the West be reimbursed by Congress; (3) that all territory not allocated for bounties for the army be considered a common fund for all the states, and that, therefore, all private purchases from the Indians be nullified[*37*].

There was opposition from the land companies to the third provision of Jones's motion, and in the congressional acceptance on October 10, that part of the proposed resolution was struck out[*38*]. The rejection of the clause invalidating land company claims was due to opposition not only from New Jersey, Pennsylvania, and Maryland. Indeed, of the eight delegates from those three states, Houston of New Jersey, Muhlenberg of Pennsylvania, and Plater of Maryland voted in favor of the full resolution[*39*]. All four delegates from New Hampshire, Massachusetts, and Rhode Island, on the other hand, voted against the resolutions, as did Madison himself and Sharpe of North Carolina. While the machinations of the land companies by no means precluded bribes of members of Congress through the granting of stock, this does not seem to account for the vote. None of the major stockholders who were at one time or another members of Congress—George Read, Robert Morris, James Wilson, Samuel Chase, and Charles Carroll of Carrollton, for example—were attending at this time. On the other hand, Middle states delegates naturally felt obliged to protect the interests of their speculating constituents.

Unfazed by congressional concern for the land companies, the Virginia Legislature made its cession on February 2, 1781, retaining the condition against the land company purchases from the Indians. Although this issue would not be settled for some time to come, the Maryland Legislature authorized its delegates to signify Maryland's ratification of the Articles of Confederation. On March 1, 1781, some six months before the effective end of the war of the Revolution, the United States had a national government in law as well as in fact.

v

The Virginia cession and Maryland ratification coincided with other dramatic developments in the executive organization and fiscal policy of Congress. Indeed, the administrative changes of late 1780-1781 were so far reaching that historians have generally interpreted this period variously as a "constructivist" reformation or a nationalist "counterrevolution"[*40*] of central significance for the analysis of the history of congressional factionalism. However, while there was an accelerating tempo of change during the winter of 1780-1781, the use of administrative boards composed of persons outside Congress as well as delegates began as early as 1777. From the outset, moreover, congressional parties vied for control of the executive apparatus.

The members of the Board of War and Ordnance, a standing congressional committee formed in June of 1776, soon discovered that it was impossible for them to function as regular members of Congress and attend fully to their duties on the Board. Thus in July of 1777, Congress resolved to appoint a Board of War consisting of three persons who were not members of Congress. As finally arranged on October 17, 1777, the Board was to keep a register of officers, maintain accounts of ordnance and supplies, superintend the building of arsenals and foundries, forward dispatches of the Congress to the states and the armies, oversee the recruitment and dispatch of land forces "in the service of the United States," make estimates for the Congress of military stores needed, and keep a record of all business transacted[41]. The Board subsequently was expanded to five members, any three of whom were to constitute a quorum, and it was instructed to sit wherever Congress happened to be. Additional appointments were made during the fall of 1777, a time of Eastern opposition to Washington and Schuyler, and the power of the Eastern party allowed them to dominate the Board.

In October of 1778, the structure of the Board of War was changed slightly in a manner that was to become the pattern used in subsequent administrative boards. Thence forward, two of the five members were to be members of Congress[42]. New appointments were made at the same time, but despite the inclusion of two Virginians, William Grayson as a noncongressman and Francis Lightfoot Lee as a congressional representative, the Board continued to have an effective Northern orientation. Timothy Pickering of Massachusetts and Richard Peters of Pennsylvania served into 1780, when Pickering resigned to replace Nathanael Greene as quartermaster general, while Jesse Root of Connecticut was appointed as the second member from Congress. As Jennings B. Sanders has pointed out, Pickering and Peters seem to have managed the Board without assistance during 1779 and 1780, and when Pickering resigned, it was dominated by Peters and Ezekiel Cornell of Rhode Island, the latter serving on separate occasions as a congressional representative and as a noncongressional member[43].

That the Board of War never obtained independence from Congress can be seen in the constant formation of special committees to consider the condition of the army, the most notable being the Committee at Headquarters. No authority over the formulation of policy was granted to the Board, and many of its relatively insignificant decisions had to be reviewed by Congress — a fact that hardly enhanced its effectiveness. This, in conjunction with the Eastern orientation of the Board during the period before 1780, was exactly what disturbed the advocates of centralization and precisely what the Old Radicals believed would preserve the integrity of the Revolution.

The Eastern party also had been most powerful in the committees on foreign and marine affairs. James Lovell managed the correspondence of the foreign affairs committee almost single-handedly during 1779—a duty which seems to have been as onerous as it was influential. Lovell complained about his gargantuan task at the same time that he assured Arthur Lee that his dispatches were being properly received. Lovell reported to Lee in June that there had been several attempts to choose a new committee rather than "filling up the old one," but nothing was done[44].

The marine committee was in many ways more controversial than Lovell's foreign affairs committee, largely because of its wider jurisdiction. It had control over the various navy boards which immediately administered the building and outfitting of ships; it ruled on prize captures either immediately or through the boards; and at times it made decisions about the importation and exportation of goods for Continental use[45]. Although the committee was composed of one delegate from each state, there was an inevitable tendency for the Eastern party to dominate its affairs. Delegates such as William Whipple had vastly more information about maritime affairs than did delegates from the South, and most of the activity supervised by the committee occurred in the North.

The administration of marine affairs also involved the periodic formation of special congressional courts to consider appeals from state admiralty courts in prize cases. It was not an entirely satisfactory arrangement. In May of 1779, a number of Philadelphia merchants, including Robert Morris, William Bradford, John Nixon, and Thomas Fitzsimmins—all associated with the Republican interest in Pennsylvania politics—complained to the Pennsylvania Executive Council about congressional management of appeals. The merchants noted that the court's membership fluctuated, and its connection with Congress resulted in shifts of location entailing inconveniences for privateers. Further, there was a lack of "fixed principles" which inhibited privateering[46].

On June 9, 1779, at the height of the campaign to purge the Lee influence from the foreign service, John Dickinson and Thomas Burke moved that the business of the marine committee be vested in commissioners[47]. On October 28, the marine committee was replaced by a new executive agency, the Board of Admiralty, a prelude to the executive reorganization of the following year. It was not an agency composed entirely of members of Congress, for the regulations for the Board of Admiralty stipulated that only two delegates from Congress could be appointed to the Board. The remaining three members would come from outside. The Board was given ample powers closely resembling those of the defunct marine committee[48]. The composition of the Board reflected both sectional and partisan factors. William Whipple of New Hampshire, Francis Lewis of New York, and Thomas Waring of South Carolina were the three members elected from outside Congress, while William Ellery of Rhode Island and James Forbes of Maryland were the congressional representatives. Whipple was a partisan of the Adams-Lee group, but he was not in Congress at the moment; Forbes, in Congress, had supported Deane but was less partisan than Whipple; Ellery, also in Congress, was attached to the Eastern party but not to the Adams-Lee core; Waring was from the Deep South, but he was unconnected with the partisan struggles of Congress; Lewis, a New Yorker, was an opponent of the Robert Morris group, but he had largely avoided the ideological controversies of 1778 and 1779.

Whether the intention of the rule that a majority of the Board should come from outside Congress had been to prevent conflicts of interest or to promote efficiency, or both, it is notable that only one of the five had never been connected with Congress. The inclusion of Lewis and Whipple illustrated the development of the beginnings of a national "establishment" which was to become more evident with innovations in adminstration organization over the next two years. After Ellery was not included in the next Rhode Island delegation, he resigned his slot and was reelected as a member from outside Congress. Again, when Congress established a court of appeals in admiralty cases shortly afterward in January, Cyrus Griffin of the Virginia delegation was elected as a judge (despite the fact that his lone vote for Virginia had been important in the thirteen roll calls recorded between January 4 and 15 in the determination of the composition and location of the court)[49]. Yet another judge of the Court of Appeals was William Paca, previously a delegate from Maryland and in 1779 a strong Deane partisan[50].

Because of the opposition to Eastern influence in naval affairs, there was a marked penetration of delegates from the Southern coalition in the new marine administration. When Waring did not arrive for the Board consultations during the spring, James Madison served in his place between March and June. The appointment of Griffin and Paca to the Court of Appeals also illustrated this tendency, as did the debates over the composition and location of the Court during January 1780. Thomas Burke and John Mathews moved that one member of the three-man Court be from New England and one member from Virginia, the Carolinas, or Georgia. Although that motion failed, there was also a successful attempt to restrict the location of the Court to the region between Hartford and Williamsburg—a maneuver naturally opposed by the Massachusetts and New Hampshire delegations[51].

An arrangement analogous to that of the War and Admiralty Boards was made for fiscal affairs on July 30, 1779, when Congress created a Treasury Board of five members, two of whom were to be delegates, the others from outside. The Treasury Board was given wide supervisory authority over the Auditor General and his assistants, the Treasurer, two Chambers of Accounts (each with three commissioners), and six auditors of the army, all elected by Congress[52]. The tendency of Congress to appoint present or past members to treasury posts was less noticeable than in the marine committee, although "connexions" were evident in Sherman's nomination of Jonathan Trumbull, Jr., to the post of comptroller in 1778 during a previous reorganization[53]. The evolution of a national "establishment" continued under Robert Morris, it might be noted. When Robert Morris, as Superintendent of Finance, attempted to collect taxes allocated by the states for the Continental account directly through his own appointees, he designated among the receivers of taxes William Whipple in New Hampshire, James Lovell in Massachusetts, William C. Houston in New Jersey, and George Read in Delaware—all of whom had been members of Congress[54].

The evolution of a political establishment was inevitable, as men such as Ellery of Rhode Island began to carve a career from officeholding in and under Congress. The evolution was necessary because of the way administration had been clogged when handled under the original committee system; yet it was deplored by many who feared the consequences of a separate, permanent bureaucracy. Indeed, it was a corrupt administration in England that had been charged with the responsibility for bringing about the Revolution, and Americans were strongly disposed to anticipate the appearance of power-hungry ministers surrounded by sychophantic placemen at the moment a national administration was created.

The fear of a concentration of power in the national government was stronger in the extremities of the Confederation than in its center—stronger in the Carolinas and New England than in Pennsylvania and New York. This was as natural as was the growth of a more systematic administration, for the capital of the Confederation inevitably would be located somewhere in the center region, which would serve as a "core area" for the closer amalgamation of the nation[55]. The mixture of necessity, fear, and Middle states dominance in the movement to centralize and improve the administration of national affairs subsequently would help shape the political controversy surrounding that movement.

VI

The half steps taken in the administration of the Admiralty and the Treasury during 1779 did not solve the crisis in national authority that became all too apparent in 1780. This was especially true in finance. Neither the reorganization of the Treasury nor the devaluation of the continental at 40 to 1 succeeded in halting the precipitous decline in the value of Continental currency. Between August of 1780 and March of 1781, a new executive structure was formed with the creation of departments of foreign affairs and war, as well as the superintendency of finance; a 5-percent impost for Continental use was recommended to the states as an amendment to the Confederation; and Congress was considering (though not recommending) a thorough revision of the Articles.

This significant, though far from total, alteration of congressional administration and authority was accomplished, not in the context of severe partisan struggles such as those over foreign policy and price controls during the previous year, but in an atmosphere of remarkable consensus. Support for the policy came from all sections and from political leaders outside Congress as well as within. A group of representatives from Massachusetts, Connecticut, and New Hampshire met at Boston in August of 1780 to frame a common policy for troop recruitment and taxation, as well as to make recommendations to Congress for the reduction of the national debt and the completion of the Confederation[56]. Among the recommendations of this meeting was the suggestion that "national concerns" of the United States be under the direction of Congress and that the Confederation should be completed with whatever states were willing to confederate. Representatives from the four New England states and New York met at Hartford in November and sent a copy of their proceedings to Congress, including the recommendation that Congress authorize Washington to use armed force against a state which refused to comply with its quotas. The New York Legislature also instructed its delegates to press for stronger authority for the Congress. Indeed, Congress should

> exercise every power which they may deem necessary for an effectual Prosecution of the War, and . . . whenever it shall appear to them that any State is deficient in furnishing the Quota of Men, Money, Provisions or other Supplies, required of each State, the Congress direct the Commander-in-Chief, without delay, to march the Army, or such Part of it as may be requisite, into such State; and by a Military Force, compel it to furnish its deficiency[57].

James Duane, a nationalist but always a discrete politician, applauded the "Zeal and publick Spirit" of the Legislature in a letter to Clinton but suggested that the "Compulsory Clause is not perhaps proper for publick Inspection"[58].

While the strongest outside pressures for national consolidation came from the North, support for a reformation in Congress came from all sections—indeed, perhaps more actively from the Middle states and the South than from New England delegations. The broad endorsement of more centralization was due in part to changes in the membership of Congress during 1780 and 1781 that have been described earlier in this chapter. But it would be a mistake to conclude that nationally oriented men had swept all before them, for a number of states' righters either remained in or entered Congress during 1780 and 1781. Samuel Adams, always an opponent of executivism and centralism, was present from late June of 1780 until April of 1781, thus serving during the controversey with the committee at headquarters, the creation of the executive departments, the appointment of Morris as Super-intendent of Finance with the powers he insisted upon, and the debates over the impost. There were other opponents of centralized authority in the Massachusetts delegation, including Artemas Ward, Elbridge Gerry (present in 1780, though not after mid-February of 1781), and Samuel Osgood[59]. In the Rhode Island delegation, neither Ellery nor Mowry shared the nation-alist convictions of Cornell and Varnum. The Pennsylvania delegation was dominated by opponents of national consolidation during 1780, as has al-ready been suggested. Thomas McKean of Delaware had been an ally, if not a core member, of the New England–Constitutionalist coalition and would later characterize Robert Morris as a "king." Further south, while Richard Henry Lee was absent his doctrines were defended by Theodorick Bland, a relative of the Lees, present during both years in the Virginia dele-gation. Finally, Thomas Burke of North Carolina, the champion of all states' righters, also served during both years.

With the exception of John Sullivan, the most active delegates in the movement to establish executive departments and augment congressional power were from the New York and Southern delegations. It was James Duane who moved on May 15, 1780, that a committee be appointed to arrange a de-partment of foreign affairs. Three months later it was Robert R. Livingston and Joseph Jones who moved that a committee of five be appointed to plan a complete new executive structure[60]. Both Livingston and Jones, and later Duane, were placed on the committee of five, which took over the work of the committee on the department of foreign affairs. The final report adopted by Congress on January 10, 1781, was drawn up by Duane. The committee report on the other Departments of War, Marine, and Finance, adopted on February 6, was also largely the work of Duane.

There were no roll-call votes requested at this time on any of the resolu-tions establishing the executive departments. A careful examination of the authority granted by Congress to the various department heads reveals why there was so little apparent argument. The Secretary for Foreign Affairs, for example, had no greater formal power than did the previous congressional committee. Instructed to reside where Congress was located and holding office during the pleasure of Congress, he was to receive and report foreign correspon-dence, collect information from abroad, and correspond with American and other ministers, and he was allowed to attend Congress that he might be better informed to execute his duties[61]. The duties of the Secretary of War were almost identical with the duties of the Board of War. He was to examine the state of troops and ordnance; keep records of the numbers of troops, arms, and supplies; make recommendations for new troop quotas, recruitments, and supplies; transmit all congressional orders; and perform other housekeeping duties. Neither department was allowed policy-making powers. The most significant innovation was that the departments would be under a single head who was not a member of Congress—an innovation that did, of course, raise the specter of executivism. But since it already had been decided that this should be the case, there was little occasion for debate[62].

Despite the radical changes brought about in monetary affairs by Robert Morris, the definition of the powers of the Superintendent of Finance did not represent an abrupt departure from the administration under the Board of Treasury. The Superintendent was to examine the condition of public finance and make suggestions for new plans, rather than formulate new policies. Although consequential powers were allocated in the settlement of accounts and implicit authority allowed in the execution of congressional policy, the office could have become a cipher in the hands of a less aggressive individual. All in all, the creation of the executive departments represented a compromise between those who supported "executivism" and those who advocated congressional control. Controversy centered not so much on the definition of the offices as on the appointments to them, in the cases of foreign affairs and war, and on the grant of additional powers to Morris. It is not without significance that the office of Secretary for Foreign Affairs was not filled until August 10, and that of the Secretary of War until October 30[63].

The appointment of Robert Morris, on the other hand, was immediate and apparently noncontroversial. Congress was looking for a financial wizard —a Necker—and Morris was the obvious choice. Only when he demanded complete authority to appoint and dismiss subordinates without congressional interference and to retain his previous business connections was there any resistance. Still, on four roll calls between March 20 and March 31, Morris won the overwhelming support of the Southern and Middle states delegations, and even some Eastern votes as well. Table 16 illustrates the point.

The almost unanimous support given Morris by the South was accented by the fact that Thomas Burke, the most ardent advocate of states' rights in 1777, either moved or seconded every resolution affecting the superintendency of finance. Burke's striking about-face has puzzled historians, but seen in the light of congressional partisanship rather than states' rights–nationalist categories, Burke's shift on this issue becomes as understandable as was his support of another stanchion of nationalism—the impost. Burke had supported the Deane faction in 1779, was a particularly vocal opponent of the Lees and the Eastern party, and had never opposed Morris. Indeed, Burke was indebted to Morris and may have been using Morris's advice on investments[64]. His role at this moment was a manifestation of both his natural activism and the concern for fiscal reformation which he shared with most Southerners who believed drastic steps were necessary to stop the British.

TABLE 16

Burke-Duane-Mathews Resolutions on Morris Conditions for Acceptance of Superintendency of Finance, March 20–31, 1781

	I	II	III	IV	V
	Pro-Morris		Middle	Anti-Morris	
N.H.				Sullivan	
Mass.	Lovell				Adams
					Ward
R.I.					
Conn.	Wolcott			Huntington, S.	
				Root	
N.Y.	Duane				
	Floyd				
N.J.					
Pa.	Clymer	Smith, T.	Montgomery		
Del.				McKean	
				Van Dyke	
Md.			Carroll		
			Hanson		
Va.	Madison	Smith, M.			Bland
	Jones				
N.C.	Burke				
	Johnston				
S.C.	Mathews				
	Motte				
	Bee				
Ga.	Few	Howly			
	Walton				

NOTES:

1. Bloc I gave complete support.

2. Bloc II supported all motions except that of March 31 to give Morris authority of appointment and removal without previous congressional authorization.

3. Bloc III opposed the above motion and the first motion to allow Morris to retain business connections (Mar. 20).

4. Bloc IV opposed all the above motions plus the second motion to allow Morris to retain business connections (Mar. 20).

5. Bloc V was in complete opposition, including opposition to the power of appointment and removal without congressional sanction (Mar. 21).

6. McKean and Van Dyke were present for only two votes and could possibly fit in Bloc III. McKean's criticism of the desire to make Morris a financial dictator four months later suggests an anti-Morris position, however. (McKean to Samuel Adams, July 8, 1781, *LMCC*, VI. 139.)

VII

Coincident with executive reformation, various resolutions were offered during 1780 to amend the Articles by granting Congress the power to collect duties on imports and exports. Again, there were precedents for such a proposal. In September of 1778 a committee of five had recommended a 2-percent duty on imported commodities[65]. The next month, however, Congress, in a set of instructions for its newly designated minister plenipotentiary Franklin, suggested he inform the French Ministry that since the Revolution had begun over the very issue of taxation, "the laying of imposts, unless from the last necessity, would be madness"[66]. That such a moment had arrived in 1780 is amply illustrated in the motion by Thomas Burke and Allen Jones of North Carolina that a 1-percent impost be collected on both imports and exports until a sum equal to the emissions provided for in the 40-to-1 devaluation of March 18 had been collected[67]. Burke's motion was a prelude to further action. On August 22, Livingston, seconded by Folsom of New Hampshire, moved for a 2½-percent impost on exports to be collected by congressional agents. The motion was submitted to a committee on ways and means chaired by the Rhode Island nationalist Cornell but subsequently was referred, on November 7, to a new committee on finance under the chairmanship of Sullivan. Sullivan's committee made its report on December 18, recommending a 7-percent duty on imports, rather than exports, and after the figure was reduced to 5 percent, it was accepted by Congress in committee of the whole on February 1. The duty was to be assessed *ad valorem* on all goods, with a few exceptions, including prizes and prize goods. The revenue was expected to amount to $600,000 or $700,000 in specie a year—not enough to pay interest on the debt, but, it was hoped, sufficient to improve confidence in Continental securities. The funds were to be allocated specifically for the retirement of the debt, and the impost would remain in force until it was liquidated[68].

As first set forth, the states were to pass laws "granting to Congress, for use of the United States, a duty of 5 per cent" on imports, thus reserving to the states the authority to legislate the impost. Thomas Burke and John Mathews moved on February 1 that the states should "vest power in Congress" to levy the duty, thereby enlarging congressional legislative authority[69]. Two days later John Witherspoon, seconded by Burke, moved unsuccessfully to go further by granting to Congress the right to regulate interstate commercial relations. The delegates balked at this audacious resolution but in a third vote did approve of the Burke-Mathews motion to recommend to the states that they grant Congress the power to levy the impost[70].

The voting on these three motions is illustrative of the varied currents of the tide of the nationalist movement. Burke's role in promoting the measures is certainly remarkable, remembering his deep commitment to states' rights in the debates over the Articles of Confederation in 1777. Burke's motions,

TABLE 17

Burke-Witherspoon Resolutions on Congressional Authority over the Impost and Interstate Commerce, February 1–3, 1781

	Opposition	Middle*	Support
N.H.	Sullivan		
Mass.	Adams, S.—Ward†		Lovell
R.I.			
Conn.		Huntington, S.	Wolcott
			Root
N.Y.			Floyd
			McDougall
N.J.		Witherspoon	
		Clark	
Pa.	Montgomery		Clymer
	Wynkoop		Atlee
	Smith		
Del.		McKean	
Md.‡			
Va.	Jones, J.		Bland
	Madison		
N.C.			Burke
			Sharpe
S.C.	Bee	Mathews	
	Motte		
Ga.			Few
			Howly
			Walton

*Most delegates in the middle group supported Burke's motions but opposed Witherspoon's, except Witherspoon, who did the reverse.

†Adams was present for two votes, Ward the third.

‡No delegates present.

and that of Witherspoon as well, were supported by such varied types as Oliver Wolcott, the strong centralist from Connecticut, and Theodorick Bland, a staunch advocate of Arthur Lee. Sam Adams, present for two of the votes, voted in the opposition, as one might expect. Lovell of the Adams-Lee faction supported the measures, however, while the nationalists Madison, Joseph

Jones, and Sullivan opposed them. Table 17 shows three blocs which emerge from the roll calls. While it is impossible to hypothesize any system of classification which can comprehend every delegate in this scale, it is immediately obvious that the nationalist-parochialist dichotomy falls far short of providing an explanation. Possibly, the best explanation evolves from the combined factors of states' rights–nationalist orientation, military peril (relevant for Georgia, North Carolina, and New York), and engagement in commerce (relevant for Massachusetts, Pennsylvania, Virginia, and South Carolina).

Just as state self-interest in western lands confused the nationalist movement, so did state self-interest complicate the acceptance of the eminently centralist instrument of congressional control over commerce. Just as military peril helped persuade Virginia to cede her western lands, so British invasion helped prompt the South to grant Robert Morris whatever terms he chose to name as preconditions for his acceptance of the superintendency of finance. The irony was that by the time the centralist movement began to develop momentum as a result of Southern support of Middle states nationalism, the war was virtually over. The essential question for those who were committed to a comprehensive nationalist policy was whether or not the multiple strands of the centralism of 1780–1781 could be woven into a whole cloth and, moreover, whether a centralist policy could be implemented in time of peace.

Notes

1 Ezekiel Cornell to Governor Greene, June 18, 1780, in William R. Staples, *Rhode Island in the Continental Congress* (Providence, 1870), pp. 295, 296. See also Joseph Reed to Nathanael Greene, June 16, 1781, Greene Papers, CL.

2 John Mathews to [Thomas Bee], Jan. 5, 1780; Mathews to Horatio Gates, Mar. 14, 1780, *LMCC*, V, 2, 72.

3 See Ezekiel Cornell to Nathanael Greene [July 21, 1780], *LMCC*, V, 281; James Varnum to Governor William Greene, Apr. 2, 1781, ibid., VI, 41–42. Burnett called Varnum one of the "strongest and most persistent advocates of enlarged powers for Congress" (*The Continental Congress* [New York, 1941], p. 504).

4 Cornell to Nathanael Greene [July 21, 1780], *LMCC*, V, 281; Varnum to Governor Greene, Apr. 2, 1781, ibid., 41–42.

5 Clarence Ver Steeg, *Robert Morris, Revolutionary Financier* (Philadelphia, 1954), p. 84.

6 Arthur Lee to Elbridge Gerry, Nov. 26, 1780, *LMCC*, V, 439n.

7 John Mathews to Thomas Bee, Sept. 22, 1778, ibid., III, 421.

8 Mathews to the President of Congress, Aug. 6, 1780, ibid., V, 309–311.

9 Irving Brant, *James Madison: The Nationalist, 1780–1787* (Philadelphia, 1948), chap. VIII.

10 James Lovell to Elbridge Gerry, Sept. 5, 1780, *LMCC*, V, 362.

11 Whitmill Hill to Governor Thomas Burke, Oct. 9, 1780, ibid., 414.

12 *JCC*, XVI, 262–267. E. James Ferguson, *The Power of the Purse* (Chapel Hill, 1961), pp. 51–52.

13 John Walker to Thomas Jefferson, June 13, 1780, *LMCC*, V, 215; William Grayson to General Smallwood, June 26, 1780, in Seventy-Six Society, *Publications: Maryland Papers*, 109; Richard Henry Lee to Henry Laurens, July 10, 1780, in James C. Ballagh (ed.), *The Letters of Richard Henry Lee* (2 vols.; New York, 1914), II, 186; E. James Ferguson, *The Power of the Purse*, pp. 65–66.

14 William Ellery to William Greene, May 23, 1780, in Staples, *Rhode Island in the Continental Congress*, p. 289. James Duane indicated he would have to return to New York early simply because he lacked money to defray essential expenses; James Duane to Governor George Clinton, [Oct. 7, 1780], *LMCC*, V, 411.

15 Samuel Johnston to Abner Nash, Nov. 6, 1780, Emmet Collection, NYPL.

16 Ezekiel Cornell to William Greene, June 18, 1780, in Staples, *Rhode Island in the Continental Congress*, p. 294.

17 Ferguson calculates that at this time a $200 certificate could be bought with bills worth as little as $65 to $100 in real value. *Power of the Purse*, pp. 68–69.

18 *JCC*, XVII, 545–548.

19 The North Carolina delegates to Governor Richard Caswell, Feb. 29, 1780, *LMCC*, V, 56–57.

20 James Lovell to Samuel Adams, Apr. 9, 1780, Samuel Adams Papers, NYPL; Nathaniel Folsom to Josiah Bartlett, Apr. 17, 1780; Nathaniel Peabody to Meshech Weare, Mar. 13, 1780; the Committee at Headquarters to the President of Congress, July 18, 1780; Joseph Jones to George Washington, June 19, 1780, *LMCC*, V, 116, 67–70, 271–278, 227.

21 *JCC*, XVII, 720. For a discussion of the Committee at Headquarters see Edmund C. Burnett, *The Continental Congress* (New York, 1941), pp. 442–471.

22 Greene thought Sherman was in "close league" with Mifflin in the new plan. Nathanael Greene to George Washington, Mar. 28, 1780, in G. W. Greene, *The Life of Nathanael Greene* (3 vols.; New York, 1867–1871), II, 275.

23 John Mathews to George Washington, Sept. 15, 1780; James Lovell to Elbridge Gerry, Nov. 20, 1780, *LMCC*, V, 372, 452.

24 *JCC*, XVIII, 961.

25 Comparative study of the emergence of nation-states has demonstrated that amalgamation often occurs around the nucleus of a dominant state. Karl W. Deutsch et al., *Political Community and the North Atlantic Area; International Organization in the Light of Historical Experience* (Princeton, 1957), pp. 72, 137–139.

26 The literature on the role of western lands in the Revolution is both vast and disputatious. The most influential studies on the topic as it relates to the Confederation are Thomas Perkins Abernethy, *Western Lands and the American Revolution* (New York, 1939), and Merrill Jensen, "The Cession of the Old Northwest," *MVHR*, XXIII (June 1936), pp. 27–48, and "The Creation of the National Domain, 1781–1784," ibid., XXVI (December 1939), pp. 323–342. Both Abernethy and Jensen stress the role of speculators from the landless states in the formulation of congressional policy. For a different view see Kathryn Sullivan, *Maryland and France, 1774–1789* (Philadelphia, 1936), and St. George L. Siousat, "The Chevalier De La Luzerne and the Ratification of the Articles of Confederation in Maryland, 1780–1781," *PMHB*, LX (October 1936), pp. 391–418. For an incisive summary of the background of the Virginia cession see William T. Hutchinson and William M. E. Rachal's note on Joseph Jones's motion of Sept. 6, 1780, in *The Papers of James Madison* (Chicago, 1962–), II, 72–77.

27 As originally formulated in the Dickinson draft of the Articles, Congress was given jurisdiction in the adjustment of state boundaries. The final version of the Articles in 1777 did not include this authority, however, Article 9 guaranteed that no state should be deprived of territory for the benefit of the nation.

28 *JCC,* XV, 1224.

29 W. W. Hening (ed.), *The Statutes . . . of Virginia* (13 vols.; Richmond, 1809–1823), X, 557–559.

30 Ezekiel Cornell to Governor Greene, June 18, 1780, in Staples, *Rhode Island in the Continental Congress,* p. 295.

31 It should be stressed again that this cooperation between Virginia and the Easterners was not a continuation of the Adams-Lee Virginia-Massachusetts axis. Had this been so, Theodorick Bland (unaffiliated in 1780) and Samuel Adams himself would have belonged to it. (While both Bland and Adams had sparse voting records in 1780, Adams's voting tendency is reasonably clear, and Bland's subsequent alignment with the Southern coalition also suggests that the materials for the Adams-Lee faction did not exist in 1780.) In all likelihood, the deviation of Jones and Madison from the Southern coalition of 1780 was a repudiation not only of regional partisanship but also of the Adams-Lee connection as well. Joseph Jones, writing from Virginia, where he had gone for a while during 1780 to see his ailing wife and to urge the western cession through Burgesses, worried constantly about a renewal of Adams-Lee factionalism. The more experienced delegate wrote to his freshman colleague asking if Arthur Lee had yet arrived at Congress and whether he was attempting to "revive the old disputes." Jones's concern was not with the Lees alone. Shortly afterward, he wrote again to Madison, warning him that Meriwether Smith, the active Deane partisan, had been reappointed to Congress. He admitted to "fears Congress will again be drawn into Sects and divisions" and urged

Madison to "check every attempt that may be made to renew former disputes." Joseph Jones to James Madison, Oct. 2, 1780, in Hutchinson and Rachal (eds.), *The Papers of James Madison,* II, 106, 148–149.

32 Joseph Jones to Governor Thomas Jefferson, June 30, 1780, *LMCC,* V, 245.

33 Madison, "Notes on Territorial Claim of New Hampshire" [1780], in Hutchinson and Rachal (eds.), *The Papers of James Madison,* II, 85.

34 Jack M. Sosin, *The Revolutionary Frontier, 1763–1783* (New York, 1967), pp. 45–52. One disturbance after the Revolution is described in an affidavit of one William White, Jan. 19, 1784, PCC, item 59, vol. 3.

35 Burnett, *LMCC,* V, lviii, lix; Woodbury Langdon to Nathaniel Peabody, Dec. 28, 1779, Peabody Papers, NHHS.

36 Robert R. Lingston to Philip Schuyler, May 21, 1780, *LMCC,* V, 159.

37 JCC, XVII, 808.

38 Ibid., XVIII, 915–916.

39 Ibid., 916.

40 Francis Wharton, in *The Diplomatic Correspondence of the American Revolution,* discussed the replacement of what he liked to call the "expulsionists" by the "constructivists," concerned with the establishment of national authority. Merrill Jensen, *The New Nation* (New York, 1950), has the best analysis of this phase of congressional politics from the viewpoint of a counterrevolution. E. James Ferguson lends support to this thesis in his analysis of the Morris fiscal program, *Power of the Purse,* chap. 6, "Counterrevolution in Finance."

41 JCC, IX, 818–820.

42 Ibid., XII, 1076–1077.

43 Jennings B. Sanders, *Evolution of Executive Departments of the Continental Congress, 1774–1789* (Chapel Hill, 1935), p. 15.

44 James Lovell to Arthur Lee, June 13 and Aug. 6, 1779, *LMCC,* IV, 264, 355.

45 Sanders, *Evolution of Executive Departments,* pp. 20–31.

46 Petition from Pennsylvania merchants to the Pennsylvania Executive Council, May 20, 1779, PCC, Pennsylvania State Papers, 1775–1791, item 69. That court of appeals judgments could be both controversial and lucrative can be seen in the drawn-out case of the sloop *Active* involving not only various claimants but also the admiralty court of Pennsylvania and the Congress. In the final judgment regarding the *Active,* the value of the ship and cargo was placed at £8,250, Pennsylvania currency. See Thomas Burke to Joseph Reed, Jan. 28, 1779, *LMCC,* IV, 45–46; JCC, XVI, 274, and other letters and resolutions between September 1779 and March 1780.

47 JCC, XIV, 708.

48 Ibid., XV, 1216–1218.

49 Ibid., XVI, 13, 17, 19, 22–24, 29–30, 32, 62–64.

50 William Paca to Samuel Huntington (President of Congress), Feb. 8, 1780, PCC, item 59, Misc. Papers, vol. III.

51 *JCC,* XVI, 17, 23, 63.

52 Ibid., XIV, 903–908.

53 It is the estimate of Sanders, *Evolution of Executive Departments,* p. 66n, that in the jockeying for appointments, "deals" were made.

54 Ver Steeg, *Robert Morris,* p. 233.

55 On the role of the "core area" in the formation of amalgamated communities, see Karl Deutsch et al., *Political Community,* pp. 72, 137–139.

56 Franklin B. Hough (ed.), *Proceedings of a Convention of Delegates from Several of the New England States, Held at Boston, August 3-9, 1780* (Albany, 1867). Rhode Island appointed delegates, but they did not attend.

57 The resolutions were adopted unanimously on October 10, 1780. *Votes and Proceedings of the Assembly of the State of New York . . .* (Poughkeepsie, 1780), p. 43.

58 James Duane to Governor George Clinton, Nov. 14, 1780, *LMCC,* V, 445.

59 If James Lovell's caustic response to past connection with the Adams-Lee faction means anything in this context, he, too, should be classified as an opponent of centralism. Lovell talked about "maggots about creating omnipotencies" in a letter to Elbridge Gerry, Sept. 5, 1780, ibid., 361–362. Jensen (*The New Nation,* p. 47) classifies Lovell as a member of the opposition to the Nationalists in this context.

60 *JCC,* XVII, 428, 791. The membership of the committee included James Lovell, John Henry, and Timothy Matlack, as well as Livingston and Jones.

61 Ibid., XIX, 43–44.

62 Ibid., 126–127.

63 For a discussion of these appointments, see Chapter 11. See especially Elisha P. Douglass, "Thomas Burke, Disillusioned Democrat," *NCHR,* XXVI (1949), pp. 150–186.

64 Burke had borrowed from Morris during his previous tenure in Congress. Writing from North Carolina in November of 1780, he apologized for not repaying Morris on the grounds that he had not been fully reimbursed for his services by the state. He indicated he expected to return to Congress and if so "will endeavour to Convert good part of my Property into money in order to be the less exposed to the Contingencies of the War, and I shall rely entirely on your friendship for directing me how to improve or employ whatever I may be able to take with me, but of this you will hear much more when we meet." Burke to Morris, Nov. 4, 1780, Morris Papers, Correspondence, 1775–1805, LC.

65 *JCC,* XII, 929.

66 Ibid., 1048.

67 Ibid., XVI, 261.

68 Ibid., XIX, 105.

69 Ibid.

70 Ibid., 111.

11 The Nationalist Dilemma: Finance, France, and the West, 1781–1782

AT the beginning of 1781, it was by no means clear that the War of the Revolution would be virtually concluded as a result of the decisive triumph at Yorktown in October of that year. The campaign of 1780 had been all but disastrous. French military assistance had been disappointing, and although there were high hopes that a French-American campaign could be launched on both land and sea during 1781, the Congress did not know even in June when it was scaling down its peace demands that Admiral DeGrasse had been ordered to move to the Chesapeake from the West Indies by August. Benedict Arnold, one of the most successful of American commanders, had defected to the British in the fall of 1780, and by the winter he was leading raids against Virginia with British naval support. General Cornwallis moved through the Carolinas almost at will, despite American resistance under the more capable leadership of Nathanael Greene. By May, Cornwallis had struck deep into Virginia with a reinforced army of over 7,000 men, and in early June, he almost captured Governor Thomas Jefferson and members of the Virginia Assembly at Charlottesville. Money was scarce, provisions were short, and there were mutinies in the Pennsylvania and New Jersey lines. The delegates in the Continental Congress, particularly those from the hard-hit South, had good cause for concern about the success of the Revolution. Rumors of a European mediation of the war under Austro-Russian auspices on the principles of uti possidetis had reached Congress by November of 1780. Since such a settlement would have allowed Great Britain to retain territory she controlled, the independence of Georgia and South Carolina seemed jeopardized. If 1779 had been a propitious time for radicals to attempt to take command of the Revolution, early 1781 was the moment for advocates of political centralization to make their move. With the ratification of the Articles of Confederation in March of 1781, at least three avenues toward centralization existed. One, the most drastic, was to scrap the Articles entirely and create a more powerful general government—perhaps in a constitutional convention. A second alternative was to call upon the states to approve amendments such as the impost granting an independent income to the Congress—an amendment which, it was generally agreed, was increasingly necessary if the Articles were to continue to function with minimal effectiveness. The third alternative was to use the existing Articles as flexibly as possible.

All these avenues toward consolidation found defenders. Immediately after the Confederation was declared in effect, John Sullivan, the centralist-minded delegate from New Hampshire, moved that Congress disband itself and leave affairs in the hands of a committee of states [1]—a provision allowed under the Articles but one which was not meant to be used in the fashion Sullivan intended, for Sullivan was most concerned with dramatizing the insufficiency of the present system. Outside Congress, Lieutenant Colonel Alexander Hamilton, a future delegate, had advocated that a convention be called to vest Congress with "complete" sovereignty over the states.

Still, most of the delegates favored working within the framework of the Articles. The more committed centralists such as James Madison did not balk at the opportunity of extracting from the Articles implied powers to coerce states that did not comply with congressional directives. But the most inviting prospect for centralists was to use the fiscal authority of Congress through the new office of the Superintendent of Finance to create an interstate community with an immediate interest in national stability and competence. In conjunction with an impost amendment, the general government might thereby gather powers commensurate with what consolidationists believed to be its responsibility.

Successful consolidation involved two requirements: it had to be effected with as much speed as possible, for the peril of 1781 had dramatically subsided by the end of the year; and it had to be effected within the partisan framework of congressional politics, for even under the most critical pressures from the British there were remnants of the "Old Radical" party which would oppose consolidation. Of necessity, the centralist movement, or "nationalist" movement as it may be called, had to be promoted through a Middle states–Southern coalition with marginal assistance from the few New England centralists who either had recently arrived in Congress or, as was less frequently the case, had shifted toward a more nationalist position.

Partly because of conflicting interests which prevented the creation of a truly cohesive nationalist coalition, partly because of delays in the implementation of fiscal reforms, and partly because of circumstances which, though seemingly unavoidable at the time, forced the very advocates of national power to virtually surrender control of American foreign policy to the French, the movement toward consolidation failed.

II

For some in Congress committed to genuine national authority, the ratified Articles of Confederation were an invitation to aggressive manipulation. This was true particularly, and perhaps naturally, for those who worked hardest for ratification, such as James Madison. Madison, in conjunction with James Duane, James Lovell, Jesse Root (a delegate from Connecticut), and John Witherspoon, led in the struggle for flexible interpretation of the Articles.

Although the ratification of the Articles of Confederation did not radically alter the manner in which Congress handled its business, strict observance of the Articles did force some changes in congressional procedures. Article 9 clearly sipulated that the votes of nine states were necessary for major decisions such as declaring war, making treaties, allocating moneys, specifying quotas from the states, and raising armies, and Article 5 required that a state be represented by at least two and not more than seven delegates. Some states had authorized a single delegate to register his state's vote, and major decisions had been made with the votes of five or six states rather than the nine states required in the Articles. After March 15, 1781, all states were forced to maintain at least two delegates in Congress if their votes were to be counted, and the passage of consequential legislation required larger coalitions of states than had usually obtained in the past.

Since a literal interpretation of the Articles created procedural barriers for proponents of a strong national government such as James Madison and James Duane, they attempted to persuade Congress to accept as flexible an interpretation of the Articles as possible. For example, Article 9 was specific about nine votes for major decisions; on other matters, presumably including the critical matter of preliminary votes on important questions, the wording of the Articles was ambiguous: "nor shall a question on any other point, except for adjourning from day to day, be determined, unless by the votes of a majority of the United States, in Congress assembled." Madison and James Duane unsuccessfully attempted to persuade the Congress that a majority of a quorum of nine, or five votes, was sufficient. Others, such as Thomas Burke and Theodorick Bland, contended that the rule meant an absolute majority of seven states. The proposal by Madison must have been alarming to many members of Congress. Thomas Rodney, recently arrived from Delaware, was distressed "to see such a Keen Struggle to increase the power of Congress beyond what the States Intended so early as but the third day after Completing the Confederation"[2].

Another question prompted by the definition in Article 13 of the Confederation brought forth even more drastic proposals by the advocates of centralism. A committee dominated by the nationalists James Varnum, Duane, and Madison contended that Congress had the authority to use military force to compel states to live up to their obligations to the general government. The committee was reporting on the meaning of Article 13, which specified that "every State shall abide by the determinations of the United States, in Congress assembled." Their report, presented on March 16, contended that "a general and implied power is vested in the United States in Congress assembled to enforce and carry into effect all the Articles of the said Confederation against any of the States which shall refuse or neglect to abide by such their determinations, or shall otherwise violate any of the said Articles . . ."[3]. The resolution went on, however, to stipulate that no "determinate and particular provision" had been made for enforcement and, because of the likelihood that this deficiency might form a "pretext" for resistance to congressional measures, an explicit grant of coercive power through an amendment to the Articles was desirable. The amendment should authorize Congress to

> employ the force of the United States as well by sea as by land to compel such State or States to fulfill their federal engagements, and particularly to make distraint on any of the effects Vessels and Merchandizes of such State or States or of any of the Citizens thereof wherever found, and to prohibit and prevent their trade and intercourse as well with any other of the United States and the citizens thereof, as with any foreign State, and as well by land as by sea, until full compensation or compliance be obtained with respect to all Requisitions made by the United States in Congress assembled in pursuance of the Articles of Confederation[4].

The amendment would go into effect as soon as all states not actually in possession of the enemy should approve.

A close reading of the proposed amendment leaves the impression that while the possibility of troops from the Continental line marching into a state capital to force funds from a state was not ruled out, the expectation was that a few frigates stopping trade until the delinquent state complied would be sufficient. Emphasis was laid upon distraining the trade of individual citizens within the state. Madison suggested precisely this the next month in a letter to Jefferson describing the proposed amendment. While he believed that "as long as there is a regular army on foot" a small detachment would serve the purpose, he continued that "there is a still more easy and efficacious mode." Two or three armed vessels employed against the trade of a state would bring prompt compliance[5].

Madison's interpretation of the amendment may not have squared precisely with that of Varnum, whose state would be particularly susceptible to such coercion, yet Varnum wrote to Governor William Greene that he hoped the amendment would pass[6]. Other nationalists, such as John Mathews, Sullivan, and Joseph Jones, also supported the measure, but, as James Varnum related, "an extreme, tho perhaps well-meant Jealousy, in many Members of Congress, especially those of a long Standing, seems to frustrate every Attempt to introduce a more efficacious System"[7]. Thomas Burke warned that the measure would alarm the states (this was a rather more restrained statement than he would have provided in 1777), but his warning was clearly accurate[8]. Whether from fear of constituent response, or because of individual convictions, Congress never seriously considered armed coercion. As the French Minister Luzerne noted, and he was not less careful an observer of congressional proceedings than his predecessor Gérard, there was a feeling for reform in Congress, but since the Articles had taken a year and a half of debate, a change in them would encounter no less difficulty: "It appears to me there is more room for desire than for hope"[9].

The report, when it emerged from the grand committee of thirteen on July 20, was entirely vitiated. Resubmitted again to a committee of three, including Varnum, Oliver Ellsworth, and Edmund Randolph, with the broad instruction to prepare an "exposition of the Confederation" and its "execution," the matter of enforcing the Articles was on the floor again on August 22, but by then the war was nearly over. All that was recommended by the new committee of three was that the states be urged to authorize Congress to lay embargos in time of war, to prescribe rules for impressing property in time of war, and to distrain the property of a delinquent state. No mention was made of the use of force to accomplish these objectives[10].

It is, of course, highly unlikely that anything like the Madison recommendation would have been approved by all the states, even if it had gone through Congress. Only the most extreme military crisis made the thought of coercion of the states even plausible. The slight attention given to the Madison resolution in the correspondence of the delegates, its submersion and dilution in various committees, and the fact that no roll call ever was recorded dealing with the issue all attest to its exotic character.

Nonetheless, any effective enduring nationalist consolidation within the structure of the Articles had to include some kind of coercion of the states. In peacetime, the likelihood of armed invasion to collect revenue would be remote, to be sure. The monetary demands upon the states would be much lighter, and in the event of the passage of the 5-percent impost, the problem of revenue collection would be markedly eased. Funds from the sale of western lands would help in the future. However, the enforcement of the wartime embargos, the application of an impost, and the observance of commercial treaties in peace as well as war all implied a measure of naval regulation under congressional auspices. The Madison amendment would have supported such requirements, especially by operating against individuals as well as states. Madison seems to have been aware of this, for in his letter to Jefferson explaining the amendment, he anticipated that if naval armament was considered "the proper instrument of general Government" (and he assumed it would), it would be maintained in peacetime. He also argued that states without maritime power had a stake in such a force, which he presumed would be made up of citizens from all the states. Such an establishment would be of particular advantage to the South not only because it would help to cultivate a merchant marine in that region but also because it could protect the Southern states against future "insults & aggressions of their N. Brethren"[11].

Madison did not specify what sort of aggression he contemplated, and it may be that he was simply trying to win the support of Virginia parochialists. Nonetheless, he raised the same issue almost two years later, in February of 1783, when he warned Edmund Randolph that should the Confederation dissolve, the rich Southern states, weak at sea, "will be an easy prey to the Eastern [states] which will be powerful and rapacious." If Southern accounts with the Continent were not squared, Madison suggested, "will they not be a ready pretext for reprisals?"[12] Earlier than many, Madison had apprehensions about the consequences of disunion—not simply because of his clear attachment to the principle of national amalgamation, but also because of a corollary concern about the security of his state and sections[13]. There were awkward contradictions in Madison's approach. It attempted (1) to generate a national income through an impost that would be collected by the states, (2) to coerce states by interrupting the trade of individuals, and (3) to achieve national consolidation through a measure that would, it was hoped, defend one region against another.

III

The Madison amendment raised the specter of civil war or another Boston Port Act. Robert Morris's program of fiscal reformation, on the other hand, was particularly appropriate as a vehicle for centralization, since it could be presented as a technical solution for problems of finance which had all but paralyzed Congress. The wide cross-factional and intersectional support Morris received in the final approval of his carefully structured conditions for acceptance of the post of financier proved that Congress was willing to embrace any design that promised success without patently violating the principles of the Revolution. Morris's establishment might lay the foundation for an effective peacetime nation-state while jealous parochialists looked willingly in another direction. Morris had the chance to simultaneously rationalize national finances, centralize administration, strengthen the national government, create institutional innovations to sustain the nationalist thrust, and cultivate a nationwide interest group of sizable proportions looking to the national government for a payoff—the latter being of central importance in any program of consolidation. The success of such a strategy depended upon a number of factors—too many, indeed, for Morris to manage effectively.

Although not openly subversive of Revolutionary principles, much of the program ran counter to the grain of the republican ideology of the Revolution. Consequently, it was of the utmost importance that it be fully launched before the end of hostilities. For the program to be effective, action was necessary in the states as well as in Congress. The impost amendment in particular required the consent of all the states, so that Morris had to rely not only upon the mood of desperation that prevailed in 1781 but also upon the nurture of sympathetic interest groups throughout the nation. In particular, he had to cultivate support where opposition was most likely to occur, as in those states which had a stake in collecting their own import duties. Above all, Morris had to demonstrate an ability to solve the practical problems of national finance at the same time that he quietly subordinated momentary economic calculations to the ultimate goal of political consolidation. Neither Morris's own experience nor mercantile tradition of that time which fused public and private enterprise was compatible with such a goal.

That 1781 was a propitious moment for Morris to undertake a nationalist program is readily apparent not only from the willingness of Congress to grant him virtually any power he requested but also from the configuration of bloc alignments of that year. As can be seen from Table 18, there was a dramatic consolidation of delegates from the Middle and Southern states. Reinforced delegations from Georgia and South Carolina, vitally concerned with their precarious link with the Confederation in the wake of the British victories of 1780, were as inclined to vote with the Middle states nationalists as they were with North Carolina and Virginia. The possibility of Austro-Russian mediation on the principle of uti possidetis which would have detached those two states from the Union made them even more amenable to centralist policy. The drift of Pennsylvania away from the New England coalition, which had begun during the tenure of the Constitutionalists in 1780, was emphatically completed with the resurgence of the conservative Republicans in the congressional delegation following the fall elections of 1780. Even James Duane had a higher level of agreement with the New England bloc than did any of the Pennsylvania delegates. The Middle-Southern coalition was strengthened not only by the persistent inclination of New York toward the South but also by unprecedented support from New Hampshire. Only Massachusetts and Connecticut offered concerted resistance to the policy of the massive coalition to the south, for the Rhode Island vote was often fractured by Varnum's opposition to Mowry (and even Mowry was only a marginal member of the shrunken Eastern party).

TABLE 18

Congressional Blocs, *1781*

	Eastern Party	Va. Bloc	N.C. Bloc	S.C.–Ga. Bloc	Pa.–Md. Bloc
			Middle-Southern Coalition		
N.H.	Livermore				Livermore*
					Sullivan
Mass.	Lovell				
	Osgood				
	Partridge				
R.I.	Mowry*				
Conn.	Ellsworth				
	Huntington, S.				
	Sherman				
N.Y.	Duane*	Duane*			Duane*
		Floyd			
N.J.					Witherspoon*
				Houston	
Pa.				Atlee*	Atlee
		Clymer*	Clymer	Clymer	Clymer
		Montgomery*		Montgomery*	Montgomery
					Smith, T.
Del.	McKean			McKean*	McKean
Md.					Hanson
				Carroll*	Carroll
				Jenifer	Jenifer
Va.		Jones, J.			Jones, J.*
		Bland			
		Randolph			Randolph*
		Smith, M.			
		Madison			
N.C.			Johnston	Johnston*	Johnston*
			Sharpe	Sharpe	Sharpe*
			Burke		
S.C.				Bee	Bee*
		Everleigh		Everleigh	Everleigh*
				Mathews	Mathews*
				Motte	Motte*

TABLE 18

Congressional Blocs, 1781

	Eastern Party		Middle-Southern Coalition		
		Va. Bloc	N.C. Bloc	S.C.-Ga. Bloc	Pa.-Md Bloc
Ga.				Few	Few
				Howly	Howly
				Walton	Walton*

* Marginal members.

Independents: Adams, S., and Ward (Mass.); Varnum (R.I.); Root (Conn.); Clark (N.J.); Middleton (S.C.).

The coalition between the Middle and Southern states did not take the form of a single bloc, but an alliance of four closely related blocs. Virginia tended to pull away from the coalition for a number of reasons. For example, when the South Carolina delegates Arthur Middleton and Thomas Bee moved that Washington be required to provide more support for the Carolina campaign by going to that theater himself or by sending part of his troops, the Virginia delegation opposed, as it had during 1780[14]. More important, however, was the position of Virginia on the terms for her western cession. She continued to demand that treaties concluded between the Indians and land companies be nullified—a policy which tended to separate Virginia not only from the Middle states (and, of course, landless Maryland) but also from the delegates from the deeper South who were intent upon supporting the nationalist policy of the Middle states. However, these internal stresses did not divorce Virginia from the coalition. Jones and Randolph were marginal members of the Pennsylvania-Maryland bloc, while Duane, George Clymer, and John Montgomery were fringe members of the Virginia bloc.

It is notable that the issue which contributed most to separating New England from the Middle-Southern coalition was not fiscal policy but foreign affairs. When Morris demanded the power to appoint and dismiss subordinates in the Department of Finance, he received a measure of support from New England, especially from Lovell and Wolcott[15]. The general alignments do reflect New England resistance to Morris's fiscal policy, but to a lesser degree than on both foreign and military affairs.

The blocs of 1781 thus indicate not so much the existence of a centralist party dominated by Morris and his congressional sympathizers as the potential for creating such a party in an atmosphere of military crisis. That the hard bargaining by Morris for his executive post was hardly discussed in the correspondence of delegates testifies to the basically nonpartisan acquiescence of Congress. John Sullivan, who voted *against* Morris's demands for appointive power, wrote to Washington: "Mr. Robert Morris has Accepted the office of Minister of Finance upon which I Sincerely congratulate Your Excellency and My Country." William C. Houston of New Jersey, chairman of the committee appointed to consider Morris's demand for exceptional powers, wrote to Thomas McKean that in the present "perplexed, deranged" condition of finance, reformation had to be the work of "one Mind." Other than such comments, and the chimerical claim by Thomas Rodney that he "prevailed in gitting Mr. Morris financier," Morris's appointment and the conditions attached to it received little attention in the correspondence of the delegates [*16*].

Morris was elected Superintendent of Finance in February and accepted the office on May 14[*17*]. Three days later, he presented his plan for a national bank, an action which strongly suggests that this nationalist-oriented fiscal institution had been carefully considered in advance as part of a broad program of financial recuperation and, in all likelihood, nationalist consolidation[*18*]. Capitalized at only $400,000 so that there would be no danger of the subscription not being filled[*19*], the Bank of North America, as it was called in its charter of incorporation issued by Congress, was to join private interest with the system of national finance. Subscriptions were received in 400-dollar shares, each conveying one vote, to be paid in gold or silver. Bank notes issued on the basis of this reserve were redeemable in specie and were receivable for all state and national government obligations as specie. Morris anticipated this would be sufficient to restore public faith in the national credit. Bank notes circulating at par would provide a stable currency for commercial transactions. Investors would be attracted to the bank, thereby augmenting capital available to the national government. The end product, Morris candidly explained to John Jay, would be "to unite the several States more closely together in one general money connexion, and indissolubly to attach many powerful individuals to the cause of our country by the strong principle of self-love and the immediate sense of private interest"[*20*]. The Superintendent of Finance would have access to all records of the bank and would closely observe its operations. Actually, Morris would, of course, determine its policy. Its president was Morris's former partner, Thomas Willing. At least four of the original board of directors had been business associates of Morris[*21*].

Opposition to Morris's plan for the bank was diffuse and anomalous. Only one vote was recorded in the Journal, and that was not over the plan itself, but the matter of incorporation by Congress. Just four delegates opposed, two of whom—Lovell and Madison—had taken nationalist positions favorable to Morris when he had demanded extraordinary powers of appointment and removal. Thomas Smith of Pennsylvania, who had also previously supported Morris, was the third. Only Artemas Ward of Massachusetts was ideologically consistent in opposing the bill. Samuel Adams doubtless would have opposed as well, but he had left Congress a month previous, never to return. Theodorick Bland was present and supported the incorporation of the bank, despite his earlier opposition to the grant of extraordinary authority to Morris[22].

During the frenetic months of the summer of 1781, Morris also secured by design or inadvertence still greater enlargement of his powers. The Marine Department was put under his control after Congress refused to allow Alexander McDougall, elected to the office of Secretary of the Marine, to continue to draw his pay and emoluments as a general in the army[23]. (McDougall also was serving as a delegate from New York at the time of his election. His explanation to Governor Clinton was "I cannot think of quitting the field, in the active part of the Campaign; while so great part of our State is in the hands of the enemy"[24].) The authority exercised by Morris over the Marine Department was not as ample as his control in finance, but it should have been sufficient to alarm Eastern parochialists who had guarded congressional powers against outside encroachments for years—above all in the highly regarded Marine. Again, the lack of serious controversy over this issue (no roll call was taken) adds to the impression that Morris could have secured whatever it was in the hands of Congress to give in 1781.

Surprisingly, in retrospect, Morris did not immediately carry on with his program of financial reformation. Indeed, having accepted his appointment in May, he did not officially take office until July. He considered January 1, 1782, as the effective date of his assuming office for the purpose of adjusting claims against the government[25]. On July 6, Congress validated some transactions he undertook as financier before taking the oath of office, but later in the month Congress ordered the Board of Treasury to continue its operations— which it did until September 20[26].

There were many reasons for the delay. Morris had not completely formed his full strategy; he was distracted by commitments to the problems of supply and finance in Pennsylvania, especially the repeal of legal tender laws; finally, his initial efforts as financier were not geared to the long-range problems of fiscal reform as much as to the provisioning and general maintenance of the army during the preparations for the Yorktown campaign[27].

Actually, Morris's delay in assuming full duties as Superintendent of Finance enhanced the success of his immediate program of stabilizing income and expenditures. By the time the financier put his full resources behind the superintendency, military requirements had abated, and the task of balancing the budget was significantly eased[28]. This fortuitous, and probably unforeseen, outcome of Morris's distraction with Pennsylvania finances in conjunction with his astute, sometimes brilliant, management of a bankrupt fiscal system produced impressive results. His conversion in the fall of 1781 of a good part of the organization of supply from the inefficient and expensive commission mode of purchasing to his preferred technique of granting contracts to the lowest bidder both eliminated waste and resulted in better fare for the army [29]. After the Bank of North America opened its doors in January of 1782, its notes as well as the so-called "Morris notes," issued in denominations of $20 and $100 from the Office of Finance in anticipation of future taxes, circulated at face value outside New England and the lower South. In the latter regions, the discount was just 10 to 15 percent, which was normal for the circulation of paper at such a distance from its place of origin[30]. When serious depreciation occurred in a given region, Morris simply stopped issuing the notes in that area. Continental officials, under close supervision by Morris, were forbidden to pay more in notes than the specie price of goods[31].

To argue that Morris's conservative policy was possible only because of the substantial decline in military requirements during 1782 is not to detract from the masterful achievement of the financier whose personal credit buoyed the whole system—the notes of the Office of Finance as well as those of the bank. At the same time, however, the diminution of hostilities gravely impaired Morris's chance to accomplish the political changes in the structure of the Confederation which were essential to the completion of his plan of reformation. Morris was convinced he could establish neither national credit nor a viable funding system without direct congressional control of revenue sufficient for those functions assigned to the national government by the Articles. At the very least, this would mean the 5-percent impost collected under national auspices and designated for national expenditures. It was estimated that perhaps $500,000 could be drawn from the impost—a sum which would not even meet interest charges on the public debt. Clearly, the stabilization of national finance which entailed payment of the public debt would require other sources of revenue. Morris recommended, and Congress obediently called for, $8 million in specie from the states for the 1782 campaign. The sum was high, but more alarming to those in states prone to resist fiscal innovations was the recommendation by Congress at the behest of Morris that the Continental revenue was to be separated from taxes for state use. Not only were state-authorized taxes to be designated specifically for Continental purposes; they were also to be collected by Continental agents responsible to Morris[32].

Recognizing potential resistance in the states, Morris made a number of remarkably astute appointments to the tax receiverships. He seems to have taken care to appoint Old Radicals to the most sensitive spots. Two stalwarts of the Eastern party in Congress, William Whipple and James Lovell, were designated for the receiverships in New Hampshire and Massachusetts. The Lovell appointment was doubly astute, for while Lovell had been a core member of the Adams-Lee faction, in actuality he was not unsympathetic with the Morris program. He had supported the full grant of authority for Morris as Superintendent and seems to have established a good relationship with the financier[33]. Morris's first choice for the receivership in Pennsylvania was none other than David Rittenhouse, the ardent Philadelphia radical. When Rittenhouse declined the appointment, Morris went to the opposite extreme by appointing John Swanwick, who was not only thoroughly sympathetic with Morris's financial program but was also his treasurer in the Office of Finance. Whatever Swanwick's affiliations, he was studiously attentive to opportunities of winning support from the political opposition. When the Massachusetts delegation of 1783 obstructed the final thrust of nationalist movement in Congress, Swanwick seized the opportunity to be of service to Samuel Holten, a Massachusetts parochialist of the Sam Adams stamp, when Holten wanted some notes processed. Swanwick profusely attested his "high esteem" for Holten and asserted it would give him "great pleasure" to obey his commands [34]. Holten later described Swanwick as a "Gentleman of Character in the City of Philadelphia & employed in public business by the Hon'ble Mr. Morris, Financier . . ."[35]. Morris did not appoint any of the Lee connections to posts in the South, recognizing that the Lees were implacable political foes[36], but he did follow a pattern of "congressional courtesy" in making some receivership appointments. He consulted the South Carolina delegation, for example, before appointing George Abbot Hall to the South Carolina post[37].

If Morris's management of receivership appointments sometimes revealed a desire to conciliate actual and potential political opposition, other appointments, such as that of Alexander Hamilton to the receivership in New York, showed a disposition to press as strongly as possible for a nationalist establishment wherever the situation permitted. He instructed his receivers to act as propaganda agents for the Continental cause and to function as sources of information by sending him political pamphlets and newspapers—actions which also attested to his desire for nationalist reformation[38].

Morris realized that his program to strengthen national finance could not be accomplished simply through more assiduous collection of taxes levied in the states for national purposes. An entirely separate program of taxation was necessary. On February 27, 1782, Morris recommended additional land, poll, and excise taxes for the funding of the public debt. The taxes were neither excessive nor entirely novel—$1 for every 100 acres of land, a $1 poll tax on all freemen and male slaves between the ages of sixteen and sixty, and one-eighth of a dollar per gallon on distilled spirituous liquors[39].

Congress referred Morris's proposal to a committee dominated by delegates of the increasingly solid knot of opposition which was developing in response to the more amply revealed fiscal program. One member was Arthur Lee, who had returned from Europe and a triumphal reception in Boston to be elected to Congress from Virginia. (One can imagine the curiosity aroused by this man who had been the vital center of the great imbroglio of 1778-1779.) Samuel Osgood, a determined parochialist from Massachusetts, unknown to the delegates in Congress before 1780, and Abraham Clark of New Jersey were the other two members[40]. Clark had served in Congress between 1776 and 1778 before coming for a second term in 1780 and had been marginally connected with the Eastern party. The committee, as could have been anticipated, reported against the proposal by Morris, thereby stalling consideration for months. The problem of additional taxes was taken up again by a grand committee of thirteen, one member from each state, appointed on July 22, and the Morris request was recommended by the committee in somewhat altered form in August. On the floor of Congress, however, none of the taxes was approved[41].

The reasons behind the rejection were symptomatic of the basic dilemma of sectional amalgamation which had cropped up during the debates over the peace terms in 1779 and would later emerge even more stridently. Delegates from more compact states, such as Rhode Island, with improved lands and a substantial commitment to commerce naturally disapproved of taxes on trade such as the impost and of taxes calculated on the basis of property values. In like manner, states such as North Carolina with a dispersed population, vast tracts of unimproved land, and little overseas trade would not tolerate a blanket tax on land. The North Carolina delegate Hugh Williamson, a transplanted Pennsylvanian who was nevertheless a core Southerner during almost his entire tenure, observed with justification that "considering the smallness of our Towns and the great tracts of broken barren and piney lands in North Carolina, we should on this plan, be charged with near double the quota of the public Debt that should in Justice fall to our share. Therefore, we are not bound in Justice to consent, nor are we bound in honor, because the Confederation expressly fixes another mode"[42].

The opposition of the North Carolinians was a portent of difficulties which would ultimately destroy the chances of Morris's financial program. In 1781, the North Carolina delegation had been in the forefront of the trend toward national consolidation, but that had been a time of dire peril for the South. By the summer of 1782, Britain had given up on a land campaign to reduce the colonies and had largely confined military pressure to naval action against American commerce. The strategic moment for success of the Morris program had passed. (See Table 19 for the structure of the congressional blocs during 1782.)

Financial policy—especially in the larger context of the nationalist program—was intricately bound with other aspects of congressional affairs. The success of the program was vitally dependent on passage of the impost, but Rhode Island was adamant in its contention that the western lands should be used instead of an impost as the source of a common fund. Morris's suggestion of a blanket land tax of $1 per hundred acres was palatable in Rhode Island and other small, highly developed states, but it was bitter medicine for the

TABLE 19

Congressional Blocs, 1782

| | Northern Party | | Southern Party | |
	Eastern Bloc	Middle States Bloc	Va. Bloc	S.C. Bloc
Mass.	Osgood			
	Partridge			
R.I.	Cornell			
	Ellery			
Conn.	Law			
	Wolcott			
N.Y.		Duane*		
N.J.	Boudinot*	Boudinot		
Pa.		Atlee*		
	Clymer*	Clymer		
	Montgomery*	Montgomery		
	Smith, T.	Smith, T.		
Del.	McKean*	McKean		
		Wharton		
		Dickinson, P.*		
Md.	Carroll, D.	Carroll, D.		
	Hanson	Hanson*		
Va.			Jones, J.	
			Lee, A.	
			Madison	
N.C.			Blount*	Blount*
S.C.			Middleton	Middleton
			Izard	Izard
				Ramsey
				Rutledge
Ga.				Jones, N.

* Marginal members.

Independents; Livermore (N.H.); Floyd and Scott (N.Y.); Clark (N.J.); Bland (Va.); Telfair and Few (Ga.).

South, with its dispersed population and extensive speculation in western lands. Morris himself and many of his friends were interested supporters of the Middle states land companies, but while this might help cement a nationalist-minded coalition of investors from New Jersey through Maryland, it was certain to offend Southerners. Edmund Randolph bluntly stated that Virginia's large share of the $8 million fund for 1782 ($1,307,594) would protect her against the assaults of smaller states attempting to void her cession terms restricting land company claims[43]. Morris's problem was to harmonize fundamentally antagonistic interests not necessarily opposed to a general proposition of increased central authority but vitally involved in specific elements of national policy. A complicated problem at the very least, perhaps insoluble by the very nature of Morris's commission to provide pragmatic solutions, the difficulty was vastly compounded by the influence of French diplomacy.

IV

Virtually all aspects of Morris's program appeared to be affected by the alliance with France. Strict compliance with financial quotas was necessary to field an army commensurate with the honor of the nation, jointly engaged as it was with France in a war against England. Contracts for supplies issued by Morris sometimes went to firms in which John Holker, the French consul in Philadelphia, was a major partner. Morris's warning that proceeds from the sale of western lands could not be relied upon to retire the national debt may have reflected his desire to draw commercial money into the funding system, but the well-known French opposition to American expansion beyond the Alleghenies raised the suspicion of complicity between Morris and Luzerne. Arthur Lee, whose credibility as an accurate chronicler is fallible but whose opinions were sure reflections of partisan sentiment, contended that congressional politics in the summer of 1781 could be summarized in a few words: "We lean entirely on the French and on Mr. R. Morris. I wish they may prove neither broken reeds, not Spears to pierce us"[44].

Lee's impression that Congress was relying upon the French and upon Morris was substantially correct, but incomplete. Morris relied upon Luzerne and the French, and Luzerne in turn relied upon the Congress as the only political body with which France could treat. Indeed, Luzerne wanted to help bolster congressional authority just as the nationalists who were promoting centralization did[45]. Luzerne had been partially responsible for the decision of the Maryland Legislature to complete the ratification of the Articles. He was very satisfied with the appointment of Robert Morris to the superintendency of finance and even put 200,000 livres at Morris's disposal before Morris accepted the office[46]. Madison contended that Morris's appointment lessened the "repugnance" of the French court to lend money to the United States[47].

Luzerne's efforts in buttressing the Confederation and congressional power were hardly disinterested. He was more sympathetic with the republican principles of the American Revolution than was his predecessor, Gérard, and his sympathy won him many more friends in Congress than Gérard had managed to cultivate, but he still had to protect French diplomatic objectives. In the pursuit of those objectives, Luzerne proceeded to manipulate congressional delegations with considerable skill. He established contacts with some of the individuals who had been useful to Gérard, such as the Maryland delegate, Daniel Jenifer. He cultivated new support as well, managing to persuade the New Hampshire delegates John Sullivan and Samuel Livermore to endorse French policy. Livermore was unacquainted with the background of the congressional struggles over foreign policy during 1779 and was more concerned with the Vermont problem than with broader aspects of congressional affairs that Luzerne was preoccupied with. To the extent that French diplomacy harmonized with New Hampshire's interest in Vermont, Livermore would be inclined to cooperate with Luzerne. More important in the defection of New Hampshire from the Eastern party was the direct influence that Luzerne had over John Sullivan, who accepted payments from the French Minister in return for a regular flow of information and a conclusive vote on issues related to the alliance. Luzerne also managed to win the support of John Witherspoon—an inflexible republican who was immune to bribery but whose attitude toward the French Minister may have been affected by the fact that Luzerne requested that his son be exchanged on the French prisoners' list[48]. Finally, the unusually full attendance of the delegations from the Deep South—all strongly disposed toward France—may have been due to funds available from bills drawn upon France[49]. By detaching New Hampshire and New Jersey from the Eastern anti-Gallican orientation and by apparently helping to ensure that the Georgia and South Carolina delegates were present to cast two safe votes, Luzerne did much to create a Gallican bloc in Congress. Those four votes, added to the votes of the traditionally pro-French delegations from Maryland, North Carolina, and New York, almost ensured the nine votes that were needed under the new rules imposed by the Articles of Confederation. The conservative Pennsylvania delegation and the Virginians also sympathized with France—the former quite completely and the latter with some reservations that were subdued by Luzerne's remarkable influence over Madison[50] and by the humiliating success of British forays into Virginia during the summer of 1781. Indeed, as the voting blocs in 1781 strongly indicate, the military situation during that year which produced the Middle-Southern coalition in Congress rendered Luzerne's task much simpler than that which had confronted Gérard.

Luzerne, acting upon instructions from Vergennes, was intent upon subordinating American diplomacy to French foreign policy. This involved a number of maneuvers, but there were two primary objectives that Luzerne had in mind: controlling the obstreperous John Adams and further limiting the terms that had been formulated in 1779 for an alliance with Spain and peace with England.

Beginning in 1780, Luzerne applied public pressure and private persuasion to (1) reduce United States insistence on navigation rights on the Mississippi in the instructions to Jay regarding conditions for an alliance with Spain and (2) void the instruction to Adams to insist on the Mississippi boundary as a sine qua non of peace with Britain. Suggesting to Northern delegates that a Spanish alliance was being impeded by selfish Southern desires in the West, Luzerne used the same strategy against the South that Gérard had employed against New England. Luzerne reported to Vergennes that the Middle states were indifferent about the West and that Maryland delegates—particularly Jenifer—were so opposed to Virginia's pretensions in the West that they would support French policy. Indeed, according to Luzerne, Jenifer was prepared to accept Spanish sovereignty over the Southwest[51]. Jenifer, in conjunction with Luzerne's secretary, the Marquis de Barbe-Marbois, later framed a set of "Observations" favoring Spanish claims to the Southwest, copies of which were sent to Vergennes and Montmorin, the French ambassador to Spain[52].

Luzerne's efforts to reduce the United States claim to navigation of the Mississippi succeeded. His victory was due not so much to his influence over Middle states delegates and members of Congress from the landless states of New Hampshire and Maryland as to the startling victories of Lord Cornwallis in the Carolinas. By November of 1780, the Georgia delegation, fearful of the rumors of a peace according to the principles of uti possidetis and desperately seeking Spanish assistance in expelling the British, moved that the navigation demand be lifted from Jay's instructions. At about the same time, Bland surprisingly urged the Virginia Assembly to repeal its resolution of November 1779 demanding navigation of the Mississippi as a precondition of a Spanish alliance—a recommendation opposed by Madison. The next month, however, Madison joined Bland in urging the change, and in January 1781 the Assembly rescinded the resolution[53]. On February 15, the Virginia delegation joined the Deep South and the Middle states in rescinding the demand for navigation below latitude 31 degrees north[54]. Thomas Burke and Johnston of North Carolina, along with anti-Gallicans in the Massachusetts and Connecticut delegations, voted against the resolution, to no avail.

Luzerne had attempted to persuade Congress to yield to Spain on the matter of the Mississippi boundary as well, but he had encountered resistance from the Southern delegations. By the end of 1780, Luzerne reported that some Southerners were willing to grant Spain a strip 100 miles wide on the east side of the Mississippi[55]. But by May of 1781, both the military situation and the threat of mediation on the basis of uti possidetis had become even more grave.

Citing the possibility of Austro-Russian mediation of the American war, Luzerne encouraged the Congress to reconsider its peace terms[56]. A committee was appointed on May 28, consisting of John Sullivan, warmly sympathetic with French policy; John Witherspoon, who believed that New Jersey would not be willing to continue the war "for the sake of boundless claims of wild uncultivated country . . ."[57]; Daniel Carroll of Maryland, and Joseph Jones and John Mathews. Witherspoon was the dominant member of the committee, and he regularly consulted with Luzerne about its recommendations to the Congress.

When the question of the peace terms reached the floor on June 6, Witherspoon, seconded by his fellow delegate William Houston, moved that the boundary ultimatum in the 1779 instructions to Adams be rescinded and that the United States insist only that it secure its independence and abide by the terms of the French alliance[58]. Witherspoon's motion was rejected, and the question was sent back to committee, but the tide was turning, for even the Virginia delegates felt compelled to offer concessions on the boundary issue. Madison and Meriwether Smith suggested that the northwest boundary be redefined so as to run from the mouth of the Miami to the headwaters of the Illinois River, and thence to the Mississippi[59]. The motion was resoundingly defeated. The Virginians frantically attempted to secure a guarantee that territory south of the Ohio would not be relinquished, but this, too, was overwhelmingly defeated. Adams was to refer to his former instructions regarding the boundaries but not be bound by them. As finally defined, the American terms required only two indispensable objectives: that the independence of the thirteen states be acknowledged and that existing treaties with France not be violated[60].

Luzerne manipulated Congress still further. Acting in accordance with instructions from Vergennes, the French Minister persuaded a subdued Congress to instruct Adams to communicate confidentially with the French court on all matters regarding the negotiations. Three days later on June 11, Congress decided that additional commissioners should be appointed and that Adams and his associates should not only consult with the French but should also "ultimately . . . govern yourself by their advice and opinion." It is not surprising that Luzerne assured Vergennes that "I view the negotiation as presently being in the hands of his Majesty except for independence and the treaties, and I myself have applauded these two reservations[61].

Congress, in its revised peace instructions, almost abdicated its authority in one of the few realms in which it was more competent than the states[62]. But, as can be seen from Table 20 (vote 2), this humiliating deference to France was possible only as the result of solid support from Georgia and the Carolinas, all of which were threatened with a loss of their independence by a negotiation on the basis of uti possidetis. John Mathews voiced the dilemma of the Deep

TABLE 20

Reduction of Peace Ultimatums, June 1781

	1	2	3	4	5	6	7	8	9	10	11	1	2	3	4	5	6	7	8	9	10	11
Richard Howly (Ga.)	x	x	x	x	x	x	x	x	x	x	x											
George Walton (Ga.)	x	x	x	x	x	x	x	x	x	x	x											
Thomas Bee (S.C.)	x	x	x	x	x	x	x	x	x	x	x											
John Mathews (S.C.)	x	x	x	x	x	x	x	x	x	x	x											
Isaac Motte (S.C.)	x	x	x	x	x	x	x	x	x	x	x											
Daniel Jenifer (Md.)	x	x	x	x	x	x	x	x	x	x	x											
Daniel Carroll (Md.)	x	x		x	x		x	x	x	x	x											
Samuel Atlee (Pa.)	x	x	x		x	x	x	x	x	x	x											
George Clymer (Pa.)	x		x	x	x	x	x	x	x	x	x		o									
William Sharpe (N.C.)	x	x	x	x	x		x	x	x	x	x			o								
William Few (Ga.)	x	x	x	x	x	x	x	x	x	x	x	o										
John Witherspoon (N.J.)	x	x	x	x	x	x	x	x	x	x	x	o										
William Houston (N.J.)	x	x	x		x	x		x	x		x	o							x			
John Sullivan (N.H.)	x	x	x	x	x		x	x	x		x	o					o					
Samuel Livermore (N.H.)	x	x	x	x	x		x	x	x		x	o					o					
Oliver Ellsworth (Conn.)		x	x	x	x	x	x	x	x	x	x	o	o									
Samuel Huntington (Conn.)			x	x	x	x	x	x			x	o	o	o								
Samuel Johnston (N.C.)	x			x	x	x	x	x	x		x	o		o	o							
Roger Sherman (Conn.)				x	x	x	x	x	x		x	o	o	o	o							
James Lovell (Mass.)				x	x	x	x		x			o	o	o	o							o
Artemas Ward (Mass.)				x	x		x		x			o	o	o	o			o		o		o
Joseph Jones (Va.)	x				x		x	x	x			o			o	o	o		o			
James Madison (Va.)	x				x		x	x	x			o		o	o	o	o		o			
Meriwether Smith (Va.)	x				x			x				o		o	o	o	o	o	o		o	
Theodorick Bland (Va.)					x			x				o	o	o	o	o	o		o	o	o	
James Varnum (R.I.)*	x	x		x		x				x		o	o						o		o	

*Varnum is a deviant.

KEY:

x = vote in support of reduced ultimatum, or enlarged peace commission.

o = vote in opposition to reduced ultimatum, or enlarged peace commission.

1. Motion to join additional peace commissioners with John Adams. June 9, *JCC,* XX, 619.
2. Instruction to Adams to "ultimately govern yourself" by the "advice and opinion" of the French ministers. June 11, *JCC,* XX, 627.

3. Instruction to Adams to use his judgment in securing as much as possible of the original boundary ultimatum of August 14, 1779. June 6, *JCC*, XX, 607.

4. Essentially similar to vote 3. June 7, *JCC*, XX, 610.

5. Use judgment in securing as much of original ultimatum as possible, but in no case yield territory south of the Ohio River or admit exclusive British claims between the Ohio, Mississippi, and Great Lakes. June 8, *JCC*, XX, 613–614.

6. Use judgment, but yield no territory south of a line from the mouth of the Miami River to the source of the Illinois River, and along that river to the Mississippi. June 8, *JCC*, XX, 611–612.

7. Motion to postpone definition of northwest boundary to future negotiation, if necessary to secure peace. June 7, *JCC*, XX, 609.

8. No cession of territory southeast of Ohio. June 8, *JCC*, XX, 613.

9. Substitute "as circumstances may direct" for "use his own judgment" in instruction to peace minister. June 11, *JCC*, XX, 626.

10. Demand only substance of independence, not formal recognition, but give up no territory in the thirteen states to Great Britain. June 9, *JCC*, XX, 618.

11. Instruct to make confidential communications with French. June 8, *JCC*, XX, 614.

South in an initial draft of a circular letter to the states drawn up on June 1. Mathews was very perturbed by the fact that the peace terms were being extracted from Congress by "hard necessity . . . at a time when these states are in a less eligible situation to enter the negotiations for peace, than at any other period of the war"[63]. Two other votes that had not been available to France in 1779 when the peace instructions were first hammered out were those of New Jersey and New Hampshire. Both were "landless" states that understandably did not wish to prolong the conflict in order to obtain western lands in which Virginia still showed a proprietary interest—particularly when Virginia itself was faltering badly in her defensive efforts against the British. Joseph Reed, president of the Pennsylvania Council, commented that "Virginia at this time affords the most remarkable Instance of Imbicillity . . . that I believe the World ever exhibited—a few thousand Men march uncontested and send forth Detachments to every part of the Country[64]. The defection of Sullivan and Livermore from the Eastern position faithfully taken by the other six delegates from New England, as well as Bland of Virginia and George Clymer of Pennsylvania, was less excusable than that of Witherspoon and Houston—particularly in the case of Sullivan. New Hampshire had not suffered from the war as New Jersey had, and it had a greater stake in maintaining Adams's freedom to negotiate.

The revision of the instructions was a master stroke by Luzerne, for in actuality the British were extremely vulnerable to a blockade of the Chesapeake. Reed was aware of the fact. He observed that "a decisive [naval] superiority for a few weeks would do the Business" but that the French were contriving to "keep us between Hope & Despair"[65]. Luzerne was better informed about impending French naval movements than was Congress, and he pressed for speedy action. Had Congress proceeded with its customary slowness, it might have anticipated the defeat of Cornwallis at Yorktown and consequently drawn up sterner instructions.

Luzerne's triumph was less than complete, for in the struggle over naming the enlarged commission, partisan alignments were different from what they were during the contest over the peace instructions. John Jay was easily elected as the second commissioner, and it was known in Congress that he had opposed relinquishing demands in the West. Had Congress really wanted to placate France, it would have chosen Franklin for the third post, but after Jay's name was put forth by Mathews, Richard Howly of Georgia nominated Henry Laurens, an anti-Gallican advocate of the fisheries. Since Laurens was then held by the British, having been captured on his way to Holland, it was necessary that he be exchanged for a major British prisoner—none other than General Burgoyne. This was moved by Mathews and endorsed by all the delegates from the Carolinas and Georgia. The only state to oppose the exchange was Pennsylvania, bound to support Franklin[66]. To further complicate the situation, Thomas Jefferson was nominated by Meriwether Smith, William Carmichael by Daniel Jenifer, and Joseph Reed by John Witherspoon[67]. In the end, it was necessary to enlarge the commission to five members: Adams, Jay, Franklin, Laurens, and Jefferson[68]. The struggle was more than a conventional contest for preferment. It reflected the traditional partisan alignments that Luzerne was working diligently to erase. Witherspoon's nomination of Reed, a man who was sympathetic with New England and suspicious of France, is an indication of the partial nature of the influence which Luzerne exerted over Congress.

By making use of the sectional and partisan divisions that persisted in the Congress, Luzerne was able to garner two more triumphs during 1781. Madison, with Luzerne's approval, succeeded in removing Adams's commission to negotiate a commercial treaty with England, and as a result of Luzerne's direct influence, Robert R. Livingston was appointed over Arthur Lee as the new Secretary for Foreign Affairs.

Observing that the fisheries were given a favored status in that they remained a sina qua non for a commercial treaty with Great Britain and that John Adams was the sole commissioner for the negotiation of such a treaty, Madison attempted in late June to add the Mississippi boundary as an equivalent ultimatum for a commercial treaty[69]. Madison's motion was soundly defeated by a vote of six to three as a consequence of opposition from the Deep South, the landless Middle states, and New England. Two weeks later, Madison, seconded by Mathews, successfully moved the revocation of Adams's commission and attached an additional instruction to the peace commissioners that they yield no commercial concessions unless they were necessary to obtain peace. If so, they were to "use their most strenuous endeavours" to secure compensation in the fisheries and the West and an additional objective—the relinquishment by Britain of any guarantee readmitting banished Tories or restoring their confiscated property[70]. At the outset of the debate, the delegations from the lower South were alarmed that England might refuse to make peace without a commercial treaty. Luzerne's secretary, Barbe-Marbois, assured them that commercial clauses could be inserted into the peace treaty. Actually, Marbois hoped that there would be no commercial agreement of any sort between Great Britain and the United States. The French hoped to edge Britain from American commerce—especially in the South. Luzerne stressed the great importance of trade between France and Virginia. He argued that while the industry and meager fortunes of the Northern region would make that area of little consequence to France, Virginia's tobacco, the indolence of Southerners (which would prevent manufacturing), their wealth, and their penchant for luxuries made Virginia a ripe market for European manufacturing nations. It was of incalculable importance that France should possess and conserve that commerce[71].

Madison's motives in making the resolution are not so clear as the motives of Marbois and Luzerne in applauding it. It is possible that he was working against commercial concessions to Britain—perhaps even trying to lay the ground for the commercial connection with France that Luzerne hoped for—and at the same time attempting to recover the Mississippi boundary. One thing is certain: he succeeded in restoring the position of the West on an equivalent plane with the fisheries, and in doing this he exacerbated the strain between New England and the South.

Concerning Luzerne's other triumph in shaping American foreign policy during 1781—the election of Robert R. Livingston to the post of Secretary for Foreign Affairs—the post had remained vacant during the first half of the year because Congress could not agree on the man to fill it. Certainly, the critical aspect of foreign policy hardly warranted inaction, but the nationalists of the Middle-Southern coalition were not entirely in agreement about a candidate. Both Madison and Robert R. Livingston were mentioned as possibilities in opposition to Arthur Lee, the anti-Gallican candidate[72]. The delay in deciding among the three men is no less interesting than the fact that Livingston should have been mentioned at all. Neither the sectional composition of the foreign service nor the qualifications of Livingston particularly recommended the New Yorker for the post. He had served in Congress between November 1779 and September of the following year, had established himself as a supporter of centralist reform, and had chaired the committee to enlarge the powers of the Congress. But during a time of inaction in foreign affairs following the convulsions of 1779, he had little to do with foreign policy, save leading a committee to receive the French fleet and army. Madison was more capable, and he had greater experience with the problems of foreign policy.

Livingston did have one major claim to the attention of the pro-French party, however: he was on extremely cordial terms with Luzerne and Marbois. Indeed, Marbois repeatedly urged Livingston to return to Congress and encouraged him to believe he would be elected to the secretaryship[73]. The enthusiastic support of Luzerne and Marbois for Livingston was not without foundation, for his attachment to the French position was as thorough as his experience in foreign affairs was incomplete. Madison's position regarding the West, on the other hand, may have prejudiced his candidacy in the eyes of the French at this moment.

The six-month delay in the election of the Secretary indicates that the Gallican party was not in complete command of Congress. Arthur Lee, whose chances for the slot were negligible precisely because of his ample but catastrophic education in diplomacy, described the election to Samuel Adams:

> Chancellor Livingston, after much manouvering was of friday last elected Minister for foerign Affairs. Upon the first vote, Massachusetts, Connecticut, Jersey, Delaware and Virginia were for Mr. Lee, and three for the Chancellor. On the second Virginia was prevaild on to throw away its vote, and the Chancellor had Hamps'e, R. Island, N. York, Jersey, S. Carolina and Georgia. Dr. Witherspoon stayed away and his Colleagues changd sides. On the third day, Mr. Smith of this State, with his senses hardly recovered from a fall that took them away entirely, was brought in and with Mr. Clymer carried the Election [74].

In his letter, Lee brooded over the machinations of the opposition in a manner reminiscent of the ancient partisan feuds, but it was clear that the power of the Adams-Lee faction had been broken. The New England bloc fractured on the first vote. Sullivan was in all probability the captive of Luzerne's bribery, while Livermore had never toed the Eastern line.

Sullivan's constant defection in foreign affairs very likely cost him an appointment to the third major executive post—that of Secretary at War. He wrote to Washington in March that he was "not Eligible" because of having "apostatized from the true New England Faith, by sometimes voting with the Southern States"[75]. For a short while, it appeared that Schuyler would be elected, a move which, in conjunction with the previous attempt to place McDougall as Secretary of the Marine, would have produced a clean sweep for the state of New York. Ultimately, a semblance of sectional balance was restored with the election of Benjamin Lincoln as Secretary at War on October 30, eight months after the creation of this office[76]. But the election of Lincoln, a Massachusetts general, was not a victory for the Eastern party. Lincoln's attitudes were more shaped by the army and more in line with the policies of the centralists than with the remaining Old Radicals in Congress.

V

By 1782, the rapid diminution of hostilities brought a marked change in the partisan structure of Congress. The massive Middle-Southern coalition of 1781 rapidly disintegrated as most of the delegates from the Middle states shifted toward an alignment with the Eastern party. A Northern coalition emerged with the capacity to muster as many as seven or eight votes against the two closely tied blocs of the Southern coalition, which had difficulty in gathering more than the four votes of Virginia, the Carolinas, and Georgia (see Table 19).

This abrupt change did not mean that the North had all of a sudden achieved total cohesion, for the coalition was a combination of two blocs which voted together with less consistency than had been true of the Middle-Southern coalition of 1781. Further, sparse attendance and deviations in the delegations from New Hampshire, New York, and New Jersey often made it difficult to secure the required seven votes for passage of an important instruction and quite impossible to muster the nine votes necessary for a conclusive decision. The formation of a Northern coalition did not indicate that partisan politics had been dramatically redefined. The coalition was formed on a relatively limited range of issues that did not touch directly upon many of the basic questions that had arisen during 1781, such as the relationship between the national government and the states. The realignment of 1782 was due to a range of factors, including finance, military affairs, and foreign policy, but the question of western claims and related matters such as Vermont produced the major divisions of 1782. Actually, the status of Vermont stimulated more roll calls than any other single question. Territorial questions of all kinds, including Vermont and western lands, accounted for well over one-third of all the roll calls for that year[77].

The issue which most contributed to the definition of the Middle states bloc of 1782 was the demand that Virginia rescind the conditions she had imposed upon her cession of the Northwest—above all the restrictions nullifying land company claims based upon treaties with the Indians. The land companies, specifically the Vandalia, Illinois, Wabash, and Indiana Companies, petitioned Congress for a validation of their claims in the fall of 1781. On November 3, a special committee recommended that the New York cession be accepted but that the cessions of Virginia and Connecticut (which also contained reservations regarding the strip of land that ultimately became the "Western Reserve") be rejected until those states removed the conditions they had imposed. The Virginians succeeded in delaying decisive action regarding both the memorials from the land companies and the cessions for a whole year. The tactics of the Virginians were varied, but they were supported in the main by the whole of the South, including delegates such as Arthur Lee, Theodorick Bland, Ralph

Izard, and John Gervais, who often opposed their Southern colleagues on other issues such as those related to finance, diplomacy, and the centralization of power[78].

It was not only delegates from "landless" Middle states who opposed the South regarding claims to the West. A substantial body of opposition came from New England as well. When Arthur Lee and Theodorick Bland moved that consideration of the petitions from the land companies be deferred until each member of Congress took an oath that he was or was not "personally interested, directly or indirectly, in any company claims against the territorial rights" of any one of the states whose cessions were being debated, the New England delegates opposed the motion by a margin of four to three[79]. Rhode Island constantly supported the Middle states on grounds that she had made clear earlier: In view of the pressing need for revenue, western lands should be sold for the benefit of the Confederation and not held in reserve for favored states. Rhode Island's interest was unusually keen in the matter, for she was under strong pressure to ratify the impost amendment which, if passed, would deprive her proportionately of much more revenue than was true of the Southern states.

The question of the cessions troubled Congress during the entire year. (Indeed, the final resolution of the Virginia cession did not occur until 1784, and Connecticut's cession was not completed until 1785.) It was a problem that was complicated further by other matters related to territory. The British invasion made it more difficult for Virginia to control her counties west of the mountains in the region south of the Ohio. As early as the summer of 1780, 1,000 residents of the Kentucky region asked that the Congress grant them separate statehood[80]. Hardly discouraged by the end of hostilities, the Kentuckians sent another petition to Congress in August of 1782. The petitioners argued that "being removed 800 miles from the seat of Government [in Richmond]," Virginia sovereignty was precarious, and the western inhabitants were in danger of losing their rights. Grounding their constitutional argument in the proposition that the charter by which Virginia claimed the West had been nullified with the dissolution of the London Company, the petitioners claimed they were under the jurisdiction of Congress which had acceded to the rights of the English crown[81].

Arthur Lee dismissed the claim as "groundless, an extravagant and idle supposition"[82]. North Carolinians, who had their own problems in the West, were quick to agree. Hugh Williamson, despite his being a transplanted Pennsylvanian, deplored that "the Spirit of making new States is become epidemic. It is certain that many of the small states or at least many of the inhabitants of those states encourage that Spirit. They look with an envious eye on the large States and wish to make us all of the Pigmy breed"[83]. Pressures to reduce the size of the states did, indeed, seem to reach epidemic proportions.

Inhabitants of western Pennsylvania, according to information reaching Congress, wanted to separate from their parent state. Samuel Wharton of Delaware seemed nonplused by the prospect, asserting that many in the Pennsylvania Legislature "are of the opinion that this State would be large enough if it was confined to the Alleghany Mountain, and it would be wisdom to acquiesce in the proposition of an independent State, if it was founded upon the admission of the rights of such as have just claim" (doubtless speculators such as Wharton himself). Wharton did, however, warn that this episode could turn into another Vermont and "be fruitful of much vexation to the National Council"[84].

While the problems in the West did much to help form the division between the Northern and Southern coalitions, the partisan politics of the Congress—and the cohesion of the Eastern bloc in particular—can be traced in great measure to the problem of Vermont. Vermont, or the New Hampshire Grants, had troubled Congress since the year of independence, but in 1781, the dispute took on new dimensions. A number of the Vermont settlers wanted status as an independent state and went so far as to send a deputation to Congress to press their cause. There were interests, in most respects utterly disconnected, which combined to support Vermont statehood. Landless Maryland, persistently poised to destroy Virginia's claim to the West and to erase her cession conditions regarding private speculations, was favorably disposed toward the precedent of scaling down state land claims. Pennsylvania and New Jersey were not unsympathetic with the pretensions of the Vermonters. Massachusetts, too, was ready to consider independence for Vermont, largely in order to augment the voting strength of the New England bloc.

The Massachusetts Legislature indicated on March 8 that it would abandon its claim to Vermont if the other two interested states would follow suit. In July, Congress appointed a committee of five to investigate the proposition and, after some delays, proposed that the Grants be divided between the Vermonters and the two major contenders—New York and New Hampshire. This is in essence what Congress did on August 21 after a conference with representatives from Vermont, Ira Allen and Jonas Fay[85]. None of the three parties was really happy with the settlement. The New Yorkers rejected the proposed boundaries, but the Vermonters used this as a handle to advance their demand for independence. After complaints from Governors Weare of New Hampshire and Clinton of New York that the Vermonters had set up their own government, were seizing lands within the jurisdiction of New Hampshire and New York, and even, worse, were plotting with the enemy, Congress again took up the Vermont issue in December of 1781[86] and ultimately referred the question to a new committee composed of a member from each state under the chairmanship of Samuel Livermore of New Hampshire[87]. The grand committee proposed on February 19 that Vermont be granted statehood if it would allow congressional arbitration of disputed boundaries with New York and New Hampshire, but the proposal was eventually defeated by New York and the South[88]. The South, consenting to generous terms for Vermont during the critical days of the late summer of 1781, was now recalcitrant. The Vermont question then hung in the balance, a constant irritant in Congress, productive of much debate and no resolution.

The cause of the Vermonters was somewhat sullied by the end of 1782 with the arrival of additional proof that there had been complicity between the self-styled government of Vermont and the British. One Christopher Osgood, a carpenter from Brookline in the vicinity of Brattleboro, presented evidence to Congress that a number of leaders of the insurgent government had been corresponding with William Smith, the one-time royal chief justice of New York[89]. Some delegates insisted that the time had come for forcible interference by Continental arms to establish congressional authority in what could be described as a rebellious province, but the Vermont cause had created a cadre of small-state sympathizers. The New Jersey Legislature, responding to a request for instructions from its delegate Elias Boudinot, resolved on November 1, 1782, that Congress had no right either to compel the allegiance of the Vermonters or to use force to precipitate a civil war[90].

James Madison, with his customary clarity, analyzed the interests involved in the controversy. In a memorandum apparently prepared for Joseph Jones to take to Virginia[91], Madison noted that the two great objects dominating congressional politics in the spring were Vermont and western lands. New England, he argued, favored Vermont's independence partly because of prejudice against New York and because of speculative interest in Vermont lands, but mostly because of a desire to augment the Eastern weight in Congress. New England was supported by Pennsylvania and Maryland in order to undermine the claims of landed states to the West—particularly the claims of Virginia. New Jersey and Delaware took the same position for the same reason, and because of the additional expectation of enhancing the influence of the small states. Madison believed that neither Pennsylvania nor Maryland wanted Vermont admitted on its own merits and that if the western problem were eliminated, they would quickly separate from the Eastern bloc. Massachusetts and Connecticut, realizing this, worked to delay resolution of the territorial question. New Hampshire was not really opposed to Vermont statehood, Madison contended. She welcomed the prospect of five Eastern votes once her claims to the Connecticut River were guaranteed, as they were in the resolution of August 21 and in subsequent congressional decisions. New York, of course, was adamantly opposed, and resistance in the South was stiffening for a number of reasons: fear of Eastern predominance, the expectation that Vermont would oppose western claims of the Southern states, opposition to admitting another state when large issues such as the peace settlement were pending, and the hazardous precedent of admitting a state carved partly from another state against its will. Madison saw Vermont and the related question of western lands as the kingpin of congressional partisan politics. Not only would Maryland and Pennsylvania drift away from their association with New England should it be resolved, but also New York would in all likelihood sever her alliance with the South and "immediately connect her policy with that of the Eastern States"[92].

The analysis of another Southerner, Pierce Butler, who was not a member of Congress but was writing from Philadelphia at the same time, was less refined but illuminating. Butler insisted, "The *Northern Interest* is all prevalent; their members are *firmly united,* and carry many measures disadvantageous to the *Southern interest.* They are laboring hard *to get Vermont established as an independent State,* which will give them *another vote,* by which the balance will be *quite destroyed*"[93].

It was coincidental that states with the soundest claims and the greatest fear of separatist movements in the West were from the South. Yet, Butler's perception of the problem demonstrated the explosive force of the Vermont problem in the context of factional realignments during 1782. To the extent that any issue reinforced the enduring latent tension between the New England and Southern interests in Congress, it threatened to crystallize party tensions. The Vermont problem did that and more. It not only involved the question of representative government which had been at the heart of the initial argument against Great Britain but also directly affected the balance of power in Congress. By exacerbating stresses between the North and the South at the same time when the peace treaty was to be negotiated, it brought into relief the sectional interests which had seriously divided Congress in 1779. Finally, it threatened to break not only the nationalist front that Morris had been carefully cultivating but, in the absence of the Old Radicals who had linked New England and Virginia, also the intersectional radical alliance of the Lees and Adamses.

VI

The issue of western lands and Vermont broke the remnants of the Eastern Old Radical party. While the power of the faction in Pennsylvania had been crushed with the Republican victory in the state elections of 1780, there were still Old Radicals scattered in various delegations as late as 1782. James Lovell served briefly from Massachusetts; Eliphalet Dyer, a marginal radical, from Connecticut; John Witherspoon and Abraham Clark from New Jersey; Thomas McKean from Delaware, and, of course, Arthur Lee from Virginia. If there were only a few original Radicals remaining in 1782, there were many delegates who automatically attached themselves to the Old Radical persuasion, either because of connections with Arthur Lee (such as Theodorick Bland of Virginia and Gervais and Izard of South Carolina) or because of parochialist, anti-Gallican, anti-Morris sentiments (such as Jonathan Arnold and David Howell of Rhode Island and Samuel Osgood of Massachusetts). The basic question which faced the Old Radical remnants in 1782 was whether they had a coherent program which could transcend the powerful but necessarily temporary cannons which had cemented the Party of the Revolution.

The issue of western lands split Radicals from Rhode Island and New Jersey on the one hand, and from the South on the other. Vermont independence won the support only of Theodorick Bland from the South; yet, to the extent that the Old Radicals relied upon the Eastern delegations for voting strength, an additional New England state had to be a major tenet of partisan strategy.

What the Radicals lacked in 1782 was a Silas Deane. Benjamin Franklin, Lee's number two enemy, almost provided a cause célèbre when he intervened in a purchasing agreement worked out by John Laurens and his secretary, William Jackson, in the Netherlands. Laurens and Jackson had used credit from a 2-million-livre gift from France and a pledge from the French Ministry that it would guarantee a 10-million-livre loan from Dutch bankers to make extensive contracts for supplies in the Netherlands. The contracts were made before any loan was arranged with Dutch bankers, however, so the purchases had to be backed with other funds. In addition, Alexander Gillon, commodore of the South Carolina navy, had overdrawn £10,000 sterling he had been promised by Franklin to buy a frigate and make extensive purchases of supplies for which he could not pay. Laurens bought supplies from Gillon and arranged to transport them on two merchant vessels purchased by the South Carolina commodore. Having overused their credit, Laurens and Gillon left before Franklin could intervene. Jackson stayed on to complete arrangements and to see to the shipment of the bullion and supplies. The French, irritated at such purchases being made in the Netherlands without a Dutch loan, refused to cover the debts beyond the original gift. Franklin, fearing impairment of United States credit should he void the contracts, instructed Jackson to use 1,500,000 livres in bullion which was to be shipped to the United States to satisfy Dutch creditors. Jackson and Franklin exchanged some acrimonious letters before Jackson left with Gillon in September of 1781. Rather than returning directly to the United States, Gillon went to the West Indies, where he captured five prizes in Jamaica, and then participated in a joint undertaking with the Spanish to conquer the Bahamas. Gillon finally arrived in Philadelphia on February 28, 1782, covered with considerable laurels, but having left a maze of fiscal difficulties for Franklin and John Adams (by then in The Hague) to untangle.

Both Laurens and Gillon were critical of Franklin's refusal to release the 1,500,000 livres of bullion, and on the motion of Bland and John Morin

Scott, a committee was set up in Congress on July 12 to investigate Franklin's behavior[94]. The committee was far from pro-Franklin in composition. Theodorick Bland was chairman, and the other two members were recently arrived Jonathan Jackson of Massachusetts and David Howell of Rhode Island. Although the committee reported to Congress as early as September 26, its report was not entered in the Journal until November 1[95]. Unsurprisingly, the report was extremely critical of Franklin. Madison described it as "one of the most signal monuments which party zeal has produced"[96]. The committee recommended that Franklin should be censured for unconstitutionally holding back the funds designated by France for use in the United States. Arthur Lee charged that Franklin's action amounted to outright theft[97]. Fortunately for Franklin, who was in the right, and for American diplomacy, which did not need another Lee-Deane imbroglio at this critical moment in the peace negotiations, the Franklin-Laurens-Gillon affair subsided with little impact. That it should have done so is an indication of the difficulties in the path of any effective revival of the Old Radical coalition.

The difficulties of the centralists were as great—perhaps greater. The centralist program had been formed of disparate elements at a time when the military crisis in the South and the bankrupt condition of Confederation finance had persuaded all but the most hard-shelled parochialists that executive reorganization and a measure of national consolidation was imperative to save the Revolution. But the reorganization resulted in an administrative establishment dominated by the Middle states—and this alarmed New England. Robert Morris's financial reforms, sensible in many respects, prompted opposition both from Northeasterners such as the Rhode Island delegates, who complained that the impost imposed an unjust tax upon them, and from Southerners, who were alarmed about his proposals regarding the taxation of slaves and vacant western lands. Forced to rely upon slim contributions from the states, Morris had to turn to the French ally for assistance—a move that exposed the centralists to increasing criticism with the abatement of hostilities.

In 1783, Samuel Osgood of Massachusetts charged that "the eagle eyed Politician of our great Ally, discovered the absolute Importance of the Aid of his Master, and the critical situation of the United States. It was then he ventured to propose that Congress should subject their Peace Commissioners to the absolute control of a foreign court . . ."[98]. Both the humiliating revision of the peace instructions of June 1781 and the revocation of Adams's commission to negotiate a commercial treaty with England demonstrated to Osgood that an intriguing system of influence existed between the French and the Superintendent of Finance. Morris had become a willing abettor of French diplomacy. Osgood's charge—doubtless exaggerated because of his fervid anti-Gallicanism—nonetheless illustrated the political difficulties that the program of the centralists would encounter once peace had been declared.

Osgood's charges also illuminated a difficulty that may have been the most serious that the centralists had to face. The American Revolution had begun as a solitary effort sustained by public virtue which did not require national organization so much as a national ideology. When that ideology seemed to fail, and when central organization was in a sense put in its place, the nation found that it depended upon outside support. There was a fundamental contradiction in the posture of centralists. They should have been able to propose a nationalist alternative to the diffuse energies of parochial enthusiasts, but because of their association with France, they seemed to debase national dignity. The question was whether or not leaders such as Morris, Duane, and Madison could be both centralists and nationalists.

Notes

1 JCC, XIX, 229.

2 Thomas Rodney, Diary, Mar. 5–6, 1780, *LMCC*, VI, 8–9.

3 PCC, no. 24, fols. 19, 25; *JCC*, XX, 469–470.

4 Ibid., 470.

5 James Madison to Thomas Jefferson, Apr. 16, 1781, in William T. Hutchinson and William M. E. Rachal (eds.), *The Papers of James Madison* (Chicago, 1962–), III, 71-72.

6 James Varnum to Governor William Greene, Mar. 16, 1781, *LMCC*, VI, 28.

7 Edmund C. Burnett, *The Continental Congress* (New York, 1941), pp. 505–517; Varnum to Greene, Apr. 2, 1781, *LMCC*, VI, 41.

8 Burnett, *The Continental Congress*, p. 505.

9 Luzerne to Vergennes, May 18, 1781, quoted in George Bancroft, *History of the Formation of the Constitution of the United States* (2 vols.; New York, 1884), I, 24.

10 JCC, XXI, 895–896. There were other recommendations pertaining to voting regulations, the establishment of a consular system, the appointment of tax collectors for funds allocated to Congress, etc., but no mention of the issue of coercing recalcitrant states.

11 Madison to Jefferson, Apr. 16, 1781, in Hutchinson and Rachal (eds.), *The Papers of James Madison,* III, 72.

12 Madison to Edmund Randolph, Feb. 25, 1783, *LMCC*, VII, 57–58.

13 Madison's position at this time contradicted his later advocacy of divided sovereignty and the coercion of law rather than arms. Yet, there is a consistent strain is his policy. Both in 1781 and 1787, he seems to have sought political harmony through countervailing powers. In *The Federalist,* Number 10, the pernicious effects of a majority faction in a state could be overcome by absorption of the faction in the larger sphere of national government empowered to operate directly upon individuals through law. In 1781, his assumption also was that wrongheadedness in a particular territory could be checked through the operation of a larger policy.

14 *JCC,* XII, 1118-1119.

15 See Table 16.

16 John Sullivan to George Washington, May 17, William C. Houston to Thomas McKean, Mar. 31, and Thomas Rodney, Diary, [July] 1781, *LMCC,* VI, 90, 40, 141.

17 Morris to the President of Congress, May 14, 1781, in Francis Wharton (ed.), *The Revolutionary Diplomatic Correspondence of the United States* (6 vols.; Washington, D.C., 1889), IV, 412-414.

18 Clarence Ver Steeg, *Robert Morris, Revolutionary Financier* (Philadelphia, 1954), p. 66.

19 Even at this relatively low capitalization, private investments were insufficient to complete the subscription. Morris had to divert $254,000 in specie from a French loan of $462,000. E. James Ferguson, *The Power of the Purse* (Chapel Hill, 1961), p. 136.

20 Ibid., pp. 66-68. Morris to John Jay, July 13, 1781, in Wharton (ed.), *Diplomatic Correspondence, U.S.,* IV, 562-563.

21 Ferguson, *The Power of the Purse,* p. 137.

22 *JCC,* XX, 547.

23 Ibid., XIX, 333, XXI, 9413. As early as June 28, Madison had framed a resolution putting the management and direction of the navy under the control of the Superintendent of Finance. Hutchinson and Rachal (eds.), *The Papers of James Madison,* III, 167.

24 Alexander McDougall to Governor George Clinton, Mar. 12, 1781, *LMCC,* VI, 26.

25 Ferguson, *The Power of the Purse,* p. 134.

26 *JCC,* XX, 723, XXI, 783-784.

27 Ver Steeg, *Robert Morris,* pp. 69-75; Jennings B. Sanders, *Evolution of Executive Departments of the Continental Congress, 1774-1789* (Chapel Hill, 1935), p. 131.

28 Ferguson, *The Power of the Purse,* p. 126.

29 Ver Steeg, *Robert Morris,* p. 165.

30 Ferguson, *The Power of the Purse,* p. 138.

31 Ibid.

32 The ordinance was passed Nov. 2, 1781; *JCC,* XXI, 1091.

33 Indeed, William Gordon warned Arthur Lee that Lovell should be watched, for on a recent trip Gordon had taken to Philadelphia, he had noticed Lovell mixing with "Deanites." William Gordon to Arthur Lee, Oct. 2, 1782, Arthur Lee Papers, HCL.

34 John Swanwick to Samuel Holten, July 4, 1783, Holten Papers, LC.

35 Samuel Holten to General Prebble, Sept. 6, 1783, ibid.

36 Lee went so far in 1784 as to invest in Morris's bank stock to the limit of voting power and then attempted to persuade as many investors to pull out at once as possible. Forrest McDonald, *E Pluribus Unum* (Boston, 1965), pp. 54–55.

37 Ver Steeg, *Robert Morris,* p. 102.

38 Ibid., p. 101.

39 *JCC,* XXII, 439. A poll tax (as well as a 2-percent impost) had been recommended by a committee under Gouverneur Morris on Sept. 19, 1778. Ibid., XII, 929.

40 *JCC,* XXII, 115.

41 Ibid., 407–408, XXIII, 545–546.

42 Hugh Williamson to Governor Alexander Martin, Sept. 2, 1782, *LMCC,* VI, 462.

43 Edmund Randolph to Governor Nelson, Nov. 7, 1781, ibid., VI, 260.

44 Arthur Lee to James Warren, July 27, 1781, Warren-Adams Letters, II, 170.

45 William C. Stinchcombe, *The American Revolution and the French Alliance* (Syracuse, 1969), p. 85.

46 Luzerne to the President of the Continental Congress, Feb. 28, 1781, in Wharton (ed.), *Diplomatic Correspondence, U.S.,* IV, 270.

47 James Madison to Edmund Randolph, June 4, 1782, in Hutchinson and Rachal (eds.), *The Papers of James Madison,* IV, 313.

48 Stinchcombe, *The American Revolution and the French Alliance,* p. 158.

49 John Witherspoon to ———, [March 1783?], *LMCC,* VII, 117.

50 Stinchcombe, *The American Revolution and the French Alliance,* p. 180.

51 Luzerne to Vergennes, June 11, 1780, quoted in Paul C. Phillips, *The West in the Diplomacy of the Revolution* (Urbanna, 1913), pp. 164n–165n.

52 Marbois to Vergennes, Montmorin, Oct. 17, 1780, ibid., 182–183.

53 Madison to Joseph Jones, Nov. 25, 1780; Hutchinson and Rachal (eds.), *The Papers of James Madison,* II, 202–204. Bland and his wife were apparently on good terms with Luzerne. Bland credited himself with persuading Luzerne to dispatch a French squadron to assist in the effort against the raids of Arnold in the Chesapeake during the winter of 1780–1781. Arthur Lee, in a letter to Bland later in 1781, inquired whether "the French and Spanish ministers [were] still at Mrs. Bland's feet?" Lee to Bland, Sept. 27, 1781, Bland Papers, LC.

54 *JCC,* XIX, 154.

55 Luzerne to Vergennes, Dec. 15, 1780. Quoted in Phillips, *The West in the Diplomacy of the Revolution,* p. 195.

56 *JCC,* XX, 560–561.

57 *LMCC,* VI, 436.

58 *JCC,* XX, 606–607.

59 Ibid., 612–613. See Table 20.

60 Instructions from Samuel Huntington to Adams, Franklin, Jay, Laurens, and Jefferson, June 15, 1781, in Wharton (ed.), *Diplomatic Correspondence, U.S.,* IV, 504–505.

61 Luzerne to Vergennes, June 11, 1781, quoted in Stinchcombe, *The American Revolution and the French Alliance,* p. 161.

62 James Lovell wrote to John Adams that America should "blush" over the "advise and consent" clause. June 21, 1781, *LMCC,* VI, 125. Lovell himself was probably embarrassed, since in a letter to Nathaniel Peabody he described the congressional action with unaccustomed brevity and dispassion: "Congress have . . . given powers to 5 Commissioners to act in Concert with our Ally." Lovell to Peabody, Aug. 7, 1781, Peabody Papers, NHHS.

63 *JCC,* XX, 586. The phrase was crossed out in the Journals.

64 Joseph Reed to Nathanael Greene, June 16, 1781, Greene Papers, CL.

65 Ibid.

66 *JCC,* XX, 647–648. Madison, Carroll, and Houston also opposed the change.

67 Ibid., XX, 628.

68 As events turned out, neither of the Southern candidates played an influential role in the peace negotiations. Jefferson declined the commission, and Laurens arrived only in time to witness the completion of the preliminary peace treaty.

69 *JCC,* XX, 713–714.

70 Ibid., 747.

71 Luzerne to Vergennes, Apr. 20, 1782, French Foreign Archives (photostat). Both Luzerne and Barbé-Marbois were struck by the difference between Virginia and New England. For the latter's impression of New England, where he arrived in August of 1779, see Eugene Parker Chase (ed.), *Our Revolutionary Forefathers: The Letters of Francois, Marquis de Barbé-Marbois . . . 1779-1785* (New York, 1929), chaps. 2, 3, and esp. pp. 76–77, 100–101.

72 As early as February 21, 1781, Gouverneur Morris wrote to Livingston that "Lee, Maddison and yourself are in nomination. I believe you will be appointed." Quoted in George Dangerfield, *Chancellor Robert R. Livingston* (New York, 1960), p. 473.

73 Marbois to Livingston, March 27 and June 29, 1781, quoted in ibid., p. 474.

74 Arthur Lee to Samuel Adams, Aug. 13, 1781, Samuel Adams Papers, NYPL.

75 John Sullivan to Washington, Mar. 6, 1781, *LMCC*, VI, 11–12.

76 *JCC*, XXI, 1087.

77 An indication of how pervasive the territorial question became in 1782 can be found in the reconsideration of the peace terms during October of 1782. After Yorktown, Congress was encouraged to redefine its instructions of June 15, 1781. (See Stinchcombe, *The American Revolution and the French Alliance*, chap. XII, esp. pp. 179–182.) While it decided against forthright instructions to its commissioners, a majority of whom (Adams and Jay) had indicated in their correspondence that they would press for the Mississippi boundary and the fisheries, Congress did consider informing the French king that it was confident he would aid the commissioners in securing the larger objectives. The main problem occurred over whether the western lands would be called the "territorial claims of these States" or the "territorial claims of these United States." See *JCC*, XXIII, 634–636.

78 See, e.g., the votes of those delegates in *JCC*, XXII, 191, 192, 193, 224, 232, 234, 240, XXIII, 552.

79 Ibid., XXII, 191.

80 The petition, dated May 19, 1780, is in the PCC, no. 48, fols. 237–244. See also *JCC*, XVII, 760, for a similar petition protesting against Virginia land speculation and engrossment.

81 Charles Thomson, "Notes of Debates," Aug. 27, 1782, *LMCC*, VI, 456–457.

82 Ibid., p. 457. It is not at all unlikely that such an informed constitutional case was concocted not by the early Virginia residents but by more recent migrants from the Middle states who had been encouraged to move by Middle states speculators—especially Pennsylvanians. This was the opinion of the recently arrived delegate from North Carolina, Hugh Williamson. Hutchinson and Rachal (eds.), *The Papers of James Madison*, V, 84n; Williamson to Governor Alexander Martin, Nov. 18, 1782, *LMCC*, VI, 545.

83 Williamson to Martin, Nov. 18, 1782, ibid. Madison wrote to Edmund Randolph the next day about reports of the "avidity of the Western people for the vacant lands and for separate Gov'ts." Madison to Randolph, Nov. 19, 1782, ibid.

84 Samuel Wharton to George Read, Nov. 17, 1782, ibid., 543–544.

85 *JCC*, XXI, 823–825; 892–893.

86 Ibid., 1159–1160.

87 Ibid., XXII, 57–60.

88 Ibid., 105–108.

89 Ibid., XXIII, 750–753.

90 *Journal of the Proceedings of the Legislative Council of the State of New Jersey* . . . (Trenton, 1783), pp. 11–12.

91 Hutchinson and Rachal (eds.), *The Papers of James Madison*, IV, 200, editorial note.

92 "Observations Relating to the Influence of Vermont and the Territorial Claims on the Politics of Congress," May 1, 1782, in ibid., 200–202.

93 Pierce Butler to James Iredell, Apr. 5, 1782, in G. J. McRee (ed.), *Life and Correspondence of James Iredell* (2 vols.; New York, 1857–1858), II 9; *LMCC,* VI, 327n.

94 *JCC,* XXII, 385.

95 PCC, no. 19, vol. III, fol. 449, *JCC,* XXIII, 700–705.

96 Madison to Edmund Randolph, Oct. 15, 1782, in Hutchinson and Rachal (eds.), *The Papers of James Madison,* V, 200.

97 Arthur Lee to Samuel Adams, Aug. 6, 1782, *LMCC,* VI, 428–430.

98 Samuel Osgood to John Adams, Dec. 7, 1783, ibid., VII, 379.

12   The Failure of the
Nationalists

BEGINNING in 1780, the advocates of centralism launched a program to strengthen the national government. Their efforts gathered momentum during the military crisis of 1781 when the South, in dire peril from British invasion and the threat of Austro-Russian mediation, which could have resulted in a peace that severed the southernmost colonies from the Union, supported the centralist policies of Middle states nationalists. That coalition weakened during 1782, however, as hostilities abated and the fate of the Deep South seemed secure. By the end of that year, information from abroad clearly indicated that a definitive peace treaty was about to be concluded—a treaty which would not only preserve the integrity of the Union but also secure virtually all the objectives that Congress had been afraid to insist upon in June of 1781, when it had revised its peace terms and reconstituted its peace commission.

The prospect of peace—especially an advantageous peace—had a profound impact upon congressional politics. The advocates of greater central authority recognized that they would have to act quickly if revenue and power were to be extracted from the states, for without military pressure from the British (which had served the centralists of the early 1780s just as it had aided the Radicals of the early years of the Revolution), there was a strong likelihood that American politics would become markedly parochial. It was imperative, therefore, that the impost be ratified by the states and that the Continental Congress and its newly created executive appendages take command of matters such as the management of the national debt and the development of the West.

No longer able to rely upon broad support from the Southern delegations, the centralists—now primarily a party of Middle states nationalists—had difficulty in securing the requisite seven votes necessary for the passage of even routine legislation. But the advocates of centralism had strengths which compensated for their weaknesses during early 1783. They had control of the executive apparatus—above all the powerful office of the Superintendent of Finance. They had exceptionally able leadership in Congress, including Alexander Hamilton, James Wilson, and James Madison. Although they could not rely upon the unfailing support of the Deep South, there was a closer relationship between the Middle states and the South than between the Middle states and New England[1]. Moreover, the centralists frequently were able to split the Eastern opposition, as is evident from the large number of independents from New England (see Table 21). Armed as they were with a positive program, this "Nationalist party" was clearly the most dynamic element in Congress.

It was in late 1782 and early 1783 that the Nationalist party came to fruition in a form that immediately suggests potential for a true "Party of the Nation-State," just as the Old Radicals had assumed the role of the Party of the Revolution. Led by young men who were to make national careers—preeminently Alexander Hamilton and James Madison—the party was tempered with the congressional experience and New York connections of James Duane, and it was enhanced by the legal wisdom and Philadelphia contacts of James Wilson. Most important, the Nationalist group was rooted firmly in the Middle states, the logical focus for a consolidating force.

It may be appropriate to note that most movements toward political amalgamation have a territorial core possessing the distinguishing qualities of the amalgamation movement—a political bureaucracy able to gather in less-organized political units, for example[2]. In the Revolutionary era, and after for that matter, that core area with the capacity to root the amalgamation process consisted of the Middle states and the northern Chesapeake, where there was a fusion of the colonial traditions of New England and the South, where the most immediate thrust for expansion into the West obtained, and where the capital was located and a large segment of the public debt was held. There were tensions within the section, of course: New Jersey was strongly in favor of the 5-percent impost, but New York and Virginia were less happy with it; Virginia was at odds with Maryland and Pennsylvania on the issue of western lands. But all the Middle states had approved the impost by the end of 1782, and the fact that Daniel Carroll, James Madison, and Joseph Jones joined the

TABLE 21

Congressional Blocs, 1783

	Eastern Party	Anti-Nationalist Bloc	Nationalist Party	Southern Party	
				N.C. Bloc	S.C. Bloc
Mass.	Higginson				
	Holten				
	Osgood				
R.I.	Howell	Howell			
	Ellery*	Ellery			
Conn.	Wolcott				
N.Y.			Duane	Duane*	Duane*
			Floyd		
			Hamilton		
			Hommedieu		
N.J.			Boudinot		
Pa.			Fitzsimmons		
			Montgomery		
			Peters		
			Wilson		
Md.			Carroll, D.		
Va.		Bland	Jones, J.*		
		Lee, A.	Madison		
N.C.				Mercer	
				Williamson	
				Hawkins	Hawkins*
S.C.				Izard*	Izard
				Read	Read
					Rutledge
					Gervais

* Marginal membership.

Independents: Foster and White (N.H.); Gorham (Mass.); Collins and Arnold (R.I.); Huntington, S., and Huntington, B. (Conn.); Clark (N.J.); McHenry (Md.).

Nationalist party demonstrates that the Chesapeake area could join the Middle states in a centralist program. The most serious weaknesses of the Nationalists were not in Congress but in the states where they failed to generate the support they needed. Virginia rescinded its approval of the impost in December of 1782, to the complete surprise of the Nationalists.

The Nationalists were in the ascendancy during the winter and spring of 1783, partly because the traditional canons of the Old Radical persuasion no longer operated to cement the Eastern party. The exhilirating anticipation of a republican reformation, of a Christian Sparta, had lost its power—perhaps even its relevance—in a time of peace and relaxation. Alexander Hamilton commented in his "The Continentalist," number six, "We may preach til we are tired of the theme, the necessity of disinterestedness in republics, without making a single proselyte . . . and it is as ridiculous to seek for models in the simple ages of Greece and Rome, as it would be to go on in quest of them among the Hottentots and Laplanders"[3]. The Old Radicals who had been at the vital center of the Eastern party during its ascendancy were missing from Congress. Sam Adams (the advocate of Spartan simplicity that Hamilton ridiculed), William Whipple, James Lovell, and Roger Sherman had all returned to New England. There were Easterners and Southerners in the Congress of 1783 who could be relied upon to oppose centralism—Stephen Higginson and Samuel Osgood from Massachusetts, David Howell from Rhode Island, Theodorick Bland and Arthur Lee from Virginia, Ralph Izard and John Gervais from South Carolina, to name the most prominent—but they were able to unite mostly out of opposition rather than in support of a policy. On questions such as Vermont and officers' pensions, they were quite at odds, as was already apparent during 1782. In addition, while there was a permanent reservoir of Eastern opposition to Robert Morris and the commercial community of Philadelphia, the hard questions of honoring loan office certificates and retiring old tenor could not help but separate Northern and Southern anti-Nationalists. There was a creditor interest in Massachusetts which no congressional politician from that state could overlook, whatever his attitude toward the political danger of funding systems might have been[4]. While there was an alliance between Howell and Ellery of Rhode Island and Bland and Lee of Virginia in the voting blocs of 1783, it was defensive in character and devoid of the constructive assurance of the Eastern coalition of the early Revolution.

Thus the end of hostilities created problems for all parties in Congress. The Nationalists had a program but needed votes. The Eastern and Southern parties had votes but were unable to unite in opposition to the Nationalists. What seemed to be evolving was a three-party system that might work to the advantage of the Nationalists, despite their shortage of votes.

II

The most familiar and fertile partisan stamping ground of Arthur Lee and Ralph Izard was the area of foreign policy. The conduct of United States commissioners and plenipotentiaries as well as the formulation of peace terms had welded the northern and southern parts of the Eastern coalition during the most heated moments of that union. Although they never would have admitted it, what the anti-Nationalists needed was a cause célèbre, preferably involving some sort of sellout in the peace negotiations by Franklin or Jay. The ground was prepared by the infamous "advise and consent" resolution of June 15, 1781—a resolution which Arthur Lee challenged on August 8, 1782[5]. According to the notes taken by Secretary Charles Thomson, there was considerable support for Lee's motion from the Georgia and South Carolina delegations, and although Lee's motion failed, the ground was prepared.

But dispatches from Jay in Spain, and in Paris after he was given leave to participate in the peace negotiations, were increasingly critical of the policies of Spain and America's ally. Jay, even more than Adams, developed a sharp distrust of Vergennes's guardianship of American peace aims. With a willing Adams and a reluctant Franklin, he disregarded congressional instructions. Together, the three commissioners negotiated with the British Minister, Richard Oswald, separately from the French during the fall of 1782. A provisional peace was formulated between the United States and Great Britain, and Vergennes was presented with a fait accompli[6]. The terms of the provisional treaty, including a secret clause which was to take effect if the British recaptured Florida from the Spanish, reached Congress on March 12.

The provisional peace was a triumph, the main clauses of which were above reproach. The boundaries which ran to the St. Croix River in Maine, the Great Lakes, the Mississippi, and the thirty-first parallel were as generous as anyone had realistically expected. Rights to the fisheries and to the navigation of the Mississippi were secured. It was a "highly pleasing" treaty, according to John Taylor Gilman, delegate from New Hamphsire, "equal to the most Sanguine Expectation"[7]. Richard Peters of Pennsylvania wrote to Horatio Gates that "These Preliminaries contain everything we ought to wish," almost as if to say the terms were too generous. William Floyd and others were slightly less enthusiastic about provisions calling for the restitution of Loyalist property, but they were quick to point out that the provisional treaty only pledged the Congress to "recommend" to the states that this be done—a necessary gesture by the Crown to preserve its honor but something the states could disregard[8].

Both the Nationalists and their opponents were placed in unexpectedly awkward positions by the provisional treaty. Arthur Lee was fully prepared to excoriate Jay and Franklin but had to applaud, with amazement one suspects, the "spirited, independent and therefore . . . most laudable" conduct of Jay as well as Adams. (He added with more conviction than evidence that the two of them were necessary "to counteract the treachery of old Franklin"[9].) Nationalists, intent upon preserving harmonious relations with France, were variously embarrassed or distressed by the actions of the commissioners who had formulated and signed the provisional articles without prior consultation with Vergennes—a violation of the spirit if not the letter of the instructions of June 15, 1781. The French court was displeased, and members of Congress who had the full text of the provisional articles before them recognized that the French Ministry would be even more upset if it had all the materials of the negotiation. The secret clause, withheld from France, defined the boundary between the United States and Florida should Great Britain regain that province from the Spanish. Indeed, correspondence from the commissioners indicated that the British had confided their intention to launch an expedition—information which, if not disclosed to Spain or at least to France, would amount to collusion with the enemy.

The situation for the Nationalists was delicate in the extreme. Robert R. Livingston, Secretary of Foreign Affairs, set forth the dilemma facing himself and Congress in a message sent to the President on March 18. The secret article meant it would be necessary either to deceive the French or to undermine the confidence of France in the peace commissioners by disclosing the article to the French court. Livingston indicated that he was certain the British were not intending to invade Florida but rather to lure the United States from her ally. The territory was of little importance, but the secret article made it an issue of the utmost gravity. The article demonstrated "a marked preference for the English over the present possessors" (the Spanish) and furthermore seemed to invite England to reconquer the territory. Livingston recommended that Congress instruct him to communicate the article to the French "in such manner as will best tend to remove any of the unfavorable impression it may make on the court of France of the sincerity of these States or their ministers"[10]. Madison also was upset with the commissioners, whose suspicions of the French court allowed the British to "decoy them into a degree of confidence which seems to leave their own reputations as well as the safety of their country at the mercy of Shelburne"[11]. Madison's colleague John Mercer, evincing what seems to have been a constant tendency of all the Virginia delegates outside the Lee circle to improve relations with France while obstructing any rapprochement with England, delivered the sharpest criticism of the commissioners. Madison recorded it in his meticulous notes of congressional debates:

> The conduct of our Ministers throughout, particularly in giving in writing everything called for by British Ministers expressive of distrust of France was a mixture of follies which had no example, was a tragedy to America and a comedy to all the world beside. He felt inexpressible indignation at their meanly stooping,

as it were to lick the dust from the feet of a nation whose hands were still dyed with the blood of their fellow-citizens. He reprobated the chicane and low cunning wch. marked the journals transmitted to Congress, and contrasted them with the honesty & good faith which became all nations and particularly an infant republic. . . . America was too prone to depreciate political merit, & to suspect where there was no danger; that the honor of the King of F. was dear to him, that he never wd. betray or injure us unless he sd. be provoked & justified by treachery on our part[*12*].

Mercer actually suggested that the commissioners should be recalled! John Adams's Eastern defenders vigorously opposed such a course. Wolcott, Osgood, Holten, Clark, and, of course, Arthur Lee urged that Congress could never censure commissioners who had procured such good terms. Even Southerners such as John Rutledge and Hugh Williamson from the Carolinas took exception to the tack of the Virginians. Alexander Hamilton proposed a middle way by which the commissioners would be commended and the article communicated to the French Minister in as casual a manner as possible. Wilson and other Nationalists also sought to extricate themselves from the thorny predicament in this fashion[*13*]. Interestingly, Wilson had never heard of the June 15 instructions before the morning of the debate—a fact that suggests that the Nationalists were not entirely coordinated in their strategy on foreign affairs. Hamilton himself, though apparently aware of the instructions, did not approve of them.

If the Nationalists were uncoordinated, this escaped the attention of the Eastern anti-Gallicans. Stephen Higginson, as complete a Massachusetts parochialist as either Samuel Osgood or Samuel Adams, informed Theophilus Parsons that Congress had long harbored a party "so thoroughly in the interest of France as to have preferred her interest to ours, whenever they came into competition." He later remarked to Samuel Adams that such persons were actually sorry that peace had taken place on such good terms that the United States was rendered independent of "foreign" (i.e., French) influence and that "these persons seize every occasion to find fault with it, to censure Our Commissioners . . ."[*14*]. It was Higginson's conclusion that this was the work of the French who wanted to obstruct any commercial treaty between the United States and England. It is unlikely that the French had such a strong influence on the pro-Gallicans, but it is highly probable that the Virginians wanted to avoid falling back into the grasp of British creditors and were hopeful of greatly expanding their trade with France. Higginson, on the other hand, like many New Englanders, was interested in reestablishing trade with England[*15*]. Regional disagreements over foreign commerce and foreign connections cropped up at the very moment that the war was won. The dispute over the commissioners abated, however, after news of the conclusion of a general peace was received on March 22. The British ordered an end to hostilities on April 9, and Congress stopped all hostilities on April 11. Congress ratified the provisional treaty on April 15, thus suppressing if not terminating difficulties with its representatives in Paris, a constant source of partisan convulsions.

III

At the same time that the peace treaty was being considered, the Nationalists were making their most serious effort to fortify the Articles and to provide Congress with enough thrust to sustain national authority after the cessation of hostilities. Events were moving so rapidly that Samuel Osgood and Stephen Higginson were convinced that a plot existed to create an aristocratic establishment centered around the person of Robert Morris and funded with French livres[16]. Osgood's distrusts were exaggerated concerning French manipulation of the Nationalist movement, but his fears of an establishment were warranted.

Moving quickly, as they could with a man like Hamilton on the floor, and as indeed they had to with the end of the war in sight, the Nationalists during the winter of 1782-1783 attempted to ram the impost through the states, establish a general system of funding the entire public debt under congressional auspices, and establish an extracongressional constituency of security holders and Continental officers so as to sustain the program. Most alarming, a few Nationalists in Congress and its administration explored the possibility of armed coercion as a means of forcing through the funding program. The mantle of aggressive, even conspiratorial, partisan action thus passed from the Old Radicals—conspicuously successful in undermining British authority in the years before independence—to the Nationalists, now intent upon reestablishing central direction. The Revolution seemed to have turned full circle.

There were three essential components available to the Nationalists: the public debt, western lands, and the army. Each had different properties which both enhanced and endangered the process of consolidating the nation-state. The public debt, substantially enlarged by Morris's policy of collecting commissary and quartermaster obligations, as well as other types of paper, was very unevenly distributed, the bulk being held in the Northern states[17]. The notion of creating a nationalist political force out of the creditors (including the army) was an obvious tactic conceived long before Alexander Hamilton became Secretary of the Treasury, but it had the distinct disadvantage of being unpalatable in areas where there were minor holdings in the debt. The army was a nationalizing force, both because it won the war and because of its unhappy status of being a public creditor. But the army, while applauded for its sacrifices during the struggle, was distrusted as an aristocratic and antirepublican force, particularly in New England, where a strong tradition of antimilitarism existed. Thus the army was a support for national cohesion only so long as it did not function politically—a fact which naturally limited its effectiveness. Of course, a military coup d'état by a disbanding unpaid army was never entirely out of the realm of possibility.

Western lands were probably the most dynamic element in the nationalist compound. The Mississippi boundary won at Paris offered a vacant territory larger than the whole region settled and developed during the 175 years of colonial past. The trans-Allegheny region was seen by many as the promise of the future—the virgin land that would extend and sustain the republican mission of the new nation. But it was also recognized that the West had divided the Republic and would continue to do so. Landed and landless states had not yet resolved all their differences. Even when Congress gained full control of the West, there were questions regarding its organization: Should the West be used as a source of revenue or social welfare? Should the institution of slavery, condemned by most Revolutionaries, be tolerated as the Republic enlarged itself? Finally, could the republican institutions for which the Revolution had been fought be perpetuated in an area so vast as that won at the peace tables in Paris? History counseled "no." Yet, the new nation, to sustain itself, had to defy history.

Most Nationalists, partly because they recognized some of these problems but mostly for other reasons, chose to promote taxation as the major instrument of national consolidation rather than organizing the West in order to secure revenue from the sale of western lands. The western issue lay dormant during most of the spring of 1783, except for a recommendation that the states speed up their cessions, while new tax systems for funding the public debt were constantly discussed. The 5-percent impost was already submitted to the states for ratification as an amendment to the Articles, so it was natural that this apparently immediate source of income should be preferred to the more distant prospect of revenue from land sales. Robert Morris was unequivocal in his insistence on the impost as the proper method for servicing the debt[18].

The Nationalist insistence on taxation as the proper mode of paying the debt was the result of political as well as economic considerations. Immediate use of western lands as a bounty for soldiers and as a source of revenue for the public debt would tend to disperse the population, whereas nationally controlled taxation would augment congressional power and help to consolidate the Confederation. Once the taxing power of Congress was firmly established, a measured advance into the West could be allowed.

There were serious flaws in the Nationalists' strategy. One was that they were using the same policies that were cited as major grievances in the constitutional argument against Great Britain a decade before. While the Continental Congress was different from the British Parliament that passed the offensive stamp tax and Townshend duties, the Nationalists were nonetheless open to the suspicion that they were contriving to make Congress into a new Parliament. Edmund Randolph reported to Madison that a number of Virginia assemblymen had a "fix'd Aversion" to giving the Congress an independent revenue which was necessary "for no other purpose" than to allow Congress to appoint its own officers and thereby gain "an undue Influence" in the states. The assemblymen also felt that "the Nature of Man & former experience justifies a Suspicion" that the moneys from a congressionally controlled impost would be used to create sinecures for "Relatives and favourites" rather than for the payment of the debt. The impost, accepted as a justifiable expedient during the war, encountered sharp distrust in peacetime[*19*]. That comparable charges came from political conservatives such as John Rutledge and Stephen Higginson as well as Old Radicals revealed a second flaw in the Nationalist plan. Neither New England nor the Deep South was prepared at this time to nationalize the Confederation, especially under the auspices of the Middle states, until they had assurance that the direction of a more consolidated nation-state would not harm their vital interests. Even if the Nationalist program were not directly prejudicial to the extremities of the Confederation, it would be mistrusted as a design to bring wealth and power to the mercantile interests of the Middle region without equivalent compensation for the other sections. Finally, since the completion of the Nationalist program required amendment of the Articles, the unanimous consent of the state legislatures was necessary, and the Nationalists were surprisingly deficient in coordinating legislation in the Congress and the states.

The Department of Finance constructed by Robert Morris alarmed the Lees and other parochialists, but it was not powerful enough to prevent the decisive rejection of the impost by the Rhode Island Legislature in December of 1782. Morris had appointed Continental receivers who were to act as agents of the national system of finance—indeed to propagandize for that system—but they were also unable to prevent the Virginia Assembly from rescinding its previous endorsal of the impost. Astonishingly, even the Virginia Nationalists were at a loss to account for the action of the Assembly. James Madison wrote to Edmund Randolph on January 22 that the repeal was "covered with some degree of mystery"[*20*]. In contrast to this puzzlement among the Nationalists, the parochially oriented opposition had worked with purpose and effectiveness.

The Rhode Island repeal was mostly the work of David Howell, the jurist and professor of mathematics at the College of Rhode Island, who was elected to Congress in 1782. Howell wrote assiduously to his correspondents and to the Governor of Rhode Island contending that the impost, which had never been popular in that highly commercial state, was unnecessary. It was later reported that he also was doing "all in his power to raise discontents" in Massachusetts. To substantiate his case, he cited correspondence from John Adams indicating that a loan would be available from Holland[*21*]. This was directly counter to the argument being circulated by Robert Morris that the impost and other general taxes he had recommended were essential because foreign loans were drying up with the cessation of hostilities[*22*].

Nationalists, indignant over the Rhode Island action, persuaded Congress to formally censure Howell for having made public privileged correspondence from abroad and to send a deputation to Rhode Island to present the Continental case to the Assembly of that recalcitrant state[23]. No sooner had the delegation (composed of the three delegates Osgood, Mifflin, and Nash) left Philadelphia than the stunning news arrived that Virginia had rejected the impost. There was nothing for the delegation to do but return.

Morris shortly afterward played his trump card. In a communication to Congress on January 24, he contended that if the states would not accept his plan for supplying adequate revenue to satisfy an underpaid army as well as foreign and domestic creditors, it was incumbent upon Congress and the states to produce the necessary revenue in accordance with the mode provided for in the Articles. The public debt should be apportioned among the states, quotas established, and contributions made as provided for in Article 8. Certain that such an arrangement would take time, if indeed it was at all feasible, he warned that if adequate funds were not forthcoming in the immediate future, he would resign by May, never having consented to become a "minister of injustice"[24].

Morris's threat—and it was a serious one that alarmed many members of Congress who were impressed with his expertise—was all the more disturbing because Congress was then hearing memorials presented by a delegation of three senior officials led by General Alexander McDougall from the army encampment at Newburgh. The complaint was that the pay was in arrears, that no provision had been made for officers' pensions, and that a settlement of accounts for rations and clothing was due[25]. A common cause thus was established between the disgruntled army and civilians who had invested in the public debt. It was a connection seen sympathetically by the Nationalists, and suspiciously by particularists and New Englanders averse to officers' pensions.

A grand committee of thirteen, which had been formed on January 6 to consider the memorials, presented a report in the writing of Alexander Hamilton on the very day Morris's letter was received, urging that Congress resolve that

> the troops of the United States in common with all the Creditors of the same, have an undoubted right to expect . . . security [for arrears of pay] and that Congress will make every effort in their power to obtain from the respective States *general* and substantial funds adequate to the object of funding the whole debt of the U.S.; and that Congress ought to enter upon an immediate and full consideration of the nature of such funds and the most likely mode of obtaining them[26].

The committee urged also that officers be given pensions either in the form of half pay for life or in a commutation of that pay to six years' full pay. After objections from the New Englanders about both the amount of back pay to be assumed by Congress (from August 1780—considered to be too early by the Easterners) and the six-year commutation, Hamilton and Fitzsimmons consulted with Morris, who insisted on the August 1780 date as being consonant with his whole policy of covering Continental debts from the time of his assuming office[27]. Such informal consultation between Morris and the congressional Nationalists was frequent and productive, in marked contrast with the tenuous contacts between Nationalists in Philadelphia and in the states.

Morris laid the groundwork for the establishment of a general fund to retire the debt by holding back on military pay. He had previously consulted with a congressional committee, arguing that no advance of pay could be made until funds were previously established—especially when Congress was being pressed by a delegation from the army—for to capitulate under pressure would establish a dangerous precedent[28]. Morris's argument seemed to place him in the ranks of the Eastern antimilitarists, but in all probability he was looking toward the manufacture of a crisis. Morris was careful to pay civilian employees under his charge, it might be noted. Whether or not this was wise policy is questionable, for Morris was criticized for this by the army at Newburgh[29].

On January 27, just three days after Morris's threat of resignation, James Wilson, seconded by Thomas Fitzsimmons, moved that general funds should be established as the only means of doing justice to the public creditors. Wilson introduced the motion with the candid observation that a public debt resting on general funds would operate as a cement for the Confederation[30]. During debate on this day and on many succeeding days, it became clear that what the Nationalists desired was a permanent revenue from a variety of taxes, including the impost, a land tax, some excise taxes, and possibly a poll tax—all to be collected by Congress.

The Nationalists were opposed on every count not only by the knot of dedicated Morris-haters but also by moderates such as Eliphalet Dyer and Oliver Wolcott of Connecticut, who opposed the collection of general taxes by Congress. Even Nathaniel Gorham of Massachusetts, who sympathized with the Nationalists, disliked the looseness of Wilson's original motion for general funds. He preferred that the taxes be specified before approving the resolution. Oliver Ellsworth, like Dyer an older member of the Eastern party, but (again like Dyer) not an Adams-Lee Radical, thought Continental funds were necessary, but he doubted that Congress could secure the unanimous consent of the states for an amendment to the Articles or that it could implement general taxes by coercing the states. His solution was the establishment of permanent state funds, recommended by Congress and linked to the retirement of the national debt[31].

The Nationalists countered these objections by stressing the inadequacy of such limitations in the face of the critical importance of maintaining the national honor in Europe and preventing discontent in the army at home. The involvement of the army in the problem was creating a crisis which seems to have been encouraged by some of the Nationalists. Arthur Lee wrote to Sam Adams, "Every Engine is at work here to obtain permanent taxes and the appointment of Collectors by Congress, in the States. The terror of a mutinying Army is playd off with considerable effecacy"[32]. It is true that the McDougall mission had stressed that "the uneasiness of the soldiers for want of pay is great and dangerous; further experiments on their patience may have fatal effects," referring to the common soldier's resentment over the arrears[33]. McDougall later told Congress, "The army is verging to that state which, we are told, will make a wise man mad"[34]. Whether or not the army was entirely opposed to having the states manage officers' pensions is problematical. The common soldiers were not in favor of pensions (for officers) when they themselves had only a meager mustering-out pay, and even some officers may not have been averse to the states assuming the responsibility for half pay for life. But the fact that an overwhelming segment of the army at Newburgh came from New England—over half from Massachusetts—doubtless persuaded many officers that their chances for half pay were better with Congress than with their home states.

Opponents of the Nationalists quickly found a strategy which seriously impaired the Nationalist argument, however. Hugh Williamson of North Carolina, by no means an anti-Nationalist, suggested that a Continental fund be set up for the foreign debt and state funds for the domestic debt. John Rutledge went one step further. Dismissing all general taxes other than the impost as unsuitable or undesirable, he moved on January 29 that the impost amendment be resubmitted to the states in a more palatable form by reserving impost funds for retirement of the foreign debt and the payment of the army, by limiting its application to a twenty-five-year term, and by giving the state in which the duties were collected credit for that amount on its quota of the whole debt[35]. Rutledge's motion did not unite the Carolinas and New England, for Wolcott and Ellsworth, as well as Williamson of North Carolina, disliked the idea of state impost credits, and the majority of New Englanders were opposed to the discrimination between domestic creditors and the army and foreign creditors. There were two other important reasons for the New England opposition: an aversion to half pay for officers and a substantial interest in the domestic debt. Massachusetts in particular had a large investment in loan office certificates and a disproportionately large amount of Continental bills of credit.

Even so, Rutledge's motion placed Hamilton, Wilson, Fitzsimmons, and their cohorts in an awkward position. Nationalist lamentations about the tragic fate of the army and warnings about the danger of a military uprising lost a measure of credibility when a twenty-five-year general fund for military pay was proposed by the opposition and supported, even by Arthur Lee, who seconded Rutledge's motion. The centralizing intentions of the Nationalists were revealed in a manner that threatened to destroy the desired union between the army and the domestic creditors. The army already was disgruntled by what appeared to them to be Morris's policy of favoring civilian employees over the men in the field.

Rutledge's proposal, endorsed in debate by Mercer, Bland, Lee, and probably others from the South who sympathized with the army but not with the public creditors from the Middle states and New England, produced some intensely partisan sectional debates. On January 30, James Wilson charged that some members of Congress were not sufficiently concerned about the many security holders in Pennsylvania and declared "with some warmth," according to Madison, that if Congress did not find the means to satisfy them, Pennsylvania would make its own provisions. Wilson's threat certainly was plausible. Pennsylvania simply could withhold its Continental quota from Congress and transfer it to holders of the national debt within the state. Wilson pleaded that Pennsylvania was "willing . . . to sink or swim according to the common fate, but . . . she would not suffer herself, with a millstone of 6,000,000 of the Continental debt about her neck to go to the bottom alone"[36]. This must have been a distasteful argument for Wilson to use, for when creditors looked to the states to service the debt, the very heart of the Nationalist political program would be destroyed.

Three weeks later Nathaniel Gorham of Massachusetts became so irate when Mercer and Lee argued that a Confederation as a rope of sand would be preferable to one as a rod of iron, that he railed at Virginia for its lack of contributions and saw no reason why Massachusetts should continue to suffer from the deficiencies of others. He "adverted with some warmth," according to Madison, who was finding many occasions to use this phrase he rarely employed, that if justice could not be found within the Confederation, "it was time this should be known that some of the States might be forming other confederacies adequate to the purposes of their safety"[37].

Possibly no member of Congress was more opposed to the breakup of the Union than Alexander Hamilton, but Hamilton was deeply pessimistic about the impasse over the public debt. When the news came on February 13 that George III had announced the provisional peace terms to Parliament, Hamilton quickly, perhaps impetuously, wrote an extraordinary letter to Governor George Clinton of New York. Doubting that the Confederation would survive the peace, and expecting that retired soldiers would be looking for new lands, he suggested that New York should set aside a tract of territory "and make a liberal allowance to every officer and soldier of the Army at large who will become a citizen of the State. . . . Should a disunion take place, any person who will cast his eye upon the map will see how essential it is to our State to provide for its own security. I believe a large part of the Army would incline to sit down among us, and then all we shall have to do will be to govern well"[38].

When Nationalists such as Wilson and Hamilton and centralists such as Gorham were turning to the states—or worse, to consideration of regional confederations—it was clear that the Nationalist program had arrived at the moment of truth. Nonetheless, Nationalists closest to Robert Morris constantly opposed funding the debt through state quotas in the manner called for in the Articles of Confederation.

Shortly after Wilson introduced his motion for general funds and Rutledge added his earmarking proposal for use of impost revenue, debate turned in the direction of the constitutional mode of securing revenue under Article 8 of the Articles. Madison, in his notes for January 31, recorded that this shift was due to the opposition of Rutledge and Bland to discussion of general funds before the regular procedure of collecting moneys on the basis of land evaluations made by the respective states was established. This diversion, in conjunction with the defeat of the proposal for commutation of officers' half pay on February 4, seems to have impelled the core of the Middle states Nationalists into action. Hamilton, seconded by Fitzsimmons, moved on February 6 that since the evaluation of lands would be both expensive and time consuming, Congress should defer the assessment until such time that money was available for evaluation by congressionally appointed commissioners applying uniform principles throughout the states[39]. His motion defeated, Hamilton, and possibly some other Nationalists closest to the financier, turned outside Congress.

IV

The occurrences of the next month between February 7 and March 10 are so shrouded in mystery that it is doubtful they will ever be entirely explained[40]. Clearly, however, the Nationalist leaders had told the delegation of officers from the Newburgh encampment of over 10,000 men that they should not rely upon the states for a settlement until all hope was lost for obtaining Continental funds. McDougall and Ogden reported to Knox: "Indeed, some of our best friends in Congress declared, however desirous they were to have our accounts settled, and the commutation fixed, as well as to get funds, yet they would oppose referring us to the States for a settlement and security, till all prospect of obtaining Continental funds was at an end"[41]. It is also apparent that Nationalists in the Department of Finance were pressing the military leadership to complement the strategy reported by McDougall. Gouverneur Morris, the Assistant Superintendent of Finance, wrote to General Knox via Colonel Brooks, returning to Newburgh, to warn against the Rutledge plan of making provision for the army apart from the other domestic creditors:

> Separate Provisions and no Provisions are tantamount in my Idea for any Laws which they can repeal they will repeal as soon as they find it expedient. The same Principle of Convenience which will lead them to take Care of the army and leave other Creditors unnoticed will operate effectually against the army when it is disbanded after a Peace. . . . the only wise Mode is for the army to connect themselves with the public Creditors to every Kind both foreign and domestic and unremittingly to urge the Grant of general permanent Funds . . .[42].

Of course, the critical question was how was the army to connect itself with the public creditors? Morris suggested that this could be accomplished if the army would apply pressure upon the state legislatures to cooperate with the Congress in creating a permanent congressional revenue, and "after you have carried the Post the public Creditors will garrison it for you"[43].

Hamilton offered advice to Washington which was comparably enig-
matic. Observing that the "prevailing opinion" in the army was that if arms
were laid down, so would the means of obtaining justice. He then went on to
argue:

> The great *desideratum* at present is the establishment of general funds, which
> alone can do justice to the creditors of the United States (of whom the army forms
> the most meritorious class), restore public credit and supply the future wants of
> government. This is the object of all men of sense; in this the influence of the
> army, properly directed, may cooperate[44].

Hamilton urged Washington not to suppress efforts of the army to secure redress but merely to keep those efforts "within the bounds of moderation." Perhaps to encourage Washington in this role, Hamilton told the commander,
with regret he said, that there were rumors in the army that Washington was
too scrupulous to defend the interests of the army with enthusiasm.

The inner workings of the Nationalist strategy, if indeed there was a
central strategy, are difficult to fix with regard to the precise role of the army.
However, Morris, who had to have been in contact with Hamilton at this point,
suggested pressure on state legislatures. Since a large majority of the troops at
Newburgh were from New England where half pay for life was most unpopular,
such a tactic made some sense. Yet how would the pressure be applied?
Hamilton suggested to Washington that he not prevent a redress of grievances
but simply keep the movements of the army within moderate bounds. But
what mode of redress was to be used?

Washington would not cooperate in any scheme involving military
pressure upon the civil governments. Knox was the ideal substitute, but he
refused to commit himself. Consequently, the army protest centered around
Horatio Gates, who was second in command and who was supported by a group
of young officers dissatisfied with Washington's defense of their claims[45].
On March 10, a circular was distributed about the camp. It was written by
Major John Armstrong, Jr., an aide to Gates, and it stressed the plight of the
troops and urged that "if the present moment be lost, your threats hereafter will
be as empty as your entreaties now. Appeal from the justice to the fears of government; and suspect the man who would advise to longer forbearance"[46].
What the memorial suggested (and it was followed by another in the same vein)
was that the army immobilize itself—refuse to fight if the war continued, and
refuse to lay down arms in the event of peace until it received its due.

The memorials apparently took Washington by surprise. He told Hamilton he had seen no discontent in the army until word reached camp from Philadelphia that the army was receiving short shrift from Congress. The man who
conveyed these rumors was Colonel Walter Stewart, recently arrived in camp as
a reactivated inspector from Philadelphia. "There is something very misterious
in this business," Washington observed, as well he might[47].

Yet, the plight of the army was genuine, and the materials existed for violent convulsion. Perhaps Washington was not completely aware of the gravity of the situation before it erupted, and perhaps Hamilton's letter, recognizing the fact, was an attempt to "coach" Washington as to his proper role. Once the memorials were circulated, however, Washington acted with firmness and rectitude. He discountenanced all "disorderly proceedings" in his general orders of March 11 and called for a meeting of all general and field officers to devise a rational course to follow. This was enough to halt radical action. It may be an exaggeration to say, as many of Washington's admirers have, that he prevented, at this moment, the creation of a dictatorship. Yet, the doleful procession of authoritarian regimes established by charismatic revolutionaries surely testifies to Washington's republican restraint in not playing the role of the opportunist.

The question may be fairly asked: Was Hamilton an opportunist? Or was Gouverneur Morris? The latter had written at the end of 1781, "I have no expectation that the government will acquire force; and no hope that our union can subsist, except in the form of an absolute monarchy, and this does not seem to consist with the taste and temper of the people"[48]. If Hamilton and Morris were not contemplating a military coup d'état, they were dangerously skirting the brink of what Washington aptly termed "a gulph of Civil horror"[49].

While no final assessment can be made on the basis of the surviving evidence, there are many aspects of the Newburgh affair which suggest that Hamilton and Morris and whoever else among the Nationalists was part of the ploy never really contemplated a coup[50]. Even their more limited designs of using the army to pressure the states and the Congress into compliance with a general revenue plan were hesitant and uncoordinated. The prominent Nationalist James Madison seems to have been unaware of any plan[51]. Washington discountenanced the protest; Knox refused to commit himself; and, in turning to Gates, the Nationalists were using a man whose congressional connections were linked entirely with the anti-Nationalists. Indeed, Hamilton was forced to consider Gates an enemy because of Washington's distrust of Gates and the ancient antagonism between Gates and Hamilton's father-in-law, Philip Schuyler[52]. While Robert Morris had to be involved in the plan, he was a major target of the dissatisfied officers at Newburgh[53].

The initial protests of the troops at Newburgh were actually directed more toward the financier than toward Congress. The first petition complained that while taxes were heavy, no part of them seemed to reach the army[54]. After the crisis had abated, Washington told Hamilton that discontent persisted, and Robert Morris was blamed for wanting to disband the army without giving them their due[55]. On April 14, Morris did indeed suggest to a congressional committee that the army should be mustered out before the settlement was completed[56]. Morris did not want to foment further discontent; he merely wanted to balance his accounts by postponing pay for the troops. This was hardly the policy to unite the army with the public creditors.

If the Nationalist strategy called for a dramatic move in the Napoleonic mode, the man at the center, Robert Morris, described by Samuel Osgood as "a good practical Merchant" but "destitute of every Kind of theoretic Knowledge"[57], was not appropriate for the task. The very circumstances surrounding his call to power mitigated against bold, truly radical moves. Appointed in the first instance to solve technical problems with the resources that existed, he was content to work within the confines of Confederation. The impost amendment was not a significant departure from those boundaries. Parochialists such as Stephen Higginson were willing to contemplate broad revisions of the Articles at the time of the Newburgh affair[58]. It is interesting, and entirely appropriate, that the most powerful man in congressional politics was more inclined to balance the budget than to seriously redirect the Revolution.

V

Partly as a result of the Newburgh alarm, the Nationalists were able to extract two concessions from a reluctant Congress: a five-year commutation of officers' half pay pensions and a much modified general revenue system with state control of collections. Clearly, the Newburgh crisis helped to set the stage for the two actions. Madison related that the disturbance at Newburgh gave a "particular awe and solemnity to the . . . moment, and oppressed the minds of Congress with an anxiety and distress which had been scarcely felt in any period of the revolution"[59]. The successful passage of the commutation measure on March 22 (for five years, rather than six) was due to a shift of the New England delegations which had always been opposed to officers' pensions[60]. The Rhode Island and Connecticut delegations were under instructions not to agree to any half pay measure, and the Massachusetts delegation was hardly sympathetic with the idea of a pension. But by February, the influential Massachusetts delegation made up of Higginson, Holten, Gorham, and Osgood hesitantly began to support a five-year commutation[61]. The explanation of this shift is not entirely clear. The four delegates knew officer pensions were unpopular in Massachusetts—though they probably did not expect to be removed in the next election, which was the case. Their gamble may have been prompted by the arguments of Madison and Wilson, who stressed that commutation at the five-year level would be cheaper than half pay for life and that despite state instructions to the contrary, half pay was a solemn obligation agreed to by Congress in October of 1780[62]. Gorham may have been convinced that commutation was part of a whole funding passage and that if the Massachusetts creditors were to be served, it would be necessary to compromise on commutation. Holten had just arrived, and, as he later confessed, he had a "predetermination against any measures for discharging the public engagements other than those pointed out in the Confederation," but he had become convinced of the necessity of a plan of general revenue[63]. If this was an indication of the persuasiveness of the Nationalists and the sense of crisis in Philadelphia, it is quite probable Holten was converted as easily on commutation. It is also not implausible that Holten, a physician without striking attainments, was as susceptible to the blandishments of the Nationalists as James Lovell, the more radical schoolteacher, had been. Lovell, it will be recalled, was seen much among the "Deanites" of Philadelphia before he became Morris's receiver in Massachusetts[64]. Holten struck up a cordial friendship with John Swanwick, Morris's highly placed assistant, who offered his services to Holten when they might be of use[65]. The conversion of the Massachusetts delegation was an example of Nationalist capacity at its best, but it is important to note that the Nationalists exhibited much more effectiveness in Philadelphia than in the outlands.

The commutation measure was worth only as much as the ability of Congress to back it up. Thus the second part of the Nationalist design, the establishment of a general revenue, was just as important as far as the officers were concerned. After three months of debate lasting from late January to mid-April, a comprehensive plan was approved for submittal to the states. It was a plan which fell far short of what the Nationalists initially had hoped to achieve.

There were two major problems in the construction of a general revenue plan. First was the ever-present distaste for centrally controlled revenues of any kind—a factor that congressmen had to take into consideration, whatever their own beliefs, when formulating a scheme that had to be unanimously approved by the states. The second problem was the ubiquitous fear that any tax would benefit certain states to the disadvantage of others. The impost would hurt Rhode Island and help North Carolina, for example. Thus other forms of general revenue had to be coupled with the impost to make it more palatable in those states which secured revenues of their own from state import duties[66]. The Nationalists decided that the best approach would be to link a number of different kinds of taxes into one general plan and to make the passage of each tax dependent upon the success of the whole package.

Robert Morris already had suggested a land tax, poll taxes, a tax on slaves, and excises as antidotes for the impost as well as means of securing additional revenue. But a tax on slaves would never be approved by the Southern states, and Maryland prohibited poll taxes in her constitution, so these two sources of income were discarded quickly by the Nationalists. James Wilson proposed that in addition to the impost (which it was assumed would bring in $1 million a year in peacetime—less than half the revenue needed to pay the interest on the debt) a land tax and an extra duty on salt be imposed, each of which he calculated would bring in another million dollars[67]. He argued that while the salt tax would hurt New England because of her use of salt in the fisheries, the land tax would press hardest upon the Middle and Southern states. Wilson's plan ran into much opposition, particularly over the land tax. A committee on the revenue dominated by the Nationalists and working under the pressure of the Newburgh affair produced a revised scheme on March 6. Discarding the land tax, it called for a 5-percent impost, duties on salt and luxury items such as liquors and tea, the imposition of state quotas as called for in the Articles, and the speedy completion of the cessions of claims to the West. In order to placate those who feared central power, the collectors of the duties and the state quotas were to be appointed by the states, but they were to be responsible to the Congress. In a deft maneuver, the committee report provided that none of the provisions would go into effect until all of them had been ratified by the states[68].

The intricacies of the Nationalist plan caused parochialists such as Stephen Higginson great concern. Higginson was alarmed that Congress was

> hammering on a strange, though artful, plan of finance, in which are combined a heterogeneous mixture of imperceptible and visible, constitutional and unconstitutional taxes. It contains the impost, quotas, and cessions of Western lands, and no part of it is to be binding unless the whole is adopted by all the States. This connection and dependence of one part of another is designed to produce the adoption of the whole[69].

The plan, when finally approved on April 18, included still further revisions. The lack of a land tax still seemed unfair to New England, and the South was unwilling to associate western cessions with a general revenue plan. Thus the "artful" device Higginson referred to was altered so as to connect only impost and the duties on luxury goods. In order to placate the more densely settled Northeast, a highly significant change was made in the method of determining state quotas under Article 8 of the Articles of Confederation. Instead of basing state quotas for the national treasury upon land values, a formula that disadvantaged the heavily populated Northeast where lands were more highly priced, the Congress agreed to base quotas upon population[70].

The difficulty with a formula for quotas based upon population was how to count slaves. New Englanders argued that if slaves were not to be counted as equals, they should be rated at at least a three-fourths ratio. Carroll of Maryland advocated a one-fifth ratio. The decision to count a slave as three-fifths of a man was a pragmatic compromise between the North and the South purporting to evaluate the worth of the labor of a slave as compared with that of a freeman in the larger context of an attempt to establish equitable quotas for state contributions to the national treasury. Four years later in the Constitutional Convention the same ratio would be used for the quite different purpose of allocating proportional representation in the House of Representatives.

Alterations of the original Nationalist plan regarding the mode of collection and the duration of the impost, duties, and state quotas were included in order to placate state fears of central encroachments. Collectors of taxes would be appointed by the states, although they would be responsible to Congress. A twenty-five-year limit was placed on the impost and other taxes. The Nationalists could take comfort, however, in the provision stipulating that the moneys were to be used for the payment of interest and for the retirement of the principal of the domestic debt as well as the foreign debt.

Hamilton, who had contributed more than any other individual to the proper congressional mood for the passage of the impost, refused to vote for the general tax measure because of these limitations, thus aligning incongruously with the Rhode Island delegates who opposed the measure for utterly opposite reasons. Hamilton did, however, recommend the general plan to George Clinton, Governor of New York, as did other delegates to their states[71].

The general revenue plan never came into effect, for while prospects for unanimous approval were good by 1787, the Constitutional Convention settled the question of national revenue. Robert Morris agreed to remain in office until the army was paid, and while there was renewed criticism of the financier from the Lee contingent, including charges that he and his associates were speculating with the notes he was issuing for soldiers' pay, there were no climactic confrontations before Morris resigned in the next year[72].

VI

By the summer of 1783, the Nationalist coalition began to erode seriously. There were many reasons, some of which have already been mentioned—the awkward, almost unpatriotic stance taken by the Nationalists who felt obligated to France when the peace terms were received, and the Southern resistance to the land tax and the poll tax in the general revenue scheme, for example. Two additional events of decisive importance may be added: (1) the problem of the organization of the West which had been successfully isolated from the general revenue bill and (2) a revolt of the Pennsylvania line in June—a revolt which occurred in the capital, not at a distant encampment, thereby actually forcing Congress to flee to New Jersey. Each problem had drastic consequences for the unity of the Nationalists. The western question split the Middle states and the South, thereby destroying the crucial alliance in the core region. The revolt of the Pennsylvania line and the inability or disinclination of the Pennsylvania Council to curb the demonstrators caused such sharp resentment in all quarters that Congress left Philadelphia never to return. Away from the congenial atmosphere of Philadelphia, Nationalists found it much more difficult to operate. Indeed, in short time they deserted Congress.

It may be a testament to the persuasive talents of Alexander Hamilton and Robert Morris that James Wilson, who was personally interested in western lands in the most vital manner, had not insisted that the Virginia cession be made part of the general revenue package as had been recommended in March[73]. Not to be permanently denied, Wilson introduced a closely related question on April 9, a week before passage of the revenue bill. In response to a petition for land on Lake Erie from some Canadians who had supported the United States during the war, Wilson moved that a committee be established to consider "proper measures" for the organization of the West[74]. He argued that population was rapidly, often illegally, moving into that region and that Congress should establish federal authority in the area in the antici-pation of new states being formed. Madison opposed, saying that all the Con-gress could do at this juncture was to urge the states with western claims to complete their cessions. Partisan alignments took a radically different shape for a moment. Wilson received enthusiastic support from Connecticut, and Madison was endorsed by his anti-Nationalist colleague, Mercer[75]. The crack in the Nationalist front would be widened significantly by the end of the year[76].

On the day of the passage of the revenue bill, the question of western lands came up again when Bland moved that the recommendation that the states revise and complete their cessions be rescinded. Virginia now received the support of South Carolina, the anti-Nationalist John Rutledge contending that if Congress questioned the Virginia cession, it should reject it. There was a possibility the cession would be approved, he maintained, and thus the recommendation would be improper. Wilson countered with the objection that Virginia never owned land north to the Ohio. Wilson's investments south of the Ohio perhaps impaired the force of his argument, but, for whatever reason, he was called to order by Joseph Jones, another Nationalist[77]. A month later, when the question of the Virginia cession was on the floor (June 10), the Nationalist coalition again split, Hamilton and Madison arguing against each other[78]. Hamilton and the other delegates who opposed Virginia's claim did not all agree over the strategy of the moment which had to do with whether there should be an immediate decision on the Virginia cession, but all supported federal jurisdiction over as broad an area as possible in the trans-Allegheny lands. Subsequent debates disclosed that the delegates from the landless states opposed not only Virginia's restrictions regarding land company treaties with the Indians and her claims for compensation in land grants north of the Ohio for the George Rogers Clark expeditions but also any title west of the Alleghenies[79]. Continuing to occupy the attention of Congress for the next three years, the western problem in its multiple facets would continue to be both a powerful lure to consolidation and a source of intense dissension.

The location of the national capital was another enduring issue that undermined the Nationalist party in 1783. Congress fled from Philadelphia after an entirely unexpected mutiny in the Pennsylvania line, which was triggered by a small group of soldiers in Lancaster who were dissatisfied at being furloughed without a final pay settlement. Demanding half of all the pay that they were entitled to as well as certificates for the other half with lawful interest and a specific date of settlement, the Lancaster troops (about eighty in number) on June 17 marched under the command of their sergeants toward Philadelphia, where they were joined by a sizable number of troops from the Philadelphia barracks. Rumors flew in advance of the marchers. It was said they planned to "rob the bank, the treasury, &c. &c."[80]. While no robbery oc-curred, there were reasons enough for alarm.

Madison recorded in his journal that the soldiers entered the city on

Friday, June 20. Congress appeared unperturbed and continued its discussion of the Virginia cession and other business. The next day, however, the Lancaster soldiers seized the Philadelphia barracks, secured the magazine, surrounded the State House where both Congress and the Pennsylvania Council sat, and presented their demands to the Council. Although the troops communicated mainly with the Council, it was rumored that Congress itself was marked for chastisement[81].

Congress appointed a committee of three (Hamilton, Richard Peters of Pennsylvania, and Oliver Ellsworth) to consult with the Council and take other appropriate measures to preserve the authority of the government. The committee obtained little satisfaction from the Council, which was convinced that the militia could be persuaded not to take arms against the soldiers of the line unless there were actual "outrages" and that it would jeopardize the authority of the government to attempt to subdue them. Congress then called upon General Arthur St. Clair, a Pennsylvanian who was in Philadelphia at the time, to persuade the troops to disperse, but St. Clair's efforts were to no avail[82].

Although the requisite number of states for a legal instruction to Washington were not present, the delegates unanimously agreed to request Washington to send some of his best and most reliable troops toward Philadelphia[83]. (This was done, and it may well have been the approach of Continental troops the next week that mainly prompted the mutineers to disperse.)

The soldiery, estimated variously at from 250 to 500 in number[84], seemed insolent and menacing. Ralph Izard moved to adjourn, but the majority decided to sit until the usual time of afternoon adjournment after three o'clock. Such heroism was the best that Congress could muster under the circumstances. The soldiers committed no violence but, in Madison's words, "occasionally uttering offensive words . . . wantonly pointed their Muskets to the Windows of the Hall of Congress." After visits to some nearby taverns, the troops grew bolder, and it seemed that they might storm the building, but they did not. Indeed, when the delegates made their departure, they were allowed to pass unmolested, although some soldiers offered "mock obstruction . . ."[85].

The rage of Congress matched its impotence. That evening, the twenty-first, with just six states legally represented, Congress passed a resolution informing the Pennsylvania Council that the authority of the United States had been "grossly insulted by the disorderly and menacing" crowd of troops and that "effectual measures" had to be taken for the protection of the national government. Both the Pennsylvania Council and the citizenry of Philadelphia had allowed the humiliation—a fact that "mortified" President Elias Boudinot. Receiving no support from the city, despite the continued occupation of the barracks by the mutineers, Congress resolved on June 24 to quit Philadelphia for Princeton, and a public proclamation was issued to that effect[86].

From the standpoint of congressional politics, the whole episode was anomalous, to say the least. Although this was the sort of pressure hinted at in Newburgh, there was clearly no connection between the Nationalists and the mutineers. There were no officers involved in the protest. Hamilton worked on the congressional committee to subdue the rebellion. If there were collaborators, it would have to have been the Constitutionalist-oriented Philadelphia militia—or, less congruously, the Pennsylvania Council chaired by the temperate John Dickinson. But all evidence suggests that the outburst was as spontaneous as the Newburgh affair was contrived.

The losers in the episode were the city of Philadelphia, to which the Continental Congress never returned[87], and the Nationalists, whose operations were severely crimped by the removal to Princeton. Because the Nationalist financial system was executed through Robert Morris, the Bank of North America, and the commercial community surrounding the financier, its geographic focus would continue to be in Philadelphia. Congressional policy had been strongly influenced by formal and informal contacts between Morris's establishment and the Nationalists in Congress, a fact that alarmed parochialists and many others—especially New Englanders. The Massachusetts clergyman William Gordon warned Arthur Lee as early as April of 1783 that Congress should leave Philadelphia to prevent the rest of the states from becoming "provinces" of Pennsylvania[88]. Samuel Osgood insisted that Congress could never be an independent body in Philadelphia. He charged, "Plans for absolute Government, for deceiving the lower Classes of People, for introducing undue Influence, for any Kind of Government, in which Democracy has the least possible share, originate, are cherished and disseminated from thence"[89]. It is incongruous that the Nationalists, far from manipulating or deceiving the Philadelphia populace, suffered from its coercion. The notion that Philadelphia was unrepublican persisted, however, and there was much sentiment in Congress for an arcadian residence removed from the taint of commercialism.

Although the New Jersey militia resolved to protect the "Honour and Safety" of Congress from all "insolence and Violence," Princeton was a small town with few accommodations. Boudinot reported to Robert R. Livingston that members were grumbling and dissatisfied with the location. More serious, there was "No great appetite for Business," and the administration was scattered: "No Minister of Foreign Affairs [a reproof for Livingston himself]—at a distance from our officers—." Both points were well taken. The administration was entirely absent, and accommodations were so crowded that Madison and Joseph Jones were forced to share one bed in a room 10 feet square[90].

Princeton was simply unsuitable as a national capital, but deciding upon an alternate location was an exquisitely difficult problem. New York had facilities Princeton did not, including vital communication lines, but it was too far north to be a permanent capital. Some considered it too corrupt and tainted with Toryism. The Virginia Assembly was eager to lure Congress to Williamsburg, going so far as to offer £100,000 Virginia currency for the construction of thirteen hotels, but there was opposition to such a southerly location. Some assumed that Northerners could not tolerate the climate even so far south as Georgetown: "The summers there will either destroy or debilitate our best constitutions," alleged Samuel Osgood. Osgood and others also objected to the aristocratic, even monarchic, tendencies of the South[91].

Congress continued to ponder its residence into the fall. Many sites were suggested: Kingston, Newport, Wilmington (Delaware), Trenton, Georgetown, and Annapolis, as well as Philadelphia and New York. On October 7, it was decided by the narrowest of margins to place the capital near or at the falls of the Delaware River, but this encountered so much resistance from Southerners advocating a Potomac location that Elbridge Gerry proposed a compromise calling for alternate residences on the Delaware and the Potomac. Temporarily, Congress would sit at Trenton and Annapolis until permanent buildings could be erected[92]. Congress did indeed move the capital to Annapolis in November of 1783 and a year later to Trenton where it resided briefly before taking more suitable northern quarters in New York in January of 1785.

Although the debate over the capital was troubled by inevitable calculations of local pride and advantage, there were dimensions of the dispute which were of the first order of importance for the maintenance of a cohesive national force. Since most of the plausible sites were located within the Nationalist heartland between the Potomac and the Hudson, strife within the Middle region impaired the cohesion of the Nationalist alliance. The New York delegates were upset over the dual residence arrangement, and the Pennsylvanians constantly urged that Congress be brought back to Philadelphia[93]. Furthermore, the designation of dual capitals accelerated the natural congressional drift toward sectional division. Despite the fact that Trenton was selected as one of the sites, Elias Boudinot, the New Jersey delegate who was President of Congress, could not help "thinking of Rome and Constantinople"[94].

There were other ways of viewing the removal from Philadelphia. David Howell remarked, "Nothing but drawn bayonetts *ever did* drive Congress out of Philadelphia and there appeared to me no sufficient reason to believe that any thing else *ever would.*" A rotating Congress would have beneficial effects, Howell believed. Indeed, it made little difference whether or not Congress ever fixed a permanent capital: "A perambulatory Congress favors republicanism," he urged, whereas "a permanent one tends to concentrate power, Aristocracy and Monarchy"[95].

It was the misfortune of the Nationalists that their program of fiscal centralism was so closely associated with the city of Philadelphia. Much of the criticism they encountered stemmed from parochial jealousy, but because of the size and wealth of Philadelphia, it was easy to translate jealousy into fears of aristocracy and monarchy. If Congress was to become another Parliament, a national legislature removed from the people and insensitive to the needs of the particular parts of a far-flung Union, it would be in the large and opulent city of Philadelphia that such a transformation would occur. Such fears were natural, partially reasonable, and anomalous. They were natural because of the vastness of the Union; reasonable because the Nationalist program *did* depend upon Robert Morris, the Philadelphia merchant; anomalous because the more democratic aspects of the financier's program were quickly rejected by anti-Nationalists in the Congress. The uniform land tax and the tax on slaves proposed by Morris would have penalized the land speculators and the slave-holding aristocracy. They were rejected probably less because they disadvantaged the landed aristocracy than because they reinforced fiscal centralism. The procedural aspects of a Philadelphia-based fiscal system caused more alarm than did the actual substance of the program. Thus seven years later, when the fiscal objectives of the Nationalists were finally attained under a new form of government, it would be necessary to locate the capital on the Potomac, rather than in Philadelphia, in order to draw enough votes to secure passage of federal assumption of state debts.

For all their resourcefulness, the Nationalists were curiously inept in attempting to tighten the bonds of the Union through their program of central-ized finance. A properly framed impost could have been ratified by all the states if the Nationalists had organized enough support within the states. But al-though they were well organized and ably led in Congress, their influence was minimal outside of Philadelphia. They were shackled not only by the Articles of Confederation, which made change extremely difficult, but also by the limitations of their program, which was narrowly conceived, relatively inflex-ible, and poorly executed. The party that began the Revolution was far more resourceful than the party that attempted to nationalize the Republic that emerged from it.

Notes

1 For example: the average levels of agreement between the delegates from Pennsylvania and North Carolina was 66%; between Pennsylvania and Massachusetts, 47%.

2 See Karl Deutsch et al., *Political Community and the North Atlantic Area* (Prince-ton, 1967), p. 72. Deutsch talks of core areas in terms of dominant political units— larger, stronger, more advanced units in terms of political, administrative, economic, educational institutions (see also p. 138). While this was not entirely true of the Middle states, the potential of the Middle region's western development fits the Deutsch model. A case can be made for the Middle region as a core area in somewhat different terms, as is suggested below.

3 *New York Packet,* July 4, 1782; *American Advertiser,* July 4, 1782; Harold C. Sy-rett and Jacob E. Cooke (eds.), *The Papers of Alexander Hamilton* (New York, 1961–), III, 103. Congressional proclamation of fast days and days of thanksgiving fell out of fashion after the war. See Samuel Holten to James Bowdoin, Oct. 31, 1785, Gratz Col-lection, HSP.

4 See, e.g., Stephen Higginson to Arthur Lee, Nov. [?], 1783, Arthur Lee Papers, HCL.

5 Charles Thomson, "Notes of Debates," Aug. 8, 1782, *LMCC,* VI, 432.

6 For a definitive account of the peace negotiations, See Richard B. Morris, *The Peacemakers* (New York, 1965).

7 John Taylor Gilman to Governor Mesheck Weare, Mar. 12, 1783, *LMCC,* VII, 72. See also William Gordon to Arthur Lee, Apr. 2, 1783, Arthur Lee Papers, HCL.

8 Richard Peters to Horatio Gates, Mar. 13, 1783, *LMCC,* VII, 79; William Floyd to Governor George Clinton, Mar. 17, 1783, ibid., 88.

9 Arthur Lee to James Warren, Mar. 12, 1783, ibid., 78. Lee must have found it galling to receive the assessment of his Massachusetts correspondent, the clergyman William Gordon, an adamant opponent of Deane and as avid a supporter of Lee, that Franklin acted in "perfect unison" with Adams and Jay. Gordon to Lee, Apr. 2, 1783, Arthur Lee Papers, HCL.

10 Robert R. Livingston to the President of Congress, Mar. 18, 1783, in Francis Wharton (ed.), *The Revolutionary Diplomatic Correspondence of the United States* (6 vols.; Washington, 1889), VI, 313–316.

11 James Madison to Edmund Randolph, Mar. 18, 1783, *LMCC,* VI, 89–90. Madison was too keen to be an unthinking admirer of France, it should be added. In December of 1782, a dispatch was received from Jay in Paris containing the copy of an intercepted letter from Marbois, Luzerne's influential secretary with whom Madison was on good terms. Marbois had written a letter opposing the United States claim to the fisheries which, "with the comments of Mr. Jay," as Madison reported it, produced visible reactions in Congress against France. The charge that France, protecting Spanish claims, also opposed United States expansion in the West was also made, and Madison recognized that if Britain gave liberal terms on these issues, the United States might alter its attitude toward both nations. In Madison's judgment, "If France acts wisely, she will in this dilemma prefer the friendship of America to that of Spain. If America acts wisely, she will see that she is, with respect to her great interests, more in danger of being seduced by Britain than sacrificed by France." Notes of Debates, Dec. 24, 1782. William T. Hutchinson and William M. E. Rachal (eds.), *The Papers of James Madison* (Chicago, 1962–), V, 441–442.

12 James Madison, Notes of Debates, Mar. 19, 1783, *JCC,* XXV, 929–930.

13 Ibid., 929–932.

14 Stephen Higginson to Theophilus Parsons, Apr. [7?], 1783, *LMCC,* VII, 122–123; Higginson to Samuel Adams, May 20, 1783, ibid., 167.

15 Stephen Higginson to Nathaniel Gorham, Aug. 5, 1783, ibid., 252. See also John Temple to Theodore Sedgwick, Sept. 2, 1784, Sedgwick Papers, MHS.

16 Samuel Osgood to John Adams, Dec. 7, 1783, ibid., 379ff.

17 Stephen Higginson protested that Congress was "swelling the number of public creditors" and would "destroy the public Credit much faster than the states can possibly establish it." Higginson to Arthur Lee, Nov. [?], 1783, Arthur Lee Papers, HCL.

18 Morris presented his most systematic argument against the use of western lands

for payment of the debt in his letter to Congress on July 29, 1782. Asserting that claims to western lands had not yet been resolved, he concluded that this would impair the usefulness of the lands as a source of credit. Further, dissent might arise from hasty decisions regarding western claims, "and a government torn by intestine commotions is not likely to acquire or maintain credit at home or abroad." Finally, if the lands were sold quickly, they would bring little revenue. (*JCC,* XXII, 445–446.)

19 Edmund Randolph to James Madison, May 4, 1783, Gratz Collection, HSP. On the changed attitude toward the impost after hostilities had ceased, see Jackson Turner Main, *The Antifederalists, Critics of the Constitution, 1781-1788* (Chapel Hill, 1961), p. 99.

20 Madison to Edmund Randolph, Jan. 22, 1783, *LMCC,* VII, 21.

21 The Howell letters were publicized in the *Providence Gazette,* Nov. 2, 1782. See also William R. Staples, *Rhode Island in the Continental Congress* (Providence, 1870), pp. 412ff. Howell's activities in Massachusetts were reported by John Lowell. Lowell to Elias Boudinot, Feb. 12, 1783, Gratz Collection, HSP.

22 E. James Ferguson, *The Power of the Purse* (Chapel Hill, 1961), pp. 148–149. Ferguson contends that Morris's communications to state legislatures were couched in an aggressive tone that may have done more harm than good.

23 *JCC,* XXIII, 772.

24 Morris to the President of Congress, Jan 24, 1783, in Wharton (ed.), *Diplomatic Correspondence, U.S.,* VI, 229. More menacingly, Morris subsequently publicized his threat to resign.

25 This was the condensation of the grievances as formulated by a grand committee which reported on January 24, the day Morris's letter to Congress was received. Madison, Notes of Debates, *JCC,* XXV, 862–863.

26 Ibid., 863.

27 Ibid., 864–865.

28 Ibid., Jan. 7, 1783, p. 847.

29 McDougall made this point in his discussion with the congressional grand committee on the Newburgh memorial on January 13. George Bancroft, *History of the Formation of the Constitution* (2 vols., New York, 1884), I, 79.

30 Madison, Notes of Debates, Jan. 27, *JCC,* XXV, 868.

31 Ibid., 868, 870, 871.

32 Arthur Lee to Samuel Adams, Jan. 29, 1783, *LMCC,* VII, 28.

33 Quoted in Bancroft, *History of the Formation of the Constitution,* I, 77.

34 Ibid., p. 79.

35 Madison, Notes of Debates, *JCC,* XXV, 882. The Rutledge resolution is not recorded in the *Journals.*

36 Madison, Notes of Debates, Jan. 30, 1783, *JCC,* XXV, 886.

37 Madison, Notes of Debates, Feb. 21, 1783, ibid., 910–911.

38 Hamilton to Governor George Clinton, Feb. 14, 1783; Syrett and Cooke (eds.), *Papers of Hamilton,* III, 256.

39 *JCC,* XXIV, 114–115.

40 See Richard H. Kohn, "The Inside History of the Newburgh Conspiracy: America and the Coup d'Etat," *WMQ,* ser. 3, XXVII (1970), 187–220, for the most penetrating examination of the Newburgh affair. Kohn admits, however, that he is forced to speculate about the identity of the group in Congress and in the Department of Finance. See esp. p. 193n.

41 Alexander McDougall and Matthias Ogden to Henry Knox, Feb. 8, 1783, *LMCC,* VII, 35n–36n.

42 Gouverneur Morris to Henry Knox, Feb. 7, 1783, ibid., 34n.

43 Ibid., 34n–35n.

44 Hamilton to Washington, Feb. 13, 1783, in Syrett and Cooke (eds.), *Papers of Hamilton,* III, 254–255.

45 Kohn, "Newburgh Conspiracy," p. 205.

46 Bancroft, *History of the Formation of the Constitution,* I, 95.

47 Washington to Hamilton, Mar. 12, 1783, in Syrett and Cooke (eds.), *Papers of Hamilton,* III, 286, 288n. Bancroft, *History of the Formation of the Constitution,* I, 93.

48 Gouverneur Morris to Nathanael Greene, Dec. 24, 1781, in Jared Sparks, *Gouverneur Morris* (3 vols.; Boston, 1832), I, 240.

49 Washington to Hamilton, Mar. 12, 1783, in Syrett and Cooke (eds.), *Papers of Hamilton,* III, 287.

50 As Kohn aptly points out, a military coup would have been virtually impossible in a nation so geographically extended and with so many levels and loci of authority. "Newburgh Conspiracy," 198.

51 Ibid., 193.

52 Ibid., 201.

53 Kohn contends that Robert Morris was at the center of the Nationalist strategy ibid., 200–201; although there is little concrete evidence to support such a contention, one gains the impression that Morris indeed *had* to be involved. John Armstrong, who discussed the event fifty years later in a letter to Jared Sparks, mentioned both Morrises and Hamilton when rejecting the notion that a *"Philadelphia Cabal"* ever existed. John Armstrong to Jared Sparks, May 19, 1833, Sparks MSS, HCL. (One also receives the impression that Armstrong in this letter was engaged in special pleading when dismissing what he called "the story" as an utter "fabrication.")

54 Quoted in Bancroft, *History of the Formation of the Constitution,* I, 77.

55 Washington to Hamilton, Apr. 4, 1783. John C. Fitzpatrick (ed.), *The Writings of George Washington* (39 vols.; Washington, 1931-1944), XXVI, 293.

56 Robert Morris to Hamilton, Bland, Fitzsimmons, Osgood, and Peters, Apr. 14, 1783, in Syrett and Cooke (eds.), *Papers of Hamilton*, III, 323.

57 Samuel Osgood to John Adams, Dec. 7, 1783, *LMCC*, VII, 379. Osgood did believe, it should be pointed out, that Morris desired to become "the first Man in the United States." It is unlikely that Osgood would have put the cast I have on his words.

58 On April 1, Higginson said in debate that he wished with Hamilton to see a general convention to revise and amend the federal government. Mercer had previously (February 27) said the situation was so critical he was ready to "new-model" in the Confederation rather than do nothing. Madison, Notes of Debates, *JCC*, XXV, 952, 916. Again, this does not mean that Higginson, any more than Osgood, thought Morris should be given more power. Higginson feared Morris and the Nationalists, whom he described as "the great man and his party." Higginson to Arthur Lee, Nov. [?], 1783, Arthur Lee Papers, HCL.

59 Madison, Notes of Debates, Mar. 17, 1783, *JCC*, XXV, 926.

60 Ibid., XXIV, 207-210.

61 Madison, Notes of Debates, Feb. 4, 1783, ibid., 889. This vote was not recorded, but see later roll calls in ibid., XXIV, 150, 154-55, 179.

62 Madison, Notes of Debates, Feb. 4, 1783, ibid., XXV, 889.

63 Madison, Notes of Debates, Feb. 27, 1783, ibid.; 917.

64 William Gordon to Arthur Lee, Oct. 2, 1782, Arthur Lee Papers, HCL.

65 See the correspondence between Holten and Swanwick during 1783 in the Holten Papers, LC. Holten seems to have been carving a career in national politics. He was definitely chagrined over being left out of the elections to the 1784 Congress and the 1786 Congress. Holten to Nathaniel Gorham, July 14, 1785, ibid. After Holten was chastised by the Massachusetts Legislature for having voted for commutation, he swung around to a more anti-Morris position, as when he seconded motions by Arthur Lee in September of 1783 pressing Morris for an explanation of why he sold clothing purchased by Congress rather than giving it to the troops. Swanwick, incidentally, was a commission agent in the sale. See Arthur Lee to James Warren, Sept. 17, 1783, *LMCC*, VII, 299.

66 See Madison's analysis of the specific interests of each of the states concerning the various kinds of public debts and taxes. Notes of Debates, Feb. 26, 1783, *JCC*, XXV, 913-916.

67 Madison, Notes of Debates, Jan. 29, 1783, ibid., 880-881.

68 Madison, Notes of Debates, Mar. 7, 1783, ibid., 920-922.

69 Stephen Higginson to Theophilus Parsons, Apr. [7?], 1783, *LMCC*, VII, 123.

70 The land tax proposed by Robert Morris and Wilson was quite different from the land

evaluation for state quotas. The former was a blanket tax of $1 per 100 acres and would have hurt large landholders and speculators; the latter was based on the market price of land as well as the size of a holding and would have penalized the more densely populated states where land had been improved.

71 *JCC,* XXIV, 261. Hamilton nonetheless recommended to George Clinton that New York ratify the plan as the best obtainable at the moment. Hamilton to George Clinton, May 14, 1783, in Syrett and Cooke (eds.), *Papers of Hamilton,* III, 355.

72 See Virginia delegates to Governor Benjamin Harrison, Aug. 1, 1783, *LMCC,* VII, 246. Arthur Lee also charged that Morris was speculating in the sale of military clothing and other articles.

73 The original report of the committee had "recommended" that states which had not unconditionally ceded their western claims "revise and complete" their cessions. Madison, Notes of Debates, Mar. 7, 1783, *JCC,* XXV, 921.

74 Madison, Notes of Debates, Apr. 9, ibid., 955.

75 Ibid., 956.

76 A committee was formed against the wishes of Virginia; it was composed of the two antagonists in the Nationalist coalition, Madison and Wilson, along with Osgood, Daniel Carroll, and Williamson. Action was taken, however, only in the spring of 1784, under the leadership of Jefferson.

77 Madison, Notes of Debates, Apr. 18, 1783, *JCC,* XXV, 962.

78 Madison, Notes of Debates, June 10, 1783, ibid., 969.

79 Madison, Notes of Debates, June 20, 1783, ibid., 973.

80 James Bennett (for the Board of Sergeants) to John Dickinson, president of the Executive Council (n.d.), Colonel William Henry to John Dickinson, June 17, 1783, in Wharton (ed.), *Diplomatic Correspondence, U.S.,* I, 17, 11.

81 Elias Boudinot to George Washington, June 21, 1783, *LMCC,* VII, 193-194; James Madison, Notes of Debates, June 21, 1783, *JCC,* XXV, 973. Edmund C. Burnett, *The Continental Congress* (New York, 1941), p. 577; Virginia delegates to Benjamin Harrison, June 24, 1783, *LMCC,* VII, 197.

82 Madison, Notes of Debates, June 21, 1783, *JCC,* XXV, 973.

83 Elias Boudinot to Washington, June 21, 1783, *LMCC,* VII, 194.

84 Curiously, the estimate of the group of mutineers declined as time passed. President Boudinot reported between 400 and 500 at four o'clock on Saturday, the 21st—the very moment the State House was encircled. Two days later, he mentioned 300 to 400. On June 24, the Virginia delegates estimated the number of 300, and Benjamin Hawkins cited 280. Boudinot to Washington, June 21, Boudinot to Elisha Boudinot, June 23, Virginia delegates to Benjamin Harrison, June 24, Benjamin Hawkins to Alexander Martin, June 24, 1783, *LMCC,* VII, 193, 195, 197, 199.

85 Ibid.

86 *JCC,* XXIV, 410, and Elias Boudinot to Elisha Boudinot, June 23, 1783, *LMCC,* VII, 195; *By his excellency, Elias Boudinot, esquire, President of the United States in Congress assembled. A Proclamation,* (Philadelphia, 1783).

87 Ezra L'Hommedieu of New York estimated that Philadelphia stood to lose $100,000 annually from the absence of Congress. Ezra L'Hommedieu to George Clinton, Aug. 15, 1783, *LMCC,* VII, 266.

88 William Gordon to Arthur Lee, Apr. 2, 1783, Arthur Lee Papers, HCL.

89 Samuel Osgood to John Adams, Dec. 7, 1783, *LMCC,* VII, 378. Stephen Higginson shared Osgood's alarm about the aristocratic character of Philadelphia. Higginson to George Clinton, Oct. 23, 1783, Gratz Collection, HSP.

90 PCC, no. 46, fols. 51–52; Elias Boudinot to Robert R. Livingston, Sept. 6, 1783, *LMCC,* VII, 299. James Madison to Edmund Randolph, Aug. 30, 1783, ibid., 282.

91 Samuel Osgood to Stephen Higginson, Feb. 2, 1784; Ephraim Paine to Robert R. Livingston, May 24, 1784, ibid., 431–432; 534.

92 The Rhode Island delegates to William Greene, Oct. 9, 1783, ibid., 326; *JCC,* XXV, 712–714.

93 Ezra L'Hommedieu to George Clinton, Oct. 23, 1783; John Montgomery to Benjamin Rush, July 8, 1783, *LMCC,* VII, 351, 216. Benjamin Rush assured John Montgomery that the Pennsylvania line meant no "insult or mischief" against Congress and urged that it return to Philadelphia. The Pennsylvania Council almost humbly assured Congress of its determination to support and protect "the honor and dignity" of the Congress. Benjamin Rush to John Montgomery, July 4, 1783, in Lyman H. Butterfield (ed.), *Letters of Benjamin Rush* (2 vols.; Princeton, 1951), I, 305; Wharton (ed.), *Diplomatic Correspondence, U.S.,* I, 33.

94 Elias Boudinot to Robert R. Livingston, Oct. 23, 1783, *LMCC,* VII, 347.

95 David Howell to William Greene, Dec. 24, ibid., 397. Stephen Higginson expressed a similar sentiment in a letter to Arthur Lee the previous month: "We are anxiously waiting to hear the choice of Congress for their temporary abode. Should their desire to conciliate carry them to Philadelphia, I fear They will not easily get from there again. The bayonet will not probably be used again to drive them out, & nothing short of the Bayonet, I suspect, will overbalance the many allurements that will be thrown in the way of the members, to retain them." Higginson to Arthur Lee, Nov. [?], 1783, Arthur Lee Papers, HCL. Lee's correspondents unanimously approved of the removal. See John Lloyd to Arthur Lee, Oct. 14, 1783, and Alexander Gillon to Arthur Lee, Nov. 29, 1783, ibid.

13 The Ascendancy of
the South: 1784-1785

THE history of partisan politics in the Continental Congress falls
naturally into three periods; an era of Revolutionary militancy during
the seventies; an attempt to achieve national consolidation during the
early eighties; and a complicated dénouement during the mid-eighties, when
Congress organized an empire—one of its most notable achievements—while
failing to correct the most conspicuous flaws in the Articles of Confederation.

The three periods were shaped by the circumstances of war and peace
and by corresponding shifts in the basically sectional composition of congressional parties. The politics of militancy were powerfully affected by the rhetoric
of the Resistance and by the ideal of republican purity. Consequently, the era
had a highly ideological tone. The politics of consolidation came about in
response to hard, practical problems—particularly in the realm of finance—
with the result that the early eighties had a more pragmatic cast, despite the
fact that many of the policies of the Nationalists had important implications
for the structure of the Republic. The politics of dénouement were more complicated, for they involved a partial redefinition of the early Revolutionary
ideology while simultaneously bringing to full term the tendency of partisan
disputes to produce three regional parties based on concrete economic interests.

The politics of militancy were dominated by an Eastern party in which
ideologues such as Samuel Adams, the proponent of a Christian Sparta, had

been most prominent. The Eastern party lost direction of the Revolution to the merchant-politicians of the Middle states led by the shrewdly competent and powerful Robert Morris, when financial problems prompted Congress to turn toward national consolidation. Intersectional coalitions among congressional delegates were important during both periods. The New Englanders, posing as a Party of the Revolution, won support from "virtuous Whigs" to the south — the Virginia Lees, the Pennsylvania Constitutionalists, and others such as Henry Laurens of South Carolina. The Nationalists of the Middle states, because of their confident management of the problems of finance, gained important endorsement from the harassed South and from some New Englanders. But these intersectional combinations proved to be temporary. The Nationalists found that much of their Southern support evaporated with the termination of the military crisis. During the final period of congressional politics, there was a tendency for New England, the Middle states, and the South to form three distinct congressional parties and for the South, more unified than ever before, to achieve the ascendancy.

There were a number of reasons for the Southern predominance. The Southern states sent able delegations, for one thing. Further, in the absence of the élan generated by the resistance against Britain, quorums were difficult to secure in Congress, and when they were attained, the requirement of an absolute majority on routine business and the votes of nine states on important matters had the dual effect of impeding action and tightening discipline within state and sectional blocs. An Adams-Lee alliance probably was impossible after 1783, but with five votes the South outweighed the other two regional clusters and was in a position to direct congressional affairs whenever it could muster temporary support from two to four states to the north. Another reason for the Southern ascendancy was the posture of the South relative to the central concerns of Congress during the mid-eighties. With certain exceptions, the South was unified on central questions having to do with the national debt, the regulation of commerce, the location of the national capital, and the defense of the frontier. The organization of the West was the most important question that Congress successfully managed during the mid-eighties, and with the exception of Maryland, the South was generally united on this problem as well.

Issues that had sharply divided Congress during the early eighties were frequently less abrasive during the remainder of the Confederation era. Morris did not resign in 1783 as he had threatened, but after the failure of the Nationalists in that year there was little reason for him to continue as Superintendent of Finance. He left office in 1784 and was replaced by a Treasury Board composed of three members. Commissioners of the treasury, of whom Arthur Lee was one, were prohibited from engaging directly or indirectly in trade[1]. With a plural administration concerned with receipts and disbursements of a scanty supply of public moneys rather than the management of a fiscal and commercial empire operated for private as well as public benefit, the question of finance became less disputatious. Of course, Congress could not eliminate financial problems. Finance was the essential difficulty, just as the West was the essential opportunity for the Congress during the mid-eighties. But arguments over finance occurred less as a struggle between nationalists and particularists than as a relatively disorganized contest over state quotas and credits for wartime expenditures. More disturbingly, the security-rich North and the security-poor South divided over depreciation schedules and interest payments on loan office certificates.

Although the politics of the mid-eighties were marked by a tripartite division, there was always the possibility that the Middle states and New England would combine against the South. The Southern ascendancy during this era was effective only so long as a Northern coalition did not materialize. By 1786, the New England and Middle states blocs, which had only loosely joined during the two previous years, combined against a remarkably unified South to produce an alarming dichotomy which threatened to break the Confederation. The issue most responsible for this sectional confrontation was the consultation between John Jay and Don Diego de Gardoqui regarding a possible commercial treaty between the United States and Spain. The Jay-Gardoqui negotiation pitted Northern commercial interests against expansive Southern agrarian interests in the most pointed fashion because of the proposal that the American right to the navigation of the Mississippi be bartered for a commercial treaty which clearly offered the greater advantage to the North. By sharpening the ever-present tension between the Eastern and Southern parties, the negotiation brought to full term the partisan antagonisms of 1779. But more than that, this issue raised root questions about the future direction of American growth and, indeed, about the very definition of the nation. So serious was the problem that it is questionable whether it could have been settled within the constitutional framework of the Confederation. Thus the dénouement of congressional factionalism involved an almost total impasse which was resolved by the Constitutional Convention.

II

Despite the enervating atmosphere of the postwar years, the membership of Congress included a number of highly competent people who were to have influential and sometimes distinguished careers in national politics. The South in particular was notable for its representation. The Southern delegates who were most active in introducing resolutions were the youthful Charles Pinckney of South Carolina (who served in 1785 and 1786), Hugh Williamson of North Carolina (a transplanted Pennsylvanian who served in 1784 and 1785), Thomas

Jefferson (who was in Congress in 1784 before leaving for his ministry in France), James Monroe (whose influence in the Virginia delegation was pre-eminent during most of his three-year term, 1784–1786), John Mercer of Virginia (whose activity was greater than the respect he won in Congress during 1784[2]), and James McHenry of Maryland (1784–1785). Arthur Lee served in the Virginia delegation during 1784 before becoming a member of the Treasury Board, and so did his brother, Richard Henry Lee, who was President of Congress in 1785. Still another Lee, Henry, whose subsequent career in the Federal Congress was notable, was a member of the 1786 Virginia delegation. The influential James Madison was disqualified by the three-year tenure rule of the Articles. Nonetheless, Madison constantly corresponded with the Virginia delegates, Jefferson, Monroe, and William Grayson (who added to the merit of the Virginia delegation during his three-year tenure, 1785–1787), and thereby helped to sustain his intelligent counsel. Correspondence between the Virginians and Edmund Randolph, George Washington, and others also testifies to a vital interest in national policy within the Old Dominion, which helps to explain the crucial role of Virginia in the politics of the mid-eighties.

If one reason for the influential position of Virginia during these years was the talent of individual delgates from that state, yet another reason illuminates the contrast between the characters of the Virginia and Middle states delegations—particularly those from Pennsylvania and New York. Virginia politics was relatively stable because it was the product of a homogeneous, aristocratic planter society[3]. The divisions in the Virginia delegation caused by the Lees and Theodorick Bland were of a different order from those within the Middle states delegations—particularly the Pennsylvania delegation, which showed the effects of what David Howell called the natural political "collisions" of the "heterogeneous materials of which that State is so remarkably composed . . ."[4]. Howell noted an exceptional degree of "ferment" and "confusion" in Pennsylvania as a consequence of the lively partisan disputes over old issues such as the Constitution of 1776 and the test oath, as well as new disagreements over state finances. Virginia tolerated divisions within her congressional delegation; the Pennsylvania Assembly did not. When the Constitutionalists won sufficient control of the Assembly to dominate the election of delegates for 1784, they radically changed the composition of the delegation, just as the conservative Republicans had previously. That such obscure individuals as Joseph Gardiner, John Bayard, David Jackson, and William Henry should have represented Pennsylvania during the mid-eighties is consonant with the antiestablishmentarian politics of the Constitutionalists. (William Henry was not entirely unknown, it might be added. It was he who was chairman of the committee which had chastised Robert Morris for breaking the price-control sanctions of 1779 in his dealings in flour under John Hoker's account.)

Not all Pennsylvanians were obscure, however. James Wilson served sporadically during 1784. Charles Pettit, formerly an aide to General Nathanael Greene in the Quartermaster Department and a major architect of the Constitutionalist fiscal program, served in Congress from 1785 to 1787. He was both able and well connected[5]. Arthur St. Clair, also a member of the delegation, was hardly inconspicuous, although his reputation after Ticonderoga and the confrontation with the Pennsylvania line in 1783 was not completely untarnished. Yet, excluding Wilson, there was a significant difference between the political talents of these men and even Mifflin (who served intermittently during 1784) and the magisterial Virginians.

Just as shifting political tides had substituted Pennsylvania Constitutionalists for the nationalist-minded Republicans, the power of George Clinton's parochial establishment in New York along with the three-year limitation on congressional tenure brought new delegates from New York. Ephraim Paine (1784), Charles DeWitt (1784), John Haring (1785–1787), John Lawrance (1785–1786), and Melancton Smith (1785–1787) were as unknown as most of the Pennsylvanians. The Journals suggest that like the latter, they stood mute[6]. These Clintonians contrasted dramatically with the elitist New Yorkers who preceded them. The imperious Philip Schuyler; his brilliant arriviste son-in-law Hamilton; the crafty Duane (almost a Tallyrand in his ability to extract political and financial fortune in treacherous revolutionary currents); the well-born, ambitious, and talented Gouverneur Morris; the aristocratic John Jay; and Chancellor Robert R. Livingston of the manorial clan were markedly different from the obscure John Haring and the low-born Smith who scratched a fortune from commissary contracts and purchases of Tory lands he helped confiscate. Unlike their predecessors, the New York delegates of the mid-eighties did not align with the South. Hugh Williamson of North Carolina lamented as early as 1784 during the tenure of DeWitt and Paine, "The Time has been, I hope it will return when the Southern States shall support or be supported by N York on Federal Questions"[7].

New England sent some new men interspersed with seasoned congressmen. One of the newcomers was Rufus King, whose abilities as a defender of the interests of his section were quickly recognized during his tenure in Congress (1785-1787). Theodore Sedgwick, another "new man" from Massachusetts was even more active than King in terms of motions resulting in roll calls. The perennial Elbridge Gerry, Nathaniel Gorham, Samuel Holten, and the acidulously anti-Southern Nathan Dane rounded out a rather powerful and generally parochial Massachusetts delegation during the mid-eighties.

From Rhode Island the able states' righters William Ellery, like Gerry a constant fixture, and David Howell, the mathematics professor from the College of Rhode Island whose stubborn opposition to the impost obscured (and indeed continues to obscure) his merits, both served during 1784 and 1785. They were replaced in 1786 by James Manning and Nathan Miller, the latter as inconspicuous as the Middle states delegates. Manning, on the other hand, was president of the College of Rhode Island and was almost as accomplished and learned as Howell, his faculty member and old companion. The Connecticut delegation included able men during this period, particularly Roger Sherman (1784) and William Samuel Johnson (1785-1787), president of Yale, both of whom attended the Constitutional Convention, as did Gerry, King, Gorham, and a number of other members of Congress.

Thus, if attendance was sparse, when Congress did have a quorum, it was not an undistinguished group of delegates who gathered at Annapolis and Trenton in 1784, and at New York City during the remainder of the period. It has not been stressed enough that the delegates during the hiatus between the war and the Constitution included two college presidents (Manning and Johnson); two future Presidents of the United States; two graduates of the medical schools of Europe (Arthur Lee of Edinburgh and Hugh Williamson of Utrecht); a professor of mathematics, natural philosophy, French, German, Hebrew and jurisprudence (Howell at the College of Rhode Island); a Royal Governor's nephew (Spaight) who took a degree at Glasgow; and a future minister to England and a candidate for the Presidency (King) whose ability in debate secured him "unrivaled influence"[8]—not to mention a large number of men who helped frame the Constitution and the policy of the Federal period.

If Congress was ineffectual in financial matters because of its impoverishment, it did pass dramatically important land ordinances in 1784, 1785, and 1787. Indeed, Jefferson, the man who coordinated the draft of the first of the three laws, was sufficiently impressed with the importance and national orientation of Congress to suggest to Madison that Virginia's "young statesmen" should be sent up. "They see the affairs of the Confederacy from a high ground; they learn the importance of the Union and befriend federal measures when they return[9].

Despite Jefferson's cordial endorsement of the federal perspective, the politics of Congress during the mid-eighties were increasingly sectional. That Congress was fragmented along regional lines after 1783 is amply evident in the fact that there were only four instances of intersectional alignment in the two years 1784 and 1785: Samuel Dick of New Jersey, a marginal member of the Eastern party in 1784; Gerry and Holten, both marginal members of the Middle states party in 1785; and John Vining of Delaware, a marginal member of the Southern party in 1785. The sectional character of the politics of the mid-eighties is also evident in the small number of independents during those years—only one from New England (the frequently deviant Gerry in 1784), just four from the Middle states, and five from the South. This may be compared with a total of twenty independents during 1779-1780 and sixteen during 1782-1783. By 1786, Congress was dichotomized in an unprecedented fashion, and only two delegates voted as independents.

TABLE 22

Independents, 1778-1786

1778	13	1781	7	1784	4
1779	11	1782	7	1785	6
1780	9	1783	9	1786	2
TOTALS	33		23		12

The drastic sectional division of 1786 was three years in the making. It began in 1784, when the Southern delegations severed most of their ties with the Middle states and New England delegations. Arthur Lee had a higher ratio of agreement with his fellow Virginians than with David Howell, with whom he had aligned against the Nationalists in 1783. In 1785, Richard Henry Lee's level of agreement with Samuel Holten, both members of the Eastern party in 1779, was 49 percent while he had a remarkably high 95 percent ratio of agreement with Monroe. The currency of the Lee interest in Virginia apparently rose during this period. Arthur Lee was assured by a Virginia correspondent, John Scott of Dumfried, that he could have a seat in the Virginia Assembly, should he want it, for it would be impossible "for Col. Grayson or any other candidate to throw you out"[10]. As it turned out, Arthur Lee went to the Treasury Board rather than the Assembly, and Grayson was elected to Congress by the Burgesses the following year. In 1785 Richard Henry Lee and Grayson agreed 85 percent of the time.

The unparalleled cohesion of the Virginia delegation (despite differences between Jefferson and Mercer) had important consequences for congressional politics, for it helped cast Virginia in its natural role as leader of a united Southern party. True, the upper and lower South still tended to diverge—especially in 1785, when the Maryland delegation separated from the Southern party. A good example of this divergence can be seen in the log-rolling arrangement between Virginia and Maryland over appointments to the Treasury Board and the Hague ministry. Maryland supported Arthur Lee for the Treasury and in return anticipated the endorsement of Virginia for its candidate for the Hague appointment, William Paca[11]. South Carolina would not join the upper South, however, and managed to secure the election of Ralph Izard as Minister to the Netherlands. Despite such differences, the South was more united than ever before, substantially more so than the North.

Of course, the North had not operated as a single interest during the Revolution, except occasionally on certain aspects of fiscal and military policy. Thus the tardiness of the merger of New England and the Middle states was natural. Another important reason for the failure of the Northern delegations

TABLE 23

Congressional Blocs, 1784

	Eastern Party	Middle Party	Southern Party
N.H.	Blanchard		
	Foster		
Mass.	Partridge		
R.I.	Ellery		
	Howell		
Conn.	Sherman		
	Wadsworth		
N.Y.		DeWitt	
N.J.	Dick*	Hand	
Pa.		Mifflin	
		Montgomery, J.	
Md.			Chase*
			McHenry*
			Stone
Va.			Hardy
			Jefferson*
			Mercer
			Monroe
N.C.			Spaight
			Williamson*
S.C.			Beresford
			Read

* Marginal membership.

Independents: Gerry (Mass.); Paine (N.Y.); Beatty (N.J.); Arthur Lee (Va.).

to unite as rapidly as the South, despite the changes in the New York and Pennsylvania delegations, was the issue of western lands and the related issues of Indian policy, frontier defense, and boundary conflicts. New England and New York divided over Vermont, as always. In addition, Massachusetts asserted in late 1783 that it had rights to lands in western New York on the basis of its original charter of 1628. The New York delegates were astonished and insisted with considerable plausibility that "no Respect ought to be paid to a State Pretention which has laid dormant more than One Hundred and fifty Years"[12].

TABLE 24

Congressional Blocs, 1785

	Eastern Party	Middle Party	Maryland Bloc	Southern Party
N.H.	Foster			
	Long			
Mass.	Gerry*	Gerry*		
	Holten*	Holten*		
	King*			
R.I.	Ellery			
	Howell			
Conn.	Cooke			
	Johnson			
N.Y.		Haring		
		Smith*		
		Lawrance		
N.J.		Cadwallader		
		Stewart		
Pa.		Gardner		
		Henry, W.		
		Jackson*		
Md.			Henry, J.	
			Hindman	
			McHenry	
Del.				Vining*
Va.				Grayson
				Hardy
				Lee, R. H.
				Monroe
N.C.				Sitgreaves*
S.C.				Bull
				Pinckney
				Read*
Ga.				Houstoun

*Marginal membership.

Independents: Pettit (Pa.); Bedford (Del.); Williamson (N.C.); Kean (S.C.); Baldwin and Habersham (Ga.).

Nonetheless, Massachusetts emigrants had settled in the region, and many more were ready to migrate[*13*]. The Massachusetts delegates compensated for the implausibility of their claim by their diligence in pursuit of it. Suspecting that New York would snatch the land away in treaties with the Indians, Samuel Osgood and his fellow delegates discarded their parochialism long enough to oppose negotiations between New York and the Iroquois within New York boundaries, claiming that this was properly within the jurisdiction of Congress. In the spring of 1784, the Massachusetts government asked Congress to appoint a federal court to settle the controversy—a course made possible by Article 9 of the Articles of Confederation. A court composed of nine judges was elected by the joint consent of agents appointed by the two states (the New Yorkers nominating mostly Middle states men and the Massachusetts agents nominating Southerners), but it proved impossible to find a quorum of judges who would accept the case. Ultimately, in late 1786, when national issues had established a communion of interest in western policy between New York and Massachusetts, the dispute was resolved in a convention between representatives of the two states meeting at Hartford. It was agreed that New York should have sovereignty over the region but that Massachusetts would have the right of preemption of the soil from the native Indians[*14*]. During the two previous years, however, the controversy caused much disagreement on both the question of title to the land and the related problem of Indian relations in the Northwest Department.

The familiar dispute between Connecticut and Pennsylvania over a similar New England penetration of the Middle states by the Susquehanna Company in the Wyoming Valley also contributed to discord between the two regions. This more ancient and corrosive controversy, which had produced bloodshed and endless litigation, erupted again in 1784 when John Armstrong, Jr., of Newburgh renown was dispatched by the Pennsylvania Council (of which he was the secretary) with 400 militiamen to restore order between Pennsylvanians and Connecticut settlers in the valley. Armstrong treated the Yankees "with bad faith and characteristic ruthlessness," according to one biographer. The Connecticut Legislature passed a resolution condemning the incident, and Governor Matthew Griswold sent letters of protest to Pennsylvania and Congress. Hugh Williamson, chairman of a committee formed to consider the Connecticut protest, remarked in a letter to Dickinson that the complaints were "sufficiently pointed and bitter. . . ." The Pennsylvania Council did offer restitution to the settlers, and the two states reached a compromise in May of 1786 whereby Pennsylvania supported the Connecticut claim to the 120-mile-long reserve in the Northwest Territory in exchange for Connecticut making no more claims and discouraging land company operations in the Wyoming region [*15*].

In addition to these disputes between Northern delegations, there were differences which arose between the small "landless" states and states with western claims when Congress finally accepted the Virginia cession in the winter of 1783–1784. This traditional division over the issue of western claims separated Rhode Island and New Jersey and, to a lesser degree, Pennsylvania from a general Northern alliance. Finally, the issue of western lands raised the question of a standing army for the defense of the frontier, a subject that was anathema in New England—especially after the defection of the Massachusetts delegates in 1783 on the question of the commutation of officers' pay. Thus the New England delegates, fulminating about the extravagance of the "Southern Gentry" and the dangers of military despotism, often disagreed with the rest of the states on the issue of a frontier establishment[16].

III

Although there were internal divisions within the North, New England and the Middle states frequently joined against the South in matters of finance and commerce—thus helping to account for the three-way division of Congress during 1784 and 1785. These were dismal years of frustration and incapacity for Congress as it attempted one expedient after another to compensate for its poverty, one plea after another for additional authority to cope with foreign commercial competition. In some respects, Congress often was united rather than divided as a consequence of its keen sense of impotence. In contrast to the days of the Morris superintendency, there were few ideological battles fought on the floor. When the impost amendment had been tied to Morris's grand fiscal system, it was more suspect than when Morris's powers were assumed by the three-man Treasury Board whose members had taken an oath against mixing public and private interest. Despite opposition in the states, congressional support for the impost as it was defined in 1783 was all but unanimous.

There were, however, disputes over servicing the public debt, over allowances for state expenditures during the Revolution, over expenditures for frontier defense, and over other specific decisions regarding fiscal policy which not only aroused controversy but also contributed greatly to the increasingly sectional dimensions of congressional partisanship. One basic cause of disputation was the fact that public securities were not distributed evenly throughout the Confederation. The Northern states, especially Pennsylvania, were security-rich by comparison with the South. This was due to many factors. Not only was there more investment capital in the North, but also there seems to have been a tradition of closer accounting of supplies in that region than in the South. Although Congress had specified rather precise regulations for the establishment of a claim against the federal account, these had frequently been overlooked during the hectic days of the Southern campaign. When the time for reckoning came after the Revolution, a large portion of Southern expenditures lacked proper validation. Irate over the narrow commercial spirit of the North, Southern delegates pressed for a relaxation of the accounting regulations, for acceptance of claims in equity, and for a lengthier time for filing abstracts with claims commissioners[17]. Hugh Williamson of North Carolina complained, "It is curious but not very pleasing to observe, that while some of the Northern states never turned out a Serjeants guard of Militia without obtaining the Sanction of Congress or of some Continental officer our State in the true Spirit of a patriot but not of an accountant has been expending Militia and raising State troops without taking any heed concerning the day of retribution . . ." [18]. Southern states had generally assumed federal debts held by individuals on liberal terms outside the rules laid down by Congress. Southern delegates, particularly the South Carolinians, urged Congress to accept those state-assumed debts as credits against the Continental account without intervention by federal officials.

Although commissioners were appointed by Congress to inspect claims throughout the states, progress in the settlements was exceedingly slow. Indeed, while individual claims were largely settled by 1787, state claims were not resolved until the 1790s, when the whole matter of the public debt had been transformed by Hamilton's fiscal program[19]. By 1785, the Southern states, hoping to gain some immediate advantage from claims, the settlement of which seemed increasingly distant, pressed for recompense for state assumption of unliquidated individual claims in the form of reduced quotas in the annual requisitions. All these aspects of individual and state claims settlements produced sectional disputes which intensified during 1785 and 1786 as Confederation finances became increasingly strained[20].

There were other sources of controversy. Virginia wanted compensation for the George Rogers Clark campaign—"a very monstrous sum," according to Rufus King[21]. Massachusetts herself, on the other hand, claimed credits for a mismanaged expedition to dislodge the British from Penobscot Bay in Maine. Virginia unsuccessfully tried to persuade Congress to allow her to claim expenditures incurred during the campaign against Lord Dunmore—a campaign which, according to Monroe, was "precisely on the same footing with the first campaign at Boston . . ."[22].

The retirement of old money and interest payments on liquidated securities also heightened sectional tensions. Massachusetts had accepted Continental bills of credit at favorable ratios to specie, with the result that large sums had flowed into that state. The Massachusetts delegates pressed for credit at a ratio of 40 to 1, which the other states (having accepted the money for taxes at disadvantageous ratios) opposed[23].

After retiring the old money and issuing the equally fragile new bills in exchange, Congress pledged to cease currency emissions—a promise largely honored after the war. Finances were put on a specie basis, and the states were called upon to make requisitions in hard money. Unfortunately, the policy proved to be unworkable, since specie was scarce and closely guarded. Because Congress was unable to cope with interest payments on the public debt, the states themselves frequently undertook the task through various devices, the first of which was the issuance of certificates receivable in taxes—a technique used by Pennsylvania in 1783[24]. After other states adopted similar expedients, the delegates were forced to recognize that the states were undertaking obligations properly belonging to Congress, and they decided to credit the states with such payments in their annual requisitions. The outcome of this policy was the "indent" system, a faltering attempt by Congress to nationalize state interest payments by issuing congressional certificates (or indents) to those states which had made payments to holders of Continental securities. The indents, after being collected by a state in taxes, could be used to satisfy a portion of the state's requisition, but the remainder—three-fourths at the outset, then one-half—had to be paid in specie. Indeed, without the full specie payment, the indents would not be accepted[25].

Unfortunately, the intention to nationalize state interest payments with indents which would presumably circulate between the states did not work out as Congress had hoped. The states were unable to meet the three-fourths specie requirement (which was finally modified to one-third, but with additional stipulations regarding the mode and timing of interest payments which vitiated the more generous ratio)[26]. In addition, many states embarked upon paper money programs which undermined the indents. Only after Congress capitulated by allowing the states to handle the public debt in their own way and receive credit in the requisitions did the indent payments become substantial[27]. This, in conjunction with the even more menacing tendency for some states to assume the principal of the public debt by establishing banks founded partially upon Continental securities, contributed to what E. James Ferguson has aptly called "the economics of disunion"[28]. In the context of congressional partisanship, it should be stressed, disunion meant not total fragmentation but the formation of regional interests—a tendency which occurred not simply because of financial distress but also because of commercial disorder.

After the resumption of peaceful commerce, it was quickly apparent that foreign powers would take advantage of Congress's inability to legislate a navigation system. There was a deluge of goods from abroad, especially from Great Britain, and the goods were quickly consumed by a population that was tired of wartime austerity. Aside from the impact of this importation on infant American manufacturers, the trade was overwhelmingly in foreign ships and, therefore, harmful to American carriers. Demands for some sort of navigation legislation to protect the American carrying trade were sent to a generally sympathetic Congress, which appointed a committee made up of Gerry, Jacob

Read, Williamson, Jeremiah Chase, and Jefferson to consider the problem. Its report, adopted with modifications by Congress on April 30, 1784, was both hesitant and bold. With the rebuff of the Nationalist program in mind, Congress contended that while its proposition "may be suspected to have originated in a desire for power," the restrictive measures adopted by the several states made national action imperative[29]. The report went on to recommend to the state legislatures that they vest Congress with the power to prohibit imports into any of the states that were not carried in American ships manned by American crews or in ships belonging to nations with which the United States had a commercial treaty[30]. The proposition won overwhelming endorsement by Congress, although the Rhode Island delegates, Ellery and Howell, objected that the states should be exhorted to pass the restrictions rather than lodging the power with Congress[31]. Howell and Ellery did recommend that the legislation provide for admitting ships from nations which allowed the United States a reciprocity in trade and for excluding ships carrying goods manufactured outside the flag under which they were registered. As finally adopted that day without a recorded roll call, the report included the Rhode Island proposal, but the regulatory power was to be given to Congress, if the states agreed. Any navigation law would have to be approved by nine states, thereby guaranteeing a regional veto[32]. Thus, with surprisingly little dissension, Congress asked for additional powers which, when added to the impost, already requested, would give substantially more content to the ideal of a national sovereignty.

The decision to ask for regulatory authority over foreign commerce generated less dispute than the question of the composition of the foreign delegation to negotiate the commercial treaties which the navigation powers sought by Congress would presumably cultivate. At this time, Franklin, Jay, and Adams were empowered to negotiate commercial treaties. Since sectional balance had been an abiding concern of the Southern delegations when the peace treaty was being formulated, the South was understandably distressed over its lack of representation abroad. Thus Samuel Hardy of Virginia and Richard Spaight of North Carolina moved on May 5, 1784, that two additional commissioners be appointed to negotiate treaties of commerce. The vote on the motion was rigidly sectional, all delegates north of Pennsylvania, with the exception of Gerry, voting in opposition[33]. A motion to appoint one more minister carried over the objection of Rhode Island and Connecticut but was lost in subsequent balloting[34]. As it turned out, the requirement of sectional balance was satisfied by the return of Jay and the appointment of Jefferson in his place, happily as the result of a nomination by his admirer from Rhode Island, David Howell.

By early 1785, British competition so disturbed the American carrying trade that there were demands from merchants, and later from the Massachusetts Legislature, for more ample national authority over commerce, both foreign and coastal[35]. As Rufus King noted, the April 30, 1784, resolution (approved by eight states when King wrote in May) gave Congress the power only to prohibit trade, not to regulate it[36]. But it was James Monroe, not King, who actively agitated for more ample congressional power over commerce as early as December of 1784. A committee chaired by Monroe was appointed on January 24, 1785, to prepare a report on the subject. The committee reported on February 16, but serious debate did not occur until summer, largely in response to the deepening commercial depression.

The committee proposed to alter Article 9 of the Articles of Confederation by submitting an amendment to the states that would give Congress the authority not only to prohibit foreign carriers and imports in American ports but also to regulate foreign and coastal trade and to levy duties on foreign imports. Monroe was fully aware of the political implication of this report. He pointed out to Jefferson that this would constitute a radical alteration of the Confederation—that it would, in itself, form "the most permanent and powerful principle in the confederation." Monroe went on to distinguish between the present "alliance" which left "the political economy of each State . . . entirely within its own direction" and the effect of the new plan, which would be "to put the commercial economy of every State entirely under the hands of the Union." Further, "The means, necessary to obtain the carrying trade, to encourage domestic by a tax on foreign industry, or any other ends which in the changes of things become necessary, will depend intirely on the union. In short you will perceive that this will give the union an authority upon the States respectively which will last with it and patch it together in its present form longer than any principle it now contains . . ."[37]. Monroe in effect suggested that the proposal (which was never approved by Congress) could substitute for the defunct fiscal nationalism of the Robert Morris era. Indeed, if the control of revenue from navigation duties were left to the disposition of Congress, the modification of Article 9 would make the 5-percent impost superfluous. Jefferson approved the revision of Article 9, adding that action on the amendment should be taken before any new states were admitted from the West, for otherwise ratification might be difficult. This was a sentiment with which Monroe concurred[38]. Time would show that ratification even of the April 1784 recommendation by the original thirteen states would be difficult enough. The proposal to alter Article 9 never left Congress.

The failure to reach agreement was due in part to the inevitable Southern fear that the Northern states would monopolize the management of Southern commerce. Richard Henry Lee, labeled by Monroe as the center of the opposition in Congress, tried to convince Madison in a letter that the amendment "would be dangerous in the extreme to the 5 Southern or Staple States, whose want of ships and seamen would expose their freightage and their produce to a most pernicious and destructive Monopoly." The South would be "at the Mercy of our East and North"[39]. James McHenry, writing to Washington just three days later, worried about the same thing: "I believe the eastern States, New York and Pennsylvania are exceedingly anxious for it [the navigation amendment] but I do not wonder at their anxiety to obtain a monopoly of the carrying trade of the union." The effect on the South would be particularly adverse, according to McHenry, for there would be not only higher carrying charges but also fewer supplies[*40*].

Paradoxically, the reason for the failure of the amendment can be attributed to the reservations of New England delegates—not only Howell of Rhode Island, who objected to the duty-producing aspects of the measure[*41*], but also King, Gerry, and Holten of Massachusetts. Rufus King argued that the danger of foreign competition to American mercantile interests was magnified and that a temporizing policy was the desirable one: "too much precipitancy may injure us, moderation and delay have ever served our true interest"[*42*].

The sentiments of King and his fellow delegates did not accord completely with those of their constituents. During June and July, the Massachusetts Legislature, at the instigation of Governor Bowdoin, passed a series of acts and resolutions establishing a state navigation system and calling upon the other states to follow suit. The Legislature further recommended that a convention be held to consider alterations of the Articles of Confederation[*43*]. The resolves, including the recommendation for a convention, were transmitted by Governor Bowdoin to the Massachusetts delegates for presentation to Congress. In a remarkable move, the Massachusetts delegation decided not to comply! Gerry, Holten, and King argued that commercial regulations should be temporary rather than permanent and tried before being incorporated in the Articles. As for the idea of a convention, any thorough alteration of the Confederation through such a device was contrary to the Articles. Moreover, a general convention would stimulate "the Friends of an Aristocracy, to send Members who would promote a Change of Government[*44*].

It is clear that the Massachusetts delegation had not forgotten the Nationalist thrust of 1781-1783, and in the case of the recently arrived King, at this time the most parochial individual in the delegation, the lack of direct exposure to the actions of the Nationalists seems to have made the specter of a central aristocratic establishment even more fearsome. It was the delegates' opinion that "many persons of elevated Views and idle Habits in these States" looked for "lucrative Employments" in an administration "which would require a standing Army, and a numerous Train of pensioners and placemen . . ."[*45*]. The Eastern delegates of the mid-eighties responded to the threat of power with the rhetoric of the early Revolution, as did the New Yorkers Melancton Smith, John Haring, and John Lawrance and the Pennsylvanian William Henry. Clearly, if congressional action was to be the answer to the economic distress and lack of political direction of the mid-eighties, it would have to be generated outside the Eastern and Middle delegations.

The Southern party was most favorably advantaged and best equipped to provide a new national focus. The South—above all, Virginia—was most concerned with wrenching free from ties with the British, and the South, especially Virginia and North Carolina, had the greatest stake in the development of the West. Consequently, the alternatives to the fiscal nationalism that had been attempted and discredited during the early eighties were more attractive to the Southern interest than to any of the other congressional parties. It was James Monroe, not Rufus King, who was most active in promoting a policy of commercial independence for the United States, and it was Thomas Jefferson who was most responsible for developing a program for expansion into the West. When Jefferson recommended that Virginia send its "young statesmen" to the "high ground" of Congress, he was talking of a terrain that was not distant from the Chesapeake, the Potomac, and the West.

IV

The undeveloped and accessible lands of the trans-Appalachian West were an irresistible allurement for the population living in the narrow settled territory east of the mountains. Some areas of the East were actually crowded, and other parts were suffering from soil exhaustion. Settlers filtered across the mountains into present western Pennsylvania, West Virginia, Kentucky, and Tennessee while the war was in progress, causing problems for Pennsylvania, Virginia, and North Carolina, which had difficulty maintaining authority in the western counties. In 1780, 1,000 petitioners in Kentucky asked the Congress for separate political status, and at about the same time settlers in the upper Tennessee Valley under the leadership of John Sevier refused to obey directives from North Carolina regarding the eviction of squatters, and some western Pennsylvanians led by Benjamin Johnson, the influential deputy surveyor of Yohogania, wanted to connect western Pennsylvania with Virginia because of easier purchase terms under Virginia law, and perhaps because Pennsylvania had just passed an act providing for the gradual emancipation of slaves[46]. Challenged by its western inhabitants, Pennsylvania, like New York, negotiated with the Indians for title to the land during the fall of 1783, but because of opposition from New England she was unable to secure congressional endorsement of her actions—a fact which did not impede her at all[47].

There were other difficulties for Congress and the states in the region northwest of the Ohio, where state cessions were creating a national domain. In September of 1783, George Washington, an investor in the West and a lobbyist of sorts for soldiers desiring western lands, warned a congressional committee on Indian affairs that white settlers would have to be separated from the Indians if war was to be averted and that some form of government should be established in a large additional western state so as to maintain order among the migrating frontiersmen[48]. Apprehensions that the Northwest—that "immense Tract of Country which is daily overrun by lawless men"—would slip from congressional control[49] helped persuade Congress to accept Virginia's cession of her claim to the Northwest, to attempt to negotiate treaties with the Indians, and to begin to develop a comprehensive plan for the whole trans-Appalachian West.

Although the famous land ordinance which formed the base of the American territorial system was not passed until April of 1784, much of the preliminary work on the ordinance was done during the fall of 1783 before Thomas Jefferson, the man who organized the final draft, even arrived in Congress[50]. Spurred on by the alluring, yet restive, situation in the West, Congress accepted the Virginia cession on September 12, subject to minor modifications which made it possible for Virginia to agree without backing away from her insistence that treaties concluded between the Indians and land companies be nullified [51]. The congressional resolution was sent to Virginia, where it was approved, and the cession was completed on March 1, 1784. In the meantime, expecting that it would soon have jurisdiction over the Northwest, and occupied with the closely related question of treaties with the Indians granting rights to the soil, Congress agreed that it should regulate migration so as to prevent Indian conflicts and make provisions for temporary and permanent republican government in a state or states to be created in the future. Congress also considered whether it should closely control territorial government during the preliminary stages of occupation through congressionally appointed officials or allow the settlers a substantial voice in their own governance[52]. Although none of these questions was settled, the inclination of Congress was to guarantee an extension of the republican form of government while keeping a close watch over the West during its early development.

The whole western question became much more complex with the Virginia cession, so it is not surprising that the organization of a territorial system should have taken time, produced disagreements, and prompted frequent vacillations. During the war years, there had been a relatively simple division of Congress between "landed" and "landless" states over the central problem of Virginia's vast claim in the West. When Virginia ceded a large part of that claim—not all of it, because she retained Kentucky—response among the landless states was varied. Pennsylvania had large unsettled tracts within her borders which she could use to help retire her debts. Maryland, New Jersey, and Rhode Island were not so favorably situated. Land speculators in the Middle states continued to oppose the terms of the Virginia cession, but the speculators had less influence in the congressional delegation from Pennsylvania in 1784 than they had previously so that the traditional Middle states speculative interest was less powerful than it had been. There was considerable cooperation between Virginia, which supported Pennsylvania's efforts to validate her trans-

Allegheny lands through Indian treaties, and Pennsylvania, which endorsed the Virginia cession with its stipulations against land company claims[53].

The demand of the landless states that Virginia give up its western claim was related not only to Virginia's disproportionate size and strength but also, of course, to the war debts. Western lands were a resource that could be used to pay off veterans and holders of federal and state public securities. Rhode Island's dogged insistence that a Continental impost be credited to the states in which it was collected stemmed from her total lack of unoccupied lands. David Howell noted that Pennsylvania had opened a land office and was accepting government obligations of all descriptions in exchange for land. He went on to complain that states which have vast tracts of wild land to dispose of may buy up the public securities and eventually reduce their sister states to the condition of tributaries. These were the states, too, which so pertinaciously insisted that the revenues to be derived from commerce should be thrown into common stock[54]. Shortly afterward Howell noted with irritation that Georgia was unrepresented in Congress because "none of their principal men dare leave the state . . . for fear of being out-manouvred" in the land jobbing in Georgia's unceded western lands. Howell wondered whether Congress would let Georgia's small population "divide among themselves that vast tract" while at the same time admitting them "to an equal participation in the revenue of an impost"[55]. It was Howell's belief that the whole of the trans-Appalachian West should be used to extinguish the public debt and that it should be done as rapidly as possible so as to avert dangerously centralizing funding systems launched for the benefit of aristocratic army officers and public creditors.

Howell's desire to settle the West and eliminate the debt, assuming it could be effected, raised a multitude of additional questions. How many states should be carved out of the West? (The Virginia cession stipulated that no less than ten states should be created from the territory north of the Ohio.) What kind of interim government was to be established? Should the settlers be given as much voice in their affairs as possible, or should Congress appoint and control temporary governments? (There were dangers in both alternatives. Arbitrary control could discourage settlement, while democracy could deprive the East of benefit from the sale of the West.) How was the land to be sold and settled? Should Congress follow the Southern tradition of dispersed occupation of choice lands under individual warrant, or should it adopt the New England tradition of prior survey and more compact, gradual settlement? What sort of society would emerge from the West? Everyone assumed it would be an agrarian society. But should slavery be allowed? The answer to that question could affect the West, and indeed the Republic, in the most fundamental manner.

The configuration of congressional attitudes toward such questions was by no means simple. New Englanders and others who wanted to protect the commercial interest feared the creation of a large number of states in the West.

Many Southerners—especially South Carolinians—worried that expansion might undermine slavery. Other Southerners—especially Virginians—hoped that expansion might help to diversify their economy and free them from dependence upon slave labor. There were expansionists who wanted sales of western lands for congressional revenue, but there were others who advocated constraint because expansion might depreciate land values in unsettled lands within state boundaries. New Yorkers, Pennsylvanians, and Virginians were concerned about depreciation; Rhode Islanders, New Hampshirites, and delegates from small, landless states tended to be interested in revenue. In addition, whether from contrivance or conviction, there were delegates who favored the development of a large number of democratic republics in the West as an antidote to actual or potential corruption of the more densely settled eastern portion of the Union. Howell and Jefferson best represented this sentiment.

Jefferson had insisted all along that the Northwest be made into a large number of states, based on the assumption that republican government required a homogeneous population and that such politics was possible only in relatively small territorial units[56]. Howell believed with Jefferson, although possibly because of different motives and assumptions, that since the future inhabitants of the West would be "cultivators of the soil," consequently "republicanism looks to them as its guardians." It is unlikely that even Jefferson could have matched Howell's paean to the West: "When the states on the eastern shores . . . shall have become populous, rich and luxurious, and ready to yield their liberties into the hands of a tyrant, the gods of the mountains will save us, for they will be stronger than the gods of the valleys. Astraea will take her flight from the tops of the Alleghany when she leaves the New World"[57]. Thus the seeding of the West was to renew the Republic, and thus the wheel had turned half circle, for it had been the cities of the East, now corrupted by ravenous importations, that had marshaled the virtue of the nation at the onset of the Revolution.

Other kinds of interests and commitments—often practical, but more often ideological—complicated the organization, survey, and sale of the land. Some congressmen, particularly New Englanders, strongly favored the development of compact settlements in order to create communities that could be given stability and coherence through the early establishment of schools and churches. This view, especially when reinforced by provisions reserving land in each township for the support of education and religion, was opposed by libertarians who objected to such corporate arrangements. The advocates of corporate development did not necessarily oppose expansion, but their policy coincided with that of the constrictionists. By the same token, democrats and advocates of rapid expansion for revenue often joined forces for different reasons. Libertarians who favored a minimum of restraint might find common cause with speculators who wanted a free hand to exploit the land. All in all, the organization of a territorial system was such a many-faceted problem that it did not accord readily with the basic partisan divisions in Congress—at least not during its early development in 1783 and 1784.

But even in the context of this profusion of interest and commitments, it was evident that the West might provide a new national focus and recapture for Congress some of its lost prestige and authority. With the completion of the cessions in the Northwest—Virginia's in 1784 and the less substantial claims of Massachusetts and Connecticut during 1785 and 1786—Congress had an independent jurisdiction over a region larger than that encompassed by any state. As the land was sold, Congress would receive an independent revenue— that critical element of sovereignty so clearly grasped by the Nationalists who failed to secure that objective through fiscal centralism. Properly managed, this vast empire might rejuvenate the republican ardor that had been so important during the early war years but which had alarmingly subsided during the early eighties. The expectation of republican renewal from the seeding of the West could transcend some of the parochialism that had always marred congressional unity. The fact that Howell of Rhode Island, Jeremiah Chase of Maryland, and Jefferson of Virginia served with apparent harmony on the committee which drafted the initial report on the governance of the West indicated good prospects for a new national concord[58]. It was assumed that much of the early migration into the Ohio Valley would come from the core region of the Confederation—from the states bordering the Potomac and the headwaters of the Ohio River. If Virginia, Maryland, and Pennsylvania could establish an accord —and there were indications that the Virginia and Pennsylvania delegations were cooperating on land policies in the winter of 1783 and 1784—an important step in the direction of national cohesion would be taken.

The Virginia cession was finally accepted by Congress on March 1, 1784, in terms that were essentially those Virginia had been insisting upon all along. Land company treaties with the Indians were invalidated; a military reservation was set aside for Virginia soldiers with land warrants issued by the state when lands in Kentucky proved insufficient; reimbursement was allowed for actual expenses incurred in subjugating the territory; a tract was set aside for George Rogers Clark and his men; and a proviso that the territory be formed into states of approximately 150 miles square was approved.

The terms were consonant with Virginia's self-interest, with regard not only to the land companies but also to the development of the region in the national context. The influx of Virginia soldiers would enhance the Ohio-Kanawha-Monongahela-Potomac river system in which Pennsylvania and Maryland, and especially Virginia, had an economic stake[59]. If Madison's hope that Virginia could develop a merchant marine were realized through the development of a major commercial center on the Potomac, perhaps at Alexandria, the tobacco economy of Virginia might be sufficiently altered to diminish her dependence on slave labor as well as on non-Virginian merchants and shippers. The prospects were too tempting for Virginians in Congress not to become closely involved with the organization of the West.

A remarkable number of prominent Virginians connected with the Continental Congress made northern and western trips during 1784. James Monroe took a trip to Lake Erie, Montreal, and New York during a congressional recess from June to November (when the device of a thirteen-member committee of the states was put into operation as required by the Articles—without success). The Virginians intended, among other things, to probe the feasibility of communication between Lake Erie and the Potomac[60]. George Washington journeyed into the interior to assess the possibilities for communication along the Potomac-Monongahela and James-Kanawha waterways. James Madison made a northern trip to Fort Schuyler during the late summer, and Thomas Jefferson seriously considered serving on the commission extending the boundary line between Pennsylvania and Virginia during April 1784 [61]. Arthur Lee was likewise interested in the Northwest, having sought, according to Jefferson, the appointment he received as one of the commissioners to negotiate treaties with the Indians in the region[62]. Arthur Lee was an early purchaser of lands in the first seven ranges surveyed, by the way[63]. Lee was not the only Virginia delegate to become interested in land purchase. William Grayson wrote to a Pennsylvania correspondent about the appointment of the five commissioners and indicated he would search for good bargains in land[64].

The movements of these Virginians, most of whom had sizable investments in western lands located in New York, Pennsylvania, and the Northwest, and particularly in the western regions of Virginia, were testaments to their abiding interest in western development. But they did not necessarily agree about the organization of the West. Indeed, as individuals their attitudes were ambivalent. Washington, Grayson, Lee, Monroe, and others were at once delighted and alarmed by the prospect of western settlement. Their hope for economic development was tempered by a sense of uneasiness over the potentially disruptive impact of turbulent populations in the loosely connected transmontane regions. The debates over the initial committee report on the land ordinance revealed that the Virginians were not alone in their uncertainty about the West.

V

The territorial system devised by Congress began to take shape in the form of two ordinances passed in 1784 and 1785. The first dealt with the political organization of the territories and their introduction as additional states, while the second defined the terms under which land was to be surveyed and sold. The two ordinances were based on reports from two committees in which Jefferson and Howell, the only delegates to serve on both, were particularly influential. (This helps to account for the fact that the committee reports were more liberal than the ordinances which emanated from them.) Congress agreed upon a form of political organization in 1784, subsequently revised in 1787, but it did not adopt a plan for surveying and selling the land until 1785.

The committee on the government of the West presented its report on March 1, the same day that Congress finally accepted the Virginia cession. Although Virginia had ceded only the area north of the Ohio, the report and the Ordinance of 1784 applied to the whole of the West, based on the expectation that all western claims would be ceded. Thus the provisions took on added significance. In accordance with the ideas of Jefferson and the stipulations of the Virginia cession, the West was to be divided into a large number of states, the bounds of which were specified in terms of two longitudinal tiers of states two degrees of latitude in extent. Thus, the committee endorsed the agrarian republicanism to which Jefferson was devoted and which Howell also endorsed. The political evolution of these western societies was to be relatively autonomous. Upon petition from the settlers in a potential state, or by its own initiative, Congress could authorize free adult males to convene to adopt a temporary government in the form of the constitution and laws of one of the original states. The legislature elected by the inhabitants during this temporary stage of government would be empowered to revise the constitution and laws as it saw fit. When the number of free inhabitants reached 20,000, a convention for creating a permanent constitution would be called, and when the number of free inhabitants equaled the number in the least populous of the original states—almost certain to be a relatively low number, since Delaware had little growth potential at the time—the state could enter the Union on an equal footing with the original states[65].

The last provision, which became a fundamental principle of subsequent continental expansion, was indispensable for the perpetuation of a republic. Congress, despite a provision in the Virginia cession calling for equal status for new states, might have worked to create colonial dependencies in the West rather than an enlargement of a confederation of equals. While this decision seems to have been hardly debated in 1784, there was opposition to admitting new states on equal terms in the Constitutional Convention, and even in the Continental Congress there were modifications of the committee's report that had a tendency to sacrifice western interests to those of the East. It would be a mistake to assume that the notion of an expanding republic was so axiomatic as to produce no opposition.

There were other liberal provisions in the report. The new states were guaranteed a republican form of government, and no possessor of a hereditary title could be admitted to citizenship. Despite the fact that two members of the committee, Jefferson and Jeremiah Chase, came from slave-holding states without serious prospect of emancipation, the committee recommended gradual abolition of slavery in the entire region west of the mountains to take effect by 1800[66]. As if to emphasize the enlightened republicanism of the report, the committee, inspired by Jefferson, recommended ten names for the new western states, most of which combined the classical bent of the Enlightenment with a fascination with the Indian as noble savage: Michigania, Cherronesus, Assenisipia, Illinoia, Sylvania, and so forth.

Congress struck out or modified some of the liberal provisions of the report. The abolition of slavery, while endorsed by Jefferson and Hugh Williamson of North Carolina, was opposed by the rest of the South and failed acceptance by one vote—that of John Beatty of New Jersey, who was sick and not present[67]. It was an enormously significant vote, but it is all but certain that slavery south of the Ohio could not have been successfully abolished by Congress. Had the resolution passed, in all probability it would have been reversed. The Carolinas and Georgia—and almost certainly Virginia—would have forced a reconsideration of the decision before ceding their western claims. The prohibition of hereditary titles was also struck down, not because of support for a western nobility but because of the assumption that the clause, designed to operate against the recently formed organization of Revolutionary officers, the Society of Cincinnati, was inappropriate for the purpose[68]. Jefferson's euphonious terminology was discarded, but the provision for a large number of states was retained. This important decision, prompted in part by the requirement of the Virginia cession, had highly significant implications. Howell calculated that fourteen new states would be created—a number precisely equal to the original confederation plus Vermont[69]. If, as Howell and Jefferson expected, the western region was to be populated with husbandmen, it stood to reason that their representatives in the Continental Congress could be relied upon to thwart the sort of centralist tendencies that Howell and other advocates of states' rights had objected to in 1783. In such manner would the purity of the Republic be sustained.

But while Congress temporarily endorsed Jefferson's objective of creating western states that would be small enough to be homogeneous republics, there were strong indications that it was not preparing to transfer power from the Atlantic seaboard to the West in either the immediate or foreseeable future. The committee's report was changed so as to give Congress the power to press measures to preserve order among the inhabitants during the first stage of settlement before a temporary government was adopted. The requirement that the temporary government be copied from a constitution of one of the original thirteen states embodied a substantial measure of congressional direction. Congress defeated a proposal that would have allowed the temporary governments to tax nonresident landowners more heavily than the actual inhabitants, despite the fact that this would have made the territories more attractive to potential settlers. With the exception of a short-lived relinquishment of Tennessee by North Carolina in 1784, the Southern states held on to their western lands throughout the Confederation era; Georgia did not complete its cession until 1802. In the end, four, not six, states were created south of the Ohio from lands gained by the United States in the treaty with Britain. In 1786, the Congress and Virginia agreed to reduce the number of states to be carved out of the Northwest to not less than three nor more than five, rather than the ten suggested by Jefferson. Finally, still greater congressional controls were imposed upon the Northwest Territory in the Ordinance of 1787. The thirteen states were far from unified in their attitudes toward the development of the West, as the vote on slavery disclosed, and as subsequent controversies over the mode of survey and sale of lands shortly revealed, but most members of Congress were momentarily concerned for the most part with the interests of their Atlantic constituents rather than their western descendants.

That Congress did not fully comprehend the meaning of the organization of the West in 1784 is evident from the many anomalies that cropped up in debates over the territorial system and policy determinations closely related to the western problem. Although the New England states favored organized settlement through corporate townships which they had been accustomed to for a century and a half, the opposition to congressional control over initial settlement came almost wholly from New England[70]. Although the South had traditionally favored an individualized system of land allotments whereby the most desirable land was claimed under individual warrants before it was surveyed, the strongest support for congressional controls during the first stage of settlement came from the Southern delegates—notably Stone and Chase of Maryland, Mercer of Virginia, Spaight of North Carolina, and Read of South Carolina[71]. Despite the fact that the introduction of a large number of western states would work to the advantage of the agrarian South rather than maritime New England, Southern delegates were the most insistent of all in reducing the number of states to be created in the Northwest[72]. And, although the Eastern delegates seemed to favor the extraction of revenue from the West, they stubbornly opposed the creation of even a small force of 1,000 Continentals for the protection of commissioners who were negotiating land cessions from the Indians[73].

Such apparent incongruities testified to the lingering impact of the division between the Nationalists and their opponents during the previous year. Although fiscal centralism had been defeated, and although Congress was safely removed from Philadelphia, most members of the Eastern party were still suspicious of any measure that tended toward consolidation. The Rhode Islanders, Howell and Ellery, were the most adamantly parochial New Englanders. Their conduct so provoked the Southerners that the Southern party tried to expel them from Congress on the grounds that their terms had expired in March under the three-year rule of the Articles. Although the attempt was unsuccessful, John Francis Mercer contended that Howell, the most notorious of the Eastern parochialists, had no right to speak or vote in Congress. Richard Spaight and Mercer, two hot-blooded members of the Southern party, went so far as to challenge Howell to a duel, but Howell scornfully laid their written challenges before Congress[74]. Such heated controversy had to do with a whole range of issues, including the impost, commercial regulations, the appointment of foreign ministers, the location of Congress, and the convening of the Committee of the States, but it also had incongruous results in debates over the organization of the West.

There were two basic dimensions to the problem of the West—the political organization of the territories and the survey and sale of the land. The debates over the survey and sale of land, the second dimension, provided a more accurate reflection of the true positions of the Southern and Eastern parties than did the discussion of political organization. Southerners were accustomed to an individualized mode of land development whereby they secured warrants for a certain amount of land which they subsequently surveyed and claimed. This system naturally led to rather rapid expansion, since the better lands were claimed and the poorer lands were left unoccupied. New Englanders, on the other hand, had a corporate tradition of settlement whereby new lands were surveyed and organized as townships before they were occupied. The township was settled at the outset by a group rather than by a succession of individuals. The New England practice was more orderly, stressed constraint rather than liberality in the distribution of land, and tended naturally to inhibit rapid dispersion of settlements.

The famous Ordinance of 1785, which laid out the method of survey and sale of the public domain, was a compromise between these two traditions, but it was a compromise that favored the New England rather than the Southern practice. As originally set forth on April 30, 1784, in a report from a committee chaired by Jefferson, that had not been so true, for Jefferson's plan called for the organization of rather large units called "hundreds" in which a purchaser could locate a claim by lot number before the lines were actually run and marked. Jefferson's plan allowed sale either by "hundreds" or by lots of a square mile, with the sale to take place in the West under the direction of congressionally appointed registrars—one for each of the new states[75]. Congress rejected the plan on May 28, and the matter was not taken up again until March of 1785, when reports from commissioners who had been appointed to negotiate with the Indians seemed encouraging. On March 16, a grand committee was formed to prepare a new plan, which was reported on April 12 by William Grayson of Virginia.

Although Grayson coordinated the recommendation of the committee, its substance was remarkably similar to the Eastern tradition. Jefferson's hundreds were replaced by townships measuring 7 square miles, later reduced to 6 square miles—less than one-third the size of the hundred[76]. The unit of sale was to be the township (rather than allowing the settler to purchase a lot if he wished), and only four "ranges," or north-south series of townships, were to be surveyed and sold at the outset. (This was later extended to seven ranges.) All land had to be surveyed before it was sold, so Congress supported the New England mode of orderly gradual expansion. Logically, the first ranges were located in southeastern Ohio along the borders of Pennsylvania and Virginia. Lands were reserved for military veterans, and in each township one section, or square mile, was reserved for the support of education and religion—a provision probably urged by Rufus King, who wrote to Elbridge Gerry that the ordinance "bears strong features of an eastern System" which he believed had "some merit"[77].

The extent to which Congress had departed from the liberal philosophy of Jefferson and Madison was evident in Madison's astonished reaction to the provision for the support of religion. He wrote to Monroe, "How a regulation so unjust in itself, so foreign to the Authority of Congress, so hurtful to the sale of public land, and smelling so strongly of an antiquated Bigotry, could have received the countenance of a Committee is truly a matter of astonishment"[78]. Grayson, who really had to shoulder the responsibility for the provision more than Monroe (who nonetheless supported the provision in two votes on April 23[79]) explained to Washington the argument of the clause's proponents, who had apparently convinced him of the necessity of the resolution: "The idea of a township with the temptation of a support for religion and education, holds forth an inducement for neighborhoods of the same religious sentiments to confederate for the purpose of purchasing and settling together" [80]. The clause in the ordinance providing support for religion was struck down as the result of a parliamentary maneuver led by Ellery of Rhode Island, but most Southerners continued to endorse this strikingly antique mode of corporate settlement[81]. It is likely that many delegates from the South and the Middle states were willing to compromise on settlement policy in order to attract presumably solid, governable citizens from New England, and perhaps from abroad[82].

But while the Southerners were willing to yield to the New Englanders regarding schools and religion, they were adamantly opposed to the sale of land exclusively by townships. After long debates, which Grayson contended would fill forty volumes[83], a compromise was reached whereby every other township would be sold in sections, that is, in lots of 640 acres. Thus were regional traditions merged in the Ordinance of 1785—the most enduring legislation yet passed by the Confederation Congress.

VI

In the wake of the failure of the Nationalist program of fiscal centralism, there were two avenues toward national consolidation during the mid-eighties. One was the regulation of commerce, and the other was the development of the West. The South, above all Virginia, had the most direct interest in both of those opportunities. The North was vitally interested in commercial treaties, but that interest did not necessarily coincide with the desires of the South to emancipate itself from its subservience to England and to develop a more balanced economy. This was one reason why the Southern delegations were so adamant about having a representative from their region abroad to participate in commercial negotiations. The North also was interested in western expansion, but the most energetic thrust into the West was emanating from Virginia and North Carolina, whose trans-Allegheny populations were rapidly approaching readiness for statehood. (And two additional states from the region south of the Ohio would improve the weight of the South in Congress, as many delegates were aware.) Even to the north of the Ohio the Virginia bounty lands as well as the general drift of population toward the accessible reaches of the river almost guaranteed a substantial Virginian influence during the early stages of settlement in the national domain. Thus, the Southern party could entice settlement from the Northeast by compromising in the Ordinance of 1785, especially since the populating of the Ohio region would improve the chances for the commercialization of the Potomac.

It was from this set of circumstances that the seemingly incongruous nationalism of the South and parochialism of New England arose. When Congress adjourned in June of 1784, the Committee of the States which was to serve in its absence was sabotaged by the Eastern representatives. Despite the fact that the South had opposed the designation of Trenton as the place in which Congress would meet in the fall of 1784, there were only four states in attendance when Congress was supposed to begin its session in November—and all four were Southern states[84]. Spaight was convinced that the Eastern states were so intent upon weakening the Union that they would shortly break the Confederation. John Mercer urged Jacob Read, who had chastised the New Englanders for endangering the "Peace and Glory of their Country" when they deserted the Committee of the States, to come to Trenton when Congress reconvened. They could at that time determine the temper of the next Congress and possibly hold together a confederation "now grown as contemptible as she ought to be respectable." Mercer went on to suggest that "if the present system won't do, some other ought." Since they were returning to their home states, they might "be useful in putting into execution any plan previously formed" [85].

Still, one of the great strengths of the Virginia blend of commercial regulation and agrarian expansion was that it could operate within the confines of the Articles of Confederation. Unfortunately, these two major props of the new nationalism being hammered out by the Virginians were turned against each other in the most exquisite fashion in 1786. It was then that John Jay who replaced Robert R. Livingston as Minister of Foreign Affairs, attempted to secure a commercial treaty with Spain in exchange for the sacrifice of American rights to the navigation of the Mississippi.

Notes

1 PCC, no. 174.

2 The most acidulous assessment of Mercer was by his colleague, Jefferson, who called him a man of vanity and ambition, whose objects and means were impure. Jefferson to Madison, Apr. 25, 1784. Julian Boyd (ed.), *The Papers of Thomas Jefferson* (Princeton, 1950–), VII, 119.

3 See Charles Sydnor, *Gentlemen Freeholders; Political Practices in Washington's Virginia* (Chapel Hill, 1952).

4 David Howell to _____, Feb. 20, 1785, *LMCC*, VIII, 38.

5 Forrest McDonald calls Pettit a brilliant financial operator in *E Pluribus Unum* (Boston, 1965), p. 49.

6 Melancton Smith, who proposed sixteen resolutions resulting in roll calls, can be cited as an exception, although in comparison with the thirty-seven motions of the intrepid Gouverneur Morris or the thirty-four resolutions of the crafty Duane, the general impression of a more subdued New York delegation must stand. This is, of course, not the only index of influence, though it is suggestive.

7 Hugh Williamson to James Duane, June 8, 1784, *LMCC*, VII, 547.

8 John Bayard to Samuel Bayard, Dec. 1, 1785, ibid., VIII, 267.

9 Jefferson to Madison, Feb. 20, 1784, ibid., VII, 450.

10 John Scott to Arthur Lee, Aug. 20, 1783, Arthur Lee Papers, HCL.

11 Samuel Hardy to Patrick Henry, Aug. 28, 1785, *LMCC*, VIII, 203–204.

12 New York delegates to Governor George Clinton, Oct. 16, 1783, ibid., VII, 340n.

13 Theodore Sedgwick, writing from Sheffield, told Peter Van Rensselaer of a rage for emigration during the spring of 1784. Sedgwick to Peter Van Rensselaer, Apr. 6, 1784, Emmet Collection, NYPL.

14 JCC, XXXIII, 623.

15 Julius Pratt, "John Armstrong, Jr.," *DAB,* I, 355–358; Matthew Griswold to John Dickinson, Dec. 20, 1784; Griswold to the President of the Continental Congress, Dec. 24, 1784, *PA,* ser. 1, XI, 447, 451; Hugh Williamson to John Dickinson, Jan. 14, 1785, *LMCC,* VIII, 6; Charles Pettit to Jeremiah Wadsworth, May 27, 1786, ibid., 368.

16 See, for example, the votes of June 1784, *JCC,* XXVII, 516, 517, 520, 521, 522.

17 E. James Ferguson, *The Power of the Purse* (Chapel Hill, 1961), pp. 184–185, 206–208, *JCC,* XXVIII, 167.

18 Hugh Williamson to Governor Alexander Martin, Sept. 30, 1784, *LMCC,* VII, 595.

19 Ferguson, *The Power of the Purse,* pp. 215–219.

20 See, e.g., the votes in *JCC,* XXIX, 548, 579, 581, 587, 708, 714, 750, 755, 758, 761.

21 Rufus King to Timothy Pickering, May 8, 1785, *LMCC,* VIII, 114.

22 James Monroe to James Madison, May 13, 1786, ibid., 377.

23 Ferguson, *The Power of the Purse,* pp. 205–206.

24 Ibid., pp. 221–227.

25 *JCC,* XXVI, 191, 194–195, 306.

26 Ibid., XIX, 768–769; Ferguson, *The Power of the Purse,* p. 225.

27 Ibid., pp. 227–228.

28 Ibid., chap. 11.

29 *JCC,* XXVI, 318.

30 Ibid., 319.

31 Ibid., 320.

32 Ibid., 322.

33 Ibid., 344.

34 Ibid., 345, 347.

35 A group of Boston merchants petitioned Congress for immediate action on May 11, 1785; King wrote to Gerry on May 19, of uneasiness among merchants and traders throughout the states (*LMCC,* VIII, 121). See also John Habersham to Joseph Clay, June 24, ibid., 151–152.

36 Rufus King to Elbridge Gerry, May 19, 1785, ibid., 121.

37 Monroe to Jefferson, June 16, 1785, ibid., 143.

38 Jefferson to Monroe, Aug. 28, 1785, in Boyd (ed.), *Papers of Jefferson,* VIII, 445; Monroe to Jefferson, Jan. 19, 1786, *LMCC,* VIII, 285–286.

39 Richard Henry Lee to James Madison, Aug. 11, 1785, ibid., 181.

40 James McHenry to George Washington, Aug. 14, 1785, ibid., 183.

41 David Howell to Governor William Greene, Oct. 29, 1785, ibid., 244.

42 Monroe to Jefferson, Aug. 15, 1785, ibid., 187; Rufus King to Elbridge Gerry, May 1, ibid., 108.

43 *Resolves of the General Court. . . . Begun May 25, 1785* (Boston, 1785), pp. 18, 31, 476; *Acts and Laws . . . of Massachusetts,* May–July 1785, pp. 289–291.

44 The Massachusetts delegates to Governor Bowdoin, Sept. 3, 1785, *LMCC,* VIII, 208.

45 Ibid., 209.

46 Jack M. Sosin, *The Revolutionary Frontier, 1763-1783* (New York, 1967), pp. 131–133; Thomas P. Abernethy, *Western Lands and the American Revolution* (New York, 1937), p. 254. James Madison advocated more courts, a separate tax depository, a separate militia, and other concessions to pacify the Kentuckians. Madison to Edmund Pendleton, Oct. 2, 1781, in William T. Hutchinson and William M. E. Rachal (eds.), *The Papers of James Madison* (Chicago, 1962-), III, 274.

47 See especially the votes in *JCC,* XXV, 591, 592, 595, 596.

48 George Washington to James Duane, Sept. 7, 1783, in John C. Fitzpatrick (ed.), *The Writings of George Washington* (39 vols.; Washington, D.C., 1931-1944), XXVII, 133-140.

49 New York delegates to Governor George Clinton, Sept. 19, 1783, *LMCC,* VII, 300-301.

50 Robert F. Berkhofer, Jr., "Jefferson, the Ordinance of 1784, and the Origins of the American Territorial System," *WMQ,* ser. 3, XXIX (April 1972), 231-262, convincingly demonstrates that Jefferson's role in the formulation of the ordinance has been exaggerated by historians. Berkhofer also contends that there is less disparity than has been generally assumed between the assumptions that guided congressmen who framed the Ordinance of 1784 and those of the Ordinance of 1787 which replaced it. I have drawn upon Berkhofer's essay while interpreting the evolution of the territorial system in the context of the partisan politics of Congress. Accordingly, there are occasional differences in emphasis between his essay and the treatment below.

51 *JCC,* XXV, 564.

52 Berkhofer, "Origins of the American Territorial System," 236-242.

53 *JCC,* XXV, 591, XXVI, 117. Indeed, George Morgan, agent for the Pennsylvania-based Indiana Company, found it convenient to operate out of New Jersey in 1784. See his petition for the Indiana claim which was delivered under the auspices of New Jersey in ibid., 111, 116. Between April 19 and 21, on ten votes concerning the Ordinance of 1784 for the organization of the West, there were seven instances of agreement and three of disagreement between the Pennsylvania and Virginia delegations. On the closely

related matter of designation of ministers abroad, Pennsylvania supported the Southern desire for regional representation on all of four votes on May 5. It was primarily finance that accounted for the separation of Pennsylvania and Virginia in the bloc structure. On eight votes dealing with finance between April 22 and 28, the two delegations agreed only twice. The same tendency obtained in 1785. On the voting on the Ordinance of 1785 between April 23 and June 6, Pennsylvania and Virginia agreed on ten of thirteen votes. Between July 18 and September 26 they agreed on only nine of twenty six votes dealing with finance. (These tabulations are from roll-call votes included in the bloc analysis and thus exclude votes in which there was less than 10 percent overall disagreement. A tabulation of all votes might show even a slightly higher agreement between the two states.

54 David Howell to Deputy Governor Jabez Bowen, Apr. 12, 1784, in William R. Staples, *Rhode Island in the Continental Congress,* (Providence, 1870), p. 488.

55 Howell to Bowen, May 31, 1784, in ibid., p. 517.

56 Berkhofer, "Origins of the American Territorial System," 243-244.

57 Howell to Jonathan Arnold, Feb. 21, 1784, in Staples, *Rhode Island in the Continental Congress,* p. 479. Astraea was the goddess of innocence and purity who had left earth to take her place among the stars as the constellation Virgo.

58 As appointed on October 15, 1783, the committee was originally composed of Madison, Duane, and Samuel Huntington (*JCC,* XXV, 694-695). On December 18 the committee was fused with another charged with the regulation of Indian trade, first appointed the same day. Subsequently, there were changes in membership on January 7 (PCC, Committee Book No. 186) resulting in the committee composed of Jefferson, Howell, and Jeremiah Chase of Maryland.

59 Jefferson to Washington, Mar. 15, 1784, in Boyd (ed.), *Papers of Jefferson,* VII, 25-27.

60 Monroe to Jefferson, Nov. 1, 1784, in ibid., 459-462; Monroe to Horatio Gates, Aug. 19, 1784, Emmet Collection, NYPL; Harry Ammon, *James Monroe; the Quest for National Identity* (New York, 1971), pp. 45-48.

61 Samuel Hardy to Benjamin Harrison, Apr. 30, 1784, in Boyd (ed.), *Papers of Jefferson,* VII, 25-27.

62 Jefferson to Madison, Apr. 25, 1784, *LMCC,* VII, 501. Lee and Benjamin Lincoln were chosen to fill the places of Stephen Higginson and Nathanael Green, who declined. The commission was thus made up of Oliver Wolcott, Richard Butler, George Rogers Clark, Lincoln, and Lee. See *JCC* for Feb. 6 and 10; Mar. 2-8, 12, and 19; Apr. 6, 7, 23, and 24; May 18; June 3; July 10.

63 Lee bought six sections for which he paid $3,205.40. PCC Misc. Papers, 1770-1789, no. 59, vol. III.

64 William Grayson to H. N. Shiell, Mar. 30, 1784. Emmet Collection, NYPL. Grayson was writing from Virginia at the time.

65 *JCC,* XXVI, 118–119.

66 Ibid.

67 Ibid., 247.

68 Ibid., 250.

69 David Howell to Jonathan Arnold, Feb. 21, 1784, in Staples, *Rhode Island in the Continental Congress,* p. 479.

70 The crucial vote was on April 21, 1784, *JCC,* XXVI, 259.

71 The pattern was established in a series of four votes, ibid., 249, 259, 275. Read was the strongest advocate of congressional controls.

72 Ibid., 391–393.

73 Ibid., XXVII, 434–435.

74 Ibid., 386, 409, 413, 415–417, 424; PCC, no. 78, fol. 311.

75 The original report was produced by a committee composed of Jefferson, Hugh Williamson, David Howell, Gerry, and Jacob Read. It can be found in ibid., no. 19, fol. 469, in the writing of Jacob Read. It is inserted in the *JCC* under April 30, XXVI, 324–330.

76 Jefferson used the geographic mile of 60,894/10 feet, a minute of latitude, rather than the statute mile used in the ordinance. Thus his square mile lot included 8,504/10 acres rather than 640 acres.

77 King to Gerry, May 8, 1785, *LMCC,* VIII, 113. See E. C. Burnett, *The Continental Congress* (New York, 1941), p. 623, for the probable role of King. See also Robert Ernst, *Rufus King: American Federalist* (Chapel Hill, 1968), p. 56.

78 James Madison to James Monroe, May 29, 1785, in Gaillard Hunt (ed.), *The Writings of James Madison* (9 vols.; New York, 1900–1910), II, 145.

79 *JCC,* XXVIII, 294, 295.

80 Grayson to Washington, Apr. 15, 1785, *LMCC,* VIII, 95.

81 While a majority of the members of Congress endorsed the provision, when Ellery moved the question "shall the clause stand?" the supporters were not able to muster the votes of seven states. *JCC,* XXVIII, 295.

82 Grayson commented to William Short that the sale of western lands would lower taxes and induce immigration from abroad and that "the want of inhabitants is perhaps our only calamity." Grayson to Short, June 15, 1785, Gratz Collection, HSP.

83 William Grayson to Timothy Pickering, Apr. 27, 1785, *LMCC,* VIII, 106.

84 Richard Spaight to Governor Alexander Martin, Oct. 16, 1784; Samuel Hardy to Governor Benjamin Harrison, Nov. 7, 1784, ibid., VII, 602–603, 607–608.

85 John Mercer to Jacob Read, Sept. 23, 1784, ibid., 591.

14 The Crisis of the Confederation

THE year 1786 was to prove the undoing of the Confederation. This was not because of the postwar depression, sometimes cited as the crisis which stimulated the Constitutional Convention. As Merrill Jensen has pointed out, the economy of the nation was on the mend by the latter half of 1786, precisely the time that the politics of the Confederation took a radically new twist[*1*]. New markets were being established in Europe and China; the trade of the Middle states was accelerating; Southern agriculture was improving. The New England states were experiencing difficulty in adjusting to the postwar economic conditions, it is true, yet the strongest pressure and the most concerted organization leading to the Philadelphia Convention came from Virginia, not Massachusetts. Indeed, if a cause-effect relationship is to be established between economic distress and the movement toward the Constitutional Convention, it would be negative rather than positive[*2*].

Rather than succumbing to the Four Horsemen of the Apocalypse, the Confederation seemed to be slowly sinking from want of attention. At the beginning of the new federal year, November 1, only ten members were in attendance at the meeting place of Congress in New York City. A quorum was not established until November 23, and from then until the end of December there were only ten days when Congress was able to transact business. During the whole winter there were seldom more than seven states in attendance, a number sufficient to hold sessions, but to pass only minor measures. Even with the appearance of the nine states necessary for the passage of a major act, unanimity was necessary. Nathaniel Gorham, the staunch nationalist who had served during the early eighties, commented disgustedly in March that "we feel all the inconveniences of the liberum Veto of a Polish Diet"[3].

The attendance problem was inherent in the congressional practice of sitting throughout the year. Most delegates had business and professional responsibilities that required periodic attention. While the problems facing Congress seemed of sufficient magnitude to demand constant application, in all likelihood more would have been accomplished with full attendance during shorter sessions.

Yet another difficulty of a much more fundamental nature was cited by Nathaniel Gorham. He was convinced that equal representation of large and small states encouraged delinquency. If the large states could expect a voice commensurate with their population or wealth, and if a majority of a quorum were established for the passage of legislation, the large states would maintain a representation to seek their interests. (Presumably the small states would be certain to be present to defend theirs[4].) This was not a characteristic reformist notion in Congress, but it does indicate that some centralists were thinking in terms of the Virginia Plan presented at the Constitutional Convention well before May of 1787.

Because of the poor attendance and other problems, many delegates feared an impending crisis. The Connecticut delegates Stephen Mix Mitchell and William Samuel Johnson wrote to Governor Matthew Griswold in April of 1786:

> Our affairs seem to indicate the approach of some great crisis. Our Trade in a very distracted situation, Britain watching for some opportune season to revenge her smarts, the fickle Indian nations ready to join those who best can supply their wants and jealous of the approach of the Americans so near their Territories, the states unwilling or neglecting to adopt almost any one Measure which can be proposed to them by Congress so as to act jointly and efficaciously for mutual Benefit[5].

The Connecticut delegates mentioned only the foreign problems (which were in some respects the most serious). For other delegates, domestic problems of finance were the most traumatic. As Henry Lee wrote to Washington, "Our foederal distresses gather fast to a point"[6]. What troubled Lee was serious indeed. New Jersey had refused to grant even "a shilling" for the requisition passed in September of 1785 until New York passed the impost, citing her own distress, the discriminatory trade policy of New York, and the latter state's refusal to grant the impost of 1783 in the manner recommended by Congress [7]. It was possible for delegates to sympathize with New Jersey's plight and even to hope as Lee did that her action would have a salutary effect on New York. Nonetheless, outright refusal to honor a congressional requisition (as opposed to negligible compliance, which had already occurred often enough) could not be ignored without imperiling the foundation of the Confederation.

Congress decided in early March to send a delegation composed of some of its most able members, Charles Pinckney, William Grayson, and Nathaniel Gorham, to appeal to the New Jersey Assembly (a tactic that would be used later in September to persuade Pennsylvania to comply more fully with the impost)[8]. The youthful and talented delegate from South Carolina made the most effective address, to judge from contemporary accounts. Pinckney appealed to New Jersey's sense of honor, which required that she attempt to fulfill her contractual obligations to the Confederation, to the public creditors and to the retired soldiers. Cleverly, he suggested as well that New Jersey had a stake in the present structure of the Confederation, which protected small states while according them equal representation. Finally raising the specter of democracy and anarchy, Pinckney and his fellow emissaries convinced the Legislature to rescind its resolution of February 20[9]. New Jersey did not, however, pass an appropriation for the 1785 requisition.

By this time there was talk about a collapse of the Confederation[10]. Charles Pettit, a Constitutionalist opponent of Robert Morris and architect of the state system of servicing the public debt in Pennsylvania, sounded the alarm with as much fervor as a dedicated nationalist. Referring to the separate fiscal and commercial policies of the states, which were "pursuing their own whimsical Schemes of dangerous Experiment, regardless of federal System, and destroying their own Strength by intoxicating draughts of Liberty run mad . . . ," as well as the failure of the states to maintain their delegations in Congress, Pettit remarked that he saw disaster in the midst of what seemed to him an unaccountable national euphoria:

> Is it possible that a great political System, however wisely formed, can be preserved and well conducted in this Manner? And yet we seem to be as supinely inattentive to our own Dangerous Situation as a flock of Sheep on their way to a Slaughter Pen. This is not an exaggerated Description of our internal Disorder, which is hastening our Political Existence to destruction, like a spreading Mortification under the lulling influence of an Opiate[11].

If the states seemed unconcerned about the plight of the nation, the same could not be said of the members of Congress—at least those delegates who attended. On May 3, Pinckney moved that Congress form itself into a committee of the whole to consider the state of the Union. Pinckney made it clear that the committee should recommend a convention to revise the Articles[12]. There was resistance to a convention from influential congressional leadership, however. Grayson thought it would be better to cope with familiar ills "than fly to others we know not of," while at the same time recognizing the serious weakness of the federal government—a sentiment penned in the wake of New Jersey's defiance of the 1785 requisition. Nathan Dane of Massachusetts was against any thorough revision, as was Rufus King, who steadfastly contended that reports that Congress and the Confederation were powerless were exaggerated[13]. Grayson wondered if Pinckney knew what he was bargaining for in recommending a convention. Writing to Madison, he commented, "Mr. Pinckney . . . will be astounded when he meets with a proposition to prevent the States from importing any more of the seed of Cain. . . ." Likewise, New York and Pennsylvania would "feel themselves indisposed" when a Potomac location for Congress was suggested. New Jersey and Delaware would be alarmed at the subject of representation which the large states would insist on taking up. Grayson wrote these speculations in part to dissuade Madison from making the upcoming conference on trade at Annapolis to which all the states were invited into the sort of constitutional convention Pinckney had urged. Nothing "decisive" should come out of the Annapolis Convention, for in that event Massachusetts would break away from the reform movement[14]. It is interesting that Grayson perceived the Annapolis meeting as an affair of the Middle region, yet another indication of the Virginia tendency to link with a core area.

Pinckney's proposal to consider the state of the Union did prompt the appointment of a grand committee on July 3 charged with the task of preparing amendments granting Congress sufficient power to serve the ends for which it was instituted[15]. Pinckney was on the committee and probably was primarily responsible for the recommendations it presented on August 7 in the form of seven articles to be added to the Confederation. They called essentially for the plan previously endorsed by Monroe and the Virginians granting powers of foreign and interstate commercial regulation, with revenue reserved to the states. In addition, the committee recommended that Congress should forcibly collect requisitions from the states. The latter provision was as interesting as it now seems cumbersome, calling as it did for various stages of congressional intervention and punishment of recalcitrant states. If a state did not pay up within a specified period, a penalty of 10 percent would be added to its quota. If a state still refused, the Congress might by-pass the state authorities and use the collection agents of the state to gather the money. If the state agents were uncooperative, Congress might use its own appointees. Opposition would be considered a breach of the federal compact. The recommendations also called for the creation of a federal court of seven justices representing the various parts of the Confederation; this court would receive appeals from state courts in cases involving foreign citizens and matters of a federal nature.

Cumbersome and inadequate as the plan might seem by comparison with the Constitution formulated the next year, it was a set of proposals which answered most of the specific difficulties experienced at the time. Presuming that such a set of amendments could win the unanimous support of the states, it is conceivable that Pinckney's plan would have been a workable form of confederation. Further, it would have been impossible to go without altering the mode of representation. Truly centralist plans such as Hamilton's fiscal system would in all likelihood have been impossible because of an additional provision that any financial plan would have to be approved by eleven states, or by eleven-thirteenths of any larger number of states in the future.

Speculation regarding the feasibility of the plan is idle, however, for it was virtually ignored—notwithstanding the fact that it was the most ambitious revision contemplated by Congress thus far. The reason for this upstaging was the shattering impact of the negotiations between John Jay, Secretary for Foreign Affairs, and Don Diego de Gardoqui, Spanish Minister to the United States with the title *Encargado de Negocios*[16].

II

Confederation diplomacy was troubled by a number of problems, including Britain's refusal to evacuate the Northwest posts and her discrimination against American trade, and also by difficulties with Spain. That nation refused to accept the 31° boundary between the United States and Spanish Florida agreed upon at Paris. She also denied United States rights to the navigation of the Mississippi. Indeed, by July 22, 1784, Spain closed the Mississippi to American commerce[17]. This naturally upset settlers and investors in the trans-Appalachian counties of North Carolina and Virginia and they demanded that Congress force Spain to reopen the Mississippi. Congress failed to persuade Spain to alter her policy—a failure that prompted some Westerners to consider separation from the United States to gain the protection of Spain. Nor was this all. Some opportunists such as James Wilkinson sought to take advantage of the main chance in the turbulent politics of the West—a mixture of land speculation, Indian trade and conflicts, contemplated expeditions against the Spanish, and intrigue with agents of both England and Spain[18].

Congress's problem with the West was not eased in the slightest by the arrival of Gardoqui in the summer of 1785. The Spanish Minister was empowered to negotiate a treaty of commerce but was instructed to stand firm on the boundary and the navigation of the Mississippi. Indeed, his mission was to secure United States recognition of Spanish claims on both counts. John Jay, commissioned as Secretary for Foreign Affairs to negotiate for the United States, was severely restricted. Not only could he enter into no agreement without prior consent of Congress; he was also required to convey in writing to Congress all proposals by him and Gardoqui during the negotiations. Jay was distressed at this, protesting "it is very seldom thought necessary to leave nothing at all to [a minister's] . . . discretion; for where that ought to be the case, the man ought not to be employed"[*19*]. The limitation of Jay's authority was perhaps due in part to the fact that Congress was for once physically able to supervise the negotiations being conducted in New York, but doubtless the major reason was the extraordinarily sensitive nature of the western question. Jay's own disposition probably caused little alarm at that point. Of all American negotiators he had once been the most pleasing to the South—the region most concerned about the West. Congress did remove the clause which so offended Jay, but in doing so it defined his instructions more precisely. He was to "stipulate the right of the United States to their territorial bounds, and the free Navigation of the Mississippi, from the source to the Ocean . . ."[*20*].

The Mississippi clause was in utter opposition to Gardoqui's instructions. The negotiations stalled, so that in early 1786 Gardoqui urged Jay to convey Spain's position on the Mississippi as soon as a sufficient representation had assembled in Congress[*21*]. Jay complied on May 29, suggesting to Congress that a committee be appointed to instruct and direct him on all subjects relative to the treaty. Ominously, he hinted at difficulties so important as to require secrecy for the present[*22*].

Jay was cryptic enough in his dispatch, but Monroe quickly surmised his intent. Writing partly in cipher to Madison, he commented, "It was immediately perceiv'd that the object was to relieve him from the instruction respecting the Mississippi and to get a committee to cover the measure." Monroe went on to describe the debates and proceedings in detail for Madison, who would himself become involved in the Jay-Gardoqui affair. Rufus King, "who is associated in this business," said Monroe, tested the disposition of Congress by deprecating the tendency of the United States to rely on France. Monroe noted in conclusion that King, Pettit, and himself were appointed to a committee to confer with Jay[*23*].

The effect of Jay's maneuver to secure new instructions, for Monroe was precisely correct, was to clarify hitherto ambivalent attitudes held by a number of important Virginians toward the West. Monroe, who previously doubted the allegiance of western settlers to the Union, and who had agreed with Jefferson and other Virginians that projects to nationalize the Articles of Confederation should be brought to full term before the admission of new western states, now sympathized with western development.

Monroe was not the only Virginian who felt constrained to shift position. Henry Lee had been even more of a constrictionist. Vitally interested in navigation of the Potomac, he actually favored giving up the Mississippi navigation in order to secure the commercial benefits of the treaty for the Atlantic states[*24*]. James Madison and George Washington also had been chary of the negative influence of new Western states on proposals for federal reform[*25*]. Yet by mid-June Madison was chastising Jay's diplomacy as "short-sighted" and "dishonorable," as "a voluntary barter in time of profound peace of the rights of one part of the empire to the interests of another part"[26]. Henry Lee, while still seeing commercial advantage in the treaty, voted consistently against it. It is true the Virginia delegates were so instructed by their legislature, but Lee also warned that giving up the Mississippi navigation might well cause such an adverse reaction that no amendment of the Articles of Confederation would be possible[27].

Such shifts of opinion were merely symptomatic of the profound effect of the Jay-Gardoqui negotiations upon congressional politics. No single issue during the entire Confederation era produced such a rigid and pervasive cleavage in Congress. Indeed, when rumors of the tendency of the negotiations reached Congress, Northern and Southern delegations separated on a broad spectrum of issues, some related to the question of the West, others not at all. When it was proposed that funds be appropriated for an Indian campaign on the Ohio, for example, there was a strong sectional division between North and South (although Pennsylvania in this instance supported the Southern desire to reduce the Indians). When the question of credits to be applied to the South Carolina quota arose, division between the North and the South was more pronounced than was usual on financial matters. There was less cleavage on the question of congressional action toward states (especially New York) which had not yet ratified the impost in the manner prescribed by Congress, but when the issue of the instructions to Jay came directly before Congress in early August, it was as if a white-hot iron were laid upon congressional deliberations. As can be seen from Table 25, the ever-present sectional thrust of partisan politics suddenly and menacingly took shape as a North-South cleavage. Delaware was absent, almost as if to dramatize the exquisite dilemma of her border position. With the exception of the first vote cast by Arthur St. Clair, who had just arrived in Congress as a delegate from Pennsylvania, and three votes cast by William Few of Georgia, Northerners and Southerners opposed each other with perfect consistency[28].

Although in some ways this episode was a reenactment of the struggles of 1779 over the fisheries and Mississippi navigation rights in the definition of American peace terms, voting in 1779 had never been so rigidly sectional. Clearly the Jay-Gardoqui question had some transcendent quality which polarized party politics.

Jay defended the treaty in a speech to Congress on August 3. He contended that a commercial treaty with Spain was more advantageous to the United States than any treaty with any other nation could possibly be. Spain consumed more than she exported and thus was forced to settle her accounts with specie from her American mines. The United States could secure a share of this specie, but only through a treaty, for Spain would not otherwise allow American merchants into the trade. The Spanish Crown had influence with the

TABLE 25

Voting by States on the Impost, Finance, Indian Affairs, and Jay-Gardoqui Negotiations, June 29–Sept. 1, 1786

	8 I	9 I	10 I	11 I	12 I	26 F	27 F	28 F	29 F	30 F	37 P	38 P
N.H.	X	N	S	N	N	N	N	N	N	N	N	S
Mass.	N	X	N	N	N	N	N	N	N	S	N	S
R.I.	N	N	S	S	N	N	N	N	S	S	N	S
Conn.		O	O	O	O	X	N	X	X	X	S	N
N.Y.	N	N	N	N	N	N	N	N	N	X	X	N
N.J.	X	N	X	N	N	N	X	N	S	S	N	S
Pa.	N	N	X	S	N	N	N	N	S	S	S	N
Del.	O	O	O	O	O	O	O	O	O	O	O	O
Md.	S	X	S	S	N	N	S	S	N	S	N	S
Va.	S	S	S	S	S	S	S	S	X	S	X	N
N.C.	S	S	S	S	S	S	S	S	X	X	N	S
S.C.	S	S	S	S	S	S	S	S	N	S	N	S
Ga.	S	N	S	S	S	S	S	S	X	S	X	X

*Numbers refer to listing of votes in Lord's Atlas of roll calls (C1408–C1459).

CODE:
N = Northern position; X = split vote; S = Southern position; O = absent; I = vote dealing with Indian affairs, F = vote dealing with finance (quotas, credits); P = vote dealing with measures toward states not complying with impost; J = vote dealing with Jay-Gardoqui negotiations.

TOTAL:

	I	F	P	J
Northern Delegations	N–21	N–22	N–13	N–76
	X– 5	X– 6	X– 1	X– 1
	S– 4	S– 7	S–20	S– 0
Southern Delegations	S–22	S–18	S–12	S–52
	X– 1	X– 4	X– 5	X– 3
	N– 2	N– 3	N– 7	N– 0

Barbary powers and could be relied upon to use its good offices to improve American trading opportunities in the Mediterranean. Moreover, a treaty with Spain would open commerce with her European possessions and with her island possessions off Africa. The treaty promised perfect reciprocity for merchants of each nation, who would enjoy trading rights as if they were subjects of the other nation. Although the West Indies and South America were not included, commercial privileges in the Philippines and an annual shipment between

39	40	41	46	47	48	49	50	51	52	53	54	56	59*
P	P	P	J	J	J	J	J	J	J	J	J	J	J
S	N	S	N	N	N	N	N	N	N	N	N	N	N
S	N	S	N	N	N	N	N	N	N	N	N	N	N
S	N	S	N	N	N	N	N	N	N	N	N	N	N
S	S	S	N	N	N	N	N	N	N	N	N	N	N
N	S	N	N	N	N	N	N	N	N	N	N	N	N
S	N	S	N	N	N	N	N	N	N	N	N	N	N
S	S	X	X	N	N	N	N	N	N	N	N	N	N
O	O	O	O	O	O	O	O	O	O	O	O	O	O
S	N	S	S	S	S	S	S	S	S	S	S	S	S
S	S	S	S	S	S	S	S	S	S	S	S	S	S
S	N	S	S	S	S	S	S	S	S	S	S	S	S
S	N	S	S	S	S	S	S	S	S	S	S	S	S
S	X	X	X	X	S	S	S	X	S	S	S	S	S

Acapulco and the Philippines might be allowed. American manufactures and productions, with the important exception of tobacco, which Spain secured from her own American colonies, might be exported to Spain and her European possessions in either American or Spanish ships. Middle states foodstuffs, and above all New England fish, would find a ready market. Further, Spain was willing to buy her masts and timber for her armed forces from the United States, making payment in specie, so long as the price was not higher than she might be charged in Europe.

In exchange for these totally beneficial provisions (for the exclusion of tobacco did not involve a sacrifice, since tobacco was already prohibited on the Spanish market), Spain insisted that the American claim to navigation of the Mississippi below the southern border of the United States be given up for the life of the treaty—either twenty-five or thirty years. Jay contended that this was not presently an important question, there being only a trickle of commerce which would go down the river until the West was more extensively populated. It was idle to think that Spain would grant free navigation of the Mississippi; the King was adamant on the point. It could be obtained only by making war on Spain[29]. Thus Jay attempted to persuade Congress that ample benefits would accrue from temporarily giving up a claim which was of little consequence at the moment.

Whether or not Gardoqui, a cagey diplomat by any standard, was consciously intending to play sectional interests against each other (as Madison for one was convinced) is of less importance than the fact that this was precisely the result of the negotiation. New Englanders were elated about the proposed treaty. Rufus King assured Gerry that American fish and flour and other produce would find a new market. All the masts, spars, and timber for the Spanish marine would be bought in the United States with specie. The gold and silver of Acapulco would be within the reach of the United States[30]. The New Hampshire delegates were so committed to the treaty that Samuel Livermore stayed in New York to see the revision of Jay's instructions through Congress even though he was due back in New Hampshire to sit on the Superior Court[31].

While the treaty was perhaps most attractive to the New Englanders, Middle states delegates hoped for benefits as well from the carrying trade and the export of provisions. Arthur St. Clair of Pennsylvania further argued in debate on August 18 that even if the treaty was of particular advantage to one section, the benefits would ultimately accrue to the whole nation. "If one state gains an advantage by foreign commerce that is quickly communicated to the rest by internal intercourse." Admittedly, the treaty would inhibit settlement of the West, but this was an advantage, not a defect in the treaty. The Atlantic states were too thinly populated to develop agriculture, much less manufacturing[32]. John Cleves Symmes of New Jersey, a speculator in western lands, was less certain about the merits of the treaty. He considered the encouragement of a population committed to the fisheries of no greater national utility than a policy devoted to populating the West. The fisheries created a useless bachelor population which was a burden on the community in its old age. At the same time, Symmes believed a shorter twelve-year relinquishment of the right to navigate the Mississippi would hardly be catastrophic. A reduction in the number of land sales could be compensated for by higher prices[33].

Symmes's suggestion of a compromise twelve-year ban on navigation was not taken up because in addition to its being unacceptable to Spain, the South was adamantly opposed to any compromise of the free navigation of the river. Pinckney, Monroe, Grayson, and others deprecated the commercial benefits in the treaty, contending that it secured nothing that could not be obtained without it[34], but their prime grievance was that the treaty sacrificed the interests of one part of the Union for the presumed advantage of another. Grayson was especially emphatic: this would "weaken if not destroy the union by disaffecting the Southern States when they saw their dearest interests sacrificed and given up to obtain a trivial commercial advantage for their brethren in the East"[35]. The "occlusion" of the Mississippi "would destroy the hopes of the principal men in the S. States in establishing the future fortunes of their families," as well as ruin the West as a fund for the retirement of the public debt[36]. Pinckney emphasized that nature had decreed that the Westerners must either be future friends or enemies of the United States, and their posture would be entirely dependent upon congressional policy toward them[37]. James Monroe went further still. It was his conviction, conveyed to Patrick Henry, then Governor of Virginia, that the Eastern members of Congress in conjunction with Jay were actually intending to make settlement in the West so unattractive that people would either not move there or, if they did, separate from the Confederation. The immediate objectives were to hold the number of Southern states at their present level, to "throw the weight of population eastward and keep it there, to appreciate the vacant lands of New York and Massachusetts"[38]. Monroe may have been inclined to ascribe such motivation to the Easterners in part because of his own awareness of New York land values, for he had invested in Mohawk lands along with Madison[39].

Monroe's charge of "interested" motives on the part of the Easterners was symptomatic of the highly charged character of the divisions and debates in Congress. Jay's role was particularly offensive to the Southerners. As Monroe perceived it, the Massachusetts delegates Gorham, King, and Sedgwick were Jay's "instruments" on the floor of Congress. Timothy Bloodworth of North Carolina contended that "all reasoning fall prostrate before Interest"[40]. Previously an advocate for the South, Jay now was an apostate who manipulated sympathizers and violated the rules of the Confederation. Monroe called the request for a change of instructions "one of the most extraordinary transactions I have ever known, a minister negotiating expressly for the purpose of defeating the object of his instructions, and by a long train of intrigue and management seducing the representatives of the states to concur in it"[41]. Further, Jay and the Eastern party were so intent upon changing the instructions that they disregarded the normal requirement of nine votes for the formulation of diplomatic instructions, contending that an alteration of instructions needed only seven votes—precisely the number they were able to secure. The spectacle of a seven-state majority (the number necessary for routine business) validating what amounted to a change in the rules of the Confederation naturally provoked intense opposition from the Southerners. Timothy Bloodworth warned that the Union would be dissolved if seven states could carry the question[42]. Nonetheless, an effort by Charles Pinckney and James Monroe to disallow a new instruction on the grounds that it did not have the votes of nine states failed by the constant margin of seven to five which characterized all the proceedings connected with the Spanish treaty[43].

Southern protests were to no avail, and on August 29 Jay was instructed that he might yield navigation rights below the southern border of the United States for an unspecified amount of time if this seemed necessary to conclude the treaty[44]. This was not all. The Eastern party in effect locked up the decision through a procedural ruling advanced on August 31 and confirmed

on September 1 that when a question had been set aside by the previous question (as was true with attempts to alter the instruction) it might not be moved
again unless the same number of states was present[45]. The New Hampshire
delegation shortly took leave of Congress, Samuel Livermore presumably to
assume his duties on the New Hampshire Superior Court[46].

Such heavy-handed, not to say unfair, tactics caused Monroe to assume
that "the party especially Jay and the principal advocates" had gone too far
to retreat. "They must either carry the measure or be disgrac'd (as the principal
already hath been by the vote of 5. States), and sooner than suffer this they
will labour to break the Union"[47].

III

Monroe had sensed previously that a movement was afoot to establish a separate confederation in the Northern states. In his letter to Patrick Henry of
August 12 he asserted, "In conversations at which I have been present, the
Eastern people talk of a dismemberment so as to include Pena (in favor of
which I believe the present delegation Petit and Bayard who are under the
influence of eastern politicks would be) and sometimes all the states south
to the Potomack"[48]. Timothy Bloodworth of North Carolina later contended
that the Eastern strategy toward the treaty threatened to dissolve the Union;
Henry Lee voiced his alarm that "gentlemen talk so lightly of a separation
and dissolution of the Confederation"[49]. Such reflections were not the product of idle threats in heat of debate. Theodore Sedgwick wrote to Caleb Strong
in Massachusetts, "It well becomes the eastern and middle States, who are in
interest one, seriously to consider what advantages result to them from their
connection with the Southern States. They can give us nothing, as an equivalent for the protection which they derive from us but a participation in their
commerce. This they deny to us." (Sedgwick doubtless was referring to the
refusal of the Deep South to support a revision of Article 9 granting Congress
authority to regulate commerce.) "Even the appearance of a union cannot in
the way we now are long be preserved. It becomes us seriously to contemplate
a substitute; for if we do not controul events we shall be miserably controuled
by them"[50].

Perhaps thoughts of disunion were more pronounced in Congress than
in the states; they were nonetheless real. The bloc alignments for 1786 illustrate the dramatic impact of the Jay-Gardoqui negotiations and the seriousness
of the talk of disunion. During that year there was not a single delegate in
either the New England or the Southern delegations who joined the opposition
or isolated himself from his sectional party. Indeed, with the exception of
William Harrison of Maryland, every Southerner qualified as a core member

TABLE 26

Congressional Blocs, 1786

	Eastern Party	Southern Party
N.H.	Livermore	
	Long	
Mass.	Dane	
	King	
	Gorham*	
	Sedgwick*	
R.I.	Manning	
	Miller	
Conn.	Johnson*	
	Sturges*	
N.Y.	Haring	
	Smith	
N.J.	Cadwalader	
	Hornblower	
Pa.	Bayard*	
	St. Clair*	
Md.		Harrison*
		Henry
		Ramsey
Va.		Carrington
		Grayson
		Lee, H.
		Monroe
N.C.		Bloodworth
		White
S.C.		Bull
		Huger
		Parker
		Pinckney
Ga.		Few
		Houston

*Marginal membership.

Independents: Symmes (N.J.); Pettit (Pa.).

of the Southern party. While there was less cohesion in the Northern bloc, with six delegates ranked as fringe members and two as independents, the union between New England and the Middle states was unparalled in the history of Congress. Further, while Sedgwick was a fringe member and Pettit an independent, both were strong Northern parochialists. Only Symmes of New Jersey qualified as a true nonpartisan in the North, and even he voted consistently with the Eastern party on the Jay-Gardoqui question.

The South had little to fear from Jay's negotiations with Gardoqui. There was no way a treaty sacrificing the Mississippi navigation rights could be ratified in Congress. If the spirit of the Articles suggested that nine states had to assent to a change in instructions, the requirement that nine states consent to the final treaty was unequivocal. It was understood by all that, barring a radical change of attitude in the South, the proposed treaty could never by consummated. Jay nonetheless continued to negotiate in a shroud of secrecy with his dubious new instruction. Monroe warned Madison at the end of September that Jay might proceed to barter away the Mississippi and that Henry Lee (who had voted with the Southern bloc but compromised in debate) might defect[51]. Monroe was correct in his assessment of Henry Lee, who explained later to Washington that a commercial treaty with Spain was vital to Virginia's "commercial aggrandizement," as well as "essentially necessary to her political happiness . . ."[52].

In order to frustrate Jay's negotiation, prevent apostasy within the Southern party, and break the Eastern-Middle coalition of the North, the Southern party—particularly Monroe and Grayson and their regular correspondent Madison—began a concerted effort within Congress, in the states, and even abroad which in its extent and complexity resembled the organization of radical resistance in the early seventies. First, the Virginia Assembly eliminated Henry Lee from its 1787 congressional delegation[53]. In the next election Madison and Joseph Jones, both of whom were committed to western expansion, were designated for Congress, along with Edward Carrington and Grayson, whose records on the Jay affair were impeccably correct. Richard Henry Lee was also elected, to the surpirse of Grayson, but since Lee had not attended Congress during 1786, he was not susceptible to the same sort of criticism that fell upon his relative Henry Lee. Ultimately, Jones declined to attend, and Henry Lee's mortification was assuaged by an Assembly sensitive to his chagrin. On December 1 he was elected to fill Jones's slot. Still, the original chastisement cannot have failed to inform Lee regarding his duty to his constituency.

If this were not enough, a subsequent resolution by the Virginia Legislature on November 29 instructed the delegates not to acquiesce to any treaty bartering navigation rights on the Mississippi[54]. The immediate source of this resolution was the insistance of the western members of the Assembly that the Legislature take a position regarding the Spanish negotiation. The presumption is surely strong that Monroe, Grayson, and Madison were the ultimate instigators of the chastisement of both Lee and Jay.

The Virginia Assembly was not the only legislature to condemn the Spanish negotiations. The North Carolina and New Jersey Assemblies also resolved that the navigation rights should not be relinquished. While the North Carolina action could be expected from Bloodworth's indignant response to congressional handling of the Jay-Gardoqui affair[55], the New Jersey condemnation was in part a triumph of Southern organization. On September 12 Monroe wrote to Madison, who was attending the Annapolis Convention, that he had heard that Abraham Clark (previously a marginal member of the Eastern party, and who was also attending the Convention) had been elected to Congress for the coming year from New Jersey. Monroe urged Madison to contact Clark about the Mississippi navigation[56]. It was Monroe's fondest hope that Pennsylvania and New Jersey might be brought into opposition to Jay—a strategy consonant both with continued resistance to Jay's policy in the context of the Confederation and with Monroe's previously articulated design of winning Pennsylvania and New Jersey away from the rumored Northern subconfederation. Monroe's letter probably did not reach Madison before the Annapolis meeting broke up, but Madison had been well apprised of the turn of events in Congress from both correspondence and a visit to New York during July and early August. Madison had many opportunities to discuss politics with Middle states leaders, for he spent the rest of August in Philadelphia, and indeed returned there after the Annapolis meeting before journeying to Richmond in late October[57]. Doubtless he discussed the Mississippi question with Clark at Annapolis and later in Philadelphia, where Clark also spent some time after the Annapolis meeting. Clark must have been won to the Southern position by Madison, with whom he corresponded sympathetically in November. Clark also lobbied with "some of the principal members" of the Pennsylvania Assembly "who appeared no ways friendly" to the revision of Jay's instructions. They were determined to propose a resolution that the Assembly instruct its delegates to oppose yielding navigation rights on the Mississippi[58]. The resolution was offered but not passed. In New Jersey, however, the instruction passed[59]. Northern support for Jay had clearly eroded within Congress and in the states. Consequently, Edward Carrington hoped and Rufus King feared that Pennsylvania as well as New Jersey "will be entirely under a *southern influence* . . ."[60].

The Southern party, led by the Virginia delegates, was so intent upon countering Jay that it contacted the French chargé d'affaires Louis Guillaume Otto (Barbe-Marbois's replacement) and suggested that France use its influence with Spain. According to Otto's report to Vergennes, a delegation of Southerners, whom Otto did not identify, urged him to persuade Vergennes to intervene in the Jay-Gardoqui negotiation to procure use of the Mississippi for exports from the United States (though not imports) and also an entrepôt near the mouth. The Southerners said that if the Jay negotiations proceeded, the West would have no recourse but to throw itself into the arms of Britain to obtain an outlet via the Great Lakes and the St. Lawrence. Britain, they suggested, would then very likely exchange Gibralter for Florida and thus make the whole interior of America dependent upon her[61]. Otto was not impressed with the veiled threat of a union between the West and England. He assured Vergennes that Americans harbored too much resentment toward the British to effect a rapprochement, that Westerners and Southerners preferred a Spanish treaty, and that the underlying reasons for Southern insistence on navigation rights were to draw population from New England and add to the Southern weight in Congress through the addition of new Western states[62]. Otto was probably right on all counts.

In committee of the whole in Congress on August 18, the Virginia delegates proposed the scheme of free navigation for exports only and the use of New Orleans as an entrepôt. The proposal failed, but the Southerners were hopeful of winning converts to the plan. Their ultimate intention was to place the negotiation in the hands of Thomas Jefferson at Madrid, acting in conjunction with the French[63]. Although this strategy, which echoed the pro-French Southern diplomacy, was never consummated, it testified to the imagination and resourcefulness of the Southern party with its Virginian leadership.

The Spanish treaty dispute coincided with the launching of the Annapolis Convention, from which Virginia nationalists—particularly James Madison—hoped a thorough revision of the Articles might evolve. Intending that the Annapolis Convention should be "subservient to a plenipotentiary Convention for amending the Confederation"[64], he was extremely distressed by the effect he believed the Jay-Gardoqui negotiations would have upon the Virginia Legislature. That Assembly was "already jealous of Northern politics and . . . composed of about thirty members from the Western waters, . . . [and] a majority of others attached to the Western Country" either personally or through their constituents[65]. Virginia's commitment to the Annapolis meeting and its sequel was crucial, as Madison well knew. Originating as a core area trade conference, it would be destroyed if that region divided at Annapolis along the same lines that obtained in the bifurcated Congress. Such a split would have an equally catastrophic effect upon Virginia's western policy. It is in this context that Monroe's comment to Madison that the Annapolis Convention was "a most important era in our aff'rs"[66] must be placed. Monroe, however, was so distraught by the events in Congress that he perceived an Eastern conspiracy to dominate the conference or, if this proved to be impossible, to separate in a Northern confederation. Pennsylvania "is their object," he insisted. "Upon succeeding or failing with her will they gain or lose confidence. I doubt not the emissaries of foreign countries will be on the ground. In short I do consider this convention as requiring your utmost exertions, in the change things will infallibly take, as well to obtain good as to prevent mischief . . ."[67]. Monroe went on to discuss the original intention behind the conference—that of promoting national regulation of trade. Monroe himself had been a strong proponent of congressional authority over trade, and he reiterated his conviction that without such power the Union would collapse. In one vital respect he altered his previous stance, however. Rather than recommending that the admission of new western states be deferred until important national decisions were consummated, he stressed the necessity of bringing "a few additional States into the Confederacy in the Southern scale"[68]. With Monroe of the Virginia delegation succumbing to the parochial syndrome, Madison's task was formidible indeed.

Scanty attendance at the Annapolis Convention precluded decisive action. The Deep South and Connecticut were unrepresented; the delegates from North Carolina and the other New England states did not arrive in time. The most that could be accomplished was deciding that a new convention should meet in Philadelphia on the second Monday of May 1787 to "take into consideration the situation of the United States to devise such further provisions as shall appear to them necessary to render the constitution of the Federal Government adequate to the exigencies of the Union; and to report such an Act for that purpose to the United States in Congress assembled, as when agreed to, by them, and afterwards confirmed by the Legislatures of every State, will effectually provide for the same"[69].

This bold, unanimous proposal, although drawn up by Alexander Hamilton, was more in accord with the previous intention of Madison and the Virginians than with Hamilton and his New York constituency. Despite Hamilton's proximity to Congress in 1786 his correspondence (or at least that which has survived) was almost entirely devoted to busniess and his activities at the bar. He seems to have been unaware of the Jay-Gardoqui negotiations which contributed so directly to the crisis atmosphere of the late summer. If he agitated for New York representation at Annapolis, this too, although briefly mentioned in his letters, was almost incidental in a curiously parochial and even nonpolitical correspondence. By comparison with the Virginians in and out of Congress—Monroe, Henry Lee, Richard Henry Lee, Madison and Washington, for example—Hamilton and many other Middle states members of the Nationalist party of 1781–1783 seemed remarkably unconcerned with national politics. There is good reason to accept Forrest McDonald's argument that the nationalist front had fragmented by 1786[70].

IV

The Jay-Gardoqui negotiations provided the critical thrust necessary to transform Annapolis from a trade conference to a staging for constitutional revolution. The linkage between Annapolis and the Constitutional Convention was also affected by the uncertainties attending Jay's diplomacy but was forged more significantly by the Shaysite insurrection in Massachusetts. If the Jay negotiations created the specter of a split in the Confederation, thus impelling certain Southern nationalists into action, the Shays rebellion threatened—or seemed to threaten—class war, thus tending to jolt certain New England parochialists toward a more sympathetic view of the Philadelphia Convention. More important, it strengthened the resolution of the promoters.

The rebellion was taking shape at the very time of the Annapolis Convention. It was the direct result of the strict policy of debt reduction in Massachusetts. The oppressive tax program brought in some $1,500,000, estimated by Rufus King to equal one-third of the income of the people of Massachusetts[71]. Consisting mostly of polls and property taxes, the program weighed heavily upon farmers and debtors whose demands for relief through paper money and debt moratoriums went unheeded by the conservative Legislature and the courts. By late summer, after the Legislature had adjourned, protest meetings demanding relief were held throughout the state. By September protesters interrupted sessions of the Supreme Court being held in Springfield. Gathering momentum in central and western Massachusetts during the fall (though no part of the state was immune from the disaffection), the resistance accelerated into what the Legislature chose to call an organized, armed insurrection. Not until an armed confrontation on January 25 between the Massachusetts militia under General William Shepherd and 1,200 insurgents under Daniel Shays was the back of the movement broken. General Benjamin Lincoln, in command of the operation, pursued the Shaysites north to Petersham, where they were finally dispersed on February 4, 1787[72].

Congress was involved at an early stage because of the existence of a federal arsenal at Springfield. Henry Knox, Secretary at War and the most ardent of the Massachusetts nationalists, responded with promptness becoming his responsibilities and his political commitments. On September 20 he warned the Congress that "some lawless people" in the neighborhood of Springfield intended "under certain circumstances" to seize the ordnance and stores and "convert them to their own 'rebellious purposes.'" He added that he had requested Governor Bowdoin to provide for the safety of the arsenal[73]. Knox sent additional communications from the war office and from New England, where he journeyed in October. His dispatches contained increasingly disturbing descriptions of the extent and objectives of the resistance. On October 18 he alarmed Congress into action: "The great numbers of people in Massachusetts and the neighboring states who avow the principle of annihilating all debts public and private" were ripe quarry for "wicked and ambitious men" who might seize command with "dreadful consequences"[74]. There was reason to believe, Knox related, that English influence might be at work. In private letters and conversation Knox, and perhaps Rufus King, who attended the meeting between Knox and Bowdoin, exaggerated the organization and size of the rebel force. Most accounts in the newspapers and in congressional letters agreed with Charles Pettit's description of "an organized Army of not less than 10,000 Men armed and Officered" ready to come forth[75].

Knox recommended that Congress organize a legionary force of 1,500 men to protect the arsenal through the winter. A committee chaired by Pettit and including Henry Lee, Charles Pinckney, John Henry, and Melancton Smith was formed to consider the crisis in Massachusetts as well as recent communications from Knox regarding Indian disturbances on the frontier[76]. It is not difficult to understand the unanimous congressional decision to send assistance to Massachusetts. Henry Lee, perhaps the most national-minded of the committee, spoke of "the horrors of anarchy and licentiousness." Edward Carrington, a Virginia centralist, later feared that even the sober Connecticut population was not free from the "infection," and like Lee, he may have been alarmed that "the contagion will spread and may reach Virginia[77]. Members of Congress, particularly the Virginians, seemed to perceive the insurrection as a kind of disease which threatened to spread throughout the Union.

Indeed, what seems now to have been a broadly based popular protest generated by legitimate grievances was matched in its confusion only by the frenetic response of conservative men of property in the entire Confederation. Henry Lee wondered how strange it was that the "sober part of mankind will continue to prefer this incertitude and precariousness" because of jealousy of centralized power "which is indispensably necessary to chastise vice and reward virtue"[78]. Lee's jeremiads were not unlike those of the Resistance era, except that imperial authority, once the cause of vice, had now become the specific to counteract vice. The same accent, though not the same conclusion, can be found in Rufus King's lament to his fellow Massachusetts parochialist Theodore Sedgwick, then resident in Stockbridge and possibly in jeopardy because of his conservatism:

> I myself have been an advocate for a Government free as air; my Opinions have been established upon the belief that my countrymen were virtuous, enlightened, and governed by a sense of Right and Wrong. I have ever feared that if our Republican Governments were subverted, it would be by the influence of commerce and the progress of luxury. But if in opposition to these Sentiments the great Body of the people are without Virtue, and not governed by any internal Restraints of Conscience, there is but too much room to fear that the Framers of our constitutions and laws have proceeded on principles that do not exist, and that America, which the Friends of Freedom have looked to as an Asylum when persecuted, will not afford that Refuge[79].

King's statement illuminates with unusual clarity the declension of the republican ideology of the Eastern wing of the Revolution. In 1776 it had been assumed that the Revolution would succeed by the virtue of the people who would sever the contaminating connection with the corrupt mother country. In 1779 it had appeared that indigenous sources of corruption had arisen from the self-interested commercial operations of merchants using the Revolution for private advantage—a new contagion perfectly symbolized by Deane and his partisans. By 1781 that decay had spread into the population at large and threatened to alter the direction of the Revolution by producing a mercantilist centralism, but the influence of commerce and luxury had been contained in no small degree because of the Eastern opposition in Congress. King himself had shunted the desire of his own constituency for political consolidation in 1785. Now it appeared that the culprits were not devious, "interested" men but the mass of people in whom that virtue which justified revolution presumably resided.

While in Boston, where he conferred with Bowdoin and Knox, King took the unusual step of personally reporting to the General Court on the state of federal affairs. In a speech devoted mostly to Confederation finance and foreign policy, he concluded with a guarded reference to the disturbances in Massachusetts, "an evil in public affairs, infinitely greater than any he had mentioned"[80]. In a logic that anticipated Madison's *The Federalist,* Number 10. King stressed that the insurrection in Massachusetts was something every member of Congress was personally involved in, realizing that his "life liberty and property" were affected by the decisions of the Legislature; that "There was a league subsisting between the States of America, to oppose every force that should arise against either of them"; and that if the Massachusetts government was supported by only a minority, "let it be remembered, that they had a majority of every State in the Union to join them"[81].

Yet King, precisely because of his commitment to Congress—the institution that had emerged from the early Revolution as the hesitant product of that suspect virtue—was unwilling to attempt radical reformation of the Articles. In the same speech in which he assured the General Court that Massachusetts did not stand alone, he rejected the Annapolis recommendation of a constitutional convention. Stressing that "The Confederation was the act of the people" and that "No part could be altered but by consent of Congress and confirmation of the several Legislatures," he concluded that "Congress therefore ought to make the examination first, because if it was done by a convention, no Legislature could have a right to confirm it"[82]. It is unlikely that this was procedural punctilio or loyalty to a body which King had established himself and had an interest in perpetuating. There is more reason to think that King, despite his doubts about the capacity of the populace for republican government, was reacting as a responsible representative of the sentiments of his constituency. Interestingly, King and the other Massachusetts delegates seem to have been less converted to the cause of consolidation by "Shays's

Rebellion" than the Virginians in Congress. Nathan Dane reiterated King's argument in a subsequent address to the Massachusetts General Court, and that Legislature refused to accept the invitation from Annapolis to convene in Philadelphia to revise the Confederation in a constitutional convention[83].

While some New Englanders, such as Henry Knox and James Varnum, both generals with a continental view, accepted the policy or consolidation before the Massachusetts insurrection, the conversion of influential Eastern leadership to the national system early envisioned by Madison was slow and uncertain. Only after the rebellion reached its peak in February did the Massachusetts legislature resolve to send delegates to Philadelphia[84]. The conversion of Rufus King, a determined advocate of national sovereignty in the Convention, is illustrative of Eastern hesitancy. By January he had concluded that "the times are becoming critical," and he was reconciled to Massachusetts involvement in the Convention, but he warned Gerry (whose misgivings persisted throughout the ratification of the Constitution) that delegates should be selected with care: "for God's sake be careful who are the men . . . a movement of this nature ought to be carefully observed by every member of the Community[85]. The next month he urged that Massachusetts should send "prudent and sagacious men" to Philadelphia, "ready to seize the most favourable circumstances to establish a more permanent and vigorous government"[86]. Just a week later, however, he confessed to Gerry that he was "at some loss" as to the wisdom of Massachusetts involvement in the Convention, for "the thing is so problematical," he said, and concluded, "I am rather inclined to the measure from an idea of prudence, or for the purpose of watching, than from an expectation that much Good will flow from it"[87].

King's vacillation was in all probability due to his indecision about the wisdom of Eastern involvement in a convention engineered by Virginians and Middle states nationalists. Virginia and New Jersey accepted the Annapolis invitation in November; Pennsylvania followed in December. North Carolina and Delaware endorsed the Convention in January and February. The Middle-Southern character of the movement was unmistakable[88], and King's parochial attachments were too strong to be discarded at will. He worried also that Pennsylvania and New Jersey were falling "entirely under a *southern Influence*" in Congress—a tendency that promised "mischief" to the public credit and the settlement of accounts[89]. Given these circumstances, and remembering always that the ultimate structure of the Constitution was totally unperceived in early 1787 and that a shift in the sectional balance had the utmost importance in calculations based on the Confederation rule of equal representation, it is not difficult to reconstruct King's apprehension.

On February 20 the New York Assembly instructed its delegates to move the convening of a separate convention for revising the Articles of Confederation. Madison believed that the New York action was designed to compete with rather than support the Philadelphia Convention. The New York instruction was framed just a day after a congressional grand committee strongly endorsed the Annapolis report, "entirely coinciding" with the Convention's opinion about "the inefficiency of the federal government" and the need for a national government "adequate to the exigencies of the Union"[90]. The Congress considered the report on February 21, at which time the New York delegates presented the New York resolution calling for a convention at an undesignated time and place "for the purpose of revising the Articles of Confederation" and reporting proposed amendments to Congress and the states[91]. While it is possible this was simply an attempt to move the Convention from Philadelphia, Madison went so far as to suggest that there was a movement afoot to dismember the Confederation "into three more practicable and energetic Governments"[92].

Both the enthusiasm of the grand committee and the flexibility of the New York resolution disturbed the Massachusetts delegates King and Dane, who were "much against the measure," according to the Pennsylvanian William Irvine. Recognizing that it would be carried without them, they offered a substitute resolution providing congressional sanction for the Philadelphia Convention "for the sole and express purpose of revising the Articles of Confederation" and reporting its recommendations back to Congress and the states[93]. Irvine anticipated that the Convention would be "a piece of patch work." Considering the congressional maneuvers endorsing the Convention, he could not have been judged wrong at the time.

v

It goes without saying that congressional politics in 1787 were vitally affected by the anticipation and unfolding of the Constitutional Convention. James Madison returned as a delegate that year—a fact that was sufficient in itself to guarantee a reciprocal influence. A number of delegates, including among others William Samuel Johnson, Madison, King, Gorham, Abraham Yates, and Charles Pinckney, were appointed to the Convention. When the question of the residence of Congress was raised again in the spring of 1787 at the insistence of the South, the proposal that Congress should relocate in Philadelphia was opposed by Madison because he was reluctant to interfere with the Convention[94]. The problem of national finance was complicated by the question of whether or not the Convention would frame a system with larger fiscal prerogatives. Finally, the passage of the Northwest Ordinance, probably the most significant piece of legislation enacted by Congress during its entire history, was intimately and intricately wound up with the Convention, in progress at the time[95].

The party politics of Congress likewise affected the Convention. Continued tension between North and South (though with some shifts of delegations on the matter of Mississippi navigation) was of particular importance. Partisan disagreements over both the Jay negotiation and the political organization of the Northwest not only created a sense of urgency at the Convention but also influenced some of its debates over the mode of representation in the lower house and led to the two-thirds requirement for ratification of treaties in the Senate. It is incorrect to think of the Convention as simply a meeting of centralists working to correct manifest inadequacies of the Articles of Confederation.

Thus the discussion below will embrace both the proceedings of Congress during the spring and summer of 1787 and some of the disputes in the Convention relevant to congressional factionalism.

Congress was plagued as much by absenteeism during the winter of 1786–1787 as during the previous year. No quorum could be obtained in the new federal year until January 17, when seven states were at last represented. The very next day attendance dropped, and not until February 2 was there another quorum. Attendance was sufficient to maintain a Congress for the next four months, but when a number of delegates left for the Convention in May Congress could not muster a quorum until July 4, when the North Carolinians and Georgians came up from Philadelphia. Congress held sessions during July long enough to pass the Northwest Ordinance and conclude the agreement with the Ohio Company for a massive land purchase in Ohio, but between August 3 and September 20 there was again no quorum. There were sessions at the end of the federal year just long enough to refer the Constitution to the states, hear the report on the budget from the Treasury Board, and make an ineffectual plea to the states to pay up their quotas. By then there was little expectation of avoiding complete bankruptcy and mortification. Congress thus during 1787 functioned in conjunction with the Convention, anticipating either a division of the Union or the substitution of an altered national form.

Despite Congress's tacit confession of incapacity and dependence on the outcome of the Philadelphia Convention, when sessions were held the old abrasive issues and party disputes which had torn Congress during the preceding year continued. When an attempt was made to elect a President on the one day a quorum was achieved in January, for example, the delegates split over Southern and Northern candidates. William Blount of North Carolina, a strong prospect, was rejected because of Northern opposition, including that of one of the "antifederal Peasants" (as Blount described them) from New York, Melancton Smith, later to be joined by other New York parochialists, John Haring and Abraham Yates. Ultimately, the Pennsylvanian Arthur St. Clair was elected on February 2 as a compromise candidate[96].

Jay's negotiation with Gardoqui remained an intolerable bone in the throat of the Southern party. Encouraged by the results of their lobbying in the New Jersey delegation and by the election in Pennsylvania of the aggressive, military-minded John Armstrong, Jr. (who was later offered a judgeship in the Northwest Territory), and alarmed by the effect the negotiation had produced in Virginia (where Patrick Henry's "disgust exceeded all measure," according to Madison[97]), the Southerners worked to redirect the negotiation with Spain. The domestic impact of the negotiation in Virginia was of critical importance even for the success of the Constitutional Convention. Patrick Henry, once a friend to federal measures, now refused to attend the Convention—in Madison's words, to keep himself "free to combat or espouse the result of it according to the result of the Mississippi business among other circumstances"[98]. Believing that Jay had not dared to proceed with the sanction of only seven states, Madison assumed the negotiation was at a standstill—which it was. Fearing, however, that some repair of the damage of the previous summer was necessary in order to prepare Virginia for a revision of the Confederation, he renewed the attempt to transfer the negotiation from Jay's hands into those of Jefferson. He urged Jefferson to contact Virginians on the matter, assuring him, "I discover, thro several channels, that it would be very grateful to the French politicians here to see our negotiations with Spain shifted into your hands and carried on under the mediating auspices of their Court"[99].

The Southern party also succeeded in instructing Jay to lay the results of his diplomacy before Congress (which Jay did on April 11, disclosing nothing of surprise)[100]. As soon as circumstances were ripe—specifically, when the Delaware delegation filled with the arrival of Nathaniel Mitchell—the Southern party, led in this instance by William Pierce and William Few of Georgia, moved to repeal the order of September 1, 1786, restricting the reintroduction of matters set aside by the previous question except by the vote of as many states as had originally voted for the previous question. The Easten maneuver which had blocked new instructions to Jay was struck down by the Southerners with the support of New Jersey (Abraham Clark and James Schureman), Pennsylvania (John Armstrong, Jr., President St. Clair, Charles Pettit, and Samuel Meredith), and Delaware (Nathaniel Mitchell and Dyre Kearny)[101]. Thus the Southern cultivation of the Middle states had paid off.

Despite the success of the Virginia design to wean the Middle states from their alliance with New England, the Southern party was not sufficiently united to carry through a repeal of the September instruction allowing Jay to give up the navigation of the Mississippi. Maryland and South Carolina, the two Southern states without significant claims south of the Ohio River, had defected on the Mississippi issue. South Carolina was represented only by Daniel Huger at the moment, so its vote would not count in any event, but Maryland's delegation was full, and it stood against the revision of Jay's instruction when an attempt was made on May 11 to forbid Jay from relinquishing rights to the Mississippi[102]. This left the Virginia-led Southern party with only six votes, even with the three Middle states.

While the frustration of the expansionist-minded Southern delegates must have been extreme, they found solace in the knowledge that they had six firm votes against any result of Jay's diplomacy. Nothing further was done on the question until September of 1788, and then the decision was, appropriately enough, to turn the matter over to the new government[103].

The success of the Southern strategy was enhanced by the sparse representation of the New England states during the entire year. Even when a sufficient number of states were available to conduct business, New England was rarely able to muster more than two votes. New Hampshire was constantly absent; Rhode Island had two delegates on the floor only briefly during April; and even Connecticut was unrepresented on over half of the roll calls between September of 1786 and September 1787. Indeed, during that year, the four New England states cast just 43 percent of the votes they might have, had their delegates all been present for all roll calls. This was notably different from the 76 percent cast by the five Southern states (Maryland and South Carolina being most frequently absent) and the 87 percent cast by the Middle states (only Delaware being significantly absent—and then mainly during September and October of 1786). The lack of representation from New England was all the more striking in view of the fact that Congress was sitting far north in New York City. Doubtless this added to the alarm expressed on so many occasions that the Eastern states were drifting apart from the Confederation.

The lack of a significant Eastern presence in Congress prompted some members of the new Southern–Middle states coalition to remove the sessions from New York. Always a volatile issue which aroused the full potential of parochial attachments, the question of the location of Congress had geopolitical and ideological implications as well which came into unnerving focus during April and May of 1787. There were compelling reasons to transfer Congress to another location farther south. Apart from the question of geographic centrality, Pennsylvania and Delaware had claim to Southern support for relocation in Philadelphia as a quid pro quo for their posture on the Mississippi negotiation. The Virginians in particular and the Southern party in general had never been reconciled to the location of the federal capital in the vicinity of Trenton and a move to Philadelphia could be used as a steppingstone to the designation of a new capital site at the falls of the Potomac. In addition, as Madison observed to Edmund Randolph, the influence of the New York location on congressional deliberations was crucial on matters such as the Jay-Gardoqui negotiations: "Had Cong's been sitting last fall at Fort Pitt," he asserted, "it is morally certain in my opinion that a sur-render of the Mississpi: wd not have had two votes . . ."[*104*].

On April 10 Dyre Kearny of Delaware and William Blount of North Carolina moved that Congress adjourn for roughly a month to remove to Philadelphia (to meet there on the first Monday in June). Rufus King excitedly wrote to Elbridge Gerry that "the injurious Influence of 1783" again stalked Congressional terrain. King's description of the proceedings is so remarkably attuned to the partisan rhetoric of 1783 that it is difficult to remember he was not present during the struggles of that year. Noting that Rhode Island, "represented by Genl. Varnum and a Mr. Arnold," had defected to the Southern side, King excoriated that delegation for abandoning "that wise policy which has been so often and so successfully opposed to political vice and Degeneracy." He feared that the Rhode Islanders "will unite in measures foreign to the true Interest of the Union, and nearly allied to cor-ruption"[*105*].

Coincident with the Mississippi navigation crisis on May 10–11, the Kearny-Blount resolution was again advanced. According to the Deputy-Secretary of Congress, Roger Alden, the relocation motion produced "some of the warmest expressions . . . I have ever heard"[*106*]. At this moment Rhode Island was unrepresented, and the defection of Schureman of New Jersey, who disagreed with his colleague Abraham Clark, prevented a seven-state majority for the resolution. A subsequent attempt to designate Phila-delphia as a temporary capital was defeated, ironically through a momentary coalition of the North and South, including Virginia, against the Middle states[*107*]. The Virginians in this instance apparently appreciated the dis-ruptive effect of such a strategy at the very moment the Constitutional Con-vention was beginning to gather. As with the question of the Mississippi navigation, the sectional discord generated by the location of the national capital would not be resolved under the auspices of the Confederation Congress. A severely divisive issue throughout the era of the Confederation, its ultimate resolution in the famous bargain between Hamilton and Jefferson over federal assumption would prove no less disputatious.

VI

Ironically, while the resolution of such volatile questions as the Mississippi navigation, the location of the capital, and the funding of the national debt had to await the creation of a more powerful and decisive national govern-ment, the infinitely more important question of the political organization of the West was not only settled by the undermanned Congress but may also have helped to make the achievement of the new federal form feasible.

The so-called Northwest Ordinance, though passed in July of 1787, had a history of continual attention dating back at least to Jefferson's Ordinance of 1784. (In the larger sense of the definition of western development, the problem of course antedated the Revolution itself.) The Ordinance of 1784 established a fundamental policy—in some respects the most fundamental policy of all—that the Republic would evolve by enlarging itself rather than through the creation of colonial dependencies west of the mountains. This principle was incorporated in the Northwest Ordinance and was followed consistently by the nation under the Constitution.

Not all members of Congress during the succeeding years subscribed to such liberal management of the turbulent West, however. In addition to the constrictionist tendencies of members representing the Atlantic seaboard, manifested in both the Northern stance during the Jay-Gardoqui negotiations and the Potomac-Chesapeake geopolitics of Virginians such as Henry Lee, there was a pervasive fear in the seaboard states that migrants to the West were at best castoffs and at worst disloyal people from the East. That the frontier should have been a scene of violence, litigation, and rumored sedition confirmed more than created the fears of the East. It was only natural that New Englanders were most alarmed about the West and least sympathetic with the plight of its "lawless Banditti which forms the Law of those Settlements"[*108*]. Yet even Monroe, after a trip to the West, concluded that the original stipulation of the Virginia cession in 1780, incorporated in the Ordinance of 1784, that ten states should be carved from the cession was impolitic. His reasoning rested partly on the assumption that much of the region was infertile and would be so sparsely populated that it would never qualify for admission. Monroe also had doubts about the wisdom of introducing a large number of states inhabited by frontiersmen whose interests would not coincide with those of the seaboard states[*109*]. This was the afterthought of the optimistic expectations of western innocence and regeneration of the Republic earlier articulated by Jefferson and Howell. Consequently, there developed a movement in Congress to subdue the western threat by tightening congressional control over the Northwest and by reducing the number of possible states and making their admission more difficult.

Largely as a result of the efforts of Monroe, Congress resolved on July 7 that only three to five states should be formed out of the Northwest [*110*]. Congressional action did not stop there, however. A committee of five (Monroe, King, William Samuel Johnson of Connecticut, Kean, and Charles Pinckney of South Carolina) was appointed to reconsider the form of territorial government for the Northwest, and on May 10 it reported a plan altering the more libertarian features of the Ordinance of 1784. Whereas the original ordinance had allowed a measure of self-direction for the early settlers, the plan of May 10 called for congressional appointment of a governor and a council of five members, the ultimate power being lodged with the governor[*111*]. A house of representatives was provided for when the number of free adult males reached 5,000, but this concession paled before a new restriction reported by an altered committee under the chairmanship of William Samuel Johnson on September 19 stipulating that before a state could be admitted into the Union it would have to have a population of free inhabitants equal to "one thirteenth part of the Citizens of the Original States." This drastic substitution for the previous requirement of a population equal to that of the least populous of the original states would have kept Wisconsin out of the Union until after 1900 and Michigan until after 1880[*112*]. By this time Monroe had reason to rue having been implicated in the whole business.

In conjunction with the constrictionist policy of the Jay-Gardoqui negotiations which generated intense partisan heat at the same time, the question of western development reinforced the general North-South dichotomy in Congress. No agreement could be reached in the fall of 1786. By March of 1787 the Virginia delegates, especially Madison, were intent upon resuming the subject. The continued irritation of Jay's negotiation, Patrick Henry's "disgust" which boded ill for the acceptance of constitutional reform in Virginia, memorials from the inhabitants of Illinois protesting speculation by land jobbers (including among others George Rogers Clark), and the absence of settled government all contributed to Madison's interest in resolving the problem[*113*].

The report of September 19 was brought forth again on May 9 for a second reading and was scheduled for a third reading on May 10, but did not receive it. Action was suspended for almost two months for the increasingly familiar reason that Congress could not achieve a quorum between May 11 and July 4. At this point events took an unusual, even bizarre, turn.

Just before Congress stalled in May, it received a memorial from probably the most famous land company in American history, the Ohio Company. It had been organized in Boston in March of 1786 with the intention of converting veteran land bounties and depreciated Continental certificates into more tangible holdings in western lands. Anticipating subscriptions to the amount of $1 million in Continental obligations translated into shares of $1,000 each, the Ohio Company, under the leadership of General Rufus Putman of Massachusetts, Samuel H. Parsons, and Reverend Manasseh Cutler of Ipswich, Massachusetts, intended to persuade Congress to modify its recently established policy of selling lands in township allotments. The Ohio Company offered what Congress was bound to accept—a major reduction of the public debt in exchange for a huge million-acre tract of land just to the west of the lands under initial survey. The company had not managed to enlist the intended number of subscribers—just 250 shares had been sold by March 1, 1787—but such a large deal attracted other influential speculators. William Duer, the erstwhile congressional delegate who had attached himself to the Southern party and who was currently functioning as Secretary of the Treasury Board, was especially interested.

Duer collected a number of influential Middle states men, New Englanders, and Europeans in a speculative scheme which functioned as a satellite to the Ohio Company project. In a plan worked out in July of 1787, Duer and his associates, organized as the Scioto Company, planned to invest in an additional 5 million acres in the Ohio country under the auspices of the Ohio Company in exchange for support for the Ohio grant in Congress and the investment of funds to make up the deficiency in the Ohio subscription. Duer's assistance could not be dismissed by the Ohio Company promoters. His contacts were as varied as they were influential. He managed to gather the support and capital of the large merchant Andrew Craigie of New York and Cambridge, Massachusetts; Daniel Parker of Boston, a major contractor for the Continental army during the war; and foreign investors in London (Smith, Wright, and Gray), Amsterdam (Van Staphorst and Company), and Paris (the Delasserts) [114]. Yet this international network of "Morrisonian"-style capitalists included as well Samuel Osgood of Massachusetts, previously an intensely parochial delegate from that state in Congress, and Melancton Smith, the arch antinationalist from New York who was presently in Congress[115].

There was no apparent connection between Duer and the Ohio Company people on the one hand and the Middle states centralists, many of whom were making their way to the Philadelphia Convention, on the other. It is true that Manasseh Cutler, the most effective lobbyist for the Ohio Company, did journey to Philadelphia at about the time he joined the fortunes of the Ohio Company with the Scioto speculation, but the ordinance and the sale were worked out in Congress rather than in the Convention, where such eminent Nationalists of the earlier period as Robert Morris, Gouverneur Morris, and James Wilson were located.

The frenetic activities of the Ohio and Scioto Companies helped in the final passage of the Northwest Ordinance of 1787 as well as in settling the contract for what amounted to 1,500,000 acres, with another 3,500,000 acres reserved for future acquisition by the Scioto investors using the Ohio Company as a screen.

Partly because Cutler insisted on an established government for the Northwest Territory as a condition of the purchase, Congress passed the Ordinance of 1787 with unaccustomed rapidity on July 13. The plan that had been hanging in limbo for four years was speeded through to completion in roughly four days under the guidance of a committee chaired by Edward

Carrington and strongly influenced by Nathan Dane. There were two good reasons for such unique dispatch—in addition to the enticement of the million-dollar sale[116].

First, the ordinance contained very little that had not already been established in principle in 1784 or hammered out through modifications of the original ordinance during 1786[117]. The establishment of the governorship and a three-man court to assume control during the first stage of settlement had already been provided for, and the creation of a legislature during the second stage of territorial evolution had been anticipated from the outset. Guarantees of habeas corpus and trial by jury as well as liberal laws governing the division of interstate estates had been essentially worked out by Nathan Dane during the previous fall. Dane indeed deserved the major credit for the ordinance, including the provision, added at the last moment on the floor of Congress in the form of a motion by the Massachusetts delegate, that slavery be excluded from the Northwest[118].

Second, an unusual accord was established between the Eastern and Southern parties in Congress, thus allowing the modified ordinance to pass. Actually, it was necessary for a number of Southern delegates to travel the 90 miles from the Convention in Philadelphia to Congress in New York in order to establish a quorum for the first time in almost two months. It was a predominantly Southern Congress that passed the ordinance, drafted in its final stages primarily by Nathan Dane under the stimulus of a New England land company. It was a Congress of delegates from eight states, only one state from New England and four states from the slave-holding South, that unanimously endorsed an ordinance including, among other things, a prohibition of slavery in the region north of the Ohio[119].

The Southern participation in the passage of the ordinance is all the more remarkable in view of the absence of almost the entire Pennsylvania delegation—including Arthur St. Clair, who was President of Congress! And the Pennsylvanian delegates were not unaware of the need of their presence. On June 20 John Armstrong, Jr., the one Pennsylvanian present, and William Grayson both wrote to William Irvine of the Pennsylvania delegation urging him to come to the Congress. Nathan Dane wrote to Gorham, a Massachusetts delegate to the Convention, to urge that delegates who were not needed in Philadelphia should travel north to Congress. Charles Thomson wrote to Samuel Meredith and to William Bingham of the Pennsylvania delegation, pleading that they attend Congress[120].

Thomson and Dane couched their appeals in tones of utmost urgency. There were rumors in New England that the Confederation had completely collapsed and that the new establishment being worked out at Philadelphia would be implemented at the point of the bayonet. It was imperative that Congress continue its sessions in order to preserve the peace and make the transition to the new federal form through due constitutional process, presuming its acceptability[*121*]. Such alarm over the continuance of the Union fits more readily with the partisan politics of the previous year than with the fact that it was the North Carolinians and Georgians, accompanying Richard Henry Lee (who was tarrying in Philadelphia, though he was not a delegate to the Convention), who answered the call from New York.

Only by perceiving the Northwest Ordinance in the context of the proceedings of the Constitutional Convention can one properly understand its passage, and only by viewing the debates of the Convention as an extension of congressional factionalism can one understand why the Convention had such a vital influence on the ordinance.

VII

The Convention was essentially a Virginia production. Despite Shay's Rebellion, New England was hesitant about the Constitutional Convention. Rufus King, probably more in touch with the pulse of the consolidationist movement than any other New Englander save Henry Knox, was skeptical of the tendency of the Convention to the very moment he arrived in Philadelphia. Knox, it is true, both approved of the Convention and pressed for Eastern involvement, but that he was the exception that proved the rule is suggested by the fact that Rufus King was the sole delegate from New England present when Madison took an informal roll call on May 25, eleven days after the Convention was supposed to convene[*122*]. By contrast, sixteen delegates from the South were in attendance. More significantly, despite the fact that such Nationalists from Pennsylvania as Robert Morris, George Clymer, Thomas Fitzsimmons, and James Wilson attended the Convention in company with the dynamic Hamilton of New York and the articulate Gouverneur Morris (now representing Pennsylvania), none of these individuals with the exception of Hamilton seems to have been involved in the interstate promotion of the Convention. Hamilton helped transform the Annapolis meeting into a platform for the Constitutional Convention, but even he, like most Middle states Nationalists of 1781–1783, seems from surviving correspondence to have been little more concerned about the Philadelphia Convention than about the Mount Vernon Conference of 1785[*123*].

The Virginia promotion of the Annapolis conference, the early and enthusiastic endorsement of the Philadelphia Convention by the Virginia Assembly, and the action of the Virginia delegates in effectively establishing the terms of discussion at the Convention through the immediate presentation of the Virginia Plan all testify to the Southern character of the Convention. Madison's correspondence immediately before the Convention was both explicit and sweeping in its discussion of reform: "Let the national Government be armed with a positive and complete authority in all cases where uniform measures are necessary . . . ," he contended to Edmund Randolph on April 8, 1787. "Let it have a negative, in all cases whatsoever, on the Legislative acts of the States, as the King of Great Britain heretofore had," he added. Madison also took care to press his radical program, including the principle of proportional representation which lay at the heart of the whole reform, upon Washington, whose influence would be all but decisive, as Madison well knew[124].

Virginia was most responsible for the organization and temper of the Convention, but the whole South enlisted in the program of radical reform more readily than other sections—particularly New England[125]. Finally, as one could anticipate, Southern delegations in the Convention had closer connections with recent proceedings in the Continental Congress. Three of the nine New England delegates in the Convention (King, Gorham, and Johnson) had attended Congress during all or part of 1786 and 1787. Of the twenty-one delegates from the Middle states, only James Wilson had been present in Congress during that interval, and then only for a few days in the spring of 1786. From the South, on the other hand, Madison, Blount, Charles Pinckney, Few, Pierce, and Houstoun were all members of Congress in 1786 and 1787. (To that group might be added James McHenry, Richard Spaight, Hugh Williamson, and Abraham Baldwin, if one counted attendance in 1785. From the Middle states and New England the only additional delegates attending Congress in 1785 were Houston, Lansing, and Gerry.)

Those Southern delegates who had experienced the traumatic bifurcation of Congress during the Jay-Gardoqui negotiations were better aware of the cutting edge of western policy, more attuned to the possibility of a division or divisions in the Confederation, and more alert to the sectional implications of constitutional decisions than were delegates who had been unconnected with national politics. This is not to say that there was a single set of Southern objectives defined entirely in terms of recent congressional partisan politics. Virginia was more intent upon proportional representation than the rest of the South— especially Maryland. The Carolinas and Georgia were more insistent that slavery and the slave trade be protected than were the Chesapeake states. Both Maryland and South Carolina had eased away from their insistence upon Mississippi navigation rights by the spring of 1787, while the other Southern states were resolved that the West should be protected. Nonetheless, the South was more unified and determined than underrepresented New England and the Middle states, fractured as before in Congress—this time on the issue of large versus small states[126].

The Southern delegations had a number of objectives, some of a defensive character, some aggressively nationalist. The three states of the Deep South were sufficiently attached to the slave labor system to refuse any revision which did not both protect the institution from national intervention and accord representation on the basis of the slave as well as free population. The latter objective, which resulted in the three-fifths rule for representation in the House of Representatives, doubtless reflected the general desire of the Southern states to achieve as full a representation as possible (and the more specific intention to recognize and thus legitimize slavery), as well as establish a protective slavery bloc in the new national government[*127*]. Thus Charles Pinckney called for three-fifths representation of slaves in the lower house and for a senate elected by the lower house to represent four districts, or sectional regions—two of which would be the South and the West[*128*]. The ultimate agreement that the slave trade would not be interfered with for twenty years and that there should be no tax on exports also reflected the Southern defensive posture.

More interestingly in the context of congressional politics, however, the Southern delegations in the Convention overwhelmingly took a "large-state" position on the issue of proportional representation in both houses. Maryland alone divided on or opposed this stance, partly because of its influential parochialist Luther Martin (never a member of Congress), and partly because of her traditional distrust of her land-rich neighbor Virginia. That Virginia led the "nationalist" force in the Convention—a force composed of four Southern states out of five and just two Northern states out of six present (eight in all)— was due not only to her supremacy in population among the thirteen states but also to her vast Kentucky holdings and her involvement in the settlement of the Northwest. That a small state such as Georgia and a middling state such as North Carolina should have joined Virginia on the very foundation of the nationalist plan, proportional representation, also testifies to the ubiquitous influence of Southern geopolitical strategy for the West in Convention proceedings[*129*].

There were, of course, other motives behind the arguments for proportional representation. It seems likely that the Virginian nationalism was partly the product of a genuine centralist political philosophy designed to subordinate the states to a degree utterly inconceivable in a confederation of equal sovereignties[*130*]. (The Virginia Plan written by Madison and presented by Edmund Randolph included, it will be remembered, a federal veto against acts of the state legislatures.) From this angle of vision the nationalist thrust surely embodied in part what Gordon Wood has aptly termed in the words of John Dickinson the struggle of "the worthy against the licentious"[*131*]. For whatever reasons, Madison and Charles Pinckney seem to have been as alarmed about paper money and Shaysites as Knox.

Yet it was not a simple matter to translate this concern, common to a large majority of the Convention delegates, into constitutional form. The

Virginia Plan provided Congress with general power, unspecified and ample, to "legislate in all cases to which the separate states are incompetent, or in which the harmony of the United States may be interrupted by the exercise of individual legislation." This was too strong to suit both Southern nationalists concerned about slavery and the staple trade and small-states delegates alarmed by the specter of large-state domination. Madison himself would not support such unenumerated authority once it became clear there would be equal representation in the Senate.

By the end of June it became apparent that equal representation in at least óne house was indisputably necessary. Oliver Ellsworth remarked that if it were denied, the Confederation would split about where they stood (i.e., on the Delaware). Throughout the proceedings there was the alarming possibility of a division, already manifestly clear from the congressional debates over the Jay-Gardoqui negotiations.

While sought by no one at the Convention, a fracture of the Union was least acceptable to Virginia. Her weight in numbers, her core region situation, and her involvement in the West all impelled her to insist upon the maintenance of the Republic as defined territorially in the Treaty of Paris. Madison worked desperately to convince the delegates from the small states that the fundamental division in the Confederation was not between large states and small, but between the North and South: "The great danger to our general government *is the great southern and northern interests of the continent, being opposed to each other. Look to the votes in congress, and most of them stand divided by the geography of the country, not according to the size of the states*"[132].

One suspects that Madison must have made this attempt to transform the debate over representation with grave misgivings. The logic of his argument could lead to the conclusion stated by Gouverneur Morris, who, though regarding the notion as "heretical," could not tolerate the implications of a Southern thrust for national policy. Having attempted to permanently control the influence of the emerging West by setting up an apportionment system which would give the Atlantic states complete discretion in admitting new states and allocating their representation apart from any fixed numerical principle, and having also discovered the solid opposition of the four most southern states to this plan, Morris was alarmed by the sectional thesis. Seeing that "the South[n] Gentlemen [as Madison reported his speech] will not be satisfied unless they see their way open to their gaining a majority in the public Councils," he concluded he would have to vote for the "vicious principle of equality" in the upper house in order "to provide some defence" for the Northern states against the South. The transfer of power from the maritime to the interior and landed interest would result in "an oppression of commerce" and a war with Spain for the Mississippi, he warned. If "a struggle between the two ends of the Union" was real (and Morris, who was out of touch with recent congressional proceedings, could not accept it as such), it was incumbent upon the Middle states to consider their position. For Morris the answer was clear: "to join their Eastern brethren." Indeed, if the distinction was genuine, Morris concluded it would be better to "take a friendly leave of each other" than to try "to blend incompatible things"[*133*].

That Gouverneur Morris, the erstwhile ally of the Southern party in Congress, could have even suggested such a subconfederation was hardly less than catastrophic for Southerners—even though his talk was couched in disclaimers. If the division of the Union had to take place, Southern security dictated that Pennsylvania, if not New York, align with the South. While the evidence is circumstantial at the very best, it is at least plausible that the constant maintenance of a Virginia delegation in the Congress at New York, along with the migration of North Carolinians and Georgians from Philadelphia to New York, was a product of Southern concern that the West be rapidly and equitably incorporated in the Union[*134*].

The appeals from Armstrong, Grayson, Dane, and Thomson for a quorum to preserve a visible head of government during the "interregnum" doubtless reached the Convention (since Dane contacted Gorham, while Grayson wrote to Blount and Hawkins on June 20) and probably prompted the Southerners to journey to Congress. Still, the fact that the Southerners made the trip and the Pennsylvanians, to whom most of the appeals were addressed, did not suggests that the Southerners were more alert to the straits of the Confederation than were the Pennsylvanians—including St. Clair, President of Congress. While such concern may have been the product of simple patriotism, the recent history of the Mississippi affair, not to mention Blount's extensive speculation in the West, suggest a more pragmatic concern. Moreover, while the call for a congressional quorum must have reached Philadelphia by June 21 or 22, the Southerners did not leave the Convention until the brief recess called on July 2. It was between June 25 and July 2 that the West was first seriously brought into the Convention debate. On June 25 Charles Pinckney stressed in a notable speech that the Convention should pay less attention to foreign precedents and more to the American situation, which was more equalitarian than Europe in its society and economy and would in all probability remain so because of the vast unsettled West. Dividing the population into professional, commercial, and landed interests, he advocated forming a government which would ensure that the latter would be the mainspring of the system[*135*]. On the same day George Read of Delaware carried the motif further. Though from a small state, Read, like many small-states delegates, was perfectly willing to accept a strong central government if there were built-in securities for the small states. (Read himself actually approved of Hamilton's quasi-monarchic plan.) Read in effect challenged the landed states to open the entire West to national sale and exploitation for the retirement of the public debt, and if this were done, he assured the "large-state" delegates that the small states would be more amenable to proportional representation[*136*]. Four days later Madison made his attempt to divert attention to the North-South division. That theme was reiterated on succeeding days, as on July 2, when Charles Pinckney stressed economic differences between the Southern staple states and the North[*137*]. Tensions were heightened by the renewed presence of Gouverneur Morris, who was as alert to the agrarian implications of the Southern-Western strategy as he was committed against it. With the debate still centered on the composition of the Senate, Morris urged the establishment of a national bond through an aristocratic Senate which would reflect a commercial interest to balance the agrarian democracy of the House[*138*]. Randolph disapproved of this, and it is probable that most Southerners did as well. It was at this moment that the delegates from Georgia and North Carolina answered the appeal from New York City.

The intricate interplay between immediate constitutional provisions for representation and regional distribution of power in the new nation was a major factor in the proceedings of the Convention—a factor only partially resolved in Philadelphia. As Staughton Lynd has hypothesized, the passage of the Northwest Ordinance provided a presumed guarantee of future power to the South, both through the admission of the new Western states on an equal basis (which Morris and Gerry, for example, tried to prevent[*139*]) and through the application of the three-fifths clause to the region south of the Ohio where slavery was not prohibited and tacitly recognized[*140*].

The critical importance of this strategy—whether fully conscious or not—can hardly be overestimated. The ordinance, passed under circumstances which added a quasi-constitutional gravity to the "covenanted" quality already lent to the ordinance by the original Virginia cession, gave to the law a character of fundamental legislation. George Bancroft, noting this aspect as well as the basic provisions of the ordinance, correctly remarked that it must stand as a state paper second only to the Constitution itself[*141*].

While the struggle over representation was the most dramatic extension of congressional partisan politics, the entire proceedings of the Convention seem to have essentially continued the geopolitical thrust of congressional politics. Sidney Ulmer's bloc analysis of Convention voting on all issues shows a configuration remarkably similar to that of Congress. Ulmer discovered four blocs: one bloc composed of Georgia and the two Carolinas, knit by slavery more than by any other factor; one essentially Middle small states bloc, including New Jersey, Maryland, Delaware, New York, and Connecticut; one New England bloc composed of Massachusetts and New Hampshire; and a bloc made up of Virginia and Pennsylvania, which Ulmer factored as a subgroup of populous, leading commercial states[*142*]. The Virginia-Pennsylvania bloc, epitomized in the two persons of Madison and James Wilson (who disagreed with Gouverneur Morris's restrictive policy toward the West), can be understood as well as a triumphant core region manifestation of the policy established by the Virginians in Congress during the preceding twelve months. Indeed, the Pennsylvania alliance was crucial, both to gain cohesion for the core region and to disarm the destructive sectional dichotomy which had obtained during the Jay-Gardoqui affair.

VIII

Congressional power was as fragile as its problems were formidable. Clearly the Confederation needed alteration, yet it would be a mistake to think that the substructure of state governments was so moribund as to require the drastic national reformation called for in the Virginia Plan and partially realized in the Constitution. The public debt was amenable to retirement under the Confederation; national revenue from a 5-percent impost was within reach in 1787; regulation of foreign trade was feasible either through an amendment of Article 9 of the Articles of Confederation or by regional compact. Shays's insurrection had raised grave doubts about the capacity of the confederated republics to maintain domestic tranquility, but the rebellion had been suppressed without recourse to aid from outside Massachusetts. From the perspective of Congress, it was the lethargy of the states and, perhaps to a lesser degree, the members of Congress that helped make the Constitutional Convention necessary. As Nathan Dane put it, "that degree of perseverance, those [measures] and exertions that carried Congress through the difficulties during the late contest would serve at present I believe for the conducting of our Federal affairs on their true principles"[143]. Yet the public virtue of the early Revolution had so visibly declined that even Easterners who once claimed such virtue as the source of their congressional influence now despaired for the Republic itself. It was thus a somewhat exaggerated sense of the dangers of licentious and turbulent democracy which also persuaded Congress and the framers of the Constitution of the necessity of surprisingly sweeping reformation. In a sense the Revolution was turned upside down. Whereas in 1774 the argument for separation from the empire had been strongly reinforced by the conviction that only through republican revolution could public virtue be salvaged, in 1787 those who directed the Confederation looked to the re-creation of a consolidated empire to cultivate a virtuous leadership and curb the populace.

Still, the most plausible polity for curbing licentiousness would have been a multiplicity of smaller, more cohesive, centralized confederations—as indeed had often been suggested. By the creation of a republican empire, the product of the Constitution and the Northwest Ordinance, the framers seemed to accentuate rather than resolve the problem of social control. Madison's skillful argument in *The Federalist,* Number 10, that majority factions would be transformed into minorities in an extended republic made more sense in the context of the original Virginia Plan with proportional representation in both houses and a federal negative over state laws than in the finished Constitution. Ironically, only the development of truly national modern political parties could accomplish the antifactional objectives articulated in *The Federalist,* Number 10. Even more ironic is the fact that party development of the 1790s began as a remarkable continuation of factionalism in the Continental Congress. The Southern and Eastern nuclei of the Republican and Federalist parties as well as the divisions in the Middle states were replications of the structure of congressional parties. The struggles over the location of the national capital, Hamilton's fiscal program, and Jay's diplomacy were re-enactments of the partisan battles of the Confederation era.

Notes

1 Merrill Jensen, *The New Nation* (New York, 1950), chaps. 9, 10.

2 This is not to say that New Jersey, a state which imported through New York and Pennsylvania, was uninterested in reform of the Confederation. Forrest McDonald, in *E Pluribus Unum* (Boston, 1965) and *We the People* (Chicago, 1958), has convincingly shown the commitment of states such as New Jersey and Delaware to a system of national revenue. Nonetheless, as will be shown below, these states and others in a comparable situation such as Connecticut and North Carolina were not connected with the organization of the Constitutional Convention, either within the Congress or outside it.

3 Nathaniel Gorham to James Warren, Mar. 6, 1786, *LMCC,* VIII, 318.

4 Ibid.

5 The Connecticut delegates to Governor Matthew Griswold, Apr. 12, 1786, ibid., 339–340. Mitchell wrote the letter, and both signed it. These sentiments were similar to those of the nationalistically inclined Johnson.

6 Henry Lee to Washington, Mar. 2, 1786, ibid., 315.

7 *JCC,* XXX, 63. New York was not alone at this time. Maryland and Georgia also had not ratified the impost.

8 The Secretary of Congress to Charles Pinckney, Nathaniel Gorham, and William Grayson, Mar. 7, 1786, *LMCC,* VIII, 319.

9 The gist of Pinckney's speech was reprinted in *The American Museum,* II, 153–159; also with variations in the *New Jersey Gazette,* Mar. 20, 1786, the *Independent Ledger* (Boston), Apr. 3, 1786, the *Massachusetts Gazette,* Apr. 3, 1786, and the *Continental Journal* (Boston), Apr. 7, 1786. Grayson also spoke, according to the

French chargé, Otto, in animated terms, asking the Legislature why it was hastening the dissolution of the Confederation which had cost all so dear. George Bancroft, *History of the Formation of the Constitution of the United States of America* (2 vols.; New York, 1884), I, 485.

10 Rufus King warned Gerry of the danger of the Confederation falling apart from inattention by the states. James Manning of Rhode Island chastized his home government for not maintaining representation in Congress (Rhode Island, along with New Hampshire, Delaware, and Georgia, had been a major offender during the winter of 1785-1786) and warned that old hands in Congress feared for the Union. Rufus King to Elbridge Gerry, Apr. 30, 1786; James Manning to Governor John Collins, May 26, 1786, *LMCC,* VIII, 346-347, 366-367.

11 Charles Pettit to Jeremiah Wadsworth, May 27, 1786, ibid., 370-371.

12 William Grayson to James Madison, Mar. 22, 1786; Thomas Rodney, Diary, May 3, 1786, ibid., 333, 350-351.

13 Grayson to Madison, Mar. 22, 1786; Nathan Dane to John Choate, Jan. 31, 1786; Rufus King to John Adams, May 5, 1786, ibid., 333, 293, 354-355.

14 Grayson to Madison, May 28, 1786, ibid., 374.

15 *JCC,* XXX, 387n.

16 Actually a plenipotentiary chargé d'affaires with full powers to conclude a treaty of amity and commerce with the United States. See Charles, King of Spain, to Congress, Sept. 25, 1784, in U.S. Department of State, *The Diplomatic Correspondence of the United States of America . . .* 1783-1789 (3 vols., Washington, D.C., 1855. [originally published in 6 vols.; Washington D.C., 1833-1837]), III, 137.

17 Thomas Perkins Abernethy, *Western Lands and the American Revolution* (New York, 1937), p. 295.

18 Ibid., chap. 24, esp. pp. 329-333.

19 John Jay to the President of Congress, Aug. 15, 1785. *Diplomatic Correspondence of the United States, 1783-1789,* III, 162.

20 *JCC,* XXIX, 658. The instruction was framed by a committee including Monroe, Pettit, Gerry, McHenry, and King. It was agreed to on Aug. 25.

21 Gardoqui to Jay, May 25, 1786, *Diplomatic Correspondence of the United States, 1783-1789,* III, 199-201.

22 Jay to the President of the Continental Congress, May 29, 1786, ibid., 202.

23 Monroe to James Madison, May 31, 1786, *LMCC,* VIII, 375-376.

24 Henry Lee to George Washington, July 3, 1786, ibid., 400. Lee favored the treaty as late as Aug. 7, when he wrote to Washington that the advantages of the treaty would be secured for nothing more than giving up a right to something the United States could not profitably use at that time. Lee to Washington, Aug. 7, 1786, ibid., 417.

25 James Madison to Thomas Jefferson, Mar. 18, 1786, in Gaillard Hunt (ed.), *The Writings of James Madison* (9 vols.: New York, 1900–1910), II, 230.

26 James Madison to James Monroe, June 21, 1786, in ibid., 254.

27 Henry Lee to George Washington, Aug. 7, 1786, *LMCC*, VIII, 417.

28 Georgia's position on some of the roll calls was ambiguous, since her interest in securing confirmation of the 31° boundary was in effect set up against the rights to Mississippi navigation, in which Georgia had less immediate interest.

29 *Diplomatic Correspondence of the United States, 1783–1789*, III, 207–212.

30 Rufus King to Elbridge Gerry, June, 4, 1786, *LMCC*, VIII, 381.

31 Samuel Livermore to John Sullivan, Aug. 26, 1786, ibid., 453–454.

32 Charles Thomson, Minutes of Proceedings, Aug. 18, 1786, ibid., 439–440.

33 Ibid., 439.

34 Monroe to Patrick Henry, Aug. 12; Charles Thomson, Minutes of Proceedings, Aug. 16, 1786, ibid., pp. 423, 427.

35 Charles Pinckney also made this point in a lengthy speech delivered on the same day in an address to Congress of Aug. 3. According to later statements by Pinckney, he was speaking for the entire Southern contingent in Congress by common consent. (Pinckney to Charles Lester, July 8, 1801, ibid., 428n.) The speech, the most informed and ably argued of all the Southern statements in opposition to the Jay strategy, is reprinted in *JCC*, XXXI, 935–948, and *AHR*, X (1905), 817–827. Thomson, Minutes of Proceedings, Aug. 16, 1786, *LMCC*, VIII, 428.

36 Ibid.

37 "Mr. Charles Pinckney's Speech in Answer to Mr. Jay . . . ," *AHR*, X (1905), 825.

38 James Monroe to Patrick Henry, Aug. 12, 1786, *LMCC*, VIII, 425.

39 Madison and Monroe attempted to persuade Jefferson to join the enterprise and to use his credit in France to help launch the speculation which at that time was underfunded. James Madison to Thomas Jefferson, Aug. 12, 1786, in Hunt (ed.), *Writings*, II, 265–267.

40 James Monroe to James Madison, Aug. 19, 1786, in ibid., 445. Earlier in the year Otto described Jay as the director of national policy; Congress was simply the organ of its chief minister. Otto to Vergennes, Jan. 10, 1786, in Bancroft, *History of the Formation of the Constitution*, I, 480. Bloodworth to Governor Richard Caswell, Aug. 24, 1786, *LMCC*, VIII, 451.

41 James Monroe to Patrick Henry, Aug. 12, 1786, ibid., 424.

42 Timothy Bloodworth to Richard Caswell, Sept. 4, 1786, ibid., 462.

43 *JCC*, XXXI, 600.

44 Ibid., 601–604.

45 Ibid., 609, 621.

46 James Monroe saw through the design behind the motion (which was moved by King and Livermore) but erroneously assumed it was the Rhode Island delegates Manning and Miller who would leave. Monroe to Madison, Sept. 1, 1786, *LMCC,* VIII, 457.

47 Monroe to Madison, Sept. 3, 1786, ibid., 461.

48 Monroe to Henry, Aug. 12, 1786, ibid., 425.

49 Bloodworth to Caswell, Sept. 4, 1786; Charles Thomson, Notes of Debates, Aug. 18, 1786, ibid., 462, 439.

50 Theodore Sedgwick to Caleb Strong, Aug. 6, 1786, ibid., 415-416.

51 Monroe to Madison, Sept. 29, 1786, ibid., 473.

52 Henry Lee to George Washington, Oct. 11, 1786, ibid., 482-483.

53 Lee, who was extremely upset about this slight, protested to Madison about his "dereliction of the friendship which existed between us" and his "abandonment of a man who loved your character to excess. . . ." (Henry Lee to James Madison, Dec. 20, 1786, in Hunt [ed.], *Writings,* II, 285n.) Monroe contended he did not wish to be elected to any vacancy left by Lee; nor was he certain how much weight attached to Lee's position in the Mississippi affair. Madison indeed assured Lee he had pointed out to the Legislature that Lee had not voted against the Virginia instructions on the Mississippi. (Madison to Henry Lee, Nov. 23, 1786, in ibid., 288.)

54 Madison to Jefferson, Dec. 4, 1786, in ibid., 290-291.

55 Bloodworth appeared before the North Carolina Assembly on Dec. 16, 1786, to denounce the negotiations. *SRNC,* XII, 899.

56 Monroe to Madison, Sept. 12, 1786, *LMCC,* VIII, 464.

57 Madison to Jefferson, Aug. 12, 1786; to Monroe, Oct. 5 and Oct. 30, 1786, in Hunt (ed.), *Writings,* II, 257, 272, 275.

58 Abraham Clark to James Madison, Nov. 23, 1786, *LMCC,* VIII, 512.

59 Ibid.; Madison to Jefferson, Mar. 19, 1787, in Hunt (ed.), *Writings,* II, 328-329.

60 Edward Carrington to James Madison, Dec. 18, 1786, *LMCC,* VIII, 523; Feb. 18, 1787, ibid., 541.

61 Louis Otto to Vergennes, Aug. 23, 1786, in Bancroft, *History of the Formation of the Constitution,* II, 384-386.

62 Otto to Vergennes, Sept. 10, 1786, in ibid., 392-393.

63 Motion of Virginia delegates, Aug. 18, 1786, *LMCC,* VIII, 440-442; Otto to Vergennes, Aug. 23, 1786, in Bancroft, *History of the Formation of the Constitution,* II, 386; Monroe to Jefferson, Aug. 19, 1786, *LMCC,* VIII, 443-446.

64 Madison to Jefferson, Aug. 12, 1786, in Hunt (ed.), *Writings,* II, 262.

65 Ibid., 262–263.

66 Monroe to Madison, Sept. 3, 1786, *LMCC,* VIII, 461.

67 Ibid.

68 Ibid., 462.

69 Charles Tansill (ed.), *Documents Illustrative of the Formation of the Union of the American States* (Washington, D.C. 1927), p. 40.

70 See in this connection Harold Syrett (ed.), *The Papers of Alexander Hamilton* (New York, 1961–), III, 643–683. Of course Hamilton's leading influence at Annapolis cannot be questioned, but without the Virginians there would have been no Convention. Madison was not the only active proponent of the Convention from Virginia. Monroe, alarmed about the talk of an Eastern confederacy, wrote to Governor John Sullivan of New Hampshire, urging that state to send delegates to Annapolis. Monroe to Sullivan, Aug. 16, 1786, *LMCC,* VIII, 430. Forrest McDonald, *E Pluribus Unum,* chap. 2.

71 Rufus King to John Adams, Oct. 3, 1786, cited in Robert Ernst, *Rufus King; American Federalist* (Chapel Hill, 1968), pp. 83–84. For a good treatment of the "rebellion" in the context of Massachusetts politics see Van Beck Hall, *Politics without Parties: Massachusetts, 1780-1791* (Pittsburgh, 1972).

72 See Richard B. Morris, "Insurrection in Massachusetts," in Daniel Aaron (ed.), *America in Crisis; Fourteen Critical Episodes in American History* (New York, 1952). pp. 21–49; Marion L. Starkey, *A Little Rebellion* (New York, 1955); Robert J. Taylor, *Western Massachusetts in the Revolution* (Providence, 1954).

73 Henry Knox to the Continental Congress, Sept. 20, 1786, *JCC,* XXXI, 675–676.

74 Henry Knox to Congress, Oct. 18, 1786, ibid., 887.

75 Charles Pettit to Benjamin Franklin, Oct. 18, 1786, *LMCC,* VIII, 487; Henry Knox to Washington, Oct. 23, 1786, in Drake, *Life and Correspondence of Henry Knox* (Boston, 1873), p. 91. Forrest McDonald had examined newspapers in all major cities and has found "some variation of the Knox letter to Washington . . . in virtually all." (*E Pluribus Unum,* p. 290.)

76 *JCC,* XXXI, 891n. The letters on Indian disturbances were delivered on Oct. 16 and Oct. 19.

77 Henry Lee to George Washington, Sept. 8, 1786; Edward Carrington to Edmund Randolph, Dec. 8, 1786; Henry Lee to James Madison, Oct. 25, 1786, *LMCC,* VIII, 463, 517, 492.

78 Henry Lee to George Washington, Sept. 8, 1786, ibid., 463.

79 Rufus King to Theodore Sedgwick, Oct. 22, 1786, quoted in Ernst, *Rufus King,* p. 86.

80 Report of the address of Rufus King before the Massachusetts House of Representatives, Oct. 11, 1786, *LMCC,* VIII, 480.

81 Ibid., 480–481.

82 Ibid., 479.

83 Bancroft, *History of the Formation of the Constitution,* I, 269–270.

84 Ibid., 274–275.

85 Rufus King to Elbridge Gerry, Jan. 7, 1787, in Charles H. King (ed.,), *The Life and Correspondence of Rufus King* (6 vols.; New York, 1894–1900), I, 201.

86 King to Gerry, Feb. 11, 1787, in ibid.

87 King to Gerry, Feb. 18, 1787, *LMCC,* VIII, 541.

88 Bancroft, *History of the Formation of the Constitution,* I, 272–273. Benjamin Hawkins to Jefferson, Mar. 8, 1787, *LMCC,* VIII, 552.

89 King to Gerry, Feb. 18, 1787, ibid., 541.

90 *JCC,* XXXII, 71–72.

91 Ibid., 72.

92 E. C. Burnett, *The Continental Congress* (New York, 1941), pp. 676–677; Madison to Edmund Randolph, Feb. 24, 1787, *LMCC,* VIII, 547–548. The idea of a division of the Confederation into two or three subconfederations had been bruited about previously, but only at this moment, Madison noted, was the notion considered in the press.

93 William Irvine to James Wilson, Mar. 6, 1787, ibid., 551; *JCC,* XXXII, 73–74.

94 Nathan Mitchell to Thomas Collins, President of Delaware, Feb. 10, 1787, *LMCC,* VIII, 537. The question of the residence of Congress persisted into the spring. It was in April that Madison explained his opposition to the move to Edmund Randolph, Washington, and Monroe, on Apr. 15, 16, and 19, respectively. Hunt (ed.), *Writings,* II, 343, 351–353.

95 The most provocative and intriguing interpretation of this relationship has been set forth by Staughton Lynd, *Class Conflict, Slavery and the United States Constitution* (Indianapolis, 1967), chap. 8.

96 Otto to Vergennes, Feb. 10, 1787, in Bancroft, *History of the Formation of the Constitution,* II, 410–411; William Blount to Richard Caswell, Jan. 28, 1787, *LMCC* VIII, 533; *JCC,* XXXII, 11.

97 Madison to Jefferson, *LMCC,* VIII, 560.

98 Ibid.

99 Ibid., 561.

100 Madison attempted to reopen the matter by referring Jay's report to a committee for consideration. This, however, was voted down on April 13. *JCC,* XXXII, 204.

101 Ibid., 279.

102 Ibid., 290; William Grayson to James Madison, May 24, 1787, *LMCC,* VIII, 600.

103 *JCC,* XXXIV, 532. (Sept. 16, 1788.)

104 Madison to Edmund Randolph, Apr. 15, 1787, *LMCC,* VIII, 578.

105 *JCC,* XXXII, 169; Rufus King to Elbridge Gerry, Apr. 11, 1787, *LMCC,* VIII, 573.

106 Roger Alden to William Samuel Johnson, May 13, 1787, ibid., 597.

107 *JCC,* XXXII, 280, 285.

108 James Manning to Hezekiah Smith, May 17, 1786, *LMCC,* VIII, 362.

109 Monroe to Jefferson, Jan. 19, 1786, ibid., 286.

110 *JCC,* XXX, 392–393. Because the original arrangement had been part of the "compact" between Virginia and the Congress in the original cession, Congress requested Virginia to revise its act of October 10, 1780 (the Secretary of Congress to the Governor of Virginia, July 11, 1787, *LMCC,* VIII, 403). See also James Monroe to Thomas Jefferson, July 16, 1786, ibid., 403–404.

111 Ibid., 404–405.

112 *JCC,* XXXI, 672. Francis S. Philbrick, *The Rise of the West, 1754–1830* (New York, 1965), p. 129.

113 Madison told Edmund Randolph that Congress found the memorials from the West "embarrassing." Madison to Randolph, Apr. 22, 1787, *LMCC,* VIII, 588.

114 Archer B. Hulbert, "The Methods and Operations of the Scioto Group of Speculators," *MVHR,* I (March 1915), p. 507.

115 Ibid.

116 *JCC,* XXXII, 334–343.

117 Burnett, *The Continental Congress,* p. 685, says "the definitive ordinance was, in nearly every fundamental feature, a development from previous proposals."

118 Philbrick, *The Rise of the West,* 130–132, stresses Dane's responsibility for the ordinance.

119 The states represented were Massachusetts, New York, New Jersey, Delaware, Virginia, North Carolina, South Carolina, and Georgia. Only one member, Abraham Yates of New York, voted against the resolution, but he was outvoted by his two colleagues Melancton Smith and John Haring. *JCC,* XXXII, 343.

120 John Armstrong, Jr., to William Irvine, June 20; William Grayson to William Irvine, June 20; Nathan Dane to Nathaniel Gorham, June 22; Charles Thomson to William Bingham, June 25, 1787, *LMCC,* VIII, 612–614.

121 Dane to Gorham, June 22; Thomson to Bingham, June 25, 1787, ibid.

122 Madison Notes of Debates, in Tansill, (ed.), *Documents Illustrative of the Formation of the Union of the American States,* p. 109.

123 Historians have not appreciated fully the extent to which the convention was a Virginia production. Most would agree with Charles Warren, *The Making of the Constitution* (New York, 1928), that sentiment for a stronger national government can be found in the correspondence of "Washington, Hamilton, Jay, Madison, Jefferson and many others, both in the South and the North" (pp. 11–12). While this is not untrue, the inference that it was these men who engineered the Convention is false — except for Madison, who of all men was most responsible for it. Warren demonstrates that Hamilton was concerned about the weakness of the Confederation and advocated changing it as early as 1780, but he can cite no letter even mentioning the Convention at the moment of truth in 1786. The reason has already been pointed out: Hamilton, despite his presence at Annapolis, was more involved in his law practice than in political reform. The same can be said with greater force about two other New York nationalists — Robert R. Livingston and James Duane, both of whom declined to attend the Annapolis Conference, even though they were elected as delegates. Most of the letters cited by Warren in his history of the background of the Constitutional Convention are from Virginians during the years 1784–1787. The same is true of Bancroft's earlier treatment, *History of the Formation of the Constitution.* Citing a larger number of letters relevant to the movement toward the Constitution than Warren, Bancroft includes a ponderous quantity of Virginia correspondence. Bancroft's collection makes it possible to calculate a rough index of involvement by tabulating all letters to and from the Middle states nationalists and comparing them with all letters to and from Virginians. Including Hamilton, Duane, Jay, Robert R. Livingston, Robert Morris, George Plater, Thomas Fitzsimmons, Gouverneur Morris, and Robert Schuyler (nine individuals), there were 34 letters cited in the indexes of Bancroft's two volumes. By contrast, eleven Virginians — Grayson, Jefferson, Joseph Jones, Richard Henry Lee, Madison, Monroe, Edmund Randolph, Washington, Edward Carrington, Cyrus Griffin, and Henry Lee — wrote or received 225 letters. Of course these data provide a rough index of involvement at best, for the 67 letters from Washington doubtless reflect the fact that his correspondence was carefully preserved. Yet it is striking that Bancroft did not include a single letter written by Hamilton, Gouverneur Morris, or Robert Morris. The 3 letters received by Hamilton may be compared with 74 sent to Madison. The conclusion that the Middle states nationalists were tending to business and the Virginians to national politics is not automatic, but it is strongly suggested from the surviving evidence.

124 Madison to Edmund Randolph, Apr. 8, 1787, in Hunt (ed.), *Writings,* II, 338; Madison to Washington, Apr. 16, 1787, ibid., 344–352. Madison was not completely confident about the outcome of the Convention at first. Perhaps fearing another abortive meeting such as the Annapolis conference, he hesitated to reassure Washington that his prestige would not be damaged by his presence at the Convention. Madison to Washington, Nov. 8, 1786, ibid., 283–284. Clearly, Madison hoped from the outset that Washington would attend.

125 The tempo of state legislative action regarding the Convention as well as the attendance of delegates illustrate this point. Virginia endorsed the Convention on October 16, 1786; North Carolina on January 6; and Georgia on February 10, 1787. Massachusetts and Connecticut did not act until March 10 and May 12, 1787, respectively. Rhode Island, of course, never sent a delegation. There were exceptions to the rule: New Hampshire endorsed the Convention rapidly on November 27, while Maryland did not act until April 23, but the New Hampshire delegates were late in arriving, and the South was present in force from the outset. Warren, *The Making of the Constitution,* pp. 41–43.

126 Rufus King was "mortified" that he was the only delegate present from New England on May 24. The New Hampshire delegation did not arrive until July 23, and Massachusetts and Connecticut generally split on the issue of representation. King to Jeremiah Wadsworth, May 24, 1787, ibid., p. 120; also p. 232. For an analysis of bloc voting patterns in the Convention see Sidney Ulmer, "Sub-group Formation in the Constitutional Convention," *Midwest Journal of Political Science,* vol. 10, no. 3 (August 1966), pp. 288–303.

127 I think this is the proper inference from William Davie's remark on July 12 that North Carolina would never confederate on terms other than three-fifths representation for slaves or more. To quote Madison, who recorded Davie's speech, "If the Eastern States meant therefore to exclude them altogether the business was at an end." Madison, "Debates in the Federal Convention," in Tansill (ed.), *Documents Illustrative of the Formation of the Union of the American States,* p. 364. Sidney Ulmer's analysis of the bloc pattern in the Convention discloses a three-state subgroup composed of Georgia and the two Carolinas, united on the factor of slavery.

128 Tansill (ed.), *Documents Illustrative of the Formation of the Union of the American States,* p. 964.

129 Virginia and its Kentucky domain amounted to roughly 103,000 square miles; North Carolina, with what was to become Tennessee, 84,000 square miles; and Georgia, with its vast western claims, fully 153,000 square miles. The three states could claim 340,000 square miles—more than double the 167,000-square-mile area of the Northwest to which Virginia had the most persistent claim. Georgia had a population of roughly 60,000 but could claim territory almost surpassing the total area of all other states excluding Virginia and North Carolina.

130 The most elaborate argument contending that Madison, Wilson, Gouverneur Morris, et al. sought and actually achieved actual national consolidation is set forth by William W. Crosskey, *Politics and the Constitution in the History of the United States* (2 vols.; Chicago, 1953), esp. chap. XVIII. See also Gordon Wood, *The Creation of the American Republic* (Chapel Hill, 1969), chaps. XII, XIII, esp. pp. 473–475.

131 Ibid., p. 475.

132 Yates's Notes of Debates, June 29, 1787. Tansill (ed.), *Documents Illustrative of the Formation of the Union of the American States,* p. 828. Interestingly, Madison is somewhat more cryptic in his report of this speech (ibid).

133 Madison, Notes of Debates, July 13, 1787, in ibid., p. 372.

134 The tentative nature of the evidence is apparent from the the fact that Morris's statement was made on July 13; his notion that the East must be secured against the West was first articulated on July 5, however. Madison, Notes of Debates, in ibid., p. 330.

135 Madison, Notes of Debates, June 25, in ibid., pp. 271–272.

136 Ibid., p. 274.

137 Ibid., p. 318.

138 Ibid., pp. 319–320.

139 On July 5 Morris tried to establish a permanent scheme of representation for the East and West, unfavorable to the latter. (Ibid., p. 330.) Gerry later failed in an attempt to provide a constitutional guarantee that the number of Western states would never exceed the number of original Eastern states. (Ibid., July 14, p. 374.)

140 Lynd's overall thesis is that the "Compromise of 1787" was between Northern merchant capitalists and Southern slave-holding elites, momentarily successful because the ordinance and the Constitution guaranteed slavery against interference. Both previous partisan struggles in Congress and the bloc voting in the Convention (Ulmer, "Sub-Group Formation in the Constitutional Convention") suggest profound sectional struggle without proving or disproving Lynd's hypothesis concerning the transcendent importance of slavery. (Lynd, *Class Conflict, Slavery and the United States Constitution,* chap. 8.)

141 Bancroft, *History of the Formation of the Constitution,* I, 115.

142 Ulmer, "Sub-Group Formation in the Constitutional Convention," pp. 294–299.

143 Nathan Dane to Samuel Phillips, Jan. 20, 1786, Continental Congress Collection of E. C. Burnett, LC.

15 Epilogue: The Genesis of the First Party System

RECOGNIZING the magnitude of the problems that the Continental Congress faced, in coping with both British military might and jealousies within the states, it would be distorting the historical record not to note its accomplishments in retrospect. Within the span of a dozen years the Congress produced the Declaration of Independence, the Articles of Confederation, the alliance with France, the Treaty of Paris which ended the war, and the basis of the territorial system—probably one of the most important sets of laws ever passed by an American legislature. If the record of Congress in managing public finance was sometimes chaotic, that chaos was a logical result of the fiscal powers it was able to employ. And if its involvement in the management of military operations was sometimes meddlesome, its concern for the preservation of civic control over the military helped to sustain a principle that guided the Republic in some of its most trying moments. Despite its frailties, the Continental Congress established a record in act and principle that has rarely been equaled during a comparable time span in American legislative history. One of its achievements was laying the foundation for the first party system.

From the first Continental Congress to the time when the Articles of Confederation were replaced by the new Constitution, congressional politics was marked by partisan alignments which, if judged by behavior rather than motive or admission, took the shape of legislative parties. Considering voting patterns, contests over the control of those appointments the Congress had within its grasp, and the intensity of partisan rhetoric, party lines were as consistently drawn and battles as sharply fought in the Continental Congress as in Congress today. That these parties were concealed rather than frankly admitted and that they were restricted for the most part to the legislature rather than embracing the populace at large were natural consequences of the desire of the leaders of the Revolution to conceal conflict in a government that was on trial. The Congress was weak in its formal powers (although it displayed remarkable strength at times in the use of those powers), and sensible men committed to the cause of independence hardly wanted to compound that weakness. Perhaps more important, it was generally assumed that republics depended upon the achievement of consensus in society and in government[1].

The existence of congressional parties was disturbing not only because it was commonly believed that stable republics depended upon consensus but also because it was assumed that consensual politics was most feasible in small geographic areas where habits and customs were similar and where the inevitable conflicts of interest that emanated from different degrees of education, attainment, and wealth could be mediated as a result of common concern for the welfare of a comprehensible community. Many believed that the states alone were sufficiently cohesive to ensure healthy republican government. In reality many of the states, particularly the larger and more populous Northern states, were becoming so economically diversified and socially pluralistic that they had lost genuine communal solidarity. But there is a frequent lag, it seems, between the fact of socioeconomic change and its translation into ideology, so if states were slow to admit the existence of conflict that somehow had to be reconciled with the ideal of a republican consensus, the existence of parties in an enlarged republic was even more troublesome to acknowledge precisely because of their predictability.

It was a stroke of genius on the part of James Madison to openly contend that many of the difficulties that had been experienced under the Confederation were due to the existence of factions (parties) within the states and that the evils of parties—particularly a majority party that tended to oppress minorities—might be checked by strengthening the national government. A national republic, according to Madison's argument in the celebrated *Federalist,* Number 10, could filter local interests and passions by channeling those interests into a centralized national legislature that would be more impartial and judicious than the separate state governments. The national legislature would naturally be composed of the "better sort," who would have a more enlightened perception of public affairs than members of the state legislatures. Whenever partial interests persisted in the national legislature, they would be canceled by opposing interests in the enlarged republic. The result of this process of refinement and cancellation would be a residuum that would constitute a filtered sense of what was acceptable to the nation, and most beneficial to its individual parts.

It was with this logic that Madison defended the Constitution, which substituted for the Confederation a massive, consolidated, democratic republic—an absurd cluster of contradictions according to the conventional political assumptions of the eighteenth century. Ironically, the Constitution sharpened rather than muted party tensions in both the states and the nation, but rather than subverting the Republic, parties helped to perpetuate it. If Madison's analysis contained errors, it also contained wisdom.

II

The first party system blossomed with extraordinary rapidity. As soon as the Federal Congress began its deliberations, voting blocs took shape[2]. By the Second Congress, firm alignments were evident to any who cared to scrutinize its proceedings. By the Third Congress, the party system was beginning to extend to the grassroots. By 1796, the year of the third presidential election, partisan politics had assumed most of the characteristics that are associated with a modern party system.

This relentless growth so contrary to the accepted precepts of stable republican government strongly suggests that the first party system was germinating during the Confederation era. Despite the fact that the House of Representatives was a popularly elected body, the initial alignments in the House showed the familiar three-way regional division that had characterized the structure of party politics in the Continental Congress[3]. New Englanders maintained a solid front; the Southerners also achieved impressive cohesion; and the Middle states divided as a section and fractured within delegations. By the Third Congress there was an increasing tendency for independent legislators to take a partisan stance and for a two-party division to take shape. The shift from three to two parties in the House produced some highly significant innovations, such as intrastate splits in delegations from the Middle states, but as the first party system crystallized, it did so basically in terms of the division between North and South that had been inherent in national politics since the beginning of the Revolution.

It was entirely natural that the first party system should have been, at least in part, an extension of the partisan politics of the Continental Congress. The major measures considered by the Federal Congresses were identical with or closely similar to the concerns that had occupied the Continental Congress. Funding the Continental debt, the location of the national capital, the development and protection of the West, and the question of diplomatic relations with England and France were the major issues during both the 1780s and 1790s.

TABLE 27

Voting Blocs in the House of Representatives, First Congress

	Eastern Bloc	Middle Bloc	Southern Bloc
N.H.	Foster		
Mass.	Ames		
	Gerry*		
	Goodhue		
	Leonard		
	Partridge		
	Sedgwick		
	Thatcher		
Conn.	Huntington		
	Sherman		
	Sturges		
	Trumbull		
	Wadsworth		
R.I.	Bourn		
N.Y.	Benson		
	Laurance		
	Silvester		
N.J.	Boudinot		
	Schureman		
		Cadwalader	
		Sinnickson	
Pa.		Clymer	Clymer*
		Fitzsimmons	
		Hartley	
		Hiester*	Hiester*
		Muhlenberg*	Muhlenberg*
		Scott	
		Wynkoop	
Del.		Vining	
Md.		Carroll	
		Gale	
			Contee
			Stone*

TABLE 27 *(Continued)*

Voting Blocs in the House of Representatives
First Congress

	Eastern Bloc	Middle Bloc	Southern Bloc
Va.		Lee	
			Coles
			Giles
			Griffin
		Madison	Madison*
			Moore
			Page
			Parker
		White*	White*
N.C.			Ashe
			Bloodworth
			Sevier
			Steele
			Williamson
S.C.	Huger*		
			Sumter
Ga.			Baldwin
			Jackson
			Matthews

*Marginal membership.

Independents: Gilman and Livermore (N.H.); Grout (Mass.); Floyd, Hathorn, and Van Rensselaer (N.Y.); Seney and Smith (Md.); Bland (Va.); Burke, Smith, and Tucker (S.C.). Burke, Smith, Tucker, and Huger of South Carolina, along with Bland and Giles of Virginia, formed a fourth minor bloc.

Further, the American Revolution did not "devour its own children"; almost two-thirds of the Senators and half of the members of the House during the First Congress had been delegates in the Continental Congress. Although that proportion declined by the mid-1790s to roughly 50 percent and 20 percent, respectively, the continued presence of leaders such as Elbridge Gerry, Rufus King, James Madison, and James Monroe reinforced the connection between the Continental and Federal Congresses. Indeed, John Jay, who was closely associated with important decisions during the entire era, was at the center of party conflict in 1779, in 1786 and in 1795.

The three-party formation of the First Congress was a natural consequence of the germination of the first party system in the Continental Congress. As has been previously suggested, communication between widely separated regions was a basic problem during the Confederation era in the United States, just as it has been a central difficulty in the achievement of cohesion in virtually all new nations emerging from colonial status. The major thrust toward amalgamation has usually emanated from a vital center, or core area, of the new nations. The foundation for such a coalition in the United States was established during the early eighties when the superintendency of finance under the direction of Robert Morris was sustained by the Middle states, with important support from the South and from a few New Englanders. This sort of central leadership continued when nationalist-minded Virginians who appreciated the centrality as well as the size of their state took the lead in promoting the Constitutional Convention and establishing the framework for the surprisingly centralized Constitution that was produced by the Convention. There was extremely close cooperation between Virginia and Pennsylvania at the Convention. Hamilton, Madison, and Jay combined to set forth the most persuasive arguments in support of the Constitution, and during the First Congress the Middle region agreed to establish the national capital at the northern border of Virginia—a vital issue that actually caused controversy in the Congress as prolonged as the controversy caused by Hamilton's program.

This germinal stage of the first party system reflected the fact that the American Revolution was in part—though not wholly, as will be suggested below—a colonial war for independence. The structure of the Articles of Confederation tended to reinforce traditional colonial tensions because of the one-vote rule, but even after the Constitution made it possible for the people to elect representatives to the House and to participate indirectly in the election of Senators and the President, regional loyalties and parochial distrusts continued to affect party affiliations. When the "three-party system" rapidly evolved into a two-party affair, traditional North-South divisions persisted[4].

There were changes, of course, in the contours and accents of party politics from the 1780s to the 1790s—changes that demonstrated that the Revolution was a civil war as well as a war for independence. But these changes cannot be comprehended unless it is recognized that the Revolution was two revolutions in one. The fiscal and commercial policies of the Federalist administration converted Eastern parochialists into nationalists, and Southern nationalists into advocates of states' rights. Parochial distrusts were hard to erase, however, and New Englanders, no longer able to contend that the Southerners who were in the forefront of the emerging Republican opposition were conspiring to create a national aristocracy, now condemned the Southerners for indolent habits that had been acquired on their slave plantations—habits which prompted them to oppose orderly government and the honoring of debts. The Southern-oriented Republicans, because of Hamilton's overbearing executivism and

TABLE 28

Voting Blocs in the House of Representatives, Third Congress

		Eastern Bloc (Federalist)	Southern Bloc (Republican)
N.H.	Smith		
Mass.	Ames		
	Bourne		
	Cobb		
	Coffin		
	Dexter		
	Foster		
	Goodhue		
	Holten		
	Sedgwick		
	Thatcher		
	Ward		Lyman*
Vt.			Smith*
R.I.	Bourn		
	Malbone		
Conn.	Coit		
	Hillhouse		
	Learned		
	Swift		
	Tracy		
	Trumbull		
	Wadsworth		
N.Y.	Gaasbeck		
	Gilbert		
	Glen		
	Gordon		
	Talbot		
	Van Allen		
	Watts		Bailey
			Tredwell
			Van Cortlandt*
N.J.	Beatty*		
	Boudinot		

TABLE 28 *(Continued)*

Voting Blocs in the House of Representative, Third Congress

	Eastern Bloc (Federalist)	Southern Bloc (Republican)
	Cadwalader	
	Dayton*	
Pa.	Fitzsimmons	
	Hartley*	
	Kittera	Findley*
		Hiester*
		Irvine*
		Muhlenberg*
		Smilie
Del.	Latimer*	
Md.	Hindman	
	Murray	
		Christie
		Sprigg*
Va.	Lee	
		Coles
		Claiborne
		Giles
		Hancock*
		Harrison
		Heath
		Madison
		Moore
		Neville
		New
		Nicholas
		Page
		Parker
		Preston
		Rutherford
		Venable
		Walker
Ky.		Greenup

TABLE 28 *(Continued)*

Voting Blocs in the House of Representatives, Third Congress

	Eastern Bloc (Federalist)	Southern Bloc (Republican)
		Orr
N.C.		Blount
		Locke
		Macon
		McDowell
		Mebane
		Williams*
		Winston
S.C.	Smith	
Ga.		Baldwin
		Carnes

*Marginal membership.

Independents: Niles (Vt.); Gilman, Sherburne, and Wingate (N.H.); Clark (N.J.); Armstrong, Gregg, Montgomery, and Scott (Pa.); Dent and Smith (Md.); Griffin (Va.); Lawson, Gillespie, and Grove (N.C.); Gillon, Hunter, Pickens, and Winn (S.C.).

because of the Federalist preference for trade and amity with England at a time when France was engaged in a republican revolution in the face of opposition from the monarchies of Europe, accused the Federalists of wanting to re-establish monarchy in America. This ideological inversion whereby Southern elitists became Jacobins and Eastern democrats became Anglophiles and monocrats was a good example of the gaps in communication that occur in a war for independence and its aftermath. The Easterners were not true "democrats" as the Southerners had originally supposed, and the Republicans were not the "Jacobins" that the Federalists feared.

Nonetheless, there was an element of truth in the distinctions that were drawn between Federalists and Republicans. Federalists did in fact believe in order, sometimes at the expense of liberty, and the Republicans were sometimes willing to tolerate disorder from a prior commitment to liberty. These different values permeated the party politics of the Continental Congress and the first party system; they persisted throughout the ideological inversion just referred to; and they were rooted deeply in that colonial past which so troubled the creation of national cohesion.

From the earliest settlement of the colonies there were basic differences in the way New Englanders and Southerners had occupied and used the land, New Englanders had settled in towns, had lived in close proximity, and had developed churches and schools centered about the town as a corporate unit— the basis of representation in the provincial assembly. In the South the land was more fertile, the climate less formidable, the attraction of quick wealth from rapid occupation of the land more alluring, the opportunity for economic gain through the use of slave labor seemingly irresistible, and the sense of community in the diffuse, expanding population less keenly present[5].

While there were undeniable differences between the Yankee of the eighteenth century and the Puritan of the seventeenth century[6], the two traditions, despite corrosion, were reinforced in the crucible of the Revolution. In New England the political organization of the Resistance centered about the town; in the South it was organized on the county level. There were comparable differences in military organization which led to relatively conventional warfare in New England and guerrilla warfare in the South. Similarly, there were regional distinctions in the accents of a broadly coherent republican ideology. The Christian Sparta of Samuel Adams was markedly different from Thomas Jefferson's republic dedicated to the pursuit of happiness. Where Easterners tended to stress individual sacrifice and restraint as a necessary foundation for the welfare of the larger community, the Southerners tended to emphasize individual liberty as the ultimate rationale for the very existence of the larger political whole[7].

These two traditions—we may call the communal and libertarian—frequently clashed. The problem of how the West should be settled and governed forced Congress to reenact the colonization of America—and thereby cast into bold relief the alternatives of town and plantation in settlement, surveillance and liberty in goverance, and restraint and exploitation in the use of the land. The Jay-Gardoqui negotiations brought to the surface many of the same tensions between liberty and restraint by pitting the interests of the settled northern seaboard against agrarian interests located mainly in the South that were attracted to the unsettled West. The problem of the West persisted for decades, and it continued to trigger disputes similar to those of the 1780s. Indeed, with the creation of a more powerful national government, the clash between the Eastern and Southern ways was intensified in this area and in many others.

As already suggested, the Eastern communal and Southern libertarian traditions were liable to startling ideological inversions. The War of Independence was a republican revolution dependent in large measure upon public support. In those terms the Eastern ideology was radically republican because it rested upon the collective will of the people to resist the enemy. But public virtue, when translated from military commitment to the honoring of public debts and the maintenance of public order as insisted upon by the preponderantly Northern (and security-rich) Federalist party, appeared coercive at the very least, and at worst, dismayingly reactionary. And when Southern Republicans encouraged public resistance to the fiscal and foreign policies of the Federalists, an aristocratic party became the party of the people.

The chance unfolding of events sometimes contributed to the alteration of party postures. The Southern party, for example, constantly tended to favor an accord with France, whether it happened to be the France of Louis XVI or the republican France of the Jacobins. Although this position was due in part to a persistent desire of Southerners who represented the most "colonial" part of the new nation to break free from British military coercion and commercial influence, the fact remains that by associating themselves with the principles of the French Revolution they were reinforcing their credibility as the party of the evolving democratic republic. Of course, the Southern Republican espousal of the French Revolution was not wholly accidental, nor was it necessarily disingenuous, but the coincidence of ideology and commercial interest that affected both North and South in connection with Hamilton's fiscal system and the furor surrounding the French Revolution conspired to cast the emerging Democratic-Republicans in the role of defenders of the liberties for which the Revolution had been fought.

The Federalists disagreed as to which party best represented the principles of the Revolution. Indeed, they claimed to be the legitimate heirs of the Revolution, just as the Eastern party had claimed to be the authentic Party of the Revolution. It was a contention that had some plausibility, particularly when connected with the charismatic leadership of Washington. But when the Federalists attempted to discredit and even to stamp out dissent—a common tendency in new nations—that contention was seriously flawed.

A major reason for the insecurities felt by the Federalists was that as the first party system matured and extended to the grassroots, the Federalists realized increasingly that they were in the minority. It was apparent that the Federalist stress upon political order and popular restraint—a derivative of the Eastern ideology—was out of tune with the ferment that accompanied the Revolution and its aftermath. The communal, corporative tradition which had sustained the Eastern party during the war was partially disfigured when it was translated into Federalism. Public virtue no longer meant sacrifices in the struggle to win the Republic but restraint in searching for opportunity now that independence had been secured. Participation in the political process had come to mean acceptance of a stratified political order rather than cooperation to regenerate a corrupt system. Consequently, Federalism was increasingly difficult to export—not simply because of its stress upon consensus, but also because of its narrowly parochial definition of the values and priorities that consensus should embody[8]. Indeed, the Federalist persuasion proved to be increasingly difficult to sustain in Massachusetts, where its most articulate exponents were located. Republican congressmen began to appear in the Massachusetts delegation by the Third Congress, and the internal tensions of Massachusetts politics filtered to the national level of politics.

III

The rejection of the Federalist argument by constantly larger segments of the whole population signified a number of important facts. Politics was becoming increasingly nationalized, for one thing, and in the process partial, parochial definitions of the political process were unacceptable to the whole of the American people. If colonial wars for independence were and are different from the classic form of internal revolution such as the French Revolution because their major problem has been the creation of a new nation rather than the destruction of a corrupt or anachronistic society, it is at least questionable whether the American Revolution fits wholly in one category or the other[9]. The American Revolution resembled a colonial revolution on the national level of politics and a series of internal revolutions within the various states. Despite the strong evidence of regional partisanship in the Continental and Federal Congresses, there were simultaneous divisions within the various states that involved sharply differing socioeconomic interests. While these interests varied somewhat from state to state, and while the conflict was serious in some areas and subdued in others, there were grave and sustained divisions between elitist and popular interests in states such as Massachusetts, Pennsylvania, and South Carolina that involved not only differing opinions about the wisdom of independence but also the implications of what the rejection of the English monarchy meant for the future of American society. Elitists wanted the perpetuation of what had been an increasingly ordered social and political system in which rank conferred esteem and position and power commanded deference. Populists challenged the revolutionary elite, and consequently they questioned assumptions that had guarded a relatively stratified society and a reasonably orderly political system. That challenge was clearly less sharp than were comparable protests in Europe. Still, America seemed to resemble Europe more and more, and the menace of changes in the relationship between men and government brought about by decisions in distant seats of power confirmed from the beginning of the Revolution that central assumption of the populists that power should be decentralized.

Indeed, the conviction that power should be rooted in local and provincial institutions rather than in any central body was so strong that there was no real controversy over the creation of a confederation that derived its energy from local rather than national sources of authority. It was this conviction that not only sustained the early war effort but also accounted for the subsequent parochialism of conservatives such as Rufus King and Theodore Sedgwick, who had strong reservations about trade conferences and a strengthened government.

But that conservatives were sometimes parochialists did not mean that there were no conflicts between interests, of course. Many good Revolutionaries believed with John Adams and Alexander Hamilton that the British constitution, purged of its monarchic elements, remained the most tested and efficacious mode of government. Others, such as the anonymous author of the essay "The People the Best Governors"[*10*], believed in a participatory democracy. The controversy was not simply rhetorical. The lower houses of assembly in the state legislatures were subjected to populist pressures resulting in legislation such as paper money laws that propertied interests considered inimical to their welfare and an open violation of public morality.

It was only gradually that it became apparent that there was a logical relationship between the existence of powerful central authority and the preservation of entrenched socioeconomic interests within the states. That recognition was well established by the time of the debate over the Constitution in 1787, but it was less fully comprehended during the middle years of the Revolution, when attempts were made to strengthen national finances. Indeed, it is unlikely that Robert Morris himself was primarily concerned with anything other than improving public credit and making a profit for himself and his friends in the process—a dual objective that was reprehensible only in terms of the highly charged imperatives of the early stages of the Revolution, and in terms of the extraordinarily volatile partisan politics of the state of Pennsylvania. In that state the struggle between a conservative colonial establishment which opposed independence on the one hand and an aggressive radical democracy which seized power to secure independence on the other produced a genuine internal revolution.

Because the Continental Congress spent most of its time in Philadelphia, and because the parties that were involved in Pennsylvania politics were tied to the battles between parochialists and nationalists in the Continental Congress during the middle years of the Revolution, it was inevitable that the internal revolution within the states which accompanied the war of colonial liberation should have been affected by the politics of the Continental Congress. It was at that time—in late 1778 and in 1779, when so many substantive issues converged with these matters of process—that the first party system began to germinate in a clearly discernible way.

Thus the first party system arose from the different ingredients that made up the American Revolution. There were regional tensions between North and South regardless of the issues of the moment, and this was a constant of congressional partisan politics. At the same time there were internal strains common to almost all the thirteen states that commanded the attention of Congress only under special circumstances—specifically, when the alleged peculations of

Deane were publicized during the Lee-Deane imbroglio; when Gérard attempted to manipulate American peace terms at the same time that he made it clear that his sympathies were with the compliant Deane rather than with the obstreperous Lee; when subsequently Robert Morris attempted to link political centralism with fiscal responsibility; when Gérard's successor Luzerne successfully maneuvered Congress to direct that American peace negotiations be directed by the French foreign office; and when menacing gestures were made by the officer corps to secure pensions at the point of the bayonet.

All these matters were highly important, and understandably controversial. But apart from their intrinsic significance in the unfolding of the Revolution, their functional importance in the development of the first party system is particularly noteworthy. Although Southerners and Easterners often shifted positions as their regional interests dictated, the radicals and conservatives of Pennsylvania were ideologically consistent during the 1780s and 1790s. The radical Pennsylvanians (the "Constitutionalists") belonged to the Eastern party during the middle years of the Revolution when that party opposed the peculations of Deane, the centralism of Robert Morris, the attempts of Gérard to dictate American peace terms, and the efforts of the army officers to secure half pay for life. In similar, that is to say, opposite, fashion, the Pennsylvanian conservatives (the "Republicans" of the 1780s) joined the Southern party—and sometimes led that party—in support of a policy that favored Morris's fiscal plans, French diplomacy, and the demands of the army. Likewise, the Pennsylvanian radicals of the 1790s joined the predominantly Southern party, which opposed Hamilton's executivism and the "monarchizing" tendencies of the Federalists. Paradoxically, the libertarian credo of the Southern party proved to be an ideology that was sufficiently spacious to absorb the social and political ferment that accompanied the Revolution in diversified societies such as Pennsylvania, and in much of the North. Consequently, the Pennsylvanian radicals shifted from the Easterners to the Democratic-Republican opposition during the Federalist decade.

IV

One of the basic problems of American politics between 1776 and 1800 was the perplexing question of whether or not it was possible to create a political structure that would at once provide cohesion in a nation of diverse parts inherited from a colonial past while at the same time absorbing the ferment associated with a civil war. Both elements of the problem seemed to invite the imposition of an authoritarian regime that could weld the nation and suppress its discontents. That the Revolutionary generation retained its republican principles by resisting the temptation to make a Caesar of its commander in chief and by establishing a stronger national authority without materially undermining the vital source of popular government in the states and at the local levels of government was a remarkable accomplishment.

That accomplishment was due in large measure, of course, to the passage of the Constitution. But it is easy to exaggerate the providential qualities of the Constitution and to underestimate the importance of the people who made it function. It is appropriate to note that Simón Bolívar warned Venezuelans not to copy the Federal Constitution of the United States because it was in his mind "a marvel" that "so weak and complicated a government" could have succeeded in the "difficult and trying circumstances of their past"[11].

The Constitution created a new national stage for the Republic, but workable government was possible only as a result of a partial transformation of the kinds of political alignments that had characterized the partisan politics of the Continental Congress and the early Federal Congresses. Regional parties had to be nationalized, and they had to be made responsive to divergent interests within as well as between states and sections. This was done, not completely— nor willingly for the most part—but sufficiently to link dissatisfied New Englanders with Virginians, and some Southerners with Northern-oriented Federalists. The most rapid and balanced nationalization of party politics occurred at the geographic center of the Union—in the Middle states, where national decisions had more immediate impact, and where parochial traditions were less distinctive and entrenched.

The provincialism that had characterized the germination of national parties in the Continental Congress was never really erased during the first system. Threats of secession punctuated the early decades of the Republic, but by 1800 it was apparent that, for the moment at least, the nation would endure. The peaceful transfer of power from the Federalists who had claimed to be the legitimate Party of the Revolution, to the Republicans, who had been chastised as being seditious, demonstrated the vitality not so much of the Constitution but of a people who had discovered the uses of party politics.

Notes

1 The assumption was almost universal, and it formed a central thread of the anti-Federalist argument against the Constituion. For an example of the argument see James Winthrop, "Agrippa, IV," in Paul Leicester Ford (ed.), *Pamphlets on the Constitution of the United States, Published during Its Discussion by the People, 1787-1788* (Brooklyn, N.Y., 1888), pp. 63-65.

2 Mary P. Ryan, "Party Formation in the United States Congress, 1789-1796: A Quantitative Analysis," *WMQ*, ser. 3, XXVII (1971), 523-542; H. James Henderson,

"Quantitative Approaches to Party Formation in the United States Congress: A Comment," ibid., XXX (1973), 307–323.

3 Henderson, "Quantitative Approaches to Party Formation," p. 315. Party politics of the Continental Congress and the Federal Congresses has been analyzed in terms of the House rather than the Senate because the continuity (and discontinuities) between the two periods was most strikingly revealed in the House, and because the House was the more dynamic and influential of the two Federal legislative bodies.

4 For an interesting commentary on the social sources of this regional division—a commentary written over 100 years ago—see Richard Hildreth, *The History of the United States of America,* (5 vols., New York, 1851), IV, 347–348, V, 415.

5 For a recent intriguing analysis of the socioeconomic distinctions between the North and the South that complements in some ways the argument of Hildreth see David Bertleson, *The Lazy South* (New York, 1967).

6 Two excellent works which make this point are Richard L. Bushman, *From Puritan to Yankee; Character and the Social Order in Connecticut, 1690–1765* (Cambridge, Mass., 1967), and Kenneth A. Lockridge, *A New England Town; The First Hundred Years* (New York, 1970). For a different view see Michael Zuckerman, *Peaceable Kingdoms: New England Towns in the Eighteenth Century* (New York, 1970).

7 Bertleson, *The Lazy South,* passim.

8 Two valuable studies of the parochial mentality of Federalism are James Banner, *To the Hartford Convention: The Federalists and the Origins of Party Politics in Massachusetts, 1789–1815* (New York, 1970), and Linda Kerber, *Federalists in Dissent: Imagery and Ideology in Jeffersonian America* (Ithaca, N.Y., 1970). Richard Buel, *Securing the Revolution: Ideology in American Politics, 1789–1815* (Ithaca, N.Y., 1972), stresses the defensive character of the Federalist ideology.

9 Thomas Barrow has suggested that the model of the colonial war of independence is sufficient to explain the American Revolution, for while strains were present both before and after independence, they were the kinds of strains that had to do with strategies rather than values—that is, conflicts between radicals and conservatives regarding the timing of independence rather than between monarchists and republicans over the basic institutional structure of American society. While I do not agree that the American Revolution can be compartmentalized so readily, there is merit in Barrow's insightful argument and in the applicability of some sort of model of the colonial war of independence for analysis of the American Revolution. Unfortunately, no clear model exists, and if it did, the American Revolution would in all likelihood contain some major anomalies. See Thomas C. Barrow, "The American Revolution as a Colonial War for Independence," *WMQ,* ser. 3, XXV (1968), 452–464.

10 "The People the Best Governors: Or a Plan of Government Founded on the Just Principles of Natural Freedom" (Hartford, 1776).

11 Simón Bolívar, address delivered at the inaguration of the Second National Congress of Venezuela in Angostura, Feb. 15, 1819, in Vincente Lecuna (comp.) and Harold A. Bierck, Jr. (ed.), *Selected Writings of Bolívar* (2 vols.; 2d ed., New York, 1951), I, 179.

Bibliography (Cited Materials)

Manuscripts

British Museum
  Additional Manuscripts, Wilkes Correspondence

Columbia University Libraries Special Collections
  Gouverneur Morris Collection
  John Jay Papers

Harvard College Library
  Arthur Lee Manuscripts
  Jared Sparks Manuscripts

Historical Society of Pennsylvania
  Dreer Collection
  Gratz Collection

Library of Congress
  Bland Papers
  E. C. Burnett Transcripts
  Force Transcripts
  Gilman Papers

Manuscripts (*Cont.*):
 Holker Papers
 Holten Papers
 Papers of Charles Thomson
 Robert Morris Papers, Correspondence, 1775–1805

Maryland Historical Society
 Gist Papers

Massachusetts Historical Society
 Dane Papers
 Higginson Papers
 Sedgwick Papers
 Thatcher Papers

National Archives
 Papers of the Continental Congress

New Hampshire Historical Society
 Bartlett Papers
 Peabody Papers

New Hampshire State Library
 Weare Papers

New-York Historical Society
 Duane Papers

New York Public Library
 Emmet Collection
 Samuel Adams Papers

William L. Clements Library, University of Michigan
 Nathanael Greene Papers
 Holker Papers

Newspapers

Connecticut Courant
Continental Journal (Boston)
Gazeteer and New Daily Advertiser (London)

Gentleman's Magazine (London)
Independent Ledger (Boston)
Lloyd's Evening Post (London)
Massachusetts Gazette
New Jersey Gazette
New York Packet
Pennsylvania Evening Post
Pennsylvania Gazette
Pennsylvania Packet
Providence Gazette
Publick Advertiser (London)
Virginia Gazette (Purdie and Dixon)

Contemporary Materials

Acts and Laws . . . of Massachusetts. Boston, 1785.
Adams, Charles Francis, ed. *Familiar Letters of John Adams and His Wife Abigail Adams.* Boston, 1875.
———. *The Works of John Adams.* 10 vols., Boston, 1850–1856.
An Address to the Merchants, Freeholders, and all other Inhabitants of the Province of Pennsylvania in particular, and the Southern Colonies in general. Philadelphia, 1768.
Allen, James. "Diary." *Pennsylvania Magazine of History and Biography.* IX (1885), 176–196, 278–296, 424–441.
American Archives. Edited by Peter Force. Ser. 4, 6 vols; ser. 5, 3 vols., Washington, D.C., 1837–1853.
Archives of the State of New Jersey, First Series, Documents Relating to the Colonial History, 1631–1800. 36 vols., Newark, 1880–1941.
Bailyn, Bernard, ed. *Pamphlets of the American Revolution.* I, Boston, 1965.
Ballagh, James C., ed. *The Letters Richard Henry Lee.* 2 vols., New York, 1914.
Bland, Richard. *Inquiry into the Rights of the British Colonies.* Williamsburg, 1766.
[Boudinot, Elias.] *By his excellency, Elias Boudinot, esquire, President of the United States in Congress assembled, A Proclamation.* Philadelphia, 1783.
Boyd, Julian P., ed. *The Papers of Thomas Jefferson.* Princeton, 1950–.
Burnett, Edmund C., ed. *Letters of Members of the Continental Congress.* 8 vols., Washington, D.C., 1921–1936.
Butterfield, Lyman H., ed. *Diary and Autobiography of John Adams.* Cambridge, Mass., 1962.
Butterfield, Lyman H., ed. *Letters of Benjamin Rush.* 2 vols., Princeton, 1951.

Chandler, Thomas Bradbury. *What Think Ye of the Congress Now?* New York, 1775.

Chase, Eugene Parker, tr. and ed. *Our Revolutionary Forefathers: The Letters of François, Marquis de Barbé-Marbois . . . 1779–1785.* New York, 1929.

Clark, Walter, ed. *The State Records of North Carolina.* 16 vols., Winston and Goldsboro, 1895–1905.

Corner, George W., ed. *The Autobiography of Benjamin Rush.* Princeton, 1948.

Cushing, Harry A., ed. *The Writings of Samuel Adams.* 4 vols., New York, 1904–1908.

Drayton, John. *Memoirs of the American Revolution.* 2 vols., Charleston, 1821.

Duane, William, ed. *Extracts from the Diary of Christopher Marshall.* Albany, N.Y., 1877.

Fitzpatrick, John C., ed. *The Writings of George Washington.* 39 vols., Washington, D.C., 1931–1944.

Ford, Paul L., ed. *Pamphlets on the Constitution of the United States, Published During Its Discussion by the People, 1787–1788.* Brooklyn, 1888.

———. *The Works of Thomas Jefferson.* 12 vols., New York, 1904–1915.

———. *The Writings of John Dickinson.* Philadelphia, 1895.

Ford, Worthington C., et al., eds. *Journals of the Continental Congress.* 34 vols., Washington, D.C., 1904–1937.

Galloway, Joseph. *The Examination of Joseph Galloway before the House of Commons.* London, 1779.

———. *Historical and Political Reflections on the Rise and Progress of the American Rebellion.* London, 1780.

Greene, Jack P., ed. *The Diary of Landon Carter.* 2 vols., Charlottesville, 1965.

Hays, I. Minnis, ed. *Callendar of the Papers of Benjamin Franklin.* 5 vols., Philadelphia, 1908.

Hening, W. W., ed. *The Statutes . . . of Virginia.* 13 vols., Richmond, 1809–1823.

Henry, William Wirt, ed. *Patrick Henry: Life, Correspondence and Speeches.* 3 vols., New York, 1891.

Hough, Franklin B., ed. *Proceedings of a Convention of Delegates From Several of the New England States, Held at Boston, August 3–9, 1780.* Albany, N.Y., 1867.

Hunt, Gaillard, ed. *The Writings of James Madison.* 9 vols., New York, 1900–1909.

Hutchinson, Peter Orlande, ed. *The Diary and Letters of Thomas Hutchinson.* 2 vols., London, 1883–1886.

Hutchinson, William T., and William M. E. Rachal, eds. *The Papers of James Madison.* Chicago, 1962–.

Isham, Charles, ed. Deane Papers, New-York Historical Society, *Collections.* XIX–XXIII. New York, 1887–1891.

Johnston, Henry P., ed. *Correspondence of John Jay.* 4 vols., New York, 1890-1893.
Jones, Thomas. *History of New York During the Revolutionary War.* 2 vols. (reprint), New York, 1879.
Journal of the Assembly of the State of New-York. Fish-Kill, 1779.
Journal of the Proceedings of the Legislative Council of the State of New Jersey . . . Trenton, 1783.
King, Charles H., ed. *The Life and Correspondence of Rufus King.* 6 vols., New York, 1894-1900.
Lecuna, Vicente, comp., and Harold A. Bierck, Jr., ed. *Selected Writings of Bolívar.* 2 vols., New York, 1951.
Lee, Charles. *Strictures on a Pamphlet Entitled "A Friendly Address to All Reasonable Americans."* Philadelphia, 1774.
McRee, G. J. *Life and Correspondence of James Iredell.* 2 vols., New York, 1857-1858.
Massachusetts Bay House of Representatives. *Journal.* Boston [various dates].
Meng, John J., ed. *Despatches and Instructions of Conrad Alexandre Gérard.* Baltimore, 1939.
Morris, Anne Cary, ed. *The Diary and Letters of Gouverneur Morris.* 2 vols., New York, 1888.
Oliver, Peter. *Origin & Progress of the American Rebellion; a Tory View.* Edited by Douglass Adair and John A. Schultz. San Marino, Calif., 1961.
Paine, Thomas. *Common Sense.* Dolphin Books edition, New York, 1960.
Pennsylvania Archives. Edited by Samuel Hazard et al. 138 vols., Philadelphia and Harrisburg, 1852-1949.
Quincy, Josiah, ed. *Memoir of Josiah Quincy, Jr.* Boston, 1875.
[Quincy, Josiah, Jr.] "Journal of Josiah Quincy, Jr., 1773." Massachusetts Historical Society, *Proceedings,* XLIX (1915-1916), 424-481.
Reed, William B., ed. *Life and Correspondence of Joseph Reed.* 2 vols., Philadelphia, 1847.
Resolves of the General Court . . . *Begun May 25, 1785.* Boston, 1785.
Saunders, W. L., ed. *Colonial Records of North Carolina.* 10 vols., Raleigh, 1886-1890.
Smyth, Albert H., ed. *The Writings of Benjamin Franklin.* 10 vols., New York, 1905-1907.
Stevens, Benjamin Franklin, ed. *Facsimiles of Manuscripts in European Archives Relating to America, 1773-1783.* 26 vols., London, 1889-1895.
Syrett, Harold C., and Jacob E. Cooke, eds. *The Papers of Alexander Hamilton.* New York, 1960-.
Trumbull Papers, Massachusetts Historical Society, *Collections.* Ser. 5, IX. X; ser. 7, II, III, Boston, 1885-1902.
U.S. Congress. *Documents Illustrative of the Formation of the Union of the American States.* Edited by Charles Tansill. Washington D.C., 1927.
U.S., Department of State. *The Diplomatic Correspondence of the United States of America, from the Signing of the Definitive Treaty of Peace* . . . *to the Adoption of the Constitution* . . . 3 vols., Washington, D.C., 1855.

Virginia House of Burgesses. *Journal.* Williamsburg [various dates].
Votes and Proceedings of the Assembly of the State of New-York . . .
Poughkeepsie, 1780.
Warren-Adams Letters. Edited by Worthington C. Ford. Massachusetts Historical Society, *Collections.* 2 vols., Boston, 1917, 1925.
Wentworth, Paul. Minutes Respecting Political Parties in America, and
Sketches of leading Persons in each Province. Edited by B. F. Stevens.
Facsimiles . . . , no. 227.
Wharton, Francis, ed. *The Revolutionary Diplomatic Correspondence of the
United States.* 6 vols., Washington, D.C., 1889.
Winthrop Papers, Massachusetts Historical Society, *Collections.* Ser. 5,
IV. Boston, 1929.
Witherspoon, John. *The Dominion of Providence over the Passions of
Men* . . . Philadelphia, 1776.

Books and Articles

Albernethy, Thomas P. "Commercial Activities of Silas Deane in France."
American Historical Review, XXXIX (1934), 477-485.
——. *Western Lands in the American Revolution.* New York, 1937.
Alexander, Edward P. *James Duane: Conservative Revolutionary.* New York,
1938.
Ammon, Harry. *James Monroe: The Quest for National Identity.* New
York, 1971.
Ashe, Samuel A. *History of North Carolina.* 2 vols., Greensboro, 1908.
Austin, James T. *Life of Elbridge Gerry.* 2 vols., Boston, 1828-1829.
Bailyn, Bernard. *Ideological Origins of the American Revolution.* Cambridge, Mass., 1967.
Bancroft, George. *History of the Formation of the Constitution of the
United States,* 2 vols., New York, 1884.
——. *History of the United States.* 10 vols., Boston, 1834-1874.
Barrow, Thomas C. "The American Revolution as a Colonial War for Independence." *William and Mary Quarterly,* ser. 3, XXV (1968), 452-464.
Becker, Carl Lotus. *The History of Political Parties in the Province of New
York, 1763-1776.* New York, 1917.
Belknap, George. "A Model for Analyzing Legislative Behavior." *Midwest
Journal of Political Science,* II (1958), 377-402.
Bemis, Samuel Flagg. *The Diplomacy of the American Revolution.* New
York, 1935.
Berkhofer, Robert F., Jr. "Jefferson, the Ordinance of 1784, and the Origins
of the American Territorial System." *William and Mary Quarterly,* ser. 3,
XXIX (1972), 231-262.
Bertelson, David. *The Lazy South.* New York, 1967.

Boyd, Julian P. "Silas Deane: Death by a Kindly Teacher of Treason?" *William and Mary Quarterly,* ser. 3, XVI, 165–187, 319–342, 515–550.

Brant, Irving. *James Madison: The Nationalist, 1780–1787.* Philadelphia, 1948.

Brown, William G. *The Life of Oliver Ellsworth.* New York, 1905.

Brunhouse, Robert L. *Counter-Revolution in Pennsylvania.* Harrisburg, 1942.

Buchannan, Roberdeau. *Genealogy of the Descendants of Dr. William Shippen, The Elder.* Washington, D.C., 1877.

Burnett, Edmund Cody. *The Continental Congress.* New York, 1941.

Bushman, Richard L. *From Puritan to Yankee: Character and the Social Order in Connecticut, 1690–1765.* Cambridge, Mass., 1967.

Chambers, William Nisbet. *Political Parties in a New Nation: The American Experience, 1776–1809.* New York, 1963.

Champagne, Roger J. "Family Politics Versus Constitutional Principles: The New York Assembly Elections of 1768 and 1769. *William and Mary Quarterly,* ser. 3, XX (1963), 57–79.

———. "New York and the Intolerable Acts, 1774." *The New York Historical Society Quarterly.* XLV (1961), 195–207.

Collier, Cristopher. *Roger Sherman's Connecticut.* Middletown, 1971.

Collins, Edward D. "Committees of Correspondence of the American Revolution." American Historical Association, *Annual Report for 1901.* Washington, D.C., 1902.

Corwin, Edward S. *French Policy and the American Alliance of 1778.* Princeton, 1916.

Crosskey, William W. *Politics and the Constitution in the History of the United States.* 2 vols., Chicago, 1953.

Dangerfield, George. *Chancellor Robert R. Livingston.* New York, 1960.

Dawson, H. B. *Westchester County, New York, during the American Revolution.* New York, 1886.

Delafield, Julia. *Biographies of Francis Lewis and Morgan Lewis.* 2 vols., New York, 1877.

Deutsch, Karl W., et al. *Political Community and the North Atlantic Area: International Organization in the Light of Historical Experience.* Princeton, 1957.

Doniol, Henri. *Histoire de la Participation de la France à l'Etablissement des États Unis d'Amerique.* 5 vols., Paris, 1886–1892.

Donoughue, Bernard. *British Politics and the American Revolution.* London, 1964.

Douglass, Elisha P. "Thomas Burke, Disillusioned Democrat." *North Carolina Historical Review,* XXVI (1949), 150–186.

Ernst, Robert. *Rufus King: American Federalist.* Chapel Hill, 1968.

Evans, Emory G. "Planter Indebtedness and the Coming of the Revolution in Virginia." *William and Mary Quarterly,* ser. 3, XIX (1962), 511–533.

Ferguson, E. James, "Business, Government, and Congressional Investigation in the Revolution." *William and Mary Quarterly,* ser. 3, XVI (1959), 293–318.

———. *The Power of the Purse: A History of Public Finance, 1776–1790.* Chapel Hill, 1961.

New York, 1901.

Freeman, Douglas Southall. *George Washington.* 7 vols., New York, 1948–1957.

Geertz, Clifford. "Ideology as a Cultural System," in David Apter, ed., *Ideology and Discontent.* Glencoe, 1964.

Gipson, Lawrence Henry. "The American Revolution as an Aftermath of the Great War for Empire, 1754–1763." *Political Science Quarterly,* LXV (1950), 86–104.

Greene, G. W. *The Life of Nathanael Greene.* 3 vols., New York, 1867–1871.

Greene, Jack P. "Bridge to Revolution: The Wilkes Fund Controversy in South Carolina." *Journal of Southern History,* XXIX (1963), 19–52.

Groce, George, C. "Eliphalet Dyer: Connecticut Revolutionist," in Richard Morris, ed., *Era of the American Revolution.* New York, 1939, pp. 290–304.

Hall, Van Beck. *Politics Without Parties: Massachusetts, 1780–1791.* Pittsburgh, 1972.

Hanna, William S. *Benjamin Franklin and Pennsylvania Politics.* Stanford, Calif., 1964.

Hawke, David. *A Transaction of Free Men.* New York, 1964.

———. *In the Midst of a Revolution.* Philadelphia, 1961.

Hazleton, John. *The Declaration of Independence.* New York, 1906.

Heimert, Alan. *Religion and the American Mind.* Cambridge, Mass., 1966.

Henderson, H. James. "Congressional Factionalism and the Attempt to Recall Benjamin Franklin." *William and Mary Quarterly,* ser. 3, XXVIII (1970), 248–267.

———. "Quantitative Approaches to Party Formation in the United States Congress: A Comment." *William and Mary Quarterly,* XXX (1973), 307–323.

Henretta, James A. "Economic Development and Social Structure in Colonial Boston." *William and Mary Quarterly,* ser. 3, XXII (1965), 75–92.

Hildreth, Richard. *The History of the United States of America.* 5 vols., New York, 1849–1856.

Hofstadter, Richard. *The Idea of a Party System.* Berkeley and Los Angeles, 1969.

Hulbert, Archer B. "The Methods and Operations of the Scioto Group of Speculators." *Mississippi Valley Historical Review,* I (1915), 502–515.

Jameson, J. Franklin. *The American Revolution Considered as a Social Movement.* New York, 1926.

Jensen, Merrill. *The Articles of Confederation.* Madison, Wis., 1940.

———. "The Cession of the Old Northwest." *Mississippi Valley Historical Review,* XXIII (1936), 27–48.

——. "The Creation of the National Domain, 1781–1784." *Mississippi Valley Historical Review,* XXVI (1939), 323–342.

——. *The New Nation.* New York, 1950.

Kohn, Richard H. "The Inside History of the Newburgh Conspiracy: America and the Coup d'État." *William and Mary Quarterly,* ser. 3, XXVII (1970), 187–220.

Labaree, Benjamin W. *The Boston Tea Party.* New York, 1964.

——. *Patriots and Partisans: The Merchants of Newburyport, 1764–1815.* Cambridge, Mass., 1962.

Lee, Richard Henry. *Life of Arthur Lee.* 2 vols., Boston, 1829.

Linn, John B. "Samuel J. Atlee." *The American Historical Record,* III (1874), 448–449.

Lockridge, Kenneth A. *A New England Town: The First Hundred Years.* New York, 1970.

Lombard, Mildred E. "James Searle: Radical Businessman of the Revolution." *Pennsylvania Magazine of History and Biography,* LIX (1935), 284–294.

Lovejoy, David S. "Henry Marchant and the Mistress of the World." *William and Mary Quarterly,* ser. 3, XII (1955), 375–398.

Lynd, Staughton. *Class Conflict, Slavery and the United States Constitution.* Indianapolis, 1967.

McDonald, Forrest. *E Pluribus Unum.* Boston, 1965.

——. *We the People.* Chicago, 1958.

Maier, Pauline. "The Charleston Mob and the Evolution of Popular Politics in Revolutionary South Carolina, 1765–1784," in Donald Fleming and Bernard Bailyn, ed., *Perspectives in American History,* published by the Charles Warren Center for Studies in American History, Harvard University, IV (1970), 173–196.

——. *From Resistance to Revolution; Colonial Radicals and the Development of American Opposition to Britain, 1765–1776.* New York, 1972.

——. "John Wilkes and American Disillusionment with Britain." *William and Mary Quarterly,* ser. 3, XX (1963), 373–395.

Main, Jackson T. *The Antifederalists, Critics of the Constitution, 1781–1788.* Chapel Hill, 1961.

——. *Political Parties before the Constitution.* Chapel Hill, 1972.

——. *The Social Structure of Revolutionary America.* Princeton, 1965.

Mays, David John. *Edmund Pendleton.* 2 vols., Cambridge, Mass., 1952.

Meade, Robert Douthat. *Patrick Henry: Patriot in the Making.* Philadelphia, 1957.

Merritt, Richard L. *Symbols of American Community.* New Haven, 1966.

Metzger, Charles H. *Catholics and the American Revolution.* Chicago, 1962.

Morgan, Edmund S. "The Puritan Ethic and the American Revolution." *William and Mary Quarterly,* ser. 3, XXIV (1967), 3–43.

Morris, Richard B. *The Emerging Nations and the American Revolution.* New York, 1970.

——. *The Era of the American Revolution.* New York, 1939.

——. *The Peacemakers.* New York, 1965.

Nelson, William H. *The American Tory.* London, 1961.

Paullin, Charles Oscar. *Paullin's History of Naval Administration, 1775–1911.* Annapolis, 1911.

Pennypacker, Samuel. "Samuel J. Atlee." *Pennsylvania Magazine of History and Biography,* II (1878), 74–84.

Philbrick, Francis S. *The Rise of the West, 1754–1830.* New York, 1965.

Phillips, Paul C. *The West in the Diplomacy of the Revolution.* Urbana, 1913.

Pole, J. R. *Political Representation in England and the Origins of the American Republic.* New York, 1966.

Pratt, John Webb. *Religion, Politics, and Diversity: The Church-State Theme in New York State History.* Ithaca, 1967.

Rossman, Kenneth R. *Thomas Mifflin and the Politics of the American Revolution.* Chapel Hill, 1952.

Ryan, Mary P. "Party Formation in the United States Congress, 1789–1796: A Quantitative Analysis." *William and Mary Quarterly,* ser. 3, XXVIII (1971), 523–542.

Sanders, Jennings B. *Evolution of Executive Departments of the Continental Congress, 1774–1789.* Chapel Hill, 1935.

——. "Thomas Burke in the Continental Congress." *North Carolina Historical Review,* IX (1932), 22–37.

Schlesinger, Arthur M. *Prelude to Independence: The Newspaper War on Britain, 1764–1776.* New York, 1965.

Selsam, J. Paul. *The Pennsylvania Constitution of 1776.* Philadelphia, 1936.

Siousat, St. George L. "The Chevalier De La Luzerne and the Ratification of the Articles of Confederation in Maryland, 1780–1781." *Pennsylvania Magazine of History and Biography,* LX (1936), 391–418.

Sosin, Jack M. *Agents and Merchants: British Colonial Policy and the Origins of the American Revolution.* Lincoln, Nebr., 1965.

——. *The Revolutionary Frontier, 1763–1783.* New York, 1967.

Sparks, Jared. *Gouverneur Morris.* 3 vols., Boston, 1832.

Staples, William R. *Rhode Island in the Continental Congress.* Providence, 1870.

Stillé, Charles. *Life and Times of John Dickinson.* Philadelphia, 1891.

Stinchcombe, William C. *The American Revolution and the French Alliance.* Syracuse, 1967.

Sullivan, Kathryn. *Maryland and France, 1774–1789.* Philadelphia, 1936.

Sydnor, Charles S. *Gentlemen Freeholders: Political Practices in Washington's Virginia.* Chapel Hill, 1952.

Thayer, Theodore. *Pennsylvania Politics and the Growth of Democracy.* Harrisburg, 1953.

Ulmer, Sidney. "Sub-Group Formation in the Constitutional Convention." *Midwest Journal of Political Science,* X (1966), 288–303.

Van Doren, Carl. *Benjamin Franklin.* New York, 1938.

Van Tyne, Claude. *Causes of the War of Independence.* Boston, 1922.

Ver Steeg, Clarence L. *Robert Morris, Revolutionary Financier.* Philadelphia, 1954.

Wells, William V. *The Life and Public Services of Samuel Adams.* 3 vols., Boston, 1865.

Wood, George. *Congressional Control of Foreign Relations During the American Revolution, 1774-1789.* Allentown, Pa., 1919.

Wood, Gordon S. *The Creation of the American Republic, 1776-1787.* Chapel Hill, 1969.

———. "Rhetoric and Reality in the American Revolution." *William and Mary Quarterly,* ser. 3, XXIII (1966), 3-32.

Young, Alfred E. *The Democratic Republicans of New York.* Chapel Hill, 1967.

Index